A Dialogue Between Law and History

Baosheng Zhang · Thomas Yunlong Man · Jing Lin
Editors

A Dialogue Between Law and History

Proceedings of the Second International Conference on Facts and Evidence

Springer

Editors
Baosheng Zhang
China University of Political Science and Law
Beijing, China

Thomas Yunlong Man
School of Transnational Law
Peking University
Shenzhen, China

Jing Lin
China University of Political Science and Law
Beijing, China

ISBN 978-981-15-9684-1 ISBN 978-981-15-9685-8 (eBook)
https://doi.org/10.1007/978-981-15-9685-8

This Springer imprint is published by the registered company Springer Nature Singapore Pte Ltd.
The registered company address is: 152 Beach Road, #21-01/04 Gateway East, Singapore 189721, Singapore

Preface

The articles in this volume grew out of the papers presented at the *Second International Conference on Facts and Evidence: A Dialogue Between Law and History* held at the Peking University School of Transnational Law (STL) in Shenzhen, China, between September and November 2019. From September 14 to 15, eight Chinese-speaking scholars held a workshop at STL to exchange views on their draft papers. On November 16 and 17, these scholars joined with more than a dozen legal scholars and historians from various universities and research institutions in Europe and the USA to expand the discussion into an international dialogue between historians and legal scholars. The *Second International Conference on Facts and Evidence: A Dialogue Between Law and History* was the second installment of a cross-disciplinary research project on facts and evidence under the auspices of the Collaborative Innovation Center of Judicial Civilization (*CICJC*), a multi-institutional research platform with its primary anchor at the Institute of Evidence Law and Forensic Science (*ELFS*) of China University of Political Science and Law (*CUPL*). The inaugural conference of this project, the *First International Conference on Facts and Evidence: A Dialogue Between Law and Philosophy*, was co-hosted by CICJC and East China Normal University and successfully convened in Shanghai, China, in May 2016.

Like their fellow researchers in other disciplines in the humanities and social sciences, historians and legal scholars and practitioners share the same interest in ascertaining "truth" in facts in their respective professional endeavors. It is generally recognized that any historical study without truthful reconstruction of historical events is fiction, and any judicial trial without accurate fact-finding is a miscarriage of justice. In both historical research and judicial process, practitioners are invariably called upon, before making any arguments or judgments, to prove the underlying facts through evidence; however, these concepts are defined or employed in different academic or practical contexts. Thus, historians and legal professionals have, respectively, developed theories and methodological tools to inform and explain the process of evidentiary proof and the core concepts of evidence, inference, interpretation and, above all, rational reasoning. Compared with other disciplines, history and law have uniquely close relationship with each other, and have developed, as demonstrated by several authors in this volume, mutually dependent and yet uneasy reliance. When lawyers and judges try to resolve a legal dispute, they first endeavor to ascertain what happened that gave rise to the dispute in recent or distant past in order to answer the "questions of fact," thus undertaking a historian's mission of fact-finding. Considering that "questions of law," the second task of resolving a legal dispute, are actually a subset of "questions of fact," it is apparent that the law determination process involves primarily questions of "historical fact." In addition, the dialogue between law and history is not just a theoretical exercise but one of enormous practical significances. For instance, because of the rise of "originalism" in interpreting the US Constitution, as explicated in at least one of the articles in this volume, getting the facts right determines the outcome in constitutional decisions by the U.S. Supreme Court.

The *Second International Conference on Facts and Evidence: A Dialogue Between Law and History* intended to bring together scholars in the legal and history disciplines from different intellectual, cultural and jurisdictional backgrounds to explore some issues of common interest in the role of fact and evidence in both disciplines. Historians and legal scholars have engaged in exchange of views on these matters for many years, especially since the second half of the twentieth century, but rarely have concerted efforts been organized to consider these issues in face-to-face dialogue or produce collection of scholarly writings in a single volume. Two prominent efforts stand out. One is *Evidence and Inference in History and Law: Interdisciplinary Dialogues* (2003), which focuses exclusively on comparison of history and law borne out of an international seminar at the Netherlands Institute for Advanced Studies, 1994–1995.[1] An older and with a broader comparative perspective beyond law and history, *Evidence and Inference: The Hayden Colloquium on Scientific Concept and Methods* also contains half a dozen articles on fact-finding in history and law.[2] In some sense, this volume follows the intellectual footprints of this tradition and expands the related efforts to include Chinese scholars in this hereto exclusively Western academic and cultural undertaking.

We are grateful to the participants of the conference and contributors to this volume for devoting time and intellectual prowess to this historic interdisciplinary and cross-cultural dialogue. We acknowledge the financial and institutional support from CICJC, EIFS, CUPL and STL that made the conference and publication of this book possible. Special appreciation is due to Profs. Ronald J. Allen and Q. Edward Wang, academic advisors to this project, who not only, respectively, helped identify leading scholars in law and history from all over the world but also provided valuable advice in developing the thematic topics of the conference. We thank all colleagues and students from CUPL and STL who have contributed in different but all helpful ways to the organization of the conference, particularly Dean Philip McConaughey

[1] *Evidence and Inference in History and Law: Interdisciplinary Dialogues*, eds., William Twining and Iain Hampsher-Monk (Chicago: Northwestern University Press, 2003).

[2] *Evidence and Inference: The Hayden Colloquium on Scientific Concept and Methods*, ed., Daniel Lerner (London: Cambridge University Press, 1962).

of STL, Professor Lin Jing of CUPL and Professor Patrick Jiang and Ms. Wang Wei of STL. We would also like to thank Springer and in particular Ms. Leana Li, Ms. Lydia Wang, Ms. Fiona Wu, Mr. Umamagesh Perumal, and Mr. Augustus Vinoth, for their hard and efficient work to ensure the publication of this book.

Beijing, China
Shenzhen, China

Baosheng Zhang
Thomas Yunlong Man

Contents

Law and History: Major Themes

History, Science, Law … and Truth: Reflections on Fact Finding in History, Science and Law 3
Ronald J. Allen

A Comparison of Fact-Finding Methodology in Evidence Law and History 11
Baosheng Zhang and Guoyang Ma

Facts and Proof: Concepts and Application

The Paradox of Proof: A Semiotic and Language-Based Critique 37
Clinton W. Francis

Facts, Evidence and Proof: The Core Concepts of Law and History 69
Guoying Shu and Xuguang Song

The Generation of Probable Facts from Testimonies in Jurisprudence and Historiography 81
Aviezer Tucker

Evidence and Facts: Perspectives from History

Why Can't Oral Testimonies be Historical Facts? The Study of "Comfort Women" and Its Challenge to Modern Historiography 99
Q. Edward Wang

Interrogating Qi Shan Again: History, Law and Evidence Science 117
Weimin Zhong and Xin Hao

Judging the Past, Blaming the Past, Hailing the Past 129
Zoltán Boldizsár Simon

Evidence and Facts: Perspectives from Law

Fact-Finding in Constitutional Cases 153
David L. Faigman

The Elaine Massacre: A Case Study in the Dialogue Between Law and History 177
Rayman L. Solomon

How to Determine the Facts of a Criminal Case 193
Ruihua Chen

Facts and Evidence: A Case Study of Developments in England's Old Bailey Criminal Court During the Eighteenth Century 211
Stephan Landsman

Case Studies in History and Law

Cleaning Up the Mess of Empire? Evidence, Time and Memory in 'Historic Justice' Cases Concerning the Former British Empire (2000–Present) 231
Berber Bevernage

On Fact Cognition and Legal Reasoning in Song Dynasty Justice from the Perspective of Intellectual Rationality 253
Jingliang Chen and Xiaokang Wang

Can Truth Be Negotiated? Rethinking Plea Bargaining at the ICTY 301
Suhao Chen

A Historical Retrial of the Socrates Trial: Who Was the Victim of Guilt Presumption? 319
Jinpeng Feng

Seeking Truth in Law and History

How We Get to Know What Aaron Burr Did? Ascertaining Past Facts in History and in Law 339
Thomas Yunlong Man and MengXuan Lu

Chasing Truth from the Perspective of History 367
Luping Zhang

Charlemagne's Imperial Title: From the Perspective of Evidence Science 399
Longguo Li

Law and History: Major Themes

History, Science, Law … and Truth: Reflections on Fact Finding in History, Science and Law

Ronald J. Allen

Virtually all intellectual disciplines, excepting only the most introspective, pursue knowledge of an external world, employing naive concepts of both truth and knowledge, and even the purely introspective disciplines (if there are any) do the same regarding the internal states of mind and emotion of the person engaging in the intellectual effort. Truth in the naive sense is captured by propositions that accurately describe whatever their referents are, and knowledge is having beliefs whose contents are in fact true propositions in that they accurately correspond to an external reality. All disciplines do so because any other form of inquiry is pointless. If there is no accessible external world, and even if there is, if one cannot explore it systematically, we are all figuratively (and maybe literally) brains in a vat, and so we may as well go have a beer and be done with it. No sane person believes any of this of course, even those who promulgate some of the more inane philosophical ramblings about skepticism, the inaccessibility of direct knowledge of the external world, and puzzle over the deep meaning of Gettier examples. In a remarkable irony that often goes unnoticed, the most radical subjectivist, the most diehard skeptic, the person most convinced that knowledge of the world is unobtainable is constantly trying to convince the rest of us that his or her arguments are correct—are actually true in the real world—that one cannot know the real world exists nor know anything about it.

Peculiar beyond belief, I say. And thus I go naively about my business in a small corner of what might be called naturalized epistemology of exploring how juridical proof actually works in western legal systems, untroubled by the philosophical meaninglessness of it all. But exploring the nature of juridical proof soon brings one into contact with the methodologies of other disciplines, and this happened in the law when in the middle of the twentieth century that stalwart of science—mathematics in general and probability theory specifically—was viewed as perhaps the solution

R. J. Allen (✉)
Northwestern Pritzker School of Law, Chicago, IL, USA
e-mail: rjallen@northwestern.edu

B. Zhang et al. (eds.), *A Dialogue Between Law and History*,
https://doi.org/10.1007/978-981-15-9685-8_1

to many of the problems bedeviling an adequate understanding of juridical proof. It turned out this was a false turn for many reasons, which I will not go into, but I want to mention the conceptual issue that causes the deep incompatibility between probabilistic explanations of juridical proof and the reality on the ground (and for that matter behind any formal theory of evidence). For probability theory to be explanatory of trials, people would need know the necessary probabilistic data to appraise evidence, such as accurate base rates and likelihoods (or belief functions, credences, etc., if one is operating within unconventional probabilistic models). But to do that, they must already know the outcome of the case being tried. Evidence at trial is obviously contingent in the sense that the implications of any particular piece of evidence is a function of all the other data relevant to the case. Litigated cases are not like pari-mutuel betting in which fully specified statistical rules determine precisely the effect of each new bet. Evidence of the existence of a dead body does not mean that a murder occurred, for example, because subsequently admitted evidence may show the death to have been accidental or in self-defense. If evidence is not contingent in this sense from a fact finder's perspective, then the fact finder already must know that there was no accident or self-defensive act, but that is exactly my point. To implement a probabilistic theory of evidence requires that the outcome already be known, which of course makes the trial itself superfluous. The hope to systematize proof is much like the futile hope that we will eventually know enough about scientific theories to make Bayesian judgments about them. That will happen in science, as in the law, only when we already know all there is to know, and thus only when scientific and legal inquiry no longer serve a purpose.

Perhaps these speculations about the nature of evidence and probabilistic approaches to fact finding do not apply to historical work.[1] But maybe they do. As Carl Hempel has noted, some historians have believed that history is concerned with the description of the particular events of the past, much like the grist of the legal mill, whereas others see the historian's task as proposing interpretations of those particular events or finding underlying "scientific laws" that explain the data. Apparently no one since the demise of the German school of history that Hempel is criticizing seems to think that the historians' task is to just chronicle the historical facts, but whether that task is to find scientific laws or provide interpretative glosses is more contested. Hempel argues that the actual historical events are mere evidence of general laws that historical work seeks to discover and not just justifications for subjective interpretations of scattered pieces of evidence from the past. One sees the implications of Hempel's approach in historiography today and its fascination with Big Data that to all intents and purposes looks like empirical science.[2] In any event, positions on historiography seem located somewhere in the range from the search for scientific laws to the proffering of interpretations.

The law has a different concern that markedly distinguishes it from both the scientific conception of historical research and the interpretive version, as well as setting it apart from scientific inquiry. At trial, the effort virtually always is to reconstruct

[1]The next few paragraphs are influenced by Allen (1994).

[2]See e.g., van Nederveen Meerkerk (2017).

a particular event, to tell things as they were in a fashion quite consistent with the Germanic conception of historiography that has been thoroughly rejected by historians. The purpose is neither to uncover general causal laws nor to articulate historical interpretations of an event. To be sure, general causal laws may be invoked intermediately as evidence that some event occurred, and themselves may be the subject of evidence. Historical interpretations, or any other kind for that matter, are the handmaidens of reconstruction rather than its result. An obvious example is that motive is always admissible but virtually never an element in a cause of action.

Interestingly, most sciences are radically unlike either law or history in that the data are virtually never problematic. What actually happened is typically the uncontroversial starting point for attempting to explain why it happened. If the data are ambiguous, experiments generally will be repeated until replication is satisfactorily achieved, thus ruling out observational insufficiencies and leaving only theoretical insufficiencies as the problem. In a sense like the interpretive approach to history, scientific theories are then advanced to explain the observations of the data but the only ones that matter are those that point to methods of confirmation—to further empirical tests of predictions made by the theory. The critical difference between science and history on this score is that the historical interpretations (like much of the debates over American constitutional law, for example) do not appear to be empirically resolvable (which may be true of Hempel's conceptions of historical laws as well; brave talk does not substitute for rigorous empirical methods). To be sure, in scientific endeavors securing the data can be difficult, as in the arduous task of searching for the Higgs Boson, but at the end of the day that data either are or are not there. In the law, and often in history, exactly the opposite obtains. Inconsistent primary data ("the light was red"—"no, it was green") are the norm, and replication is generally impossible. In legal decision making, controversy virtually always settles on what happened. Why something happened (whatever did happen) may be evidentially controversial, by which I mean parties may advance varying and conflicting generalizations for the benefit of the fact finder (consider again motive), but they will be advanced in an inferential structure leading to a conclusion about a fact or series of facts rather than about a universal, a principle, or a theory.

At least one other significant difference between science and law—and I diffidently suggest history as well—obtains. Regardless of the process of discovery, scientific knowledge is organized in a hypothetico-deductive fashion. General principles are taken as assumptions under which are organized principles of increasing specificity. This organizes not only the knowledge but also the efforts of researchers. Work focuses on either systematizing further the deductive structure of preexisting knowledge through the elimination of anomalies (empirically or theoretically) or on the modification or replacement of the conceptual structure of the field. While some philosophers of science see these activities as quite distinct, their respective practitioners have much in common. Both share a well-organized body of substantive and methodological knowledge, although they may disagree about the explanatory power of that knowledge. Still, the disagreement typically exists over well-defined issues and is swamped by the scope of agreement. Even those assaulting the conceptual foundations of a field typically share with those doing work within a field methodological and mathematical principles, agree on what counts as evidence, and are able to express their scope of disagreement comprehensibly. And it is precisely the scope of agreement and disagreement that generates highly specific research efforts that occur at multiple sites simultaneously that actually bring about, in Harman's phrase, a change of view (and which also puts a lie to a considerable extent to the Kuhnian tall tales of incommensurability).

This description of the activity of scientific research does not describe factual inquiry in the legal process, although for a counterintuitive reason. The difference is not that scientific inquiry is highly complicated and lay judgments about ordinary life quite simple, but the exact opposite. Scientific progress in large measure proceeds through the simplification of phenomena, in particular through controlling as many variables as possible, which the hierarchical structure of scientific knowledge facilitates. Judgments about ordinary events, by contrast, virtually never are and cannot be recast as the results of controlled experiments. Too many variables are constantly and necessarily in play. And factual judgments at trial are even more resistant to domestication because the complicating features of the trial process are draped over the bubbling cauldron of real life.

Consider a simple example. Suppose a witness begins testifying, and thus a fact finder must decide what to make of the testimony. What are some of the relevant variables? First, there are all the normal credibility issues, but consider how complicated they are. Demeanor is not just demeanor; it is instead a complex set of variables. Is the witness sweating or twitching, and if so is it through innocent nerves, the pressure of prevarication, a medical problem, or simply a distasteful habit picked up during a regrettable childhood? Does body language suggest truthfulness or evasion; is slouching evidence of lying or comfort in telling a straight forward story? Does the witness look the examiner straight in the eye, and if so is it evidence of commendable character or the confidence of an accomplished snake oil salesman? Does the voice inflection suggest the rectitude of the righteous or is it strained, and does a strained voice indicate fabrication or concern over the outcome of the case? And so on.

The list of relevant variables goes far beyond credibility issues, of which demeanor is only one. When a witness articulates a proposition, the fact finder must determine what the proposition is designed to assert. That task, too, involves an immense number of variables. In addition, the fact finder will possess some knowledge based on its observations leading up to the first articulated proposition by a witness, acquired from the lawyers for example. And there are many more examples. For the law to proceed as a science would require that many of these variables be in a deductive structure with their necessary and sufficient conditions spelled out. No such structure could be created; it would be too complex. Moreover, the "thing" being theorized is adaptive, and thus would immediately begin to change, making the deductive structure outdated before it could even begin to do its work.[3]

Although we see that the structures of scientific and lay knowledge differ both in organization and acquisition, implicit in them both is the inability to state a priori

[3] See, e.g., Allen (2011, 2013).

the necessary and sufficient conditions for knowledge. Lay knowledge is, somewhat counterintuitively, an a fortiori case because of its complexity and the resultant lack of organized attempts to eliminate agreed-upon ambiguity. In the lay world, hordes of laymen do not descend in an organized fashion on well-articulated problems to resolve them in a fashion analogous to the work of scientists. This is not primarily because the problems are trivial but instead because the scope of ambiguity is far too wide. I think it fair to say, at any rate, that we lack consensus over the extent of our knowledge of conventional affairs (some people know, or believe they know, matters that elude others) or in what order aspects of it should be studied (some people regret ambiguity about wine more than ambiguity about truthfulness at trial; others do not). And of course, it is not obvious, outside of legal disputes, what the payoff might be for investing greater resources than we presently do in an organized effort to eliminate conventional ambiguity.

How does historical work fit into this? I am not sure. I suspect that it exploits the complexity of the human condition with which the law struggles. There is always more evidence of the past to be considered, and thus to be reordered. I look forward to comments on this matter.

There is also a critical difference between history (and science for that matter) and law, and that is the explicit adversarial nature of the American legal process. The adversarial process does much more than structure the trial process; it also structures the investigatory process. It delegates to the individuals with knowledge of the underlying events and the proper incentives to invest the socially optimal amount in further investigation the responsibility to collect and adduce the evidence. In American civil trials, this is facilitated by open and complete discovery, which mandates that the parties share all the pertinent information with each other. In criminal trials, even more starkly the parties are obligated to search out the pertinent evidence, and have the right incentives to do so, to not over or under invest in the production of evidence. Obviously, there are slips between the cup and the lip, and parties can behave strategically, which diminishes the beneficial effects of the adversarial process. But those effects remain large. Investing anyone else with investigatory responsibility means some third party (usually a government official) must duplicate the costs of learning the facts that the parties have simply by virtue of being involved in the relevant transaction, and of course the third party will be a government bureaucrat whose incentives will rarely include the socially efficient production on information. The bureaucrat will not be spending his or her own money, and may be more concerned about their own interests than those of the parties.

The superior knowledge of the parties not only guides evidence collection but presentation. The parties' obligations extend to constructing the best explanations for the evidence and presenting judge or juror with plausible inferential links and chains. In the condition of access to all the evidence, a priori this structure has the greatest chance of generating the socially optimal decisions over time. However, without access to the evidence, the system becomes less efficient, which is seen in some civil cases where parties attempt to exploit the transaction costs of discovery for personal gain and in criminal cases generally in which in the U.S. open discovery is not the norm.

There is one other critical distinction between law on the one hand and history and science on the other. Not deciding a case is not an option for a civilized legal system, because not deciding a case is to decide it. The status quo favors someone, and not deciding a case leaves the status quo intact. Notwithstanding the wide-ranging and intractable ambiguity of the human condition, domesticated however much by the adversarial process, decision must be made. But, there is not and could not be (otherwise trials would be superfluous) a formalized theory of evidence that generates accurate outcomes, and thus legal systems can only locate the decision over what is true somewhere and more or less live with the results. This locus is the fact finder, judge or juror. Virtually all proffered material is admissible at trial; trial judges affect admissibility very little, and the formalities of the rules of evidence even less. The proffered data become evidence if they influence a fact finder. Whether they do is determined by the sum total of that person's experiences at the moment of decision, experiences which will by that time include the advocates' efforts to enlighten the fact finder about the implications of the material produced at trial and all the other observations generated by the trial.

In the law, then, evidence is not a set of things; it is instead the process by which fact finders come to conclusions about the past. This concept is banal in the sense that it reduces to the proposition that a disinterested fact finder reconstructs the past based on all the observational inputs available at the moment of judging but the banality contains genius in the twin recognition that there is no alternative except official orthodoxy on conventional matters and that the probability of gathering the necessary information for an accurate reconstruction of the past increases astronomically with the size of the fact finding body and not just with the size of the evidentiary proffer at trial. Each fact finder is in essence a solitary scientist constantly reducing conventional ambiguity. This type of ambiguity is treated differently from the scientific variant because resources would be wasted by attempting to reach explicit agreement on its contours prior to the existence of a dispute, and so we do not organize assaults on it. It differs from the historical variant because again motive (historical laws and interpretations) may be relevant but is never a material fact. When a dispute arises involving factual ambiguity, a small set of individuals is gathered, from one (a judge) to twelve (an historical jury), to pool its members' knowledge in order to make sense of the evidence adduced. Given the lack of a social justification for organizing conventional knowledge on a scientific model, the law achieves an analogous result by holding a convention of lay scientists and requiring that they deliberate long enough to reach agreement.

Notwithstanding the differences in fact finding among science, law, and history, one commonality stands out: without accurate fact finding, the rest of the process is useless. Scientific theorizing to explain the cosmos with the earth at its center was just a colossal waste of time, as would be the construction of historical interpretations or laws based on mythologies rather than reality. In the law, every single conception of a right depends on accurate fact finding. Rights are meaningless without accurate fact finding. In the West, much is made of the political side of the Enlightenment that inverted what was thought to be the natural order of things that the people were subservient to their rulers to make the rulers subservient to the people. But the epistemological side of the Enlightenment that replaced dogmatic knowledge with empirical knowledge was the necessary foundation for that political revolution. Facts matter, and facts can only be found in free and open inquiry where no a priori limits on investigation are imposed. No topic is taboo. The stain of slavery on the western world is one example, as is the abuse of young people in particular by the clergy. Or the inquiry into corruption, political or personal, the long struggle for minorities and women for equality. Without free inquiry, one does not do science; one does witchcraft. Without free inquiry, legal systems do not dispense justice but injustice. And without free inquiry, historians create children's stories rather than accurate chronicles of the past, which are unlikely candidates for any intellectually compelling interpretation or theorizing. Thus, even if the ancient conception of history as chronicling the past has fallen from favor, it remains the necessary first step in any systematic historical thinking.

At least that is the view in the West. What is it in China? How do you conduct historical research aimed at the truth in a society that is apparently forbidden to discuss publicly such things as universal values, freedom of speech, civil society, civil rights, the historical errors, crony capitalism, and judicial independence? Hopefully, the next few days will generate some answers to these and other important questions.

References

Allen, Ronald J. 1994. Factual Ambiguity and a Theory of Evidence. *Northwestern Law Review* 88: 604.

Allen, Ronald J. 2011. Rationality and the Taming of Complexity. *Alabama Law Review* 62: 1047–1068.

Allen, Ronald J. 2013. Taming Complexity: Rationality, the Law of Evidence, and the Nature of the Legal System. *Law, Probability and Risk* 12: 99–113.

van Nederveen Meerkerk, Elise. 2017. Big Questions and Big Data: The Role of Labour and Labour Relations in Recent Global Economic History. *Internationaal Instituut voor Sociale Geschiedenis*, 95.

A Comparison of Fact-Finding Methodology in Evidence Law and History

Baosheng Zhang and Guoyang Ma

1 Evidence Is a Common Problem Faced by History and Law

Evidence is a common phenomenon in the process of human knowledge exploration. "All disciplines, from archeology to zoology, from history to astronomy, from statistics to decision theory, have largely shared problems of evidence and inference" (Anderson et al. 2005, 46). According to Twining's article *Evidence as a Multi disciplinary Subject* (Twining 2003), some recent developments have greatly strengthened the case for making evidence a multi disciplinary field in its own right. "In this context, 'Evidence' is preferable to 'Evidence Science'." In 2005, Schum (2005) published *Thoughts about a Science of Evidence,* emphasizing that evidence is a common problem faced by many disciplines. But "there is no single discipline known to [Schum] that provides all answers regarding the properties, uses and discovery of evidence" (Schum 2005). Therefore, it is necessary to carry out interdisciplinary research on "evidence science" to solve the common problems of evidential reasoning and knowledge acquisition faced by various disciplines. In this sense, knowledge acquisition in history and law belongs to the same exploration of evidence science.

B. Zhang (✉)
Qian Duansheng Professor, Collaborative Innovation Center for Judicial Civilization and the Key Laboratory of Evidence Science, China University of Political Science and Law, Beijing, China
e-mail: bensenzh@cupl.edu.cn

G. Ma
China University of Political Science and Law, Beijing, China

B. Zhang et al. (eds.), *A Dialogue Between Law and History*,
https://doi.org/10.1007/978-981-15-9685-8_2

1.1 Historical Facts Are the Common Research Objects of History and the Evidence Law

Fact is one kind of actual existence, which we can grasp by means of perception and mind (Zhang 2018, 1). All facts occur in a certain time and space. In the time dimension, facts can be in the past and present tense, but not future tense. Wigmore pointed out that "a fact is any act or condition of things, assumed as happening or existing" (Garner 2004, 628). In the past tense, facts are existing things or things that have already happened, which we could call historical facts. What is happening or facts in the present tense are not the object of study in history or law.

Once a historical fact has occurred, it has a feature that cannot be changed, which is called "accomplishment" (Peng 1996, 74–78). "Facts cannot be changed. When we talk about changing some facts, we just mean that we wish the facts in the future to be different from the facts before us or in the past. Facts are always accomplished or happening" (Jin 2011, 817). The accomplishment of fact is the same as its historicity. That means, once some fact has happened, whether you like it or not, it is an irrevocable historical fact or historical event. The common sayings "water under the bridge", "the die is cast", "it is no use crying over spilt milk" are all wonderful notes on accomplishment. In litigation, the facts that triers of fact should find are irrevocable historical facts. In the study of history, all the facts that need to be studied by historians are fait accompli.

1.2 The "Mirror of Evidence" Doctrine of Historical Fact-Finding

For historical facts, because of the lack of direct knowledge, the fact-finder can only rely on the "mirror of evidence" to infer the facts indirectly. This means that in the process of evidential reasoning, the cognitive means of fact-finders have some natural limitations. This is shown in the following aspects:

First, evidence is prerequisite for historical fact-finding; it is the sole "bridge" connecting the subject with the object. Evidence is just like a mirror that reflects the facts of past cases. Without this "mirror of evidence", it is impossible to ascertain what happened in the past. Yet the images shown by this "mirror" may be illusory, like "flowers in the mirror" or "moon in the water". Therefore, whether historical facts can be found accurately depends not only on how many pieces of evidence can be obtained but also on the ability to identify the authenticity of the evidence. Generally speaking, the more relevant evidence, the higher the accuracy of fact-finding. However, if there are problems in the authenticity or credibility of the relevant evidence, it will seriously affect the accuracy of fact-finding. Therefore, Simon (1973) said that "in a world of this kind, the scarce resource is not information; it is processing capacity to attend to information." Regarding the relationship between historical facts and historical materials, the former is a real event, while the latter is the documentary record left behind when real events occur. However, it is doubtful to many historians how much documentary evidence describes the "real past". For example, in the male-centered social culture, historical records are often about men's activities, and how these records differ from the facts becomes a problem. Therefore, in the academic awakening of "postmodernism", documentary historical materials are regarded as "texts" or "narratives". Scholars begin to pay attention to pluralistic, marginal and unusual sources, such as conflicting narratives in social memory and social identity, and exploring the significance of social situations and personal feelings in these evidentiary analyses. Wang (2001) has held that the study of historical memory is not to deconstruct our existing historical knowledge but to treat historical materials with a new attitude, regard them as a relic of social memory, and reconstruct the understanding of "historical facts" in the analysis of historical materials. The "historical materials" preserved in records are only a small part of these "past facts". They are selected, organized, even altered and fictitious "past". Therefore, documentary historical materials cannot be regarded simply as the carrier of "historical facts". They are the products of social memory under various subjective emotions, prejudices and social power relations. Obviously, it is the basic function of the cognitive subject to find the facts accurately, distinguish the authenticity of the evidence and make evidential reasoning.

Second, the logic of historical fact-finding is induction and abduction. The finding of historical facts is an inductive reasoning process from evidence to inferred fact, to fact of consequence and essential elements (Allen et al. 2011, 143). In the chain of reasoning according to Twining and others, the nature of inductive reasoning of fact-finding is reflected in different levels, from evidence to interim probanda, penultimate probanda and ultimate probandum (Anderson et al. 2005, 60–63). Among them, "generalizations" such as experience or common sense knowledge are associated with each link in the chain of reasoning, and they supply justifications for each reasoning link, allowing the inference from evidence to the penultimate probandum. Whether the evidence is relevant to the proof of the fact of consequence, or how much it has probative force, is generally not governed by a set of rules set by the legislator in advance, but only by the "logic and general experience" of the fact-finder (judge or jury). This determines that fact-finding is a process of inductive reasoning (Allen 2011). Likewise, Hu (2013, 197) believed that traditional Chinese textology methods are only applicable to the study of known materials; they seem powerless in unknown fields, because "evidence in historical science cannot be reproduced". He summarized three basic views about textology methods in the Qing Dynasty: (1) It is not forbidden for people to have independent opinions in the study of ancient books, but for each new opinion, there must be evidence of materialism. (2) Sinologists' "evidence" are nothing more than "anecdote". (3) Proof by example is an inductive method. If there are not many examples, it is merely proof by analogy. If there are many examples, then it is a proper induction.

Different from the reasoning process in which induction leads to general knowledge from specific evidence, abduction works in the other direction. As another typical method of evidential reasoning, abductive reasoning can be used not only in investigative activities but also in historical studies. For example, Hu Shi applied the method of "inferring the cause from the result and producing evidence to infer the result" to classical academic textology and the study of China's modernization (Xi 2016). "Inferring the cause from the result" is Huxley's method of inferring unknown facts from known facts. This method of doubt, or "strictly distrusting everything without sufficient evidence", is also known as the "method of history". "Producing evidence to infer the result" comes from Dewey's "experimental method" or the method of producing evidence. Hu Shi holds that the commonality between historical science and experimental science is "to do evidence-based discussion", but the difference between them is that "'evidence' in historical science cannot be duplicated. Historical scientists have to look for evidence, and they cannot create or reconstruct evidence (by experimental methods)." But we can use the experimental method of "producing evidence to infer the result" to prove the hypothesis about the unknown field and expand our knowledge. Therefore, "experimentation is to create appropriate 'causes' to pursue the imaginary 'results'". Hu (2005, 187) used these evidential reasoning methods to study the history of Chinese literature and found the law of dual evolution and dual development.

Third, as the "ideological product" of evidential reasoning, truth is probabilistic. The nature of inductive reasoning determines the probabilistic nature of fact-finding. Because the historical fact-finder cannot take past facts as the research object directly, evidential reasoning becomes the basic method of historical fact-finding. There will always be problems in the fact-finding, such as the quantity, authenticity and other problems of evidence, so the truth derived from evidential reasoning is just a cognitive achievement or "ideological product" formed in the mind of the fact-finder. According to the correspondence theory of truth, "when the object and subject, during the course of integration, could match up to a degree of more than 50%, such cognition is featured as having found the truth" (Shu 1993, 206). Of course, reconciling historical truth with the correspondence theory of truth will produce a dilemma: that is, because the fact-finder cannot observe the cognitive object (historical facts) in the sense of "objectivity", he can only reconstruct the historical facts in his mind through the processing of evidence information, which will make it impossible to judge the "subjective and objective agreement" (degree of correspondence between truth and historical fact). Twining (1985, 15) said that "the application of the principles of induction to present evidence makes it possible to assign a probable truth value to a present proposition about a past event". Because the historical fact-finding must go through a process of induction from evidence to probandum, the finding of truth is a judgment of the probability of the factual propositions. In fact, the judgment of factual propositions can never reach absolute certainty. The probability of fact-finding is mainly reflected in five fundamental reasons illustrated by Twining, along with others (Anderson et al. 2005, 246). First, the evidence is always incomplete. Second, evidence is commonly inconclusive. Third, the evidence is often ambiguous. Fourth, Bodies of evidence are commonly dissonant. Fifth, evidence comes to us from sources whose credibility, to some degree, is less than perfect. These five reasons are not only the reasons for the probabilistic nature of historical truth but also the causes of the "mirror of evidence" principle.

1.3 *Both History and Evidence Law Are Facing Scientific and Technological Challenges*

The development of contemporary science and technology not only provides a powerful means for exploring historical facts but also brings serious challenges to it. An editorial in *Nature* (2016) described how scientists were using genetic evidence to theorize about patterns of ancient human migration, although some historians were still skeptical about this methodology. However, the editorial cited Patrick Geary as saying that historians will be left behind unless they learn to accept the scientific tools of genetics. "If historians do not get involved and engage with this technology seriously, we're going to see more and more studies that are done by geneticists with very little input from historians", he said.

Compared with the application of DNA evidence in historical research, scientific evidence invaded the legal field earlier. In the second half of the nineteenth century, open consideration of evidence replaced formalistic evidence theory in civil law countries, opening the door for the use of scientific evidence. Radbruch (2012, 145) says that the status quo of scientific evidence theory is that: On the one hand, psychological analysis is applied to witnesses to assess their credulity and misunderstandings in order to minimize their probative value. On the other hand, improved techniques are employed in the analysis of fingerprints, bloodstains and many other observed targets so that the probative value of physical evidence can be enhanced. The extensive use of scientific evidence in trials have solved many hard cases, helped many innocent people to eliminate the injustice of wrongful conviction, and brought the hope of "scientization of factual inquiry" (Damaška 1997, 143) to mankind. However, just like the "double-edged sword" of science, scientific evidence not only helps the courts reduce the number of wrongful convictions but also creates a lot of wrongful convictions. In March 2016, *Science* published a series of articles on forensic science research, one of which said that a report published in 2009 by the U.S. National Research Council found that forensic analysts had long overstated the strength of many types of evidence, including footprints and fingerprints, tire tracks, bullet marks, blood splatters, fire, and handwriting (Enserink 2016). The title of another article, *When DNA is Lying*, is even more sensational. The article said that DNA evidence has helped exonerate hundreds of wrongly convicted people, but it has also landed innocent people in jail (Starr 2016). According to updated data from the American Innocence Project (2019), the misapplication of forensic science contributed to 45% of wrongful convictions in the United States proven through DNA evidence. The so-called "misapplication of forensic science" or "misuse or misleading use of scientific evidence" includes: (1) unreliable scientific principles or lack of factual basis; (2) scientific methods whose validity have not been fully proven; (3) misleading testimony of expert witnesses; (4) errors in the process of testing and (5) misconduct by forensic scientists. Obviously, in the face of the "invasion" of scientific evidence into the legal field, judges, as "laymen" of science, have not been fully prepared. They tend to have a superstition of scientific evidence, which will inevitably lead to a kind of blind obedience (Chen 2010), thus compromising their ability to examine and judge scientific evidence. However, since there is no presupposed probative force in any evidence, scientific evidence does not necessarily have reliability or credibility. In addition to the "general acceptance" of scientific principles and methods, the use of scientific knowledge in courts depends on experts. Experts may help fact-finders to correctly understand evidence or adjudicate disputed factual issues. They may also misuse scientific principles and technical methods to make inferences, thus misleading judges and juries to make wrong decisions. In this regard, historians and judges are in the same situation. Historians can use the lessons learned from evidence law to keep an appropriate vigilance against the possible drawbacks of the application of scientific evidence.

2 Differences Between Fact-Finding in History and Law

History and evidence law are two similar subjects. Both of them aim to find out the truth of history to the greatest extent. But they have the following differences.

2.1 *The Difference of Subject Responsibility: Judicial Finality and the Endless Exploration of History*

As the final means of dispute resolution in human society, judicial results have finality. Firstly, it manifests in the principle of judicial final settlement; that is, the judiciary holds an authoritative position in a variety of dispute resolution systems, and it is the final procedure for dispute resolution and the last line of defense for justice. In a country under the rule of law, it is necessary to ensure that every organization and individual respects the final judgment of the court, and that the validity of a court's legal judgment cannot be overridden by any means. Secondly, in litigation procedure, the finality of the court's ruling is reflected in two legal principles: "ne bis in idem" in civil law systems and "the rule against double jeopardy" in common law systems. Article 14(7) of the United Nations International Covenant on Civil and Political Rights expresses the basic requirements of these two principles: No one shall be liable to be tried or punished again for an offence for which he has already been finally convicted or acquitted in accordance with the law and penal procedure of each country. These principles have not been clearly stipulated in the current procedural law of China, and many practices in judicial practice violate these principles. The finality of adjudication is of great significance to ensure the authority and public credibility of justice.

The purpose of history is to discover the truth of history through the exploration of historical facts. In historical research, any acquired historical knowledge has a certain degree of fallacy and therefore needs to be continuously subjected to new tests or falsifications (such as archeological discoveries). In other words, any historical knowledge belongs to the "temporary" proposition, which needs to be revised according to newly found evidence. In the study of history, it is a normal phenomenon to argue about historical knowledge, which shows the relativity of historical knowledge. This kind of academic debate can promote the progress of historical science. From another point of view, a reasonable academic debate can be solved through further research (including the improvement of methods). By contrast, Twining (2003, 92) believes that the duty of the judge is to come to a firm decision in adjudication. "This pressure for decision has led the law to develop important ideas about presumptions, burdens of proof and standards of proof as aids to decision". Martin (1998) has quoted some scholars' viewpoint that in terms of social timeliness, there is no time limit for historical study, but the administration of justice has to solve urgent issues. Historians are surprised to find that judges only consider a small amount of "facts" in their convictions so that the trial can be continued. Lagarde believed that judicial evidence is formed in the procedure provided by law and leads to irrevocable conclusions. These are two reasons why they are different from historical evidence (Martin 1998).

2.2 *Different Attitudes Towards Hearsay Are Determined by the Differences in Probandum*

The main research objects of evidence law are the facts of court cases. Although trial facts are also historical facts, they are very recent in comparison with historical research objects. Usually, the parties (especially the defendant) and witnesses are still alive, and the real evidence has not been corrupted. However, the probandum in history is generally more remote, and historians have to rely on hearsay evidence.

Thayer (1898, 264) wrote in *A Preliminary Treatise on Evidence at the Common Law* that when we talk about "evidence" in evidence law, it does not have the main meaning given to it by ordinary discourse. This is a forensic procedure term. It imports something put forward in a court of justice. When people talk about historical evidence, scientific evidence and the evidences of Christianity, they are talking about different things. The evidence law is concerned with the furnishing to a court of matter of fact for judicial investigation. In the law of evidence, only testimony from witnesses and exhibits are evidence (Allen et al. 2011, 7–8). According to the hearsay rule, "hearsay" means a statement that the declarant makes outside of the current trial of hearing, and a party offers it in evidence to prove the truth of the matter asserted in the statement.[1] The law of evidence excludes hearsay mainly on the basis of the "testimonial triangle" theory.[2] Considerations include: the hearsay declarant does not make an oath, the fact-finder does not observe what is being

[1]See FRE 801.

[2]The testimonial triangle concept was first popularized for the academic legal community by Professor Laurence Tribe in his article Triangulating Hearsay, 87 Harv. L. Rev. 957 (1974). For

declared, and the other party does not have the opportunity to cross-examine the hearsay declarant. Therefore, there are some problems associated with hearsay, such as dangers of sincerity, narrative ambiguity, perception and memory. These are the main implications of the definition of hearsay in the U.S. Federal Rules of Evidence 801 and the rule against hearsay in 802.

By contrast, historical studies are based primarily on hearsay, because the witnesses (including the parties and witnesses) of historical events have already died. Historians can only reconstruct historical facts based on hearsay, and they cannot cross-examine historical figures. This situation has led to a change in the methodology of archaeology from "documents" to "cultural relics". In Foucault's view, in the past, history relied on documents and thus claimed to be the proof of the collective memory of the ages, and regarded itself as an anthropology. Therefore, traditional historical studies mainly record the relics and articles of the past. They turn the relics and articles into "documents", and use and question the documents. Scholars not only discuss the narratives in documents but also want to know whether the facts in documents are true and under what conditions can they be believed. Are the documents correct, or have they been tampered with? Therefore, documents have always been regarded as a language with expressive function, or as a faithful record of the truth that the document recorder wished to reflect. Foucault's Archaeology of Knowledge advocates that documents should be turned into "cultural relics". Their primary task is no longer to explain the meaning of documents, or to judge the authenticity and value of documents, but to organize and arrange documents, to distinguish and arrange the relevant and irrelevant, to discover their internal elements, and to describe their various relationships. At the same time, people should inspect the interior of the document and find its significance. That is to say that Foucault's archaeology regards literature as "relics". Archaeology only considers the object's own value, not its instrumental value. It only reveals its complex internal relationships, regardless of time and the past. Archaeology freezes time, and it deals with the internal layers of a particular knowledge system (any of the various humanities systems) (Huang 2006). In this sense, documents are only evidentiary material through which historians reconstruct human past behavior. New Historiography or Archaeology of Knowledge tries to explore some relations in the composition of documentary evidence itself through evidential reasoning.

Since historical studies are mainly based on hearsay, or even hearsay of hearsay, in order to distinguish the truth of hearsay and avoid false hearsay, a Multi-Evidence Method has been developed. Ye (2009) discussed the connection between anthropology and traditional Chinese textology, which developed from the two-way evidence of the early twentieth century to three-way evidence in the 1990s, and then to four-way evidence in the twenty-first century. He laid out the four stages of evolution, i.e., trust in, suspicion of, interpretation of and multi-dimensional interpretation of ancient scholarship.

---

a much earlier version of the triangle, see Charles Kay Ogden and Ivor Armstrong Richards, The Meaning of Meaning 10–12 (1927).

1. One-way evidence: documentary evidence. In the view of modern scholars, the so-called saints' books, such as *The Book of Songs, The Book of History, The Book of Rites, The Book of Changes*, which were elevated to "classics", are actually based on oral hearsay, rather than texts that directly record historical facts. Modern scholars have developed an all-round movement of suspicion and discrimination against the early history of documentary evidence. This is an unprecedented challenge to the one-way evidence theory of traditional Chinese academic study, and also a great subversion of the 3000-year-old belief in sacred writing.
2. Two-way evidence: archaeological materials. Wang Guowei put forward the idea of "two-way evidence" in *New Evidence for Ancient History*, calling on scholars to verify "material on paper" with "underground material" (oracle bone inscriptions). He said that "we are fortunate to have access not only to textual materials but also to new materials underground. It is through underground materials that we can correct texts or check the contents of ancient books. Even suspected sources may be facts. The two-way evidence can only begin now". Wang Guowei's "evidence" here refers to "historical data from different observations", while "two-way evidence" refers to "mutual verification of two bodies of historical data from different observations" (Zhang 2003).
3. Triple evidence—ethnological materials. Yang Xiangkui put forward the idea of three-way evidence. He believed that if there is insufficient evidence from documents, more should be obtained from archaeological materials. If it is still insufficient, more can be obtained from ethnological research. In view of the unbalanced social development of ethnic groups in China, ethnological materials, including oral narrative and ritual narrative testimony or extrinsic evidence, can make up for the deficiencies of documentary evidence. Therefore, in the study of ancient history, three-way evidence has replaced the old two-way evidence.
4. Four-way evidence—real evidence or image evidence. On the basis of summarizing the "seven materials" theory of Li Ji's ancient history research, Ye Shuxian simplified the "five ways" theory advocated by Zhang Guangzhi into the "four-way evidence". Finally, he used the division of testimony and real evidence in the law of evidence and five types of narrations of cultural text in anthropology or semiotics to reorganize the respective roles of the four-way evidence. He also interpreted the respective functions of the four-way evidence (see Tables 1, 2).

2.3 *Fact-Finding in History Lacks the Concept of Materiality*

Materiality is the main component of the relevance of judicial evidence. Relevance is the attribute of evidence that helps to prove or disprove the consequential probandum. The consequential fact mentioned here is the requirement of materiality, that is, the issues to be proved by using the evidence belong to the consequential facts that need to be proved according to law. Suppose, in the case of Zhang San's murder of Li Si, the prosecution asked Zhang San's mother to testify about the beriberi of Zhang

Table 1 Functional comparison between textology and the law of evidence

Classification of textology methods	Classification of evidence law	Five types of cultural text narration in anthropology or semiotics
One-way evidence	Documentary evidence (indirect)	Text narrative
Two-way evidence	Documentary evidence (indirect)	Text narrative
Three-way evidence	Testimony or extrinsic evidence	Oral narrative and ritual narrative
Four-way evidence	Real evidence or image evidence	Object narrative and image narrative

Table 2 Comparison between five types of cultural text narration in anthropology or semiotics and the four-way evidence

Five types of cultural text narration in anthropology or semiotics	Classification of textology methods	Classification of evidence law
Text narrative	One-way evidence and two-way evidence	Documentary evidence from testimony
Oral narrative	Three-way evidence	Documentary evidence from testimony
Image narrative	Four-way evidence	Real evidence
Object narrative	Four-way evidence	Real evidence
Ritual (rites and music) narrative	Three-way evidence and four-way evidence	Testimony and real evidence

San. This testimony is relevant to the fact that Zhang San has beriberi. However, although this factual claim is also a probandum, it is not a consequential fact. It is not material for the trial (whether Zhang San murdered Li Si or not). But if a witness provides an invoice to prove the factual pleading that Zhang San bought the murder weapon, the factual pleading has a "material" relationship with the consequential fact of the litigation. Therefore, relevance refers to the relationship between evidence and factual pleading, while materiality refers to the relationship between factual pleading and trial elements, and the definition of relevance includes these two relationships (Zhang 2018, 14–15). Therefore, when judges judge whether a piece of evidence is relevant, they must consider two questions: First, whether the evidence is related to the consequential facts in proving a case—this issue is called "materiality". Second, whether the evidence presented has the function of proving the material issue, that is, whether the evidence is helpful to establish the material issue. When the evidence makes a consequential fact "more or not more" probable, it is relevant (Allen 2010).

Twining (Anderson et al. 2005, 104) believes that historians share with lawyers a concern with particular past events, but historians lack the concept of materiality.

Trials are typically past-directed and hypothesis testing; they are concerned with inquiries into particular past events in which the hypotheses are defined in advance by law. This concept identifies in advance the hypotheses to be proved or negated and helps to formulate and anchor disputed issues of fact in advance with precision and specificity. Through a specific case, we will analyze the differences between the focus of law practitioners and historians in fact-finding. In the famous Sacco-Vanzetti case, Nicola Sacco and Bartolomeo Vanzetti emigrated from Italy to America in the early 1900s. Their work was respected, but at the same time they were also implacable anarchists. In 1920, they were charged with felony murder in a commonplace but ruthless crime. But there are still some arguments about whether they were convicted for being murderers or for being anarchists. One major element of the argument is that they were wrongly convicted because of a problem in the authenticity of certain firearms evidence against Sacco. At the time of their arrest, Sacco was carrying a 32-caliber Colt automatic pistol. At the trial, a police officer testified: "Sacco attempted on several occasions to put his hand under his overcoat in spite of being warned [by Connolly] not to do so." In the later trial, the prosecutors spent a long time proving that a bullet had been fired through the 32-caliber Colt automatic that was alleged to belong to Sacco. The court allowed prosecutors and defenders to test-fire bullets through Sacco's 32-caliber Colt automatic, but ballistic experts on both sides disagreed. Obviously, in the above-mentioned case, the testimony of the police that "Sacco attempted on several occasions to put his hand under his overcoat in spite of being warned [by Connolly] not to do so" did not make it more possible that Sacco shot at the police, so the testimony lacked relevance. Similarly, the prosecution and defense ballistics experts disagreed about whether the bullet had been fired through Sacco's 32-caliber Colt automatic, so the scientific evidence lacked relevance.

By comparison, historians study this case from a different perspective. They are often involved not only in establishing what happened but also explaining why it happened. This is often a more difficult and more interesting problem. Furthermore, historians are typically interested in questions that go beyond establishing and explaining a particular event. For example, a lot of historical research literature about the Sacco-Vanzetti case treats as straightforward or assumes the question of their innocence in order to explore many issues related to the political, social and legal background at that time (Twining 2003). Martin (1998) quoted many scholars' opinions to compare the fact-finding of historians with the fact-finding of judges. Two points aroused the greatest interest of the author: Firstly, to the degree of detail of fact-finding, history aims at memory and identity construction, while justice aims at social peace to settle disputes. For example, historical facts about the number of victims of Nazi concentration camps in World War II, human experimentation sites and the attribution of responsibility involve the most detailed historical techniques. In order to prevent people from forgetting this human experience, it is necessary to emphasize that the memory of Auschwitz is "indispensable". In contrast, the prosecutor declared that they are not historians, and these detailed searches should be completed by historians. For them, it is enough to collect one or two pieces of evidence that prove the facts and that cannot be refuted by contrary evidence. Secondly, in the case of urgent collective memory and society, only the judiciary can confirm a very important fact by judgment.

Because the consequential fact in judicial fact-finding is regulated by substantive law, the process of judges or juries using evidence to find the truth of the case is not arbitrary, but strictly limited by law. In this sense, in a judicial case, what is the consequential probandum and what is the relevant evidence are determined by law, which is the role of consequential materiality. However, historians cannot be limited by any rules and regulations in the study of a historical case, so they can study historical facts from multiple perspectives and draw many different conclusions.

2.4 Historical Evidence Analysis Lacks the Concept of Admissibility and the Definite Goal of "Justice-Seeking"

The principle of admissibility highlights the legal characteristics of evidence. In the field of litigation, admissibility refers to "the quality or state of being allowed to be entered into evidence in a hearing, trial, or other proceeding" (Garner 2004). "Admissible evidence is relevant and is of such a character (e.g., not unfairly prejudicial, based on hearsay, or privileged) that the court should receive it" (Garner 2004). Admissibility first involves relevance, i.e., the exclusion of irrelevant evidence. "Irrelevant evidence is not admissible."[3] Therefore, relevance is a necessary condition for admissibility. But Thayer (1898, 264–266) said that "it is obvious that, in reality, there are tests of admissibility other than logical relevancy." These other tests include value considerations such as fairness, harmony and efficiency. Twining et al. (Anderson et al. 2005, 87) held that, in addition to the rules of relevance, most of the remaining rules of evidence can be viewed as falling into three categories—rules for justifying the exclusion of evidence on the ground that it has improper prejudicial effect that exceeds the probative value, rules that direct or reflect cost-benefit analysis in order to prevent excessive delay or time consumption, and rules that reflect external policies that are considered to go beyond the purpose of ascertaining the truth. Assuming that there should also be some exclusionary rules of evidence in historical studies, it is obvious that only irrelevant evidence should be excluded in order to achieve the goal of truth-seeking. However, in addition to the goal of seeking truth, the law of evidence also has the goal of seeking justice, including guaranteeing procedural justice and human rights. Examples include rules that exclude illegal evidence and rules that protect specific social relations and values, such as privilege rules, etc.

In the law of evidence, the pursuit of truth (truth-seeking) and values (justice-seeking) are two sides of a coin, which co-constitute the justification of an evidence rule. Cohen (1986, 54) held that truth is the main object of intellectual inquiry. Therefore, the truth of a proposition, if it is relevant to our concerns, is the best reason for us to accept it into our stock of stored information. In other words, in

[3] See FRE 402.

this respect, truth is a kind of reason, just as justice is a kind of reason. The unity of value and truth determines the dual functions of evidence law: one is to promote the discovery of truth, that is, truth-seeking; the other is to maintain universal social value, that is, justice-seeking. These two functions are competitive. "The goal of truth is in competition with other goals, such as economy, preserving certain confidences, fostering certain activities, and protecting constitutional norms" (Posner 1993, 206). Truth-seeking is only one of the basic values of the law of evidence, not all of them. Evidence rules should pursue the unity of various objectives.

Compared with judicial pursuit of justice, due to the lack of adversarial proof procedure in historical research, the analysis of historical evidence lacks the concept of admissibility and usually has no clear rule for excluding evidence. Hu (2000, 14–26) pointed out when comparing the differences between historical textology and the law of evidence, the development of "the law of evidence" in modern countries is largely due to the fact that both litigants are allowed to have the right to refute the evidence put forward by the other party. Because of the refutation of the other party, it is not easy to use false evidence and irrelevant evidence. In contrast, no opposing party stands in front of a textology scholar to refute his evidence, so he often refuses to examine strictly whether his evidence is reliable and relevant. The main reason why the method of textology is far less rigorous than the judge's judgment is the lack of a conscious refutation of its own standards.

However, historians, being cognitive subjects under specific historical conditions, cannot get rid of the restrictions of social and cultural background when determining the truth or falsehood of evidence, evaluating evidence or applying evidential reasoning. They can only, as Sima Qian said, "form their own unique theory" in the process of "exploring the relationship between natural phenomena and human society and being familiar with the process of historical development" (Ban 1962, 2735). The so-called "forming their own unique theory" is undoubtedly the product of value judgment. Yu (2008) analyzed this problem from two aspects: (1) No historians have personally experienced the historical facts that have long disappeared, they can only reconstruct the historical facts conceptually through the media of historical materials. As Becker (1967, 47) said, there is a most important distinction to be made: the distinction between the ephemeral event which disappears, and the affirmation about the event which persists. (2) The historical facts regarded by any historian as the object of study are only a part of the sum of historical facts, or even a negligible part. As Toynbee and Urban (1974, 10) said, any study of human affairs is bound to be selective. Supposing someone had all the newspapers published in the world, and supposing he had a guarantee that every word reported was true, he would still have to select, and, even if he reproduced all the facts, he would have to highlight some and devalue others.

Therefore, although historical research lacks the concept of admissibility and the clear goal of justice-seeking in the process of using evidential reasoning, historians all live in a specific social and historical environment, which inevitably makes their historical research have certain value selectivity. Historians use the specific value standards given to them by their specific society to reorganize historical facts. This will naturally lead to a serious tension between the pursuit of truth and the choice of value in the study of history. Moreover, this tension is not the same as that clearly derived from the legislator's demand for justice-seeking in law. Therefore, there is no lack of malicious falsification of history in historical research and social practice.

3 Explanation Theory of Historical Facts in History and IBE of the Evidence Law

Evidential reasoning is needed in the ascertainment of historical facts, which is the same as the induction used in the truth-seeking of the court. However, it has been found that modern historiographic research often falls into its own social and cultural barriers when it uses various historical materials and knowledge of other disciplines to explore "historical facts" through "analogies" and "similarities". For example, in our cognitive rationality, ideas like how to define "similarity", how to find "relevant" evidence, and how to "recall" are often difficult to isolate from the influence of social culture (Wang 2001). As mentioned above, in the law of evidence, whether the evidence is relevant to the probandum is decided by substantive law. However, in the study of history, the relevance of a piece of evidence to the probandum may be subject to a historian's own interpretive theory, based on a certain value or methodology.

Yu Wujin believed that the historical facts discussed by historians are not self-sufficient and unconditional, but they appear through a certain theoretical perspective. He quoted the classic explanation of "perspectivism" of Fay (1996, 72). Perspectivism is the view that all knowledge is essentially perspectival in character; that is, the assessment of knowledge always take place within a framework, which provides conceptual resources in and through which the world is described and explained. According to perspectivism, no one can directly observe the reality as the reality itself, but approach it with their own slant, which contains their own assumptions and preconceptions. Historians observe historical facts from a certain theoretical perspective, and the facts are distorted by this theoretical perspective. Historians pay too much attention to some historical materials while making evidential reasoning but ignore others, so they are full of selectivity of explanation. Because historians are always engaged in history study under the guidance of certain theoretical perspectives, "they must be conscious of their limitations, that is, they can never face all historical facts 'fairly', but can only face those historical facts by their theoretical perspectives. The idea that someone can face all historical facts freely and fairly without any constraints of theoretical perspectives is always a naive dream" (Yu 2008).

The process of historians discovering historical facts through a certain theoretical perspective is a process of evidential interpretation or evidential reasoning. In this regard, Peng (2010) analyzed three viewpoints in twentieth century western historiography theory: reconstructionism, constructionism and deconstructionism. (1) In the view of reconstructionism, historians' history is as close as possible to historical reality, so historical facts themselves will show significance and dominate historical interpretation. As long as new interpretations for the same object are reasonable, they will eventually be incorporated into a sounder interpretation as elements. (2) In the view of constructivism, historians' history is an understanding of a certain aspect of history from a specific perspective of a particular historian, whose construction of historical facts contains explanatory factors. People may interpret the same historical point differently by using different theoretical tools. However, as long as these interpretations are not fallacious but based on historical methods, they will not have real conflicts on the same plane. Wang Mingke (2001) remarked that, in the West, there has been a discussion on modern national identity and related cultural construction. Some scholars believe that the "old" nation and its traditional culture are often modern constructions. For example, in this analytical model, the saying that "Huangdi is the common ancestor of the Chinese nation" is considered to be the collective imagination and construction of modern Chinese intellectuals. In this sense, all history is contemporary history. (3) In the view of deconstructionism, historians can only write literary texts, not the truth. White (1995) discussed the difference between "event" and "fact" thus. The "events" happened in the past, which are "given" to historians, rather than constructed by them; the "facts" are quite different, they are constructed in the documents attesting to the occurrence of events, which are constructed by historians. Therefore, historical facts eventually emerge in the form of linguistic structures, rather than mere facts. On the one hand, facts contain interpretation, and it is difficult to completely separate facts from interpretation. To some extent, interpretation dominates facts. On the other hand, facts and interpretations can be transformed into each other. Historians can propose several possible models, none of which can claim a more "substantial" basis than other models. The progress of history means that new interpretations of the same topic are constantly emerging. In the view of deconstructionism, people are not facing the same past; interpretation dominates the facts, so the pluralism of interpretation cannot be avoided.

Based on the above analysis, the law of evidence is undoubtedly against constructivism. On the one hand, constructivism is too subjective, and the principle of evidential adjudication requires that there must be a certain relationship of conclusive evidence by evidential reasoning between the factual premise and the judgment conclusion. This will help "consolidate the intellectual infrastructure that is needed for systems of social organization within which disputes are reflected in argument and counter-argument, rather than in the use of threat of violence" (Cohen 1986, 61). On the other hand, the basic value orientation of rights protection of the law of evidence plays a strong role in controlling the process of proof. For example, the right of confrontation limits the admission of hearsay evidence. And the principle of presumption of innocence requires that the conviction of the defendant must meet the "proof beyond a reasonable doubt" standard, or else the presumption of innocence must be maintained.

Just as the discovery of historical facts requires evidential interpretation, hard cases of fact-finding in law also need evidence interpretation. On the one hand, when both parties use evidence to prove their own factual pleading or refute the factual pleading of the other, they need to interpret the evidence. For example, in the Simpson murder case, one of the arguments or consequential probandum was whether Simpson had a chance to commit the crime. Evidence suggested that there was about 40 min between when the victims were murdered to when Simpson re-appeared at his home to leave for the airport (Schmalleger 1996, 1–432). Therefore, Allen (2011) said that the testimony and exhibits in the trial are meaningless before being explained by human observers. Moreover, the interpretation of any piece of evidence cannot be determined in advance, because it is the function of the background and experience of the fact finder.

In the development of theories of judicial proof, some scholars have attempted to interpret evidence with a probabilistic approach. The problem of probabilistic interpretation is that evidence modeling by presumptive probabilities might result in ridiculous conclusions. In the Collins case (1968),[4] the prosecution prosecuted the two defendants based on probabilistic calculations. This approach received criticism from jurists. Tribe (1971) stated that quantitative analysis is politically unacceptable when it comes to the risk of conviction for innocent people. Allen (2014, 110) proposed a solution, for "inference to the best explanation" (IBE) or "plausibility" to substitute for probabilistic interpretation. This is a method of holistic accounts. Holistic accounts mean that the trier of fact should not confine himself to the specific evidence; on the contrary, he must concentrate on the whole case or story formed by evidence. IBE consists of three steps: Firstly, the party who bears the burden of proof should produce evidence and provide a compelling interpretation. Secondly, the opponent should produce a competing version of the incident to interpret the evidence. Finally, the fact-finder is entitled to construct his/her own interpretation. In a civil case, IBE can be applied to allow the fact-finder to compare. Is the plaintiff's story better than the defendant's story? Or not? Whichever is more plausible should win. In criminal case, if there is no plausible story of guilt, the person is innocent; if there is a plausible story of guilt, and no plausible story of innocence, the person is guilty. If there is a plausible story of guilt and a plausible story of innocence, the person is innocent (Allen 2011). For instance, in Nian Bin case,[5] the key issues were not proved, such as the source of poison and the method to spread the poison. In that case, there was no plausible story of guilt; therefore, the person was innocent.

In short, as long as there is evidential reasoning, it will inevitably involve the issue of interpretation of evidence. Not only in the process of inductive reasoning do we need to use generalizations to interpret evidence and make common sense reasoning, but also in the process of abductive reasoning, we need to formulate possible interpretation for the evidence, hypothesis, the proposition to be proved and so on. It is the interpretation function that endows the creativity of evidence reasoning. Of course, IBE may not be applicable to the study of history, because the study of history does not need to follow the principle of presumption of innocence and the principle of favoring the defendant.

[4]People v. Collins (1968 Cal. 2d 319).

[5]See Incidental Civil Judgement of the High People's Court, Fujian (2012) No. 10, Min criminal Zhong Zi.

4 Fact-Finding from the Perspective of Mutual Reference Between History and Law

The basic function of comparative research is to discern similarities and differences, to see similarities from differences and to see differences from similarities (Liu 1996). Among them, the comparison of differences in similarity is to clarify the development characteristics and approaches of each discipline, while the comparison of similarities in difference is to promote mutual learning and reference between disciplines. History and evidence law have the basis of mutual reference. As Hu (2000, 14) said: "The textology is to use evidence to test the past facts, historians use evidence to test whether the facts are true or false, right or wrong, the same as the detective investigation responsibility and the judge's trial responsibility, and the rigor of the method should be the same." Obviously, the similarity between history and law in fact-finding not only provides a basis for their mutual reference but also puts forward new possibilities for improving the accuracy of fact-finding.

4.1 A Situation of Majority of Evidence Owned by One Party and Resolution Measures

Draft Declaration on the Right to a Fair Trial and a Remedy stated that "In criminal proceedings, the principle of equality of arms imposes procedural equality between the accused and the public prosecutor: (a) The prosecution and defence shall be allowed equal time to present evidence; (b) Prosecution and defence witness shall be given equal treatment in all procedural matters; (c) Evidence unlawfully obtained shall not be used as evidence against the accused or against any other person in any proceeding." In fact, this reveals the principle of equality between the prosecution and the defense in the judicial trial, that is, the prosecution and the defense are equally armed. However, in modern litigation, especially in procedural litigation, as long as the state funds and organizes the prosecution, the principle of "equality of arms" in adversarial trials will be undermined. In criminal cases, defendants may except help from the prosecution in supplying some information which otherwise they might find difficult or impossible to uncover (McEwan 1992, 17–26). An important reason is that the gap between the resources (evidence) held by the defendant and the resources held by the other party is too large, which leads to the problem of "majority of evidence owned by one party" caused by the differences in the ability to obtain evidence and distance from the evidence. The impact of this problem is very serious. According to statistics, 29 of the 250 innocent people who were exonerated in DNA testing found evidence hidden by prosecutors after the trial (Garrett 2011, 169). In the case of Zhao Zuohai[6] and Yu Yingsheng,[7] the concealment of evidence was an important reason for the flawed fact-finding. In order to change the imbalance of prosecution and defense caused by this problem, fact-finding in the legal field should change the imbalance of resources through institutional means, such as a discovery system. However, the problem of "majority of evidence owned by one party" is still a difficult problem in judicial activities.

History provides a new way to solve this problem. This is mainly reflected in the question of whether archaeological materials are trustworthy relics of the past. This issue is enlightening to the study of evidence law. In archaeological research, archaeological materials have long been regarded as more objective and trustworthy relics than historical documents, because they can more objectively reflect past human behavior and social structure. However, contemporary archaeologists do not simply regard an archaeological relic as a relic of "past facts" but as a series of ancient garbage generated by social and natural activities. All archaeological data potentially represent a cycle of four (ideally consecutive) stages of behavior: acquisition, manufacture, use, and deposition (Sharer and Ashmore 1987, 72–75). According to Wang (2001), bronze inscriptions of the Western Zhou Dynasty mainly reflected the social and historical memory that an aristocrat considered important and worth preserving in the political and social environment of the Western Zhou Dynasty. And pre-Qin literature was mainly about early Warring States and Han Dynasty people's memories of the Western Zhou Dynasty. Bronze materials are precious and time-consuming to produce, so only those who possess social power and resources can record their collective memory and support their advantageous social status. Therefore, as a kind of bronze inscription of social memory, its contemporary and social significance is produced in the process of "using". It is also strengthened and preserved in the memory of some dominant social groups under the operation and counterbalance of social power. Relatively speaking, other people's memories are lost or discarded. Of course, all of this does not mean that we should discard the evidence but that we should examine them again. On the one hand, historical research should be more careful to verify the authenticity of evidence. In this sense, Hu (2000, 10) argued that the way of textology is like a judge's judgment today. He sits in the court and listens to the lawyers of both sides present their evidence. He brings up his pen and declares that evidence of one side is insufficient and loses the lawsuit; evidence of the other side is sufficient and wins the lawsuit. His position is only to judge the ready-made evidence, and he cannot judge beyond the existing evidence. On the other hand, historical research should not be superstitious towards the known evidence but should look for "unusual cases", that is, to understand the resource allocation, competition background, the corresponding human social identity and discrimination system and power relationship when the evidence was produced (Wang 2001). For example, on

[6]See Intentional Homicide by Zuohai Zhao. http://www.pkulaw.cn/case/pfnl_a25051f3312b07f36fc427f7da394b487078f987098f23c5bdfb.html?keywords=%E8%B5%B5%E4%BD%9C%E6%B5%B7&match=Exact. Accessed December 16, 2019.

[7]See Guiding Case No. 25 from the Supreme People's Procuratorate of the people's Republic of China: Appeal by Yingsheng Yu.

July 14, 1789, the Bastille in France was captured, but the historical evidence left by the incident may be different due to different situations. Different people have made different records according to different angles.

In historical research, the investigation of historical evidence has no institutional regulations, so historians need to explore carefully according to different scenarios. Their work may begin by discovering the surface of an event, but it can never end there; they must always remember that the event was an action, and that their main task is to think themselves into this action, to discern the thought of its agent (Collingwood 1936, 25). This is instructive for solving the problem of "majority of evidence owned by one party". In the process of trial, one party will make use of superior resources and social power to produce evidence or memory that is beneficial to himself, while the other party's evidence and memory will be discarded. Therefore, the fact-finder needs to deal with the evidence in a situational way, and make a comprehensive judgment on the content of the evidence in combination with the situation of evidence acquisition. For example, the concept of "digital innocence" (Fairfield and Luna 2013) requires that all kinds of data information should be applied to prove innocence, not just guilt. The main consideration is that in the era of big data, the gap between the prosecution and the individual defendants in terms of their ability to access data has further increased. Evidence can be true or false, which is an important way to distinguish evidence from facts. This requires that all kinds of evidence be treated more rationally in judicial activities, with relevance rather than objectivity as the fundamental attribute of evidence (Zhang and Yang 2019).

4.2 The Feasibility of Historical Interpretation of Evidence Rules

Evidence law is a science that studies the rules of evidence and the rules and methods of fact-finding (Zhang 2018, 15). The rules of evidence, like other legal rules, require the judge to explain their meaning when necessary in the application process. However, in practice, due to (1) human cognitive defects; (2) the ambiguity of legal language; (3) the diversification of legal meanings in different contexts (Wei 2016), interpretation of legal rules will produce certain conflict. As Bentham (1823, 10–11) said that anyone who wants to discuss the law will inevitably become an Expositor or Censor. The task of Expositor is to show us what the law is. The task of Censor is to observe to us what law should be. Obviously, in the case of the above conflicts, history provides a reasonable way of historical interpretation.

For the evidence law, there is a certain time period between its generation and application. In this time period, it is likely that changes in technology, economic relations, social structures, social values and constitutions will raise questions about how the old rules apply in the new context. In order to solve this problem, it is necessary to analyze the context of the law and determine the normative content and normative purpose at the time that it first arose. This is historical interpretation (Rüthers

2003, 340). For example, in the judicial interpretation of Article 52 of the Criminal Procedure Law of the People's Republic of China, "nobody shall be forced to attest his own guilt", the purpose of the legislator at the time of the legislation may be explored. That would include (1) the need to prohibit torture to extract confessions, to prevent unjust and false convictions; (2) to strengthen the protection of judicial human rights; and (3) to implement the provisions of the International Covenant on Civil and Political Rights (Lang 2012, 116). Cardozo said that "history, in illuminating the past, illuminates the present, and in illuminating the present, illuminates the future" (Cardozo 1946, 53). However, with the deconstruction of historical interpretation by postmodernism, the crisis of historical interpretation appears in the scope of legal interpretation (Chen and Kong 2006). This kind of crisis has led people to gradually forget the significance of historical interpretation to law. The neglect of legislators will lead to a decline in respect for legal texts, then trigger a public credibility crisis (Liu 2010, 217). Therefore, reference to the historical interpretation method is of great significance for the improvement of evidence law.

First, historical interpretation can free judges from the imprisonment of text when applying the rules of evidence. With the rapid development of society, it is clearly impossible to adapt to the requirements of the times by relying only on text. Therefore, a mode of thinking of "flexible application in the spirit of the law" has gradually been accepted by people (Chen 2018). Historical interpretation is an important way for judges to be flexible. The reason is that an accurate history of the purpose of a law can often give a more reliable answer than a literal or textual interpretation (Rüthers 2003, 344).

Second, historical interpretation can set limits for judges' discretion and avoid their abuse of power. If the interpreter should not be allowed to interpret by himself, but should do so in a way that can be reviewed afterwards, we must provide some interpretation standards that can be used as criteria for the interpreter (Larenz 2004, 199–200). Thus, historical interpretation as a standard can limit the discretion of judges. For example, according to Article 56 of the Criminal Procedure Law of the People's Republic of China, where the material evidence or documentary evidence is obtained against the legally prescribed procedure, which may severely impair judicial impartiality, supplements and corrections or reasonable explanations shall be made; if the above-mentioned measures cannot be taken, the said evidence shall be excluded. In deciding whether to allow correction and whether to adopt the evidence after correction, there is a question of delimiting the boundary of the discretion of judges. It is necessary to restrict the discretion of judges through the method of historical interpretation: Historical interpretation raises a question for judges, that is, whether judges should understand the evaluation of legislation, or whether they can consider it necessary to violate the evaluation of legislation (Rüthers 2003, 344). Even when the judge finally decides to interpret beyond the standard of historical explanation, he must give a more convincing justification.

Finally, historical interpretation can increase the acceptability of judges and maintain social fairness and justice. The modern judicial system embodies the principle of democracy and realizes the transition from the "monologue" of inequality between subject and object to the "dialogue" of equality between subjects (Nie 2011). The essence of this "dialogue" trial is to increase the acceptability of the judgment. In the process of the interaction among the prosecution, the defense and the trial, the judge processes the evidentiary information of the prosecution and the defense. Through rational reasoning, the abstract probandum become specific facts clearly grasped in the subject's thinking (Zhang 2018, 59–60). As the fact-finder, the judge needs to provide reasons for the "cognitive achievements" of fact-finding. Historical interpretation provides a reasonable framework for the interpretation of the reasons for the fact-finding. The more different reasons that a legal decision or legal proposition can be supported, the less arbitrary, more rational, more definite, more predictable and acceptable the legal decision is (Wang 2009). Therefore, historical interpretation can not only increase the acceptability of the case results to the parties, it can also increase the identification of the society with the case results, thus enhancing the judicial public credibility.

5 Conclusion

From the perspective of interdisciplinary comparative research, studying the similarities and differences between the methods of fact-finding in evidence law and history is a form of evidence science research initiated by Professor Twining in the UK and Professor Schum in the US. The preliminary study of this article on this topic is only an attempt, but it has gained some results, for example, the understanding of the common research objects of history and evidence law (the accomplishment of historical facts and the probability of historical truth). Both history and the law of evidence are restricted by the "mirror of evidence" and challenged by the scientific and technological revolution. Of course, we also found that administration of justice and historical research are subject to different time constraints. Finality is of great significance to ensure the authority and credibility of justice, but the exploration of history is endless. They hold different attitudes towards hearsay. The principle of evidentiary adjudication requires that there must be a certain corroboration relationship between the factual premise and the judgment conclusion that has been proved by evidential reasoning, which inevitably requires a strict attitude against hearsay evidence. The probandum in historical studies are generally much older, so they have to rely on hearsay, even hearsay of hearsay. In order to distinguish the truth and falsity of the asserted matters in hearsay and avoid spreading false information, historical research has developed a Multi-Evidence Method to corroborate hearsay evidence. Finally, facts in the field of history lack the concept of materiality, and historical evidence analysis lacks the concept of admissibility, etc. Through interdisciplinary research, the mutual reference of history and law will provide new ideas for judicial problems and the application of historical explanation to judicial activities.

History must be illustrated by the laws, and the laws by history (Montesquieu 2001, 339). For historical fact-finding, in a sense, law and history are of the same origin, and it can even be said that history is the source of law (Wang 2003). Compared with history, historical fact-finding in the field of law is even more austere, as it also needs to be restricted by judicial justice and timeliness.

References

Allen, Ronald J. 2010. Relevancy and Admissibility. *Evidence Science* 3: 365–382.

Allen, Ronald J. 2011. Evidence and Inference/Probability and Plausibility. *Evidence Science* 1: 113–126.

Allen, Ronald J. 2014. The Nature of Juridical Proof. In *Professor Allen on Evidence*, vol. I, ed. Baosheng Zhang, 87–116. Beijing: China Renmin University Press.

Anderson, Terence, David Schum, and William Twining. 2005. *Analysis of Evidence.* Cambridge: Cambridge University Press.

Ban, Gu. 1962. *Han Shu.* Beijing: Zhonghua Book Company.

Becker, Carl Lotus. 1967. *Detachment and the Writing of History: Essays and Letters of Carl L. Becker*. New York: Cornell University Press.

Bentham, Jeremy. 1823. *A Fragment on Government.* London: E. Wilson.

Cardozo, Benjamin N. 1946. *The Nature of the Judicial Process.* New Naven: Yale University Press.

Chen, Xuequan. 2010. Scientific Treatment of Probative Force of DNA Evidence. *Tribune of Political Science and Law* 5: 50–61.

Chen, Jinzhao. 2018. How the Law Adjusts the Changing Society: An Interpretation of the Thinking Mode of Adhering to the Rules of Flexible Application in the Spirit of Law. *Tsinghua University Law Journal* 6: 79–93.

Chen, Jinzhao, and Guangning Kong. 2006. Crisis of "History" and Rebirth of "Meaning": Historical Methods (Factors) in Legal Interpretation. *Journal of Henan Administrative Institute of Politics and Law* 2: 95–104.

Cohen, L. Jonathan. 1986. *The Dialogue of Reason: An Analysis of Analytical Philosophy.* New York: Oxford University Press.

Collingwood, Robin George. 1936. *Human Nature and Human History*, vol. 22. New York: Ardent Media.

Damaška, Mirjan R. 1997. *Evidence Law Adrift*. New Haven, CT: Yale University Press.

Enserink, Martin. 2016. Evidence on Trial. *Science* 351: 1128–1129.

Fairfield, Joshua A.T., and Erik Luna. 2013. Digital Innocence. *Cornell Law Review* 99 (2013): 981–1076.

Fay, Brian. 1996. *Contemporary Philosophy of Social Science: A Multicultural Approach.* Oxford: Blackwell.

Garner Bryan, A. 2004. *Black's Law Dictionary.* St Paul: Thomson West.

Garrett, Brandon L. 2011. *Convicting the Innocent: Where Criminal Prosecutions Go Wrong.* Cambridge, MA: Harvard University Press.

Geary, Patrick J. 2016. Geneticists and Historians Need to Work Together on Using DNA to Explore the Past. *Nature* 533: 437–438.

Hu, Shi. 2000. *Scholarly Methods.* Liaoning: Liaoning People's Publishing House.

Hu, Shi. 2005. *The Oral Autobiography of Hu Shi.* Trans. Degang Tang. Anhui: Anhui Education Publishing House.

Hu, Shi. 2013. Research methods of the scholars in the Qing dynasty. In *Hu Shi's Selected Collection*, ed. Zhesheng Ouyang. Beijing: Peking University Press.

Huang, Hui. 2006. An Analysis of Foucault's Theory of Knowledge Archaeology. *Etudes Francaises* 2: 30–34.

Innocence Project. 2019. Overturning Wrongful Convictions Involving Misapplied Forensics. https://www.innocenceproject.org/causes/misapplication-forensic-science/. Accessed 3 July 2019.

Jin, Yuelin. 2011. *On Knowledge*, vol. II. Beijing: The Commercial Press.

Lang, Sheng. 2012. *Amendment and Application of the Criminal Procedure Law of the People's Republic of China*. Beijing: Xinhua Publishing House.

Larenz, Karl. 2004. *Methodology of Law*. Trans. Aie Chen. Beijing: The Commercial Press.

Liu, Jiahe. 1996. Comparative Study of History and History of the World. *Journal of Beijing Normal University (Social Science Edition)* 5: 46–51.

Liu, Yacong. 2010. *Fact and Explanation: Between History and Law*. Beijing: China Law Press.

Martin, Jean-Clément. 1998. La démarche historique face à la vérité judiciaire. Juges et historiens. *Droit et société* 38: 13–20.

McEwan, Jenny. 1992. *Evidence and the Adversarial Process: The Modern Law*. Cambridge, Ma.: Blackwell Publishers.

Montesquieu. 2001. *The Spirit of Laws*. Kitchener: Batoche Books.

Nie, Changjian. 2011. The Role Transformation of "Speaker" and "Listener": Procedural Thinking on the Acceptability of Judicial Judgment. *Tribune of Political Science and Law* 2: 95–104.

Peng, Yilian. 1996. *On Facts*. Guangxi: Guangxi Normal University Press.

Peng, Gang. 2010. Historical Facts and Historical Interpretation: A Survey in Light of 20th Century Western Historical Theories. *Journal of Beijing Normal University (Social Sciences)* 2: 47–55.

Posner, Richard A. 1993. *The Problems of Jurisprudence*. Cambridge, MA: Harvard University Press.

Radbruch, Gustav. 2012. *Rechtsphilosophie*. Trans. Jian Mi. Beijing: Law Press.

Rüthers, Bernd. 2003. *Rechtstheorie*. Trans. Xiaoding Chun and Yue Wu. Beijing: China Law Press.

Schmalleger, Frank. 1996. *Trial of the Century: People of the State of California vs. Orenthal James Simpson*. Upper Saddle River, NJ: Prentice Hall.

Schum, David. 2005. Thoughts About a Science of Evidence. http://128.40.111.250/evidence/projects/integrated/index.asp. Accessed 29 Dec 2015.

Sharer, Robert J., and Wendy Ashmore. 1987. *Archaeology: Discovering Our Past*. Mountain View, CA: Mayfield Publishing Co.

Shu, Weiguang. 1993. *The General Design of Scientific Epistemology*. Changchun: Jilin People's Publishing House.

Simon, Herbert A. 1973. Applying Information Technology to Organization Design. *Public Administration Review* 33: 268–278.

Starr, Douglas. 2016. When DNA is Lying. *Science* 351: 1133.

Thayer, James Bradley. 1898. *A Preliminary Treatise on Evidence at the Common Law*. Boston: Little, Brown & Co.

Toynbee, Arnold Joseph, and G.R. Urban. 1974. *Toynbee on Toynbee: A Conversation Between Arnold J. Toynbee and GR Urban*. New York: Oxford University Press.

Tribe, Laurence H. 1971. Trial by Mathematics: Precision and Ritual in the Legal Process. *Harvard Law Review* 6: 1329–1393.

Twining, William. 1985. *Theories of Evidence: Bentham & Wigmore*. Stanford, CA: Stanford University Press.

Twining, William. 2003. Evidence as a Multi-Disciplinary Subject. *Law, Probability and Risk* 2: 91–107.

Wang, Mingke. 2001. Historical Facts, Historical Memory and Historical Mentality. *Historical Research* 5: 136–147+191.

Wang, Hongzhi. 2003. On the Same Origin of Ancient Chinese History and Law. *Tribune of Political Science and Law* 2: 170.

Wang, Xiahao. 2009. The Justification Standard of Legal Decision or Judgment: From the Perspective of Legal Argument. *Legal Methodology* 8: 56–80.

Wei, Zhixun. 2016. Why Rule by Law Inevitably Calls for Legal Interpretation? *Seeking Truth* 6: 96–105.

White, Hoyden. 1995. Response to Arthur Marwick. *Journal of Contemporary History* 30: 233–246.

Xi, Yunshu. 2016. Hu Shi's Philosophical Methodology and its Source. *Tribune of Social Sciences* 6: 21–48.

Ye, Shuxian. 2009. A Methodological Criticism of Evidences Law in Chinese Academic Tradition and its Prospect—From the Method of One Way Evidence to the Method of Four Ways Evidences. *Evidence Science* 4: 389–404.

Yu, Wujin. 2008. Historical Facts and Objective Law. *Historical Research.* 1: 4–12+190.

Zhang, Hengjun. 2003. The Application of Wang Guowei's 'Bi-way Evidence' in Historical Research. *Economic and Social Development* 5: 152–154.

Zhang, Baosheng. 2018. *Evidence Law*. Beijing: China University of Political Science and Law Press.

Zhang, Baosheng, and Ping Yang. 2019. Criticism on the Objectivity of Evidence. *Tsinghua University Law Journal* 6: 1–34.

Facts and Proof: Concepts and Application

The Paradox of Proof: A Semiotic and Language-Based Critique

Clinton W. Francis

1 Introduction

The limits of our Modern system of judicial proof are being tested and evaluated. Critics, who question the adequacy of conventional models of juridical proof and the law-fact distinction, highlight a growing awareness of paradox in our Modern-based system.[1] Decisions regarding new forms of digital-based evidence submitted in trials show that our current courts and rules of evidence are struggling to accommodate emerging digital-based technology and social practice.[2] These emerging digital phenomena are also challenging transaction planning that is structured around proof based on written agreements. Advanced cyber systems, which test hypotheses embedded in algorithms against live feeds of information (as illustrated by developments in relation to online valuation networks, smart contracts, and block chain technology), offer a dynamic alternative to static written agreements. They promise more optimal social outcomes through greater transparency, context-sensitivity, and lower transaction costs, which expand the social conception of what is adequate proof beyond the limits of conventional legal understanding.

[1]For example, criticism of the law-fact distinction as indefensible describes the unstable nature of the distinction in terms that are consistent with the conclusion that this major structuring feature of the common-law legal system is a paradox. *See* Allen and Pardo (2003). Critical analysis of conventional theory of juridical proof reveals contradictions in the theory, which suggest it can also be viewed as paradox. For instance, the conventional theory separates the legally-defined elements and the potentially counterintuitive outcome that results when the probability of proof assigned each disaggregated element are combined seems reminiscent of the classic Zeno's paradox. *See* Allen (1993–1994).

[2]*See generally* Roth (2017), Sites (2018, 2014), Guo (2017) and Chin (2016).

C. W. Francis (✉)
School of Law, Northwestern University, Evanston, IL, USA
e-mail: cwfrancis@law.northwestern.edu

B. Zhang et al. (eds.), *A Dialogue Between Law and History*,
https://doi.org/10.1007/978-981-15-9685-8_3

The paper posits that a socially-optimal legal system needs to develop in parallel to the society it regulates and when a legal system's development fails to effectively reflect social progress, inefficiency and injustice results. It claims that a gap has grown between our current system of judicial proof and contemporary society, whereby the complexity of technology platforms and social networks in contemporary society exceed, at an accelerating rate, the complexity of the legal system which regulates it. The result is a misalignment of our Modern-based legal system with our social reality. A symptom of this is the growth of legal paradox within the evidentiary system, suboptimal trial outcomes, and the development of alternative systems of proof that operate outside of our conventional judicial model.

The proposed model uses semiotics and a theory of language development to provide an analytic of proof that roots these problems in the historical origins and limitations of our text-based judicial system. It further looks to our emerging digital-based society for solutions that mitigate paradox and produce more optimal social outcomes. The defining characteristic of the model is that it purports to legitimate itself through greater complexity, and therefore greater capacity to communicate, at a meta-level—meta-communication—about the contextual history of the underlying content communication.

The model interprets the development of law and proof within social history, and reflects upon the historical conditions and processes that influence this development. In so doing, it re-conceptualizes the identity, institutions, and legitimation of proof to align more effectively with the dramatic social changes in contemporary, Post-Modern society. This new conceptual framework provides the context to reduce the complexity gap between our current system of judicial proof and the contemporary society it regulates, in an attempt to decrease paradox, reconfigure trial practice, produce more socially optimal judicial outcomes, and expand our social conception of adequate proof.

2 Semiotic Model of Proof

From the semiotic perspective central to this paper, judicial trials can be interpreted as verification and validation of statements composed of a complex arrangement of signs designed to convince the arbiter of fact or law. Furthermore, it is claimed that this analysis can be extended to interpret proof outside the legal system. Semiotic analysis is not familiar to a legal audience, so it is useful to provide a brief description of the basic elements of a sign system, after which the paper applies them to an interpretation of proof, with a focus on judicial trials.[3]

---

[3] *See generally* Saussure (1986), Barthes (1994) and Eco (1979, 1984).

2.1 Evidence as Signs: Indexes, Icons, and Symbols

All signs involve "stand-for relationships", where a "signifier" stands for something—its "referent"—with an assigned meaning referred to as the "signified." For this reason, all signs are a form of evidence of their referent. Signs evolve in separate structures of differentiation and relationship ("networks") that are developed in the practice of their articulation ("statements"). To successfully operate as the basis for social communication, networks, and the characteristics and operation of their component symbols, have to be accepted as conventions whereby they become mutually recognized. When a statement is articulated, "signification" occurs, whereby a relationship of predication is created between a subject and its predicate, and thus meaning becomes possible—for example: "this is a breach of contract." Our social and economic exchanges are structured around complex statements which are synthesized into forms of narrative. The paper posits that this semiotic progression of language development leads to narrative constructions which form the basis of all evidence and its ultimate comprehension (Fig. 1).

Classical semiotics differentiates signs into three classes: indexes, icons, and symbols. All three types are routinely adduced as evidence in trials: fingerprints and signatures as examples of indexes; photos, maps and sound recordings as example of icons; and written texts and witness testimony as example of symbols. The signifiers in all three types of signs consist of a presented physical trace—the physical fingerprint, the photograph, the document, or the verbalizing witness. The types of signs differ based on the manner in which the signifier stands to its referent, measured along a continuum between "motivated" to "arbitrary."

Indexes are highly physical traces of, or pointers to, a specific referent and are accordingly described in semiotic analysis as "motivated" (Saussure 1986)—the relationship between the signifier and its referent is motivated because fingerprint

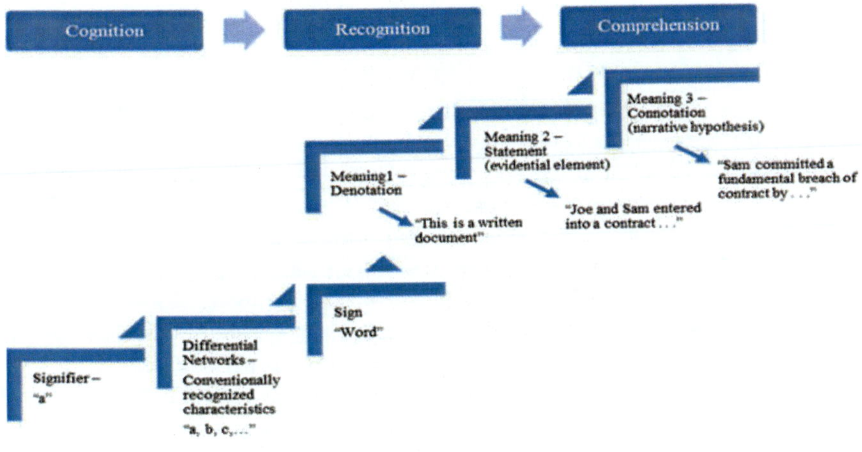

Fig. 1 Semiotic elements of communication

bears the mark of the person and provides a concrete basis for attribution to that person. The physical and motivated nature of indexes makes them relatively stable. While they may still be contested at trial or elsewhere, their relative stability makes them a fundamental element of all proof.

Icons are signs whose signifiers are depictions of their referent, for example, an image, map or sound recording, offered in evidence. While the physical nature of the signifier's depiction of its referent provides a stable base for examination, its verification and validation may be compromised because signifiers are not direct physical traces in the way indexes are, but are rendered by a person or machine acting as an intermediary between the signifier and its referent.

The statements of witnesses or proffered text are examples of symbols, the third type of sign. A symbol contains no indexical trace or iconic depiction—the word "man" bears no discernible relation to its referent and the corresponding term in Chinese is entirely different from its English translation. For this reason, a symbol is described as standing in an "arbitrary" relationship to its referent—it is not motivated by its referent. Unless there is an accompanying hand-written text, signature, voice recognition or the like to provide an indexical reference, symbol-based proof validation is accordingly negatively impacted by its lack of motivation. It is important to note, however, that while proof validation is a greater challenge for symbol-based evidence, it has a potentially much broader scope of context reference than that based in indexes or icons—for example, testimony can potentially address both time and space detail and emotive overlay. In contrast, indexical and iconic proof typically do not address the context in which the sign was created and largely offer only a discreet piece of evidence, which in the course of a trial will need to be supplemented by, and placed in relation to, other evidential signs.

2.2 The Semiotic Cycle

While the three types of signs differ in their semiotic structure, when viewed from the perspective of proof, it is proposed that discerning proof for all three involves the same process, which I explain in terms of a "Semiotic Cycle" model. In order for signs to operate as proof they have to be both verified and validated (and we require them to be so in all contexts, whether in trials or everyday occurrences). Verification is the first step in proof and requires confirmation that the proffered sign stands for a member of a class whose characteristics are conventionally defined—determining that the proffered sign is in fact a fingerprint, the image of a person, or a verbal statement, etc. This conventionally defined verification establishes the sign's "denotation." Denotation occurs prior to, and is indispensable in establishing, its later attribution to someone, something or an event. In the trial context, verification justifies admissibility if the denotation is relevant to the legally-defined cause of action. But this is far from establishing proof, which involves the additional step of validation. Validation requires confirmation of a proof hypothesis whereby the verified sign is attributed to a specific member of the class of referent—"this is the image of Jill." If the hypothesis is successfully proved this validates the specific meaning assigned to the proffered sign.[4]

In order to be verified and validated, each sign is processed through the Semiotic Cycle that can be analytically broken into three successive steps:

1. *Presentation*, which involves the proffering of a physical mark that is a potential trace of something; the sign signifier always has a presentational physical trace, whether it be an index, icon or symbol. For this step to be completed there has to be "cognition," and assuming the fact arbiter has normal cognitive function in most cases this is not controversial.
2. *Representation*, which involves recall of prior learning whereby the fact arbiter recognizes that the proffered sign denotes some *non-specific* member of a conventionally defined class of referent—"this is the video of a person," or "this is a financial record." When "recognition" occurs, the signifier is verified as a sign with conventional denotation. But the process of proof is not complete, because the sign has not been confirmed as standing for a specific member of the class—"this is a photo of the accused," or "this is a financial record of the defendant." Representation, and hence verification of the sign, will become problematic in circumstances where there is a dispute as to whether or not the presented trace is a sign, for example, whether the blurred image is a person, or the list of numbers is a financial record.
3. *Simulation*, which involves proving that the sign is attributable to a *specific* member in the context of a hypothesis—"this is the defendant's image, blood, fingerprint, signature, and it indicates ... etc." If positively validated, the specific assigned meaning is proved, the desired signification is complete and recognition matures to "comprehension." In this case, the meaning of the sign proceeds from denotation to the connotation attributed by the hypothesis (Fig. 2).

Simulation, the third step, involves comparison of the sign to its referent and is the most challenging aspect of proof. It requires validation of the proof hypothesis by testing the sign(s) to establish whether or not it is an accurate "index" of the "original", i.e., validation that the sign in fact points to the alleged referent. The sign—whether index, icon, or symbol-based—is tested by comparison with a sample of the alleged referent posited as the "original". For example, comparison of blood to sample presentation of the original, of a photo to a presentation of the original, of a signature to sample presentation of the original, or of testimony to the hypothesized event. This implies that adequate proof, no matter what type of sign it is based on, passes through all the steps in the posited Semiotic Cycle, from presentation to

[4]The concepts of verification and validation applied in the context of computer simulation provide some insights that are useful in understanding the proposed Semiotic Cycle. Computer simulation models are imitations of real-world systems, and their approximations are verified and validated to the degree needed for the models intended application. In this context, verification of the simulation model is conceptualized as a process of confirming that it is correctly implemented with respect to conventional specification and assumptions associated with the purpose of the conceptual model, and validation of the simulation is conceptualized as checking the accuracy of the model's representation of the real system. *See generally* Naylor and Finger (1967) and Banks et al. (2010).

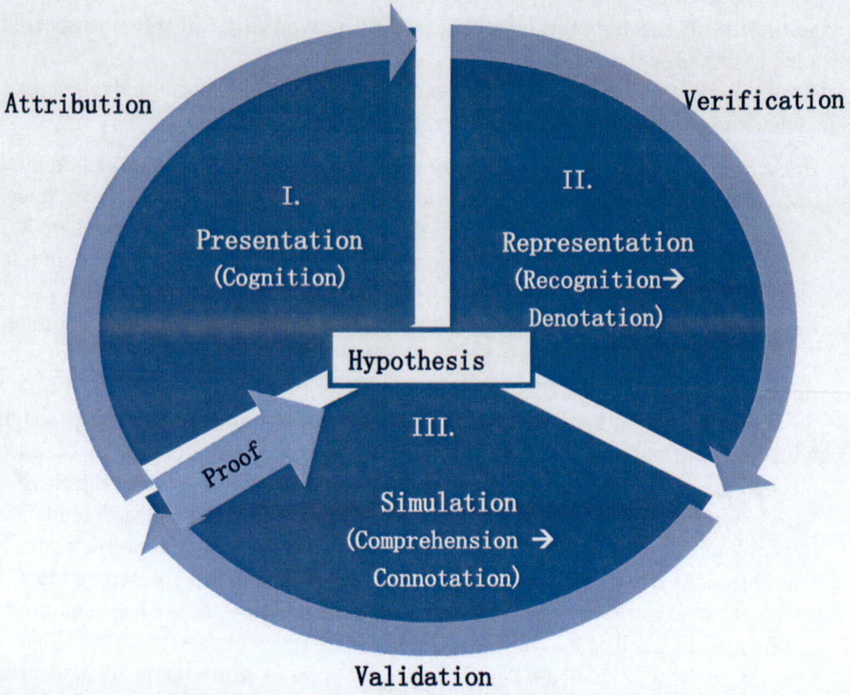

Fig. 2 The Semiotic Cycle

representation to simulation, and that in the final simulation stage it loops back to test itself at an indexical level. It underscores that indexes are the most primal and most provable element of signification and reflects the ontological reality that physical signs—indexes—are subject to the least chance of degradation and the highest level of scrutiny. (For this reason science focuses on indexes, using their stability to facilitate reproducibility as the basis of proof of its hypotheses, and accordingly, as a basis of legitimation.)

In the absence of corroborating witness testimony, witness statements offered in testimony are especially difficult to prove through comparison. Accordingly, additional techniques are used to determine whether witness testimony is a valid index of the original event it claims to stand for, for instance by checking witness testimony for consistency through cross examination. Another is to cross reference testimony to accompanying physical signs offered by the witness's body language—a process of layering of signs that can be used to bolster all forms of evidence.[5] Viewed from this perspective, the hearsay rule of evidence can perhaps be interpreted as designed to ensure the indexical integrity of testimony, by ensuring the close, presentational

[5] Often we rely on parallel sign processing that functions to confirm attribution to the same referent, and we adduce this evidence in trials to bolster proof. *See* Allen (1993–1994). For example, the movement of lips synchronous with verbal sound confirms the attribution to the speaker, a photo reinforcing a verbal statement, or a rating reinforcing a specific assigned value.

proximity of the witness to the referent, which is a defining characteristic of an index; accordingly, testimony from a witness who does not have a direct presentational relationship to the event but is separated by an intermediate representation is typically excluded.

Interpreted in terms of the Semiotic Cycle model, proof of the complex hypotheses typical of judicial trials involves a complicated interrelationship of iterative sequences of the model. A judicial trial normally requires proof of a number of elements placed in relationship to one another, and this requires complex proof starting with validation of discrete signs with discrete hypotheses—proof of the defendant's signature or specific action. The process then inevitably advances to the validation of a complex narrative-type hypothesis—that the defendant breached the contract, caused the harm, etc. We can conceptualize this as successive iterations of the Semiotic Cycle that progressively establish the elements and relationships that interact in increasingly complex layers. Successful validation at each iteration will tend to reinforce the preceding validations and support more comprehensive validation of progressively more complex hypotheses. This may involve the conjunctive proof of the attribution of commission, causation, and/or calibrated action to the defendant depending on the nature and complexity of the ultimate narrative hypothesis—for example, "the defendant moved the ladder which caused the fall, and the defendant's act was negligent behavior." Employed in this fashion, the Semiotic Cycle provides an interpretation of trials that serves as an alternative to conventional juridical theory, which conceptualizes fact finding as probability-based proof of disaggregated elements.

3 The Paradox of Proof

Any critique of our current legal system, and legitimation of a model that purports to discern a superior level of proof producing more socially-optimal outcomes, confronts the paradox of self-validation. It justifies its own value in teleological fashion because, similar to the current evidentiary system, it selectively filters evidence and frames the basic hypotheses to prove its own legitimacy. Such paradox is an inevitable feature of any system which hermetically creates its own identity and structure to legitimate itself. Our legal system and any model that critiques it—necessarily including the model and resulting critique presented in this paper—confronts this challenge. It is posited, however, that this inherent paradox can be mitigated by increasing the meta-communicative capacity of the critique or proposed model, whereby it increases self-awareness of the conditions that inform its articulation and increases the rigor of its self-legitimation.

The proposed analysis attempts to achieve greater meta-communicative capacity by means of the positioning of the Semiotic Cycle, outlined above, within a model of language development whereby the resulting semiotic analysis seeks to legitimize itself by testing its validation in the examination of its own history. All language systems use a semiotic foundation, so that use of language development as the basis for increased meta-communication harmonizes explanation of judicial proof and the social history that frames its development, and in the process helps address the integration of historical and judicial proof.

It is suggested that understanding the history of language development is central to understanding the increase in society's meta-communicative capacity. As society moves through the stages of language development, from *oral* to *written* to *digital*, at each stage an additional level of language code and translation is added, the earlier level being nested in the subsequent to form a dependent hierarchy of language—digital founded on written, which is founded on oral. Each new level represents the prior level(s)—a statement at the new level simultaneously represents both the general operational principles of the earlier level (often precociousness) and the specific reference it articulates (consciousness). Fluency in the new language level in practice requiring successively more complex translation from one level to the next, and with each new epistemic change the essential role of semiotics is brought closer to consciousness. It should be noted that the building of this dependent hierarchy through the successive layering of language codes that characterizes social development is further reproduced in individual human development, with, in normal development, the oral language capability preceding reading and writing, which precedes digital fluency.

The proposed model posits that meta-communicative capacity (and the associated theme of conscious realization of the fundamental function of semiotics) potentially increases with the addition of every new level, and necessarily results in a corresponding increase in language complexity. In the context of social development, as fluency in the new level of language spreads through the population it expresses itself in social practice which reinforces its effect. As the dependent hierarchy of language increases its complexity corresponding with the social development of a new level of language, the structure of signification is changed, and accordingly there is a change in epistemology that (re)sets the parameters of meaning.[6] Technology, politics, law, etc., are all transformed as derivatives of this change in meaning, and changes in these derivative forms form a feedback look with changes in social practice to reinforce the effect of the new language system at a cognitive and psychological level. This feedback helps actualize, in social and psychological practice, the increased meta-communicative capacity of the new language system. In the process, the lens through which people experience the world and the structure of value by which they assess it and themselves is radically reconfigured.

[6]The increase in system complexity associated with each evolutionary step creates a dependent hierarchy of language—digital founded on written, which is founded on oral, which is founded on genetic, which is founded on electro-chemical—with the creation of each successive system level being accompanied by a new, more complex language system that represents the system that preceded it. The notion of a dependent hierarchy of language helps us understand this complexity and its underlying meta-communicative capacity. It also helps us understand that the dependent hierarchy of language establishes an immutable direction of natural development for our world. The violation of this natural hierarchy, when for example we elevate society above nature, is arguably the source of some of the most profound and damaging paradoxes. Understanding this natural hierarchy helps navigate fundamental issues regarding framing of logical types and accordingly mitigate the paradox which is a symptom of the pathology associated with inversion of the nature-based hierarchy.

Use of a model of language development as the structuring heuristic of the proposed model receives support from the growing evidence (accepted in conventional material, biological and social science) of the central role that language performs in the evolutionary move from electro-chemical, to genetic, to social (and within the social from oral, to written, to digital) systems. As we embark on the challenge of creating an adequate interpretative model, I believe it is useful to consider that this challenge parallels that which is confronted in biology, i.e. modeling the relationship of the history of the individual organism to the history (ontogeny) of the evolution of a set of species (phylogeny). In the context of biology, notions of increased complexity are regularly used to address evolution and the relationship of ontogeny to ontology, and for this reason we may be able to borrow learning from this endeavor.[7] In order to help our application of this learning, it is useful to explore the possible equation of phylogeny to the evolution of social history (the different types of legal systems as "species" that punctuate this evolution) as related to equation of ontogeny to development of each specific type of legal system (viewing the developing characteristics of that particular legal system as a phenotypic expression of its specific ontogeny). These correlations can help us to position legal systems and their development within a larger framework that may better allow an evaluation of their effectiveness in practice (or, as in the case of biology, their ability to thrive or ultimately survive).

4 A Language Development Model

The proposed model based on language development incorporates the Semiotic Cycle, placing it in an evolutionary framework in order to interpret the effect of historical changes in epistemology on the system of judicial proof. As explained, the goal of the model is to reduce paradox in proof and increase the social optimality of proof outcomes using the evolution of language development to interpret changes in legal complexity and meta-communication. After elaborating the model, this section of the paper explores its application to the analysis of the historical development of proof, focusing in particular on our current controlling models of judicial proof (Fig. 3).

The model employs three levels—*language system*, *signification system*, and *historical phases*—and can be read either statically or dynamically.[8] From a static perspective, the levels form an analytic ladder, starting with language system progressing to historical phases, with each analytic level being a step upon which the

[7] *See generally* Bateson (1972, 1988) and Wilden (1972, 1987).

[8] This corresponds with the dual perspectives familiar to semiotic analysis: (1) paradigmatic, from which perspective the levels form static logical types each defining a class; and (2) syntagmatic, from which perspective the levels are viewed as the dynamic articulations of speech. *See* Saussure (1986).

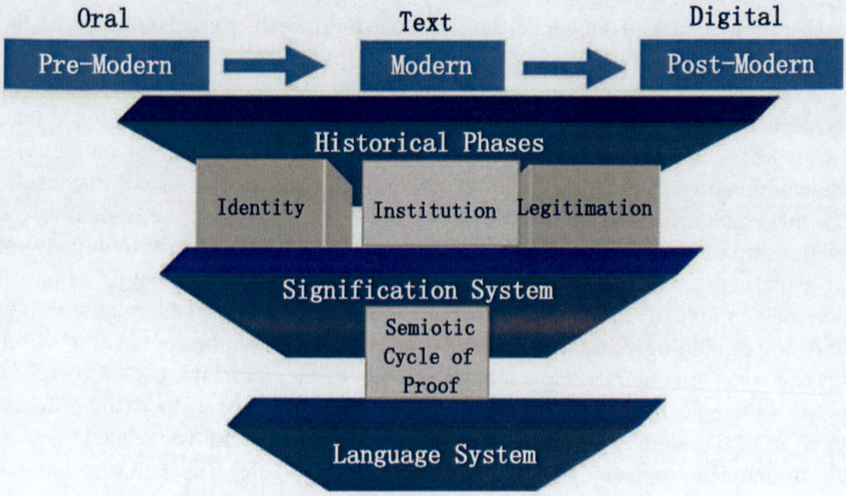

Fig. 3 Language development model

next level depends. From a dynamic perspective, the levels form a feedback loop, with the level above having feedback effects that impact the level(s) below.

The Language System level (bottom level) represents the basic semiotic function that underlies all language. In the context of proof this is characterized by the proposed Semiotic Cycle model, which is posited as the process of proof across all phases of history. While changes in the levels above result in the assembly of radically different types of social statements, the same semiotic elements involved in the Semiotic Cycle continue to be articulated, albeit in increasingly more complex form.

Signification System (middle level) describes the particular structure of conventional meaning (or epistemology) that accompanies the particular types of language system, as they evolve through history.[9] For the purposes of the language development model, we analyze this structure in terms of three variables: the identity the system provides itself ("*identity*"), the institutional form of its practice ("*institutions*"), and how it legitimates itself ("*legitimation*").

Historical Phases (top level) represents major social changes and is characterized by three broadly-defined social paradigms that punctuate the evolution of society, and in turn the context of law, which are labelled as: *Pre-Modern*, *Modern*, and *Post-Modern*. A radical innovation in language system presages the emergence of

[9]The Signification System middle level of the model can also be viewed in terms of narrative boundaries, which set "biases" Language System. These biases operate on the structure of predication of social statement through "principles of selection" and "principles of economics". The principles of selection operate in regard to the paradigmatic pole of language to define objects. The principles of economics operate in regard to the syntagmatic pole of language to define the relationships among objects. The complex predications that are compiled in the narrative statements are structured by these dual principles working through the poles of language. Together the principles set the bias on meaning whose structure is expressed in the identity, institutions, and legitimation of the social system and its derivative sub-systems.

each new historical phase, each successive system being a more complex system that builds upon the earlier one: the Pre-Modern is based on an oral language platform, the Modern is based on textual language, and the Post-Modern is based on digital language. An epistemic social change is represented at this third Historical Phases level by the movement of social history from one phase to another. This recalibrates the Signification System (middle level), which in turn recalibrates the Language System (lower level). The recalibration produces a discontinuity that privileges a new perspective, changing the signification system that controls meaning while expressing itself in transformed social identity, institution and legitimation.[10]

Implicit in the model are three important premises. The first premise is that a principal driver of historical change in epistemology is the evolution of language, which recalibrates the structure of the dominant social signification system—expressed as changes in the system's identity, institutions, and legitimation. The next premise, is that society frames its legal system, so that when the dominant language system of society experiences disruptive change the conditions exist for a corresponding epistemic change in the judicial system. Associated with this premise is the assumption that, while proof always involves passing through all three steps involved in the proposed Semiotic Cycle (presentation, representation, and simulation), the controlling system of proof associated with each of the historical phases privileges one of the successive steps involved in the cycle: the Pre-Modern, oral-based language system favors a presentational model of epistemology, which structures interpretation in terms of indexes; the Modern, text-based language system favors a representational model of epistemology, which structures interpretation in terms of icons; the Post-Modern digital-based language system, favors a simulation model of epistemology, which structures interpretation in terms of symbols. A further premise is that meta-communicative capacity is positively correlated with an increase in language complexity, and therefore increases with the social evolution of language. As the proposed model originates within the signification system associated with the Post-Modern, digital-based language, it claims to incorporate the greater meta-communicative capacity needed to justify its critique of the Modern, text-based legal system. This meta-communication is imperative to mitigate the paradox inherent in theory and to legitimate a framework that proposes a more socially-optimal system of proof.

The following sections analyze the changes in the system of judicial proof associated with each historical phase. They briefly describe the Pre-Modern, and focus principally on the Modern and the emerging Post-Modern.

[10]Each phase in the sequence is amply described by anthropologists and historians, and the exponential changes in meaning that accompany them is interpreted by Post-Modern writers. *See generally* Foucault (1966) and Baudrillard (1981, 1989).

5 The Pre-modern

The Pre-Modern phase in social history is defined by oral language as the dominant language system. During the Pre-Modern, oral-based proof was conceptualized in presentational terms, which collapsed all three stages of the Semiotic Cycle into a single, monadic expression that was presentational in effect. The world was understood in terms of indexes where objects and events were believed to carry their meaning on the face of themselves, with the features of their surface being interpreted as indexes linked by networks whose relationship to other objects and events was defined by surface similarity.

Proof was tested and judged based upon a view that all signs carried their own inherent meaning and therefore were self-validating. Trial by ordeal was the prototypic form, and apocryphal children were beaten to embed an enduring memory of an important event. Theory and practice merged, and the identity, institution, and legitimation that structured the system of signification converged into a tight nexus: the gods resided in all things and truth was immutable, the tribe was the dominant institutional form, judgment was legitimated by charisma, and the social networks that mediated the process of proof were based on the qualities of the person rooted in blood-line inheritance and close familial relationships of the community.

6 The Modern

The Modern phase, which framed the development of our current system of judicial proof, is text-based. Text was revolutionary in that it allowed society to represent the world in symbolic depictions (signs) allowing a departure from face-to-face communication. Once social conventions were established regarding symbol-based signs, the possibility of expert-controlled discourse arose to refine their meaning.[11]

6.1 Textual Representation and the Subject-Object Dyad

Early in the Modern phase, René Descartes explained Modern epistemology in terms of a central opposition of subject and object, whereby the subject is an observer (possessed of consciousness and unique personal experience) and an object is an a priori thing, or entity that exists outside the observer. While the philosophic merit of the opposition has been subsequently much debated, the opposition is arguably an accurate empirical description of how Modern representation operated and for this reason it haunts Modern philosophy to the present day.

[11] The units of measure could be alpha, numeric, or possibly other types of symbols, the relationships among which create a set of distinctions that can be used to "map" the referent they describe or measure.

From the perspective of the present semiotic and language analysis, the Cartesian subject-object opposition was a projection of the limitations which text's symbol-based statements placed on Modern meaning. Far from being a neutral and transparent form of language, Modern text-based representation filtered its content in the image of its own semiotic structure and within the limits of the conception of time and space that it projected. It reproduced the disembodiment of meaning associated with the disembodying movement of language from the oral speaker to the text as an *opposition*, which it imbued in the very interpretations it rendered regarding any subject matter. The explanation which Modern philosophy provided did not identify the semiotic origin of the opposition; it focused on the philosophic merits of the opposition while ignoring that the "opposition" was an empirically accuracy description of the meaning generated by use of text-based language. From the perspective of the present analysis, the subject-object opposition is an empirically accurate description of the structure of Modern meaning. However, rather than the origins of the opposition lying in indelible philosophic truth, it is a construct that projects the semiotic identity of text representation onto the world it represents.

Whereas in Pre-Modern society the world was viewed in terms of indexes that were essentially one-dimensional pointing in a specific direction, by way of contrast, in Modern society the world was constructed in terms of icons that were two-dimensional. These icons added a sense of distance or depth into representation, which was noticeably missing from the Pre-Modern. But they lacked an inherent sense of time—in particular, the historical contingency of the meaning these representations rendered and of the temporal feedback relationship between text-based signs and the world they stood for.

In the Pre-Modern there was only one level of semiotic code translation involved in recognition—oral language. In the Modern, a second level of code translation was inserted—text language—which augmented the coding of oral language allowing an increase in dimensionality. The subject-object opposition posed a paradox, whereby in the abstraction of Modern philosophy the identity given to meaning was a recapitulation of the text-based, representational, semiotic process. Expressed from a more practical perspective, text representation allowed the observer to stand outside its referent and represent it in icon-based models. Indeed, the subject-object opposition was an iconic representation of the very relationship it projected—the "object" being the subject matter of representation and the "subject" being the observer standing separate from the subject matter. Textual representations projected this opposition onto the world representing it in inherently iconic form. Absent from the icon-based models that characterized the Modern was an understanding of the effect of a language system's operation on the model it represents. An understanding that was to become implicit in the epistemology of simulation that followed in the Post-Modern—the effect of language complexification on meaning, the disruptive effect of an increase in complexity accompanying the historical emergence of an additional level of language, the link between increased language complexity and growth in meta-communication, and the feedback between language articulation and the world it models.

Our current, Modern-based legal system is a creature of the world of text representation that expresses itself in forms that are derivative of the semiotic structure of icon-based representation, and is accordingly largely blind to the effect of the effect of this on its operation. It reproduces the subject-object opposition within itself, and as a consequence within its system of judicial proof. As a result, the identity, institutions, and legitimation of the Modern system of judicial proof are premised upon a series of oppositions that are derivative of the subject-object opposition. From this perspective, the "law-fact" opposition, which reserves issues of law for the judge and the appellant court, is a derivative that structures Modern legal identity. Centralization, which places authority outside litigants (and associated with this, bureaucratization, which separates person from position), is a derivative that structures Modern legal institutions. The concept of a qualified legal professional, which separates lawyer and judge from lay person, is a derivative that structures the legitimation of the legal profession and judiciary (and simultaneously places in question the legitimacy of the lay jury which stands in opposition to, or other than, the figure of judicial authority).

Text-based representation and its expression in these subject-object derivatives—legal phenomena with no inherent sense of their own history, and of the history and effect of the language development that enabled them—control all aspects of the Modern-based system of judicial proof. Trials occur inside the established centralized institutions whose constitution is memorialized in text. Judicial proceedings are commenced through pleadings that are typically written. Rules derived from textual sources define the elements that need to be proved, and the admissibility and relevance of evidence adduced to prove them. Proceedings are managed by formally appointed judges who use the law-fact distinction to regulate the jury. The testing of the legal professionals who have the exclusive right to practice law and expert witnesses who are privileged to provide testimony, prioritizes text-evidenced and text-structured learning as the basis for their qualification. Appellant review is based on the judicial record rendered in text. Transaction planning focuses on text and looks to text-recorded legal statutes and precedent for guidance in interpretation. In other words, the very structure of the Modern-based system of judicial proof is built on text and its expression in the associated subject-object derivatives that define its identity, institutions, and legitimation.

6.2 The Manifestation of Paradox in the Modern: The Law-Fact Dyad and the Conventional Theory of Juridical Proof

From the perspective posited in this paper, paradox is more than a logical contradiction; it is a statement or experience with artificially collapsed levels of history—the statement or experience contradicts the historical conditions that enable or verify the statement. Logical analysis examines paradox from an ahistorical perspective characteristic of the Modern, with the result that paradox is amenable to identification and description, but arguably never outright explanation. Following from the historical language-development view of the paper, paradoxes such as those exemplified in the operation of Modern legal system are amenable to explanation when they are seen as signs of the limits of a system's capacity to meta-communicate about its relation to its own historical framework.[12]

The structuring of our Modern system of judicial proof around a text-based, subject-object dyad creates the conditions for paradox. The textual foundation of, and the projection of derivative forms of the associated subject-object dyad within, the identity, institutions, and legitimation of the judicial system, limits the system's understanding of its contingent position within history and of the underlying evolution of language.[13] So long as the Modern text-based signification system dominates larger society, the expression of its derivative subject-object dyad within the legal system has empirical merit; the two-level code of text semiotics which controls legal

---

[12]Paradox ensues when there is an inversion of natural and historical dependencies because the member contradicts its membership in its class. An inversion occurs, and paradox results, when something is, or announces itself, at one level as a member of a class upon which it depends, but at another level defies the class definition and the rules of construction of the class.

"This statement is untrue" is a simple illustration of how a paradox can be produced by a logical inversion of a natural, dependent hierarchy, in this case an inversion of the natural, dependent hierarchy that is traced by the history of language. The statement is paradoxical in that it contradicts its implicit truth claims as a meaningful utterance. At one level the statement uses conventional syntax and word denotation to produce a grammatically correct statement. At another level, the resulting a self-referential meaning undermines the very conventions and historical development of the syntax and denotation that precede it and upon which it depends. The paradox accordingly results because the statement defies the very social conventions of language that support, and developmentally precede, its truth claims.

Paradoxes are thus the symptoms of a process of logical typing that, when applied to classifications of the world, potentially subvert the dependence of the human subject on a hierarchy laid down by a developmental sequence—a dependent hierarchy in which the lower levels (nature) developmentally precede the higher levels (human culture). The potential for inversion is realized when the dependent hierarchy becomes represented in a classification that constructs a hierarchy of logical types that runs in the opposite direction to the dependent hierarchy. The criticisms leveled against the controversial theory of intelligent design, for example, seem to be implicitly based on the argument that the theory performs such an inversion—the natural world is explained by the theory as the product of human-like intelligence and this, the critics argue, contradicts the Darwinian-based idea that natural world evolutionarily precedes human culture.

See Francis (2009).

[13]The Modern-based legal system struggles to position its own development within social history that structures it—to position its ontology within the phylogeny that frames it. (Indeed the versions of original-intent debate that plague Modern legal systems suggests it cannot even satisfactorily position itself inside its own development, i.e. it cannot position its phenotypic characteristics within its ontology.) As a corollary of this, the Modern-based legal system exhibits limited self-awareness of the industrial-aged origins of the institutions and text-based technology that serve as its foundation. It moves painfully slowly to try to adapt to change and often applauds its conservative nature as a basis of legitimation. Its ideological and structural inability to position itself within history arguably limits its theory and practice, and in turn shackles the capability of the society it regulates. A symptom of this is acceleration of paradox and suboptimal outcomes.

meaning resonates with the social practice it structures. However, once this text-based system is no longer controlling and the larger society changes, the inherent paradox represented by the legal system becomes more apparent.

Viewing Modern proof in these semiotic and historical terms arguably brings a different perspective to bear on the features of the Modern system of judicial proof and the current debates that surround it, and helps elucidate the source of the paradoxes within the system that are now being identified by critics. Much has been recently written about the relationship of determinations of law and fact, and there is a strong academic critique that challenges the distinction and describes it in terms that are consistent with paradox; close analysis has led commentators to conclude that the processes involved in trials of law and trials of fact strongly resemble one another, and this has fueled their conclusion that the law-fact distinction is not defensible in theory or practice (Allen and Pardo 2003).

But what the critiques fail to explain is why understanding of this similarity is defied by the entrenched judicial practices that persist in their allegiance to the law-and-fact paradox. From the perspective of this paper, the two forms of trials—law and fact—are indeed similar, because they both involve articulation of the same Semiotic Cycle. However, the persistent allegiance is explained because they are, projections of the subject-object opposition inherent in the text-based epistemology of the Modern judicial system. This not only limits legal cognition, but furthermore has become strategically leveraged by the legal profession and its politico-economic beneficiaries. From this strategic perspective, the resulting derivative forms—and central to these is the law-fact distinction—have become indelibly fixed within the design of the Modern legal system for its own strategic purposes stemming from concurrent definitions of identity, institutions, and legitimation.

The similarity between trials of law and fact should accordingly not obscure understanding of why allegiance to the difference persists—and this understanding risks getting lost for the purposes of this paper if a semiotic and language-development perspective is not maintained. Analyzed in semiotic terms, while the internal processes associated with hearings on issues of law and trials of fact are similar, they are opposed for a reason. Their opposition is arguably as an expression of text semiotics, i.e. "law" stands to "fact" as a text-based signifier stands to its referent. This relationship, we have seen, is mirrored in the subject-object dyad that is projected across the identity, institutions, and legitimation of the Modern system of judicial proof, and it is this relationship that is reproduced in the law-fact opposition. The hierarchical relationship whereby trials of issues of law stand above those of fact recapitulates this phenomenon and, it is posited, is accordingly a projection of text semiotics and mirrors the relationship of the observer-subject to their observed object.

Legal history research shows that the law-fact opposition and associated derivatives was seized as the basis of hegemonic control and that their strategic and practical usefulness served as a feedback to accelerate expanded allegiance to the text paradigm and its associated subject-object dyad. Early-Modern political systems used the law-fact distinction and centralization as the instrument of control and a growing culture of experts exploited the system, using it for personal gain and legitimation. For example, the central, English common law courts in the sixteenth through nineteenth centuries were led by a judiciary, backed by the legal profession, which used this text-based hegemony to design a system that controlled a huge volume of litigation using a small judicial body (Francis 1983, 1986). Central to this system was the formal divide of issues of law and fact, and the procedural separation of the two. Cases were initiated using a highly formalized system of text-based, formal pleadings, which were required to reduce the case to a single, certain issue of either law or fact. The pleading process was rigorously monitored by the courts, with all issues of law and procedure reserved for the central courts *en banc*. Only issues of fact were sent to the jury, with less than five or six percent ever reaching this level—the bulk of the cases being settled before trial due to rapidly spiraling court costs (that on average ran to around five times the amount at stake) and fear of procedural demur based on a matter of technical pleading.[14]

The analysis proposed in this paper arguably also brings a new perspective to the current debate regarding the justification for the conventional theory of juridical proof, which similar to the law-fact critique is been characterized by commentators as replete with paradox. In particular, the conventional theory separates the legally-defined elements and critics have characterized the potentially counterintuitive outcome that results when the probability of proof assigned each disaggregated element are combined in terms that are as reminiscent of the classic Zeno's paradox (Allen 1993–1994). Close testing of the theoretical rigor and practical reality of trials of fact have led the same critics to conclude that the current system of judicial proof can best be described using a bifurcated model of "structure of proof" and "theory of evidence". Accepting this conclusion, it may be valuable to consider whether this bifurcation is another manifestation of the two paradox-like faces of language—semantic and syntactic—and therefore provides further confirmation of the semiotic underpinnings of the system of proof.

The Semiotic Cycle provides a model of trials that is alternative to that offered by the conventional theory, and in the process purports to resolve the paradox inherent in the theory. The Modern, conventional model of juridical proof conceptualizes trial outcomes as disaggregated proof of the separate elements of the legally defined cause of action, each assessed according to the required level of probability. Alternatively, the Post-Modern-based, Semiotic Cycle model conceptualizes trials as an iterative simulation with aggregate, feedback-supported proof of an expanding hypothesis. Complex proof involves iteration of the Semiotic Cycle, where the hypothesis expands to a narrative-like statement that maps the elements and their relationship as prescribed in the substantive law that defines the cause of action—for example, the elements and relationships in a negligence or fraud action. With each iteration a new sign is offered in evidence and placed in relation to earlier evidence in the context

[14] An interesting evidential control on the central common law experience is provided by the practice and history of the English Court of Equity. While Equity was centralized and text-based similar to the common law courts, it used a system of interrogatories to regulates its proceedings in place of the common law system of pleadings. As a result, Equity litigation developed into giant rambling narratives where, in marked contrast to common law proceedings, the boundary between law and fact was ill-defined. I argue elsewhere that this developed because judicial control was differently defined as a type of "market differentiation" relative to the common law. *See* Francis (1986).

of the evolving hypothesis. Successive iteration creates a cumulative valuation, such that growing success in proof of the expanding hypothesis can feed back to bolster successful proof at an earlier stage, leading the adjudicator of fact to conclude, for example, "in view of all the evidence, I believe it was the defendant at the scene of the crime". Therefore, in the Modern, representational model, it is the *evidence* that is proved, whereas in terms of the proposed Post-Modern, simulation model, it is the *hypothesis* (the sign with its attributed characteristics) that is proved.

6.3 The Growth in Textual Literacy and the Rise of the Expert

Viewing our Modern system of judicial proof through the lens of the proposed model may also provide a new perspective on the elevated status and role our system affords experts. Historically, the Modern emphasis on experts appeared in the vacuum left by the displacement of oral society. Growth in textual literacy accelerated the breakdown of familial cultures and defined the Modern era by allowing transactions to be represented outside the time and space boundaries of the local community. Social anonymity followed in the wake of this, and the expert appeared (generally across society, and in the context of trials as the expert witness) to synthetically draw connections and interpretations amongst dissolving traditional social networks of proof. In place of the network of face-to-face, presentational relationships that characterized legitimation in the Pre-Modern, there appeared networks of experts whose legitimation was based on heavily text-dependent formal training and certification. Recognition always involves learning—you learn the signification associated with a specific denotation and recall it in the act of recognition. However, text reconfigured the learning process a phenomenon especially evident in relation to all aspects of the identity, institutions, and legitimation of the Modern system of judicial proof.[15] Text allowed the learning that defines the legal profession and the experts admitted into trials of fact to be formally structured and controlled using text.

The privilege afforded to text representation, and the strategic leverage of vested politico-economic interests that feed back to support this, arguably impedes the Modern legal system's ability to assimilate the notion of digital-based networks and expert systems that have emerged in Post-Modern society. The Modern system of judicial proof does not think in terms of networks of information and expert systems: rather, it thinks in terms of writings and experts. Our Modern-based system projects this thinking onto trials to question the admissibility of proffered evidence generated by these new systems, often referred to as "machine evidence". The resulting decisions slow the development of new methods of proof that harness the potential

[15]This development was foreshadowed in the early text-based societies of classical Greek and Roman times.

of these innovative digital-based systems, causing the information economy to be shackled by the service economy.[16]

6.4 *The Impact of Documentary Evidence on Transaction Planning*

The text-based underpinnings of our Modern-based system of judicial proof, has also profoundly affected how proof has been traditionally handled in ex ante transaction planning where the parties are concerned about future proof, the prototypic example being planning of enterprises, transfers, investments, or asset dispositions. From its inception, the Modern legal system was amenable to documentary evidence—physical documents were accepted in evidence and the attached signatures provided index-based validation. This made Modern courts a useful companion to social change; written agreements and dispositions operated in anonymous environments allowing memory to extend beyond the face-to-face networks of local communities, and the growth of Modern commerce and industry relied on them, with networks of experts soon appearing to draft, attest, and interpret the documents.

From the perspective of transaction planning, the evidentiary emphasis on the documentation of transactions dramatically affects the time and space dimensional reach of the information assessed during the planning process, by forcing the past and future to be compressed within the document and all terms to be fixed at the specific date of signing. Representation clauses contained in agreements attempt to pull the past into the present, warranty clauses attempt to project the present into

---

[16]Despite evidentiary gatekeepers (such as the rule against hearsay), certain types of financial information and financial expert testimony have found their way into the courtroom. For example, to admit financial records courts have relied on the business records exception to the rule against hearsay, which is embodied in Rule 803 of the Federal Rules of Evidence. *See* United States Code Service Federal Rules Evidence. R. 803; *See also* In re WorldCom, Inc. Sec. Litig., 2005 U.S. Dist. LEXIS 2215, *19 (S.D.N.Y. February 17, 2005), Kwestel (1999).

With the increase in complex financial documents entering the courtroom, courts began to allow financial experts to testify as expert witnesses. *See* Dionne et al. (2018), Hopkins et al. (2010) and Hill et al. (2009). *See also* California v. Sutter Health Sys., 130 F. Supp. 2d 1109 (N.D. Cal. 2001) (financial expert testified as to defendant's accounts receivable); Steiner Elec. Co. v. Maniscalco, 2016 51 N.E.3d 45, 54 (financial expert testified as to the value of a customer list); In re Commercial Fin. Servs., Inc., 350 B.R. 520, 529 (Bankr. N.D. Okla. 2005) (discussing the qualifications of a financial expert).

However, while initially courts were more lenient on admitting financial expert witnesses, as opposed to being stricter on other types of expert witnesses (medical, engineering, etc.), there has been a push to heighten the standards for when a financial expert should be allowed to testify. *See* Adrogue and Ratliff (2000) and Lloyd (2007).

Furthermore, when confronted with advances in data analytics and machine automation, courts have struggled with the issue of whether machine generated testimony (such as analytics of a company's internal controls) should be admissible in a court of law, and as such have demonstrated unwillingness to allow this type of evidence. *See* Roth (2017) and Sites (2014, 2018).

See generally supra note 2.

the future, and covenants attempt to constrain the future. No matter how tightly a document is drafted, the time-space reach of the document is fallible given the limits of textual determinism and the parties' foreseeability. But so long as text is the primary and most advanced language technology used for transaction planning, the limits of documentary evidence are unavoidable, and the capacity of the Modern-based system of judicial proof is not put into question.

Accompanying the development of documentary evidence law was the development of Modern substantive law principles whose use in transaction planning was largely contingent on written agreements. Contract law developed to elaborate the principles applicable to agreements containing all types of subject matter, where the early appearance of Statutes of Fraud confirmed the importance of written proof. Property law developed to turn valuable assets into protectable "objects", with writings forming the principal form of recording property ownership and serving as the required form of substantiating evidence. Importantly, property could be transferred by contract (via contract sale, license, mortgage, easement, etc.), and as a result contract and property law developed in parallel with, and reinforcing, one another to become the principal vehicles for transaction planning of allocation of risk, financial return, and control. With the growth in number of asset classes, both tangible and intangible, the reach of contract and property extended deep into society.

From a semiotic perspective the development of contract and property law was highly correlated with growth in the language platform of text. They operated as the fundamental elements of symbolic, text-based predication—contract standing to property as verb to noun—and their incorporation in documented agreements permitted the drafting of complex allocative statements. Further, within this perspective, corporate law—which arrived as a mid-Modern development—allowed for the textual creation of artificial or virtual entities whose signatory and ownership rights qualify them to make these statements. This represented another shift away from Pre-Modern society, whereby the virtual corporation stands to an individual as text does to oral, being both disembodied and more complex than its referent. While these substantive law developments were not the direct products of the Modern system of proof, the amenability of their documented form into the Modern system of judicial proof emphatically bolstered their legal development and use in practice.

6.5 Credit Bureaus as a Foreshadowing of the Future

The Modern system of judicial proof facilitates the use of text-based networks of contracts and property to stand in place of face-to-face networks of proof that broke down in the anonymity of the growing urban and industrial society. But the suitability of these writings to handle the new types of networks that break the tradition of text representation is questionable, and their sub-optimal adaptation foreshadows a more overtly simulation-oriented system.

Starting in the mid-nineteenth century and growing rapidly in the twentieth century was the appearance of credit bureaus whose writings recorded the reports of creditors concerning the payment history of their debtors, which were used as the basis for creditors' future decisions regarding creditworthiness. Their growth revolutionized the credit industry and transformed the landscape of litigation.[17] Before the development of credit bureaus, credit-collection cases accounted for the vast bulk of cases filed in court, but during the course of the twentieth century, the number of credit-collection lawsuits plummeted, largely attributed to the expansion of credit bureaus. While increase in the use of written contracts and possible improvements in the Modern judicial system may have contributed to this dramatic change in the profile of court dockets, it was evidently principally driven by the development of the credit bureaus as a new form of proof that operated in a new type of verifiable network beyond the courts. Not only was this innovation outside the epistemology and imagination of the Modern system of judicial proof, but the evidence also it produced was largely excluded because of the hearsay rule, which had developed based on assumptions regarding face-to-face social networks.

The credit bureau experience highlighted the limits of Modern judicial proof and anticipated the rise of new systems of proof. It pointed to the possibility that the expansion of such systems of proof could be the driver for new types of social networks with a new approach to proof—networks that might spawn new methodologies for transaction planning that would non-plus our traditional notions of contract, property and corporate law. The discussion in the following section of the emerging Post-Modern, digital-based era elaborates this topic.

7 The Post-modern

7.1 Digital Language, Triadic Thinking, and Computer Embodiment: Meta-Communication, Simulation, and the Semiotic Cycle

The appearance of digital language produced a triadic language system that has re-characterized our society, spawning new approaches to proof and transaction planning that are challenging the effectiveness of our Modern-based judicial system. Digital language represents and supersedes text language, translating the levels of oral and textual language upon which it depends. The computer developed as a

[17]For example, in the English common law courts around 95% of cases filed in the hundred years before the mid-nineteenth century were credit collection suits. Further, in the first year of operation of the English County Courts in 1844 their dockets were completed dominated by credit-collection lawsuits, with around 500,000 initially filed, growing to one million by the end of the century. *See* Francis (1986).

technologic derivative of this new three-level system of language, with its architecture and operational structure similarly exhibiting a three-level structure—hardware, middleware (operating system), and software—arranged in a dependent hierarchy.

The triadic form of digital language and its derivative technological expression in the use of computers was not an accidental innovation. These innovations were the expression of nascent triadic thinking that arose during the course of the Modern era and which allowed for new meta-communicative thinking that brought history into interpretation. Signs of triadic thinking appeared on many fronts. For example: in Modern research within the work of Darwin, Marx, Freud, Einstein, Eisenberg, and Crick, to name a few; in commerce as demonstrated by the twentieth-century growth in credit bureaus; and in technology evidenced by early electric-based systems of communication that developed express code functions to represent and facilitate telephonic and later telegraphic communications. All of these innovations involved nesting representation in history—of society, biology, physics, commerce, and technology. As the Modern epistemology began to exhaust itself, it produced a growing paradox and suboptimal outcome, and this type of triadic thinking appeared as a reaction to the conventional dyadic epistemology, arguably propelled by both the practical need and curiosity for resolution of the associated contradictions.[18]

The embodiment of digital language in computers gives automated expression to the inherently meta-communicative power of the new triadic language system. It allows information about the translation of content code to be simultaneously represented in parallel meta-code, and its automated-machine quality not only facilitates these translations but also simultaneously represents them in meta-statements. Text-based representation, in comparison, possesses a very limited capacity to record the history of the code translations involved in its production; the "scrivener" of hardcopy is unable to stand outside himself to record the context of his transcription at the time he performs it. The hardcopy document can be manually dated and signed, and if the document is subsequently physically transferred it can be endorsed by its transferor to provide a record of the transfer, but this is the limit of its meta-communicative capacity.

Computers provide a platform with exponentially greater meta-communicative capacity, and after the launch of the internet, which places computers in a network relationship with one another, gives new effect to the meta-communicative potential of the digital language system. This in turn spawns social applications where communications can record and prove the history of their content and thereby become the basis for proving attribution to individual people and validation of their history—think of a simple email whose meta-text allows recording attribution to a particular author/sender and details of the time and space context simultaneously with the communication. The reconfiguration of the social identity, institutions, and legitimation of proof (examined below) that accompany the emergence of the Post-Modern

[18] Paradox and suboptimal outcomes are symptoms of epistemological exhaustion that are not unique to the Modern. They accompanied the decline of the Pre-Modern and will arguably reappear when the current Post-Modern runs its course. However, paradox has different manifestations across the historical phases, and their current manifestation are specific to our Modern-based system of judicial proof.

are arguably an outgrowth of the advancement in attribution of information propelled by this new level of meta-communication.

The development of digital language, embodied in cyber-based technology, moves epistemology from representation to simulation, and the nature of how the world is modelled from icon to symbol. It provides the platform for socio-information networks that offer an exponentially greater time-space reach, detail and accessibility. This allows expression in theory and practice of the role of simulation and the Semiotic Cycle in relation to social proof. This includes:

- Internet-based user and product rating systems that provide community-subscribed, alpha-numeric indices of past performance as a digital-expression of the network-based systems of proof pioneered by credit bureaus, for example, eBay, Uber and Yelp;
- Open-system, product development networks that provide digital-based rating networks as a replacement for text-based certification of expertise, for example, the Linux operating system where developers freely contribute attributed code and where they achieve reputation status based on their code's quality and functionality; and
- Block-chain technology that provides validation of asset transfers in otherwise anonymous markets as a digital-based, algorithmic substitute for proliferated and inefficient government filings or large, institution-based financial or commodity exchanges.

7.2 *Disruptive Change in the Identity, Institutions, and Legitimation of Proof*

The shift from representation to simulation, and the corresponding increase in meta-communicative capacity driven by digital language, reconfigures the system of signification, manifesting itself in disruptive changes in the structure of the identity, institutions, and legitimation of proof (Fig. 4).

7.2.1 Post-modern Identity of Proof

Identity is based upon how proof is conceptualized, and in the Post-Modern people begin to comprehend proof in terms that are amenable to the proposed Semiotic Cycle. They theorize proof, not as representations that are icons of that which they stand for, but in terms of more complex simulations that are symbol-based models that feedback on their referent. Arguably proof always has to pass through all stages of the Semiotic Cycle and this has been the process across all phases of the history of society. Once the signs offered in evidence are verified in the representation stage (and are recognized in terms of the conventional paradigms of denotation), their proof passes to the simulation stage where the sign is placed in a hypothesis which is tested

	Identity	Institutions	Legitimation
Pre-Modern (Oral)	• Presentation • Monadic • Immutable truth • God(s) in everything	• Tribe • Person → position	• Blood-line inheritance and close familial inheritance • Charisma
Modern (Text)	• Representation • Dyadic • Law-fact opposition • Issues of law reserved for judiciary	• Centralization • Person separated from position • Proof outside litigants	• Qualified judiciary and professionals • Expert witnesses • Judiciary and professionals separated from lay • Documentary evidence reinforced by contract, property, and corporate law
Post-Modern (Digital)	• Simulation • Triadic • Semiotic Cycle and History of Language brought to consciousness	• Distributed networks built on digital platforms • User and developer-based certification	• Algorithms with live feeds of data • Networks validate integrity of algorithms and channels of information • Contract out of legal system process and substantive law

Fig. 4 Disruptive change in the identity, institutions, and legitimation of proof

and judged—"this fingerprint does/does not stand for the defendant". The hypothesis invariably involves attribution of the sign to someone or something and successful proof involves a simulation wherein validity of the hypothesis is tested by comparing the sign to the original referent to which it is attributed, with the comparison test being fundamentally indexical in nature—for example, do the characteristics of the sign placed in evidence "point" to the defendant? If the comparison of the sign to the original is affirmative the hypothesis is validated and proof is successful.

But only in the Post-Modern are the conditions ripe for the Semiotic Cycle to move from unconscious or pre-conscious, to conscious operation. The protocols of verification and validation used in digital development map the very process of the Cycle, and our contemporary experience of growing social use of digital-based platforms and networks are arguably signs of conscious understanding of this. The technology of simulation is increasingly being brought to bear on all aspects of our lives. Accompanying this there appears to be a recognition that proof operates like simulation within which representation and presentation are nested as earlier steps in its three-stage process. Representation dominated Modern epistemology, where proof operated like an icon standing passively outside that which it modelled with no explicit recognition that this proof actively altered the reality it stood for. However, the Post Modern is accompanied by a growing recognition that proof operate in a feedback relationship with its referent—the hypothesis-based simulation and the referent it models being both semiotic in nature and by virtue of this co-exist in inseparable communication with one another.

The Semiotic Cycle that is expressing itself in an expansion of the social conception of adequate proof, holds the potential to change conventional trial theory and practice. It offers a re-conceptualization of proof and how it is handled in trial practice: of evidence in terms of semiotics; of proof as a Semiotic Cycle in which the elements of a hypothesis are assembled in presentation, verified in representation, and validated in simulation; of the role of attribution, which cycles back to indexical evidence within the simulation process; and of trials as iteration of the Semiotic Cycle.

How this potential might manifest itself in trial practice is unclear and the topic extends beyond the scope and expertise of this paper. However, possible directions of change include understanding: of evidence in terms of their operation as indexes, icons or symbols to enhance understanding of their semiotic operation and effectiveness; of the difference between verification and validation, and the roles of cognition, recognition and comprehension; of the need for careful structuring of the hypothesis of proof in anticipation of its validation in simulation; of the role of attribution in simulation and the fundamental nature of indexical proof in establishing this; of trials as iterative validation of complex hypotheses; of the narrative nature of these hypotheses and the possible use of different tropic form in their construction[19]; and of the role of proof in the context of discrediting "fake news" and checking false acusations.[20]

---

[19]Exploration of the use of different tropic form to categorize trial narratives is beyond the scope of this paper. However, a possible direction for research would involve examination of the correlation of the different semiotic forms of evidence with the different forms of trope—the principal types being metonymy, synecdoche, and metaphor. One possible hypothesis is that indexes, icons, and symbols correspond with the narrative use of metonymy, synecdoche, and metaphor respectively. Another possible hypothesis is that the epistemology of the Pre-Modern, Modern, and Post-Modern, correspond with the dominant use of metonymy, synecdoche, and metaphor respectively.

[20]Interpretation in terms of the Semiotic Cycle that holds the potential to change conventional trial theory and practice, also holds the potential to change how we view proof in our larger politico-economic society. Viewed in terms of this emerging perspective, the phenomenon of "fake news" that circulates in the contemporary can be seen as presaging conscious recognition of this semiotic interpretation. However, in contemporary society where the social interpretation of mass media communication is still strongly invested in the Modern epistemology, there is cause for concern regarding the motives surrounding this phenomenon. In particular, there is manipulation associated not only with the creation of fake news, but also with the false allegations of fake news, both of which can be skillfully used to fabricate or discredit proof and create dangerous feedback cycles within public sentiment.

7.2.2 Post-modern Institutions of Proof

The structure of the institutions of proof have begun to change dramatically with the emergence of the Post-Modern, in parallel to the changes in the identity of proof. Centralization of proof in judicial institutions is the norm of the Modern. The Modern courts claim a monopoly on judicial enforcement, and assemble themselves in pyramid fashion around a ladder of appeals, the law-fact distinction is used by the judiciary (and the legislature) to exercise hegemony over the lay jury and lower level courts, documentary evidence is the principal form of ex ante transactional proof, and expert testimony is privileged. With the emergence of the Post-Modern, there are signs of a growing awareness that proof is no longer the exclusive domain of the judicial system but is increasingly moving away from centralized institutions, becoming distributed across networks built on digital platforms. Running parallel to this, the preeminence of documentary evidence is gradually being challenged by the appearance of block chain-type systems where complex algorithms check the veracity of asset transactions across networks of encrypted exchanges. Furthermore, the status and role afforded experts is being threatened by digital-based expert systems.

7.2.3 Post-modern Legitimation of Proof

The structure of legitimation of proof has also begun to change in the Post-Modern. Legitimation based on a culture of experts and officially certified documents, wherein networks of legal and other experts are used to validate law, facts and judicial process, is pervasive in the Modern-based legal system. In the Post-Modern, network-based systems, structured with varying degrees of openness that assess users, producers, and products, develop as alternative systems of proof whose legitimacy rivals the culture of experts. Further, as an economy of information increasingly develops (separate from the economies of goods and services), the value of information, its principle of selection and assessment, and its channel of communication is tested in digital networks. These networks of exchange, which validate information by checking the integrity of algorithms that organize it and verifying the channels that carry it, increasingly serve as alternative systems of proof whose legitimacy rivals documentary evidence.

7.3 Dynamic Transaction Planning and Re-conceptualizing the Boundaries of Proof

The emergent changes in the Post-Modern system of proof have potentially far-reaching effects on transaction planning and the accompanying principles of substantive law. Innovative application of digital technology to transaction planning allows the parties to progressively move proof outside our judicial system in the interests of greater transparency, information integrity, and lower transaction costs compared with use of written agreements and ex post litigation. As a result our notions of the boundary of our legal system are being re-conceptualized, and the concept of an adequate system of proof is no longer being equated with written text and judicial trials.

Simultaneously, the limits of our Modern-based system of judicial proof are being tested as demonstrated by its difficulty in accommodating these new practices. Alternative forms of transaction planning built around digital-based, expert systems have begun to challenge the Modern nexus of written agreements and substantive law. As discussed above, the Modern substantive law used to guide ex ante transaction planning was arguably reinforced by the status afforded to textual documentary evidence in the representation-oriented system of judicial proof. Contract, property and corporate law developed around the use of the written agreement as the primary form of proof of transactions, and the resulting text forced transactions to be compressed in time and space into the form of a two-dimensional representation fixed at a specific date. In place of this system of transaction planning based on text-based representation, the parties involved in transactions have begun to use overtly simulation-oriented systems, whose form resonates with the Post-Modern change in proof. Instead of compressing a transaction into the static language of an agreement executed at a set date, the new, innovative system moves the focus of planning to formulation of algorithms that dynamically regulate the parties' allocation of future risk, reward, and control based on live feeds of information. The role of representations, warranties, and covenants is progressively reduced in favor of channels of information whose content maps onto and is tested relative to the hypothesis expressed in an automated, underlying algorithm. Thus proof begins to be transformed in a new, real-time system of transparency.

The sub-optimal nature of Modern principles of proof and substantive law is highlighted by a growing trend for parties to contract outside of the judicial system, using systems of alternative dispute resolution and sophisticated smart contracts that create alternatives to the mechanisms provided by classic Modern-based commercial, corporate, and bankruptcy laws. These new systems overcome static predication, in which contract, property, corporate and other elements of text-based statements are replaced by systems of dynamic predication that produce fluid systems of allocation whereby the transaction context is repeatedly tested against an algorithmic hypothesis. In the process, social conceptions of time and space are reconfigured and the conditions for new levels of transparency arise, where proof is rooted in expert-system simulations that articulate a simulation matrix of digital-based platforms and networks.

The resulting digital-based innovations have made changes in relation to the fundamental role of index-based proof in simulations by using technologically advanced systems to increase the capacity to attribute the source of the information that feeds the simulation. These attribution systems include identity validation based on biometric indicators for human users, RFID-type trackers for goods, and standardized-data formats that facilitate system harmonization and carry meta-statements that attribute authorship and locational source, which can be tested against deep archives that record and assess historical performance. The systems bring the power of Post-Modern digital technology to bear on the attribution imperative that is central to the process of hypothesis validation within the simulation-stage of the iterative Semiotic Cycle. The result is a system of integrated networks that represent transaction history using simulations that embody an implicit understanding of the operation of the Semiotic Cycle. This in turn advances a meta-communicative understanding of the role of the Post-Modern as the triadic phase in a history driven by language development.

7.4 *Testing the Limits of Evidence*

Modern rules of evidence that show initial signs of sensitivity to the semiotic underpinnings of proof and the operation of the Semiotic Cycle are now ironically blocking innovation of more semiotic-informed approaches to evidence. In the context of the above explanation of the Semiotic Cycle, important examples of Modern rules were characterized as symptoms of a nascent sensitivity to the semiotic underpinnings of proof. These examples exhibit this sensitivity by virtue of their recognition of index-based testing and of hypothesis formation which the Semiotic Cycle describes as fundamental to the simulation stage, and relates to the need for rendering hypotheses in a form that makes them amenable to discrete iterations of the Semiotic Cycle. We saw that the hearsay rule excludes testimony that was not based on direct, index-rich, face-to-face presentation. The character-judgment rule, which excludes testimony that is characterized by a particularly error-prone subjective assessment, is a further exemplification of this idea. While the narrative rule excludes testimony that tends to dilute the narrative, it exemplifies recognition of the importance of hypothesis formation and testing in judicial trials. Collectively these examples attempt to validate witness testimony or assimilate it to the Modern system of proof, by excluding signs that: stand distant from their referent, reference networks that cannot be validated, or are not amenable to hypothesis validation of because of their compound or rambling nature.

In ironic fashion, it is these very Modern-era legal rules of evidence that are now blocking the developments of digital-based solutions to the limitations they were originally intended to address; they evolved in pragmatic response to challenges confronted in regard to verification of proof, but because they were not articulated with consciousness of their semiotic ramifications they have arguably confronted the limits of their understanding. New digital networks provide a powerful index of the veracity of a witness by creating more transparency regarding a witness's past behavior and their community reputation as a better predictor of the validity of their testimony. The advanced networks accomplish this objective by validating character through social networks and by recording financial, social, and indexical narrative-based hypotheses through their greater surveillance and complexity. But the Modern-based rules of evidence are resisting the probative value of many of these advanced, technological statements. In this respect these rules actively work to frustrate Post-Modern innovation in the system of proof.

8 Conclusion

The paper proposes a model that interprets judicial proof in terms of a Semiotic Cycle and the evolution of language in historical phases in order to help unravel the paradoxes that have appeared in our current, text-based system of judicial proof and to provide the framework for evaluating associated evidence outcomes. The model assumes that a major change in the dominant social system of language is a disruptive event that generates and propels a new historical phase that tests the then-current, socially constructed legal system's adaptive suitability in terms of social alignment. It views the rise of digital language as such a disruptive event, and accordingly looks to emerging Post-Modern, digital-based, innovations as the basis for social regulation that expands proof and validation beyond the bounds of our current, Modern-based judicial system.

The use of semiotics and language development is justified as the foundation of the model on the assumption that they encode societal identity, institutions and legitimation, and provide an ever-present, common denominator throughout the phases of social history. In the context of the development of the Modern system of judicial proof, the controlling, text-based signification system expressed itself in identity, institutions and legitimation in ways that were adaptive to the conditions of industrial society. But with the advent of Post-Modern, digital-based society, a complexity gap has appeared between the Modern system of judicial proof and the underlying social context. The result is a misalignment of law and society. This misalignment is evident in growing awareness of paradox in academic discourse, increasing signs of a decline in adaptive suitability of our Modern-based system of judicial proof, and accelerating technological change that expands the concept of proof beyond the exclusive domain of our judiciary and their static rules of evidence.

In order to substantiate its interpretation, the proposed model confronts the paradox of proof whereby the principle in question controls its own judgment, i.e., definition of the hypothesis to be tested, selection of the evidence that is proffered in its defense, and the process of its validation. Viewed in terms of the Semiotic Cycle, when an idea judges itself and thereby evaluates its own legitimacy, it controls every aspect of the cycle as it engages in its self-judgment. The model proposes to mitigate paradox and increase optimal social outcomes by increasing meta-communication. It attempts to accomplish this by ensuring that whenever an issue is presented for judgment, information depicting the historical conditions impacting its interpretation are carried simultaneously as a meta-statement. This mirrors the way digital systems attach descriptive meta-tags to content in order to document the history of this content.

The proposed Semiotic Cycle views evidence as proffered signs, and trials as verification of these signs and validation of the hypothesis they are posited to prove.

Verification tests signs relative to the conventional denotation they are alleged to represent, and validation tests the sign-based hypothesis relative to the plausible narrative it is alleged to simulate. Proof of complex hypotheses involves multiple iterations of this Semiotic Cycle, each of which tests hypothesis plausibility in a process the privileges index-based signs. It is suggested that analysis of trials in terms of the Semiotic Cycle may shed new light on trial practice and provide the framework for future research that could have positive implications for practice and theory of judicial trials. Further, when the Semiotic Cycle is examined in the context of the history of language development, it points to changes in the social concept of adequate proof that marks a significant departure from the Modern-based system of judicial proof. This is illustrated in the emergence of innovative, digital-based social networks that facilitate simulations by assigning and attributing value to information at the same time as communicating its content. Understanding this departure and the historical evolution of proof provides a perspective that can perhaps reform the laws of evidence that will allow our current system to better accommodate new forms of evidence, thereby better promoting the socially optimal outcomes they promise.

Finally, use of powerful algorithms within these digital-based social networks provides new platforms for transaction planning that can expand beyond the limits of written agreements, which confine allocations of future reward, risk, and control to the compressed time and space of textual representation. These new platforms offer the possibility of more transparent, context-sensitive and real-time transaction planning at lower cost. Their algorithms express hypotheses, agreed by the parties, which define live feeds of information to provide feedback validation of the hypotheses. The resulting automated simulation of the agreed transaction plan is a conscious expression of the Semiotic Cycle, which expands the concept of socially-adequate proof beyond the exclusive bounds of our judicial system. Further, the practice of contractually opting out of adherence to our current judicial system—its substantive laws as well as its trial procedures—that is accompanying use of these innovative, digital-based transaction-planning platforms, suggests that the contract, property and corporate legal principles that subsequently developed relying upon the evidential status afforded written agreements are declining in importance.

References

Adrogue, Sofia, and Allan Ratliff. 2000. Kicking the Tire After Kumho: The Bottom Line on Admitting Financial Expert Testimony. *Houston Law Review* 37: 431.

Allen, Ronald. 1993–1994. Factual Ambiguity and a Theory of Evidence. *Northwestern University Law Review* 88: 604–640+616+626.

Allen, Ronald, and Michael Pardo. 2003. The Myth of the Law-Fact Distinction. *Northwestern University Law Review* 97: 1769–1807.

Banks, Jerry, John S. Carson, Barry L. Nelson, and David M. Nicol. 2010. *Discrete-Event System Simulation.* London: Pearson Education.

Barthes, Roland. 1994. *The Semiotic Challenge.* Trans. R. Howard. Berkeley: University of California Press.

Bateson, Gregory. 1972. *Steps to an Ecology of Mind*. Chicago: University of Chicago Press.
Bateson, Gregory. 1988. *Mind and Nature: A Necessary Unity*. Broadway: Random House Publishing Group.
Baudrillard, Jean. 1981. *For a Critique of the Political Economy of the Sign*. Trans. C. Levin. St Louis: Telos Press.
Baudrillard, Jean. 1989. *From Marxism to Postmodernism and Beyond*. Trans. D. Keller. Stanford: Stanford Press.
Ching, James. 2016. *Is Blockchain Evidence Inadmissible Hearsay?* http://www.law.com/sites/jamesching/2016/01/07/is-blockchain-evidence-inadmissible-hearsay. Accessed 29 Aug 2019.
Dionne, Paul, et al. 2018. The Role of the Corporate Finance Expert in Debt-Equity Litigation: Lessons From. *Journal of Taxation* 128: 24, WL 1666390.
Eco, Umberto. 1979. *A Theory of Semiotics*. Bloomington: Indiana University Press.
Eco, Umberto. 1984. *The Role of the Reader: Explorations in the Semiotic of Texts*. Bloomington: Indiana University Press.
Foucault, Michel. 1966. *The Order of Things: An Archaeology of the Human Sciences* (1971 ed.). New York: Pantheon Books.
Francis, Clinton. 1986. Practice, Strategy, and Institution: Debt-Collection in the English Common-Law Courts, 1740–1840. *Northwestern University Law Review* 83: 807–955+847.
Francis, Clinton. 2009. Language System 3.0: An Agenda for a Model of Innovation Valuation. *The Role of Intellectual Property Rights in Biotechnology Innovation*, ed. David Castle, 178–201. Cheltenham: Edward Edgar Publishing.
Francis, Clinton. 1983. The Structure of Judicial Administration and the Development of Contract Law in Seventeenth-Century England. *Columbia Law Review* 83: 35–137.
Guo, Angela. 2017. Blockchain Receipts: Patentability and Admissibility in Court. *Chicago-Kent Journal of Intellectual Property* 16: 440–452.
Hill, John W., et al. 2009. Increasing Complexity and Partisanship in Business Damages Expert Testimony: The Need for a Modified Trial Regime in Quantification of Damages. *University Pennsylvania Journal of Business Law* 11: 297.
Hopkins, Sheryl L, et al. 2010. Corporate Governance: An Expert can Make a Difference in Litigation. *New York State Business Journal*.
Kwestel, Sidney. 1999. The Business Records Exception to the Hearsay Rule—New is Not Necessarily Better. *Missouri Law Review* 64: 595.
Lloyd, Robert M. 2007. Proving Lost Profits After Daubert: Five Questions Every Court Should Ask Before Admitting Expert Testimony. *University of Richmond Law Review* 41: 379.
Naylor, Thomas H., and J.M. Finger. 1967. Verification of Computer Simulation Models. *Management Science* 14: 92–107.
Roth, Andrea. 2017. Machine Testimony. *Yale Law Review* 126: 1972–2053.
Saussure, Ferdinand. 1986. *Course in General Linguistics*. Trans. R. Harris. Chicago: Open Court Classics.
Sites, Brian. 2014. Rise of the Machines: Machine-Generated Data and the Confrontation Clause. *Columbia Science and Technology Review* 16: 36–102.
Sites, Brian. 2018. Machines Ascendant: Robots and the Rules of Evidence. *Georgia Law Technology Review* 3: 1–27.
Wilden, Anthony. 1972. *System and Struct Structure: Essays in Communication and Exchange*. Abingdon: Routledge.
Wilden, Anthony. 1987. *The Rules are No Game*. Londres and New York: Routledge & Kegan Paul.

Facts, Evidence and Proof: The Core Concepts of Law and History

Guoying Shu and Xuguang Song

1 Introduction: Analogy Between Law and History

Law (mainly evidence law) shares many common concepts and ideas with history, and has similar methodological bases. First, "facts", "evidence", "proof" and other concepts "are the key words of historians and judges" (Ginzburg 1991, 79); second, the core concern of law and history lies in the proof or inference. There are many similarities between the rule of evidence in law and the rule of textual research in history (Zhang and Sun 2010, 122); third, both evidence law and history involve the exploration of what happened in the past, so they will encounter similar problems. For example, can we discover the truth of the past? If so, how can we find such a truth? How can we be sure that we have discovered the truth? If not, does it mean that the facts are not objective, but a subjective "construction", so it will inevitably be affected by the subjective judgment (even prejudice or intentional fabrication) of the subject? These issues will form the core of this paper.

2 The Concept of "Fact" in Law and History

Both evidence law and history focus on the past. In this regard, there is no difference between legal facts and historical facts, but there are some differences between them in many specific features.

G. Shu (✉)
China University of Political Science and Law, Beijing, China
e-mail: shuguoying@263.net

X. Song
Shenzhen University Law School, Shenzhen, China

B. Zhang et al. (eds.), *A Dialogue Between Law and History*,
https://doi.org/10.1007/978-981-15-9685-8_4

2.1 Similarity Between Legal Facts and Historical Facts

There is always a dispute between "objective facts" and "legal facts" in the law community. The former refers to the objective natural facts, while the latter refers to the facts evaluated and identified by law. Similarly, some historians believe that "historical facts" should be distinguished from "objective facts". The former is a subjective fact and a relative fact (Zhang and Sun 2010, 124).

First of all, two things need to be distinguished: First, the objective facts that are supposed to exist in the past are "what actually happened at a particular time and place" (Allen 1993, 622); second, in the sense of epistemology, fact is "the conscious extraction and collection of the situation or things in the external world made by the cognitive subject by using special cognitive means.... It's people who 'tear it off' from the matrix of the world" (Chen 2017, 31). Although there may be controversy about the past, and deviations from the truth, existence of objective facts cannot be denied. Historical facts are first presupposed as a state of a real event or object that has happened in the past, and it must be based on truth. Legal fact-finders must also presuppose an objective fact that has actually occurred. The "case facts" are presupposed to be acts or events that have actually occurred, and the legal norms should be evaluated as such a fact (Shu and Song 2018, 43, 45, 47, 49, 50).

Secondly, as for the task of historians, some people think that it is mainly to restore or discover the objective truth, which has at least two presuppositions: first, the past can be rediscovered or restored; second, in the process of discovering historical facts, historians can achieve complete value neutrality (Peng 2010, 47–48). But these two conditions are difficult to realize. Historians cannot go back to the past, but can only reconstruct or reproduce the past in various ways, which cannot be completely objective and cannot get rid of the subject's perspective and limitations. Some people also think that since it is impossible to trace back to the past and reconstruction cannot be objective, the inevitable conclusion is that human beings cannot understand the past at all, but only some subjective ideas (Peng 2010, 48), which leads to relativism. There are also similar arguments in law. Some people think that fact finding must be committed to finding objective facts; others think that facts are facts recognized by the court. In fact, the pursuit of truth is only an ideal dimension, not an inevitable requirement under unideal conditions. Subject to the lack of evidence and limited rationality, fact-finders cannot be completely determined that the "fact" that is ultimately identified is the completely unchangeable truth. "The past is, by definition, a datum which nothing in the future will change" (Bloch 1953, 58). '"Truth" may be "truth," but that's no guarantee that a court will find it' (Steiner-Dillon 2020).

2.2 The Difference Between Legal Facts and Historical Facts

First of all, historical facts are usually related to major events with specific political, social and military significance, and often record the deeds of great historical figures, which are relative to the state and the nation; legal facts are often related to individuals, in theory, and all individuals can become the subject of legal acts, while usually the state cannot become the subject of litigation (Ginzburg 1991, 86).

Second, historical facts span a longer time than legal facts. Because of the length of time, it is not so important to explore the details. What historians need to confirm is often the context of major events. Unlike the foregoing, due to the limitation of prescription of action and so on, cases appearing in court are often recent acts or events, and the specific circumstances of the cases are very important for the judgment.

Third, students in the early years of law school know that not all the facts of life, but only those events or behaviors that have legal significance can be dealt with by the law. Moreover, the determination of factual circumstances also depends on the constituent requirements of legal norms. For example, to prove the fact that Zhang San intentionally killed Li Si, the court needs to determine not only whether Zhang San killed Li Si, whether he killed intentionally or by mistake, but it needs to be determined whether he killed deliberately or passionately, what motivation existed, what means or tools were used, when and where the incident happened, and Zhang San's responsibility capacity (such as age, mental state, etc.) and whether he had other justifications (self-defense, emergency avoidance, etc.).

In addition, law and history often need to evaluate facts. The biggest difference may be that legal issues and factual issues are intertwined, and legal evaluation will affect the determination of the facts of the case itself. In addition, sometimes there are some evaluation elements or words in the elements of legal facts, such as "malicious collusion", "public order and good customs", "honest credit", etc. It cannot be determined without value judgment whether the specific facts of the case correspond to the corresponding fact paradigm; but logically, only when the historical facts are confirmed can there be historical evaluation, and historical evaluation cannot affect historical facts; at most, it can only affect the choice between different historical narratives. For example, whether Fei Yue and Tianxiang Wen are "national heroes" (a kind of historical evaluation) may be different in different periods and in the eyes of different historians, but the historical investigation of Fei Yue and Tianxiang Wen must be aimed at seeking truth.

Finally, the identification of legal facts is often accompanied by the impact on substantive rights, which is essentially an action with some practical consequences, but the identification of historical facts is only a decision (Twining 2006, 253), unless a specific subject takes other actions with practical consequences on the basis of this decision. For example, when the court finds that the fact of Zhang San's intentional killing is true, the corresponding legal consequences will follow.

2.3 *Facts and Stories: What Can Law Learn from History?*

The past has become history, and it can only reappear in the present time and space in the form of stories. As the historian Keith Jenkins said: "that the world/the past comes to us always already as stories and that we cannot get out of these stories (narratives) to check if they correspond to the real world/past, because these 'always already' narratives constitute 'reality'" (Jenkins 1991, 11). Such stories may come from historians' assumptions, from the dictation of some direct witnesses, or just some legends. Therefore, sometimes there are different versions of the story about the same person or the same event. For example, the story about the "Three Emperors and Five Emperors" has different versions.

In fact, in a lawsuit, the facts of a case appear in the form of "telling stories" (narratives) at first (Zhang 2017, 114), which often come from the narrations of the litigants or witnesses. Sometimes, the integrity and authenticity of the story may be more important than the inference of the evidence. For example, studies have shown that "American juries determine 'the truth' about alleged past events mainly by constructing and comparing stories rather than critically evaluating arguments from evidence" (Twining 2006, 336). The story will be true or false as well as right or wrong. Both law and history have developed a set of theories and methods to solve such uncertainty.

In the judicial process, when the quality of a story is good and it is properly supported by the existing evidence, we can conclude that the story is true (Verheij and Bex 2008, 76). Therefore, the truth of this story can also be refuted from three aspects: first, the quality of the story (i.e., it is incomplete, inconsistent, and the causal relationship is not clear); second, the appropriateness and relevance of the evidence (i.e., the evidence is forged or incomplete, or the evidence is inadequate to support the relevant conclusions); third, the legality of the procedure (i.e., the acquisition of evidence is illegal, and the procedure for the fact finding is illegal).

3 The Concept of "Evidence" in Law and History

Many people point out that there is much contrast between the use of evidence in law and history.[1] In this regard, the work of historians is similar to that of the judges of the court in the first instance: they all need to carefully determine the authenticity of the story according to the evidence materials. To a certain extent, the determination of facts is actually a process of seeking the best interpretation based on evidence (Zhang 2017, 128–129).

3.1 Similarity Between Judicial Evidence and Historical Evidence

First of all, many kinds of evidence are universal, such as direct evidence and indirect evidence, documentary evidence and non-documentary evidence (Collingwood

[1]For example, Jeremy Bentham, John Henry Wigmore (Rescher and Joynt 1959, 561).

1994, 277), material evidence and verbal evidence. For example, there are the testimony of witnesses in the judicial context, the evidence of "IOU" and "bloody knife", various archaeological sites and existing cultural relics in history, etc. Also, there is another kind of reasoning evidence. This kind of evidence cannot prove any facts on its own, on the basis of reason or common sense, it can deduce certain factual claims. For example, "a witness without interest is usually honest" and "what is recorded in the official history is generally true". Although such inferential evidence can be overturned, it is the key to linking up the whole network of proof.

Secondly, the use of evidence must comply with some basic principles, for instance, the authenticity (or credibility) and relevance of evidence must be critically examined. For example, generally speaking, the evidentiary force of verbal evidence requires mutual confirmation of other material evidence. Ancient Chinese textual studies emphasize that if there is only one piece of evidence supporting a certain conclusion, this conclusion is unacceptable, so the main evidence is often listed at first, followed by the circumstantial evidence (Zhang and Sun 2010, 122). Robin George Collingwood also suggested that only when the testimonies of authoritative persons are strengthened by other evidences can we regard them as historical knowledge (Collingwood 1994, 256–257). This is consistent with the "Corroboration Rule" of modern evidence law, that is, the nature or probative power of a single piece of evidence determines that it cannot prove the facts of a case alone, so it is necessary to supplement other materials as evidence.

Thirdly, there are similarities between the two in the process and methodology of emphasizing the supremacy of evidence. For example, for the collation of historical data, as Hu Shi said, "collation is a legal term, which contains the meaning of trial" (Hu 1998, 300). Ancient collation and judicial procedure are similar. Collation is divided into two parts: verification and judgment. Verification refers to the basic texts used for reference and comparison in collating documents, which need to be compared by various methods. But only relying on them often cannot solve the text collation. The key lies in judgment, that is, the careful judgment of historians.

3.2 *The Difference Between Judicial Evidence and Historical Evidence*

The biggest difference between judicial evidence and historical evidence is that the former is based on specific circumstances. That is to say, evidence collection, review and judgment all take place in the context of trial, so it must be bound by many factors such as substantive law, procedural law, time and space scenarios.

First of all, in addition to relevance and authenticity, judicial evidence must also meet the requirements of legitimacy: The exclusionary rule of illegal evidence will exclude some evidence that does not meet the requirements of legitimacy. But in history, the ability of evidence to form the basis of proof often depends only on itself, even if sometimes the means or methods of obtaining evidence may violate professional ethics or law.

Secondly, in the determination of legal facts, hearsay evidence should be excluded in principle on the grounds that "statements made without oath outside the court are usually unreliable"; "the presenter has not been cross-examined in court, so the loophole in his statement is not can be found"; "the jury may give a high rating to the rumors", and so on (Hu 1998, 297–301). This rule guarantees the accuracy and completeness of the testimony, but for historical research, it is meaningless (Yi 2008, 75, 79), even if there is a court that judges historical facts.

Moreover, sometimes, there may be problems in the qualification of witnesses in judicial decisions (Rescher and Joynt 1959, 572). For example, in ancient China, there was a tradition of "no criminal responsibility for concealing crimes for one's relatives", which obviously would not be considered in history.

Finally, history is more skeptical of evidence than law. In terms of historical research, most of the evidence is to some extent inaccurate, incomplete, biased, and even distorted due to private interests. Therefore, all evidence should be treated with caution and any conclusion should be regarded as temporary. Many people agree with the view that the editor of historical materials should be regarded as biased unless it can be proved that he is fair and objective (Lomas 1990, chapter evidence). Because of the pressures of time and procedure, for the proof of evidence, a judge cannot face evidence like a historian, and a judge usually presumes that evidence is proficient unless there is a contrary claim. For example, when a witness begins to narrate, he has promised the authenticity of what he says. When the evidence is presented in court, it is presupposed to be true. Unless there is contrary reason or evidence, the proceedings will regard these statements as evidence.

3.3 On Evidence: What Can Law Learn from History?

In terms of language habits, "evidence" sometimes refers to a kind of material, for example, when we talk about "evidence", "witness testimony", "tender evidence", "suppress evidence", "forge evidence" and "destroy evidence"; and it sometimes refers to a kind of fact proposition, for example, when we talk about "the authenticity, legality and relevance of evidence".

Evidence must appear as an externalized form of material before it can be recognized by human beings. However, because evidence itself cannot speak, its ability as evidence, that is, its role in proving activities, is determined by its content. History tends to view evidence from the first perspective. For example, Collingwood once said: "Everything is evidence which the historian can use as evidence. But what can he so use? It must be something here and now perceptible to him: this written page, this spoken utterance, this building, this finger-print" (Collingwood 1994, 246–247). Of course, the materials, information or data here must have content: "Although things or articles often appear as evidence in the argument, they can only play a role in the form of facts" (Shu and Song 2018: 44). Facts that need to be reshaped or identified no matter what period of time they exist, i.e. the establishment of past facts, in essence, comes from some inference made according to the facts of today, which is the appearance of those evidences in front of us.

Proof can only rely on evidence that can be directly (or with the help of scientific tools) perceived by human senses. For example, when a knife is placed in front of us and someone states the course of an event face to face, the existence of these materials is usually hard to deny, but whether the contents of these materials are true, and whether their contents can establish inferential relations with the fact that they claim to support need to be verified. For example, when the evidence is "a knife with the blood trace of the victim and the fingerprint of A", the first topic to be verified here is not "A stabbed the victim with this knife", but "this knife does exist", "it does have the blood of the victim", "it does have the fingerprint of A", so we can make a conclusion: A is likely to have stabbed the victim with this knife. Of course, this kind of inference can only be a probability and often needs the support of other evidences.

In short, the evidence must first be presented to us in a form that can be perceived by human beings. Secondly, it must express or support a certain factual claim itself. This is the dual essence of evidence.

4 The Concept of "Proof" in Law and History

The core issue of judicial proof and historical proof is how to prove that a certain (objective) fact has happened or existed, so it is necessary to support the authenticity of a certain fact on the basis of various evidence. "The common element is the idea of the evidential role of linking data to hypotheses or probanda through inferential reasoning" (Twining 2006, 438). This is also the professional responsibility of historians and judges (Bloch 1953, 138–139).

4.1 Similarity Between Judicial Proof and Historical Proof

As mentioned above, proof is based on the facts expressed or directly supported by the evidence itself to support the facts to be proved. However, the so-called evidence fact can only be a clip tailored according to the cognitive purpose, and cannot be all the facts reflected in the evidence materials. Because the content of facts is infinite in theory, and from different perspectives, there may be many differences in these contents. In the process of recording, recalling or restating these contents, there must be many plots intentionally or unintentionally missed. As E. H. Carl said, "It used to be said that facts speak for themselves. This is, of course, untrue. The facts speak only when the historian calls on them: It is he who decides to which facts to give the floor, and in what order or context" (Carr 1964, 11). Therefore, the evidence facts must have the judgment of the subject, and also must be limited by some tailoring criteria.

In most cases, the supporting relationship between the evidence facts and the to-be proven facts is not an inevitable deductive relationship, but an inductive relationship depending on experience, which often involves degree or probability issues (Rescher and Joynt 1959, 561–562). In law and history, there is a set of mechanisms to ensure the realization of practical rationality. For example, the reason why the so-called "Twenty-four Histories" is regarded as a history of faith may be that the writing of these historical books relied on some relatively reliable historical materials, which were often from first-hand materials recorded by authoritative historians. The personality, qualification and character of the creators of these historical books are worthy of trust. The contents recorded in these historical books are supported by other historical books or materials. In law, the reason why we believe in the power of proof of witness testimony is that empirical reason tells us that, in the absence of interest, rational people usually do not tell lies, so we can acquiesce to the power of this kind of evidence. But because we cannot guarantee that witnesses do not tell lies at all, we put forward many specific standards to guarantee the authenticity of testimony to a greater extent. For example, the witness must appear in court to testify, the witness must swear, the testimony must be cross examined, and the content of the witness's testimony must be confirmed by other evidence, etc.

4.2 The Difference Between Judicial Proof and Historical Proof

Historical knowledge is not a simple accumulation of facts. Historians often need to classify and compare these facts in some way (Aron et al. 1958, 13–15). Sometimes, they also need to explain the causes and consequences of the incidents and explain them in a larger historical context. But in trials, this understanding and interpretation is largely irrelevant (except for persuasion matters) (Allen 2014, 129). In addition to the truth, jurists will also pay attention to the causes and consequences of the incident, for example, the motive of the crime, the social harm caused by the criminal act, etc., but these factors may not need to be proved in the court. The focus of the court trial is the authenticity of the circumstances related to the constituent elements (Allen 1993, 623–625).

In the study of history, the ideal goal of pursuing truth is the absolutely priority, and it is not affected by other goals or values. Even if doubtful stories were written into history for various reasons (for example, history is written by the winner), they can no longer obtain the legitimacy of history when they are found to be in doubt. However, although proof itself requires truth-seeking, in the entire judicial process, the pursuit of truth is only one of the values that it seeks. Its deeper goal may be to achieve other legal values such as dispute resolution and justice based on the facts of the case. For example, in the judicial practice of the United States, values such as Life, Individual

Liberty, Stability, Due Process, Truth, Judicial Economy, Federalism, Health and Safety are all goals that the rules of evidence seek to promote (Bergland 1973, 165–166). These other values are not necessarily based on truth-seeking. Due to factors such as procedural restrictions and legal regulation, the settlement of disputes and the realization of justice may be based on some unrealistic "case facts".[2] For example, when the litigation claim has passed the statute of limitations, the key evidence in the criminal proof is excluded as the "fruit of the poison tree" (illegal evidence). At this time, the goal of "seeking truth" is not so important, and even the litigation participants no longer try to prove what the "truth" is.

In a word, the most important difference between historians and jurists in the pursuit of truth may be that the normative frameworks behind them are different. Jurists, whether they are judges or parties and their defenders, must be bound by the legal normative framework in their attempts to prove the truth of a case. For example, according to the exclusionary rule of illegal evidence, evidence collected illegally cannot be adopted. According to the requirements of legal norms, the circumstances other than the legal elements do not need to be proved. Only proof meeting the standards of proof can be established, and the standards of proof needed in different legal fields are different. In historical research, there are some similar normative requirements, but these requirements are often given by the academic community. For example, in the interpretation of history, how to survive, how to progress civilization and other issues may become the research framework that must be accepted in the interpretation of history. There are many obvious differences between historical proof and judicial proof due to the different normative frameworks.

4.3 *Proof: What Can Law Learn from History?*

With regard to proof, historians and jurists naturally have many places to learn from each other. For example, Shiming Zhang proposed that historical studies can learn at least three points from the judicial referee methodology (as the saying goes, "people with rich experience can judge right and wrong quickly and accurately"): First, there should be a spirit of suspicion. Examine all kinds of materials and theories with keen insight and rich experience. Second, attach importance to evidence. Third, emphasize legal reasoning. There should be evidence as well as proof (Zhang 2015). It is not hard to see that what historians can learn from judges is more a kind of professional rationality and technology, but in fact, the professional rationality of justice may be overestimated. The role of cognitive subject and the book of irrationality such as

[2]Though according to the requirements of history, the value of justice seems to be the pursuit of historians as well, this kind of justice must be based on a record of truth. For example, Shen Xu's *Shuo Wen Jie Zi* (≪说文解字≫, literally: 'Explaining Graphs and Analyzing Characters'), an early-2nd-century Chinese dictionary from the Han Dynasty, said that "史，记事者也。从又持中。中，正也", which means, the task of ancient historians is to record all sorts of things objectively with the numerous materials in hand. Actually, justice in history is truth, which is very different from that in law.

imagination are intentionally ignored in the methodology of judgment, and the work of historians can give some enlightenment to jurists.

The first question concerns the subject in the identification of legal facts. Perhaps because of the limitations of the legal system and judicial responsibility, the active role of the judge in proof seems to have been intentionally ignored, but history seems to be willing to recognize the role of historians. "The past has occurred. It has gone and can only be brought back again by historians in very different media, for example in books, articles, documentaries, etc., not as actual events. The past has gone and history is what historians make of it when they go to work. History is the labour of historians" (Jenkins 1991, 8). The handling of facts has not always been the strength of legal persons. Judges often accept the training of legal knowledge and legal methodology but lack training on factual issues. If the role of the subject cannot be ignored in the identification of legal facts, it is possible to construct a series of procedures or systems about the identification of facts only by recognizing the active role of the subject.

Second, history often emphasizes the role of imagination. In the eyes of British philosopher Collingwood, historical inference is essentially an imagination, which is indispensable. Without it, there would be no history. It is relying on this imagination that those plots in history can be constructed. In order to pursue the truth, this structure must accept the guidance of three methodological rules: "First, his [the historian's] picture must be localized in space and time"; "secondly, all history must be consistent with itself"; "thirdly, and most important, the historian's picture stands in a peculiar relation to something called evidence" (Collingwood 1994, 246). However, in the field of law, "based on facts" and "based on evidence" have been widely accepted. It seems that the space of subjective imagination has been completely eliminated, but in fact, there are also such imagination problems in legal proof. People's memories are not always accurate. They may be mixed with the imagination of many subjects in their narratives, consciously or unconsciously. However, we cannot always find out which narratives are purely out of imagination. Therefore, we must use the rationality of common sense, the integration of logic and many other factors to make rational judgments. It is often required that such a narrative must be corroborated by other evidences. In this sense, Collingwood's conditions are equally meaningful in judicial proof: First, the map constructed by the judge must have existed in a certain time and space, not in the existence of virtual space. Second, it should comply with requirements for logical consistency. The plots of narrative cannot conflict with each other and must be consistent with the overall historical background. Third, the judicial narrative ultimately depends on evidence.

5 Conclusion

It is easy to conclude from the above analysis of concepts such as fact, evidence and proof that the analogy between law and history is a useful catalyst, which facilitates law practitioners to clarify many controversial or unnoticed issues. While law has always emphasized that judicial judgment shall be based on facts, and truth judgment shall be based on evidence, law practitioners can see from historical wisdom that those facts (incidents or acts) to be judged by judges are essentially a kind of past event, and they appear in court as a form of story or narration and thus cannot be totally true. In order to substantiate the truth of these stories, the supporters will propose many evidence materials which cannot substantiate themselves, and therefore judges must verify and determine the truthfulness of such stories and the evidential value of the truthfulness of such stories. It is important not to ignore the usefulness and imagination of persons who determinate the truthfulness of the facts. These are places where law practitioners can learn from historians.

References

Allen, Ronald J. 1993. Factual Ambiguity and a Theory of Evidence. *Northwestern University Law Review* 88: 604–640.

Allen, Ronald J. 2014. Relevancy and Admissibility. In *Professor Allen on Evidence*, vol. I, ed. Baosheng Zhang, 116–143. Beijing: China Renmin University Press.

Aron, Raymond, Suzanne, Keller, and Judith K., Davison. 1958. Evidence and Inference in History. *Daedalus* 87: 11–39.

Bergland, David P. 1973. Value Analysis in the Law of Evidence. *Western State Law Review* 1: 162–184.

Bloch, Marc. 1953. *Historian's Craft (Apologie pour l'histoire ou métier d'historien)*. Trans. from the French by Peter Putnam. New York: Vintage Books.

Carr, E.H. 1964. *What Is History?* 2nd ed, ed. R.W. Davies. London: Penguin.

Chen, Bo. 2017. "Taking Fact as Basis" or "Taking Evidence as Basis"?: Philosophical Reflection on Scientific Research and Judicial Trial. *South China Quarterly* 7: 22–39.

Collingwood, Robin George. 1994. *The Idea of History: With Lectures 1926–1928*. Oxford: Oxford University Press.

Ginzburg, Carlo. 1991. Checking the Evidence: The Judge and the Historian. *Critical Inquiry* 18: 79–92.

Hu, Shih. 1998. Scholarly Methods of Qing Dynasty Scholars. In *Collected Works of Shih Hu 2*, ed. Zhesheng Ouyang. Beijing: Peking University Press.

Jenkins, Keith. 1991. *Rethinking History*. London: Routledge.

Lomas, Tim. 1990. *Teaching and Assossing Historical Understanding*. London: The Historical Association.

Peng, Gang. 2010. Historical Facts and Historical Interpretation: A Survey in Light of 20th Century Western Historical Theories. *Journal of Beijing Normal University (Social Sciences)* 2: 47–55.

Rescher, Nicholas, and Carey B. Joynt. 1959. Evidence in History and in the Law. *The Journal of Philosophy* 56: 561–578.

Shu, GuoYing, and Xuguang Song. 2018. "Taking Evidence as Basis" or "Taking Fact as Basis": Exchanging Views with Professor Chen Bo. *Journal of Political Science and Law* 1: 43–52.

Steiner-Dillon, James. 2020. *Is Truth Truth*? (March 6, 2020). Available at SSRN: https://ssrn.com/abstract=3550212 or http://dx.doi.org/10.2139/ssrn.3550212. Accessed 3 Apr 2020.

Twining, William. 2006. *Rethinking Evidence: Exploratory Essays*. Cambridge: Cambridge University Press.

Verheij, Bart, and Floris Bex. 2008. Accepting the Truth of a Story about the Facts of a Criminal Case. In *Legal Evidence and Proof: Statistics, Stories, Logic*, ed. Henry Prakken, Hendrik Kaptein, and Bart Verheij. Aldershot: Ashgate.

Yi, Yanyou. 2008. The Hearsay Rule: Its History, Rules, Rationale and Tendency. With Discussions on the Theory of Transplanting Hearsay Rule to China. *Tsinghua Law Review* 4: 72–100.
Zhang, Baosheng. 2017. Facts, Evidence and Ascertaining the Facts. *Social Sciences in China* 8: 110–130.
Zhang, Shi-ming, and Zhe Sun. 2010. The Historical Facts and the Legal Facts: Sima Guang's "Tong jiankaoyi"'s Approach, Status and Enlightment. *Journal of Historical Science* 2: 115–125.
Zhang, Shiming. 2015. Rule of History as Rule of Law: Into Knowledge History of Historical Textology and Sources of Law. *Guangming Ribao.* March 25.

The Generation of Probable Facts from Testimonies in Jurisprudence and Historiography

Aviezer Tucker

1 Introduction

Philosophers have distinguished five and only five sources of knowledge: Empirical, from the senses; a priori, from reason; testimonial from the information we receive from other people; memorial, from our memories; and self-knowledge, from intuition (Audi 2002). Historiographic and legal evidence is mostly, though not exclusively, testimonial. It is a hallmark of unreflective historiographic thought to believe that historiography is an empirical science—when was the last time a historian perceived Napoleon through the senses?! Even people who experienced events associated with historical processes like the French Revolution did not perceive more than aspects or parts of them. Historiography and jurisprudence are founded on the *epistemology of testimony* (cf. Coady 1992; Tucker 2004; Lackey 2008; Gelfert 2014; Shieber 2015; Tucker 2016). They generate knowledge of the past mostly, though not exclusively (since there are also inferences from material evidence, remnants and so on), from testimonies, from what people, live and dead, testified had happened, orally or in writing. This reliance on the epistemology of testimony distinguishes jurisprudence and historiography from the empirical sciences that infer knowledge from sense data, and from mathematics and logic that infer a priori knowledge from reason.

Understanding testimonial inferences requires the abstract conceptual tools that epistemology in general and the epistemology of testimony in particular have developed. Being a dolphin does not make one into a marine biologist. Athletic accomplishments do not result in expertise in human physiology. Success in business does not imply insights into economic theory-Jeff Bazos is not likely to win the Nobel Prize in economics anytime soon. Similarly, accomplished historians, police investigators and judges are not necessarily experts in understanding why they are accomplished,

A. Tucker (✉)
Davis Center for Russian & Euasian Studies, Harvard University, Cambridge, USA
e-mail: avitucker@yahoo.com

B. Zhang et al. (eds.), *A Dialogue Between Law and History*,
https://doi.org/10.1007/978-981-15-9685-8_5

in modelling their best epistemic practices. Practitioners possess *tacit* knowledge of their practices. Philosophers and other theoreticians strive to achieve explicit theoretical knowledge that can be taught explicitly rather than through practice and imitation (Collins 2010).

By *knowledge* I mean *propositions with sufficiently high probability in a context of inquiry*. Very probable knowledge is often considered to be "factual". *Epistemic Contextualism* suggests that what we consider knowledge depends on context (cf. Ichikawa 2017). In different contexts different probabilistic thresholds are required for propositions to be considered knowledge. In common law, there are different standards for criminal law (guilt beyond reasonable doubt), civil law (the preponderance of evidence), and in licensing cases (presumption of guilt). The probabilistic threshold generally correlates with the context, with the severity of the consequences of establishing the facts to the accused. In criminal cases that may result in incarceration or worse, the probabilistic threshold is high. In civil cases, where the worst outcome for the accused is substantial financial loss, it is lower. In cases of licensing, where the worse outcome is a moderate fine, the probabilistic threshold is even lower (Ho 2008). For example, in the US, celebrities O. J. Simpson and Robert Blake were acquitted of murdering their wives in a criminal court, but were held responsible for killing them in civil suits brought by the families of the victims. The juries found the probability of their committing these crimes lower than beyond reasonable doubt, but sufficiently high according to the preponderance of the evidence. Within criminal law itself, there are different probabilistic thresholds for judgment. In common law legal systems, convictions demand higher probabilistic thresholds than acquittals. Therefore, the estimated rate of error in judicial acquittals in the United States is several times that of errors in convictions. Systems of justice can manipulate the ratios of rates of error in acquittals to convictions by adjusting the laws that regulate due process and admissibility of evidence (Tucker 2011).

In most historiographic contexts, the standard of proof is comparable to that in civil cases, the preponderance of evidence. Still, when historiographic research may seriously affect lives, it may require a higher probabilistic threshold for truth, comparable to "beyond reasonable doubt". It is acceptable to infer from the preponderance of the evidence that someone was an informer for Cardinal Metternich in the Habsburg monarchy; but similar preponderance of the evidence may not suffice for branding a *living* person an informer in Communist Czechoslovakia (Tucker 2014).

I argue in this article that *multiple independent testimonies* can *generate* probable knowledge in historiography and jurisprudence even when unreliable. For this reason, much of the practices of historians, detectives, and triers in general consist of the search for coherent and independent testimonies. Single testimonies without corroboration can at most *transmit* their own reliabilities. I open the discussion with a critical analysis of previous epistemic models of the inference of knowledge from multiple testimonies. I criticize in particular the attempt to model the inference of knowledge from testimonies in one neat algorithm, whereas in fact the inference is a series of inferences that sometimes do not have sufficient evidence to advance to the end of the series. I further criticize prevailing conceptual analyses of *coherence* between testimonies, the *independence* of testimonies, and their *reliability* to argue that all these concepts are best understood as aspects of the *flows of information* from events to testimonies. I present then a new alternative modular model that fits the actual veritistic best practices of historians, triers, and detectives, who infer knowledge from multiple testimonies.

Arguably, though Bayesian algorithms that infer probabilities of hypotheses from evidence such as testimonial evidence represent pure reasoning, most people including triers and historians are challenged by quantitative reasoning and are less than proficient in probability theory. When presented with probabilistic results or when instructed in them, they fail to comprehend the theory and misinterpret or ignore it and its results because it confuses them (Faigman and Baglioni 1988). Still, rule following behavior is distinct of the precise, abstract and explicit articulation and understanding of rules. For example, the linguistic practices of most people obey the grammatic and syntactic rules of their native tongue. Some make mistakes, especially in complex linguistic contexts. But generally, people follow grammatic and syntactic rules and can correct each other when they make mistakes because they know the rules implicitly. Expert grammarians who can formulate and apply precise rules are few. The same holds for simple logical rules and their application. Some, perhaps most, triers and historians cannot understand, formulate or teach the concepts of probability. Yet, Bayesian reasoning does not have to be quantitative or precise. It may be conceptual and fuzzy, if the gaps between competing probabilities are sufficiently large. For example, if a probabilistically illiterate person wonders on the way home whether their spouse is already at home, if they see the light on as they approach their home, they will infer that the spouse is at home, and vice versa if the light is off. It is not impossible that the light was left on by mistake from the previous night or that the spouse is sitting in the dark, but these alternative hypotheses have sufficiently low prior probabilities to be ignored. The result of this Bayesian reasoning is then conceptualized in non-probabilistic deterministic terms, the spouse is or is not at home. Similarly, it is not entirely impossible that George Washington was not the first president of the United States and that all the immense volume of documentary evidence that testifies that indeed he was the president was planted by some deceptive agency. But the gap between the very high probability that Washington was indeed the president and the existence of the deceptive documentary agency is so huge that historians conclude in deterministic terms that Washington was the first president, though it would have been more precise to say that the probability that he was the president is very high, but just short of 1. As a historical entity, the existence of George Washington is hypothetical (cf. Murphey 1973), though highly probable, beyond any reasonable doubt. When gaps between the probabilities of competing hypotheses are closer, triers and historians need to inspect the Bayesian reasoning behind the assignments of probabilities and then there would be ample opportunities for confusions and ignorance to manifest themselves. But such cases are outliers in historiography and "easy" cases in jurisprudence. Friedman (1987, 2004, 46–70) presented a Bayesian interpretation of rules of evidence which is quite convincing, though he did not go much into the significance of multiple testimonies as I will. I explain in this paper why often there are wide gaps between competing hypotheses in historiography and in easy cases of adjudication. When there are no significant gaps, the hypotheses are underdetermines, and historians and triers must conclude that they do not have sufficient testimonial evidence for knowledge.

2 Generation of Knowledge from Testimonies Versus Its Transmission

The *transmission theory* of testimony considers testimony to exclusively *transmit* rather than *generate* knowledge. Transmission theory views testimonies as analogous to coins that, once minted, can only be passed from hand to hand, or be lost. If single testimonies are unreliable, the information they transmit is insensitive to the information transmitted by their origins, and they cannot transmit knowledge they do not possess (Lackey 2008, 94). Plantinga (1993, 84) and Wright (2018) denied that the probability of beliefs supported by testimonies may exceed the reliability or justification of any single testimony. If testimonies can only transmit their reliabilities, the primary task of historians and jurists is to collect testimonies, find grounds to evaluate their reliabilities, discard the unreliable ones, and then base their judgements and historiographic narratives on the sufficiently or most reliable testimonies. Collingwood (1956, 257–261; cf. Tucker 2004, 132–133) called this methodology "cut and paste" historiography.

The rudimentary method for guarding against false or unreliable testimonies since ancient times was the requirement for at least two independent witnesses, *testis unis, testis nullus*. Roman law quantified the strength of legal proofs from multiple testimonies by adding fractions: "[T]he corroborative testimony of two unimpeachable eyewitnesses constituted a complete proof," (Daston 1988, 42) if more witnesses of inferior quality, represented by lower fractions, were available, their testimonies could still add up to a "full proof". The article about *probabilité* in the *Encyclopédie* in 1765, written probably by Diderot, formulated the advantage of multiple witnesses in generating knowledge as 1-(1-reliability rate)^2. The article recognized the lower reliabilities of hearsay evidence and oral transmission, and the greater reliability of written records. However, it did not consider the prior probabilities of the testimonies, how surprising they were, and did not mention the independence of the witnesses as a necessary condition (Daston 1988, 318–320).

Leopold Ranke's older contemporary, Laplace, introduced in his treatise on probabilities (1840, 136–156) probabilistic Bayesian models of inferences from testimonies. Laplace demonstrated first that the posterior probability of a hypothesis (that determines whether it is considered knowledge in context or not) supported by a single testimony is the reliability of the testimony multiplied by its prior probability (its probability before the presentation of the testimony; for example, the same ancient historian with the same reliability may generate knowledge when testifying to a battle and fail to generate knowledge when reporting a supernatural occurrence, because the prior probability of the second is lower than the first). Single testimonies *transmit* their epistemic properties. Then, Laplace showed how coherent multiple independent testimonies can *generate* knowledge by inferring together beliefs that have higher probabilities than the reliabilities of the testimonies that infer them. The lower is the prior probability of what the testimonies cohere about, the more surprising are the testimonies, the higher is the posterior probability of what the testimonies agree on. For example, the prior probability of any number winning the lottery is very low. When an unreliable witness (a toddler for example) testifies which number won, that witness cannot generate knowledge. But if there are multiple independent unreliable testimonies (for example of two or more toddlers who never met) and they cohere (agree on the winning number), they generate knowledge despite the low individual reliabilities of the testimonies. The lower the prior probability in such cases, the higher is the posterior probability, for example, if independent unreliable testimonies agree on a phone number, its posterior probability is much higher than if they agree on the area code. Lewis (1962, 346), Bovens and Hartmann (2003, 117–119), Olsson (2005, 24–26) and Tucker (2016, 2018) reaffirmed Laplace's conclusions in the context of the epistemologies of testimony and memory. Triers may convict beyond reasonable doubt on the exclusive basis of the multiple independent testimonies of criminals who are individually unreliable, as long as the prior probabilities of their testimonies are low (e.g. because they are very detailed). Historians look for testimonies in archives and for corroborating independent testimonies irrespective of the individual reliabilities of the sources. Common to all these expert institutional practices is the inference of knowledge from coherent and independent multiple testimonies that can be individually unreliable or whose reliability cannot be estimated.

As noted above, these values do not have to be estimated precisely or even quantitatively. For example, if detectives obtain two or more independent eye witness testimonies to a crime and the witnesses agree that the perpetrator had dark hair, and most members of the population have dark hair, the prior probability is too high for inferring knowledge. But detectives would then interrogate the witnesses to obtain more details (age, built, dress, gait, unusual traits & etc.) until they reduce the prior probability sufficiently to make the testimonies useful for the generation of knowledge. The precise quantitative values do not matter.

This Bayesian model of inference of knowledge from multiple testimonies solves puzzles about the epistemology of testimony: Coady (1992, 30–32) considered a jury that hears testimonies with identical propositional content from four witnesses. After hearing three witnesses the jury may have a higher degree of belief in the content of the testimonies than the fourth witness, who did not hear the previous three testimonies. How can this marginal testimony increase the degree of belief of the jurors in its content? The answer is that testimonies can increase the posterior probability of what they testify to beyond their own reliability or the degree of belief of the witnesses in their own testimonies. Coady (1992, 36–37) wondered further why the testimony of a child was inadmissible in common law, while the testimonies of multiple children were admissible. This is not puzzling, considering that the reliability of a single testimony by a child is low and it transmits this low reliability to the probability of any belief based exclusively on it. But if the prior probability of what the children testify to is sufficiently low, and the testimonies are independent, they can *together* generate highly probable knowledge.

The social outcome of the generation of knowledge from multiple testimonies is egalitarian: Some philosophers and historians and sociologists of science (e.g. Shapin and Schaffer 1985; Shapin 1994; Fricker 2007) claimed that evaluations of the reliabilities of testimonies have been epistemically unjust, biased by social hierarchies. Still, if the prior probabilities are sufficiently low, independent testimonies whose reliabilities are underestimated can generate knowledge, as long as they are not excluded altogether, dismissed as having zero reliability, in what Fricker (2007, 130) called "pre-emptive testimonial injustice".

3 Conceptualizing the Bayesian Model

Though the above Bayesian model is clear, it may have conflicting conceptual interpretations that disagree on:

1. What type of *coherence* between multiple testimonies can generate knowledge?
2. What type of testimonial *independence* is necessary for the generation of knowledge from multiple testimonies?
3. How do historians and triers measure the *reliabilities* of testimonies?
4. How do historians and triers actually *infer knowledge* from multiple testimonies?

4 Coherence of What?

Testimonies must be coherent to generate knowledge. Bovens and Hartmann (2003, 9–13) examined the assumption that the coherence *between the propositional contents of testimonies* generates knowledge. For example, if there is an 80% statistical correlation between properties P and Q (for example, yellow Mercedes and taxis) in a population, and if one witness testifies that A was P (the thief drove a yellow Mercedes), and another independent witness testifies that A was Q (the thief was a taxi driver), the testimonies are 80% coherent. *Ceteris paribus,* the more coherent are the testimonies, the higher is the posterior probability of the hypothesis they support. Bovens and Hartmann rejected this Bayesian Coherentism because it is *insufficient* for the inference of knowledge from sets of testimonies. Olsson (2005, 97) also concluded that coherence underdetermines truth even when the witnesses are reliable and the priors are sufficiently low because "[t]he witnesses… may have fudged their story into agreement … the posteriors [are] severely underdetermined by facts of coherence, 'severely' because considerations of coherence alone do not even allow us to make comparative assessments of the height of the posterior" (2005, 135–136).

Propositional coherence is also *not necessary* for the inference of knowledge from multiple testimonies because some propositionally incoherent testimonies can generate knowledge. For example, testimony can mean its opposite by adding a wink or its verbal equivalent (O'Brien 2007) or because the proposition is sarcastic or ironic. Some testimonies convey—P by (P & Q) where Q is patently false. For example clever victims of coercion who are forced to bear propositionally false testimony, can include in their testimonies or "confessions" blatant falsities like testifying about collusion with fictional literary characters or dead people to discredit their own testimonies. Other testimonies may be "encoded" and require a hermeneutic "cipher" to interpret their surface propositional meanings. Jurists and historians specialize in generating knowledge from such propositionally *incoherent* testimonies.

It is possible to avoid these drawbacks by interpreting the concept of coherence of multiple testimonies not as describing the relation between *propositional contents*, but as describing the relation between *information* units preserved in testimonies. Coherent testimonies preserve coherent information that may or may not be expressed in propositional contents. Testimonies may also preserve coded information that has no propositional content and can be inferred only with the aid of theories that link properties explicit in the information signal with information that is "nested" in it. For example, information may be transmitted by what the testimonies *do not* say, or say ironically, or is deliberately false. Testimonies receive and transmit *information* in its Shannon (1964) sense of diminishing uncertainty. Information coherence accommodates the above cases where propositional coherence was not necessary. Information coherence is necessary, but it is not sufficient for the inference of knowledge from multiple testimonies. Several other conditions must be satisfied, most notably testimonial independence. Independence too is of *information* flows.

5 Testimonial Independence

The *independence* of testimonies can be interpreted in terms of *conditionality*, *causation*, or the *flow of information*. These three interpretations are distinct because some conditional relations are not causal; the world is full of conditional correlations that do not result from causal relations. When causes overdetermined their effects (for example the assassins of Caesar overdetermined his death), causes are neither necessary nor sufficient conditions for their effects. Some effects do not preserve information about their causes. For example, the "perfect crime" leaves no traces in its effects. Not all information transmissions have effects that are conditioned by them, for example, testimonies that transmit information that the receiver already possesses. The detection of information transmission does not require the discovery of a causal mechanism (Dretske 1981, 26–39).

Frequentist conditional interpretations of testimonial independence demand the satisfaction of Reichenbach's (1956, 157–167) "screening conditions." "A1, …, An are independent pieces of evidence for H if and only if A1, …, An are probabilistically independent of each other both on condition of H and on condition of ~H. The idea is that once the truth or falsity of the hypothesis is given, the independent pieces of evidence are probabilistically independent of each other since there is no direct link between them" (Shogenji 2007, 264). Earman (2000, 56–61; cf. Tucker 2019) noted that these screening conditions are satisfied only rarely between testimonies and even when they are, it is difficult to prove it, because the frequencies of testimonies are difficult to compute.

The testimonies that historians and jurists consider independent and useful for the generation of knowledge are often conditional on, or caused by, other independent testimonies. For example, when some witnesses would not testify unless other witnesses testified first. Generally, independent testimonies can be causally and conditionally affected by each other if they only trigger the *expression* of the testimony but do not affect the content of the *information* they transmit.[1] Such testimonies are independent of each other in the sense that the *information flows* that generated each of them did not intersect, but were traceable back to common origins. Accordingly, *testimonies that retransmit information that they received from other testimony or testimonies are dependent on it, or them. Otherwise, they are independent*. It may be possible to trace back the information transmitting processes extending backward from each testimony "genealogically" (Jardine 2008, 170–171). For example, the police attempts to solicit testimonies from eye witnesses to crimes before they can communicate with each other about it and instructs them not to communicate with each other about their testimonies until they testify in court, to preserve their independence. Historians search for testimonies to events from people who could not have transmitted information to each other, for example because they were on opposing sides in a conflict.

6 Reliability

High testimonial reliabilities are crucial for inferring knowledge from *single* testimonies. Reliabilities are important in the generation of knowledge from multiple testimonies when the prior probability of that knowledge is very *high,* for example, if two eye witnesses to a crime can only remember that the perpetrator had dark hair, in a population that has mostly dark hair.

[1]Cohen loosened the required screening conditions, allowing independent testimonies to increase but not to decrease each other's probability, as long as each testimony, by itself, "independently," increases the probability of the hypothesis (Cohen 1977, 101–102). Cohen's account can thus accommodate cases when testimonies increase each others' probability. Still, independent and coherent testimonies can conditionally reduce each others' likelihoods but still generate knowledge together: Suppose there are several eye witnesses to a crime. They all feel that the police should be informed about the crime, but they are also afraid of criminal retaliation. They prefer that somebody else testifies. Though their testimonies would be coherent if expressed, if one witness testifies to the police and other witnesses know it, the likelihood of their testimonies decreases without affecting their independence.

There are four interpretations of testimonial reliability: Frequentist, rule-governed, endogenous, and genealogical. I reject the first three and endorse the last.

The interpretation of reliability as truth frequency goes back to Bernoulli in the late seventeenth century (Daston 1988, 312). Reliabilities are interpreted as conditional probabilities that connect testimonial representations and *facts* (Bovens and Hartmann 2003, 14). Similar approaches interpret reliability as truth telling and unreliability as randomization. Olsson (2005, 133), Plantinga (1993, 78–82) and BonJour (2010, 155) correctly doubted the availability of evidence for independently testing the reliabilities of many testimonies in this sense. The reliabilities of witnesses and types of testimonies, as gauges of the reliabilities of particular testimonies, may vary from one context to another (Fricker 1994; Bovens and Hartmann 2003, 17). If the testimony is one of a kind, or one of a very small class, frequencies are statistically meaningless. If testimonies transmit information via untrue propositional content (P by means of –P + irony), this interpretation of reliability is also too narrow.

Thagard interpreted reliability in frequentist terms as "the ratio of claims by X on topic T that turned out to be true to all the claims made by X on topic T" (Thagard 2005, 307). He argued that since available data rarely allows the calculation of frequencies of true testimonies in the class of claims made by somebody on a given topic, it is often impossible to evaluate the reliabilities of testimonies. "Objective probabilities... are well-defined only for frequencies of occurrences in specified populations of events"[2] (Thagard 2005, 311). Thagard argued that even when the data for assessing testimonial truth frequencies is available, historians and triers rarely bother to calculate frequencies because "there are a number of different non-enumerative ways of inferring credibility" (2005, 307). Lackey (2008) too argued that there are methods, other than frequentist comparison of testimonies with "facts," for the evaluation of testimonial reliabilities. Lackey's *rule governed* examples were of the reliabilities of mundane testimonies that transmit information about the time of day or one's name. By contrast, reports on the achievements of one's children are unreliable because they tend to be exaggerated. It may be possible to attempt to generalize Lackey's examples to general rules. For example, "testimonies that speakers know are easy to check tend to be reliable," or "when witnesses do not have a personal interest in the effects of their testimonies, they tend to be reliable." Other rules may generalize about physical indicators of dishonesty or the frequent use of words like "honestly, ..." and about the competences of witnesses to detect the kind of information they convey (Fricker 1994; Goldman 1999, 123–125). Still, universal, context independent, rules or statistical generalization for the determination of reliabilities of testimonies have been elusive (Coady 1992, 210–211; Fricker

[2]Thagard argued that estimates of the credibility of types of testimonies vary from their truth frequencies, even when ascertainable. For example, a single "big" lie may plunge the credibility of a witness to zero from near a unity, even if the frequency of true testimonies by this witness remains high.

2007, 72–76). Jardine (2008) demonstrated that many such rules would be necessary, each would have obvious exceptions, and taken together without contexts, they would be inconsistent.

The *endogenous* approach to reliability (Bovens and Hartmann 2003, 56–88) infers the reliabilities of testimonies exclusively from their coherence, independence, and low prior probabilities, without resorting to external information or evidence. "[A]greement on something relatively improbable will make it relatively likely that the reporters are reliable and, given a certain level of improbability, relatively likely that what is reported is true" (Olsson 2005, 46–7). Olsson (136) rejected the endogenous interpretation. Likewise, Walton and Reed (2008) noted that the reliabilities of independent testimonies are independent of each other. Reliabilities are based on exogenous information and inferences, as historians and triers know well.

I suggest that testimonial reliability is *the ratio of information that is preserved by the testimonies at the end of a transmission process to the information that was transmitted at its origin.* Jardine (2008) proposed that the evaluation of the reliabilities of individual testimonies follows their *genealogies*, their pedigrees, the historical information transmission processes that generated them. External evidence, much of it testimonial, can infer these genealogies. Historians trace the genealogies of testimonies from eye witnesses to historians to copiers to later historians and so on (Kosso 2001). It is possible to draw a model of the transmission of information as a flow chart that looks like a tree or a bush. These models of genealogies can estimate the reliability of transmission of information from information "parent" to its "descendant". Gaps and other disruptions in the transmission of information question the genealogical relation and consequently the reliability of the testimony. For example, historiography of the ancient world questions how later sources could have gained knowledge of events that happened centuries earlier, how could the information been transmitted, or not. Since testimonies infer each other's' reliabilities, testimonies as sources of knowledge form a network of inferences that affect each other holistically, in Quine's sense of a web of beliefs.

7 Modular Generation of Knowledge from Multiple Testimonies

Historians, detectives, and triers separate testimonial information from noise, trace information signals back to their origins, and infer properties of the origins from the signals they sent to the present. The major mistake of previous modelling of inferences from multiple testimonies has been in expecting there to be a single simple precise algorithm that would generate the desired inference in one fell swoop with testimonial input and doxastic output. There is no such algorithm. But the absence of this algorithm does not imply that there can be no Bayesian modelling of inferences of knowledge from multiple testimonies that models the best practices of historians and triers. I have argued (Tucker 2004, 2016) that historiographic and legal inferences from testimonies are modular; they proceed in several stages. They are not, and do not need to be precise when the probabilistic gaps between competing hypotheses are sufficiently large to eliminate all the hypotheses except one at each stage. When there is no such obvious wide gap, the process of inference is halted, sometimes in the middle of the process of inference.

The process of generation of knowledge from multiple testimonies proceeds in three consecutive stages, each conditionally dependent on its predecessor:

1. A comparison of the likelihoods of a set of testimonies that transmit coherent information given *some common origin* of the coherent information, and given *no common origin.*
2. If it is more probable that there was some common origin of the testimonial coherent information, historians and triers compare the likelihoods of the testimonies given alternative types of information flow nets. This comparison also ascertains the independence or dependence of the information flows.
3. Once information flow nets from common origins to independent testimonies are determined, it is possible to attempt to compare the likelihoods of the testimonies given competing hypotheses that specify properties of the information origin or origins.

7.1 Stage I

Types of testimonies that tend to *preserve information reliably* are most useful for demonstrating high likelihoods of a common origin. The emphasis on primary sources in general and eye witness reports in particular, the requirement that witnesses testify exclusively to firsthand knowledge, and the exclusion of hearsay in Common Law exclude testimonies that are likely to lose information (equivocation) and/or mix it with too much noise, signals that did not originate in the common origin of the testimonies. Some theories, or at least generalizations, about types of information transmission and preservation in time must be assumed in the selection of the most likely to be reliable testimonies. Historically, many of these generalizations were introduced simultaneously in historiography and jurisprudence around the turn of the nineteenth century (Tucker 2004, 46–91).

The first stage in the generation of knowledge from multiple testimonies attempts to prove that the coherent information the testimonies convey more probably preserves information transmitted from *some common information origin whose properties are not specified* than from different sources whose properties are specified. For example, if several historical testimonies cohere in claiming that an emperor was corrupt, they may have some common origin, or different historical testifiers may have had different grudges against the emperor and the easiest traditional slur against any emperor was that he was corrupt.

When the gap between the likelihoods of the testimonies given the two hypothesis, of common and different information origins, is sufficiently large, quantitative precision is unnecessary. Since the "common" and "different" information origins hypotheses are exhaustive and mutually exclusive, the improbability of one implies that the other is likely. The vanishing likelihood of detailed, information rich, surprising, sets of testimonies that have low prior probability given different information origins favors the probability of a common origin. For example, information rich detailed testimonies to a murder (how, when, where, and so on) probably share *some* common origin because it is unlikely that different origins of information would generate coherent *detailed* testimonies. By contrast, generic, information poor, testimonies to a murder that just allege "Smith murdered Jones" may have no common origins. They are likely given different desires and interests of witnesses to blame or frame the same person. For this reason, the police seeks as many details, as much information, from witnesses even when the details are not directly relevant for the crime, for example, how the criminal was dressed, their height, and hairstyle, how they arrived and left the scene of the crime and so on. They are irrelevant for the crime, but they are instrumental in eliminating the likelihood that witnesses simply accuse a common rival without a common origin for the information. Similarly, historians collect detailed information from different primary sources, to eliminate the likelihood of the evidence without a common origin.

The false intuition that surprising or information rich, detailed, single testimonies are more reliable than expected ones (Bovens and Hartmann 2003, 112–113) originates with the psychological association between testimonial detail and a common origin of information in the first stage of generation of knowledge from *multiple* testimonies. It is exploited by con-artists, pathological liars, and forgers both in the worlds of crime and historical forgery to associate their *single* false testimonies with the high probabilities of coherent information rich, detailed, *multiple* testimonies given a common origin (Grafton 1990).

The likelihoods of testimonies that convey coherent information given different origins of information is assessed by considering the various advantages—material, psychological, and so on—that the testimonies conferred on the witnesses. This assessment requires background knowledge, much of it testimonial again, about their circumstances and social context. Testimonies that were disadvantageous for testifiers or at least had no value for them are not likely given different origins. For example, if the witnesses' interests and loyalties would have motivated them to suppress Smith's guilt (because they are members of his family, partners, friends and so on), it is unlikely that they would all testify he was a murderer without some common origin. The likelihood of testimony that conflicts with the interests or biases of witnesses is low; the likelihood of a set of such testimonies, given different origins of information, is vanishing.

Multiple testimonies often *increase the posterior probability of a common information origin by decreasing exponentially the posterior probability of its only alternative, different origins.* Since a small number of detailed and surprising testimonies that convey coherent information is usually sufficient to decrease the likelihood of the testimonies given different origins to close to zero, additional testimonies are redundant. This "economy of witnessing" is implicit in the practices of plea bargains, when prosecutors grant criminals who agree to testify against their accomplices reduced sentences. After obtaining two or three independent testimonies, they cease offering plea bargains because the likelihood of few detailed testimonies given different origins is negligible and the interest of the prosecutor is to keep deals with criminals to the minimum necessary for conviction. Even when the testimonies are "free", from innocent witnesses, the prosecution does not burden the court with more than a few coherent testimonies.

Historians, detectives, and triers estimate the prior probabilities of common and different origins of testimonies according to the probability that the information signals that led to the testimonies could have intersected. This requires tracing back information signals from the testimonies. For example, if two testimonies report that the emperor was corrupt or that Smith murdered Jones, the prior probability of a common source depends on whether the two testimonies can be traced back to a point in time when the two information could or could not have intersected, in events such as the corruption of the emperor or the murder or in a meeting where the witnesses agreed to frame the emperor or Smith. This tracing can be less detailed and precise than the kind of information flow tracing that is undertaken in the second stage of inference of knowledge from multiple testimonies.

7.2 *Stage II: Alternative Information Flow Nets*

If it is probable that a set of coherent testimonies had a common origin, historians and detectives attempt to trace the information flows and distinguish independent signals from dependent noises. For example, the art of textual critics is to detect information signals that indicate the temporal-historical and special-geographical origins of composite testimonial documents by looking for discontinuities in vocabulary grammar and syntax, style, conceptual framework, and implicit values; internal contradictions, gaps in narratives, and parts that are inconsistent with the alleged identity of the author (Grafton 1990; Tucker 2004, 46–91). Some testimonies may mention explicitly their origins or preserve linguistic, terminological, or conceptual inconsistencies that can be used to separate texts into their constitutive documents that can be compared with other documents to infer their provenance. Historians, detectives, and triers are particularly interested in learning whether testimonies were independent. Dependent testimonies are no better than a singular testimony that can at most transmit its reliability. Only independent coherent multiple testimonies can be used to generate knowledge that is more probable than their reliabilities.

There is no single algorithmic or theoretically based methodology for this second stage. Rather, historians and detectives and jurists must discover external and internal to the testimonies evidence that should allow them to trace the information signal. Independent evidence about the testimonies from other testimonies is often essential. Testimonies then "bootstrap" each other to create a coherent net of beliefs about what happened in the past.

7.3 Stage III-Knowledge from Multiple Testimonies

The final stage in the generation of knowledge from multiple testimonies compares the likelihoods of the independent testimonies that preserve information from a common origin, given competing hypotheses about the properties of their common information origins. Sometimes, the likelihood of the testimonies given a particular origin is so obvious and high that there would be no seriously competing hypotheses, e.g. in simple cases when the most probable origin is described by the coherent propositional contents of the testimonies. If two independent credible witnesses agree on the detailed properties of the perpetrator of a crime or on the course of a battle, the only plausible hypothesis is that the perpetrator had indeed the properties they described and the battle proceeded according to their narrative. In other cases, information theories and prior probabilities should discriminate between competing hypotheses. For example, if eye witnesses to a crime offer descriptions of the perpetrator that may fit a range of individuals, the one individual who already has a criminal record relating to this kind of crime is more probably the criminal than suspects without motives or criminal records.

If the posterior probabilities of several inconsistent hypotheses about the properties of the common origin of the coherent testimonies are close, they are underdetermined. For example, when police investigators collect coherent and independent testimonies about a crime that do not transmit enough information to discriminate between several possible suspects. Surviving historical documents may underdetermine a range of possible historical events. For example, there is no historical evidence to the death of Saint Paul. But he must have died within a certain range of years and his death must have been natural or he was executed by the Romans.

If there are multiple incoherent testimonies, investigators group the testimonies in sets that share coherent information and follow the above three stages to infer a posterior probability for each hypothesis. The hypothesis with the highest posterior probability becomes "knowledge". If the posterior probabilities of beliefs generated by inconsistent testimonies are close to each other, they are underdetermined.

8 Historical and Legal Institutions and the Epistemology of Testimony

Institutional-professional norms enforce the rules that underlie the above model of inference from multiple testimonies at least tacitly through the rules of evidence and the expectation that historians display epistemic diligence and collect the relevant evidence in archives, compare the testimonies, and base their conclusions on multiple independent sources, while carefully considering the reliabilities of single testimonies. These rules are enforced much like the rules of grammar and logic, when professionals correct each other without necessarily having an explicit knowledge of the rules or being able to abstractly state them. Historians employ transparent processes of inference from multiple testimonies that are traceable through their footnotes. If a historian strays from the norms, if the testimonies referred to in the footnotes do not exist or do not contain the information the historian imputed to them, other historians will expose it and the community will enforce its professional norms (Evans 1999, 100–110). Triers who adhere to due process and the rule of law, like historians, follow the above process of inference from testimonies. In systems with an independent judiciary, the appellate system allows for the correction of errors in inference. But there is no error free judicial system. In common law systems, the rules of evidence tend to shift the direction of error to acquit the guilty at the expense of convicting the innocent (Tucker 2011).

Testimonies that convey coherent information are more likely to have had common than different origins when they are information rich, surprising, and detailed. It is necessary to trace the information transmission nets, to check the reliabilities of witnesses and where and how they received their information. Transmission flows that link the common origin with the testimonies should not intersect for the testimonies to be independent. It is possible then to infer knowledge of events that generated information signals from testimonies that preserved that information, and obtain highly probable knowledge, which most people consider historical truth (Tucker 2014).

References

Audi, Robert. 2002. The Sources of Knowledge. In *The Oxford Handbook of Epistemology*, ed. P. Moser, 71–94. New York: Oxford University Press.

BonJour, Laurence. 2010. *Epistemology: Classic Problems and Contemporary Responses*, 2nd ed. Lanham Maryland: Rowman & Littlefield.

Bovens, Luc, and Stephan Hartmann. 2003. *Bayesian Epistemology*. Oxford: Oxford University Press.

Coady, C.A.J. 1992. *Testimony: A Philosophical Study*. Oxford: Oxford University Press.

Cohen, L.Jonathan. 1977. *The Probable and the Provable*. Oxford: Oxford University Press.

Collingwood, R.G. 1956. *The Idea of History*. Oxford: Oxford University Press.

Collins, H.M. 2010. *Tacit and Explicit Knowledge*. Chicago: Chicago University Press.

Daston, Lorraine. 1988. *Classical Probability in the Enlightenment*. Princeton: Princeton University Press.

Dretske, Fred I. 1981. *Knowledge and the Flow of Information*. Cambridge MA: MIT Press.

Earman, John. 2000. *Hume's Abject Failure: The Argument Against Miracles*. Oxford: Oxford University Press.

Evans, Richard J. 1999. *In Defense of History*. New York: Norton.

Faigman, D.L., and A.J. Baglioni. 1988. Bayes' Theorem in the Trial Process. *Law and Human Behavior* 12 (1): 1–17.

Fricker, Elizabeth. 1994. Against Gullibility. In *Knowing from Words: Western and Indian Philosophical Analysis of Understanding and Testimony*, ed. Bimal Krishna Matilal, and Arindam Chakrabarti, 125–161. Dordrecht: Kluwer.

Fricker, Miranda. 2007. *Epistemic Injustice: Power and the Ethics of Knowing*. Oxford: Oxford University Press.

Friedman, Richard. 1987. Route Analysis of Credibility and Hearsay. *Yale Law Journal* 96: 667–742.

Friedman, Richard D. 2004. *The Elements of Evidence*, 3rd ed. St. Paul MN: Thomson West.

Gelfert, Axel. 2014. *A Critical Introduction to Testimony*. London: Bloomsbury.
Goldman, Alvin. 1999. *Knowledge in a Social World*. Oxford: Oxford University Press.
Grafton, Anthony. 1990. *Forgers and Critics: Creativity and Duplicity in Western Scholarship*. Princeton: Princeton University Press.
Ho, H.L. 2008. *The Philosophy of Evidence Law: Justice in the Search for Truth*. Oxford: Oxford University Press.
Ichikawa, Jonathan Jenkins. 2017. *The Routledge Handbook of Epistemic Contextualism*. New York: Routledge.
Jardine, Nick. 2008. Explanatory Genealogies and Historical Testimony. *Episteme* 5: 160–179.
Kosso, Peter. 2001. *Knowing the Past: Philosophical Issues of History and Archeology*. Amherst NY: Humanity Books.
Lackey, Jennifer. 2008. *Learning from Words: Testimony as a Source of Knowledge*. Oxford: Oxford University Press.
Laplace, Pierre-Simon. 1840. *Essai philosophique sur les probabilités*, 6th ed. Paris: Bachelier.
Lewis, C.I. 1962. *An Analysis of Knowledge and Valuation*. La Salle IL: Open Court.
Murphey, Murray G. 1973. *Our Knowledge of the Historical Past*. Indianapolis: Bobbs-Merrill.
O'Brien, Dan. 2007. Testimony and Lies. *The Philosophical Quarterly* 57: 225–238.
Olsson, Erik J. 2005. *Against Coherence: Truth, Probability, and Justification*. Oxford: Oxford University Press.
Plantinga, Alvin. 1993. *Warrant and Proper Function*. Oxford: Oxford University Press.
Reichenbach, Hans. 1956. *The Direction of Time*. Berkeley: University of California Press.
Shannon, Claude Elwood. 1964. *The Mathematical Theory of Communication*. Urbana IL: University of Illinois Press.
Shapin, Steven, and Simon Schaffer. 1985. *Leviathan and the Air-Pump: Hobbes, Boyle, and the Experimental Life*. Princeton: Princeton University Press.
Shapin, Steven. 1994. *A Social Theory of Truth: Civility and Science in Seventeenth Century England*. Chicago: University of Chicago Press.
Shieber, Joseph. 2015. *Testimony: A Philosophical Introduction*. New York: Routledge.
Shogenji, Tomoji. 2007. Why does coherence appear truth conducive. *Synthese* 157: 361–372.
Thagard, Paul. 2005. Testimony, Credibility, and Explanatory Coherence. *Erkenntnis* 63: 295–316.
Tucker, Aviezer. 2004. *Our Knowledge of the Past: A Philosophy of Historiography*. Cambridge: Cambridge University Press.
Tucker, Aviezer. 2011. Scarce Justice: The Accuracy, Scope and Depth of Justice. *Politics, Philosophy, and Economics* 11 (2012): 76–96.
Tucker, Aviezer. 2014. Historical Truth. In *Forms of Truth and the Unity of Knowledge*, ed. Vittorio Hosle, 232–259. South Bend IN: Notre Dame University Press.
Tucker, Aviezer. 2016. The Generation of Knowledge from Multiple Testimonies. *Social Epistemology*, 30: 251–272.
Tucker, Aviezer (2018) Memory: Irreducible, Basic, and Primary Source of Knowledge. *Review of Philosophy and Psychology*, 9 (1): 1–16.
Tucker, Aviezer (2020) The Inferences of Common Causes Reduced to Common Origins. *Studies in History and Philosophy of Science Part A*, 81: 105–115.
Walton, Douglas, and Chris Reed. 2008. Evaluating Corroborative Evidence. *Argumentation* 22: 531–553.
Wright, Stephen. 2018. *Knowledge Transmission*. New York: Routledge.

Evidence and Facts: Perspectives from History

Why Can't Oral Testimonies be Historical Facts? The Study of "Comfort Women" and Its Challenge to Modern Historiography

Q. Edward Wang

Historically speaking, historiography and jurisprudence were intrinsically connected not only because they shared an identical epistemological basis, but also because they, at least with regard to the European experience, had had a shared history in their developments into modern academic disciplines. Little wonder, therefore, that Donald Kelley, one of the leading intellectual historians in the English-speaking world, chose to begin and build his career around the entangled histories of law and history in early modern Europe. In his early writings, Kelley examined comparatively how the two disciplines in their formative stages mutually influenced each other in improving their methodology. Indeed, Kelley's works stress that historiography, or the research and writing of history, and jurisprudence, the study and practice of law, both need to establish and ascertain facts as the point of departure for their service to society.[1]

In modern times, or more precisely, from the nineteenth century onward, what Kelley finds in his research of the histories of law and history in Europe began to exert its influence around the world and became accepted as a paradigmatic model for others to follow suit and establish both as academic disciplines. Indeed, insofar as the history of historiography is concerned, many similar characteristics were developed, informing the practices of historical writing around the world. Granted, historians outside the English-speaking world continue using their own native languages in delivering their research findings, even though more and more of them nowadays have also chosen to publish in English. But with regard to research method, academic standard and writing style, historical writings produced across the world have shared

[1]Kelley (1970, 1984a, b).

Q. E. Wang (✉)
Rowan University, Glassboro, NJ, USA
e-mail: wangq@rowan.edu

Peking University, Beijing, China

B. Zhang et al. (eds.), *A Dialogue Between Law and History*,
https://doi.org/10.1007/978-981-15-9685-8_6

many commonalities. This is not only true to the regions, such as Africa and Latin America, where preferences for recording history in writing were a modern development, but it is also true to countries like China and Japan where historical writings had had a long history.

This is however until now. In more recent days, the seeming universal acceptance of the European model of historiography around the world has witnessed some notable dissension, prompting us to reevaluate our received notion of facts in the practices of both history and law. In the following, I will use one example in the Japanese study of the so-called "comfort women" in the Japanese army in World War II to illustrate how the recent advances in memory studies and women's history have challenged both historians and legal scholars to reconsider the definition and understanding of facts for the studies of historiography and jurisprudence at present and for the future. I have several reasons to take this approach in writing this paper. The first is that it enables us to see meaningful progress in the field of history and other neighboring disciplines and how they pose new challenges for us to reconsider the notion about facts. In fact, the "comfort women" issue in World War II has received attention from both jurists and historians as well as among scholars in other disciplines.[2] The second is that by focusing on a Japanese case, I hope to transcend the binary consideration in areas of comparative historiography and comparative cultural studies, prevailing in both China and elsewhere, in which comparisons between the West and China have usually received the most attention. (I believe this is a much-needed experiment as I initially presented this paper in China, the country where China-West dichotomy has often dominated scholarly discussions.) The third is that by drawing on my own knowledge of the history of historiography, I would like to point out that while historiography and jurisprudence had indeed shared perhaps a common origin, pace Donald Kelley's valuable research, they later, or more specifically, from approximately the second half of the nineteenth century, have embarked on different routes of development. And this divergence occurred because modern historians came to rely increasingly more on written records than oral testimonies for establishing and ascertaining factuality in their writing. And lastly, by drawing on Ueno Chizuko's challenge, which is comparable to yet also distinct from the criticisms of modern historiography rendered by Holocaust studies in the West,[3] to Japanese historians' obsession with textual evidence over oral testimonies in their studies of "comfort women," I will discuss briefly how new developments in the history field, marked by the rise and influence of memory studies—the study of "comfort women" included—have challenged historians to reconsider the issue of "facts" in historical research. This reconsideration will, I hope, perhaps renew the tie between historiography and jurisprudence, its former ally in epistemology and methodology.

[2]See, for example, Dolgopol and Paranjape (1994), Henry (2013), Sarah Soh (2008), Kumagai (2016), Tanaka (2002) and Norma (2016).

[3]See, for example, Langer (1991), Hutton (Summer 2005) and Lawson (2010), especially its "'Holocaust Testimonies': The Ruins of Memory and Holocaust Historiography" chapter, 270–304.

1 Where Is the Written Evidence?

Let us begin by reviewing the historiography of "comfort women" in Japan. During the last quarter of the last century, the issue of "comfort women" in the Japanese army during WWII was thrust into public attention, resulting also in the publications of serious scholarly works in Japan. The term "comfort women" was a euphemistic expression (hence it is put in quotation marks throughout this paper), coined by the Japanese army before and during the war to refer to the army prostitutes who satisfied the sexual needs of Japanese officers and soldiers. Among the prostitutes, some, especially in the early days, were recruited Japanese prostitutes whereas many others came from Korea and Taiwan, the two colonies Japan had annexed into its empire at the turn of the twentieth century. Then after WWII broke out in Asia, they were also joined by Chinese, Pilipino, Javanese and Dutch women. With few exceptions, as research finds, most of the "comfort women" were either cajoled or coerced into the service, yet, as argued at least by some, whether or not the Japanese army had directly played a role in forcing the women into the service remains unclear. Nonetheless, from the early twentieth century, these women's miserable experiences became recalled and remembered in songs, movies, memoirs and novels, which were also followed by mentions, often in passing, in historical works in the postwar period. In the 1970s, novelist Senda Kakō (1924–2000) published a bestseller, carrying a sensational title, *Military Comfort Women: Eighty Thousand Accused, No Voice of Women*, which was later adapted into the same-titled movie. The successes of his novel, which had a sequel, and movie helped draw public attention to the hidden and shameful experience many women had suffered under the Japanese military empire in WWII.

But it was not until the 1990s that historical communities in Japan began to treat the phenomenon seriously as a subject of research, for two main reasons. One was due to international pressure, for from the late 1980s, assisted by Korean scholars, some former Korean "comfort women" broke out of their long silence and publicly denounced Japan for their suffering, which helped kick off the study of "comfort women" in South Korea, followed also by mainland China and Taiwan. The other was domestic disputes between left-wing and right-wing politicians and intellectuals. In the face of the lawsuits, historians on the left, such as Yoshimi Yoshiaki, then a history professor at Chuo University, collected and published sources on "comfort women", established Center for Research and Documentation on Japan's War Responsibility and, more importantly, published the influential book *Jūgun ianfu* (Military comfort women) in 1995, which has been sold well over 80,000 copies. Yoshimi supported the claims by the former "comfort women" in Korea and elsewhere that they had been abducted into the "comfort stations" (*ianjo*) against their will and suffered rape and other forms of sexual violence by Japanese soldiers. The research done by Yoshimi and his colleagues might have prompted Japanese politicians to make apologies to their counterparts in South Korea, in which the so-called "Kōnō Statement", made on August 4, 1993, is most well known. As Japan's then Chief Cabinet Secretary, Kōnō Yōhei admitted that the Japanese army was involved in forcibly recruiting the "comfort women", for which he sincerely apologized to the victims (Yoshimi 2000, 33–35).[4] In 1994, the Asian Women's Fund was also established whose purpose was to pay reparations to the "comfort women".

However, the story was far from over. First of all, not all former "comfort women" chose to receive compensation from the Asian Women's Fund. Second, the Japanese government's apologetic position agitated the country's right-wing groups, in which some scholars are also included. For example, Nishio Kanji, a literary critic known for his writings on German culture and history, criticized the works by such left-wing historians as Ienaga Saburō (1913–2002) who, while not working specifically on "comfort women", exposed nonetheless their horrific existence in his histories of the war. Drawing examples in modern German history, Nishio argued that it was unfair to criticize Japan for not apologizing as sincerely as did Germany for its war responsibilities. Then from 1995, Fujioka Nobukatsu, a Tokyo University professor, published a series of essays, promoting what he called a "Free View of History" (*jiyūshugi-shikan*) on Japan's modern past in hopes of confronting and challenging the studies by Ienaga, Yoshimi and other left-wing historians. To Fujioka and Nishio, the left-wing and Marxian historians in postwar Japan propagated a "Masochistic View of History" (*Jigyaku-shikan*) of Japan's modern past, whose influence permeated the writing of history textbooks. The consequence of this "Masochistic View of History", they charged, was that it did not raise the national spirit of Japanese youth, nor did it do justice to postwar Japan's remarkable sociopolitical and economic transformation. In 1996, Nishio, Fujioka and others cofounded Japanese Society for History Textbook Reform (*Atarashii Rekishi Kyōkasho wo Tsukuru Kai*), which produced new history textbooks that implement their "Free View of History" against the "Masochistic View of History", or in the alliterated Japanese expression, "*jiyūshugi-shikan*" versus "*Jigyaku-shikan*". In the name of promoting national pride among the Japanese, their textbooks whitewashed the atrocities the Japanese army committed against their Asian neighbors in WWII. With respect to the "comfort women" issue, the Society members could not deny its existence but insisted that all the women involved in the service had not been done so against their will. That is, they voluntarily joined it—no coercion had ever occurred. And their attempt achieved some success: from 1997, the majority of history textbooks used in Japanese schools no longer mention "comfort women" (Kohihama 2018, 58–70).[5]

To rebut the counterattack by the right-wing political forces, left-wing historians have continued to search for and reveal evidence in the army and government archives. But they have also faced an enormous challenge. Toward the end of WWII, Japanese army headquarters ordered the destruction of documents, which means that few direct proofs could be located in the official sources that contained specific orders given by the headquarters to establish the "comfort stations" in the battle zones and also staff them with unwilling women by force.

[4]For the "Kōnō Statement", see https://en.wikipedia.org/wiki/Kono_Statement, accessed October 9, 2019.

[5]For a brief introduction to the debate on the "comfort women" issue in the Japanese academe, see Sand (Fall/Winter 1999). A more recent critical survey is by Li (Winter 2020).

Worse still, fellow historians have published works that dispute Yoshimi Yoshiaki's conclusion. And these historians who oppose Yoshimi are equally enthusiastic for grounding their research on government sources. One example is Hata Ikuhiko, a respected WWII historian in Japan with a number of publications that already earned him an international reputation. In 1997, Hata published *Comfort Women and Sex in the Battle Zone*, which is an expansive study with over 400 pages. Without question, Hata aimed to offer a final and definitive work on the subject, hoping to put an end to all the disputes around it. To a degree, it seems Hata has achieved this goal: In 2018, his work was rendered into English and received endorsements from a few US-Japan scholars. For instance, in his blurb, Kevin M. Doak, a chair professor of Japanese history at Georgetown University, states exactly that Hata's work "should be the definitive study" as well as "an essential work for historians, policy analysis, political scientists, politicians, and anyone who wants to truly understand a sad chapter in modern history."[6]

In his Afterword for the English version of his work, Hata declares:

> In writing this book, I did not include emotionally charged or politically driven arguments. I have not included personal views or proposals. I believe this is the only way to impartially lay out the facts. I would like to leave it up to each reader to make a personal interpretation and draw their own conclusion after reading the book. (Hata 2018, 344)

Hata Ikuhiko's statement, or disclaimer, clearly reminds us of the famous quote by Leopold von Ranke (1795–1886) in his preface to the *Histories of the Romance and Teutonic Peoples* that his writing of the book was only to show "what actually happened" (*wie es eigentlich gewesen*). Perhaps, it is due to this Rankean statement made by him that his book has been considered by some as a "factual" account of "comfort women" studies. To display his "impartiality", Hata includes in his book a chapter on testimonies by former "comfort women" across Asia, including those by a few Dutch victims, though without any by Japanese "comfort women". In his Afterword, he also explains why he did so:

> In studying this topic, it is essential to listen to the accounts of those who were involved—former comfort women, brothel operators, military police and doctors who supervised comfort stations, and soldiers who used the facilities—in addition to consulting existing documents and materials.

What he says above seems to suggest that his work has attempted to transcend the confines of written sources, and government archives in particular.

However, Hata is certainly not "impartial" toward his sources. With respect to oral testimonies, while he included those by former "comfort women", he admits that he trusts more of the testimonies by Japanese military policemen. "Many members of the military police", he argues, "were high achievers chosen from among soldiers. Their accounts can provide excellent material to substantiate or refute claims made about comfort women. I obtained more cooperation than I had expected". In other words, he regards the oral testimonies by "comfort women" as untrustworthy, needing to be corroborated by the military police, for the latter had recruited and managed them!

---

[6]See Kevin M. Doak's blurb on the back cover of Hata (2018).

And of all the sources he utilized in producing *Comfort Women and Sex in the Battle Zone*, it is also quite clear, by examining the book's structure and the trust of its argument, Hata favors written documents over oral testimonies. For instance, immediately following chapter six on the "comfort women's" testimonies, he presents chapter seven, "The Confabulations of Yoshida Seiji", in which he supplies evidence to refute Yoshida's testimony on Japanese army's mistreatment of "comfort women". Indeed, many have credited Hata with exposing Yoshida's account as falsified. Attaching the chapter after the testimonies by "comfort women" may be deliberate, for he perhaps wants to caution the reader about the validity of these women's recollection. Then in chapter eleven, entitled "Five Points of Contention: Q&A", which constitutes evidently the main point of his book, Hata addresses several key questions in the study. The very first one is whether or not the Japanese government or army had been involved in running the "comfort stations" by forcibly recruiting women into the services. His counterargument is based on that in the postwar trials, no Class B and C defendants confessed to such sex crimes. That is, he bases his argument on the fact that no official records suggesting the operations of "comfort stations" were "either under the orders of, or with the tacit approval of, the higher military command". In sum, Hata not only overrates official records, but he also considers the war criminals' testimonies more credible than that of their victims' (Hata 2018, 272–273). Nonetheless, Hata's book is still damaging to Yoshimi and his supporters, for it attacks the latter's finding in its own game, so to speak. That is, while different in their positions and interpretations regarding the nature of the "comfort women" system and its relationship with the Japanese army, both sides share one key similarity, which is to see government records, or written documents, as more valuable sources than the "comfort women's" oral testimonies.

2 Rhetoric, Relics and Archives—"Facts" in Modern Historiography

The question, of course, is why? In other words, why Japanese historians, whatever their ideological differences, regard oral testimonies as inferior to written documents, and government archives in particular? This question is especially pertinent to our comparative study of the concept of "facts" in legal and historical practices, for in court trials, oral testimony, whether it is by the defendant, plaintiff or witnesses, remains critical for establishing facts. When did historians begin to downplay the factual value of oral testimonies? The answer, a bit ironically, seems to lie in the early modern period when historiography, as Donald R. Kelley informs us, was coeval with jurisprudence in transforming itself into an academic discipline. In his many writings, Kelley offers quite a persuasive account of the paralleled developments of historiography and jurisprudence in early modern Europe. Agreeing with others, Kelley states that the idea and practice of historicism of the nineteenth century, a term which we will define and discuss below, characterized the formation of history as a bona fide academic discipline. Yet he quickly notes that there were "precursors" of historicism in an earlier period; indeed, he believes that some of the early, or pioneering, "historicists" had appeared in the Renaissance. "The humanists were the first men", writes Kelley, "to make a conscious and concerted effort to revive a dead past with some appreciation of temporal perspective and willingness to examine antiquity in its own terms". And, more importantly, Kelley thinks that the humanist endeavor to recover and revive the classical past was aided, among all other disciplines, mostly by the study of law. "The marriage of legal and historical studies in the sixteenth century", he declares, "provided one of the most enduring elements in the continuity of historicism from that age down to the present (Kelly 1970, 7, 9–10)".

Without question, Kelley's work is noteworthy in displaying the intimate alliance between history and law in European history, which deserves a closer look here. But if history was related to law, then such a relationship had occurred earlier. As is well known, before history was morphed into an independent academic pursuit in the period on which Kelley focuses his attention, history had been an integral branch of rhetoric; the latter constituted one of the *Trivium* from ancient to medieval Europe. Moreover, that rhetoric should perform an important part in one's education had been a pearl of received wisdom from classical times. For instance, Cicero, the famed Roman senate and orator, who had conferred the title "father of history" to Herodotus, had given rather extensive thoughts on the benefit of history to the study of rhetoric. To Cicero, history was primary to the study and practice of oratory. He and Quintilian, his follower in this regard, regarded history as essential to the improvement of rhetoric, or oratory, in both content and style. The content of history, which is replete with ample examples from the past, helps an orator to advance his exhortation whereas the style of history enables him to see the full range of linguistic tools available at his disposal.

Rhetorical knowledge and skill, of course, are crucial in legal practices, past and present. More specifically, as Matthew Kempshall in his recent study shows us, the benefit of history to improving rhetoric was demonstrated in the three forms of rhetoric developed through the Middle Ages, or between 400 and 1500. These three forms were "demonstrative or epideictic rhetoric", "legal or judicial rhetoric" and "deliberative rhetoric". All of them have some relevance to our consideration of the close collaboration between history and law. By "demonstrative or epideictic rhetoric", Kempshall refers to the speeches that either praise or blame the character of an individual, which were common strategy lawyers still use today in arguing for or against the case under trial. If "demonstrative or epideictic rhetoric" was used to describe a person's moral worth, then "legal or judicial rhetoric" pursued a more specific goal, which was to defend or prosecute an individual on trial. And lastly, "deliberative rhetoric" refers to the speeches that address or argue for political action; and political actions and their consequences constituted, customarily, the mainstay in the European tradition of historical writing (Kempshall 2011, 133–264).

If in medieval Europe, history and law were connected in rhetoric, then from the Renaissance onward, the two converged in their search for an improved methodology. Or more exactly, the interest in studying Roman law and restoring its authenticity that prompted the humanists to turn to history, which they regarded as indispensable for the endeavor to reconstruct history. In the words of Baudouin, who is regarded by Donald Kelley as the pioneer in advancing the method of history in the era, one needed to study the nature of law through philosophy, the meaning of law through philology and the origin of law through history. Drawing on the emphasis on eyewitness account in the legal practice, Baudouin also came to stress the importance of using primary sources in historical study. And, perhaps more importantly, the interest that gave rise to the historical school of law in France, of which François Baudouin, a jurist (1520–1573) was a forerunner in Kelley's reckoning, also turned the attention of its members to archival sources. Of all the sources available to the research of history, quoting Baudouin again, "the noblest and fullest will be … the records of the kingdom of France and the court of the parlement of Paris". One of his reasons for advocating the value of archival sources, with no surprise, was that they were used by legists and historians (Kelley 1970, 120, 216). Ironically, it was also the interest in archival materials that eventually polarized the two disciplines, for the use of archival materials was more for the study of legal history, not for legal trials. Indeed, in the mid-sixteenth century when Baudouin praised the value of archives, as Kelley reminds us, "archives constituted an untapped source for legal and institutional history". Moreover, he notes, the emergence of the interest in archives among legists and historians coincided with the "rising wave of antiquarian enthusiasm", for the collection of such materials had started in ancient Rome (Kelley 1970, 216). How the rise of antiquarianism came to shape historiography is outside Kelley's scope of research. For that subject, we should turn to the works of Arnaldo Momigliano and, more recently, that of Peter N. Miller. In his "Ancient History and the Antiquarian", one of his many important works on the subject, Momigliano writes that antiquarian research "meant a revolution in historical method". What he means is that it was due to the antiquarians' attention on authenticating ancient objects that a new awareness began to emerge in the Age of Antiquaries, which was termed as "the distinction between original and derivative authorities". According to Momgliano, the Age of Antiquaries probably reached its height in the eighteenth century but it had occurred in the wake of the Renaissance (Momigliano 1950, 285–315). Peter Miller concurs by focusing his research on Nicholas-Claude Peiresc (1580–1637), who was born a few years after François Baudouin's death and identified by Momigliano as the "archetype of all antiquarians". Sharing Momiglino's lament that antiquarianism had become a thing of the past, Miller nevertheless thinks, by publishing a new book on the subject in 2017, that "studying objects as evidence", the endeavor that had characterized the work of the antiquarians from that bygone era, is worthwhile, especially in considering "the current wave of material culture studies" (Miller 2012, 2017).

All the same, it is true that while helping turn historical writing into academic research, antiquarianism itself became replaced by archaeology in the following nineteenth century. But its influence was consequential: by drawing attention to objects as evidence, it gave confidence to the historian that they could reconstruct the past better than those who had lived through the age and written about it. In other words, armed with material remains from the past, modern historians could rewrite history. In the case of Roman history, for instance, this means that modern historians would and could do better than did Livy, Tacitus and other ancient Roman authors in telling us about the Roman past. In 1812, when Barthold Niebuhr (1776–1831) published his two-volume *Roman History*, he was credited with raising "history from a subordinate place to the dignity of an independent science", which set a model of inspiration for all the "greatest historians of the succeeding generation". Niebuhr received such accolades because he went beyond the work of Livy in writing about "regal and republican Rome". But Niebuhr did that by using "songs" and "funeral panegyrics" among others, which were, of course, oral sources (Gooch 1959, 14–20). Niebuhr's example suggests that by the early nineteenth century, historians had been persuaded by the notion, reflecting the antiquarian influence and interest, that they needed to rely on "original authorities", not "derivative" ones even if those were narratives from ancient authors. But they had not established the preference for written sources over oral ones as the base for their writings.

Then came Leopold von Ranke (1795–1886), an admirer of Niebuhr who tried to emulate the latter's success in principle, but not in the same area. Different from Niebuhr, Ranke was not a historian of the ancient world, even though he, a trained philologist, had lectured on such related subjects as a school teacher at a gymnasium. From early on, Ranke was more interested in the formation of modern nation-states, as shown in his writing of the *Histories of the Romance and Teutonic Peoples*, his first publication in 1824, which consequently earned him a professorship at the newly founded Berlin University. But like Niebuhr, described G.P. Gooch, Ranke believed that historical writing needed to use original sources, or that "the nearest witness to the event was the best, and that the letters of the actors were of more value than the anecdotes of the chronicler". It was perhaps in search of the "letters of the actors" that turned Ranke into the archives. While teaching in Berlin, Gooch wrote, Ranke's "greatest joy was in the archives". From then on to the end of his life, archival sources accompanied his writings of many histories (Gooch 1959, 75–76).[7] In 1874 when publishing the new edition of "Criticisms of Modern Historians", which was initially an appendix to his first book, the seventy-nine-year-old Ranke recalled that at the time when he wrote his *Histories of the Romance and Teutonic Peoples*, information drawn on archival sources was considered "new knowledge", but afterwards, he quickly added, this "new knowledge burst out like a fountain of spring that provided the base for my subsequent writings" (von Ranke 1984, 150).

Indeed, when Ranke wrote his first book, *Histories of the Romance and Teutonic Peoples*, he had not used archives to a full extent. The sources he had used for the writing comprised "memoirs, diaries, letters, legation reports, and original accounts from eyewitnesses", not all of them were necessarily found in the archives. But in his preface, he had already made the famous statement that pointed to the direction of his future scholarly pursuit. "To History has been given the function of judging the past, of instructing men for the profit of future years. The present attempt does not aspire such lofty undertaking. It merely wants to show how it essentially was (*wie es eigentlich gewesen*)". The use of archives became a way for him to achieve his goal,

[7] Kasper R. Eskildsen argues that it was in the 1830s that an "archival turn" occurred in Ranke's career, (2008).

for, as he stated in the introduction to his *History of England*, "to comprehend this period (of English history) we must approach it as closely as possible" because "to introduce the interests of the present time into the work of the historian usually ends in its restriction of free execution". It was in the archives, Ranke admitted it with pride, that "I have sought and found much that was unknown and which I needed for obtaining insight into events" (von Ranke 2011, 86, 96–101).

3 The Primacy of Written Records in Japanese Historiography

Leopold von Ranke, therefore, was instrumental in turning archival sources into the foundation of historical writing. But despite his widespread global influence, which occurred a decade or so after his death, Ranke's emphasis on strictly presenting archival materials in historical writing was not the only model cherished and followed by historians, even among his German compatriots. In 1868, for instance, when Gustav Droysen (1808–1884), who was about a generation younger than Ranke, wrote his *Grundriss der Historik*, a seminal text that later shaped the teaching of historical methodology, archival sources were not regarded as primary. Instead, Droysen favored "relics" (*Überreste*) and "monuments" (*Denkmäler*) to "written documents" (*Quellen*) (Droysen 1882, 13–16).[8] So the question we need to ask, returning to the theme of this paper on the study of "comfort women" in Japan, is how and why modern Japanese historians prioritize the use of government documents over oral and other sources. To answer this question, we need to review briefly the development of historical study as an academic discipline in modern Japan. It is commonly recognized that Japan's route to modernity began in 1868, for, in the wake of Commodore Matthew Perry's visit from the US in the previous decade, Japan in that year witnessed the Meiji Restoration, which resulted in a change of power on top. In the very next year, the new or Meiji government established the Historiography Bureau, whose function was to produce an official history of the country, following, as Meiji Emperor's decree indicated, the example of the compilation of "standard histories" (*zhengshi*) in imperial China. From the perspectives of both history and historiography, therefore, Japan's modernization combined both influences: while it aimed to catch up with the changing trend set by the modern West, it invariably also resorted to wisdom from the Asian tradition, in which Chinese culture figured centrally. As time went on, however, the former, or the Western influence, gained more and more weight, overwhelming the latter. But Asian cultural traditions did not go away completely but continued to play its role in shaping Japan's modernization process, either covertly or clearly in different time periods during the Meiji era (1868–1912).

[8]For German historians' reservations of and critical reactions to Ranke's emphasis on archive use, see Eskildsen, "Leopold Ranke's Archival Turn", 432–433.

The work at the Historiography Bureau from the late 1860s to the Bureau's eventual demise toward the end of that century reflected this syncretic process of cross-cultural mingling. As its original purpose was to extend the Chinese model of dynastic-history writing, the Historiography Bureau in Japan was initially mostly staffed by scholars known for their knowledge and training in sinology, such as Shigeno Yasutsugu (1827–1910) and Kawada Takeshi (1830–1896). The two, however, had different ideas in mind for compiling an official history for Japan. More exactly, while both believed that the compilation should begin with source collection, which had been the established way of practice in dynastic-history writing, they differed in their evaluation of the validity of certain texts from the past, hence debated on whether or not these should be included. As prominent sinologists of the time, Shigeno and Kawada both boasted a good knowledge of the Chinese scholarly tradition, its historiography included. But as we know, intellectual traditions in China had experienced notable changes over the periods. Between the two Japanese sinologists in the Historiography Bureau, Shigeno was more versed than Kawada in the scholarly trend in Qing China (1644–1911), featured by the rise of "evidential learning" (*kaozheng xue*). Advocating the principle of "seeking truth from facts" (*shishi qiushi*), Qing evidential scholars conducted textual and historical criticisms of the existing body of the Chinese written tradition, hoping to restore its authenticity and validity by detecting and correcting previous misunderstandings as well as winnowing out outright forgeries. Toward the end of the eighteenth century, this Qing intellectual trend had also reached Japan that constituted a major part in Shigeno's early education. Much more concerned than Kawada regarding the validity of facts in historical sources, Shigeno, while working at the Historiography Bureau, decided to exclude some texts from use because of their dubious content, for which he clashed with Kawada because the latter saw in those texts certain didactic values. In the end, Kawada left the Bureau, leaving Shigeno in charge of the project (Keiji 2005; Numata 1961).

Shigeno Yasutsugu's belief in "seeking truth from facts" not only motivated him to debate with Kawada but also determined, to some extent, the subsequent development in Japanese historiography during the Meiji period. As the Meiji government opened Japan's door to the outside world, modern Western culture flooded into the country, exerting a dominating influence in the decades from the late 1860s to the mid-1880s. Buoyed by the trend of Westernization, Shigeno also hoped to acquaint himself with Western historiography. To this end, he not only read Augustus Mounsey's *The Satsuma Rebellion: An Episode of Modern Japanese History*, but, as now head of the Historiography Bureau, also commissioned George Gustav Zerffi (1820–1892), a Hungarian diplomat and a self-made historian working in London at the time, to write a survey of the history and characteristics of "scientific history" in the West. Through Zerffi's work, Shigeno and his colleagues became impressed by the critical historiography advanced by the German Rankean School. Out of their impression of and interest in modern German historiography, they invited Ludwig Riess (1861–1928), a distant disciple of Leopold von Ranke's, to teach in Japan in 1887. In the following fifteen years while teaching at Tokyo University, Riess taught a range of courses, but "Historical Methodology" was the flagship one that largely constituted his legacy in Japan.

In other words, through Riess, Japanese historians in the Meiji period merged the two historiographical traditions: from Qing evidential learning, they learned skills and techniques in textual criticism for ensuring the validity of written sources, whereas from Rankean historiography via Ludwig Riess' teaching, the emphasis on using primary sources and taking a neutral, or objective, point of view when reconstructing the knowledge of the past. In 1888, together with Riess, Shigeno and his colleagues at the Historiography Bureau became professors of history at Tokyo University. Following the German/European model, they organized the historical association and published *Journal of History* (Rekishi zasshi) in 1889. Shigeno Yasutsugu was elected president of the association. In his inaugural speech, he stressed that as a historian, one should keep a "fair and detached attitude" toward historical figures and events in the past, suggesting his acceptance of the principle proclaimed and practiced by the Rankean School in modern European historiography (Brownlee 1998, 73–80). Thanks to Ludwig Riess, therefore, the professionalization of history in Japan began in tandem with other Euro-American countries. While Germany led the process in 1857, the UK followed it in 1886 and the American Historical Association in the US was not formally established and the *American Historical Review* did not go into publication until 1895.

If Japan became the first country in Asia to catch up with the trend in modernizing and professionalizing historical study, its historians achieved it, as discussed briefly above, by combining the Asian tradition and Western influence. The end result of this combination was that historical study in Japan, from the Meiji period onward to more or less this day, became increasingly depended only on the use of written documents, which they believed as containing most reliable facts. Tsuboi Kumezō (1859–1936), who was a teaching assistant for Riess at Tokyo University and later studied four years in different European universities before returning to take over the "Historical Methodology" course in Japan, published his lecture notes. In his discussion of historical sources, Tsuboi regarded "relics" (*ibutsu*) as the first type, which however was understood as including not only material remains but also various kinds of historical documents. The second was "tradition", which was equally comprehensive, ranging from historical books, historical images to legends, tales and songs. He emphasized that one should remember that texts were not the only sources for historians. But in the following chapter on "The Auxiliary Disciplines of History", he first discussed in detail philology (*gengo-gaku*) and paleography/diplomatics (*komonjo-gaku*), then proceeded to geography (*chiri-gaku*), archaeology (*ākiorojī*), chronography (*nendai-gaku*) and genealogy (*keifu-gaku*), suggesting, nonetheless, his preference for written sources (Tsuboi, 77–295). That is, critical evaluation of written documents via methods of philology, paleography, etymology and phonology, advocated and advanced by evidential scholars in Qing China, to ascertain their authenticity and validity constituted the main part in Tsuboi's teaching of historical methodology.

By comparing Tsuboi Kumezō's *Historical Methodology* with Ludwig Riess' same-titled course notes, written in English and kept at Tokyo University, one sees more clearly how Tsuboi modified Riess's original position concerning different types of historical sources. Influenced by Gustav Droysen, Riess considered "relics" the primary one and defined it broadly to include not only physical artifacts but also "state papers, writs, bills, letters, dispatches". Then the second kind were "monuments" and the third was simply termed as "sources", which, according to Riess, included "chronicles, annals, biographies, memoirs" and "historical songs, proverbs, anecdotes". Riess thus was more interested than Tsuboi in the relics of the physical kind, or material remains from the past. In the following chapter (lecture?), entitled "Historical Critiqu", Riess also chose to first talk about how to evaluate "piece of material" for checking its authenticity before moving on to "Criticism of Sources" (*Quellenkritik*), or the examination of written documents (Ludwig, 26–62). What differed Riess more from Tsuboi was that in his course notes, Riess did not discuss auxiliary disciplines of history, nor did he foreground the studies of philology and paleography as essential methods in historical research. In a word, in teaching the same course, Tsuboi covered a good deal more of textual materials as sources for historical study. And compared with Riess, Tsuboi's influence was greater and more far-reaching in Japan's historical circles: After appearing first at the end of the nineteenth century, his *Historical Methodology* was reprinted a number of times in Japan throughout the first half of the twentieth century.

4 Ueno Chizuko's Critical Challenge and Its Implications

Fast forward—or returning—to the study of "comfort women" in 1990s Japan. While Japanese historians seemed to be caught in a deadlock over their differences in interpreting the written sources on the "comfort women" question, then entered Ueno Chizuko, a prominent sociologist and feminist in today's Japan. From 1995, Ueno published a series of essays on memory studies as a way to look at Japan's recent past, especially from a feminist and gender perspective. In 1997, she collected the essays into an anthology entitled *The Politics of Memory*, in which some of the chapters deal with "comfort women". In the same year, Ueno participated in a conference organized by Yoshimi Yoshiaki and others at the Center for Research and Documentation on Japan's War Responsibility, at which she articulated her position regarding the "comfort women" experience and criticized Yoshimi's approach as inadequate, lopsided and outmoded. Ueno acknowledges that Yoshimi and his supporters are "conscientious" scholars who have worked diligently on finding sources in their study of "comfort women". But they also appear inadequate in fending off effectively the attacks by Fujioka in the latter's proposing of the "Free View of History". One main reason for this inadequacy, Ueno believes, is that Yoshimi and others failed to realize what she called a "paradigm shift" in contemporary historiography. In her opinion, the "shift" or "transformation" (*tenkan*) resulted from the post-structuralist critique, or the "linguistic turn", that had posed a serious challenge to the received notion of "facts" in positivist historiography. Regarding historical methodology, Ueno thinks that Japanese historians have faced three challenges: (1) challenge to its "written-source fetishism"; (2) challenge to the myth of "objectivity and neutrality" in scholarship and; (3) the challenge of oral history, oral traditions and oral testimonies. In short, Ueno argues that without recognizing and taking into account of the above challenges, then historians would and could not come up with a fuller understanding of the historicity about the "comfort women". For if one adheres to "written-source fetishism" and excludes the oral testimonies by the victims who had experienced the suffering, then this "objectivity and neutrality" are themselves quite biased as they basically follow and implement the "rule of the victor".[9]

In her presentation at the conference, Ueno Chizuko enunciated four specific points about the oral testimonies by former "comfort women". First, one should understand that testifiers are not the same as tapes used in the tape-recorder that one can replay the same content over and over again. Second, testimonies are mutually created in the dialogue between an interviewee and an interviewer, which means that once the interviewer is different, then the testimony would be different too. Third, every time a testifier gives a testimony, she/he usually tries to fit with the mainstream discourse. As such, if her testimonies are inconsistent or contradictory, the researcher should see them as manifesting exactly the truth, which Ueno also prefers to call "reality". Elsewhere, she has argued that the "reality" is multifaceted, so "realities" may be a better term of description (Chizuko 1999, 2002). And fourth, the creation of the testimonies is only possible when the interviewer and interviewee have gained mutual understanding and reliance. By contrast, the so-called "true testimony" under oath in front of a judge at a court could be viewed as an oppressed form of testimony. For, to the testifier, her testimony is not simply for revealing "facts" but for recalling and reminiscing a hidden, suppressed and discriminated past in order to reconstruct the entirety of her life.[10]

There are several ways to read and interpret Ueno Chizuko's above points. In the following, I shall limit my discussion to three areas. First, it goes without saying that by making these points about the nature and characteristics of oral testimonies, Ueno makes her intention rather clear, which is to problematize the received notion that in historical study, oral testimonies are supplementary and secondary to written documents. For while holding diagnostically opposing positions on the "comfort women", both Yoshimi Yoshiaki and his opponent Hata Ikuhiko nonetheless share the same notion that whether or not those women were forcibly recruited into the service depended on finding of official documents. As discussed above, Hata made his case on the lack of such direct government "order" whereas Yoshimi has continued in searching for it through the years, even though he already found a mention of the Japanese army's involvement in recruiting "comfort women" (Argibay 2003; Yoshimi 2000). To Ueno, this persistent search for and relentless emphasis on written

[9]Ueno Chizuko's presentation "Junda-shi to rekish-gaku no hōhō" (Gender history and historical methodology), in Nihon no sensō sakinin shiryō sentå (Center for Research and Documentation on Japan's War Responsibility), ed., *Shimpojium nashonarizumu to "ianfu" mondai* (Symposium on nationalism and "comfort women" issue) (Tokyo: Aokisha, 1998), 21–29.

[10]Ueno Chizuko, "Junda-shi to rekish-gaku no hōhō" Symposium, 27–28.

sources in reconstructing the history of "comfort women" is deeply flawed, for it overlooks and devalues the victims' actual experience. And, that the victims, in this case, happened to be women, which is to her, speaks volumes about the essential and significant contribution made by the advances of women's and gender history to the study. In a word, Ueno hopes to establish that in reconstructing the historicity of "comfort women", these women's recollections and testimonies ought to be considered the primary source for researchers.[11]

Second, if testimonies can be regarded as primary sources for reconstructing historical reality, then this directly relates to the theme this paper hopes to address here, which is about the intrinsic and historical connection between legal and historical study, or jurisprudence and historiography. As discussed at the beginning of this paper, I have observed that there was a shared epistemological origin of the two disciplines at their formative ages. In fact, if one looks further back, tracing from the very beginning of the history of Western historiography, then one can readily find that oral sources were essential for such ancient historians as Herodotus and Thucydides, or the founding fathers of the history discipline, in constructing their historical accounts. Granted, oral testimonies by plaintiffs, witnesses and defendants are not the only sources used in legal practices for establishing evidence. But these oral testaments are essential and, from time to time, even indispensable for both the defendant and plaintiff. Thus viewed, Ueno's stance on oral testimonies as the primary source for historical research is not radical or extreme, but points to a direction for us to renew the tie between historiography and jurisprudence by reconsidering what "fact" is and how "fact" is construed and constructed in both fields. Meanwhile, reevaluating the worth of oral testimonies in historical study would, in my opinion, also helps reveal the perceived flaw in modern historiography, exposed and criticized also by scholars in Holocaust studies, in (over) emphasizing the coherence for constructing a historical narrative at the expense of survivors' account and experience. It would thus be a useful way to diversify historians' narration and reunite the alliance between history and memory in remembering the past (Hutton 2005; Lawson 2010).

Third, though perhaps latent in her presentation, Ueno's emphasis on the importance of including oral testimonies of former "comfort women" reflects her intention to reintroduce morality into historical study. In my opinion, she values these women's oral testimonies not only because they had gone through the war and had had first-hand experience, which made their testimonies extraordinary and irreplaceable, but also because these are testaments by the "victims" in the war. That is, Ueno takes a moral position in her research by siding with the "victims" without hesitance or ambivalence. And, by patently upholding this moral position, she attacks the notions of "objectivity and neutrality", which were hailed traditionally as the ideals in modern historical scholarship. In this regard, I believe, her approach, too, helps reunite historiography and jurisprudence. Indeed, in legal practices, the search, collection and verification of facts constitute the main part of the work, which makes the whole process rather similar to the work of the historian. Then impartiality and objectivity

[11] A similar position is explored by Maki Kimura in her *Unfolding the "Comfort Women" Debates: Modernity, Violence and Women's Voices* (Houndmills: Palgrave Macmillan, 2016).

are also deemed critical for the jurors and judges in examining and evaluating the facts. Yet there has been a key difference between jurisprudence and the historiography of modern times: while the former seeks to convey and communicate justice through the process, such as the victim receives proper reparations and perpetrator a fit punishment, the latter's goal, at least as it was conceived by the followers of Rankean historiography, is to only offer a balanced and impartial account in which moral judgment should be absent.

By way of conclusion, it is perhaps necessary to note that over the past several decades, or even over the past century, the Rankean model of "objective" historiography has been under relentless scrutiny and critical reevaluation. Contrary to the image of Ranke being a value-free historian holding a detached position in constructing his narratives, many valuable studies have pointed out that Ranke not only had a vision, or a historical outlook, but that his ideas of history also reflected and extended his religious belief, German idealism, and political persuasion.[12] Indeed, from the later part of the last century, historical writings have experienced notable changes, thanks to the flourishing of memory studies and robust feminist scholarship, among other significant developments. Having examined the tradition of Japan's historical writing from the feminist perspective, Ueno Chizuko's challenge to what she called "written-source fetishism" among Japanese historians in studying the "comfort women" reflects a formidable force that is reshaping the landscape of historical scholarship around the world. As historians reevaluate the notion of facts, reexamine the epistemological base and reconsider the function of their discipline, it would perhaps lead to a new and beneficial alliance between historiography and jurisprudence in the years to come.

References

Argibay, Carmen M. 2003. Sexual Slavery and the 'Comfort Women' of World War II. *Berkeley Journal of International Law* 21: 375–389.

Braw, J.D. 2007. Vision as Revision: Ranke and the Beginning of Modern History. *History and Theory* 46 (4): 45–60.

Brownlee, John. 1998. *Japanese Historians and the National Myth, 1600–1945*. Vancouver: UBC Press.

Chizuko, Ueno. 1999. The Politics of Memory: Nation, Individual and Self. *History and Memory* 11 (2): 142–144.

Chizuko, Ueno. 2002. Rekishi gaku to feminizumu: 'josei shi' o koe su (Historiography and Feminism: Transcendence of Women's History). *Sai no seiji gaku (Politics of differences)*: 56–89.

Dolgopol, Ustinia, and Snehal Paranjape. 1994. *Comfort Woen: An Unfinished Ordeal, Report of a Mission.* Geneva: International Commission of Jurists.

Droysen, Gustav. 1882. *Grundriss der Historik*. Leipzig: Verlag von Veit & Comp.

Eskildsen, Kasper R. 2008. Leopold Ranke's Archival Turn: Location and Evidence in Modern Historiography. *Modern Intellectual History* 5 (3): 425–453.

Fitzsimons, M.A. 1980. Ranke: History as Worship. *Review of Politics* 42 (4): 533–555.

Gooch, G.P. 1959. *History and Historians in the Nineteenth Century*. Boston: Beacon Press.

[12]See, for example, Iggers (1962), Fitzsimons (Oct. 1980) and Braw (Dec. 2007).

Iggers, Georg G. 1962. The Image of Ranke in American and German Historical Thinking. *History and Theory* 2 (1): 17–40.
Hata, Ikuhiko. 2018. *Comfort Women and Sex in the Battle Zone.* Trans. Jason Michael Morgan. Lanham MD: Hamilton Books.
Henry, Nicola. 2013. Memory of an Injustice: The 'Comfort Women' and the Legacy of the Tokyo Trial. *Asian Studies Review* 37 (3): 362–380.
Hutton, Patrick. 2005. Quickening Memory and the Diversification of Historical Narratives. *Historical Reflections/Réflection Historiques* 31 (2): 201–216.
Keiji, Nagahara. 2005. *20 seiki Nihon no rekishi-gaku (20th Century Japanese Historiography).* Tokyo: Yoshikawa Kōbunkan.
Kelley, Donald R. 1970. *Foundations of Modern Historical Scholarship: Language, Law and History in the French Renaissance.* New York: Columbia University Press.
Kelley, Donald R. 1984a. *Historians and Law in Prerevolutionary France.* Princeton: Princeton University Press.
Kelley, Donald R. 1984b. *History, Law and Human Sciences: Medieval and Renaissance Perspectives.* London: Variorum Reprints.
Kempshall, Matthew. 2011. *Rhetoric and the Writing of History, 400–1500.* Manchester: University of Manchester Press.
Kohihama, Rui. 2018. Women's History at the Cutting Edge in Japan. *Women's History Review* 27 (1): 58–70.
Kumagai, Naoko. 2016. *The Comfort Women: Historical, Political, Legal and Moral Perspectives.* Trans. David Noble. Tokyo: International House of Tokyo.
Langer, Lawrence. 1991. *Holocaust Testimonies: The Ruins of Memory.* New Haven: Yale University Press.
Lawson, Tom. 2010. *Debates on the Holocaust.* Manchester: University of Manchester Press.
Li, Yang. 2020. Reflections on Postwar Nationalism: The Debates and Challenges in the Japanese Academic Critique of the 'Comfort Women' System. *Chinese Studies in History* 53 (1): 41–55.
Miller, Peter N. 2012. *Peiresc's Orient: Antiquarianism as Cultural History in the Seventeenth Century.* Farnham: Ashgate.
Miller, Peter N. 2017. *History and Its Objects: Antiquarianism and Material Culture since 1500.* Ithaca: Cornell University Press.
Momigliano, Arnaldo. 1950. Ancient History and the Antiquarians. *Journal of the Warburg and Courtauld Institutes* 13: 285–315.
Norma, Caroline. 2016. *The Japanese Comfort Women and Sexual Slavery during the China and Pacific Wars.* London: Bloomsbury.
Numata, Jiro. 1961. Shigeno Yasutsugu and the Modern Tokyo Tradition of Historical Writing. In *Historians of China and Japan*, ed. W.G. Beasley and E.G. Pulleyblank, 264–287. Oxford: Oxford University Press.
Riess, Ludwig. *Methodology of History* (No publication place and date, preserved at Tokyo University).
Sand, Jordan. 1999. Historians and Public Memory in Japan: the 'Comfort Women' Controversy. *History and Memory* 11 (3): 116–128.
Sarah Soh, C. 2008. *The Comfort Women: Sexual Violence and Postcolonial Memory in Korea and Japan.* Chicago: University of Chicago Press.
Tanaka, Yuki. 2002. *Japan's Comfort Women: Sexual Slavery and Prostitution during World War II and the US Occupation.* London: Routledge.
Tsuboi, Kumezō. *Shigaku kenkyuhō (Historical Methodology)* (Tokyo: Waseda University, no publication date but most likely in the 1890s; Available as a digitized text in Japan's National Diet Library).

von Ranke, Leopold. 1984. *Zur Kritik neuerer Geschichtschriber*. Leipzig: Verlag von Duncker & Humbolt.

von Ranke, Leopold. 2011. *The Theory and Practice of History*. ed. & intro. Georg G. Iggers. London: Routledge.

Yoshimi, Yoshiaki. 2000. *Comfort Women: Sexual Slavery in the Japanese Military during World War II*. Trans. Suzanne O'Brien. New York: Columbia University Press.

Interrogating Qi Shan Again: History, Law and Evidence Science

Weimin Zhong and Xin Hao

The name of evidence science has risen to great debate since the twenty-first century. The scope of discussion includes its specific title, definition, research object, subject nature, theoretical system, etc. This debate comes from the field of law (mainly in the field of judicial practice). Firstly, there is an outburst about whether its title is "evidence law", "evidence science" or "Evidence" (Fei 2015). The dispute over the fundamental issues of the evidence science has risen a controversial topic. The general point of view could be divided into two sides: One will be the evidence science in a narrow sense, which is the theory and method of collecting evidence, fact-finding and other procedures in the field of law. It's field includes the evidence law, forensic science and the mutual coincidence and coherence of these two. Another example is the evidence science which is also called "General Study of Evidence" or "the great revolution of evidence law" (Zongzhi 2006; Pei 2010, 2015; Yang 2017). It covers all subjects under humanities, social sciences and natural sciences that require evidence and proof (Zhang 2019). It is a methodology viewed by the world, just like "science of sciences". The purpose of evidence science is to avoid the uncertainty and arbitrariness of fact-finding as far as possible regardless whether it is viewed from a narrow or broad perspective. And preconditioned that there is a unified reality in the past, which requires discovery and understanding in the appropriate way. Evidence science is a subject of standardizing the process of evidence and fact-finding, so as to obtain the truth of the past reality.

However, according to the practice and theories of history containing generalized identification of evidence science, it's narrative subject is inevitable, and the truth or reality of history has a different manifestations at different levels and angles.

W. Zhong · X. Hao (✉)
Tsinghua University, Bejing, China
e-mail: 734374690@qq.com

W. Zhong
e-mail: weiminzh@mail.tsinghua.edu.cn

B. Zhang et al. (eds.), *A Dialogue Between Law and History*,
https://doi.org/10.1007/978-981-15-9685-8_7

Historical evidence is indeed the start of historical research. In my opinion there is no “unified reality”; historical materials are narrative interpretation, resulting to the unavoidable subjectivity. The analysis and proof process of historical materials have experienced the retention, trade-off, subjective analysis and interpretation of historians. In addition to it’s discipline norms and relative objectivity requirements, it is emotional, aesthetic, moral and other human factors which makes it possible for the historical research. The theory of historical research is also deeply influenced by its practitioners (historians) with their own historical research paradigm, ideology and the trend of the times. History should not try to avoid it’s subjective narrative level, it is meant to be a set of human factors that work within a vitality lifestyle to leave behind a legacy. In fact, in terms of the logic of theory and practice, Law is the same as History, which both should not be called as evidence science in the absolute sense.

1 Subjectivity of Evidence (Historical Materials)

Similar to law, history is also a subject that includes the past to obtain evidence in order to get some kind of cognition. There is a relatively common cognition that history is a form of evidence science, whose main purpose and task are to restore historical facts and reality with the help of evidence. Leading to the inevitable consistency of the results of historical research which holds the only truth to ontological reality. However, let’s take the various researches and evaluations of Qi Shan (琦善) by the mainstream historians from the post-war to the founding of the people’s Republic of China, as well as Jiang Tingfu (Tsiang Ting-fu)’s and Mao Haijian’s as an example. Qi Shan, was an imperial commissioner and a representative of the Chinese side in the first Opium War. He was put in charge of the military commander-in-chief. He left a great deal of historical evidence behind when he negotiated with the British representative. However, historians from a different historical timeline, through the analysis of the evidence, had an entire different evaluation of Qi Shan in their studies.

He was a “traitor” who largely led to the defeat of the war in the eyes of those traditional historians.[1] On the contrary, Jiang Tingfu highly praised Qi Shan as a diplomat who were “far beyond the times” (Jiang 1931), while Mao Haijian regarded him as just an “ignorant official” (Haijian 1995, 16). They all followed the academic norms in historiography and had a fair view point to an extent regarding towards historical materials. However, their understanding and cognition were so different towards the same object. It is because that history is mainly a story-telling craft rather

[1]In the late time of the Qing Dynasty, a lot of people held negative attitudes towards Qi Shan, such as ‘*Daoguang yangsou zhengfu ji*’, ‘*Yifen wenji*’, ‘*Zhongxi jishi*’ and so on. For a long time after the founding of the People’s Republic of China, the mainstream view was that Qi Shan was against Lin Zexu, and a capitulationist as well as a ‘traitor’ who advocated ‘relaxing the ban of opium’. The representative scholars and works are: Fan Wenlan. 1948. *Zhongguo jindaishi shangbian di1 fence (Modern history of China vol. 1)*. Xinhua shudian; Lin Zengping. 1979. ‘*Zhongguo jindaishi (Modern history of China)*’. Changsha: Hunan renmin chubanshe. etc.

than evidence science in the first place, inheriting principles and theories which are similar to those of law. On the basis of the normative requirements, they are subjects to put their own understanding and interpretation into the historical materials or evidence to tell a single coherent story. At the practical level of the two subjects; from the formation of historical materials or evidence to the result presented in the form of essays or the court decision, it is impossible to avoid the gap between the evidence and the truth. To some extent, both subjects produce or reconstruct a set of narratives, so they are not absolute evidence science.

Such examples can be found mostly within historical research. Let's take Li Hongzhang (李鸿章) as another example. The traditional view is that Li Hongzhang is an executioner because he killed a lot while leading the troops to suppress the rebellion of the Taiping Heavenly Kingdom. He is also regarded as a traitor in modern Chinese history, because he gave up the nation's interests and rights in order to promote the Westernization Movement. Moreover, he signed many "unequal treaties" on behalf of the country. However, in the past two decades, great changes have taken place in the academic evaluation of Li Hongzhang. Many scholars believe that Li Hongzhang is an outstanding politician in the modern history of China, and he made great contributions to the modernization of China. Additionally, he protected a lot of national rights for China in the negotiations with the foreign powers. We can see many thorough changes in historical research; from the beginning to the end of history research, all aspects have shown that although the exploration of historical truth and facts are one of the logical starting points and objectives of historical research. It is an individual interpretation and analysis that bond the historical materials into a complete logical chain of narrative for the historical research. Hence, achieving a different perspective from different historians.

Historical materials, being the evidence in historical research, are the only window for historians to peep into the facts of the past, are the foundation of historical research. The production process of historical materials itself is a result of interpretation. During the negotiations between Qi Shan and the British representatives, Admiral George Elliot and Captain Charles Elliot, the diplomatic notes about each other and the Imperial Pronouncements correspond with the replies of Daoguang Emperor and Qi Shan. All of them are the history materials formed by recorders under their own observation and judgment of the situation. After the fall of Humen, the impeachment of ministers must also have been from the analysis of the status and summed up their own judgment. Such historical records, do not emphasize on comprehensiveness and objectiveness, which are more or less mixed with the subjective factors because of the recorder's self-position. During the Battle of Chuenpi, which has a significant impact on Qi Shan's evaluation, it can be seen that in the early reports of China and Britain, they claimed that their defeat was at a smaller scale compared to the other side (Zhongshan daxue 1965, 700; Haijian 1995, 152). It is clear that these biased records are caused by the identity and interests of both sides. If those are used directly without discrimination, the research will deviate further from the historical truth.

Therefore, the limitations of historical materials require the effort to compare and verify by researchers. Some minor differences may lead to an entire different understanding, such as achieving different conclusions due to the difference in locations of historical materials. Historians Chen Shenglin and Mao Haijian compared the documents collected by Masaya Sasaki in the British Archives and "Chouban Yiwu Shimo" (筹办夷务始末), which is commonly used by historians. They found that the "Chouban Yiwu Shimo" of Qi Shan's note dated 2nd September 1840 was misplaced chronologically after the memo of August 17. This hence led to a misunderstanding of Qi Shan, who acted in accordance with the emperor orders, as the person who first proposed to punish Lin Zexu (Chen 1990, 113; Haijian 1995, 11). This is also the correction of most arguments claimed by historians that Qi Shan was against Lin Zexu and requested Qi Shan to advocate surrender. Historians face not only the possibility that historical materials could be biased, but also often encounter the situation that historical materials themselves could be totally wrong. Guangdong inspector Wang Tinglan's letter, was sent to the emperor, regarding Qi Shan's corruption of accepting bribes from Captain Charles Elliot. After close scrutiny by Jiang Tingfu, he came to a conclusion that the events and time in the letter were inconsistent. Therefore, the credibility of the text content is greatly reduced.

Furthermore, the discovery of historical materials is also a gradual process, and none of the researchers are able to read all the historical materials before carrying out the research. Jiang Tingfu copied and collected the archives of the Palace Museum for a long time in the late 1930s, and published it as "Chouban Yiwu Shimo", which played a vital role in his research on Qi Shan. These archives were impossible for the people from Qing dynasty to comment on Qi Shan after the end of the war. It happens often that the historical materials cannot be completely adequate for the topic researchers to study. In the meeting and daily communication between Qi Shan and the British, we are unable to understand and speak from Qi Shan's point of view, let alone his inner thoughts might be equal, humble or arrogant. Historians needs to use reasonable logical analysis and imagination to fill in the blanks of historical materials. When Mao Haijian wanted to discover the truth, he started with the exploration and analysis of his psychological activities, and obtained a more reasonable explanation (Haijian 1995, 15–21). Historical materials have great subjectivity, arbitrariness and uncertainty. Besides showing the relevant historical materials of one topic: "Let the historical materials speak for themselves", historians have to also use their analysis to tell a story. The value of history study lies in the retention and trade-off of historical materials, selecting evidence from the vast dispersion of irrelevant historical materials through their own interpretational choice into a single coherent narrative. Otherwise, historians are more likely to collect and search for historical materials and just exhibit their treasured historical materials, which are not included for an academic research.

2 Subjectivity of the Process of Analysis and Proof

Because of the different position of different historical materials, they are often orientated to several possibilities and not restricted to one. Besides applying their own logical analysis and empirical principles to examine and revise historical materials, historians need to establish their own interpretation for the results and paths of their research. When there are discourses with different meanings, historians need to choose and explain them according to their own cognition and principles. When studying Qi Shan's attitude towards Britain, Mao Haijian saw detracting terms such as "yixing quanyang 夷性犬羊" "barbarians, ignorance of etiquette 野蛮之人, 礼义不知" in Qi Shan's memorials. In a note given to Captain Charles Elliot, he also stated that only when the British "shows signs of obedience", he will then "act on behalf of emperor's kindness". Mao Haijian thought that it is completely adhering to the arrogant and ignorant attitude of Qing Dynasty (Haijian 1995, 7–9). Jiang Tingfu saw that although there was criticism quoted "Ying Yi (啖夷)" in Qi Shan's report, he quoted "your country (贵国)" "your commander (贵统帅)" which pronounced equality in his notes to the British. Comparing with the arrogant attitude of the whole empire, Jiang Tingfu regarded him as the "first foreign minister in the last ninety years", who are "beyond the contemporaneity" (Jiang 1931, 3). Tao Yuanzhen, on the other hand, through the British's criticism towards Qi Shan from "Zhongxi jishi (中西纪事)", had an opinion that Qi Shan's attitude is in fact "overly humble" (Yuanzhen 1935). Even faced with the same historical material, historians have different explanations. Jiang Tingfu attributed the pacification policy of Daoguang Emperor to the translation problem of British official documents, which led Qi Shan and Daoguang misunderstanding the British's intentions for pleading injustice (Jiang 1931). Dealing with the similar content, Mao Haijian, combined with his understanding of the later edicts of Daoguang Emperor, believed that the lost in translation was not an issue. Moreover, Daoguang's decision was scrutinized carefully under much considerations, such as pacifying the war, having financial stability and so on (Haijian 1995, 176–179). Without any strong evidence to explain that these explanations are wrong, it is impossible to conclude which perceptions are right or wrong. It is the complexity of history that different truths exist in different ways at all levels.

The analysis, interpretation, supplement and integration of historical materials are influenced by researchers' own critical thinking, logical deduction and their life experience. Most people had a difficulty of understanding the great disparity between China and Britain during the first Opium War, and the awkward role of Qi Shan mediating between the two countries, from Qi Shan's historical timeline to the end of the Qing Dynasty. It is reasonable that they cannot understand why Qi Shan, the "mighty" Chinese representative, advocated a compromise. Only can they looked for the answer within the familiar thinking logic of political collusion between officials in the traditional bureaucracy, resulting in the uproar of Qi Shan's "bribery" rumor without any evidence.[2]

[2]The opinion that Qi Shan was bribed by the British was quite popular. During the Opium War. Zuo Zongtang mentioned it in his letter to his teacher. See Zuo Zongtang, *Zuo Wenxianggong quanji*

Historians' intellectual ability and life experience could lead to the interpretation and cognitive differences in the analysis of historical materials, and the deeper influence is caused by the general trend of the times and the historical theory of historical view. Historical background and historical view play an indelible role in the study of history. The comments and analysis of the Opium War that appeared right after the end of the war, such as "Daoguang yangsou zhengfu ji (道光洋艘征抚记)", "Yifen wenji (夷氛闻记)", "Zhongxi jishi (中西纪事)" and so on, have viewed Qi Shan in a negative position. It was certainly inseparable from the environment in which Confucianism dominated the whole country at that time. With strict etiquette and hierarchy rule, the decisions made by the emperor could never be criticized by his subordinates. It is also impossible for the majesty of China to be defeated by barbarians, so the defeat could only be caused by the minister with great responsibility. By this logic, Qi Shan, who carried out the decree and even had the intention of compromise, only required to play the role of the bad side in the traditional "loyal and traitor" moral model. As Mao Haijian said, not only the autocracy of Confucian traditional ideology, but also the internalization consciousness and self-discipline for a long time forested this way of thinking. It is the cultural influence from which it could not be separated from in the late imperial China (Haijian 1995, 16–20). Jiang Tingfu, on the other hand, in his article "Qi Shan and the Opium War", thought that Qi Shan had reached the position of "far beyond the time", which was also inseparable from the historical context at that time. Jiang Tingfu has been classified by many scholars as one of the historians serving the mainstream ideology, and many people think that his research on Qi Shan also had contemporary relevance. This article was published two months after the Mukden Incident. It was a time when the whole national situation became chaotic and the northeast territory was in danger. Meanwhile, it is a time when the Chinese people are in a dilemma of having an anti-Japanese war and also avoiding such great loss towards national strength. It cannot help but remind the readers of the compromise made by Qi Shan at the time of the national chaos in the late Qing Dynasty. Therefore, many readers think that Jiang Tingfu's article is alluding to the current situation through raising the evaluation of Qi Shan, and also to express his views on resisting imperialism through diplomatic means.[3] Influenced by Marxist

71 Zuo Wenxianggong gongshudu 1 (Zuo Wenxianggong 71 Zuo Wenxianggong slips 1). Guangxu 16nian keben. Daoguang Emperor also heard that. he had secretly told Yi Shan to check whether Qi Shan had 'private gifts', and mentioned it again in the later trial. See Qi Sihe et al. 1964. *Chouban yiwu shimo Duangguang 2.* Beijing: Zhonghua shuju chubansh: 824, 999–1001; Zhongguo diyi lishi danganguan. 1992. *Yapian zhanzheng dangan shiliao 3 (historical Materials of the Opium War Archives3.,* Tianjin: Tianjin guji chubanshe: 459, 475. Under the same logic, when Yi Buli got demotion, Daoguang Emperor also doubted whether he had accepted bribes. Therefore, it can be regarded as the thinking inertia of that time, which is analyzed in detail in Haijian's book (1995). However, according to the research of many scholars, there is no evidence or motivation that Qi Shan has accepted bribes.

[3]Wang Yujun. 1986. 'Tiang Tingfu xiansheng dui zhongguo jindaishi yanjiu de changdao (Jiang Tingfu advocacy for the study of modern Chinese history)', *Jindai zhongguoshi yanjiu tongxun* 1:17. Scholars have also discussed the specific metaphor of Qi Shan in his article: Cai Lesu compared the historical process at that time with the Qi Shan image described by Jiang Tingfu, and also considered Jiang Tingfu's political attitude. He argued that the reference of Jiang Tingfu in writing Qi Shan

view of history, the historical academicians emphasized the theory of imperialist aggression, oppression and also class struggle after the founding of the Pcople's Republic of China According to the behavior in the Opium War. The upper class was divided into the surrenders and resistors, so Qi Shan was accused of advocating the surrender to imperialism, and later became the critical object. Mao Haijian's relevant research and evaluation of Qi Shan since the 1980s were closely related to the atmosphere of China's rapid modernization after the reform and opening up. Under the historical modernization paradigm, Mao Haijian's assessment of Qi Shan's "failure to do anything useful for China's change" was directly linked to his contribution towards China's modernization (Haijian 1995, 561). Therefore, the analysis of historical evidence proved that even under the strict discipline norms, historical research is still telling a story that belongs to every scholar. The truth behind every history is shown at different levels in the stages of different narratives.

3 The Subjectivity of the Theory of History

The different explanations and various perspectives by historians are not only reflected in the study of Qi Shan, due to the different stages of time. The changes of the interpretation system and research perspective have an extensive and profound impact on the historical study of other events and scope. History is not evidence science, which is also related to the theory of history itself. In China, historians have not simply viewed objectivity with much importance since the origin of history. From the narrative of "Confucius compiled The Spring and Autumn Annals chastising evil deeds and urging people to do good deeds", Sima Qian's ultimate ideal goal is "creating a philosophy of my own", the obligation of ancient historian officials was to educate people to learn from the past. They explained historiography from the beginning, shouldered with the responsibilities of education and even propaganda. Therefore, the description of historical materials and the study of history are not only the summarization of objective facts and the excavation of historical truth, but also instructions and orientation to the present. Nevertheless, in ancient China as mentioned earlier, is also an example of changing process of Qi Shan's evaluation that shows characteristic and nature of history which are continuously present in history research. Although some historians try to emphasize the objective factor of history, the other aspects of the nature of history such as subjectivity cannot be ignored and denied.

---

should be Wang Jingwei. See Cai Lesu, and Yin Yuanping. 2008. 'Fankang diguo zhuyi de ling yitiao lu: lun Jiang Tingfu de Qi Shan yanjiu (another way to resist imperialism: Jiang Tingfu's study of Qi Shan)', *Hunan daxue xuebao* 6: 37–40. Through Jiang Tingfu's book 'Zhongguo jindaishi (Modern History of China)' written six years later during anti-Japanese war, comparing the different evaluations of Qi Shan and Lin Zexu with his book and article, many scholars think that Jiang Tingfu had a new view on the political choice in the anti-Japanese war. As a result, the evaluation of Qi Shan in the book is obviously lower than that in the previous article.

The subject narrative in historical research does not indulge researchers in their own overwhelming emotion and boundless imagination. The most important feature of history is based on existing historical materials, and at this point historians should make reasonable and logical deduction. It is precisely that that historical research is extremely vulnerable to subjective factors such as the ages with time, ideology, individual emotions and so on. Historians should always keep their own consciousness and be aware of their limitations. Otherwise, it is easy to cross the boundary of reasonable norms and draw conclusions beyond the present of historical materials. This is also the reason why Mao Haijian's research caused a big controversy. Perhaps it is because Mao was overly influenced by the modern paradigm; pouring too much "nationalist emotion historians born with" into his study. The purpose and method of his research are "to choose the Opium War, which should have been the starting point of China's modernization. Analyzing what mistakes the Chinese people, especially the policy makers, had made and how it led to their mistakes" (Haijian 1995, 25–26). Just by considering the extent of modernization development as the only standard of research, then the researchers must find modern Chinese history obtaining such "mistakes"; thoughts and behaviors were conservative, the development of economy, science, technology and politics lag behind in all aspects. However, before modifying the errors of ancient people and history process, it is necessary to consider whether researchers have been influenced by the contemporary context, concurrently presupposed the premises and assumptions of inevitable mistakes for them, before discussing whether they made mistakes or not (Luo 1999).

The misconception that history is evidence science may be influenced by the history of western historical theories. As a modern discipline, history was born in Germany in the late nineteenth century. Under the creed of freedom and reasoning, advocation and belief since the Enlightenment, historical research, as a "science", has been professionalized and concentrated in universities and research centers. The core of its discipline is the same as other specialized sciences which is "the truth that lies in the conformity of knowledge with objective reality" (Iggers 1997). When it comes to the work of historians, according to Ranke: "wie es eigentlich gewesen",[4] one of the reasons why many people misunderstand that history is evidence science. Before the first half of the twentieth century, it was widely believed that researchers could restore the truth of history with sufficient evidence. As long as the historical materials are dealt correctly, an objective and unified historical reality will naturally emerge. Therefore, the focus of historical research is to find and examine historical materials, with the belief that historical development has a single direction and a pattern. The understanding of history from other disciplines is mostly about this positivism which might have been agreeable by others.

[4]Although, as many studies have shown, Ranke's own methodology had a deep philosophical background, not only concerned with the critical examination of historical materials. However, it is widely circulated that Ranke rejected all philosophy theories, paying only attention to the naturalism and positivism of facts, and to some extent the latter version of historical view becomes the characteristic of European and American historical research at the end of the nineteenth century and the beginning of the twentieth century.

However, the objectivity and positivism of history subject, which generally had been believed to be the subject nature. They have been greatly challenged twice in the development of western historiography theory: the historical relativism trend in the 1920s and 1930s and the postmodernism trend since the 1960s and 1970s. The traditional value and belief that history is evidence science have been questioned. The understanding of history as a subject has been changed tremendously, and the nature of narrative history has been recognized and valued exponentially (Gang 2008).

As mentioned earlier, several historical materials could be retained and used by historians as time passes by. Therefore, it is impossible to obtain overall information with an incomplete data. Researchers are unable to give up their subjectivity in the application and interpretation of historical materials. This is basically how the relativism overcome the objectivity of traditional history in the 1920s and 1930s. With the decline of speculative historical philosophy and the rise of analytical historical philosophy, historians have made a qualitative leap in historical epistemology. For example, Collingwood's viewpoint that "all history is the history of thought" and Benedetto Croce's words that "every true history is contemporary history" emphasize the subjectivity of historians, and that the mind-set of these characters are an indispensable element in the study of historians. They assumed that history written by historians is not the presentation of objective history, however historians believed otherwise that objective history had great ideological impact.

Following that after, the kind of professional history was transformed into various types of histories, which were influenced by all kinds of social science in the twentieth century. In this spectrum of histories, whether it was used in quantitative, sociological and economic research methods, or the structuralism from the Annales school, class analysis of Marxism, history theory valued natural science as a model, on the contrary of the 1920s and 30s, they tried to become more "scientific" and objective. Its hypothesis and premise were still a kind of continuity and direction in the development of history. However, such an optimism foundation for the modern world was deeply challenged and undermined by the primary changes in the structure of the industrialized society, and there was a rebound from the concept of modern scientific progress in the 1960s and 1970s.

Hayden White's masterpiece Metahistory: The Historical Imagination in Nineteenth-Century Europe published in 1973, as a vital symbol and the rise of post-modernism historiography in the 1960s and 1970s. The former grand narratives which historians focused on, such as politics and economy, were replaced by the understanding of the culture of daily life and experience from the lower class. Narrativism is a typical expression of postmodernism. The most prominent feature of narrative theory is thoroughly textualization of history, which refers to the shift towards the concerns and theoretical reflection of historians on historical text. While the focus of relativism was the selectivity and subjectivity of historical materials as the constituent elements of historical texts, narrativism in the post-modern trend emphasizes that the comprehensive meaning of the text is greater than the sum of individual elements through historical story-telling. Historical text containing language and fiction starts from the evidence as basis for the work of historians. The whole procedure of history is from the understanding and interpretation of historians to the readers' understanding of it. In this process, the appropriateness and rationality of the text cannot be measured by the traditional standard of objectivity of evidence. To some extent, historians and novelists put in the same effort to tell a story by choosing and arranging statements. Nowadays, the understanding of most historians about the discipline of history compliments to what He Zhaowu quoted, "history is a subject of humanities" (Zhaowu 2007, 10). History is essentially an interpretation and narration, not a social or natural science, nor can it be covered by evidence science.

4 Law Is not an Absolute Science of Evidence

"The role of an objectivist historian is equivalent to a judge who adheres to neutrality or impartiality" (Novick 1993, 1–2), similar to a typical expression of history as evidentiary science. However, whether the discussion and controversy on this issue in historical theory, or the case study of Qi Shan's judgment by historians at the practical level, it has been proven that historians do not play the role of so-called "objective" and "neutral" judges. And judges and law in reality, as historians believe, should be "objective" and "neutral" compared to historians? The conclusion is apparent because law research and judge verdict actually operate under a logic similar to historical research through the analysis and understanding of evidence, pursuing truth and objectivity, and resulting to a research or verdict. Therefore, it is necessary to reflect on the view that law is evidence science.

The principle that judges and lawyers rely on evidence is somewhat true. Evidence is the starting point of fact-finding, and the premise of judicial justice. However, in the practical process of obtaining and utilizing the evidence, we can find that the gap between legal and objective fact cannot be eliminated. The basis of judicial decision reply on this evidence, but there is a possibility that existing evidence is insufficient. Therefore, people can only acquire these evidence that has been selected along a certain time and various factors. It is difficult to reflect all the facts and truths objectively and neutrally through a limited set of evidence. As far as lawyers are concerned, they will naturally take the initiative to select and arrange the evidence accordingly to their value preference and interest tendency, accompanied by speaking for the plaintiff or the defendant. Therefore by using the selected evidence, lawyers will form a reasonable selected narrative in favor of one's side, and depict this story to others. In this sense, their work is no different from that of historians. On the other hand, based on the stories presented by both plaintiff and defendant, the judge uses this discretion to test the verification of the evidence. By using both sides to the story, the judge will establish a final verdict with legal facts to support it. To a certain extent, the source of evidence for judicial proof is more "indirect" than historical evidence. Although the law has a principle of legality, authenticity and relevance for the judge to exclude illegal evidence, the judge still has a lot of space in fact-finding, such as deciding verification of single evidence and judging mutual confirmation among all kinds of evidence. It forms the individual difference and subjectivity by the standard of free evaluation of evidence through inner conviction. The academicians also admit that there must be a set of differences between the legal and actual facts. It is impossible to pursue 100% true facts when the judge comes to a conclusion. But with the standard that the evidence reaches high probability to be verified, judges make their own identification of a chain of evidence and narrative stories. As far as many cases of appeal and sentences which may alter the reality, the narratives and subjectivity in the administration of justice often do not lead to only one understanding.

In terms of philosophy of law, quoted by a famous judge, Holmes, "The life of the law has not been logic", which strongly criticized legal formalism, academics began to pay attention to the importance of the judge's individual experience in discretion and judgment. The linguistic turn in philosophy in the twentieth century not only triggered the narrative tendency of history, but also had a paradigm influence on jurisprudence under the frame of postmodernism. This symbolizes the representative of legal analytical positivism, H.L.A. Hart argued the "open structure" of language. It has given a rise in discussion of interpretation of legal rules. People lost in belief in the certainty and objectivity of law, but started to focus on the interpretation of law from the perspective of language or experience.

Since history and law have a strong characteristic in narration, we could conclude that both are not pure evidence science. Since the Enlightenment, science, rationality and objectivity have been generally promoted to a sacred position, the scientific and ideological revolution were carried out under the ideological trend of rationalism. On the other hand, the subjective factors of humanities, such as emotion, aesthetics and ethics, are belittled and obliterated for "non-scientific" reasons, as if the former is advanced and meaningful, while the latter is backward and meaningless. However, from the disciplinary nature and sources of history and law, as well as the research practice, the connection between historical materials and truth, evidence and facts cannot be separated from the subjective humanistic factors of interpretation and narration. There have been an increase in awareness by researchers towards the significance of subjective factors to history and law. It is the interpretation and narration of history that makes it a "living history". Otherwise, history is only a list of historical materials. It is the humanity of historians and the pursuit of human nature that makes the research interesting at the aesthetic level. Similarly, the free evaluation of evidence also eases the tension between the stable law and the changing reality, by leaving the space for moral tradition and human customs, and opportunity to improve the law. Otherwise, once the law is formulated, the duties of jurists, lawyers and judges are only able to act in accordance with the existing law. While clarifying the misunderstanding that history and law are evidence science, we should not ignore the normative basic condition of historical materials and evidence. To prevent from moving towards the other extreme of subjectivity in history and law. On the contrary, the norms and methods of discipline practice have been strengthened in the development of these two disciplines. That is the concept of objectivity of history and law that has a deeper and richer purpose under the continuous reflection and discussion of scholars.

References

Cangling, Pei. 2010. Zhengjuxue de da geming zailun shizhi zhengjuguan (The Great Revolution of Evidence Law—Further Discussion of Substantial Evidence View). *Falv kexue* 3: 87–97.

Cangling, Pei. 2015. Lun zhengjuxue de xueke dingwei (The Disciplinary Orientation of Evidence Science). *Huanqiu falv pinglun* 1: 5–19.

Chen, Shenglin. 1990. *Lin Zexu yu yapian zhanzheng lungao (Lin Zexu and the Opium War).* Guangzhou: Zhongshan daxue chubanshe.

Fei, Zheng. 2015. Zhengju kexue de yanjiu xianzhuang ji weilai zouxiang (Research Status and Future Trend of Evidence Science). *Huanqiu falv pinglun* 4: 146–165.

Gang, Peng. 2008. Xiangdui zhuyi, xushi zhuyi yu lishixue keguanxing wenti (Relativism, Narrativism and The Question of Objectivity in History). *Qinghua daxue xuebao* 6: 27–41.name

Haijian, Mao. 1995. *Tianchao de bengkui: yapian zhanzheng zai yanjiu (The Collapse of China: A Restudy of the Opium War).* Beijing: Shenghuo dushu xinzhi sanlian shudian.

Iggers, George G. 1997. *Historiography in the Twentieth Century. From Scientific Objectivity to the Postmodern Challenge.* Middletown, Connecticut: Wesleyan University Press.

Jiang, Tingfu. 1931. Qi Shan yu yapian zhanzheng (Qi Shan and the Opium War). *Qinghua xuebao* 6 (3): 1–26.

Luo, Zhitian. 1999. Tianchao zenyang kaishi bengkui—yapian zhanzheng de xiandai quanshi (How to Start the Collapse of 'China'—A Modern Interpretation of the Opium War). *Jindaishi yanjiu* 3: 9–24.

Novick, Peter. 1993. *That Noble Dream, The 'Objectivity Question' and the American Historical Profession.* Cambridge and New York: Cambridge University Press.

Yang, Jiwen. 2017. Da zhengjuxue de zhengming yuanli yanjiu (Research on the Proof Principle of 'General Study of Evidence'). *Zhengju kexue* 6: 709–718.

Yuanzhen, Tao. 1935. Du Qi Shan yu yapian zhanzheng (After Reading 'Qi Shan and the Opium War'). *Judu yuekan* 88: 7–11.

Zhang, Baosheng. 2019. *Zhengju kexue lungang (A Preliminary Outline of Evidence Science).* Beijing: Jingji kexue chubanshe.

Zhaowu, He. 2007. *Lishi yu lishixue (History and History Theory).* Wuhan: Hubei renmin chubanshe.

Zhongshan daxue lishixi zhongguo jindai xiandaishi jiaoyanzu, yanjiushi (Abbreviated to "Zhongshan daxue"). 1965. *Lin Zexu zougao zhong (Lin Zexu Drafts).* Beijing: Zhonghua shuju chubanshe.

Zongzhi, Long. 2006. Da zhengju xue de jiangou jiqi xueli (The Construction and Theory of 'General Study of Evidence'). *Faxue yanjiu* 5: 82–98.

Judging the Past, Blaming the Past, Hailing the Past

Zoltán Boldizsár Simon

1 Ethical Relations to the Past (In Historical Culture)

This essay attempts to understand how we became preoccupied lately with the question of "Who's to blame?" when talking about the past. At first sight it may seem that there is not much to discuss. One may argue that looking for past culprits to blame for the shape of our present is simply a correlate of carrying out historical judgment. Not a necessary correlate perhaps, but one that accentuates certain types of judgments passed on the past. And true enough, we rather habitually judge the past in our everyday life and in public debates. Furthermore, judging the past is arguably an integral feature even of scholarly modes of approaching the past. Debates on objectivity as opposed to historical judgment and on the relativity of historical interpretations to the ethical and political values of historians have accompanied the formation of academic historiography since its institutionalization to the present day (Novick 1988; Ginzburg 1991; Vann 2004).

Our recent investment in blaming the past, however, emerged outside the framework of those long-standing debates on judging the past. Hence the claim I wish to advance: blaming the past is not simply a more strident way of judging. We would better conceive of it as an emerging relation to the past in its own right. But what does this mean exactly? And what relation to the past in the first place? For, as Mark Day (2008) claimed more than a decade ago, relations to the past are manifold. Although we tend to attribute primary importance to epistemic ones that revolve around the conditions of producing knowledge of the past, Day (2008: 419) thinks that we should go beyond the epistemological focus as historians also "evaluate the past in studying past actions and works, criticising or praising them on intellectual, ethical, or other grounds". I agree.

Z. B. Simon (✉)
Bielefeld University, Bielefeld, Germany
e-mail: zoltan.simon@uni-bielefeld.de

B. Zhang et al. (eds.), *A Dialogue Between Law and History*,
https://doi.org/10.1007/978-981-15-9685-8_8

The kind of relations to the past I would like to map in this essay belong to the larger family of evaluative relations Day mentions. More specifically, I am interested in exploring certain ethical or ethico-political relations to the past. This does not mean that other types are less relevant or that they are independent from ethical ones. As Herman Paul (2015) argued more recently while embracing Day's agenda, kinds of relations to the past—epistemic, moral, political, aesthetic—are often intertwined. On this premise, exploring ethical relations to the past has the additional benefit of enabling us to catch a glimpse into how the ethical is entangled with other kinds of relations to the past, including judicial, temporal, and even epistemic ones.

As to the specifics, two of the relations I wish to explore have already been mentioned above: judging the past and blaming the past. In situating the two and in arguing for the distinctness of the latter, I will also introduce a third ethical relation as a counter-relation of blaming: hailing the past. All three prevail in broader socio-cultural practices just as well as in scholarly undertakings, meaning that the scope of this essay is not limited to investigating how historians relate to the past.

What then is the adequate scope of studying relations to the past? Whereas Day's project is committed to studying the knowledge production of historical studies, Paul's approach is more inclusive. It is "based on the assumption that 'history' needs not be limited to academic historical studies, but can also include histories of the kinds one encounters in museums, newspapers, parliaments, novels, life-stories, computer games, and tourist guides" (Paul 2015: 457). In other words, it intends to encompass our entire "historical culture". And there is nothing surprising in this extension. It seems to be part of a larger reorientation in studying history and historical thinking. As Grever and Adriaansen (2017: 75) argue in their brief history of the "umbrella concept of historical culture", the notion emerged in the 1980s in German history didactics to denote the "historical component of political culture". By today, however, it has achieved its broadest meaning as "people's relationships to the past" (Grever and Adriaansen 2017: 73). What this means is that historical theory, leaving behind a focus on questions of historiography, has joined forces lately with history didactics, history education, and even public history in studying historical culture understood as relations to the past.[1]

But back to a specific historical theory approach, the scope of the notion of "historical culture" may be broadened further. Paul's understanding is premised on investigating that which is explicitly "historical": that which is either deliberately produced as "historical" in one sense or another (such as a tourist guide or a computer game) or that which understands itself as having to do with "history" (such as museums or newspapers). In my view, if we want to understand how we relate to the past today, we need to pay equal attention to that which is not explicitly and deliberately "historical", both in society and in the scholarly world. In academia, much knowledge production exhibits relations to the past without claiming affiliation with professionalized historical studies. Constructionist approaches throughout the entire scholarly

[1] Studying historical culture does not exhaust all approaches within history didactics, public history, and the theory and philosophy of history. What I try to indicate above is only a recent point of convergence of these fields.

landscape, for instance, typically appeal to a sense of historicity without appealing to the more conventional practice of historical studies (Simon 2019b). The same applies to the societal sphere where relations to the past inform socio-cultural practices that we typically do not think of as "historical" ones. This is largely due to yet another point I wish to make, namely, that even what we call "historical" is not confined to relations to the past, but also to the future. For history, at its broadest, is a matter of relating past, present, and future to each other. And relations to the future imply relations to the past, for which the best examples may be imaginaries of impending catastrophe scenarios due to human activity.

In fact, one of the examples through which I will approach ethical relations to the past is a correlate of the scientific future scenario in which the Earth system escapes conditions that support human life on the planet at worst, or tends towards conditions that likely trigger societal collapse in more modest scenarios. In this respect, what I try to explain is a prevalent line of the humanities' reception of the notion of the Anthropocene. The other example will be the demands of the Rhodes Must Fall Movement. The two cases could not possibly be more different; they seem to belong to different orders of things. Yet, both are invested in the question of who exactly is to blame for the present condition, and the relative distance of the cases from each other is in fact the best indicator of the extent to which the phenomenon pervades our current social practices, both in wider society and in academic scholarship.

The four-step argument of the coming pages will begin with a more detailed introduction of the two cases as seen within the context of a societal engagement in seeking social justice. After sketching the specific historical milieu of the emergence of past-blaming, the second step will elaborate on the conceptual distinction between blaming the past and judging the past. This then provides the basis for the third step that maps the merits and shortcomings of past-blaming by investigating the different notions of responsibility invoked by judging and blaming the past respectively. Finally, the fourth step introduces the equally omnipresent phenomenon of hailing the past as the counter-relation of blaming. Instead of a firm conclusion, this will lead to the question whether we are content with the way in which the extremes of blaming and hailing seem to have been overtaking debates about the past.

2 Seeking Social Justice

Ethical relations to the past can be profoundly related to epistemic ones. Even the extra-epistemological question at the heart of this essay begins by addressing an epistemic situation in which evidence is already consulted and facts are settled. For, to be clear, this is hardly the end of the story. The past is fiercely debated even when facts are agreed upon and evidence is accepted. Hence the question: how to account for the sheer existence of such extra-factual and extra-evidential debates about the past?

The answer leads to the realm of ethics, and, inasmuch as the question is directed at the most cardinal extra-evidential debates of our own times, it leads to the post-WWII convergence of a quest for social justice and an increasing involvement of historical knowledge at judicial processes. As to the first half of the equation, ranging from the rise of the civil rights movement and the women's liberation movement to the emergence of gender and subaltern studies, the second half of the last century witnessed a new wave of emancipatory politics seeking social justice both as a wider societal phenomenon and as a scholarly project. As to the second half of the equation, the same period also brought about a growing appeal to historians' expert witnessing before the court. The cases are extremely diverse and range from gender discrimination (Jellison 1987) and the ethics of human experimentation (Rothman 2003) to the large-scale setting up of truth commissions and historical expert commissions to investigate historical injustice (Hayner 2001; Torpey 2003; Barkan 2009; Pettai 2018).

This intersection of historical knowledge and the quest for social justice constitutes the background of the emergence of the phenomenon I would like to address. Today, it seems to me, in engaging with historical injustice, we do not merely judge the past by seeking historical truth. More and more frequently, we point our fingers to culprits and past wrongdoers who we suspect are responsible for bringing about the present condition we conceive of in negative terms. We increasingly blame those culprits in both societal and academic debates, and we tend to deem their deeds unforgivable by passing a moral sentence.

This is what I would like to call *blaming the past*, and I would like to introduce a few clarifications right away. Rather obviously, blaming does not literally concern the past as an abstract entity. Instead, it concerns specific past actions, social groups, social forces, ideas, and behavioral patterns that we think of as effective in bringing about dire present conditions and remaining effective in their wrongdoings in the present. Just like the much better known operation of *judging the past*, it is best conceived of as an evaluative and ethical relation to the past. Distinguishing between the two (more on the distinction in the next section) does not mean that in our ethical evaluations of the past we either judge or blame, that we do only one at a time. Nor does it mean that they are opposites. In fact, judging and blaming the past may share just as many features as those that distinguish them, and the two typically blend into each other in our ethical evaluations of the past. Finally, it is equally important to keep in mind that my focus is on negative evaluations. While the past is oftentimes evaluated positively, what I am interested in here is the difference between negatively judging and blaming, because it seems to me that blaming is not simply a harsher negative judgment.

All this being cleared up, it is time to bring some concreteness to the issue by introducing two examples. One of the most famous recent instances of approaching the past in dominantly evaluative terms may very well be the debate about statues at university campuses. The debate was kicked off by the Rhodes Must Fall protest series, starting in 2015 at the University of Cape Town, with students demanding the removal of the statue of Cecil Rhodes, a British imperialist and former prime minister of the once British colony of Cape of Good Hope (1890–1896). The protests quickly broadened their scope toward institutional racism in general and spread over other universities in South Africa and the University of Oxford.[2] Spin-off protests also followed at other universities in the English-speaking academic world with local targets. Harvard Law School witnessed protests against the school's crest derived from the coat of arms of the slaveholder family of Isaac Royall Jr., while protesters at Princeton University demanded the removal of Woodrow Wilson's name from murals and from the School of Public and International by calling out the former president's racist legacy.

Addressing present legacies of past wrongdoings, the protests targeting past figures are not simply about the past; they are about the present being infused with the past. Theories and philosophies of history developed several concepts to make sense of the situation in which the past is perceived as surviving in the present. With or without explicitly framing the conceptual innovations within the framework of historical injustice, the notions of "presence" (Runia 2006), the presence of the past (Lorenz 2010), the irrevocable past (Bevernage 2012), and the past that haunts (Kleinberg 2017) may all be instrumental in indicating how the barriers between past and present break down and how the past does not simply go away with the passing of time.

Berber Bevernage's politically-oriented theory of history is most explicit about the temporal stakes involved in addressing historical injustice. In the view of Bevernage (2014, 2015), we should shift the focus of the debate on transitional justice in particular and on historical injustice in general from the context of truth-telling and reconciliation to the context of the "politics of time". For the way we relate the past to the present is thoroughly political, and a strict division between them may result in two undesired scenarios that point to opposing directions. First, giving in to what Bevernage calls "temporal Manichaeism" may result in a perception that injustices are now a thing of the past; and second, claiming that the past should not be seen through the filters of present-day sentiments may result in a "temporal relativism" that prohibits us to form ethical judgments on the past.

In the Rhodes Must Fall Movement, however, neither is the case. Judgments on the past are passed from a present viewpoint (no "temporal relativism"), while the past is considered as surviving in the present and not something we are done with (no "temporal Manichaeism"). Yet, the issue seems to boil down to the question of time, as Victoria Fareld (2019) emphasizes in her analysis of the protests. To understand what this means, let's stay for a moment with Bevernage's undesired scenarios while changing the context. Claire Norton and Mark Donnelly (2018) make a point similar to Bevernage's in discussing the general character of slavery reparation debates. They argue that that taking sides in slavery reparation debates involve differing views on the question of the survival and continuing effectiveness of the past in the present. In the words of Norton and Donnelly (2018: 96), "the debate concerns the boundary between past and present; whether the injustices of

[2]The interpretive context of the protests entangle issues such as the decolonization of universities, slavery reparations, the persistence of racial inequalities, memory politics, the question of black presence, and many others. See, for instance, Mbembe (2016), Prinsloo (2016), Nyamnjoh (2017), and Shilliam (2019).

slavery still have repercussions today or whether they remain securely in the past". More importantly, they also make a point that, I think, is of crucial significance: that "there is no real disagreement between those arguing for or against reparations over the fact that slavery was a horrific crime" (Norton and Donnelly 2018: 96).

What interests me here is the extent to which there is a debate in the first place, even though both sides unanimously judge the past in the very same way as "a horrific crime". This is not merely an epistemic, but clearly an evaluative agreement, which makes me doubt whether the debates are as straightforward as Norton and Donnelly suggest, with the camps delineated so easily. It looks a bit too schematic to assume that everyone judges the past in the same way, so there is only one major split between advocates of reparations who perceive the past as surviving in the present and those against reparations who automatically think that the past is no longer effective. I suspect that there are deeper and more complex fissures that may divide even those who otherwise agree about the survival of the past in the present, even those who do not posit a strict division between past and present.

That there is an evaluative measure beyond judging the past, that this measure is blaming, and that past wrongdoings can actually be considered as effective in the present by almost all participants in a broad discussion, is even more apparent in my second major example: the Anthropocene debate. The notion of the Anthropocene has originally been proposed to denote a potential geological epoch in which human activity transforms the Earth system (that is, our planet conceived of as an integrated system) on a geological scale (meaning that traces of such transformation manifest in stratigraphic data). It points to a gloomy future scenario in which anthropogenic changes may trigger abrupt transformations of the Earth system, threatening to escape the Holocene conditions of the planet which are known to support human life.[3]

By now, there seems to be a growing agreement across disciplines that the Anthropocene may best be conceived of as a wider predicament with social, cultural and political constituents that must be explored together with the scientific Anthropocene. Given the multidisciplinary appeal of the notion on the one hand, and the prevailing disciplinary understanding in the scholarly world on the other, this is not an easy task. No wonder that a group of researchers from Finland (Toivanen et al. 2017) even distinguishes between four major notions of the Anthropocene that are in use today—geological, biological, social, and cultural—while nevertheless arguing for the necessity of transdisciplinary approaches.

At the same time, an influential line of humanities reception questions even the very term Anthropocene on the ground that it features a universal notion of the 'human' (*anthropos* in Greek). According to Claire Colebrook (2016: 83), the problem with the scientific naming of the Anthropocene is that "to refer to 'anthropos' is to forgo asking just who within humanity was the agent of destruction". To understand what this means, let's begin with the fact that being conceived of as an agent on a planetary scale is part of an ongoing redefinition of figure of the human as kicked off by the sciences. As historian Julia Adeney Thomas (2014) notes (without

[3]The Anthropocene literature is vast by now. For a brief glimpse into the fundamental scientific ideas see the report of the Anthropocene Working Group, Zalasiewicz et al. (2017).

questioning the term Anthropocene), as soon as such redefinition enters the realm of values, the humanities and the social sciences are better positioned to articulate the stakes. Lövbrand et al. (2015: 211–212) reason along similar lines in making the case for social sciences joining the discussion. They point to the fact that "the Anthropocene concept represents a tremendous opportunity to engage with questions of meaning, value, responsibility and purpose in a time of rapid and escalating change".

There are of course several ways of articulating stakes concerning values. What I wish to call attention to is the specific way in which a prominent line of humanities and social scientific scholarship aiming at social justice situates the scientific discourse on anthropogenic planetary changes with the question of values. Just like in the previous case, what interests me here is the *mode* in which social justice issues are raised. While virtually everyone agrees that there is an extent to which the Anthropocene predicament compels us to address and rethink questions of social justice, the demands of such rethinking oftentimes exceed the realm of judgment, and gesture towards the realm of blaming.

This happens in a less straightforward way than in the Rhodes Must Fall case. Typically, it requires two steps: first, attributing the act of blaming the entirety of humanity to the Earth system science perspective by entailment; and second, stepping up and directing blame toward more specific targets. According to Bonneuil and Fressoz (2016: 66), "the anthropocenologists' [note the derogatory label] dominant narrative of the Anthropocene presents an abstract humanity uniformly involved—and, it implies, uniformly to blame". But "species thinking on climate change," concurs Malm (2015), "only induces paralysis. If everyone is to blame, then no one is." In the name of social justice, the culprits need to be specified, as Bonneuil and Fressoz (2016: 71–72) seem to suggest when saying that

> the challenges of the Anthropocene demand a differentiated view of humanity, not just for the sake of historical truth, or to assess the responsibilities of the past, but also to pursue future policies that are more effective and more just; to construct a common world in which ordinary people will not be blamed for everything while ecological crimes of the big companies are left unpunished [...].

The problem with this interpretation is of course not its social justice agenda but the act of blaming "ordinary people" that is attributed to the Earth system science view. In reality, scientific papers, to my knowledge, are hesitant even to attribute clear causality to human activity when it comes to planetary change. They typically feature sentences like this: "Correlation in time does not prove cause-and-effect, of course, but there is a vast amount of evidence that the changes in the structure and functioning of the Earth System [...] are primarily driven by human activities" (Steffen et al. 2015).

Inferring blaming from such statements seems more than just a bit of a stretch. It likely reflects more of a growing investment in blaming within humanities and social scientific scholarship than within the targeted scientific agendas. As soon as scientific approaches to the Anthropocene are presented as blaming an undifferentiated humanity, pointing to the fact that certain social groups and social forces linked to those groups have more to do with altering planetary conditions and launching catastrophic prospects than others, and, more importantly, directing blaming toward such social groups and forces, appear as reasonable interventions. But, as to the former intervention, no one really doubts that the wealthy, the rich, industrialization, capitalism, and the Global North have more to do with bringing about the present planetary condition than others in a differentiated human world. Nor does anybody really doubt that the social forces and groups of such past wrongdoings are effective in the present. If blaming as an additional intervention still enters the picture, it comes as an excess to an otherwise largely unchallenged judgment on the wrongdoings of the past in which the wrongdoers are already identified.

There may be countless other examples of blaming the past for lingering injustices (in particular) and for dire present conditions (in general). Examples can be found in all segments of the political spectrum, ranging from blaming postmodernism for the emergence of post-truth politics to blaming the Empire for post-independence conditions. I chose the examples above because they represent two of the most crucial instances of addressing historical injustice today, motivated by ethical concerns that must be voiced.[4] What I think has to be explored are the merits and shortcomings of the way such concerns are expressed today. Not with the intention to discredit, let alone, to blame blaming, but with the aim of gaining a conceptual understanding of an emerging "historical" phenomenon and a new relation to the past—in order to open a discussion about it.

3 Judging the Past and Blaming the Past

Let me begin with what I think is the common ground of both judging and blaming the past: the attribution of responsibility. Engaging in the quest for social justice—either in humanities and social scientific scholarship or in popular forms of social action—is hardly possible without addressing the question of responsibility and without translating causality to ethics. Although this does not dismiss causality, it clearly establishes an order of importance in which the ethical relation to the past overpowers one that is primarily interested in making causal connections. Such translation is even inevitable in making the case for the necessity of action. Claiming with logic that certain past events, actions, ideas, behavioral patterns and occurrences likely contributed to the constitution of the present does not yield action the same way as claiming with ethics that those past events, actions, ideas, behavioral patterns and occurrences are *responsible* for shaping the present condition. As an example, consider the Anthropocene debate. When Dipesh Chakrabarty (2018: 13) claims that "the translation of physical 'force' into the very human terms of 'power' and 'responsibility' may be seen to be at work in all texts searching for a planetary

[4]This does not imply affiliation with available popular political positions. In fact, I think that the entire political domain is out of sync with present-day realities. For more on this see Simon (2019a).

human ethics in the present time",[5] he associates the translation of scientific terms to concepts in the humanities with the aim of bringing responsibility into the picture precisely in order to create the possibility of action.

Entering the realm of ethics by attributing responsibility to past events, actions, ideas for shaping the present is thus a precondition of both judging and blaming the past. To continue with indicating the breadth of the common platform of judging and blaming, *legal liability* is not a prerequisite of either past-blaming or past-judging in moral terms. It is possible to judge capitalism or to blame it for the Anthropocene without taking the case to court. Yet some of the most interesting new developments in evaluating the past are related to the interference of legal and moral responsibilities when bringing past wrongdoings to present-day recognition and reconciliation. History plays a crucial role in situating those measures. To begin with, an appeal to "justice" is an appeal to a notion that is both legal and ethico-political. Then, in case truth commissions are set up, justice is attempted to be achieved through bringing the notion together with the notion of "truth", entailing the invocation of the controversial legal concept of "the right to truth" (Naqui 2006; Walker 2010). And because truth means "historical truth" in the sense of truth about past wrongdoings, history inevitably enters the picture, often in the practical way of assigning historians with the task of carrying out historical investigations as part of a legal procedure.

Needless to say, tasking historians with unearthing the truth about the past and thereby lending support to judicial processes is a controversial idea. Those arguing for the compatibility of historical and legal procedures may point to shared features such as the careful weighing of evidence that the ideal forms of both historical and legal inquiries require. Difficulties, however, enter at a more fundamental level of temporality. In exploring the question of whether historical injustices can plausible brought to present-day justice in the first place, Bevernage (2012: 2–3) already noted the conflicting imperatives behind the reversible "time of jurisdiction" and the irreversible "time of history". But even if it were possible to reconcile the temporalities of legal and historical processes, there remains a practical difficulty in invoking history to seek justice. According to Norton and Donnelly (2018: 126), "history as a mode of knowledge is incapable of providing a neutral or agreed-upon platform for justice because its method will always be ideologically weighted in favour of those political interests that possess and control archives".

What to do with history then in judicial processes? In the view of Norton and Donnelly: nothing. They base this view on the examination of the case of a representative suit filed by the Kenya Human Rights Commission in 2009 in the British High Court, seeking reparations for human rights abuses during the Mau Mau Uprising in the middle of the last century against British colonialists (with historians giving evidence during the trial). After reviewing the case, Norton and Donnelly (2018: 126) end up claiming that "the more ethically defensible position" on the role of history "is one which recognises that no one should *need* a history as a support for

[5]For a broader argument concerning the necessity of joint work across the scientific and humanities landscapes in developing an understanding for the Anthropocene, and, especially, for an argument about how this entails a way to able to see the work of one in terms of the other, see Robin (2018).

their political claims or appeals for justice", because what the five original claimants needed were not history but "competent lawyers and the support of the Kenya Human Rights Commissions".

I do not wish to thoroughly discuss the views of Bevernage and Norton and Donnelly. They are summoned here to testify to the extent that the intersection of historical and legal measures is constantly questioned and debated. The only critical remark I would like to make is that legal procedures are just as much prone to political interests in their own way as historical procedures are. And if this is indeed the case, there is no reason to dismiss one procedure and trust in the other in the way Norton and Donnelly do when they favor legal support in reconciliation claims. More importantly, reconciliation may not be the end of the story. Compensation, recognition or reconciliation though legal and historical procedures is not necessarily what victims of historical injustice actually want, which is the point that finally leads to the question of how blaming escapes the realm of judgment.

Before addressing the excess toward blaming, let's again bring some concreteness to the issue. Let's consider the case Norton and Donnelly examined, the reparations for abuses in the Mau Mau Uprising in the 1950s against British colonial rule in Kenya, as a case of judging the past.[6] The first thing to note is that the legal procedure of 2009—with a representative suit filed on behalf of five survivors of detention camps—was initiated on the basis of Caroline Elkins's history book, *Imperial Reckonings* (2005). Regardless of the criticism and the controversies within the profession, legitimate historical scholarship kicked off a legal procedure. In turn, the legal procedure itself heavily relied on weighing historical evidence, especially after the disclosure of previously unavailable documents—stored in a Home Office repository—which backed up many of Elkins's oral sources on abuses. The case concluded in a legal settlement in 2013, with The Foreign Secretary's statement (2013) acknowledging the "torture," the "abuses" and the "ill treatment" of the colonial administration, which provides "recognition of the suffering in injustice that took place in Kenya," but denying the liability of the UK Government for the actions of colonial administration.

In the Mau Mau case, the past is unanimously judged by victims and perpetrators alike. Even though the UK Government disputes legal liability, it does not deny that wrongdoings have taken place. Nor does it dispute the establishment of responsibility for past wrongdoings by acknowledging that these have been committed by colonial administration. What it disputes is the continuity of legally associating past perpetrators with present institutions, while still remaining silent concerning the continuity of moral responsibility. Yet the sheer fact of reaching a legal settlement is carried out on the establishment of the continuity of both moral and legal responsibilities (regardless of the view of the UK Government on the question), which was already implied by victims' point of view and by the act of initiating the legal case.

[6]The 2009 case is the first of two cases, the second one being a group litigation starting in 2012 and concluding unsuccessfully in 2018. For a more detailed account on the judicial processes of the Mau Mau cases see the book of Norton and Donnelly just as well and Bevernage's contribution to this volume.

Now, how does an excess to judging go beyond the establishment of responsibility? To begin with, establishing responsibility is not necessarily what victims seek. Nor do they necessarily conceive of their own needs in terms of legal and historical support—including a weighing of historical evidence—in the act of attributing responsibility. The mission statement of The Rhodes Must Fall Movement at the University of Cape Town (2015) is very clear about the fact that their claims and demands need no support, investigation or debate. The statement calls "infuriating" the efforts of the university management's attempt "to open up a process of debate through their 'Have Your Say' campaign" and "absurd that white people should have any say in whether the statue should stay or not". This is only one of the instances of the statement repeatedly claiming exclusivity in both defining and handling the case. Further instances include: first, welcoming "participation in radical action as a sign of solidarity, so long as that participation takes place on our terms"; second, pointing at the fact that "our pain and anger is at the centre of why the statue is being questioned, so this pain and anger must be responded to in a way that only we can define"; and third, rejecting "the notion that the university has any decision to make here" and asserting that "our pain should be the only factor taken into consideration".

Unlike in the case of truth commissions and representative suits, victims here take direct action and make a stand against the involvement of third-party mediation in determining both "historical truth" and responsibility. They have no intention to investigate or debate whether historical injustice took place, and, if so, whom responsibility should be attributed to. The "truth" about the past is already established by Rhodes featuring in the mission statement as "a man who was undeniably a racist, imperialist, colonialist, and misogynist", and his enduring legacy is already held responsible for present institutional racism, as a result of which the statue appears as an enduring "act of violence".

All this, I think, points beyond the realm of judgment and gestures towards blaming the past inasmuch as it proclaims a moral sentence presented as undisputable. As an evaluative act, blaming the past knows no "but" and no shades. Hence the fact that it condemns instead of merely judging. A recourse to the pros and cons of legal or historiographical measures, or, for that matter, a recourse to any third party or a viewpoint other than present-day lived experience, could likely tone down the moral sentence. Whether there is a way to take such cases of historical injustice to court, cases in which reconciliation is not sought, is an open question. It is also hard to answer the question whether the lack of intention to recourse to third party mediation or the lack of adequate judicial and historical modes of addressing the issues amplifies the moral sentence. Either way, the claim of self-sufficiency in evaluating the past clearly goes against how both legal liability and moral responsibility is established in judging the past through an appeal to a weighing of evidence and the recantation of pro and con arguments. The judgment can be pre-conceived before handling the pros and cons, interpreting the evidence may be biased, but in past-judging there is an appeal to the authority of a third party—evidence, legal or historical expertise, etc.—between the one who carries out the judgement in the present and the past actions, figures, groups, attitudes, social forces that are judged.

The question of third-party mediation is the first major difference between the Mau Mau case and the Rhodes Must Fall Movement. The second has to do with the question of temporality and the perception of the past as surviving in the present. Although the past is perceived as surviving in both cases, there is a difference in the way this takes place. In the Mau Mau case, past wrongdoings and injustices are clustered in a period left behind, and the present seeks justice and reconciliation for them. In the Rhodes Must Fall Movement, however, the point of departure is a perceived present injustice that is traced back to the survival of past injustices. The difference lies in the emphases of the primary temporal location of injustices and the direction of continuity. In the Mau Mau case the past, that is, the colonial origin, is the primary location of injustices from where the continuity is extended to the present. Contrary to this, the Rhodes Must Fall Movement locates primary injustices in the present which are traced backwards to their colonial origin.

The question of temporality brings to light the potentially positive side of blaming the past (including its condemnatory tone): the fact that it is directed toward the past. Because the logic of establishing the past-present continuity starts from the present, it is clear that the primary target of social critique is not the past, but the present. Blaming the past in facing present-based injustices stands as a proxy for applying harsher measures to the present. Accordingly, the responsibility for past wrongdoings is also a proxy for a responsibility attributed for present wrongdoings. It channels sentiments towards Rhodes as a figure of the past instead of present wrongdoers. More on this later.

For now, to gain a better understanding, I would like to situate the phenomenon with the distinction between "historical truth" and "historical wounds" that Chakrabarty (2007) developed within the context of subaltern studies. At first blush, it may seem reasonable to align what I call blaming the past with a specific way of dealing with what Chakrabarty calls "historical wounds", especially because Chakrabarty links the latter notion with victims of historical injustice and with the surviving legacy of past wrongdoings in the present. Among other things, the overlaps concern the way in which both are verified by historical research in the sense of broad academic and social consensus that injustices took place in the past, and the way in which both nevertheless challenge the conventional disciplinary codes of professionalized historiography by virtue of being anchored in victims' appeal to present lived experience.

Yet there is an extent to which blaming the past does not enable an association with "historical wounds". It is connected to Chakrabarty's claim that historical wounds "are not permanent formations", meaning that "the social consensus on which they are based is always open to new challenges". To support this claim, Chakrabarty (2007: 78) points at the "concerted attempt" in Australia "to dislodge the consensus around certain historical truths on which the aboriginal sense of historical injury is founded". Now, there may clearly be attempts to challenge the social consensus on certain "historical truths", even in the Rhodes Must Fall case. But this typically does not happen, and even critics acknowledge past wrongdoings.

The interesting and perhaps most revealing aspect concerns here the assumed longevity not of the consensus about "historical truth" but the longevity implied by the evaluative measures. For in blaming the past there is *a tendency towards permanence with respect to the moral sentence* presented as indisputable. Unlike historical wounds, it is not meant to go away. Historical wounds may go away when historical truth is pulled out from under it, as Chakrabarty claims, even though this is not a welcomed scenario. At other times, historical wounds might go away precisely because historical truth stands: truth-telling, according to Margaret Urban Walker (2010), can by itself qualify as a reparation measure aiming at reconciliation.[7] And Walker, I think, may be right inasmuch as reconciliation and recognition is the aim and inasmuch as the primary location of injustices is the past and not the present. Furthermore, Chakrabarty (2007: 77) also considers recognition and the ability "to speak of the wound or to speak in its name is already to be on the path to recovery". Either way, wounds are meant to be healed. Contrary to this, blame and the moral sentence are attributed in order to make them stay forever, to prevent further harm, and reconciliation is not what is sought for in the first place.

Inasmuch as the moral sentence of blaming the past gestures towards permanence, it carries a temporality that Fareld (2018) calls the time of the *imprescriptible*. Although Fareld discusses the emergence of the temporal category in the context of the debate on the Statute of Limitations and in opposition the idea that twenty years after the fall of the Nazi regimes its crimes would expire, I would like to advance the claim that the conceptual outlook of imprescriptibility resembles the aforementioned positions in today's reparations debates.

In reviewing Vladimir Jankélévich's critique of the Statute, Fareld (2018: 61) notes that the time of the imprescriptible is the time of the victim: pitched against "society's time" that passes and "makes us forget and forgive", the time of the victim is a "time that does not pass". "Time has no hold on the crimes", meaning that, according to Fareld (2018: 61), "the chronological temporal scheme that situates the crime as something belonging to the past is simply ruled out" and "the past is reclaimed as an ethical space where past, present and future coincide". This, I believe, aptly describes also the temporality underlying today's reparations positions which proclaim the undisputable moral sentence on a past that is conceived as surviving in the present. To be clear, I do not wish to suggest that the debate on the crimes of the Nazi past would share substantial features with more recent debates on lingering historical injustices. The only thing I want to point out is that the time of the imprescriptible informs the moral sentence in the latter context too, although with a crucial qualification.

In Fareld's account, the emergence of the imprescriptible is criticized by historians on the ground that it erases the distinction between the time of justice and the time of history. To illustrate the difference, Fareld (2018: 62) claims that "the judge always has the final say" and "her task is to close the case, settle the conflict", while "the task of the historian is rather to keep the case open". I am not sure that the resistance of historians to imprescriptibility is a resistance to closure through judging. Bringing closure to the legal case simply does not entail that the closure is not only temporary. When the judge has the final say, that final say is a final say in the judicial process, not

[7]For another view that emphasizes the necessity for reparations measures beyond truth-telling, see Lean (2003).

an eternal judgement. Legal cases can in fact be reopened just as well as dominant historical interpretations can be revisited. If imprescriptibility is nevertheless at odds with any historical sensibility, this is likely because it exceeds the realm of judging, which otherwise is an integral feature of historical thinking.

4 Responsibilities

To render this claim plausible, I want to elaborate on the notions of moral responsibility informing judging and blaming the past, respectively.

4.1 Past Wrongdoings, Present Responsibility

Again, let me begin with that which is common to judging and blaming the past: the responsibility attributed for past wrongdoings is a *present responsibility*. The phrase does not simply refer to the fact that the question of responsibility is addressed in the present. In a more substantial way, present responsibility means that whatever and whoever is held responsible for past wrongdoings is conceived of either as being still operative in the present or as having the potential to become so (a threat that calls for pre-emption).

Present responsibility for past wrongdoings is anchored in the perception of the past as surviving in the present. As mentioned earlier, the notions of the irrevocable, the present, and the haunting pasts are conceptual innovations that try to make sense of the surviving past. These notions are invaluable in emphasizing how the conflation of temporal layers abandons the idea of a historical distance between past and present (Phillips 2013; Phillips et al. 2013). I would nevertheless like to draw attention to the other side of the equation, namely, the extent to which certain pasts, depending on the needs of the present, may be more prone to make their way to the present than others. And, like it or not, this has something to do with temporal distance in the attribution of *present responsibility*. Typically, although not necessarily, the more distant the past is, the less likely it is to be seen as surviving in the present. And the less the past is considered to be (potentially) operative and effective in the present, the less we are inclined to talk in terms of present responsibility about past wrongdoings. Slavery in Ancient times and serfdom in the medieval world are less likely to facilitate heated discussions of present moral responsibility than the question of slavery in the more recent history of the United States. Similarly, whereas a discussion of systemic injustices under Alexander the Great is more likely to be discussed in terms of causality than in terms of moral responsibility, the latter comes to the forefront in debating the systemic injustices of colonization. Or, in the context of the Anthropocene debate, pointing at the domestication of animals thousands of years ago as an early instance of human activity interfering with planetary processes hardly invokes debates as hotheaded as our current ones about the present responsibility attributed to capitalist modes of production and industrialization. Whether this *should* be the case is open to debate, but it seems plausible to claim that the case *is typically* so in both societal and academic debates.

The question of historical distance connects to the question of the direction of reasoning between the temporal dimensions in attributing responsibility, mentioned in the previous section. When there is no perceived temporal distance to injustice, and when the present is the primary location of injustice, the excess to judging becomes far likelier. When wrongdoings are present wrongdoings above all, when the continuity between past wrongdoings and present wrongdoings is established by looking backwards from the vantage point of the present, then past wrongdoings are proxies for present wrongdoings. Harsher measures than judging enter the picture here precisely because of this proxy function. Blaming the past channels ethical evaluations that, in case they would be more explicitly targeted toward present injustices, could cause irremediable societal rifts and deepen already existing present conflicts. Directing blaming toward past injustices (identified as ones with legacies surviving in the present) tones down potential conflicts and serves as a measure to avoid outbursts of violence in the struggle for social justice in the present.

None of this means that more distant past injustices are not talked about in evaluative terms. It only means that the way we look at the presently ineffective past in moral terms (such as medieval serfdom) differs from the way we look at those actions and social formations that we think are still effective in the present (as in the Rhodes Must Fall protests). It is in the latter cases that we typically attribute present responsibility for past wrongdoings, raising the question of *what exactly to do with the wrongdoers effective in our very own societal space and time.*

Attributing responsibility for surviving past wrongdoings in the present makes no sense without assuming that the wrongdoers—be they persons or impersonal social forces—are either still operative in the present or can potentially reappear and become operative again (which must be prevented). What is more, in cases of harsher ethical measures of blaming when the responsibility attributed for past wrongdoings is a proxy for present wrongdoings, *the wrongdoers to whom responsibility is attributed may also be proxies for present wrongdoers.* Institutional racism, or, again, capitalist production in the context of the wider Anthropocene debate may be instances of presently operative wrongdoers. The best examples of preventing agents of past wrongdoings potentially becoming operative again are failed regimes whose crimes truth commissions are tasked with investigating after regime changes. In those cases, truth-telling about the crimes of the past may indeed qualify as a reparations measure. My focus here nevertheless lies with cases when truth telling alone does not suffice because past wrongdoings appear as a *presently pressing actuality*, and not merely a potentiality. Then the question arises: what does present responsibility entail when perpetrators are still among us?

4.2 *Responsibility for Bringing About the Present Condition, Responsibility for the Future*

Regardless of whether one judges or blames the past, present responsibility for past wrongdoings is equally implied. When asking the question of what to do with perpetrators among us, however, judging and blaming part ways as they assign different responsibilities for moving ahead toward a future condition that can be considered as better.

Blaming the past has serious difficulties in this respect. Even though the motives behind the moral sentence are positive inasmuch as they aim at liberation, the liberatory aims are closer to what Berlin (2002) defined as negative liberty as distinguished from positive liberty. They are closer to an idea of liberty as being free from constraints and obstructions than to one aimed at self-mastery within the larger frame of a societal vision of the future. To avoid misunderstanding, I do not claim that past-blaming is *based* on Berlin's notion of negative liberty. Being rooted in the lived experience of victimhood, blaming the past is not founded in any *concept* whatsoever. What I want to point out with this parallel to negative liberty is only the sheer fact that blaming the past entails a limited sense of responsibility for the future. Its vision of the future consists of being free from the measures, thought patterns, behavioral attitudes and social forces of the past which are perceived as surviving in the present.[8]

The reason why blaming the past has difficulties with stepping out of a negative kind of responsibility for the future and moving towards a positive societal vision leads back to the time of the imprescriptible. When the moral sentence carries the weight of eternity, and when it concerns perpetrators among us, a dilemma arises. To begin with, pledging responsibility for a positively stated societal future requires a "society." But if the past of wrongdoings survives, then such "society" inevitably means a community that includes wrongdoings and their wrongdoers among us. Should they be included then in the common societal future that can reasonably be called better? If so, they come with their crimes; if not, there is a future only for part of the society.[9]

The dilemma that arises from this situation goes as follows: we either give up on blaming, tone down the moral sentence we pass, and thereby risk legitimizing the

---

[8]The combination of negative liberty with a surviving past brings to light an interesting twist, often overlooked in historical theory: the survival of the past is precisely what the prospect of liberation wants to liberate from. Ultimately, the responsibility for the future boils down here to a responsibility of getting rid of the surviving past. The past may be present or may haunt the present as is adequately captured by the concepts of historical theory, and the temporal barriers between past and present may indeed be broken down in historical injustice, but the ultimate aim of achieving social justice is precisely the restoration of those barriers between past and present.

[9]To be clear, none of this exempts perpetrators from past and presents wrongdoings. As Shilliam (2019) argues in situating the Rhodes Must Fall Movement with the theme of Black presence in British higher education, societal exclusion is, in the first place, the practice of wrongdoers on the assumption of "Black cognitive incompetency". And this is precisely why the imprescriptible moral sentence is passed on them.

ideas and behavioral patterns that we deem unacceptable and hold responsible for wrongdoings, or we opt for the imprescriptible to prevent escalation of wrongdoings, thereby risking the possibility to uphold a positively stated shared future of all. Is this a no-win situation? Or can there be other options? We'll see. Facing the dilemma, making choices or trying to find resolution will likely be at the center of debates on historical injustice in the near future.

4.3 *Responsibility of the Few, Responsibility of All*

Inasmuch as blaming the past struggles with upholding a societal future of all, it must also struggle with articulating a shared responsibility of all. To illustrate this point, the debate on anthropogenic climate change seems more instrumental than the politics of reparations. In the climate context, typically not individuals or social groups, but socio-economic forces and patterns of thought are identified as responsible for past wrongdoings that brought about the present condition of the Earth system. No one really doubts that this means a *responsibility of the few*. At the same time, nor does anyone doubt that the future of all is at stake on the largest planetary scale. Doubts emerge when it comes to the question of the responsibility for the future of all. As long as the primary relation to the past is blaming, the *responsibility for the future of all* is anything but the *responsibility of all*, while it remains unclear whose responsibility it actually might be.

In less abstract terms, when wrongdoers are held responsible for past and present wrongs, it is hard to assign them a role in a sense of shared responsibility of all for the future. Blaming capitalist production or ideas of human mastery and technological advancements associated with the project of Western modernity for the climate crisis oftentimes result in the argument that "solving" the crisis means getting rid of that which is blamed. As a concrete example, consider the proposed solution of Slavoj Žižek (2010: 334), according to which "one can solve the universal problem (of the survival of the human species) only by first resolving the particular deadlock of the capitalist mode of production". Or, in the context of holding ideas of human mastery, human supremacy and human exceptionalism responsible for the current climate and biodiversity crisis, consider the stand of Eileen Crist (2018) against the "dominant framework of technofixes" and the "techno-managerial portfolio" (including immense endeavors such as geoengineering and off-planet colonization), associated with the "Promethean impulse to sustain human hegemony". Against "technofixes", Crist (2018: 1244) thinks that we need to "scale down" and "pull back" "the human factor", and open "our imagination toward a new vision of humanity no longer obstructed by the worldview of human supremacy".

If the wrongdoer is the capitalist mode of production (Žižek) or the idea of human supremacy and its project of technological mastery (Crist), it is difficult to assign them a role in the responsibility for the future.[10] On the logic of such arguments, the responsibility for the future cannot also be the responsibility of those who are blamed for launching terrible conditions in the first place. Even if it seems extremely unlikely that we can act on a planetary scale to avoid future catastrophe without invoking the very large-scale technology that is blamed for the crisis in the first place, on the logic of blaming the past it is hard to assign a role to such technology.

Thus, the question with which blaming the past struggles is: "Whose responsibility is the responsibility for future?" It seems to me that past-blaming does not have an answer to this question. But to be clear, I do not wish to suggest that judging the past, unlike blaming it, does have a clear answer. My claim is only that whereas blaming the past excludes such responsibilities, judging the past does not. Whereas past-judging, in principle, can have *corrective* measures applied to past wrongdoers (capitalism and technology may remain the examples here) and keep on including them in a vision of the future of all in a corrected shape, past-blaming does not seem to be content with corrective measures.

5 Blaming the Past, Hailing the Past, and the Rise of Moralizing

Remember that the argument of this essay does not concern two clear-cut and easily separable relations to the past. In our negative evaluations of the past, judging and blaming typically occur fused with one another. Distinguishing between the two on a conceptual level serves the purpose of gaining a better understanding of the stakes involved in blaming the past. The more we gesture towards blaming the more we find ourselves grappling with the questions and dilemmas outlined above.

I reckon that this may not sound like a spectacular conclusion, but providing easily digestible takeaway messages never was the goal here, and there is still one last point to address: the question of counter-relations. The best way to indicate that blaming is not simply a harsher version of judging the past is to point to the fact that it has its own counter-relation to the past, which may be called *hailing the past*. Steven Pinker's *Enlightenment Now* (2018) is probably the perfect example. Bill Gates calls it his "new favorite book of all time" on the cover, while my Twitter feed was flooded with criticism from academics in the humanities and social sciences upon its release. In fact, humanities scholars, and especially historians, do not merely criticize the book. Oftentimes they also mock and ridicule Pinker's endeavor to retell the story of the triumph of Enlightenment ideals (or what Pinker thinks those ideals are) through cherry-picked graphs and charts (Harrison 2018; Riskin 2019). Needless to say, this is not how Pinker himself conceives of his own undertaking. The self-conception of his enterprise is rather that he attempts to counter the overwhelming skepticism

[10]Embracing the technologies held responsible for launching the catastrophe also in fixing the situation is associated with the ecomodernist pole most strongly in the Anthropocene debate. See Asafu-Adjaye et al. (2015).

and cultural pessimism among intellectuals about progress in the human world by arguing that there is a measurable advancement in "human flourishing" over time, resulting not only in longer and healthier lives but also in better ones.

For the purposes of this essay, it is not important to dive into the controversies surrounding *Enlightenment Now*. What matters more is to indicate how the book represents the inverse of past-blaming inasmuch as the premise of Pinker's entire endeavor is grounded in a perception of the present as better than ever, and inasmuch as Pinker thinks that past patterns of Enlightenment thought are responsible for bringing about such better present conditions. The message is that we should embrace the past of great ideas that already resulted in a present perceived as terrific in many respects, and we should pursue those past ideas further for potentially even greater benefits. Just like in past-blaming, the legacy of the past is upheld as that which is responsible for the shape of the present, except that, in hailing the past, the present condition is perceived in the opposite terms: not terrible but terrific.

What to make out of all this? How is it that the way we look at the past seems to be tending towards the extremes of full-blown admiration or complete repudiation (even though both camps seem to be aware that an effort to grasp a bigger picture would hardly allow such one-sided advocacies)? It seems to me that this has a lot to do with a change in the structure of the political field in the last few decades, which, in turn, can be linked with the exhaustion of the idea of history as we know it.

In *Politics Out of History*, Wendy Brown (2001) argued already almost two decades ago that "morality in politics" has been overtaken by "political moralism" in the shape of what is oftentimes referred to as identity politics or cultural politics. What I describe in terms of blaming as an emerging relation to the past, Brown (2001: 22–23) considers—in a more heavily loaded vocabulary—as a "reproachful moralizing sensibility" and a "moralizing politics" that attests to a "crisis in political teleology" and is "a symptom of a broken historical narrative to which we have not yet forged alternatives". What I describe as the lack of a responsibility of all and the lack of a responsibility for a positively stated societal future, Brown (2001: 29) sees as "moralism" becoming "a hegemonic form of political expression" that marks "both analytic impotence and political aimlessness—a misrecognition of the political logics now organizing the world, a concomitant failure to discern any direction for action, and the loss of a clear object of political desire".

The point I want to make by reciting Brown is that the emergence of blaming the past is an accompanying phenomenon of the rise of moralism in the political domain. Such moralism is not confined to injustice-driven politics as analyzed by Brown. It pervades all socio-cultural practices which affiliate with political engagement (including academic ones), and it equally informs efforts that raise the question of past wrongdoings and efforts like Pinker's ambition to reaffirm the "broken historical narrative" as if, well, nothing ever happened to it. This is the kind of politics we have, or at least one of the dominant kinds. And if theoretical discussions of history in the last decades were right in claiming that history is inescapably political and linked with power, then the history—be it academic or public—and the general sense of historicity we have is necessarily entwined with the kinds of politics we have.

It is in the clash of moralizing poles, nurtured in the growing vacuum left by a nonetheless growing skepticism toward the modern idea of history, that our ethical relations to the past take the shape of blaming and hailing. While blaming the past inhabits that vacuum with an ahistorical appeal to imprescriptibility, hailing the past simply tries to refill the vacuum with that which was there before. Once we understand this, once we begin to understand what the new phenomenon means, we can ask the question whether we are content with the situation. Once we identify the potential shortcomings (such as difficulties with upholding a societal vision of the future based on togetherness) and benefits of blaming the past (such as channeling accumulated sentiments by functioning as a proxy for blaming present wrongdoers), we can assess its desirability. Or, alternatively, we can try to look for other options against the backdrop of the fusion of the ethico-political, the historical, and the judicial domains in raising questions of social (in)justice in new ways, both on the societal and the scholarly level.

One thing is nevertheless inescapable. As soon as we ask the question of social (in)justice, we navigate in the realm that inevitably situates these three domains. The particular understanding of the intertwinement of historical, ethico-political and legal matters in recent relations to the past as sketched in this essay is of course open to debate. But in case it finds resonance, in case it looks plausible, then the question whether we are content with the way in which blaming and hailing the past increasingly dominate our evaluative relations to the past must be asked. So, here it is: Are we?

Acknowledgements I thank Berber Bevernage for reading and commenting on an earlier version of this essay, originally prepared for *The Second International Conference on Facts and Evidence: A Dialogue between Law and History*, held at the School of Transnational Law in Shenzhen, China, 16–17 November 2019.

References

Asafu-Adjaye, John, et al. 2015. *An Ecomodernist Manifesto.* Available at: https://static1.squarespace.com/static/5515d9f9e4b04d5c3198b7bb/t/552d37bbe4b07a7dd69fcdbb/1429026747046/An+Ecomodernist+Manifesto.pdf.

Barkan, Elazar. 2009. Introduction: Historians and Historical Reconciliation. *American Historical Review* 114 (4): 899–913.

Berlin, Isaiah. 2002. Two Concepts of Liberty. In *Liberty: Incorporating Four Essays on Liberty*, ed. Henry Hardy, 166–217. Oxford: Oxford University Press.

Bevernage, Berber. 2012. *History, Memory, and State-Sponsored Violence: Time and Justice.* London and New York: Routledge.

Bevernage, Berber. 2014. Transitional Justice and Historiography: Challenges, Dilemmas and Possibilities. *Macquarie Law Journal* 13: 7–24.

Bevernage, Berber. 2015. The Past is Evil/Evil is Past: On Retrospective Politics, Philosophy of History, and Temporal Manichaeism. *History and Theory* 54 (3): 333–352.

Bonneuil, Christophe, and Jean-Baptiste Fressoz. 2016. *The Shock of the Anthropocene: The Earth, History and Us.* Trans. David Fernbach. London: Verso.

Brown, Wendy. 2001. *Politics Out of History*. Princeton: Princeton University Press.
Chakrabarty, Dipesh. 2007. History and the Politics of Recognition. In *Manifestos for History*, ed. Keith Jenkins, Sue Morgan, and Alun Munslow, 77–87. London and New York: Routledge.
Chakrabarty, Dipesh. 2018. Anthropocene Time. *History and Theory* 57 (1): 5–32.
Colebrook, Claire. 2016. What is the Anthropo-Political? In *Twilight of Anthropocene Idols*, ed. Tom Cohen, Claire Colebrook, and J. Hillis Miller, 81–125. London: Open Humanities Press.
Crist, Eileen. 2018. Reimagining the Human. *Science* 362: 1243–1244.
Day, Mark. 2008. Our Relations with the Past. *Philosophia* 36: 417–427.
Elkins, Caroline. 2005. *Imperial Reckonings: The Untold Story of Britain's Gulag in Kenya*. New York: Henry Holt.
Fareld, Victoria. 2018. History, Justice and the Time of the Imprescriptible. In *The Ethos of History: Time and Responsibility*, ed. Stefan Helgesson and Jayne Svenungsson, 54–69. New York and Oxford: Berghahn.
Fareld, Victoria. 2019. Coming to Terms with the Present: Exploring the Chrononormativity of Historical Time. In *Rethinking Historical Time: New Approaches to Presentism*, ed. Marek Tamm and Laurent Olivier, 57–70. London: Bloomsbury.
Ginzburg, Carlo. 1991. Checking the Evidence: The Judge and the Historian. *Critical Inquiry* 18 (1): 79–92.
Grever, Maria, and Robbert-Jan Adriaansen. 2017. Historical Culture: A Concept Revisited. In *Palgrave Handbook of Research in Historical Culture and Education*, ed. Mario Carretero, Stefan Berger, and Maria Grever, 73–89. London: Palgrave.
Harrison, Peter. 2018. The Enlightenment of Steven Pinker. *ABC Religion and Ethics*, Feb 20. Available at: https://www.abc.net.au/religion/the-enlightenment-of-steven-pinker/10094966.
Hayner, Priscilla B. 2001. *Unspeakable Truths: Confronting State Terror and Atrocity*. London and New York: Routledge.
Jellison, Katherine. 1987. History in the Courtroom: The Sears Case in Perspective. *The Public Historian* 9 (4): 9–19.
Kleinberg, Ethan. 2017. *Haunting History: For a Deconstructive Approach to the Past*. Stanford: Stanford University Press.
Lean, Sharon F. 2003. Is Truth Enough? Reparations and Reconciliation in Latin America. In *Politics and the Past: On Repairing Historical Injustices*, ed. John Torpey, 169–191. Oxford: Rowman & Littlefield.
Lorenz, Chris. 2010. Unstuck in Time. Or: The Sudden Presence of the Past. In *Performing the Past: Memory, History, and Identity in Modern Europe*, ed. Karin Tilmans, Frank van Vree, and Jay Winter, 67–102. Amsterdam: Amsterdam University Press.
Lövbrand, Eva, et al. 2015. Who Speaks for the Future of Earth? How Critical Social Science Can Extend the Conversation on the Anthropocene. *Global Environmental Change* 32: 211–218.
Malm, Andreas. 2015. The Anthropocene Myth. *Jacobin Magazine*, Mar 30. Available at: https://www.jacobinmag.com/2015/03/anthropocene-capitalism-climate-change/.
Mbembe, Achille Joseph. 2016. Decolonizing the University: New Directions. *Arts & Humanities in Higher Education* 15 (1): 29–45.
Naqui, Yasmin. 2006. The Right to the Truth in International Law: Fact or Fiction? *International Review of the Red Cross* 88: 245–273.
Norton, Claire, and Mark Donnelly. 2018. *Liberating Histories*. London and New York: Routledge.
Novick, Peter. 1988. *That Noble Dream: The "Objectivity Question" and the American Historical Profession*. Cambridge: Cambridge University Press.
Nyamnjoh, Anye. 2017. The Phenomenology of *Rhodes Must Fall*: Student Activism and the Experience of Alienation at the University of Cape Town. *Strategic Review for Southern Africa* 39 (1): 256–277.
Paul, Herman. 2015. Relations to the Past: A Research Agenda for Historical Theorists. *Rethinking History* 19 (3): 450–458.

Pettai, Eva-Clarita. 2018. Historical Expert Commissions and Their Politics. In *The Palgrave Handbook of State-Sponsored History After 1945*, ed. Berber Bevernage and Nico Wouters, 687–712. London: Palgrave.
Phillips, Mark Salber. 2013. *On Historical Distance*. New Haven: Yale University Press.
Phillips, Mark Salber, Barbara Caine, and Julia Adeney Thomas (eds.). 2013. *Rethinking Historical Distance*. Basingstoke: Palgrave.
Pinker, Steven. 2018. *Enlightenment Now: The Case for Reason, Science, Humanism, and Progress*. New York: Viking.
Prinsloo, Estelle H. 2016. The Role of the Humanities in Decolonising the Academy. *Arts & Humanities in Higher Education* 15 (1): 164–168.
Riskin, Jessica. 2019. Pinker's Pollyannish Philosophy and Its Perfidious Politics. *Los Angeles Review of Books*, Dec 15. Available at: https://www.lareviewofbooks.org/article/pinkers-pollyannish-philosophy-and-its-perfidious-politics/.
Robin, Libby. 2018. Environmental Humanities and Climate Change: Understanding Humans Geologically and Other Life Forms Ethically. *WIREs Climate Change* 9: e499.
Rothman, David J. 2003. Serving Clio and Client: The Historian as Expert Witness. *Bulletin of the History of Medicine* 77 (1): 25–44.
Runia, Eelco. 2006. Presence. *History and Theory* 45 (1): 1–29.
Shilliam, Robbie. 2019. Behind the Rhodes Statue: Black Competency and the Imperial Academy. *History of the Human Sciences* 32 (5): 3–27.
Simon, Zoltán Boldizsár. 2019a. *History in Times of Unprecedented Change: A Theory for the 21st Century*. London: Bloomsbury.
Simon, Zoltán Boldizsár. 2019b. Historicism and Constructionism: Rival Ideas of Historical Change. *History of European Ideas* 45 (8): 1071–1090.
Statement to Parliament on Settlement of Mau Mau Claims. 6 June 2013. Available at: https://www.gov.uk/government/news/statement-to-parliament-on-settlement-of-mau-mau-claims.
Steffen, Will, et al. 2015. The Trajectory of the Anthropocene: The Great Acceleration. *Anthropocene Review* 2 (1): 81–98.
Thomas, Julia Adeney. 2014. History and Biology in the Anthropocene: Problems of Scale, Problems of Value. *American Historical Review* 119 (5): 1587–1607.
Toivanen, T., et al. 2017. The Many Anthropocenes: A Transdisciplinary Challenge for the Anthropocene Research. *Anthropocene Review* 4 (3): 183–198.
Torpey, John (ed.). 2003. *Politics and the Past: On Repairing Historical Injustices*. Oxford: Rowman & Littlefield.
UCT Rhodes Must Fall Mission Statement. 2015. Available at: https://www.jwtc.org.za/resources/docs/salon-volume-9/RMF_Combined.pdf.
Vann, Richard T. 2004. Historians and Moral Evaluations. *History and Theory* 43 (4): 3–30.
Walker, Margaret Urban. 2010. Truth Telling Reparations. *Metaphilosophy* 41 (4): 525–545.
Zalasiewicz, Jan, et al. 2017. The Working Group on the Anthropocene: Summary of Evidence and Interim Recommendations. *Anthropocene* 19: 55–60.
Žižek, Slavoj. 2010. *Living in the End Times*. London: Verso.

Evidence and Facts: Perspectives from Law

Fact-Finding in Constitutional Cases

David L. Faigman

1 Introduction

The Constitution is a visionary document. Its meaning is not generally thought to be found in empirical details. Indeed, when most people think of the Constitution they become romantics. The Constitution transcends time. The Constitution expresses eternal truths, such as freedom, equality, liberty, and due process. These are not concepts mired in factual disputes or scientific debate. They are normative principles that soar.

Of course, brief reflection on the subject quickly reveals that the Constitution is a product of the times. Constitutional questions tend to be packaged in terms of contemporary circumstances. It could be no other way. The Constitution is a practical document, despite the romance that surrounds it and the tendency of courts and constitutional scholars to ignore the practicalities of implementing it. It may be, as Chief Justice Earl Warren said in *Brown v. Board of Education*,[1] that "segregation is inherently unequal." But even such seemingly obvious truisms of principle will sometimes give way to compelling factual circumstances. Is segregation inherently unequal when warring gangs are physically separated in state prisons?[2] And is segregation inherently unequal so that the Constitution always prohibits public funding of women's colleges?[3]

[1]347 U.S. 433 (1954).

[2]See *Cruz v. Beto*, 405 U.S. 319, 321 (1972) (per curiam).

[3]See *United States v. Virginia*, 518 U.S. 515 (1996).

D. L. Faigman (✉)
Hastings College of the Law, University of California, San Francisco, CA, USA
e-mail: faigmand@uchastings.edu

B. Zhang et al. (eds.), *A Dialogue Between Law and History*,
https://doi.org/10.1007/978-981-15-9685-8_9

The Constitution, in fact, is an admixture of soaring principle and brute fact. Free speech principles loom large, yet a state can regulate adult entertainment establishments if they lead to dilapidated neighborhoods, drug abuse, and prostitution.[4] Whether it is "cruel and unusual" to execute defendants who killed before they turned eighteen years-of-age depends on psychological and physiological developmental differences between minors and adults.[5] Informed consent and twenty-four-hour-waiting provisions in abortion regulations may be unconstitutional if they create "substantial obstacles" to the exercise of the right of reproductive choice.[6] The medical fact of when a fetus is viable—i.e., can survive on its own outside the womb—establishes the point in time when the government can prohibit abortions. Psychological predictions of violence are constitutional prerequisites to the civil commitment of alleged "sexually violent predators."[7] In virtually every constitutional case, the soaring language of the Constitution is brought down to earth by plain facts.

Despite the conspicuous role facts play in constitutional discourse, the Court has yet to develop a philosophical framework to describe their role in constitutional doctrine or developed evidentiary procedures by which facts could be systematically incorporated into constitutional decisions. Philosophically, the Court veers between two incompatible world-views. It sometimes approaches the empirical world as a scientific realist, seemingly taking facts seriously and premising constitutional doctrines on them. More often, however, the Court views facts as social constructs, and treats them as products of interpretation rather than discovery. Procedurally, constitutional facts come to the Court's attention haphazardly (Larsen 2012, 1255–1312). Factual claims are found in legislative records, introduced through expert testimony at trial, set forth in the parties' briefs, asserted in amicus briefs, and, on occasion, the subject of original research by judges. Rules of admissibility, burdens of proof, and standards of appellate review are rarely discussed, often ambiguous or vague, and not infrequently inconsistent across constitutional contexts. Both philosophically and practically, therefore, fact-finding in constitutional cases is a slapdash affair.

Although justices have displayed different degrees of empirical ignorance—or, perhaps, avoidance—over time, the phenomenon has been pervasive throughout the Court's history. Indeed, individual justices are alternatively faithful and feckless to factual concerns. For example, Justice Anthony Kennedy, writing for the Court in *Ashcroft v. Free Speech Coalition*,[8] invalidated a federal law banning virtual child pornography (i.e., computer generated or other facsimile that purports to depict children in pornographic situations). He found the lack of data connecting this material to violence to be dispositive: "The Government has shown no more than a remote connection between speech that might encourage thoughts or impulses and any

[4]See *City of Renton v. Playtime Theatres, Inc.*, 475 U.S. 41 (1986).

[5]See *Roper v. Simmons*, 543 U.S. 551 (2005).

[6]See *Planned Parenthood of Southeastern Pennsylvania v. Casey*, 505 U.S. 833 (1992).

[7]See *Kansas v. Hendricks*, 521 U.S. 346 (1997).

[8]535 U.S. 234 (2002).

resulting child abuse. Without a significantly stronger, more direct connection, the Government may not prohibit speech on the ground that it may encourage pedophiles to engage in illegal conduct."[9] Yet, five years later, Kennedy wrote the opinion in *Gonzales v. Carhart*,[10] which upheld a federal law banning an abortion procedure, partly on the basis of assertions that were supported by no data. Kennedy hypothesized that "some women come to regret their choice to abort the infant life they once created and sustained" and suffer "[s]evere depression and loss of esteem" as a result. Kennedy, however, admitted that he could "find no reliable data to measure the [hypothesized] phenomenon."[11] In both *Free Speech Coalition* and *Gonzales*, challengers asserted the protection of fundamental rights against governmental interference, and data were unavailable on pivotal empirical concerns. Kennedy thus found the government's bald assertion of fact insufficient to overcome a publisher's free speech right to publish child pornography but sufficient to overcome a woman's due process right of reproductive freedom.

The Court's erratic approach to its constitutional empirical jurisprudence, however, serves a political function. Facts have the disturbing tendency to change, either because our knowledge of them changes or the facts themselves change. Resting constitutional doctrine on a changing factual landscape, then, presents the danger of putting constitutional law on uncertain terrain. Taking facts seriously would permit the Constitution's meaning to change as the facts change. The Court has generally avoided this result by using facts to serve its more general interpretive goals. Facts are interpreted, not found. In subsequent cases, if the facts on which precedent sits change, the Court ignores, reinterprets, or elides them.

The Supreme Court approaches fact-finding much as the Catholic Church did in the sixteenth century. Facts are a constituent part of doctrine. The Court employs empirical claims to buttress its reading of the constitutional text, but later scientific refutations of these claims have little or no effect on the Court's continuing adherence to the doctrines built upon them. But just as the Church lost credibility when it was dismissive of science, the Court endangers its legitimacy by maintaining a jurisprudence that is inattentive to scientific advances. Failure to place constitutional law on a rational and realistic empirical foundation, even one that evolves with changing times and progressing technology, threatens the legitimacy of the Court's pronouncements. The Constitution was founded upon enlightenment principles, yet the Court's approach to the empirical world remains mired in the Dark Ages.

This article sets forth a framework for an enlightened constitutional jurisprudence. The Constitution is an eminently practical document that must address the exigencies of the times. Transcendent concepts such as equality, liberty, and free speech are not self-executing terms, but must be interpreted and applied to a dynamic empirical world. This article addresses the question, to borrow from the words of John Marshall,

---

[9] Id. at 253–254.

[10] 550 U.S. 124 (2007).

[11] Id. at 159.

how can a constitution "intended to endure for ages to come" be "adapted to the various *crises* of human affairs"?[12]

2 A Unified Theory of Constitutional Facts

To be coherent, a constitutional fact jurisprudence must have two basic characteristics. One is that courts consider constitutional facts in a realistic fashion, so that they are understood to exist largely independent of the normative principles embodied by the Constitution. The second is the availability of a systematic procedural structure by which constitutional facts might enter the legal process so that findings can be absorbed over time and across jurisdictions. This article endeavors to fulfill both of these characteristics, and thus provide a blueprint for constitutional fact-finding.

2.1 The Need for an Empirically Sophisticated Judiciary

If facts are ever to perform the lead role contemplated for them in a scientific realist vision, judges will have to assume directorial duties. This is, after all, their charge in all other aspects of constitutional litigation. Yet the case of empirical evidence places substantial burdens on them. This is especially so when complex scientific facts are involved, since so little of a lawyer's training prepares the lawyer to deal with the statistical and methodological technicalities of high-quality research. However difficult the task, in the twenty-first century judges cannot fulfill their constitutional responsibilities if they do not critically understand the methods of fact-finding, whether involving history or histology.

Law requires judges to be generalists. While the law is a distinct institution with its own goals and objectives, it constantly interacts with the world and institutions around it. The law is at bottom an empirical and practical profession. It receives input from a variety of sources, digests it through the legal process, and applies the output with the expectation of effecting some result. These steps require judges to have extraordinarily broad understanding of an assortment of professional disciplines. In constitutional law, history is essential, since original intent is an often-cited authority for determining the Constitution's meaning. A court considering the original intent of the warrant requirement in the Fourth Amendment, for example, would have to wade through volumes of historical documents and debate.[13] And unless a true consensus among historians existed—a rare occurrence—the court could not defer to experts on this matter. The judges would, in effect, be operating as "amateur historians." This would simply be a requirement of the job and no one would

[12] *McCulloch v. Maryland*, 4 Wheat (17 U.S.) 316, 415 (1819) (emphasis in original).

[13] See, e.g., *Kyllo v. United States*, 533 U.S. 27 (2001); see *also District of Columbia v. Heller*, 554 U.S. 570 (2008).

seriously doubt its necessity. Moreover, it would be extraordinarily disconcerting if any judge decried the prospect of being an amateur historian or professed ignorance of the subject. Similarly, judges must sometimes be amateur political theorists, psychologists, neuroscientists, economists, linguists, and sociologists—all without complaint.

Yet when it comes to science, and particularly statistics, judges stumble, wondering whether it is truly part of their responsibility to know the details of scientific methods. Perhaps the most explicit attempt to reckon with the realities of the interface between law and science came in the evidentiary context of *Daubert v. Merrell Dow Pharmaceuticals, Inc.*[14] In *Daubert*, the Court held that judges are gatekeepers who must evaluate the methodological bases of proffered scientific evidence under Federal Rule of Evidence 702.[15] In a subsequent case, *Kumho Tire Co. v. Carmichael*,[16] the Court extended this injunction to all expert opinion, whether it be from rocket scientists or real estate agents. This mandate requires judges to have some understanding of research design and statistics, since they must examine the methods and principles underlying the expert's opinion. In *Daubert*, however, Chief Justice Rehnquist complained that this responsibility would require federal judges "to become amateur scientists."[17] He meant it derisively, but it turns out to be a prerequisite for the judicial role.[18] Although judges' success at becoming amateur scientists under *Daubert* has been mixed, it is generally believed that this obligation is now a core component of a judge's evidentiary obligations (Faigman et al. 2019–2020).

Judges, however, resist undertaking similar obligations in constitutional cases. Indeed, judges sometimes proudly declare their ignorance of the subject, cavalierly stating that knowledge of science and statistics is not necessary to constitutional analysis. In a particularly egregious example of this, in *Craig v. Boren*,[19] the Court applied intermediate scrutiny to strike down an Oklahoma law that prohibited men younger than twenty-one years of age from purchasing "nonintoxicating" 3.2% beer while permitting women older than eighteen years of age to buy it.[20] Oklahoma had justified the discrimination on the basis of statistical studies indicating that young men account for a disproportionate share of drivers arrested for driving while intoxicated.[21] Justice Brennan initially dismissed the studies as methodologically weak and of little use.[22] But rather than rely on the cogency of his statistical critique, Brennan added an apologia:

---

[14]509 U.S. 579 (1993).

[15]Id. at 592–593.

[16]526 U.S. 137 (1999).

[17]*Daubert*, 509 U.S. at 601 (Rehnquist, C.J., concurring in part and dissenting in part).

[18]For further discussion of the judicial imperative to know science, see Faigman (2006).

[19]429 U.S. 190 (1976).

[20]Id. at 210.

[21]Id. at 200–201.

[22]Id. at 201–203.

> There is no reason to belabor this line of analysis. It is unrealistic to expect either members of the judiciary or state officials to be well versed in the rigors of experimental or statistical technique. But this merely illustrates that proving broad sociological propositions by statistics is a dubious business, and one that inevitably is in tension with the normative philosophy that underlies the Equal Protection Clause.[23]

This is a remarkable statement in so many ways. Imagine substituting "historical" for "experimental or statistical." Would it be "unrealistic to expect the judiciary to be well versed in the rigors of historical technique"? Moreover, the Court applied intermediate scrutiny, which required state officials to prove that the liquor law was "substantially related to achievement of [important governmental] objectives."[24] The statistical studies provided, at least in part, this proof. In effect, the Supreme Court struck down a law legitimately enacted by Oklahoma on the basis that the state provided insufficient justification for the law, though the Court disdained knowing the experimental or statistical bases for that justification. This display of scientific disinterest gives new meaning to the "counter-majoritarian difficulty."[25] If the Court's power depends on its judgment rather than control of the purse or sword, this failure to provide an explanation for invalidating a duly enacted state law undermines the Court's legitimacy.

Those lacking scientific training often make the critical mistake of thinking of scientific knowledge as categorical or certain. But brief reflection by even the most scientifically naive should dispel this notion. Applied science, in particular, is almost invariably probabilistic in nature. Anyone who has ever checked a weather forecast knows this basic lesson. Yet courts regularly ignore this component of scientific information. The Supreme Court is particularly guilty of adopting a myth of scientific certitude. In *Roe v. Wade*,[26] for instance, the Court held that a state's interest in the potential life of the fetus became "compelling"—and thus sufficient to ban abortions—at "viability."[27] But viability is a statistical prediction of survivability that varies widely over many weeks during the second and third trimesters (Faigman 2008). The Court never so much as mentioned the statistics associated with this new bedrock of constitutional law. The same has occurred in a wide variety of contexts, including in regard to predictions of violence in sexually violent predator cases, brain function in people in a "persistent vegetative state, the clinical need for so-called partial-birth abortions, and the list goes on and on.[28] Ignoring the statistical bases for empirical statements, however, does not make them any less probabilistic. Instead, it conceals the policy choices embedded in the probabilities and allows the Court to shirk responsibility for deciding the tough cases around the margins. The empirical

[23] Id. at 204.

[24] Id. at 197.

[25] See Bickel (1986) (coining "counter-majoritarian difficulty" as a term for the problem of reconciling judicial review with democratic principles).

[26] 410 U.S. 113 (1973).

[27] Id. at 163.

[28] Id., Chaps. 1, 3, 4.

uncertainties of factual statements are as important as the statements themselves and should be part of the legal calculus.

As a general matter, judges and lawyers are well acquainted with the basic task of allocating costs of error. Procedural mechanisms such as burdens of production and proof are directed at managing the costs of error in different substantive legal contexts. In criminal cases, for example, in which false positives (i.e., convicting the innocent) pose the greatest risks, the "beyond a reasonable doubt" standard applies (Sundby 1989, 457–510). This stringent standard generally reflects the well-known colloquialism that it is better to let ten guilty men go free than to convict one innocent man (Sundby 1989, 460). This maxim simply states the legally acceptable ratio between false negatives and false positives. Implicit in this statement is that the ratio selected between these two errors inevitably affects the power of the criminal trial process to identify true positives and true negatives. In particular, all things being equal, reducing the number of false positives will also reduce identification of true positives—a real and substantial cost to society.

Statistical statements associated with research studies, however, do not correspond neatly to ordinary conceptions of the burden of proof for a variety of reasons. First of all, the analogy itself may not be apt. No clear relationship exists between burdens of proof and probability estimates. We can say generally that the "preponderance of the evidence" standard is akin to a probability estimate greater than fifty percent, but such a description is ambiguous and misleading. Both the probability estimate and the burden of proof are subtle and complex statements, culturally tied to statistics and law, respectively, with only some overlap in meaning. Burdens of proof in law are not quantified and, at best, reflect an intuitive judgment regarding the degree of proof needed in light of the gravity of the decision to be made. They operate as rough and ready guidelines and are not intended to have true quantitative correlates. In science, by comparison, probability estimates are objective statements, albeit packed with a wide assortment of explicit and implicit assumptions. If the underlying assumptions hold, the probability estimate is set forth as an accurate statement about some specifically defined empirical proposition.

In addition, the burden of proof operates on the ultimate question of fact, whereas scientific evidence tends to be relevant to one or more individual component facts of that determination. In cases involving the civil commitment of sexually violent predators (SVPs), for example, two empirically based determinations must be found under the Constitution: (1) mental abnormality and (2) likelihood of future violence.[29] Both present substantial empirical challenges. For instance, the Court defined mental abnormality as "serious difficulty in controlling behavior,"[30] a neuro-psycho-physiological fact of great complexity. In many cases, moreover, the scientific research does not speak specifically to the legal issue in dispute. For example, statistical tests used to predict future violence in SVP cases are based on general population data, and typically are combined with individualized clinical data to make assessments regarding particular defendants (Fisher et al. 2015, 685–753).

---

[29] *Kansas v. Hendricks*, 521 U.S. 346 (1997); *Kansas v. Crane*, 534 U.S. 407 (2002).

[30] Id. at 413.

Statistical statements regarding a person's likelihood to be violent, therefore, must be integrated into the other evidence available and, in combination, can be said to support or not support the applicable burden of proof. Rarely, if ever, will the probabilities of empirical research directly correspond to legal burdens of proof.

Complicating matters greatly, the complex statistical statements discussed above are only the tip of the empirical iceberg. In practice, statistics are only as good as the research methods used to generate them. Shoddy research methods produce feeble statistics. Virtually every context in which scientific research is employed in the law presents issues involving the quality and quantity of the underlying research. Consider, for example, the conundrum of what lineup procedures are best employed under the Due Process Clause. A key question debated in this area concerns the choice between the traditional simultaneous lineup (sometimes referred to as a "six-pack," as six "suspects" are displayed to the witness at one time) and the alternative procedure whereby witnesses view one suspect (photograph or person) at a time, known as a "sequential lineup."[31] Most of the research conducted in this area has been done in the laboratory and has involved contrived circumstances and college-age subjects. In 2006, however, Illinois sponsored a major test of this hypothesis.[32] The Illinois research was a "field study," in which the two lineup procedures were compared in real cases. Field studies have the advantage of real-world verisimilitude, but suffer the messiness and potential confounds of actual practice.

Laboratory research in this area had seemed to settle the question regarding the advantages and disadvantages of the two procedures. The data generally indicated that sequential lineups were less sensitive than simultaneous lineups, meaning that they resulted in fewer accurate identifications (i.e., fewer true positives), but also fewer misidentifications of subjects (i.e., fewer false positives) (Wells and Olson 2003, 277–295).[33] One theoretical explanation for a simultaneous lineup's greater power was that witnesses might be inclined to pick "the best suspect" from a comparative analysis of the suspects standing side by side, whereas sequential lineups avoided such comparative judgments by requiring a yes or no decision with each person shown (Wells and Olson 2003, 288).[34]

The Illinois field study, however, failed to replicate the findings from the laboratory studies. Indeed, the Illinois research found that sequential procedures "resulted in an overall higher rate of known false identifications than did the simultaneous lineups."[35] Sequential lineups resulted in a 9.2% rate of false identifications, compared to a 2.8% rate for simultaneous lineups, while simultaneous procedures resulted in a higher rate

---

[31] See *generally* Mecklenburg (2006).

[32] Id. at 4 n. 5.

[33] For a meta-analytic comparison of sequential and simultaneous line-ups, see *generally* Steblay et al. (2001).

[34] Another possible explanation for differences between lineup procedures is that subjects use a different selection criterion for sequential lineups than they use for simultaneous lineups. See Meissner et al. (2005).

[35] Illinois Report, *supra* note 31, at iv.

of true identifications than did the sequential lineups, which was consistent with laboratory findings. Witnesses who viewed simultaneous lineups identified the suspect 59.9% of the time, whereas those who viewed sequential lineups identified the suspect forty-five percent of the time.[36] Hence, in a test of the hypothesis in the field, simultaneous lineups appeared to both maximize the identification of perpetrators ("true positives") and minimize the misidentification of innocents ("false positives").[37] What should one make of this research?

The weight of the statistics depends on the strength of the research methods used to produce them. The fact that the Illinois study was a field study gives it greater power in some respects, while undermining it in others. The concerns with the Illinois study, however, are not specifically associated with it being field research. Although many complaints might be made, as is true with all empirical research, two in particular undermine the value of any lessons that might be drawn from the Illinois findings. First, the measure of success for identifications was whether the suspect was correctly identified, not whether the perpetrator was correctly identified.[38] The study made no attempt to establish the veracity of the suspects as the perpetrators, even in a subset of the sample where DNA or other definitive evidence might have been available.[39] This is especially problematic because a high positive identification rate (i.e., true positives) should be found if simultaneous lineups lead to comparative selections among the lineup participants, as critics contend (Wells and Olson 2003, 288). However, this defect would not explain why simultaneous lineups also led to fewer mistakes (i.e., had lower false-positive rates). A second defect in the research method might explain this latter finding. The Illinois study compared blind sequential lineup procedures to nonblind simultaneous lineups.[40] Many researchers believe that when administrators of lineups know the suspect's identity, there is a risk that they will provide subtle (or not so subtle) clues to the witness as to which one is the "correct" choice.[41] Failure to blind the administrator in the simultaneous lineups while blinding administrators of the sequential lineups is a substantial confound that might explain the lack of correspondence between the field research and the laboratory studies.

As the Illinois example makes clear, statistics cannot be viewed independently from the research methods used to generate them. Even when adequate research methods have generated robust statistics, this empirical work must be applied to some policy decision. What are the policy implications—either for a state legislature or a court considering the due process implications of lineup procedures—of research

[36] Id. at 38.

[37] Id. at 61.

[38] See id. at iii.

[39] Although there was no concerted effort to establish that the suspects were in fact the perpetrators, the researchers did report that "many suspect identifications recorded in the Illinois Pilot Program were corroborated by independent evidence." Id.

[40] See Illinois Report, supra note 31, at v.

[41] Although it is widely believed that lineup administrators sometimes give implicit or explicit clues to witnesses regarding the "correct" choice, research has yet to fully demonstrate this hypothesis. See Haw and Fisher (2004).

comparing simultaneous and sequential lineups? Even if the research studies were relatively clear, the policy choices are not.

Assume that the Illinois study's results are an artifact of the confounding variables and that the laboratory work best describes the policy choice presented by sequential and simultaneous lineups. Suppose, in particular, that simultaneous lineups are more sensitive than sequential lineups, thus producing more true-positive identifications, but also more false positives. This might lead some to advocate sequential lineups on the basis that, on balance, it is much worse to convict the innocent than to free the guilty. Others might advocate simultaneous lineups, arguing that they are a more powerful tool for law enforcement and that other evidence or cross-examination at trial can discern incorrect identifications.

A third possibility exists which does not require a blanket choice of one procedure over the other. The data in this example support the proposition that simultaneous lineups produce more positive identifications, of both the true and false varieties. But in some cases false positives may be less worrisome, and the more powerful (albeit less discerning) test might be preferable. For instance, in sexual assault cases in which forensic DNA evidence is available, we should prefer a lineup procedure that would maximize positive identifications because subsequent DNA testing will clear anyone who is wrongly accused. There are certainly significant costs associated with wrongful accusations that result in arrest and DNA testing, but these cost are relatively minor compared to wrongful convictions (i.e., false positives) and the failure to apprehend the perpetrators (i.e., false negatives). In contrast, in cases in which eyewitness identification is likely to be the best or only substantial evidence available, sequential lineups might be a better policy choice. In those cases, reduction of false identifications might very well be of paramount importance. As this example illustrates, constitutional practice can be shaped by close examination of, and due regard for, the lessons and limitations of mature research programs.

The empirical world is inevitably central to the practice of constitutional law, whether in setting the contours of doctrine, giving practical effect to the dictates of that doctrine or, when ignored, frustrating that doctrine's implementation. It is incumbent on judges, therefore, to understand the sum and substance of the vast empirical component of constitutional cases. This might include matters ranging from, on the one hand, the debates of the Virginia ratifying convention to, on the other hand, the neuroscience of "mental abnormality." Throughout its history, however, the Court has paid constitutional facts little attention. It has, at best, used facts heuristically, with little regard for their role in the process of interpreting or applying the Constitution. Moreover, the Court has completely disregarded the procedural aspects of fact-finding, receiving and deciding factual questions in a slapdash manner. Although fact-finding in constitutional cases will never be the relatively well-ordered process found in ordinary trials, it could be considerably more coherent than current practice. The next section provides a roadmap and process by which constitutional facts might be found.

2.2 A Proceduralist's Guide to Constitutional Fact-Finding

Up to this point, the core concern has been to establish the need for constitutional fact-finding that is based on scientific realist principles and which takes into account the complexities of constitutional jurisprudence. The main lesson is that it is eminently possible for the interpretation and application of the Constitution to be empirically sophisticated. To accomplish this objective, however, requires fidelity to a host of procedural guidelines for receiving and deciding constitutional facts. This section endeavors to describe these guidelines in a straightforward and clear fashion.

2.2.1 Three Types of Constitutional Facts

The essential starting point for the success of any set of procedural guidelines is the definition of terms. In constitutional cases, facts come in three basic varieties: doctrinal, reviewable and case specific. Doctrinal facts are relevant to interpreting the Constitution and thus affect the definition of the rules or standards used to implement the Constitution. Most commentators believe, for example, that the historical meaning of the phrase "freedom of speech" is relevant to defining the reach of First Amendment protections. This is a factual question that depends on an interpretation of historical sources. The second kind of constitutional facts are reviewable facts. Reviewable facts become relevant under particular interpretations of the Constitution and must be found pursuant to some applicable rule or standard. For example, the Court has found that nude dancing is a form of expression that is covered by the freedom of speech guarantee. At the same time, however, the Court has recognized a state's substantial interest in avoiding the crime and neighborhood deterioration that allegedly accompanies nude dancing establishments. The general empirical relationship between adult dancing parlors and neighborhood degradation is a reviewable fact. Finally, the third kind of constitutional fact is case-specific. Staying with the nude dancing example, the secondary effects created by a particular adult establishment in a specific neighborhood would be case-specific facts.

As defined, therefore, doctrinal and reviewable facts are general in nature and accordingly transcend individual cases. Case-specific facts, as the name connotes, are relevant only to the respective cases in which they arise. The determination regarding which kind of constitutional fact is implicated in the first instance is itself a subject of constitutional interpretation. The Court must determine at what level of generality the constitutional fact ought to be resolved. This choice has significant ramifications for constitutional jurisprudence. In *Brown v. Board of Education*, for example, the challengers of segregated schools introduced two kinds of research findings regarding the deleterious consequences associated with segregation. The first type was Kenneth Clark's general research findings, originally published years before the onset of the litigation. The second type was data collected from the individual school districts involved in the litigation. Those data indicated that the negative effects of segregation observed generally were occurring in the locales involved in these cases. The decision over what "frame of reference" to use in deciding the matter—nationwide or individual school district—was endemic to the broader inquiry regarding the meaning of the Equal Protection Clause. By choosing a nationwide perspective in *Brown*, the Court largely established a national rule that could not be relitigated from place to place or in case after case. In effect, the Court considered the policy of school segregation facially and found it invalid based on, among other things, its empirical consequences.

The question of ***what*** must be proven is a matter of substance and depends on the meaning of the Constitution. The question of ***how*** a particular kind of fact should be proven is a matter of procedure and involves the proper application of the Constitution. Application, however, is inextricably linked to interpretation, so that the former inevitably shapes the latter. Procedure in constitutional cases, therefore, must cohere to basic constitutional norms and conform to basic constitutional principles. In effect, just as is true more generally, procedure should serve to deploy constitutional meaning to concrete cases in ways that are faithful to that meaning. The procedural mechanics suggested here are crafted to do just that.

2.2.2 Proving Constitutional Facts

The most basic consideration presented by constitutional facts concerns the question of proof. Specifically, what evidence is allowable—that is, admissible—to prove each kind of constitutional fact and what decision rules apply to resolve conflicting evidence? Doctrinal, reviewable, and case-specific facts present very different issues in regard to empirical proof and thus must be considered separately.

Doctrinal Facts

Doctrinal facts tend to be the grandest but most amorphous kinds of facts found in constitutional cases. Their uncertain character and their relevance to determining the meaning of specific provisions of the Constitution largely exempt them from the adversarial process. Although the parties are likely to address doctrinal facts in their briefs and oral arguments, these facts would rarely be the subject of expert testimony at trial. Courts have as much latitude to find doctrinal facts on their own as they have to research case law.

As a practical matter, the line between doctrinal fact and embedded principle is indeterminate. Courts use doctrinal facts rhetorically, typically combining empirical assertions and normative claims to support particular interpretations. While the Court has been known to treat reviewable and even case-specific facts this same way, the complex and amorphous nature of doctrinal facts support this untidy treatment. Federalism, for instance, might or might not promote "laboratories of experimentation," but falsifying this fact would not have any appreciable impact on the Court's holding in *New York v. United States* that the federal government cannot "commandeer" state legislatures under the Tenth Amendment.[42] The Court's view that the federal government violates state sovereignty when it takes over legislative or executive apparatuses was indeed supported by the belief that this would undermine their ability to operate as laboratories of experimentation. Disproving this premise, however, would not alter the outcome. The rule of "no commandeering" is based on a large number of premises, some textual (e.g., the reach of the Tenth Amendment), some normative (e.g., the need for electoral accountability), and many empirical (e.g., continuing efficacy of federalism's checks and balances to guarantee individual liberty). Whether a particular congressional action operates to "commandeer," of course, is a reviewable fact, and whether it commandeered a state apparatus in a particular case is a case-specific fact. These are matters of application. But in defining the constitutional rule of "no commandeering," empirical arguments necessarily combine with textual, precedential, and normative, and they cannot be separated out for purposes of procedural proof. Doctrinal facts, therefore, do not operate as proof in any conventional sense of that term.

Burdens of proof, therefore, are largely inapplicable to the processing of doctrinal facts. Doctrinal facts are a constituent part of defining the Constitution. As such, they are ultimately within the province of courts to decide. No particular procedural rules should apply to them. They can be found at any stage of the legal proceedings and through any means by which the applicable law might be determined. They thus might come in during argument at trial, through amicus briefs on appeal, and by judges' own research at any time throughout the process.

Reviewable Facts

Reviewable facts are general in nature and transcend particular disputes. They have precedential effect. Unlike doctrinal facts, however, they can largely be defined free of normative or textual considerations. They can be isolated for purposes of saying whether they are so, or not. In the case of reviewable facts, there is a fact of the matter that can be the subject of proof. While the Court too often fails to be faithful to its own statements, it regularly describes reviewable facts as truly empirical propositions to which there are at least approximate answers. The Court has thus seriously contemplated factual concerns such as the onset of viability, whether a twenty-four-hour waiting provision substantially interferes with the abortion right, the effects of virtual child pornography, the mental competency of minors, and so on.

Proof of reviewable facts comes to a court's attention in many ways. It is proffered through expert testimony, embedded in record transcripts of legislative or administrative agency hearings, argued in the briefs and memoranda of the parties and amici, and discovered through independent judicial research. Moreover, reviewable facts are introduced and analyzed at every level of court. Historically, there has been no practice or tradition that reviewable facts originate first at trial, meet any

---

[42]See *New York v. United States*, 505 U.S. 144 (1992).

particular threshold admissibility requirements, or otherwise survive the rigors of the adversarial process.

When evidence of reviewable facts is offered at trial, ordinarily it is through the testimony of experts and must meet threshold requirements of admissibility. In most state and federal courts, rules of admissibility are designed to ensure that the basic foundation for this proffered testimony is valid. This is true whether the admitting court evaluates the methodological bases for the expert opinion or simply considers whether the basis for the evidence is generally accepted among professionals in the particular field from which it comes. In federal courts, Rule 702 and the decision in *Daubert v. Merrell Dow Pharmaceuticals, Inc.* apply to the reception of expert evidence. Under *Daubert*, the proponent of expert testimony has the burden to demonstrate that the basis for the opinion is more likely than not valid. *Daubert* stands for the proposition that the probative value of expert evidence is proportionate to the quality and quantity of the data and the research methods that support it. *Daubert* largely incorporates the critical perspective associated with the methods of good empirical investigation, whether it comes from scientists, historians, or auto mechanics. Courts should take a similar approach to questions of reviewable facts, whether or not they come to the court's attention through expert testimony at trial.

Judges should measure empirical claims in accordance with the methods on which these claims are based. Inevitably, knowledge about the empirical world will be known with greater or lesser confidence. The more complex the phenomenon, the more difficult it will be to study. Very often in constitutional cases too little will be known about relevant reviewable facts. When this is so, the normative principles of the Constitution allocate the risk of error. In short, the Constitution establishes rules of decision for fact-based inquiries. The Constitution ought to be understood as allocating burdens of proof for reviewable facts.

Reviewable facts are readily amenable to standards of proof. In *Casey*, for example, the Court stated that laws that "unduly burden" the right of abortion are unconstitutional. This was operationally defined as any law that created a substantial obstacle to the exercise of the right. The undue burden standard contains both an empirical and a normative—i.e., cost of error—component. The question of when a law interferes with the right is an empirical matter. That it must be substantial, rather than merely tangible, is a normative statement of weight. But the Court has not been consistent or clear regarding the meaning of the substantiality requirement in this or other contexts. Similarly, in Commerce Clause cases, the Court has long held that Congress has the authority to regulate commerce if it "substantially affects interstate commerce." Indeed, in *United States v. Lopez*,[43] the Court emphasized the substantiality component of the test. Yet the Court has been distressingly unclear regarding whether Congress has any affirmative obligation to produce proof of this matter or, more particularly, what it means to "substantially affect" commerce rather than simply "affect" commerce. In effect, defining these sorts of terms would make clear which party bears the costs of error. If, as had been assumed after 1937, the costs of error for "exceeding" the commerce power do not lie with Congress, then

[43] 514 U.S. 549 (1995).

the challengers of federal power should bear the burden of proof to show that the subject of congressional legislation does not substantially affect interstate commerce. The greater the deference owed to Congress in this matter, the greater should be the burden shouldered by challengers of the law. There is no intractable reason why such clear statements of the law could not be made, other than the Court's apparent nonrealist approach to the subject of constitutional application.

Case-Specific Facts

In the area of case-specific facts, the Court has been more attentive to evidentiary standards and the challenges associated with allocating burdens of proof. To a large degree, this is simply because case-specific facts fit the Court's preconceived notions of "fact-finding." Whether decided by judge or jury, case-specific constitutional facts are subject to ordinary rules of evidence and are neither the subject of additional proof through memoranda and briefs nor a proper subject of independent judicial research. Moreover, burdens of proof apply to case-specific facts either as a routine matter, based on the context in which they arise—i.e., civil or criminal case—or because the Court has established the proper burden of proof on the basis of special circumstances dictated by normative constitutional considerations.

In *New York Times v. Sullivan*,[44] for example, the Court held that public officials cannot prevail in a libel action brought against critics of their official conduct unless they could prove "actual malice." This required proof "that the statement was made with ... knowledge that it was false or with reckless disregard of whether it was false or not."[45] The Court explained that this demanding standard of proof was necessitated by the guarantees implicit in the First Amendment. "[E]rroneous statement is inevitable in free debate," the Court asserted, so that even false statement must "be protected if the freedoms of expression are to have the breathing space that they need ... to survive."[46] The Constitution is committed "to the principle that debate on public issues should be uninhibited, robust, and wide-open, and that it may well include vehement, caustic, and sometimes unpleasantly sharp attacks on government and public officials."[47]

The Court showed a similar level of empirical accountability in *Addington v. Texas*,[48] in which it considered the proper burden of proof in civil commitment cases. The Court explicitly contemplated the proper allocation of "the risk of error" when a state seeks to involuntarily commit a person to a mental hospital for an indefinite period. Traditionally, courts chose between the preponderance of the evidence standard used in most civil cases and the criminal standard of proof beyond a reasonable doubt. The Court believed that neither of these standards would properly allocate the

[44] 376 U.S. 254 (1964).

[45] Id. at 279–280.

[46] Id. at 271–272 (internal quotation marks and citation omitted).

[47] Id. at 270.

[48] 441 U.S. 418 (1979).

costs of error between the parties. It stated that commitment hearings, which pose "a significant deprivation of liberty," require more than a preponderance of the evidence. At the same time, the Court determined, the criminal standard of proof beyond a reasonable doubt was not appropriate in ordinary civil commitment cases. The Court explained, "It cannot be said … that it is much better for a mentally ill person to 'go free' than for a mentally normal person to be committed."[49] The *Addington* Court, therefore, settled on the intermediate standard of clear and convincing evidence to best allocate the costs of error in this area.

2.3 *Judicial Review of Constitutional Fact-Finding*

An inherent and necessary consideration in establishing processes to control constitutional fact-finding is the matter of judicial review. Boiled down to its essence, this concerns the question of when, if ever, particular courts are obligated to defer to the factual findings of other bodies or institutions. The issue largely divides along two tracks, with the first involving judicial review of juries, legislatures, and administrative agencies, and the second concerning appellate review of lower courts. Conventionally, three factors of importance might determine what deference is due. The first is the identity and competencies of the institution in question. The second is the kind of fact implicated in the decision (i.e., doctrinal, reviewable, or case specific). The third is the importance of the constitutional values implicated in the case. Upon close examination, however, it turns out that only the second and third factors should have any determinative value. In constitutional cases, the identity of non-judicial fact finders and their greater or lesser competence to find facts, is largely irrelevant on the issue of deference. Moreover, this lesson is basically the same regarding setting appellate standards of review. Consideration of the strengths and weaknesses of juries, legislatures, administrative agencies, and lower courts demonstrates that judicial and appellate review should depend exclusively on the kind of fact in dispute and the importance of the constitutional principle that the disputed facts implicate.

2.3.1 Constitutional Fact-Finding by Trial Courts

Most constitutional facts enter the judicial process through the trial court, and for case-specific facts, it is the only gateway. It is not at all unusual, however, for reviewable and, especially, doctrinal facts to be introduced first on appeal or even be posited by amici or discovered through independent judicial research. In conventional trial-process discourse, substantial attention is devoted to the line of demarcation that theoretically divides fact and law. This debate has substantial practical effect, since it largely defines the parameters of the jury's function. In constitutional cases, however, this conversation has considerably less theoretical interest. As an initial matter, both

[49] Id. at 430.

doctrinal facts and reviewable facts are, for all intents and purposes, treated as matters of law by trial courts. Case-specific facts, however, can present somewhat more controversy in the choice between judge and jury. In the end, though, there is nothing inherent in a constitutional case-specific fact that renders it obviously appropriate for one or another trial-court decision maker. As with other determinations concerning constitutional facts, this matter depends on an interpretation of the Constitution. Some facts—such as whether a statement defames a public figure or a photograph is obscene—should be decided initially by juries, whereas other facts—such as whether Nazis marching in Skokie will incite violence[50] or the city of Hialeah lacked a secular purpose in banning animal sacrifice[51]—should be decided initially by the trial court.

A somewhat more interesting issue concerns the vertical relationship between juries and the courts they serve. In particular, should courts be deferential to constitutional fact-finding when it is done by juries? Two arguments, in particular, support such deference. The first is that juries are themselves creatures of the Constitution, specifically guaranteed in criminal and civil cases by the Sixth and Seventh Amendments, respectively. The second is that juries are closer to the evidence than appellate courts and thus can assess demeanor. Upon close inspection, neither of these arguments for deference is convincing in constitutional cases.

In virtually all cases in which juries are called upon to decide constitutional facts, a basic or fundamental right is implicated. This responsibility is at odds with the institutional role of the jury. The jury's primary function is to represent the community from which its members are drawn and to faithfully apply duly enacted laws. The jury is thus an essentially majoritarian institution. This role clashes with the counter-majoritarian values guaranteed by the Constitution. Although juries are justly celebrated for sometimes operating to check government tyranny, the institution remains fundamentally majoritarian. When juries defend liberty they, in effect, operate as a check and balance on the majoritarian decision making of the legislative and executive branches of government just as those branches operate to check each other. Juries are not encouraged to nullify the law generally, and outside certain celebrated historical examples, this exercise of power is not acclaimed.

Beyond the constitutional arena, a venerable principle of evidence law is that triers of fact (either jury or judge) deserve deference from appellate courts because they have the opportunity to observe witnesses, measure their demeanor, and thereby assess their credibility. It is far from clear that there is any truth to conventional beliefs about demeanor, and some research calls it into question entirely (Burgoon and Dunbar 2016). But even if there is some value to assessing demeanor, the nature of constitutional litigation is such that it is probably not enough to justify blanket deference to front-line triers of fact. In ordinary litigation, case-specific fact-finding has little impact beyond the case at hand. Although case-specific facts do not reoccur in constitutional cases, by definition, they nonetheless contain some amount of precedential import. They tend to be cited by other courts as exemplars of the reach and limits of constitutional doctrine. Moreover, the resolution of case-specific facts

[50] See *National Socialist Party of America v. Village of Skokie*, 432 U.S. 43 (1977).

[51] See *Church of the Lukumi Babalu Aye v. City of Hialeah*, 508 U.S. 520 (1993).

resolve the constitutional rights and liabilities of particular persons. When basic constitutional rights are implicated, whether in free speech or other contexts, independent appellate review of case-specific facts is necessary to protect those rights and to help establish the parameters of applicable doctrine for other cases.

2.3.2 Constitutional Fact-Finding by Legislatures

Although much ink has been spilled on the question of the judiciary's obligation to be deferential to legislative fact-finding, this subject may be the simplest conceptually to address. Indeed, much of modern constitutional jurisprudence embodies the essential balance that underlies the clash of majority will (i.e., government interests) and individual liberty. Legislatures, of course, are the quintessential voice of the majority and thus, speaking classically, it is their tyranny that the Bill of Rights was intended to block. When legislative action treads upon basic liberties, the Court is obliged to closely scrutinize the legislature's justifications for acting. This, by necessity, means that courts must independently assess the empirical bases for legislative action. Otherwise, legislatures could avoid judicial holdings simply by finding facts differently than the courts.

Over the years, the Court has sought to construct myriad tests to guide its efforts in reviewing government action, including those of state and federal legislatures. These have ranged from tiered scrutiny to multi-factor tests. Increasingly, these tests have begun to break down and there appears to be an expanding chaos in the standards of review the Court uses (Massey 2004, 945). In *Lawrence v. Texas*, for instance, the Court struck down a state sodomy law without specifying what kind of scrutiny applied.[52] In *Gonzales v. Carhart*,[53] the Court did not say what level of review it was using in upholding a federal law that banned so-called partial birth abortion without including a health exception. In *Grutter v. Bollinger*,[54] the Court upheld race-based affirmative action using a diminished form of strict scrutiny. In *United States v. Virginia*,[55] the Court invalidated VMI's exclusion of women using a supercharged intermediate scrutiny test. Although it has not happened completely yet, many of the classic forms of constitutional analysis are disappearing and not being replaced by new forms.

Despite the growing murkiness of the tests used, the Court has never shrunk from the task of reviewing a legislature's constitutional fact-finding when basic constitutional values are at stake. Over the last thirty years, the Court has exercised its oversight muscle in cases arising across the constitutional spectrum. With changing membership on the Court resulting in a more conservative makeup, the sorts of cases in which legislatures are second-guessed might change from the Fourteenth Amendment to the Second Amendment, or from due process to interstate commerce, but

[52] *Lawrence v. Texas*, 539 U.S. 558 (2003).

[53] 127 S.Ct. 1610 (2007).

[54] 539 U.S. 306 (2003).

[55] 518 U.S. 515 (1996).

the Court's willingness to independently review legislative fact-finding is an abiding truth.

Yet the Court regularly extols the virtues of legislatures' fact-finding abilities. Legislatures have a wide variety of institutional advantages in this regard. They have greater resources than courts, for instance, to sponsor research, hold hearings, and call expert witnesses. They have the power to define research questions and the flexibility to follow them up by redefining the scope, direction, and size of any inquiries. These institutional strengths have repeatedly led the Court to express its preference for legislative fact-finding and point out its own limited capacity to match the resources legislatures have at their disposals.

While legislatures might indeed have great power and leeway to gather facts, this does not necessarily affect the standard of review courts bring to legislative fact-finding. Courts, too, are fact finders. Legislatures may excel in defining and framing research, but the courts should excel at hearing controverted evidence and coming to a decision free of partisan influence. Adopting a standard of independent review in some constitutional cases will not dissuade legislatures from compiling a full record. Indeed, a legislature that anticipates confronting a rigorous standard of review when the matter reaches the courts should be expected to do more to ensure a compelling factual record.

2.3.3 Constitutional Fact-Finding by Administrative Agencies

Administrative agencies are a sort of constitutional hybrid, sharing characteristics of both legislatures and trial courts (including juries). They very often have responsibility over the full panoply of constitutional facts—doctrinal, reviewable, and case specific. Administrative agencies, unlike legislatures or courts, usually possess technical expertise that is highly tuned to their respective areas of specialization. If any institutional context called for judicial deference on the basis of technical competence, it would be the administrative agency. Outside of constitutional cases, such deference is largely the rule.[56] In the context of constitutional litigation, however, the issue of judicial deference to administrative agency fact-finding is primarily a function of the kind of fact involved and the constitutional implications associated with the finding of the respective fact.

No deference is owed administrative agency findings of doctrinal facts, as these facts concern the Constitution's meaning and must be resolved by courts. Reviewable and case-specific facts present more challenging issues. In many contexts, agency expertise will far outstrip judicial understanding of complex or technical subjects. Nonetheless, this expertise is not enough to offset courts' obligations to independently define and apply constitutional safeguards. Agencies, like juries, derive their authority, if not their identity, from majoritarian values. This fact alone demands judicial oversight when basic constitutional values are in play. Moreover, in the case of reviewable facts, the potential practical difficulty of different agencies deciding

---

[56]See *Chevron U.S.A., Inc. v. Natural Resources Defense Council*, 467 U.S. 837 (1984).

the same fact differently augurs for non-deferential review. Case-specific facts do not pose this particular difficulty but, as was true in the trial context, they set the parameters and establish the contents of constitutional claims. Administrative agencies, like legislatures, have the resources to establish the best empirical case to support their decisions. Courts should give due respect and careful attention to these factual matters. In the final analysis, however, courts have an obligation to independently review administrative agency fact-finding when those facts are integral to the definition or application of fundamental or basic constitutional principles. The pivotal issue in this regard is not the institutional expertise of the agency, but the inherent constitutional import of the rights and interests affected by the facts in dispute. When an administrative agency finds facts that implicate core constitutional values, courts should review those findings independently.

2.3.4 Lower Court Review of Higher Court Fact-Finding

Perhaps the most difficult aspect of the law and science connection for lawyers to understand is the different perspectives the two fields employ regarding authority. The law's approach to authority is premised on established precedent and hierarchy. Although the law progresses through changing times, it does so reluctantly and often in denial of the fact. It is also stolidly hierarchical, being defined by ascending levels of courts in which the highest court's pronouncements prevail by dint of rank rather than the power of its ideas. Science operates very differently. Although science sometimes gets mired in existing paradigms, its leitmotif is the discovery of new knowledge. New ways to understand and control the world may not always be an unalloyed good, but it is what science does. Also, while science can be rigidly and thoughtlessly hierarchical, it is operating dysfunctionally when it does so. Science, at its mythological best, is democratic, a society in which the lowliest patent office clerk can revolutionize settled views. The law has no real equivalent.

If courts are ever to employ facts in a scientifically realist fashion, these clashing perspectives must be reconciled. Somehow, the law's top-down pronouncements must be amenable to bottom-up revision when substantial new information is available. Ideally, any process employed to accomplish this integration of venerable constitutional principle and cutting-edge knowledge will maintain the strengths and benefits each side brings to the matter. Constitutional law is a steady, slow-moving omnipresence for good reason. It is informed by transcendent normative principles that are properly seen as steadfast and set in the bedrock of American society. Quickly changing understandings of basic constitutional principles would send shockwaves through the foundations of the state. At the same time, constitutional doctrine mired in the empirical beliefs of the past has similarly disruptive consequences. Modern tools of empirical research, especially in the social and behavioral sciences, can provide insights and knowledge scarcely imagined even fifty years ago, much less more than two hundred years ago. Modern tools of behavioral researchers, such as powerful computers, genetic screening, functional magnetic resonance imaging (fMRI), statistical modeling and many more, have completely transformed entire fields. It is safe to predict that much more is to come. The question is not whether the law should have to devise ways to incorporate new knowledge into constitutional decision making, but how it will do so.

The answer to this question depends primarily on the kind of fact—doctrinal, reviewable, or case specific—that is at issue in the case. The rigid hierarchy of the law should be maintained in the situation of doctrinal facts, but modified substantially in the case of reviewable facts. In short, lower courts should have the power to revisit higher court authority when the factual basis of that authority depends on reviewable facts that substantial research indicates have changed. Lower courts should not have this authority for doctrinal facts, and they already have this power for case-specific facts.

The power to reconsider precedent when the reviewable facts on which it is based have changed would not give lower courts the freedom to overturn higher court authority with which they merely disagree. A lower court's distinguishing higher court authority would have to be supported by findings that the changed fact was necessary and sufficient for the earlier ruling and that new research unequivocally supports the new findings of fact.

Many benefits would come from adopting a procedural rule whereby lower courts could reexamine precedent when research demonstrates that the predicate facts supporting the earlier decision have changed. Perhaps foremost, it would advance the legitimacy of constitutional practice by keeping it in line with contemporary knowledge of the facts underlying constitutional decisions. Constitutional doctrine should fit the facts as they are known today. Also, giving lower courts the power to revisit reviewable facts will have a salutary effect on the Supreme Court's sometimes haphazard reliance on such facts in its jurisprudence. The knowledge that other courts will seriously evaluate the empirical data behind its decisions will lead the Court to be more serious in its evaluations of the data. Moreover, a general trend toward taking facts seriously in constitutional discourse would likely increase the amount of, and improve the use of, empirical data. Researchers long disenchanted with the Court's empirical legerdemain would almost certainly notice and quickly begin to devote considerable resources to studying subjects of interest to the courts. There would be a renaissance of sorts in the amount and diversity of information produced and in efforts to capture judicial attention. To be sure, this research would not all be valuable, and much of it would be worthless, but in time the cream would rise to the top. The lower courts would be the gateway for this work. Over time, they would develop the sophistication to recognize important findings and help draw attention to them, thus speeding the dissemination and incorporation of new and valid findings into constitutional law.

3 Conclusion

The Supreme Court has never sought to impose any systematic order on its reception of facts in constitutional cases. Although facts are a pervasive presence in the Court's opinions, there is no logic or order to their use. The Court treats them as rhetorical devices, to be used or withheld as the normative circumstances of the case dictate. While this practice gives the Court great latitude in its interpretation and application of the Constitution, it also weakens that institution's rightful authority. It privileges power over logic. It elevates faith over reason. Holdings premised on hollow empirical propositions are nothing more than pronouncements. They persuade by virtue of the Court's prestige, not by the power of its analysis.

The Court's use of fact-based arguments in place of the true grounds for its decisions undermines the very pillars of constitutional democracy. Although the Court has the duty to say what the law is, the people of the United States have ultimate responsibility for their government. In a very real sense, the Court answers to the people. The people are sovereign. In *McCulloch v. Maryland*, John Marshall explained that the "government of the Union … is, emphatically, and truly, a government of the people. In form and in substance it emanates from them. Its powers are granted by them, and are to be exercised directly on them, and for their benefit."[57]

The Court should have to state plainly the true reasons for its decisions. Informed constitutional democracy is not possible without this probity. Constitutional jurisprudence is unlikely to be effective if it is applied in sustained ignorance of the world. Being blind to the factual antecedents and consequents of the Constitution can only lead to unsalutary outcomes.

Many of the founders were men of science who relied on Enlightenment philosophers to inform their political philosophy. Benjamin Franklin was elected to the Paris Royal Academy of Sciences and both James Madison and John Adams were well read in the natural philosophy of the day. Thomas Jefferson was nearly an entire science department unto himself. It is ironic that those entrusted with their handiwork have such an unenlightened approach to the empirical world. Knowledge of the factual world cannot dictate constitutional values. But such knowledge is a tool upon which the Court must sometimes rely to ensure that those values are realized.

Enlightened constitutional practice can be neither solely normative nor exclusively empirical. It requires a blending, an integration, of the two. This cannot be accomplished other than through brute practicality. However unromantic it might seem, an informed empirical jurisprudence depends on the systematic use of procedural guidelines. Only such procedures can manage the reception and employment of good quality research.

Many scholars and judges are attracted to constitutional law by the romance of it. Principles of liberty, equality, freedom of speech and the free exercise of religion are values that inspire lawyers to poetic heights. Slogging around in the procedural trenches of evidence law, burdens of proof, and statistics is not what the average

[57] *McCulloch v. Maryland*, 4 Wheat (17 U.S.) 316 (1819).

constitutionalist joined up to do. To be done right, however, those details are what can make the Constitution soar. The poetry lies in the details.

The Constitution does not protect theory or abstract generalities. It ensures practical and substantive rights. It is a blueprint for a nation in action. The romance of liberty or equality must take concrete form in the arrangements of real people. Freedom of speech is guaranteed in particular contexts against counterclaims of public necessity. The great principles of humankind and good government enshrined in the Constitution depend on knowledge of brute reality to be realized. The guarantees of the Constitution are merely words on paper until they take shape in the real world. It is, therefore, incumbent on the Court to have a good understanding of that world if it is to give the Constitution effect.

References

Bickel, Alexander M. 1986. *The Least Dangerous Branch: The Supreme Court at the Bar of Politics*. New Haven, Connecticut: Yale University Press.

Burgoon, J., and N. Dunbar. 2016. Accuracy of Distinguishing Truth from Lie. In *The Social Psychology of Perceiving Others Accurately*, ed. J. Hall, M. Schmid Mast, and T. West.

Faigman, David L. 2006. Judges as "Amateur Scientists". *Boston University Law Review* 86: 1207.

Faigman, David. 2008. *Constitutional Fictions: A Unified Theory of Constitutional Facts*. Oxford, UK: Oxford University Press.

Faigman, David, Edward Cheng, Jennifer Mnookin, Erin Murphy, Joseph Sanders, and Christopher Slobogin. 2019–2020. *Modern Scientific Evidence: The Law and Science of Expert Testimony*, Chap. 1.

Fisher, Carl E., David L. Faigman, and Paul S. Appelbaum. 2015. Toward a Jurisprudence of Psychiatric Evidence: Examining the Challenges of Reasoning from Group Data in Psychiatry to Individual Decisions in the Law. *University of Miami Law Review* 69: 685–753.

Haw, R.M., and R.P. Fisher. 2004. Effects of Administrator-Witness Contact on Eyewitness Identification Accuracy. *Journal of Applied Psychology* 89: 1106–1112.

Larsen, Allison Orr. 2012. Confronting Supreme Court Fact Finding. *Virginia Law Review* 98: 1255–1312.

Massey, Calvin. 2004. The New Formalism: Requiem for Tiered Scrutiny? *University of Pennsylvania Journal of Constitutional Law* 6: 945.

Mecklenburg, Sheri H. 2006. Illinois State Police, Report to the Legislature of the State of Illinois: The Illinois Pilot Program on Sequential, Double-Blind Identification Procedures. Available at: https://eyewitness.utep.edu/Documents/IllinoisPilotStudyOnEyewitnessID.pdf.

Meissner, C.A., C.G. Tredoux, J.F. Parker, and O.H. MacLin. 2005. Eyewitness Decisions in Simultaneous and Sequential Lineups: A Dual-Process Signal Detection Theory Analysis. *Memory & Cognition* 33: 783–792.

Steblay, Nancy, Jennifer Dysart, Solomon Fulero, and R. C. L. Lindsay. 2001. Eyewitness Accuracy Rates in Sequential and Simultaneous Lineup Presentations: A Meta-Analytic Comparison. *Law and Human Behavior* 25: 459–473.

Sundby, Scott E. 1989. The Reasonable Doubt Rule and the Meaning of Innocence. *Hastings Law Journal* 40: 457–510+460.

Wells, Gary L., and Elizabeth A. Olson. 2003. Eyewitness Testimony. *Annual Review Psychology* 54: 277–295+288.

The Elaine Massacre: A Case Study in the Dialogue Between Law and History

Rayman L. Solomon

Lawyers and historians both have a goal of creating "persuasive" narratives out of facts. Their professional roles, however, produce differing constraints and possibilities for constructing "accurate" histories of events. One obvious difference is their temporal contexts. Given statutes of limitations, lawyers are writing histories based on research that is immediate, and they may be totally unaware of important sources, such as government records that are classified and unavailable. The historian's craft, on the other hand, is accretive. It may be written decades or even centuries later and have available prior research, factual detail, and archival sources that would have been inaccessible to a lawyer.

Lawyers and historians are both instrumental in their efforts to be persuasive. Again, their professional roles cause distinctive differences. In their classic article on the relationship between "questions of law" and "questions of fact" Professors Ronald Allen and Professor Michael Pardo argue convincingly that there is no analytical difference between the two. Rather, it is a functional classification that allocates decisional roles to either judges or juries. However, they state that the relationship has important consequences (Allen and Pardo 2003, 1769–1807). One of those is that lawyers will "shape" facts to favor what they perceive to be "the law". Details may be omitted or buried in a narrative if the lawyer thinks that it will be more likely to convince a judge or a jury that her case fits within the holding of the controlling precedent or creates a compelling case to change that precedent.

Even if historians at one time believed they could write the "true" history of an event, that day has long since passed. There is probably a consensus that all histories are partial. Historians may all agree on certain facts—the American Revolution's open warfare with the British began in April, 1775. However, historians disagree

R. L. Solomon (✉)
Rutgers Law School, Camden, NJ, USA
e-mail: raysol@law.rutgers.edu

Peking University School of Transnational Law, Shenzhen, China

B. Zhang et al. (eds.), *A Dialogue Between Law and History*,
https://doi.org/10.1007/978-981-15-9685-8_10

about when the Revolution "began" and its causes. Historians attribute the causes to economic, social, political, and intellectual influences. Each of these emphasize certain facts and omit others in order to make their arguments persuasive. While each is a partial explanation of the event, they make no pretense to be "definitive", as the accretive nature of the professional enterprise makes such claims indefensible. Although there are some tendentious books or articles written that deliberately ignore facts or falsify records to advance a certain thesis or narrative, these are considered outside the professional norms of the historian.

In order to explore these issues, I will examine the history of the Elaine Race Massacre, which was one of the largest, if not the largest, race massacres in the United States, and resulted in an important U.S. Supreme Court case, *Moore v Dempsey*[1] in 1923, that altered both criminal due process and civil rights litigation.

1 The Background

The Massacre occurred 100 years ago, September 29–October 2, 1919 in Phillips County, Arkansas. The county seat, Helena, is a Mississippi River port that had a self-perception and reputation as a "progressive" city, where there had been no previous lynchings. The county is the beginning of the Mississippi River delta on its western bank; that is, the topography south of Helena is flat, and the soil extremely fertile, which is ideal for cotton. Beginning around 1900 northern lumber companies began to clear-cut the virgin forest lands in the south county. They would ship the timber by train to Helena, mill it, and then sell it in the north. The cleared land would then be planted in cotton. These were large land holdings; 2000–5000 acres.[2]

Following the Civil War and the passage of the Fifteenth Amendment slavery ended in the United States. Throughout the South, white plantation owners developed a system of peonage farming to control the large mostly African-American labor force needed to grow cotton. These mostly Black farmers were called sharecroppers. They rented land from the plantation owner, bought cotton seed and supplies on credit, and then sold the cotton they grew to the landowner. This was all done through contract, though they might well be called contracts of adhesion—there was no opportunity to bargain meaningfully over terms. The white plantation owners set all of the prices and the interest charged on the credit given the sharecroppers. The result of this arrangement was that sharecroppers were systematically and continually cheated. Accountings were infrequently given, and sharecroppers were rarely able to get out of debt (Whitaker 2008, 74).

In order to understand why violence erupted in Elaine two developments should be discussed. First, the price of cotton, which had been steady around 12 cents a pound for many years, rose precipitously during World War I and reached a high of

[1] *Moore v. Dempsey*, 261 U.S. 86 (1923).

[2] As will be discussed there are many sources for the history of the Elaine Massacre. The most comprehensive and authoritative history is Whitaker (2008). On Phillips County see Chap. 4.

49 cents a pound in 1919. The second is that there were a number of young African American sharecroppers from Phillips County who had served in World War I. Upon their return from the War, they expected that the segregated social system in the South should change, including the grossly unfair peonage sharecropping system. These young men, together with their elders, began to agitate to get their fair share from the large landowners near Elaine (Whitaker 2008, 72).

They pursued two means of addressing their grievances. First, they hired a white, former U.S. Attorney, Ulysses S. Bratton, to represent them against the plantation owners. He began to make demands for information about the sharecroppers' accounts under their contracts. This both angered the plantation owners, and made them anxious about the militancy of the African Americans. The sharecroppers also began to talk to labor organizers for the Progressive Farmers and Household Union. The organizers convinced several of the influential Black leaders in the area that the only way to get a fair share of the profits from their labor was to become members of their union (Whitaker 2008).

On the night of September 30, 1919 the union organizer, Robert Hill, a Black veteran of World War I, arranged a meeting of about 100 Black men, women, and children at Hoop Spur Church, which was 3 miles north of the town of Elaine, in south Phillips County. That part of the county was reachable only by one road and railroad tracks which went from there to the lumber mills. The sharecroppers feared violence and had armed guards protecting the church. The county sheriff sent a deputy and a railroad security officer by car to the church to monitor the situation (Whitaker 2008, 83–88).

What happened next was that shots were fired, the security officer died, and the deputy was wounded. I have stated this in the passive voice as at this point two narratives begin: one white and one Black. The white narrative is that the car stopped as it had a flat tire, the Blacks fired first attacking the two whites who defended themselves. The Blacks stated that the two whites fired first and began to shoot up the church, and they defended themselves. When gunfire erupted the sharecroppers in the church escaped through windows and the back door.

The next day rumors spread throughout Helena that there was a Black uprising in south county and that the union members had a list of white plantation owners and others they intended to murder. The sheriff formed a posse comprised of members of the American Legion who had served in World War I. They were joined by volunteer posse members from other Arkansas counties and from Mississippi. They traveled toward Elaine and began indiscriminately to murder Blacks. Two whites in the posse were killed, which further inflamed the situation. Business and professional elites in Helena wanted to end the "riot" as soon as possible, so they requested the Arkansas governor to send troops. He did so immediately and on the second day these U.S. Army troops, armed with machine guns, arrived (Whitaker 2008, 89–126).

The terrified Black sharecroppers fled their homes and hid out in the surrounding forests and swamps. Two soldiers were killed, apparently by friendly fire, but this led to the commanding officer to give 'shoot to kill orders' to the troops. However, upon seeing the soldiers many of the Blacks, who thought the soldiers were there to protect them, were murdered as they came out of hiding. Meanwhile, the posses were also hunting down and killing Blacks not only near Elaine, but also in the northern parts of the county, where Blacks had played no part in the union organizing campaign. Four members of a prominent Black family in Helena, who were returning on a train from a hunting trip, were taken off the train in Elaine, put in a sheriff's car, then murdered, and left on the roadside (Whitaker 2008, 89–126).

The systematic killing of the Blacks was documented by reporters who accompanied the posses and the soldiers. After five days (October 3rd) most of the violence stopped, although it took several more days before it completely ended. Beginning on October 2nd, as the killings decreased, the Army began to take sharecroppers into custody and hold them in Elaine. After the violence subsided they transferred the 300 arrested Blacks to Helena where they were held in jail cells (Whitaker 2008, 122).

Before turning to the legal proceedings several points should be made. First, no whites were ever arrested and tried either in state or federal criminal courts or military tribunals for the murder of the African Americans. Second, as we will see when discussing the historiography of the Massacre, the most disputed "fact" was the number of Blacks who were killed, and no definitive answer has ever been provided. Estimates vary from no more than 25 to over 850, but the best estimates are between 100 and 225 (Whitaker 2008, 123–126). Third, the Massacre occurred during the height of time to pick cotton, and many planters were in desperate need for labor. Half of the men and women arrested were vouched for by their planters, released, and never faced a trial. Fourth, although the Massacre is part of America's violent summer of 1919, its causes were local. The incidents were about the control of labor and the unionization was not related to any national movement. Neither the planters nor those in Helena connected the union or sharecroppers to Bolshevism.

Fifth, and most important, the two narratives continued. The white narrative posited that the entire event was an insurrection orchestrated by the union leaders which was designed to kill white plantation owners and take their land. The most active Black unionists were considered the ringleaders and were the ones targeted to be made an example of, so that the existing peonage system should never be challenged again. The Black narrative, which as we will see was backed by investigations by the NAACP's Walter White, as well as the prominent Black journalist Ida Wells-Barnett, denied that any conspiracy existed. They argued that the sharecroppers were engaged in no illegal conduct, rather they were employing legal means to enforce their contractual rights, and only sought justice and fair treatment (Whayne 1999, 285–313).

2 The Lawyers' Case: The White Narrative

150 Blacks remained jailed in Helena. Unlike countless stories throughout the Jim Crow South, there was no mob attack on the jail where the Black prisoners were taken out and hanged. The Helena business and political elite formed a Committee of Seven to deal with the mob. As mentioned previously, they wanted to keep the

city's reputation as being progressive. When a mob formed in the streets before any trials started and threatened to lynch the prisoners, the white leaders made a deal with them. There would be no lynchings and in exchange the Blacks would be quickly tried, convicted, sentenced to death, and executed (Whitaker 2008, 161).

All of the elements of what we today consider a sham or unfair trial then occurred. The Blacks were tortured and beaten in order to force confessions. The defendants were given defense attorneys who were part of the white establishment. They did not interview their clients nor did they prepare a defense for each. At trial these lawyers did little to assist the defendants through their arguments or questioning of witnesses. The juries were all white males, a number of whom had participated in the Massacre by serving in the posses which had formed to put down the supposed insurrection in south Phillips County. Trials began a month after the arrests. Each one took a little over one hour, and juries deliberated for less than half that. All trials ended in convictions (Whitaker 2008).

Such tactics as confessions obtained through torture, non-de jure exclusions of Blacks from the jury, and ineffective assistance of counsel strike at the very truth-seeking function of a trial. Here the forced confessions implicated the union organizers by claiming they were planning the murder of white planters, and linked men to the murder of the five whites, when no real evidence existed to implicate them. However, once these biased jurors found the defendants guilty, the factual questions were settled. The white narrative was established. The bargain the Committee of Seven struck with the mob was delivered. The only questions for review by an appellate court were questions of law. But in 1919 when these trials occurred U.S. constitutional law had not evolved to overturn convictions based on the use of these criminal trial tactics. It was not until a decade later and beyond that the U.S. Supreme Court in a series of cases declared that each of these was unconstitutional.

Seventy-five of the defendants were sentenced to prison and twelve were sentenced to death. Saving these twelve became a national cause célèbre both in the Black press such as the *Chicago Defender* and the *Crisis*, and in the northern press, especially in Chicago and New York (Whitaker 2008).

It took four years to spare the lives of these twelve men. The story has all the plot twists and cliff-hanging moments of a movie thriller or novel. However, this real-life drama was a product of brilliant legal tactics by the defense, mistakes made by the initial prosecutor and then the Arkansas Attorney General, and the courageous acts of two judges, one state and one federal. It also has an unlikely hero, Scipio Africanus Jones, a former slave who had become an important Black attorney in Little Rock. It was his tireless work and skill—and his personal courage and refusal to give up—that kept these men alive. He was aided, especially with national publicity and fundraising, at critical times by the fairly young organization, the NAACP, which had engaged in an anti-lynching legislative campaign over its first decade. The NAACP contributed funds to help Jones begin to work on the appeal and to pay for direct filing and other costs (Stockley 2001).

Immediately after the convictions of the twelve, Jones worked on post-trial motions to the trial court; all of were quickly denied. He then had sixty days to file the direct appeal to the Arkansas Supreme Court. The Supreme Court heard the appeal on March 22, 1920 and one week later it issued its ruling. The Court upheld the convictions of six of the convicted men, these became known as the Moore 6, The Court held that the defendants had received a fair trial and ruled that the trial was not "an empty ceremony." It set an execution date for these men for July 23, 1920. However, for the other men, known as the Ware 6, the Supreme Court overturned their convictions and ordered that they receive new trials. These six had been found guilty of "murder" rather than either 1st or 2nd degree murder, which was required by Arkansas law (Whitaker 2008, 222–223).

I believe it would be clearer if, rather than chronologically shifting back and forth between these two groups of six, I will first detail how the Ware 6 escaped being electrocuted, and then turn to the Moore 6. Scipio Jones had only six weeks to organize the retrial of these six. He decided that it would be best to have a white establishment lawyer to be lead counsel at the trial in Helena, and was able to convince an ex-Confederate Col., George Murphy, to take the case. Two days into the first trial Murphy had a heart attack, and Jones had to conduct the defense himself. By all accounts Jones defended the men masterfully. He also displayed amazing personal courage by walking up the courthouse steps each day alone. He introduced evidence that cast doubt on the prosecutor's narrative that the Black men had a list of white planters that they intended to murder, and he skillfully cross-examined the prosecution witnesses. Nevertheless, the all-white juries again convicted all six. However, the trial judge erred in not calling the jury commissioner to testify that the exclusions of Blacks from the jury had not been based on their race, as required by the U.S. Constitution. Jones' appeal to the Arkansas Supreme Court was successful and in December, 1920 for a second time the Court overturned the convictions and ordered a new trial (Whitaker 2008, 224–229).

Over the next several months Jones sought to delay the start of the new trial. As we will see, during this time a new execution date, June 10th had been set for the Moore 6, and Jones believed that as long as he delayed the Ware 6 trials he could keep the executions from taking place. The argument was that since the twelve were supposedly all involved in the same conspiracy, if half were found not guilty it would not make sense to execute the others. The State also wanted to delay, as they were afraid of the same thing, and they did not want the execution to take place before the retrial. In May, 1921 Jones implemented the delay strategy by making a motion for a change of venue—seeking to move the trial from Helena to Marianna, in the adjacent county. When the execution date moved from June to September, the trial court granted the change of venue. Since passions still remained high and physical danger was real, the prisoners were required to be transferred from the state prison in Little Rock to Marianna by stealth in the dead of night, for fear a mob would stop the train and lynch them (Whitaker 2008, 235–247).

Because an appeal in the Moore 6 case was pending in the U.S. Supreme Court, in October, 1921 the trial judge granted a delay at the prosecution's request. As the Supreme Court case was still pending in October, 1922 the prosecutor again sought and received a delay. Here was the brilliant tactical move by Scipio Jones. In neither instance did he ever formally consent to the delays. Arkansas law was that if the state did not try a defendant in two consecutive court terms, prosecution was barred.

Jones petitioned the Arkansas Supreme Court to order the six released because of the violation of what could be called the "Arkansas speedy trial act", and on June 25, 1923 the Arkansas Supreme Court agreed and the defendants were ordered to be released. Fearing that a mob might try to lynch them, the Ware 6 were secretly transferred without any restraints to the Little Rock prison, where they were freed that night to rejoin and rejoice with their families (Whitaker 2008, 296–298).

Let me now turn back to the Moore 6. Following the Arkansas Supreme Court's affirmance of their convictions and the setting of July 23rd execution date, Scipio Jones filed a direct appeal to the U.S. Supreme Court, which everyone knew was unlikely to be successful. However, it did stay the execution. On October 11, 1920 the U.S. Supreme Court denied certiorari (Whitaker 2008, 233). The Arkansas governor set an execution date of June 10, 1920. Jones had no appeals left, but he devised a strategy to file a writ of habeas corpus with Judge John Martineau, who then sat as a Chancery Court judge in Little Rock. In an extraordinary move, on June 9th, the Judge granted a hearing on the writ which had the effect of staying the execution. It is clear that this was a last ditch effort to block the executions, as the chancery court had no jurisdiction over criminal matters and the Arkansas Supreme Court had already once reversed the Judge when, in another case, he had done a similar thing. One week later the Arkansas Supreme Court reversed, and the Governor set another execution date; this time September 23, 1921. The tactic worked and bought the men another three months, and allowed Jones time to devise one last effort to save the men (Stockley 2001, 190–191).

Two days before the scheduled execution Jones filed a writ of habeas corpus in the Federal Court in Helena before Judge Jacob Trieber. In order to understand what happened next one needs to understand the prior history of the writ of habeas corpus. The writ is used to challenge the jurisdiction of the state to keep a person incarcerated. In this instance it is asking the federal court to review convictions of a state court. Since the Civil War, the Supreme Court had never granted the writ to challenge a state court conviction. Basically, if there had been any semblance of a trial, and there was a state process to review the initial trial, the federal courts would not interfere. The factual basis of guilt or innocence was not at issue. This was the state of the law, despite the legislative history of the federal statute which authorized habeas corpus. That history makes clear that it was passed during Reconstruction so that there could be federal review of state convictions of African Americans. Like other protections of Blacks, the Supreme Court had cut back on these rights during the Jim Crow period (Stockley 2001, 205–206).

Given this history, the only glimmer of hope that Scipio Jones had was provided by the Leo Frank case, which the U.S. Supreme Court had decided in 1915. In a 7-2 opinion the Court refused to grant the writ and free Frank, who was subsequently lynched by an Atlanta mob. The majority held that the Georgia appellate process had adequately reviewed the trial of Frank and found it to be fair, and thus there was no violation of Frank's constitutional rights. In the majority opinion Justice Mahon Pitney did, however, say that if a trial was "mob dominated" and the state review did not correct this, the writ could be granted. Justices Oliver Wendell Holmes and Louis Brandeis both dissented.[3]

Jones scripted his fact allegations in his federal habeas to try to fit through the small opening that the Court had created in *Frank*. He argued that the trial was a sham because the deal the Helena elites had made with the mob in order to prevent the lynchings was in effect the "trial" and that the mob "thronged the area". He also was able to get evidence to support the Black narrative of events into the record. He obtained the statements of two of the white members of the posse who were also present during the torture of the defendants, and had been instructed by the prosecutor before they testified at trial not to say anything that might be exculpatory. The motives of the two former posse members are not clear, but it appears they were moved by their consciences, as they were both immediately fired from their jobs and had to leave the state to avoid physical harm (Whitaker 2008, 258–264).

At this point the Arkansas Attorney General made an understandable, but tactical error, which had the effect of eventually securing victory for the Moore 6. In response to Jones' petition, rather than denying the allegations, the State demurred; that is, they admitted the facts as true, but relied on *Frank* and the prior law case law to argue that as a matter of law the trials violated no constitutional rights. There had been full state appellate review and the Arkansas Supreme Court had found the trials fair; this case was exactly like *Frank*, the Arkansas Attorney General argued (Whitaker 2008, 258–264).

Judge Trieber, having scheduled a hearing, which stayed the scheduled execution, recused himself, as he had lived in Helena for much of his life and was a friend and colleague of many of the business and professional leaders who were involved in the Massacre. An Oklahoma federal judge was brought in to hold the hearing, and although he stated that the alleged facts were disturbing, the U.S. Supreme Court's case law was clear. He denied the petition for a writ of habeas corpus. The judge did authorize an appeal of his decision to the U.S. Supreme Court. On October 21, 1921, two years after the Massacre Jones filed the appeal with the high Court (Whitaker 2008, 258–264).

The Court agreed to take the case, *Moore v. Dempsey*, but because of its backlog, the case was not heard until January 9, 1923.[4] The NAACP, which helped to finance the appeal, convinced the prominent white liberal attorney and Supreme Court veteran, Moorfield Storey, to be the first chair at the oral argument. However, instead of having Scipio Jones as second chair, the NAACP asked the white former U.S. Attorney, Ulysses Bratton, who had been the sharecroppers original attorney in 1919 when they were seeking to challenge their treatment by the planters. It appears that Jones would have been able to sit at the counsel's table, but he was unable to get to Washington in time for the hearing.

At oral argument both the State and Storey stuck to their briefs. Storey and Bratton reiterated the narrative of mob domination, which Jones had created, and the State

[3] *Frank v. Mangum*, 237 U.S. 309 (1915).

[4] *Moore v. Dempsey*, 261 U.S. 86 (1923).

relied on the precedent of the *Frank* case. However, when the State sought to contradict the narrative of mob domination, Chief Justice Taft cut the Arkansas Attorney General off and reminded him that because the State had demurred to the petition, all the facts must be taken as true (Whitaker 2008).

The Court handed down its decision in *Moore v. Dempsey* on February 19, 1923. Justice Holmes, the dissenter in Frank, wrote the majority opinion which was joined by his fellow dissenter in *Frank*, Justice Brandeis, and Chief Justice Taft, as well as three other justices. Justice McReynolds, perhaps the most racist of all twentieth century justices, along with Justice Southerland, dissented. The Court reversed the district court and ordered a hearing on whether the allegations could be proven.

Holmes wrote:

> The case stated by the petition is as follows, and it will be understood that while we put it in narrative form, we are not affirming the facts to be as stated, but only what we must take them to be, as they are admitted by the demurrer...if the case is that the whole proceeding is a mask – that counsel, jury and judge were swept to the fatal end by an irresistible wave of public passion, and that the State Courts failed to correct the wrong, neither perfection in the machinery for correction nor the possibility that the trial court and counsel saw no other way of avoiding an immediate outbreak of the mob can prevent this Court from securing to the petitioners their constitutional rights.[5]

He concluded:

> We shall not say more concerning the corrective process afforded to the petitioners than that it does not seem to us sufficient to allow a Judge of the United States to escape the duty of examining the facts for himself when if true as alleged they make the trial absolutely void.[6]

McReynolds basically reiterated Frank and argued that the Arkansas Supreme Court's review was thorough and that the majority was opening a door for all future defendants to prolong receiving the punishment that they were due by introducing a new level of federal review of state proceedings. He concluded:

> The fact that petitioners are poor and ignorant and Black naturally arouses sympathy; but that does not release us from enforcing principles which are essential to the orderly operation of our federal system.[7]

At this point the difference between a "legal" fact and an "historical" fact became critical. Despite the dramatic victory in the Supreme Court the Moore 6 were not yet freed. Scipio Jones now had to prove that the mobs "thronged" the proceedings. He was not at all certain he could do that. He could easily prove the existence of a deal between the Committee of Seven and the mob and hostility in the courtroom, but proving that a mob "thronged" the proceedings would be difficult, if not impossible. There were no newspaper reports or other evidence that after the trials began that a mob had formed either outside or inside the courtroom (Whitaker 2008, 298–299).

Jones again proved his tactical mastery, his personal courage, his perseverance, and most of all his commitment to the Elaine sharecroppers. He had to negotiate

[5]*Moore v. Dempsey*, 261 U.S. 86 (1923) at 87.

[6]*Moore v. Dempsey*, 261 U.S. 86 (1923) at 92.

[7]*Moore v. Dempsey*, 261 U.S. 86 (1923) at 102.

between two irreconcilable parties. The State and the Helena elite did not want to make a deal that would in any way imply that the men were innocent. The NAACP did not want any settlement that implied guilt or that the men had been treated fairly. Jones traveled to Helena, which carried personal risks to his safety, he convinced the legal and business leaders that a settlement would avoid a public trial highlighting the torture and the mob intimidation, which could only damage the image Helena was trying to promote. The prosecution would also have difficulty trying to prove the existence of the list of planters to be murdered. He had the same message for the governor. On the other side he convinced the NAACP that the most important thing was to save the lives of the Moore 6, which could only be insured by a settlement. He persuasively argued that anything short of death or life imprisonment would be seen by the public as a victory (Whitaker 2008, 300–306).

On November 2, 1923 Jones reached a settlement with the governor and then the NAACP. There would be no pardon, the sentences would be commuted to twelve years, which would allow parole after four years. However, one year later the governor seemed to be reneging on the deal. Jones again got together with all of the Helena leaders, including the prosecutor, and their petition strongly urged the governor to follow through. On his last day of office, January 13, 1925 Governor McRae in his last act as governor furloughed the Moore 6 and the defendants who had been convicted of non-capital crimes and were serving sentences in the Arkansas prison. As of that date the last of 87 men who had been tortured, convicted, and spent over five years incarcerated were now free (Whitaker 2008, 300–306).

3 The Historians' Case: The Black Narrative

A comprehensive study of the Elaine Massacre's history was not produced for over 80 years. Rather, historians focused on the ramifications of *Moore vs. Dempsey.* The consequence of this was that the "facts" of the Massacre were not investigated. Rather, Scipio Jones' allegations of fact as presented in his brief to the Supreme Court were taken as the history. The exception to this was the investigation by two northern Blacks who traveled to Phillips County months immediately after the Massacre: Ida B. Wells-Barnett and Walter White. Wells visited the prisoners while they were on death row and gathered factual information about their treatment and demonstrated through her calculations the extent to which they had been cheated by the planters. She self-published a 19-page pamphlet, *The Arkansas Race Riot*, which circulated widely in the North and served as a major piece of the publicity campaign to free the Moore 6 and the Ware 6 (Giddings 2008, 604–613).

In the weeks following the Massacre, Walter White, who had recently joined the NAACP staff, traveled undercover to Arkansas to investigate and determine how or whether the organization should get involved in defending the sharecroppers. Being light-skinned he could pass for white and posed as a Chicago reporter. Even though in his autobiography White exaggerated the degree of danger he faced, it required great bravery to accomplish this mission and established him as a major force in the organization. His articles in the *Chicago Defender* and other Black newspapers also brought the plight of the sharecroppers to the attention of northerners. Both White and Wells-Barnett were able to document the unfair trials of the prisoners and reinforce the Black narrative that Jones had created in his brief. Their articles helped to raise funds throughout the North to pay for the appeals (Janken 2003, 49–55).

Among the first articles to examine *Moore* were two a decade after the decision by the Dean of the University of Arkansas Law School, J. S. Waterman. In one he discussed the subsequent fate of the Elaine defendants following the Supreme Court opinion. However, he completely accepted the white narrative. He began his article by stating, "The indictments came as a result of an alleged negro 'insurrection' near Elaine, Phillips County, Arkansas, which began on September 30, 1919." The footnote reads, "Most available discussions of the Elaine conflict have been decidedly biased, and are as a rule favorable to the negroes." In the other article Dean Waterman argues that *Moore* stands for the proposition that in reviewing state court convictions, a district court must independently determine the facts of the allegations. The federal court cannot rely on the state court's findings (which the Dean seems to object to), but minimizes the effect of the ruling by emphasizing that the district court cannot rely solely on allegations (Waterman and Overton 1933a, b).

During the 1930s in a series of cases the U.S. Supreme Court followed the *Moore* precedent and continued to expand criminal due process. In 1932 the it required states to provide counsel in death penalty cases. In 1935 it overturned a conviction where African Americans were barred from juries. In 1936 the Court held coerced confessions were inadmissible at trial. This expansion continued for the next forty years. As scholars examined this they focused on *Moore*. This point may be made best by looking at historian Michael Parrish's book, *The Supreme Court and Capital Punishment: Judging Death*. The first words of Chap. 1 begin, "Phillips County, Arkansas lies along the Mississippi River…" and the Chapter ends:

> For the first time since the adoption of the Fourteenth Amendment, the justices had effectively overturned a state criminal conviction on grounds of due process and expanded the possibilities of reviewing state criminal trials by means of habeas corpus. Moore v. Dempsey had initiated the redesign of the jurisprudence of death in America. (Parrish 2010, 27)

The very Chapter heading reinforces this. Chapter 1 is entitled "Before Moore v Dempsey" and the next chapters detail the use of the *Moore* precedent in redesigning federal oversight of state trial procedures and the incorporation of the federal constitutional rights and procedures into state proceedings.

The *Moore* opinion was also influential in another important way. In due process cases prior to *Moore*, the Supreme Court was deferential to statutory or historical precedent before mandating a process that had not been prescribed by the legislature. Frank Easterbrook, now judge on the U.S. Court of Appeals for the Seventh Circuit, has argued that Holmes' opinion in *Moore* was the first to break with that tradition. Holmes posits as a matter of natural law that a trial dominated by a mob is unconstitutional. Easterbrook states that "The case is significant because of the way it reached the result: It is the first departure from the Court's (prior reasoning)". While, Easterbrook is not among the scholars who approve of Holmes' method, whereby Holmes arrogated to the Court the power to determine what procedures were required to meet constitutional standards, it is what led to the expansion of criminal due process rights and to procedural rights in civil cases as well. *Moore* was the trunk from which all of these branches grew (Easterbrook 1982, 105).

There is a second genre of writing about *Moore* that involves the writing of the history of the National Association for the Advancement of Colored People (NAACP). The organization was most influential and successful in ending de jure racial segregation in the United States. Historians of the organization focused on *Moore*. The NAACP had been formed in 1909, and had spent most of its advocacy in anti-lynching efforts. They had by 1919 been unsuccessful both legislatively and through the courts. *Moore* was the organization's first major victory. Additionally, Walter White's personal involvement in investigating the Massacre, had a profound effect on the future. One of White's biographers wrote, "Ever since he directed the successful appeal to the Supreme Court of *Moore v Dempsey* in the twenties White asserted a prerogative to be involved in the association's legal matters (Janken 2003, 327)." This makes the point that the success of *Moore* was a key factor in the decision to use the federal courts to attack de jure segregation. Richard Kluger in his magisterial history of *Brown* makes the point that, "White was a shrewd enough social analyst to see that the courts were the arena where the Black man's fight for equal rights might be most effectively waged as the Thirties got underway. He would remain a law buff and amateur attorney throughout his twenty-three-year reign at the NAACP (Kluger 1975, 173)." A recent book by Megan Ming Francis directly makes the argument that *Moore* was the progenitor of *Brown*. She wrote:

> The ability of the Supreme Court to siphon power away from the states in the 1950s and 1960s was connected to its criminal procedure revolution that was set in motion by *Moore v Dempsey*. Indeed, if *Brown* was the spark, as a legion of scholars have argued – and if we can trace a straight line *from Moore v. Dempsey to Brown v. Board of Education*, as I have argued we can – then it seems logical to consider this case (*Moore*) the foundation of the civil rights state. (Francis 2014, 166–167; Cortner 1988)

It was White's personal involvement in the Elaine Massacre, together with the catalyzing effect on the NAACP and its supporters of the Supreme Court's intervention on behalf of African Americans for one of the few times since Reconstruction in the *Moore* opinion, that provides the link that Francis asserts. My major disagreement with her and the others who have written from the NAACP records, is that by focusing entirely on them, she has missed almost entirely the heroic efforts of Scipio Jones in saving the lives of men unjustly accused and sentenced to die.

Neither the historians of the criminal due process revolution nor the historians of the NAACP explored the general history of the Massacre. Other than Dean Waterman, they accepted the Black narrative either through the facts in the brief or the NAACP records. The only exception to this was the short article written by Dr. J. W. Butts, who was a participant in the events in Elaine. In 1961 he published an article in the Arkansas Historical Quarterly that he based on interviews with eyewitnesses and newspaper accounts. It completely followed the white narrative. He argued that the "Negros" were the aggressors and started the trouble by firing on the deputy sheriff; the troops fired on the sharecroppers only after being fired on; the sharecroppers had never made any peaceful attempts to settle their differences with the planters; all trials were fair; and no mob attempted to do violence (Butts and James 1961, 95–104).

In 2001 a Little Rock lawyer, Gil Stockley, who had grown up in Eastern Arkansas, wrote a comprehensive history of the Massacre. His monograph, *Blood in their Eyes* looked at much of the documentary evidence and refuted the main points that the Butts' article had made. Stockley noted that the survivor of the night car ride to the Hoop Spur church testified inconsistently. He first said that the stopped the car because of car trouble, but then later testified that they stopped to relieve themselves. Although not conclusive, he argued that it made it more likely that the deputy sheriff had instigated the firefight, rather than being the victims. He examined the accounts of the military and was the first person to find that not only did the sharecroppers not initially fire on the soldiers, but it was likely that most of the four whites who died the days following the deputy's death, were likely shot by friendly fire. He detailed how the sharecroppers had in fact attempted peacefully to secure their fair share of the profits from their contracts with the planters by hiring their lawyer and joining together with the union. He also found no evidence that the union had drawn up a list of planters to be murdered. Stockley examined the trial records and testimony and established beyond a reasonable doubt that the trials had been a sham and were so procedurally inadequate as to make it impossible to "prove" the existence of a conspiracy to murder planters or to tie any of the Ware 6 or Moore 6 to the murders of which they were convicted (Stockley 2001).

Seven years later the journalist, Robert Whitaker, published *On The Laps of Gods*. It built on the prior work of Stockley and the others. He was able to examine some federal military records that Stockley had not, and had access to some other manuscript archives. Whitaker produced the most comprehensive social, political, economic, and legal history of the Massacre. His findings did not differ from those of Stockley except in one significant detail. Whitaker was able to construct the most accurate estimate of the number of Blacks who were murdered. The white version was that there were no more than 25 Blacks who died. There are journalistic accounts which range as high as 856. Both Stockley and Whitaker agree that an exact count will never be known. This reflects both the then current attitudes of the state and federal governments, as well as the press and white elites, about the value of the sharecroppers lives. However, by a careful examination of the military, legal, eyewitness, and journalistic records, as well as testimonies (including the depositions introduced by Scipio Jones in the habeas proceedings) Whitaker was able to document twenty-two killing fields. He has estimated that the number of deaths was at a minimum 100, and possibly several times higher, although it will never be accurately known. Only twelve names of Black victims are known, but all five white names are (Whitaker 2008).[8]

[8] Whitaker (2019).

4 Conclusion

The examination of the history and historiography of Elaine has demonstrated some of the differences between lawyers' use of evidence and the historians'. *Moore* began a fifty-year effort of the U.S. Supreme Court to police the state courts in an attempt to ensure that evidence of guilt would be as accurate as possible. The reaction to the state's use of torture and biased juries, together with ineffective counsel and fear of mobs, began the process of federal oversight of criminal trials. The Supreme Court demanded fair procedures so that, to the extent possible, accurate evidence could be presented to impartial factfinders to determine guilt or innocence. *Moore* also demonstrates how a lawyer can try to shape the facts to the law, although in this case he was aided by the procedural rules. When the State demurred, the defendants' allegations were taken as true, even when proving the most important facts of the "mob thronging" the trial would have been difficult, if not impossible.

Writing about the historiography of the Elaine Massacre in 1999, a prominent Arkansas historian wrote, "Historians, struggling with a mass of rich but contradictory and even tainted evidence, have failed to arrive at a common narrative of events (Whayne 1999, 286)." As we have seen the two narratives, one white and one Black began almost as soon as the violence ended. The white version was needed to support the prosecution's theory, and the Black version was recounted by the northern journalist investigations weeks after the Massacre. Historians over the century have expanded our understanding of the importance of the events by focusing on the legal reforms and the role of the *Moore* decision in ending de jure segregation. But it was only in the past decade that the accretive process of history produced what appears to a comprehensive history of the event. So far, the historians who continue to work on the history of the Elaine Massacre are making findings that further add to our knowledge of events, such as where the twelve who were spared execution moved after they were freed, but do not seem to be significantly altering the facts of the Massacre or our understanding of the causes.

The legal and historical legacies of the Elaine Massacre are varied and complex, but it provides a case study to examine the craft and professional norms of both the lawyers who helped create those legacies, and the historians who have documented them.

References

Allen, Ronald J., and Michael S. Pardo. 2003. The Myth of the Law-Fact Distinction. *Northwestern University Law Review* 97: 1769–1807.

Butts, J.W., and Dorothy James. 1961. The Underlying Causes of the Elaine Riot of 1919. *Arkansas Historical Quarterly.* 20: 95–104.

Cortner, Richard C. 1988. *A Mob Intent on Death: The NAACP and The Arkansas Riot Cases.* Middletown: Wesleyan University Press.

Easterbrook, Frank H. 1982. Substance and Due Process. *Supreme Court Review* 1982: 85–125.

Francis, Megan Ming. 2014. *Civil Rights and The Making of the Modern American State*. New York: Cambridge University Press.

Giddings, Paula J. 2008. *Ida: A Sword Among Lions*. New York: HarperCollins Publishers.

Janken, Kenneth Robert. 2003. *White: The Biography of Walter White, Mr. NAACP*. New York: New Press.

Kluger, Richard. 1975. *Simple Justice: The History of Brown V. Board of Education and Black America's Struggle for Equality*, vol. 1. New York: Alfred A. Knopf Inc.

Parrish, Michael E. 2010. *The Supreme Court and Capital Punishment: Judging Death*. Washington: CQ Press.

Stockley, Grif. 2001. *Blood in Their Eyes: The Elaine Race Massacres of 1919*. Fayetteville: The University of Arkansas Press.

Waterman, John S., and Edward E. Overton. 1933a. *The Aftermath of Moore v. Dempsey. Washington University Law Review* 18: 117–126.

Waterman, John S., and Edward E. Overton. 1933b. Federal Habeas Corpus Statutes and Moore v. Dempsey. *University of Chicago Law Review* 1: 307–327.

Whayne, Jeannie M. 1999. Low Villains and Wickedness in High Places: Race and Class in the Elaine Riots. *The Arkansas Historical Quarterly* 58: 285–313.

Whitaker, Robert. 2008. *On the Laps of Gods: The Red Summer of 1919 and the Struggle for Justice that Remade a Nation*. New York: Three Rivers Press.

Whitaker, Robert. 2019. *Discovering a Hidden Past: How Do We Know That a Massacre Occurred?* https://pryorcenter.uark.edu/event.php?thisEvent=WHITAKER-Robert-20190919-ElaineSymposium&eventdisplayName=A%20Symposium%20on%20the%20Elaine%20Massacre%20%20Robert%20Whitaker%20%20Discovering%20a%20Hidden%20Past:%20How%20Do%20We%20Know%20That%20a%20Massacre%20Occurred? Accessed 20 Mar 2020.

How to Determine the Facts of a Criminal Case

The Relationship Between Subjective Elements and Objective Elements in the Standard of Proof

Ruihua Chen

1 Introduction

China's *Criminal Procedure Law* adopts an "objective standard of proof", asking the judge to satisfy an external goal or requirement of proof when determining case facts. It lacks specific requirements on the extent to which the evidence producer needs to convince the judge or the extent to which the judge needs to be convinced. However, this objective standard of proof has been changed since 2010. For the first time, the standard of "beyond a reasonable doubt" has been introduced into China's judicial interpretations by the Supreme People's Court as one of the standards to judge whether the evidence in death sentence cases is "solid and sufficient" (Zhang 2010). Furthermore, the *Criminal Procedure Law* (2012 Amendment) formally introduced "beyond a reasonable doubt" into the standard of proof as one of the three legal conditions of "solid and sufficient evidence" (Lang 2012; Jiang 2013). The newly added "beyond a reasonable doubt" standard has introduced "subjective elements" into the original standard of proof, i.e. explicit legal requirements on the degree of inner conviction when the judge is determining case facts, or the basic meaning of the principle of "discretional evaluation of evidence". The renewed standard of proof is subjective and internal, rather than objective and external.

On that account, this paper intends to conduct a preliminary study on the introduction of the subjective elements into the standard of proof by analyzing the objectification of the previous standard and its main limitations, discussing the significance of bringing subjective elements into the standard of proof, and providing corresponding insights on the integration of subjective and objective standards. The central

R. Chen (✉)
School of Law, Peking University, Beijing, China
e-mail: chenruihua88@sina.com

B. Zhang et al. (eds.), *A Dialogue Between Law and History*,
https://doi.org/10.1007/978-981-15-9685-8_11

argument of this paper is that the introduction of subjective elements is a legislative effort to overcome the defects of the objective standard of proof. In order to successfully "activate" it, it is necessary to integrate subjective elements and objective elements appropriately.

2 Reflection on the Objectification of the Standard of Proof

It is a tradition of China's evidence legislation to set up an external and objective requirement of proof for judges to determine the facts of cases. As a standard of proof outside the subjective cognition of the judge and independent of the inner conviction of the judge, the standards of "clear facts" and "solid and sufficient evidence" belong to an unattainable goal of proof. Before 2010, China's *Criminal Procedure Law* did not give any specific interpretation of this standard of proof, and the theoretical and practical understanding was completely fragmented. The Supreme People's Court promulgated and applied the Criminal Evidence Rule in 2010, which explained the meaning for the first time.[1] The *Criminal Procedure Law* (2012 Amendment) clearly defined "solid and sufficient evidence" to have three specific elements.[2] In general, the *Criminal Procedure Law* and judicial interpretation concretize the definition of the standard of proof and introduce subjective elements such as "beyond a reasonable doubt". But relatively speaking, the introduction of subjective elements into the criminal evidence law is far less important than the large emphasis placed on the objective elements of the standard of proof. To some extent, it can be said that the development of the criminal evidence law is the process of concretizing the objective standard of proof.

2.1 The Concretizing of the Objective Standard of Proof

From the Criminal Evidence Rule in 2010 to the *Criminal Procedure Law* (2012 Amendment), China's judicial practice and legislation have made a lot of efforts in concretizing the standard of proof. These authoritative documents adopted a large number of theoretical results and converted existing theoretical interpretations into legal norms. Especially for the standard of "solid and sufficient evidence", criminal

[1]In 2010, the Supreme People's Court, the Supreme People's Procurement, the Ministry of Public Security, the Ministry of State Security and the Ministry of Justice jointly formulated the Provisions on Several Issues Concerning the Examination and Judgment of Evidence in Death Sentence Cases. Its Article 5 clearly defines the conditions of "solid and sufficient evidence".

[2]According to the Article 53 on the Criminal Procedure Law, Evidence is solid and sufficient when the following conditions are met: (1) All facts for conviction and sentencing are supported by evidence; (2) All evidence used to decide a case has been verified under legal procedures; and (3) All facts found are beyond reasonable doubt based on all evidence of the case.

evidence law now incorporates a series of external and objective legal elements and strengthens the objectification of the standard of proof in the following six aspects.

Every fact of the case is proved by evidence. That "all facts for conviction and sentencing are backed by evidence" is regarded by the criminal evidence law as the first condition of "solid and sufficient evidence". In other words, any fact without evidence is untenable and cannot be used as the basis for conviction and sentencing. Moreover, every fact of the constitutive elements of a crime and every circumstance of the sentence must be proved by evidence. Otherwise, these elements of fact and sentencing circumstances cannot be valid.

Every piece of evidence has probative value and admissibility. "All evidence used to determine the case have been verified through legal procedures". This is actually a comprehensive requirement on the probative value and admissibility of evidence. The probative value of evidence includes two basic requirements of genuineness and relevance. That evidence is "verified" is the requirement for genuineness. That the evidence has the function of "determining the case" is the sign of its relevance. The process of collecting, examining and judging evidence should go through legal procedures, which means that evidence must have the statutory qualifications and conditions, that is, have the admissibility of evidence. As the standard of proof required by the judge to determine the case facts, "solid and sufficient evidence" includes the qualification requirements for the probative value and the admissibility of every single piece of evidence.

Evidences corroborate each other. The mutual corroboration of evidence means that the case facts are proved by two or more pieces of evidence that overlap with each other. Different pieces of evidence that reveal the same fact or information are generally regarded as mutually corroborating, and their genuineness are also thus verified. On the contrary, if there are inconsistent or even contradictory facts or information, then the evidence cannot be regarded as mutually corroborating, and their genuineness cannot be verified. If the evidences used to determine a case fail to corroborate each other, and there is contradiction between difference pieces of evidence that cannot be ruled out, the evidence shall be determined as "insufficient".

Entirety of the evidence forms a complete and systematic proof. A systematic proof, also known as an "evidence chain", generally means that the entire body of evidence under verification is consistent and fits together, forming a chain of evidence (Zhang 2010). As an external standard of proof, "solid and sufficient evidence" requires not only sufficient quantity of evidence but also a complete and systematic proof for the facts. In the case where there is only indirect evidence, judicial interpretation clearly requires that the evidence should form a "systematic proof". If direct evidence and indirect evidence exist at the same time, and the direct evidence is determined to be not credible, the judge should still examine whether the indirect evidence can meet the above requirements.

Direct evidence is corroborated by other evidence. In cases where there is direct evidence, the main condition for "solid and sufficient evidence" is whether the genuineness of the direct evidence can be corroborated by other evidence. Specifically, for direct evidence that points to a relatively complete set of criminal facts, as long as the genuineness of the direct evidence is corroborated by other evidence, then all factual information contained in the direct evidence are deemed verified. Therefore, corroboration of the genuineness of direct evidence is not only the way to verify the genuineness of the direct evidence, but also the way to guarantee that the facts contained in the direct evidence are proven.

The conclusion is exclusive and sufficient to eliminate all reasonable doubts. The Criminal Evidence Rule requires that the conclusion be exclusive and sufficient to eliminate all reasonable doubts. If, according to the evidence, there exists both possibilities that the defendant has or has not committed the criminal act, then the conclusion is not exclusive. "Eliminating all reasonable doubts" means that, after comprehensive examination of the case evidence, two possibilities have been ruled out: one is that the act is not a crime, or the crime did not happen; the other is that the defendant did not commit the criminal act, or others have committed the criminal act.

2.2 Evaluation of the Objective Standard of Proof

Since 2010, a series of operable normative requirements have been adopted with regard to the most important standard of proof, "clear facts, solid and sufficient evidence". Compared with the original legislative expression which was too abstract, the new legislative model plays a positive role in accurately clarifying the standard of proof, regulating and restraining the judge's discretion. However, this legislation still promotes the external objectification of the standard of proof, that is, it does not adopt some requirements that restrain the discretion of the judge when it comes to inner conviction. For this legislation to achieve the concretization of the standard of proof, it is necessary for us to rethink on a theoretical level.

"Solid and sufficient evidence" is not an operable "standard" of proof. In philosophical epistemology, "clear facts, solid and sufficient evidence" means that the objective facts of the case have been found and have reached the level of objective truth. In the context of judicial judgment, this standard of proof with philosophical epistemological meaning displaces an operable standard of proof with an idealized goal, which forces the court to determine case facts without an operable standard. The standard of proof of "clear facts, solid and sufficient evidence" formulated by China's *Criminal Procedure Law* is often regarded as a "requirement of proof", but it can hardly serve as a "standard" of proof. From an objective perspective, it is impossible to determine whether all the evidence is sufficient to determine the case facts according to this requirement. From the subjective perspective, it is impossible to judge whether the judge's determination of the case facts has reached the degree of inner conviction (Zhang 2003). Therefore, there is a natural limitation to this legislative effort, which tries to concretize the standard. The more the legislator tries to concretize the standard of proof from the objective level, the easier it is to formulate some requirements of proof with the tendency of formalization, to set the standard of proof as an ideal goal close to the "truth of facts", and to deviate from the original meaning of the standard of proof.

The conditions under which a single piece of evidence is converted into the basis of a final decision are not equal to the standard of proof. The *Criminal Procedure Law* (2012 Amendment) set "all case facts are backed by evidence" and "all evidence has been verified through legal procedures" as the legal conditions for the standard of "solid and sufficient evidence". This way of expression is worthy of reflection. The original meaning of "all case facts are backed by evidence" is that all case facts should be verified based on the evidence, but there is no specific requirement for this specific standard. If a certain case fact is not proved by the evidence, it is a typical example of "unclear facts" or "insufficient evidence". And even if all the factum probandum are proved by evidence, it is still not enough to constitute "clear facts" or "solid and sufficient evidence".

As for "all evidence has been verified through legal procedures", it is a condition that must be met for all evidence to be converted into the basis for a final decision. In principle, all evidence being converted into the basis for a final decision must have both the probative value of evidence and the admissibility of evidence. However, even if all the evidence in the whole case has the probative value of evidence and the admissibility of evidence, it may not be enough to determine the case facts. The judge should make a comprehensive evaluation of the evidence to judge whether it is sufficient to reach the highest degree of inner conviction. It can be seen that the *Criminal Procedure Law* sets the requirements for the probative value of evidence and the admissibility of evidence as the legal conditions of "solid and sufficient evidence", which clearly confuses the standard of proof with the conditions for converting evidence into the basis for a final decision.

The objective standard of proof cannot measure the degree of the judge's inner conviction. "Clear facts, solid and sufficient evidence" puts too much emphasis on the objective aspect of the standard of proof and ignores the subjective aspect, the judge's inner conviction. In other words, the legislator only cares whether the ultimate facts of the case are found, not whether the judge is being convinced. Since 2010, more and more detailed judicial interpretations about "solid and sufficient evidence" have helped resolve the deficiency of the standard of proof, which is too philosophical, yet they still strengthen the objective aspect of the standard of proof. For example, "evidence corroborating each other" requires that there be no unexplainable contradictions between different evidence, and so it has an obvious objective overtone. "System of proof" is interpreted to mean that the evidence used to determine the case must be sufficient in quantity. The standard of proof with formulaic overtones is still an objective standard, which is external to the subjective cognition of the judge. The so-called "corroborated confession" is actually another name for the confession being corroborated, which is a kind of proof requirement outside the inner conviction of the judge. Moreover, the "exclusive conclusion", although it is related to the subjective cognition of the judge, still belongs to an external requirement of proof.

It can be seen that the criminal evidence legislation in China always avoids defining the subjective cognition of the judge in the process of concretization of the standard of proof. The criminal evidence legislation obviously ignores the problem of defining the degree of the judge's inner conviction.

The lack of specific standards of proof tends to make judges interpret "clear facts" arbitrarily. In reality, in the wrongful convictions disclosed in recent years, almost all of the guilty sentences rendered by the court have claimed "clear facts, solid and sufficient evidence." After these wrongful convictions are remedied, the same court often draws the conclusion of "unclear facts and insufficient evidence" based on the same evidence.[3] This shows that the judge has great discretion on whether the case meets the standard of proof.

At first sight, the criminal evidence law has adopted more and more detailed standards and conditions for "solid and sufficient evidence", which seems to mean that the judge's discretion in determining case facts can be effectively constrained. But in fact, the law does not set any operational measures for the judge's inner conviction and subjective cognition. This kind of legislation, which establishes the requirements of proof only from an external perspective, makes the judge decide the case and apply the rules mechanically.

The lesson of the "wrongful convictions" shows that the enhancement of the objective standard of proof from the external perspective cannot form an effective constraint on the subjective cognition of the judge. In fact, in the proceedings of these cases, the judge generally had a reasonable doubt and was unable to form inner conviction. However, such subjective cognition did not become the direct basis for factual decisions. Under the influence of various factors, judges determined the case facts not according to experience, rationality and conscience. They applied mechanically the "evidence corroborating each other", "contradiction being eliminated", "formation of evidence chain", "exclusivity" and other external requirements of the standard of proof. After many "wrongful convictions" were disclosed, it could be seen that the original judges did not follow their own inner judgment in determining the case facts, but only blindly followed the external, formalized requirements of proof, which resulted in misjudgment.

3 The Introduction of Subjective Elements

Since 2010, China's criminal evidence law has gradually introduced some subjective elements into the standard of proof. In the *Provisions on Several Issues Concerning the Examination and Judgment of Evidence in Death Sentence Cases* promulgated in 2010, the Supreme People's Court first proposed the subjective standard of "beyond a reasonable doubt",[4] according to which, the conclusion from the case facts determined by indirect evidence needs to be "exclusive and sufficient to eliminate all

[3]Around 2000, three well-known criminal wrongful cases had occurred in China, namely the Du Peiwu case, the She Xianglin case and the Zhao Zuohai case (Zeng and Wang 2003; Sun et al. 2005).

[4]In 2010, the Supreme People's Court, the Supreme People's Procurement, the Ministry of Public Security, the Ministry of State Security and the Ministry of Justice jointly formulated the Provisions on Several Issues Concerning the Examination and Judgment of Evidence in Death Sentence Cases. Its Article 33 firstly defines the standard of proof "beyond a reasonable doubt".

reasonable doubts". After the implementation of the *Criminal Procedure Law* (2012 Amendment), "beyond a reasonable doubt" was extended to apply to all criminal cases and was regarded as a legal condition of "solid and sufficient evidence".

3.1 The Introduction of "Beyond a Reasonable Doubt"

Some judges on the Supreme People's Court claim that "beyond a reasonable doubt" is equivalent to "exclusive conclusion", that is, "only the defendant is found guilty of the crime; others are completely excluded from the possibility of committing the crime" (Zhang 2010). According to this opinion, there is no substantial difference between the objective and subjective standards of proof established by the *Criminal Procedure Law*. In judicial practice, "clear", "solid" and "sufficient" are all subjective judgments on the standard of proof while "the objective elements correspond to subjective elements. For instance, 'clear facts, solid and sufficient evidence' corresponds to the subjective standard of 'inner conviction'" (Zhang 2010).

However, this interpretation of judges on the Supreme People's Court did not substantially change after the implementation of the *Criminal Procedure Law* (2012 Amendment), and no specific interpretations on meaning of "beyond a reasonable doubt" or how to apply this standard of proof has been made in subsequent judicial interpretations. Then there is a question, on what account did the legislature introduce the subjective element of "beyond a reasonable doubt" into the *Criminal Procedure Law*? Some officials who participated in the revision process of the Criminal Procedure Law clearly stated that "beyond a reasonable doubt" means that there is no reasonable or well-founded doubt about the determined facts, and in fact inner conviction is achieved. Only when the aforementioned conditions are met can the evidence be found to be "solid and sufficient" to decide the case. The introduction of "beyond a reasonable doubt" does not aim to modify the standard of proof in China's criminal proceedings but to further clarify the meaning of "solid and sufficient evidence" from the perspective of subjectivity (Lang 2012).

It is obvious that both the judges of the Supreme People's Court and the officials involved in the legislative work believe that "beyond a reasonable doubt" is a subjective standard of proof and is difficult to be specifically interpreted. They also believe that the introduction of a subjective element neither replaced the original "solid and sufficient evidence" standard nor reduced the whole standard of proof in criminal procedures. A related article in the *Criminal Procedure Law* (2012 Amendment) seems to confirm this view, according to which, "beyond a reasonable doubt" is clearly identified as one of the statutory conditions for "solid and sufficient evidence", in parallel with to two other conditions ("all facts for conviction and sentencing are supported by evidence" and "all evidence used to decide a case have been verified through legal procedures"). However, the other two conditions mainly represent the principle of evidentiary adjudication and the condition for the transformation of evidence into basis for deciding a case. Only the "beyond a reasonable doubt" standard can reveal the substantial meaning of "solid and sufficient evidence".

3.2 "Beyond a Reasonable Doubt" in Its Original Sense

"Beyond a reasonable doubt" is a standard of proof transplanted from the Anglo-American law of evidence. As for the meaning of "beyond a reasonable doubt", *Black's Law Dictionary* notes that it refers to "an abiding conviction, a moral certainty and the truth of the charge" and can be viewed similarly to terms like "clear", "accurate", "undoubted", etc. To be more specific, "beyond a reasonable doubt" is nothing less than "achieving moral certainty", and is consistent with the jury's judgment and conviction. As a rational person, the member of the jury has reached such a high degree of inner conviction based on the evidence that it is impossible to come to any other reasonable conclusion.

The interpretation in *Black's Law Dictionary* almost equates "beyond a reasonable doubt" with complete inner conviction, while Anglo-American case law rarely gives a direct explanation for the term. However, "reasonable doubt" is concretely and clearly defined. It is generally believed that "reasonable doubt" is not an imaginary doubt or a suspicion based on speculation, but a "real" and "substantial" doubt which comes from the evidence, or facts and circumstances proved by the evidence, or the lack of evidence. "Reasonable doubt" is a situation where, after a thorough consideration of all evidence, members of the jury cannot say that there is an acceptable conviction, based on the truth of the allegations, or their confidence that they know the truth (Ronald 2006).

Although "beyond reasonable doubt" is rarely clearly explained in Anglo-American case law, there are at least four basic understandings: (1) "Beyond a reasonable doubt" is a negative standard of proof, which tries to tell the jury what "reasonable doubt" is and that no conviction can be made in the presence of "reasonable doubt"; yet its own connotation is not accurately described. (2) "Beyond a reasonable doubt" is a subjective standard of proof, which encourages the adjudicator to listen to his or her inner conviction based on the trial when deciding whether the standard of proof has been reached and whether the accused is guilty. (3) "Beyond a reasonable doubt" does not go as far as absolute certainty or mathematical certainty of case facts, nor does it mean that all doubts should be excluded. "Everything related with human affairs is open to some possibility or imagined suspicion". Therefore, it is unnecessary and impossible to exclude all doubts. (4) "Beyond a reasonable doubt" depends on a judge's inner sense and is a description of the judge's knowledge of case facts. It is not equal to the external and objective requirement of "restoring the truth of the facts", but belongs to the judge's inner and subjective standard.

Both "beyond a reasonable doubt" in Anglo-American case law and "inner conviction" in civil law belong to subjective standards of proof, which indicates the judge's understanding of case facts. However, the "beyond a reasonable doubt" standard focuses on defining the judge's subjective judgment from negative perspectives, while the "inner conviction" standard focuses on positive perspectives. Although the civil law requires judges and juries to base their judgments on rationality, experience, and conscience, "discretional judgment" is not arbitrary; at the very least, it is bound by the principle of in dubio pro reo. According to this principle, as long as there is a reasonable doubt about whether the defendant is guilty or not, the adjudicator should render an acquittal. The principle of "in dubio pro reo", together with the principle of "discretional evaluation of evidence", has led to the formation of a standard of proof similar to the principle of "beyond a reasonable doubt" in civil law countries (Floyd et al. 2006).

3.3 The Intention to Introduce Subjective Elements

The introduction of "beyond a reasonable doubt" helps overcome the over-idealization of the original standard of proof. The original standard of "clear facts" is closely related to "seeking truth from facts" in philosophy, which is only an objective goal of cognition and is incapable of playing a role in the standard of proof. The original standard of "solid and sufficient evidence" is only a qualitative and quantitative requirement for the proof of the facts without specific measures. However, the introduction of "beyond a reasonable doubt" offers adjudicators a measurable standard with which to find case facts. There is no doubt that "beyond a reasonable doubt" is the highest standard in the range of human subjective cognition. Although there may be different opinions on the specific meaning of "beyond a reasonable doubt", it is easy to reach a consensus on the content of "reasonable doubt", a measurable standard. Therefore, compared with the ideal goal "solid and sufficient evidence", "beyond a reasonable doubt" has more certainty and operability. To some extent, the introduction of "beyond a reasonable doubt" stands for the first real standard of proof in China's *Criminal Procedure Law*.

The introduction of "beyond a reasonable doubt" helps overcome the excessive objectification of the original standard of proof. Both "clear facts" and "solid and sufficient evidence" are standards of proof from the external perspective and cannot automatically transform into standards for the adjudicator's subjective cognition. If there are only objective standards of proof in law, the judgment on whether the defendant is guilty will vary from people to people depending on different cognitions of the case. The introduction of "beyond a reasonable doubt" fixed this situation by encouraging the adjudicator to examine whether his/her inner conviction has been reached. After a complete courtroom trial and a comprehensive examination of the evidence, if the adjudicator has formed an inner conviction, he/she can directly give a verdict of guilty, and vice versa. Compared with objective elements such as "seeking truth from facts" and "discovering the truth", on the requirement of inner conviction, it is easier for adjudicators to eliminate differences and reduce disputes, thus achieving maximum consensus.

The introduction of "beyond a reasonable doubt" can play a similar role to "in dubio pro reo". In China's mainstream theory of criminal procedure, "in dubio pro reo" is regarded as an inevitable element of the presumption of innocence, and it is the basic criterion for judicial authorities handling cases in doubt. In China's past judicial practice, the standard of "clear facts, solid and sufficient evidence" was often interpreted from an objective perspective while the circumstance of "unclear facts and insufficient evidence" was often understood from a subjective perspective. For example, in a case of bribery, say there is a clear contradiction between the testimonies of the briber and the bribee. Under the circumstance that the testimonies cannot mutually prove each other, the judge will announce "a contradiction between the evidence" and "a reasonable doubt" in this case. Then the judge will eventually conclude that the defendant did not commit bribery. To some extent, the introduction of "beyond a reasonable doubt" means that after comprehensively examining the evidence of the case, if there is still a reasonable doubt, the adjudicator must follow the principle of "in dubio pro reo" and render an acquittal. Conversely, to convict the defendant, the standard of "beyond a reasonable doubt" must be met.

4 The Relation Between the Objective Elements and Subjective Elements

Despite the authoritative interpretation of the "beyond a reasonable doubt" by legislation and judicial practice, there are still some debates. Some scholars support the view that "beyond a reasonable doubt" is no different from "solid and sufficient evidence". "Beyond a reasonable doubt" does not replace the standard of "solid and sufficient evidence", and it is not a new standard of proof that is lower than "solid and sufficient evidence" (Wei 2013; Li 2013). However, some scholars argue that "solid and sufficient evidence" necessarily means "beyond a reasonable doubt", but "beyond a reasonable doubt" does not mean "solid and sufficient evidence". At least in some cases, the standard of "beyond a reasonable doubt" is lower than "solid and sufficient evidence" (Long 2012, 2013). Moreover, there is an innovative view that the introduction of "beyond a reasonable doubt" is a requirement for the extent to which evidence is used to find the facts of a case, and it is a new interpretation of the standard of proof (Fan and Zhang 2012).

The criminal evidence law introduces both objective and subjective elements into the standard of proof, which will inevitably lead to discussions about the relationships between the two. However, both the *Criminal Procedure Law* and the relevant judicial interpretations only give a rough interpretation about the relationship. The Supreme People's Court can make a specific judicial interpretation or a concrete interpretation about the standard of proof through guiding cases. But no matter which method is applied, the Supreme People's Court must find the logic of the judgment to determine the extent of the judge's inner conviction. For the viewpoints mentioned above, this article will make some reflective comments and provide some corresponding opinions on the integration of subjective and objective standards.

4.1 The Subjective Standard is Equal to the Objective Standard

Both legislative officials and judges of the Supreme People's Court regard "beyond a reasonable doubt" and "solid and sufficient evidence" as the same standard of proof. In reality, those who hold this view fundamentally neglect the essential difference between "beyond a reasonable doubt" and "solid and sufficient evidence", and lack sufficient understanding of the fundamental defects of China's original standard of proof. In principle, "beyond a reasonable doubt" and "solid and sufficient evidence" are standards on different levels, and it is impossible for the two to be the same. Firstly, the former is a subjective standard of proof, which is set to establish a certain standard for the judge determining case facts, while the latter is an objective standard establishing a more ideal goal of proof for the judge. Secondly, "beyond a reasonable doubt" does not need to achieve absolute certainty, that is to say, the judge does not need to eliminate all reasonable doubts in the case, while "solid and sufficient evidence" is synonymous with "seeking truth from facts", which requires the judge to "restore the truth of the facts". Finally, "beyond a reasonable doubt" requires judges to examine their inner convictions through experience, rationality, and conscience. This shows respect for judges' inner judgments, which is inherent in the independence of the judiciary. "Solid and sufficient evidence" is an external requirement from the law for a judge determining the facts. It sets obvious restrictions on the discretion of judges and establishes a basis for an external authority to review the judgments.

Obviously, "beyond a reasonable doubt" and "solid and sufficient evidence" are not standards of proof on the same level. And the view that the two are the same cannot give a reasonable explanation for the development of China's criminal evidence law in recent years.

Since 2010, the standard of "beyond a reasonable doubt" has gradually been introduced into China's criminal evidence rules and finally into the *Criminal Procedure Law*. By introducing the standard of "beyond a reasonable doubt", legislators attempted to solve the problems caused by the original standard of proof and establish a yardstick to measure the inner conviction of the judge. For the provisions of the *Criminal Procedure Law* (2012 Amendment), "beyond a reasonable doubt" has become the core condition of "solid and sufficient evidence" and serves to concretize the latter. To some extent, if we want to set a label for the standard of proof in China's criminal proceedings, it is still "solid and sufficient evidence". However, regarding the standard for judges determining facts, it is necessary to further examine the inner conviction of the judge. Only upon reaching "beyond a reasonable doubt" can the judge draw a conclusion of "solid and sufficient evidence". Obviously, the introduction of "beyond a reasonable doubt" not only explains the requirements of "solid and sufficient evidence", but also to some extent changes the meaning of the standard of proof in China. That is a significant change from "external objective elements" to "internal subjective elements", replacing the original abstract requirements of proof with the judge's inner conviction. Without a doubt, this change is a major transformation of the standard of proof in China's criminal procedure.

4.2 The Subjective Standard is Lower Than the Objective Standard

Some scholars believe that "beyond a reasonable doubt" is an inevitable requirement of "solid and sufficient evidence", and that the latter has more and higher requirements than the former. However, this view ignores the substantive difference between "beyond a reasonable doubt" and "solid and sufficient evidence". In fact, these two standards of proof are not on the same level, and neither the legislator nor judges of the Supreme People's Court will accept to reduce the standard of proof by introducing "beyond a reasonable doubt". They can at most accept the introduction of subjective elements to remedy the deficiencies of the objectification of the standard of proof.

If "beyond a reasonable doubt" is regarded as a standard lower than "solid and sufficient evidence", it would mean that after the introduction of "beyond a reasonable doubt", China's courts only need to meet the level of truth about 95%. However, in the face of the increasing number of "wrongful convictions" disclosed in recent years and the increasing pressure in criminal trials, how can the standard of proof in criminal proceedings be reduced? A logical criminal policy should raise the standard of proof and strictly control discretion in judicial proof, and it cannot make the standard of proof lower. From the perspective of policy and morality, courts need to reach 100% in truth-finding, and it is impossible to accept any compromise.

In fact, "beyond a reasonable doubt" and "solid and sufficient evidence" are different standards, which means that neither one of them is not higher or lower than the other. The former is a standard that measures the degree of inner conviction of the judge from an internal and subjective perspective, while the latter is from an external and objective perspective. The main purpose of the introduction of "beyond a reasonable doubt" is not to reduce the standard of proof but to overcome the shortcomings of the original objective standard of proof, in order to set a suitable standard for judges to avoid wrongful convictions.

4.3 The Integration of the Subjective and Objective Standards

By responding to the two views above, it can be found that "beyond a reasonable doubt" is neither equivalent to nor lower than the standard of "solid and sufficient evidence". The introduction of "beyond a reasonable doubt" adopts a new way of measuring the degree of inner conviction of the judge. This subjective standard has the possibility of overcoming the shortcomings of the standard of "solid and sufficient evidence".

However, if the standard of "solid and sufficient evidence" appears to be too ideal and abstract, "beyond a reasonable doubt" does not have a very clear and specific meaning either. How can we prevent the judge from abusing the standard of "beyond a reasonable doubt"? The experience of Anglo-American evidence law shows that a direct definition of "beyond a reasonable doubt" does not work. However, it is possible to define the meaning of "reasonable doubt", although Anglo-American law does not define it very well. On the contrary, the development of China's criminal evidence law shows that although "solid and sufficient evidence" is indeed an external and ideal goal of proof, it is not impossible to define the meaning of "solid and sufficient evidence". In recent years, the developments of the standards of proof in China's criminal evidence law, such as "evidence corroborates each other", "indirect evidence forms a complete and systematic proof", "direct evidence is corroborated by other evidence", "the conclusion is exclusive" and so on, are beneficial explorations of concretization upon the standard of "solid and sufficient evidence".

If we combine the definition of "beyond a reasonable doubt" with "solid and sufficient evidence", will it create a new way to make the standard of proof concrete?

Compared with "beyond a reasonable doubt", the definition of "reasonable doubt" is more explicit and concrete. Relative to "solid and sufficient evidence", "insufficient evidence" also has a specific yardstick. If it is difficult to draw an equation between "beyond a reasonable doubt" and "solid and sufficient evidence", is there a closer correlation between "reasonable doubt" and "insufficient evidence"? In other words, in circumstances of "insufficient evidence", will the judge have "reasonable doubts" about the facts?

To take some cases for examples, firstly in a bribery case, when some evidence cannot be corroborated with each other, a major contradiction exists between the evidence, and witnesses and defendants make inconsistent statements at different times, such situation makes it easy for the judge to form a reasonable doubt about the facts found. In these circumstances, we usually conclude that there is "insufficient evidence". Consequently, we can conclude that "the evidence cannot be corroborated with each other" is equivalent to "reasonable doubt".

Secondly, suppose there is a murder case with only indirect evidence. The existing evidence is not enough to form a complete and systematic proof or chain of evidence. A contradiction exists between the evidence. Some facts of constitutive elements of the crime are not proved by the evidence. And the judge had a reasonable doubt about this case. Therefore, "indirect evidence used to determine the case cannot form a complete and systematic proof" can also be regarded as a "reasonable doubt".

Thirdly, suppose there is a case with direct evidence such as the defendant's confession or eyewitness statement, and the other evidence can at most prove that the defendant had the motive and time for committing the crime but cannot corroborate the criminal facts contained in the direct evidence. People have reasonable doubt about the authenticity of the direct evidence, and naturally it is impossible to determine the case based on the direct evidence. Therefore, "direct evidence cannot be corroborated" can also be considered as another form of "reasonable doubt".

Fourthly, suppose in the trial of a theft, when the victim has not been found, there is no victim's statement about the case, and no stolen objects are found. The judge thinks that the possibility that "the theft did not happen" cannot be excluded. In another murder case, although the defendant makes a guilty confession and the evidence in the case proves that the defendant had a motive and time for committing the crime, the crime scene investigation and examination prove that a third person other than the victim and defendant left bloodstains, body fluids, and fingerprints at the crime scene. This clearly shows the possibility that other people have committed crimes in this case, and it is impossible to fundamentally exclude the possibility that "the defendant has not committed a crime". "The possibility of not committing crimes or other people committing crimes cannot be excluded" can also be considered as another form of "reasonable doubt".

Obviously, under the so-called standards of proof, such as "evidence corroborates each other", "indirect evidence forms a complete and systematic proof", "direct evidence is corroborated by other evidence", "the conclusion is exclusive" and so on, the conclusion that the defendant commits the criminal act seems to be an abuse of rules of experience and logic, and they can easily cause the judge to determine the case mechanically. In fact, even if a case meets the above standard, there is still a question about whether the judge has formed an inner conviction and whether there is a reasonable doubt. On the contrary, if there are some opposite circumstances, for example that "the evidences do not corroborate each other", "the direct evidence cannot be corroborated" or "the conclusion is not exclusive", we can generally consider there to be "reasonable doubt", and it consequently cannot meet the standard of the "beyond a reasonable doubt". Obviously, this circumstance is equivalent to "insufficient evidence".

The interpretation that regards the objective situation of "insufficient evidence" as "reasonable doubt" is increasingly accepted by the judges of the Supreme People's Court. The *Criminal Justice Reference* jointly edited by the five criminal courts of the Supreme People's Court has defined "beyond a reasonable doubt" based on the objective manifestation of "insufficient evidence". That is, taking all of the case evidence together, as long as the case has not yet met the standards that "other possibilities are excluded", "the key evidence cannot be corroborated with each other", or "the possibility of the defendant's innocence is greater than the possibility of guilt", the judge can directly determine that the case has not been proved "beyond a reasonable doubt".

In general, the integration of "beyond a reasonable doubt" and "solid and sufficient evidence" is only possible on the level of "negative fact finding". The so-called "negative fact-finding" refers to the maximum avoidance of mistakes and the prevention of misjudgments. The interpretation of the specific meaning of "reasonable doubt" can find clues and seek inspiration from the objective circumstance of "insufficient evidence".

4.4 External Constraints upon the Subjective Standard: The Independence and Legitimacy of Judicial Adjudication

To prevent the judge from abusing the standard of "beyond a reasonable doubt" and to prevent the misjudgment of facts, other than introducing some measures from the objective aspect, it is necessary to introduce external constraints. These institutional constraints contain a wide range of content, but in summary, the core is that judicial adjudication should be independent and justified.

When judging whether a case has been proved "beyond a reasonable doubt", the judge can normally make a general judgment based on rationality, experience and conscience. However, in a case with "reasonable doubts" about the defendant's criminal facts, whether the judge dares to render an acquittal is another question. According to the judicial practice in China, almost all criminal cases that have later been proved to be "wrongful convictions" have formed some degree of "reasonable doubt" in the trial process. These doubts are either reflected in contradictions between the evidence, which cannot corroborate each other, or that the same witnesses or defendants have made contradictory statements, or that the evidence cannot be integrated to form a chain of evidence, or that "the possibility that the defendant did not commit the criminal act, or others have committed the criminal act, cannot be excluded". Regrettably, even the presiding judge who has a reasonable doubt about the case cannot change the conclusion of a guilty sentence, because the judge does not have true independent jurisdiction over the case, and it is impossible to make the final adjudication based on his/her inner conviction. The court's internal administrative approval of the case, the trial committee's discussion about the case, and various forms of judicial intervention outside the court have led the court to hand down guilty sentences in the cases, which have not been proved "beyond a reasonable doubt". Naturally, sometimes in cases where the defendant cannot be acquitted, due to external intervention, the court will also render a guilty sentence with "flexible verdicts".

For a judge without independent jurisdiction, it is of no practical significance to establish a standard of "solid and sufficient evidence" or "beyond a reasonable doubt". To transition from the original judicial proof system that paid too much attention to objective standards, to the subjective standard of proof that values the inner conviction of the judge, at a minimum the independence of the judge should be guaranteed. In this respect, the independence of adjudication should be ensured to give the judge independent authority to render an acquittal when "reasonable doubt" cannot be eliminated.

In addition to maintaining independence, the legitimacy of the court's adjudication also needs to be highly valued, especially with regard to the legitimacy of the trial proceedings. In order to avoid the judge's abuse of inner conviction, it is necessary to fully establish the principle of direct and verbal trial, so that the judge can completely eliminate the reliance on the case files of the public prosecution and determine the facts from the evidence, cross-examination, and debates of the evidence in the court. At the same time, the defendant's right to counsel should be fully guaranteed to ensure that they can effectively exercise the right of cross-examination in the investigation of every piece of evidence, that is, to question their witnesses and cross-examine the prosecution's witnesses in court. Then, the judge will have the opportunity to form an inner conviction of the case facts by personally listening to the witness's statements in court and the cross-examination from both parties. Moreover, the judge should give a full judgment reasoning based on the facts, so that the higher court can conduct a comprehensive review of the adjudication made by the lower court at second instance, the panel of judges can conduct a full and fair debate on the facts to make a decision based on the opinions of the majority, and so on. If these institutional arrangements can be realized, the introduction of the "beyond a reasonable doubt" into the standard of proof will also have a good external institutional environment.

5 Conclusion

Introducing "beyond a reasonable doubt" into the original standard of proof in China's criminal evidence law is an important legislative attempt to focus on the degree of judges' inner conviction instead of external and objective requirements. It is neither a simple explanation of "solid and sufficient evidence" nor a reduction of the standard of proof, but a re-establishment of the standard of conviction from the subjective perspective of judges. To some extent, although the previous standard of proof, i.e. "clear facts, solid and sufficient evidence", still remains in China's criminal evidence law as a form, its core has been replaced by "beyond a reasonable doubt".

Replacing objective requirements with subjective elements is not an arbitrary act by legislators but has profound reasons and significance. In general, the original standard of "solid and sufficient evidence" raised the standard of proof to the point of "seeking truth from facts" and "objective truth", which was just an ideal and abstract goal without the function of setting a yardstick for the finding of case facts. What is more, measuring a judge's facts-finding activities with an external, objective standard of proof does not have minimum operability and easily leads to confusion among judges. On the contrary, the standard of "beyond a reasonable doubt" tends to measure a judge's subjective understanding of case facts from the degree of inner conviction and encourage a judge to render a conviction or acquittal according to whether there is "reasonable doubt", which is obviously more scientific and reasonable than "seeking truth from facts" and "objective truth", the original abstract standard of proof. Though there may be difficulties in defining "beyond a reasonable doubt", it is not difficult to reach a consensus on the meaning and form of "reasonable doubt" as long as we resort to experience, rationality, and conscience.

For now, there is no specific explanation for the meaning of "beyond reasonable doubt" in China's criminal evidence law. In sharp contrast, more and more statutory standards for "solid and sufficient evidence" are set, including "evidence corroborating each other", "the indirect evidence forming integrated complete and systematic proof", "the direct evidence being corroborated by other evidence", "the conclusion from the case facts being exclusive", etc. In order to make the standard of "beyond reasonable doubt" take root in China's criminal evidence law and be successfully "activated" in judicial practice, it is necessary to truly integrate the subjective and objective elements. Among them, an appropriate "grafting" of the standard of "reasonable doubt" and the manifestation of "insufficient evidence" might be a beneficial attempt at this integration. In addition to setting operable internal factors, an effective external restriction mechanism should also be established to prevent the abuse of "beyond a reasonable doubt", and ensuring the independence and legitimacy of judicial adjudication should be its main content.

References

Fan, Chongyi, and Zhong Zhang. (2012). Beyond a Reasonable Doubt: The New Standard of Proof. *Procuratorate Daily*, May 16.

Floyd, Feeney, Herrmann Joachim, and Liling Yue. 2006. *One Case—Two Systems: A Comparative View of American and German Criminal Justice*. Peking: China Legal Publishing House.

Jiang, Bixin (ed.). 2013. *The Comprehension and Application of the Interpretation of the Supreme People's Court on the Application of the Criminal Procedure Law*. Peking: China Legal Publishing House.

Lang, Sheng (ed.). 2012. *The Revision and Application of the Criminal Procedure Law of the People's Republic of China*. Peking: Xinhua Law Press.

Li, Rong. 2013. Viewing the Standard of Proof in the New Criminal Procedure Law form the Rise and Fall of Legal Evidence's Standard of Proof. *Nanjing University Law Review* 40 (2): 269–283.

Long, Zongzhi. 2012. "Beyond a Reasonable Doubt" in Chinese Law. *Peking University Law Journal* 6: 1124–1144.

Long, Zongzhi. (2013). *The Way of Judicial Proof*. In The Guideline of Criminal Justice, ed. Peng Dong, 62–91. Peking: Law Press.

Ronald, J. Alan. (2006). *Evidence: Law, Problems and Cases*. Trans. Baosheng Zhang, et al. Peking: Higher Education Press.

Sun, Chunlong, et al. (2005). Examining the case of murdering a wife in Province Hubei. *Oriental Outlook*, April 14.

Wei, Xiaona. 2013. "Beyond a Reasonable Doubt" is a Lower Standard of Proof? *China Criminal Science* 9: 57–63.

Zeng, Yuexing, and Daren Wang. (2003). *The Appeal of Justice*. Peking: Law Press.

Zhang, Weiping. 2003. The Utopia of the Construction of the Standard of Proof. *Chinese Journal of Law* 4: 60–69.

Zhang, Jun (ed.). 2010. *The Comprehension and Application of Criminal Evidence Rules*. Peking: Law Press.

Facts and Evidence: A Case Study of Developments in England's Old Bailey Criminal Court During the Eighteenth Century

Stephan Landsman

1 Introduction

Between the late seventeenth century and the early years of the 1800s, English serious-crimes prosecution underwent a remarkable change in its approach to the gathering of evidence.[1] Because of the existence of a reasonably reliable journalistic record called the Old Bailey Session Papers (OBSP),[2] it is possible to trace how the judges and, somewhat later, lawyers, of those times transformed criminal trials form rudimentary judge-driven inquiries into sophisticated legal proceedings dedicated to the examination of a wide range of testimonial and documentary evidence. In this transformation it is possible to trace the way legal professionals sought to grapple with the challenge of finding facts in what was increasingly perceived to be a setting where certainty was hard to establish. Eighteenth century evidence treatises[3] describing changing attitudes about what proofs were admissible at trial shed additional light on this transformation.

The changes that occurred at the Old Bailey provide a case study of the way lawyers have sought to address the challenges arising out of judicial fact finding. Of course, as a case study, this paper is focused on a single court, in one nation, at a particular moment in history. Yet, in these developments may be glimpsed a broader

[1]This history is explored in detail in Landsman (1989–1990, 496).

[2]For an analysis of the historical value of the OBSP see Langbein (1978, 263). For a persuasive argument regarding its accuracy see Langbein (1983, 1).

[3]The most important evidence treatises of the era included Gilbert (1754) (facsimile of the 1754 ed. Published by Garland Publishing, Inc. 1979), Peake (1801), Evans (1826), Philips (1814).

S. Landsman (✉)
DePaul University, Chicago, IL, USA
e-mail: SLANDSMA@depaul.edu

B. Zhang et al. (eds.), *A Dialogue Between Law and History*,
https://doi.org/10.1007/978-981-15-9685-8_12

set of insights about the way lawyers, when authorized to do so, go about finding, organizing and presenting evidence in situations where accuracy is deemed essential but certainty is hard to achieve.

2 English Criminal Trials Around 1700

The British legal historian, Cockburn (2008, 109), has described the criminal trials of Tudor and Stuart England as "nasty, brutish and essentially short." Virtually none took more than 20 min to try and as many as 25 might be heard by a judge and jury in a 12 h sitting (Cockburn 2008, 124–125, 137–138). Although Smith (1906) wrote in the middle of the sixteenth century, his description of a typical criminal case has been viewed as representative of proceedings as late as 1700.[4] Smith described the courtroom contest in the following terms:

> The judge first after they be sworne, asketh first the partie robbed, if he knowe the prisoner, and biddeth him looke upon him: he saith yea, the prisoner sometime saith nay. The partie pursuivaunt giveth good ensignes verbi gratia, I knowe thee well ynough, thou robbedst me in such a place, thou beatest mee, thou tookest my horse from mee, and my purse, thou hadst then such a coate and such a man in thy companie: the theefe will say no, and so they stand a while in altercation, then he telleth al that he can say: after him likewise all those who were at the apprehension of the prisoner, or who can give any indices or tokens which we call in our language evidence against the malefactor. When the Judge hath heard them say inough, he asketh if they can say any more: if they say no, then he turneth his speech to the enquest. (Smith 1906, 99–100)

The first thing of note occurring at this trial was the administration of the oath, the alleged victim being "sworne" at the outset. Some seventeenth-century courts, when the oath was reserved for prosecution witnesses exclusively, went so far as to declare it to be the most important factor in a finding of guilt (Cockburn 2008, 121). The judge was the dominant figure in the proceedings. He[5] was in charge of the interrogation of the victim, the defendant and the other witnesses (Green 1985, 138) and presided over the "altercation." He orchestrated the trial and when he "hath heard them say inough" he drew the case to a close by instructing the jurors ("turneth his speech to the enquest"). He was the only lawyer in attendance and the examiner who extracted what he believed to be the information pertinent to the jury's decision. The parties, as a general matter, did not adduce proofs but simply participated in the altercation's free-flowing disputation. This was not an orderly presentation of testimony but an argument. The jury decided on the basis of what it heard in the altercation, what the judge said in his "speeche" and whatever private knowledge it might have (Green 1985, 245).[6]

---

[4]See, e.g. 9 Holdsworth (1944, 3rd ed., 225), Plunkett (1956, 5th ed., 434), Langbein (1974, 29).

[5]The male pronoun is being used exclusively throughout this article because all the judges of the era were men.

[6]The jury's private information was, by the late seventeenth century, likely only to involve the reputations of the parties and witnesses.

Trials in the early years of the eighteenth century were not very different from those described by Smith one hundred and fifty years before. A typical case reported in the OBSP of May, 1717, went as follows:

> Mary Stephens, alias Bird, alias Gilbert, of St. Dunstans Stepney, was indicted for assaulting Edward Davis on the highway, and taking from him 5 Guineas and 14 s. 6 d. in silver, the 13th of November last. The Prisoner [sic] said, An it please your Excellency, I had received the Money at Chelsea-College, and was drinking in a Brandy-shop in Rose-mary-lane, having the Guineas in my Phobb and the Silver in my Pocket. The Prisoner came in there, and said she would conduct me to my lodgings, and led me, I don't know where, into a by-place, and there threw me down, and fell upon me, and took my money. Being asked whether it was not the Brandy that threw him down, he reply'd An it please your Excellency perhaps that was a help. There was no positive evidence that the Prisoner was the Woman, but only the Prosecutor deposed, that she sent one of her Concerns (meaning her Consorts) to him, to offer him 2 Guineas to make it up; and it being about 10 a clock at Night, and his sight perhaps as dark as the season, the Jury acquitted her.[7]

Again, it was the judge who directed and dominated the proceedings. He interrogated the victim and highlighted his intoxication ("whether it was not the Brandy that threw him down."). This was common practice in an era when judges used their power of "lawful menace" (Cockburn 2008) to uncover what they considered the key information for decision. As in the proceeding described by Smith, the parties did not generate the trial evidence or interrogate the witnesses. Despite some suspicious activity on the defendant's part (her alleged, but unproven, offer "to make it up") the absence of convincing proof led to an acquittal. The one possible difference in the Stephens case from what had come before was the seemingly heightened desire for "positive evidence that the Prisoner was the woman."

One thing absent from virtually all criminal trials in the early 1700s was lawyers representing the parties. Few cases were prosecuted by attorneys and defendants were barred by law from having counsel (Langbein 1983, 307–314). The first formal step toward removing this prohibition did not come until 1696, when Parliament granted defendants in treason trials the opportunity to employ counsel.[8] Well into the 1730s, lawyers were an extremely rare sight at the side of the criminally accused in the Old Bailey. My examination of the OBSP for every fifth year between 1717 and 1732 identified only two such instances; one in 1717, and the other in 1732 (Landsman 1989–1990, 607). On the prosecution side there appeared to be three appearances by counsel between 1717 and 1727, and a jump to six in 1732 (Landsman 1989–1990, 607).

The absence of lawyers, particularly on the defense side, meant the case was really in the judge's hands. There was no one to investigate or organize a presentation. What was heard was statements from those identified by the magistrate or justice of the peace who issued the indictment.[9] At trial there was no one other than the judge to

[7]This article follows John Langbein's suggested citation form for OBSP reports. The case name is that of the first listed defendant. It is followed by OBSP, as the name of the source publication. Then comes the month and year of the proceeding. In the case of Mary Stephens, the appropriate citation is: Stephens, OBSP (May 1717), at 5.

[8]See 7 and 8 Will. 3, Ch. 3 (1696).

[9]On the indictment process see the Marian Committal Act of 1555 which read as follows:

interrogate the witnesses. He knew nothing of the matter other than what he heard from the witnesses in attendance. There were no counsel to provide alternative views of the case, to challenge witnesses by cross-examination, or insist on the enforcement of rules of evidence. The absence of consideration of any rules of evidence meant that hearsay (out-of-court statements used to prove what they claimed) was considered without objection. This may be observed in the Stephens case where the victim quoted the alleged "consort'[s]" offer "to make it up." That said, the hearsay material was, apparently, disregarded as "no positive proof" and the defendant acquitted.

Modern English and American criminal trials are fundamentally adversarial. They feature three key elements: party control of the presentation of proof, judicial neutrality and relative passivity and highly structured forensic procedure (Landsman 1988, 2–5). None of these elements was in place in the Old Bailey trials of 1700. The parties did not control the proof process. They, generally, did not organized the appearance of witnesses or conduct the examination of witnesses who did appear. The judge was intensely active, literally the central player in the questioning. Virtually no rules of evidence were invoked, let alone enforced. Litigants' efforts to pursue an adversarial strategy were looked on with disapproval. The editor of the OBSP said as much in the case of Margaret Brown in 1727:

> The Prosecutor was very resolute in her Deposition, and charged the Prisoner with more heat than became her in a Court of Justice; it being the Prosecutor's Place only to swear to the best of their Knowledge, and that too, with Decorum, Caution, and a calm undisturbed Disposition of Mind, not forward to give their own Opinion, but with reverence submit their own Judgment to that of the Court, who are not to be dictated by a Witness, but informed of the Circumstances relating to the Affair, that Justice may be executed with Ease, and a due Regard shewed to those in Authority.[10]

Here the judge was in charge and the "Prosecutor" was expected to behave simply as one among several witnesses.

The evidence rules of the era reflected reluctance to use trials for a party-driven in-court probing of proofs. The reigning conception of evidentiary principles in the early eighteenth century was that provided by Gilbert (1754) in his treatise authoritatively published in 1754, some 26 years after his death.[11] Gilbert's central evidentiary tenet was that "[t]he first … and most signal Rule, in Relation to Evidence, is this,

---

That from hence forth such Justice or Justices before who any Person shall be brought for Manslaughter or Felony, or for Suspicion thereof, before he or they shall commit or send such Prisoner to ward, shall take the Examination of such Prisoner, and Information of those that bring him, of the Fact and Circumstance thereof, and the fame, or as much thereof as shall be material to prove the Felony, shall put in writing within two Days after the said Examination: and the same shall certify in such Manner and Form, and at such Time, as they should and ought to do, if such Prisoner so committed or sent to ward had been bailed or let to mainprise. See 2 and 3 Phil. and M., ch. 10 (1555).

[10]Brown, OBSP (Aug 1727), at 3.

[11]Jeremy Bentham said that Gilbert's work was "the grand fountain of legal instruction on the subject of evidence" that had to be demolished if a better system were to be built. 1 Bentham (1827, 5 vols., 6) [Facsimilie of the 1827 ed. Published by Garland Publishing, Inc. 1978]. See Twining (1985, 1).

That a Man must have the utmost Evidence, the Nature of the Fact is capable of" (Gilbert 1754, 5). For Gilbert this "best evidence" rule was the key (Twining 1982, 211, 213). It led him to favor written over oral proof and view the trial as a judicial search for a single determinative piece of evidence. In line with this view Gilbert devoted three times as much space to documentary evidence as oral proof (Landsman 1989–1990, 592). Where the testimony of witnesses was to be considered, a series of witness exclusions was emphasized (Landsman 1989–1990, 593) along with special emphasis on the importance of the oath. As Gilbert put it: "The first and lowest Proof is the Oath of one Witness." (Gilbert 1754, 106) In line with such arithmetic reductionism he declared: "The second Degree of Credibility is from the Oaths of two several Witnesses, and one Step higher than the Credibility that arises from the Oath of one Witness only" (Gilbert 1754, 108). Cross-examination was of little importance to Gilbert and was never directly addressed in his treatise. When credibility had to be assessed "Figure and Rank" were the guiding principles (Gilbert 1754, 110–112). The trial was, for Gilbert (1758), a cabined process strikingly similar to the Continental Roman Canon system with which he was familiar[12] and which required the testimony of at least two witnesses to the gravamen of an offense or the confession of the accused to secure a conviction (Langbein 1978, 129–139).

3 English Criminal Trials 1770–1815

The late eighteenth century saw the development of the criminal trial into a robust presentation of proofs, often undertaken by counsel, and the testing of those proofs by vigorous cross-examination. The simple in-court altercation directed by the inquiring judge was replaced by an adversarial contest prepared and pursued by the litigants. Two examples may help illustrate the new approach coming to dominate the courtroom.

3.1 Case Studies

In December of 1771, William Davis[13] was tried on a charge of having stolen mail from the "Isle of Wight-bag." The prosecution was directed by Crown counsel who called an astonishing 39 witnesses. In their testimony the witnesses traced the purloined letters, several containing negotiable bills of exchange, from the hands of their authors into the post, through a number of intermediate postal stations and then to the moment of their theft from a mail cart on which the defendant had hitched a ride. Crown witnesses then detailed the defendant's efforts to collect on several of

[12]Gilbert was well acquainted with the approach through his writing about Chancery practice which shared many of its characteristics.

[13]Davis, OBSP (Dec. 1771), at 16.

the bills of exchange. Finally, the prosecution's witnesses turned to the defendant's arrest and the identification procedures used once he was in custody. The prosecution bolstered its case with a substantial number of authenticated documents that corroborated the Crown's proof.

The defendant had counsel who conducted vigorous cross-examination, most particularly about the post-arrest identification. The defendant's lawyer explored whether the identifying witness had previously selected someone other than the defendant or been exposed to suggestive information regarding the defendant's name. Th court then turned to Davis and asked him to present his case. He said: "[I]llness renders me entirely incapable; therefore I must submit the circumstances of my defense to my Council."[14] The court allowed counsel to proceed. After the defendant's lawyer made a number of legal points concerning the indictment he offered 17 witnesses to the defendant's good character. The jury convicted and Davis was sentenced to death.

Here counsel on both sides took up the task of gathering the evidence necessary to address a complex series of events. Counsel did not simply stand up in court and question the witnesses made available as a result of the indictment process. Plainly, the case had been carefully investigated and each step the letters took was demonstrated in the testimony of a knowledgeable witness. Crown counsel not only presented the witnesses and documents but dealt with the evidentiary challenges posed by defense counsel's cross-examination concerning identification. The judge was not the chief interrogator but the moderator of a proceeding in which each party's counsel was given the opportunity to make his case. Defense counsel challenged and tested the prosecution's witnesses and sought, through the offering of 17 character witnesses, to undermine the credibility of the Crown case.

A second example of the new approach developing in the Old Bailey was the burglary prosecution of John Knowles and John May in 1782.[15] Counsel for the prosecution began by questioning a chambermaid who identified certain goods found in the defendant May's lodgings as having come from the victim's burgled home. Then came the constable, watchman and neighbor who testified that a break-in had occurred. Up to this point all the evidence was circumstantial-in other words, there was no testimony directly asserting the defendant's criminal conduct. That changed with the appearance of the fifth prosecution witness, Henry Hart, who claimed he had been the defendant's accomplice in committing this burglary. Before he could begin his testimony, defense counsel challenged Hart's competency to testify because he was a convicted felon barred by law from testifying unless his sentence had been remitted. "The court said they should reject his evidence, if [a] letter was not produced from the Secretary of State's office ordering the remission of [Hart's] sentence."[16] Prosecuting counsel was prepared for this evidentiary challenge. He immediately called Duncan Campbell of the Secretary of State's office to the witness stand. Campbell produced the required letter.

---

[14] Id. at 25.

[15] Knowles, OBSP (Feb. 1782), at 213.

[16] Id. at 215.

With the preliminaries satisfied counsel turned to Hart's direct examination. The witness testified to being a member of a gang of five, including the defendants, that committed a number of burglaries together. He stated that after he was arrested he led the authorities to Knowles's and May's lodgings, where some of the goods previously identified as having been stolen were found. He was then cross-examined by defense counsel as follows:

[Hart.] I was three years and seven months upon the hulks, it was the first time.

[Defense Counsel.] How soon did you take to this course?

[Hart.] I cannot tell.

[Defense Counsel.] How many days might it be?

[Hart.] It might be November or December.

[Defense Counsel.] Not begin directly?

[Hart.] No; I had two guineas and a half to spend, Mr. Campbell gave me; I worked at my business a little, at a glass maker's; I have not been tried here above once or twice.

[Defense Counsel.] You cannot tell really?

[Hart.] Am I obliged to tell it.

[Defense Counsel.] Tell the truth if you can?

[Hart.] I was never cast but once; I was tried upon another wrong affair; I was took up in Park Street for this robbery, in the middle of the street I was seen coming out of a house, I thought it the best way to give evidence when I was taken up and my life in danger, May, Knowles, and Munday, and Best there, and myself.

[Defense Counsel.] This was just three weeks after you came out?

[Hart.] It was a week after Christmas; none of the property was found upon me; about three weeks or a month after the robbery was committed I was taken up; I never gave no information before this. I cannot guess how many robberies I have been concerned in during the three weeks, I believe but three or four, which I am to appear to.

[Defense Counsel.] You understand you cannot be tried for this?

[Hart.] If I make my evidence good I believe I am safe.

[Defense Counsel.] You understand by swearing against those men, your life is safe?

[Hart.] Yes, surely.

[Defense Counsel.] You don't mean to begin again?

[Hart.] No, not to go any more.[17]

Here, again, counsel played the decisive role in addressing the credibility of the evidence. This time, however, it was to challenge the testimony offered by the prosecution. Defense counsel artfully set before the jury all the reasons why one might doubt Hart's testimony. He was a recidivist ("I have not been tried here above once or twice.") who, within a month of his release from confinement ("I was three years and seven months upon the hulks"), had joined a gang and committed, by his own testimony, "three or four" burglaries. He was testifying against the defendants to save himself ("your life is safe"). In the jury's mind, it would appear, the cross-examination had undermined the witness's credibility. One of the jurors is reported to have asked Hart about the sale of some of the allegedly stolen goods. This seemed to be an

[17]Id.

effort to find corroboration for Hart's testimony, the reliability of which had been thoroughly shaken. After one more prosecution witness, but no real improvement in its circumstantial case, the prosecution rested.

The court then turned to the defendant Knowles and directed him to present his case. He denied knowing Hart or being involved in a burglary. May followed with a similar declaration. Their counsel then produced two witnesses (both related to May) who claimed that the goods the chambermaid had said came from the burgled house were their family's property and had ben brought from the family's home in Lincoln four or five years earlier. Next, counsel presented four witnesses to vouch for May's good character. These were followed by three witnesses who testified to Knowles's upstanding reputation. In sum, the defendants presented a vigorous defense featuring nine witnesses as well as powerful cross-examination of the alleged accomplice, Hart. Without corroboration about the goods or the crime, the jury rejected Hart's accusation and acquitted the two defendants. This outcome so shocked prosecuting counsel and the court that when these same two defendants were later tried for a second burglary, the prosecutor and judge did everything in their power to bolster Hart's accusations, including recalling a number of witnesses to corroborate various aspects of Hart's testimony. This time Knowles and May were convicted.[18]

Neither of these cases can be said to have been entirely typical. The number of witnesses produced was unusually large. Counsel appeared on behalf of defendants in only about 20% of the OBSP-reported cases in 1782 (Landsman 1989–1990, 607). Yet, what was reported in these cases was clearly part of a new approach to fact-finding coming to dominate criminal trials. The search for a single definitive item of evidence either documentary or vouched for by oath had given way to an in-court testing of the credibility of each piece of evidence. That testing was not carried out by an inquiring judge but by parties, ever more frequently represented by counsel, whose job it was to find evidence, present it in court and challenge the proofs offered by opposing parties.

3.2 *The Role of Counsel*

Much of this change may be traced to the growing presence of counsel. Lawyers were rarely reported to be present in the Old Bailey before the 1730s. In that decade a trend toward the appearance of counsel may be seen—lawyers being remarked in, perhaps 5–15% of cases (Landsman 1989–1990, 607). There things, more or less, stood until the 1780s when the percentage of cases with counsel moved toward 30%. In the 1790s the percentage increased still further (Landsman 1989–1990, 607).

The OBSP provides information on how lawyers worked their way into the trial process. In a hard-fought 1742 case involving a defendant named Annesley,[19] the session papers reported:

---

[18]Id. at 217.

[19]Annesley, OBSP (July 1742), at 1.

> Mr. Hume Campbell, of Council for the Prisoners, said, that although he knew by the Course of the court at Old Bailey, he was not at Liberty to observe the Prosecutor's Evidence, yet he apprehended that for the Ease of the court, he might just open the Nature of the Defense, without making any Observations upon it.[20]

This approach opened the way for defense counsel to speak. Such presentations could easily morph into a more encompassing discussion of the evidence. This appeared to be the case in the 1747 Tickner case,[21] where counsel began by talking about the law regarding the running of uncustomed goods but soon was declaring, "For my part I don't know what uncustomed goods are. Here's nothing appears that these are any goods. Here's carrying something in bags …"[22]

As the courtroom doors began to open to counsel, courts became more liberal in affording defendants latitude in turning their cases over to their lawyers. This was the situation in the Davis prosecution, discussed above, when the accused declared: "Illness renders me entirely incapable."[23] The court allowed counsel to proceed in adducing the evidence. In cases dating from the 1750s on, some defendants, without excuse, began declaring to the court: "I leave it to my counsel."[24] The exact limit of what counsel could do was in flux. In the 1777 Russen case[25] the court outlined the limit as follows:

> Your counsel are not at liberty to state any matter of fact; they are permitted to examine your witnesses; and they are here to speak to any matters of law that may arise; but if your defence arises out of a matter of fact, you must yourself state it to me and the jury.[26]

This was the approach displayed in both the Davis and Knowles cases with which this section began.

One of the ways counsel promoted heightened scrutiny of evidentiary issues was by investigating cases before trial. This is clearly what occurred on the prosecution side in the case involving the purloind Isle of Wight letters. The 39 witnesses were sought out with methodical thoroughness so as to demonstrate the movement of the stolen letters and the utterance of the bills of exchange. Some counsel went beyond witness identification and visited the scene of relevant events. Such was the story in the Brownrigg case in 1767,[27] where counsel for the Crown in the midst of the cross-examination of one of his witnesses interjected: "I saw them [hooks used to restrain the victim] there two or three days ago."[28]

---

[20] Id. at 19.

[21] Tickner, OBSP (Oct. 1747), at 262.

[22] Id. at 265.

[23] Davis, OBSP (Dec. 1771), at 25.

[24] See, e.g., Brezeau, OBSP (Jan. 1752), at 63 ("The rest I leave to management of my counsel."); White OBSP (Jan. 1762), at 56; Trout, OBSP (Dec. 1760), at 12; Smith, OBSP (Jan. 1772), at 97; Bolland, OBSP (Feb. 1772), at 126.

[25] Russen, OBSP (Oct. 1777), at 374.

[26] Id.

[27] Brownrigg, OBSP (Sept. 1767), at 258.

[28] Id.

The OBSP records suggest that this investigative work was on occasion, performed not by trial counsel but by that category of English lawyers called solicitors. These lawyers were not permitted to advocate in the Old Bailey, where audience was limited to barristers (Robson 1959, 1; Beattie 1986, 278), but were frequently employed to do the critical pretrial preparatory work of finding witnesses and outlining the questions trial counsel should pursue. In the previously mentioned Annesley case, John Patterson was called to testify. His job as an "attorney" for Annesley was to attend the magistrate's inquest in the case: "I had not time to enquire into the Fact, and prepare for Mr. Annesley's Defense, I could do him but little service more, than by cross-examining the Witnesses for the Crown and making Observations on their Evidence".[29] Here a legal professional was probing the testimony at the inquest and understood his job to include "enquir[ing] into the Fact".

In a 1762 case,[30] the solicitor Robert Want explained his pretrial work on behalf of a defendant in an earlier case[31] and why he could so clearly recall the testimony in that case. He said: "I'll tell you why I can: I examined all the witnesses myself, separately and apart, in order to prepare for that [prior] trial."[32] Want then explained how his evidentiary findings were communicated to the barrister trying the case: they "were stated particularly in the brief [pretrial instructions to the barrister], and asked from the brief."[33] Whether performed by a barrister or solicitor, this intensive focus on the scene, the witnesses and the testimony at the preliminary hearing all prepared trial counsel to present the strongest evidence and dig into the reliability of evidence offered by an opponent.

3.3 Cross-Examination

As is apparent from the cases with which this section began, cross-examination was a critical tool in counsel's arsenal for testing the reliability of evidence offered in trials at the Old Bailey. By the middle of the eighteenth century it had become a staple of trial proceedings. Through cross-examination counsel came to replace the court as the chief tester of the quality of the proof. The interrogation could be vigorous, even combative. While it may have tested the quality of the witness's testimony it could also distort the fact-gathering process. One of the celebrated advocates of the day, William Garrow, made his reputation by powerful cross-examination.[34] This sometimes raised decision maker concerns. In the Cox case, in 1792, Garrow sharply

[29] Annesley, OBSP (July 1742), at 25.

[30] Tyrrell, OBSP (Sept. 1762), at 171.

[31] Sibson, OBSP (May, 1762), at 117.

[32] Tyrrell, OBSP (Sept. 1762), at 171.

[33] Id.

[34] On Garrow's career, see 7 Dictionary of National Biography 907–908 (1968) (22 vols.) ("Garrow was a consummate advocate. Remarkable alike for his acuteness and tact, he was unrivalled in the art of cross-examination.")

cross-examined a young witness. His approach troubled at least one member of the jury, who said to the great barrister: "We consider it only the evidence of a child, Mr. Garrow, and you should not try to draw things from him."[35] Garrow's response neatly illustrates counsel's commitment to the aggressive use of cross-examination:

> Mr. Garrow. There was no intention to draw anything from him but what is the truth; you do me great injustice to suppose me capable of doing any such thing; but it is my duty, and the duty of everyone else, to get at the fact: however, gentlemen, it is in your hands, and much good may come of it.[36]

Cross-examination had become one of counsel's tools of choice "to get at the fact."

3.4 *Rules of Evidence*

Another one of counsel's tools was the growing body of evidence rules. These could be seen at work in the Davis case when, to all appearances, they motivated crown counsel to present the elaborate chain of custody for the stolen letters. They could also be seen as raising the remission barrier to the accomplice Hart's testimony in the Knowles case. In each, the effort to satisfy evidentiary restrictions was designed to assure, at least minimally, that the proffered proofs were reliable. Garrow, the consummate trial lawyer, described his profession's view of the importance of evidentiary rules: "The King cannot break down, or infringe, or invade any one of the rules of evidence, he has no prerogative to say that innocence shall not be protected."[37]

3.5 *The Judge's Role*

As the parties and their counsel assumed an ever greater role in the trial process the judge's part in proceedings shrank. While judges still presided, ruled on evidence questions and summed up the proof to the jury, they no longer took the lead in interrogating witnesses, at least when counsel appeared. There were a number of factors that influenced this shift. Revulsion at the behavior of the partisan and sarcastic judges of the Stuart reign led to a profound political backlash capped by the Act of Settlement[38] which, in 1701, guaranteed that judges' commissions would remain valid during good behavior. The objective was to block royal interference with the courts and protect their independence (Cockburn 2008, 259–261). In the context of the termination of the Stuart monarchy and the rejection of its manipulation of the

[35] Cox, OBSP (Jan. 1792), at 83.

[36] Id. at 84.

[37] Reilly, OBSP (Sept. 1787), at 1073.

[38] Act of Settlement, 12 and 13 Will. 3, Ch. 2 (1701).

courts, the Act of Settlement carried the strongest message that judges should remain neutral in word and deed. By the 1760s, if not a good bit sooner, this had become the general expectation. In explaining it, the pre-eminent legal analyst of the era, William Blackstone, provided a sweeping justification. He said that judges, no matter how well-meaning, have "an involuntary bias towards those of their own rank and dignity: it is not to be expected from human nature, that the few should be always attentive to the interests of the many" (Blackstone 1765–1769, 379).

This remark from the judge who was the most influential legal scholar of his day, described an approach to fact finding that was far different from what had come before. The viva voce examination of witnesses by the litigants was now viewed as the best way to "sift out the truth" (Blackstone 1765–1769, 373). This made sense not only because of the concerns about bias but because of the judge's lack of knowledge about the facts of the case. As the evidence scholar William David Evans, writing in 1806, put it: "[T]he judge, acting only upon the impressions of what has already been disclosed, cannot by any possibility anticipate [what might be critical in each witness's knowledge]." (Evans 1826, 234). The implication with respect to counsel's role in cross-examination was clear to Evans: "The benefits of cross-examination are sometimes defeated by the interposition of the court, to require an explanation of the motive and object of the questions proposed, or to pronounce a judgement upon their immateriality: whereas experience frequently shows that it is only by an indirect, and apparently irrelevant inquiry, that a witness can be brought to divulge the truth which he had prepared himself to conceal ..." (Evans 1826, 234). Jeremy Bentham, writing in his monumental evidence treatise at the beginning of the nineteenth century would sum up what should happen in court and why the trial should be in the hands of the parties:

> When the business, the proper business, of both parties, is taken out of the hands of both parties, and lodged in the hands of the judge: so far as depends upon the state of the affections, of motives and interests, the business is as badly arranged as possible. General deficiency of zeal, variegated by occasional excess of zeal, and that on one side only: general carelessness, variegated by occasional partiality, both of them almost without control: such is the natural result of so incongruous a state of things. (Bentham 1827, 407)

3.6 The Establishment of an Adversarial Process

What was developed in the English courts of the eighteenth century was an adversarial system of justice—one where the parties, most particularly through counsel were responsible for adducing the proofs in open court upon which the legal decision would be based. The judge in this system was to preside in an evenhanded manner and a neutral jury was to decide the case on the basis of what it heard at trial. The proceedings were safeguarded by forensic rules, most particularly regarding evidence, that the judge was to enforce (Landsman 1988, 2–5). In this system the door was opened wide to the testimony of witnesses who the parties identified and presented. Their testimony was then to be subjected to robust cross-examination. The OBSP records bear out a pattern of growth of witness offerings. In 1717 and

1722 prosecutions in the Old Bailey involved one or two witnesses about 70–80% of the time (Landsman 1989–1990, 609). By the 1790s this percentage had dropped to about one third (Landsman 1989–1990, 609). Cases with six or more prosecution witnesses grew from about two percent to about ten percent (Landsman 1989–1990, 609). The growth in the number of witnesses when coupled with the presence of counsel meant more elaborate and lengthy trials that provided decision makers with a great deal more information. The pattern of witness offerings on the defense side during the eighteenth century was more variable, though the percentage of defense cases with no witnesses trended downwards (Landsman 1989–1990, 609).

3.7 Why the Change Took Place

From the observations of the judges and evidence scholars writing in the latter part of the eighteenth century it would appear that heightened focus on the production and testing of evidence was, in significant part, motivated by a belief that such an approach improved the quality of fact-finding. Lord Mansfield, perhaps the leading courtroom figure of the period between 1760 and 1790, in Walton v. Shelly, promoted the new expansive approach, declaring: "The old cases upon the competency of witnesses, have gone upon very subtle ground. But of late years the courts have endeavored, as far as possible, consistent with these authorities, to let the objection go to credit, rather than the competency of a witness."[39]

Contemporary evidence scholars explained the justification for this shift. Perhaps the most outspoken was Bentham (1827, 6) who produced his five volume Rationale of Judicial Evidence in the 1820s. In his usual pungent style he argued: "Evidence is the basis of justice: to exclude evidence is to exclude justice." (Bentham 1827, 490). Though not as outspoken as Bentham, others made a similar point. Thomas Peake described the method of decision making to which the courts aspired:

> In almost every case which presents itself for the consideration of a Court of Justice, some fact is disputed by the litigating parties, and the truth being unknown to those who are to decide, recourse must be had to the testimony of others. As this is corroborated or opposed, by the good or bad character of the witnesses, by their concurrence or contradiction of each other, or by the circumstances and probabilities of the case, the mind of the hearer arrives at a greater or less degree of certainty; and weighing these considerations together, is enabled to pronounce on the truth or falsehood of the fact in dispute. As to the weight which may belong to any evidence which is admitted by the Court, it must ever depend more on reason than authority to decide; but even here some lines have been drawn, and some known rules established: as far as decided cases have defined these rules, it is the peculiar business of the Lawyer to know, and abide by them. (Peake 1801, 1–2)

The final measure of the effectiveness of courtroom activity according to William Evans, another prominent evidence scholar, "must consist in requiring as much certainty and regularity as is consistent with general convenience" (Evans 1826,

[39]99 Eng. Rep 1104, 1106 (K.B. 1786).

124). Certainty could only arise from consideration of what the parties found and proffered.

In the criminal courts there was also an intensely practical reason for the shift regarding the discovery and presentation of evidence. Faced with an outcry about crime on the highways, Parliament, in 1692, passed a statute establishing a reward of £40 (a huge amount at the time) for the apprehension and conviction of highway robbers.[40] This legislation was followed by similar measures regarding burglary, horse theft, coining and a number of other offenses (Radzinowicz 1948–1968, 57–68). In response, a group of, more or less, professional "thief catchers" came into existence (Landsman 1989–1990, 572–580). They sought out suspects, brought them before magistrates and pressed the prosecution case at trial in the Old Bailey. One of the most notorious of all thief catchers was Jonathan Wild who plied his trade until he, himself, was prosecuted and hung in 1725 (Howson 1987). Wild was so remarkable a character that he inspired both operatic and novelistic treatments of his doings.[41] His mode of operations was to locate and produce witnesses claiming to have been victims of reward-designated crimes and then to support their accusations with alleged accomplices given immunity for their testimony (Beattie 1986, 366–367). The cases were often bolstered with corroborating witnesses like people who claimed to have seen the accused with the accomplice[42] or stable hands who had noted the defendant's hiring of a horse under suspicious circumstances.[43] Wild would complete the prosecution case by testifying, often by quoting alleged out-of-court admissions either by the defendant or his relatives.[44] This formula worked remarkably well until it became apparent that Wild and his colleagues were fabricating cases to frame innocent defendants in order to collect the reward (Howson 1987, 81). He was, eventually, prosecuted and hanged. His execution did not end the thief catching industry and there were periodic scandals well into the 1750s (Radzinowicz 1948–1968, 326–346).

The thief catcher problem caused the courts to become more cautious in their assessment of testimony in criminal cases. This led to heightened probing of the evidence offered. Where a defendant could produce evidence of his good character[45] or a solid alibi he was likely to be acquitted by a jury skeptical of venal bounty hunters. This heightened caution reinforced the adversarial values being embraced in the courts and provided a concrete example of the need to scrutinize testimony with care. The tool most energetically applied was cross-examination.

---

[40] 4 W. and M., ch. 8 (1692).

[41] Wild's story provided the basis for Gay's *The Beggar's Opera*, as well as Defoe's *Moll Flauders* and Fielding's *Jonathan Wild*. Radzinowicz reports that Wild claimed responsibility for the capital conviction of more than 70 defendants. 2 Radzinowicz *supra* note 79, at 34 n. 5.

[42] Fox, OBSP (Dec. 1721), at 6.

[43] Id.; Wright, OBSP (Dec. 1721), at 8.

[44] Id.

[45] See, e.g., James, OBSP (Feb. 1722), at 6.

3.8 *Risks Posed by the New Approach to Trials*

The new lawyer-driven trial procedure posed its own risks. While it may have responded to a heightened desire for a wider array of evidence and its testing by vigorous interrogation, it dramatically increased the cost and length of proceedings. Fact finding in the Old Bailey became more expensive and slower. These costs were apparently accepted as the price for decisions affording a greater assurance of reliability.

Counsel were at the heart of the new approach. Their zeal in investigation and questioning were critical. It was, however, easy for zeal to tip over into excessive partisan behavior. This possibility worried the era's evidence scholars. David Evans decried the risk of excessive witness preparation as "[s]ome practicers, to insure the success of their cause, interrogate the witnesses again and again" (Evans 1826, 209). Here the adversarial desire to prepare the strongest case was perceived as posing a danger to accuracy and candor. Evans was also concerned about cross-examination which could undermine an honest witness, depriving the court of accurate information through an "intimidating and acrimonious course of inquiry" (Evans 1826, 216). Bentham, perhaps in hyperbolic terms, summarized the problem:

> For one occasion in which, under the spur of the injury, the injured witness has presented himself to my conception as overstepping the limits of a just defence,—ten, twenty, or twice twenty, have occurred in which the witness has been suffering, without resistance and without remedy, as well as without just cause, under the torture inflicted on him by the oppression and insolence of an adverse advocate. (Bentham 1827, 86–87)

It was difficult to curb such excesses. Evans noted that too vigorous judicial control of adversarial cross-examination might result in "destroying the liberty upon which the benefits" of such examination might be gained (Evans 1826, 233).

3.9 *Reflections on This Case Study*

What should we make of the Old Bailey eighteenth century history? In some ways it reflects the special conditions of England in that era. The conflict between King and Parliament triggered legislation pushing judges from active inquiry to presiding over a contest managed by counsel. The activities of thief catchers, most particularly, their corrupt pursuit of bounties led in the same direction. Yet, the Old Bailey story may contain some insights about reforming and strengthening evidence-gathering processes. Faced with serious challenges to integrity English judges and litigants turned to lawyers—not on just one side but for all parties. This employment of legal professionals heightened the prospect of a thorough investigation. When lawyers were imported into the courts they brought zealous effort on behalf of their clients. Of course, this meant two perspectives on and arguments about the law. But, it also had a profound influence on evidence gathering. Lawyers visited the scene of events, searched for witnesses, prepared those witnesses for trial, presented their testimony in court and tested the testimony of opposing witnesses through cross-examination. Where factual development is weak or partisan the bilateral introduction of lawyers can help secure an expanded flow of information and the testing of information when presented.

Importing counsel can also help address the challenge of judicial bias. As Blackstone observed, all judges have biases. Further, as William David Evans noted, judges have only the most limited information about the cases being tried before them and are often incapable of asking the questions that will reveal the critical facts. When lawyers assume the central role more penetrating examination is facilitated and the judge's blind spots avoided. Moreover, lawyer involvement can help the court maintain its neutrality. The judge is not compelled to develop and test a personal theory of the case. The court can leave that job to counsel until all the evidence has been produced. As Fuller (1961), along with Thibaut et al. (1972, 386) have pointed out, keeping the judge out of the interrogation effort generally reduces the risk of bias and unfairness in proceedings.

Arrangements relying on lawyers to develop and present the evidence offer other benefits. When the state serves only its own interests in judicial proceedings it is unlikely to encourage robust use of the court system. Inga Markovitz, some years ago, examined the East German labor courts. What she found was that they were unpopular and little used. The key reason was that they did not give participants any sense that their interests, rather than those of the state, were being considered (Markovitz 2004, 95). When processes cede significant control to the parties to pursue their interests, use is likely to increase. Ceding significant control can do more than simply encourage use. Tyler (2006, 375) has found that when parties are given the opportunity to make their case their satisfaction with and belief in the fairness of courts is substantially enhanced. Tyler (2006, 375) calls the opportunity to make ones case "voice" and identifies it as a key ingredient, win or lose, in a litigant's sense of satisfaction. What this all adds up to is the powerful enhancements of the legitimacy of the courts. Legitimacy of this sort influences onlookers as well as participants and is a valuable asset in promoting the rule of law. There are, however, risks to an approach that relies on lawyers to run the fact-finding process. They must be available and their services must be of adequate quality to insure effective adjudication. Unfortunately, governments have not always been willing to provide sufficient resources to assure such services. Insightful analysts have also noted that placing control in counsel's hands can create a group of "insiders … professional repeat players who dominate criminal justice" (Bibas 2006, 911–912). That domination can result in counsel's pursuit of "self interest" to the detriment of fair representation. To counter such inclinations publicity and transparency in criminal proceedings are essential (Bibas 2006, 917).

References

Beattie, John M. 1986. *Crime and the Courts in England*. Princeton: Princeton University Press.

Bentham, Jeremy. 1827. *Rationale of Judicial Evidence*. New York: Garland Publishing Inc.

Bibas, Stephanos. 2006.*Transparency and Participation in Criminal Procedure*, 86 N.Y.U. L. Rev. 911

Blackstone, W. 1765–1769. *Commentaries on the Laws of England*. Chicago: University of Chicago Press.

Cockburn, J.S. 2008. *A History of the English Assizes 1558–1714*.

Evans, William David. 1826. *On the Law of Evidence*. In *A Treatise on the Law of Obligations, or Contracts*, ed. M. Pothier, trans. W. Evans, 2 vols. New Jersey: The Lawbook Exchange, Ltd.

Fuller, Lon L. 1961. *The Adversary System*. Washington: U.S. Information Agency.

Gilbert, Geoffrey. 1754. *The Law of Evidence*. New York: Garland Publishing, Inc.

Gilbert, Geoffrey. 1758. *The History and Practice of the High Court and Chancery: In Which is Introduced an Account of the Institution and Various Regulations of the Said Court: Showing Likewise the Ancient and Present Practice Thereof, in an Easy and Familiar Method*. Washington: W.H. & O.H. Morrison.

Green, Thomas Andrew. 1985. *Verdict According to Conscience*. Chicago: University of Chicago Press.

Holdsworth, William S. 1944. *A History of English Law*. London: Methuen & Company.

Howson, Gerald. 1987. *It Takes a Thief: The Life and Times of Jonathan Wild*. London: Ebury Press.

Landsman, Stephan. 1988. *Adversarial Justice: The American Approach to Adjudication*. Eagan: West Publishing Company.

Landsman, Stephan. 1989–1990. Rise of the Contentious Spirit: Adversary Procedure in Eighteenth Century England. *Cornell Law Review* 75.

Langbein, John H. 1974. *Prosecuting Crime in the Renaissance*. Cambridge: Harvard University Press.

Langbein, John H. 1978. The Criminal Trial Before the Lawyer. *University of Chicago Law Review* 45.

Langbein, John H. 1983. Shaping the Eighteenth-Century Criminal Trial: A View from the Ryder Sources. *University of Chicago Law Review* 50.

Markovitz, Inga. 2004. Exploring Law Reform—But Will It Travel? *Cornell International Law Journal* 37.

Peake, Thomas. 1801. *A Compendium of the Law of Evidence*. Massachusetts: Thomas & Thomas.

Philips, S.M. 1814. *A Treatise of the Law of Evidence*. A. Strahan, Law-Printer to the King's Most Excellent Majesty.

Plunkett, Theodore Frank Thomas. 1956. *A Concise History of the Common Law*. New Jersey: The Lawbook Exchange, Ltd.

Radzinowicz, Leon. 1948–1968. *A History of English Criminal Law and Its Administration form 1750*. London: Macmillan.

Robson, Robert. 1959. *The Attorney in Eighteenth Century England*.

Smith, Thomas. 1906. *De Republica Anglorum*, ed. L. Alston. Cambridge: Cambridge University Press.

Thibaut, John, Walker Laurens, and Lind E. Allen. 1972. Adversary Presentation and Boas in Legal Decision Making. *Harvard Law Review* 86.

Twining, William. 1982. *Well and Truly Tried: Essays on Evidence in Honour of Sir Richard Eggleston*. Edited by Enid Campbell and Louis Waller. Sydney: Lawbook Co.

Twining, William. 1985. *Theories of Evidence: Bentham and Wigmore*. Redwood City: Stanford University Press.

Tyler, Tom R. 2006. Legitimacy and Legitimation. *Annual Review of Psychology* 57.

Case Studies in History and Law

Cleaning Up the Mess of Empire? Evidence, Time and Memory in 'Historic Justice' Cases Concerning the Former British Empire (2000–Present)

Berber Bevernage

1 Introduction

Since the start of the new millennium, and most notably since around 2010, colonial injustices and their legacies have been the central stake of a quickly increasing number of lawsuits in and against the UK.[1] Because colonial injustices from a legal perspective are often considered 'antique' or 'historic', their adjudication contributes to a relatively new legal phenomenon which challenges the conventional temporal boundaries of the law and can be called 'historic justice'.[2]

The best known historic justice experiments are undoubtedly the criminal law cases concerning the Holocaust that have taken place since the 1980s—think, for example, of the trials of Barbie, Touvier and Papon in France or the trials against John Demjanjuk in Israel and Germany. Much has indeed been written about the judicialization of history and historicization of jurisdiction in the context of criminal law (e.g. Douglas 2001; Wilson 2005; Golsan 2018).

In this article, however, I focus on an important phenomenon that, thus far, has received far less scholarly attention: namely the use of civil litigation in historic justice. Although they often concern very serious wrongs (including torture, illegal

[1]I would like to thank Ramses Delafontaine, Eline Mestdagh, Walderez Ramalho, Kate Temoney, Marie-Gabrielle Verbergt and Rafael Verbuyst for their ideas and critical comments. They have helped me a lot in writing this article. This chapter was previously published in *Storia della Storiografia*.

[2]I am opting for the term 'historic' rather than 'historical' in order to indicate that this type of justice should not be confused with attempts to do justice by revealing the historical truth about certain crimes or providing a historical representation of the victim's experiences. In many ways, the 'historic justice' which I will analyse in this article can be considered anti-historical in the sense of how it generally relates to issues of 'historical expertise', 'historical truth' and 'historical context'.

B. Bevernage (✉)
Department of History, Ghent University, Ghent, Belgium
e-mail: berber.bevernage@ugent.be

B. Zhang et al. (eds.), *A Dialogue Between Law and History*,
https://doi.org/10.1007/978-981-15-9685-8_13

detention and extra-legal executions), most of the lawsuits in the United Kingdom (UK) concerning colonial injustices are based on civil law. They are generally either involve torts law—civil law regulating the (monetary) compensation of personal or other harms—or requests for 'judicial review', whereby judges are asked to legally assess governmental (in)actions. Some of these lawsuits have been successful or at least made it high up in the hierarchy of the British (and European) court system. Others lawsuits were dismissed almost immediately and never reached the stage of full trial. Nearly all of them, however, were in the first instance treated by the same court—the so-called Queen's Bench Division of the High Court of England and Wales. This means that the entry of (post-colonial) historic justice cases into the British legal system is regulated by a select set of gate keepers.

This article analyses how this small group of gate-keeping judges, have dealt with recent post-colonial historic justice claims and to what extent they have embraced or rejected the law's new role in cleaning up the mess of empire. I will discuss some of the advances as well as challenges and setbacks of the historic justice experiment. I will thereby especially focus on evidentiary challenges and disputes.

My central thesis is that despite some remarkable successes most of the post-colonial historic justice cases in the UK remain unsuccessful and that, with some notable exceptions, most British judges remain highly sceptical about them. The general scepticism of most judges manifests itself clearly in quite heated and distinct disputes about evidence. I will argue that although civil law is based on the balance of probabilities and thus has a lower evidentiary standard than criminal law with its 'beyond reasonable doubt'-rule, the evidentiary challenges for those championing historic justice remain very high and often unsurpassable.

I will identify six major evidentiary challenges that characterize the experiments with (post-colonial) historic justice in British civil cases: (1) legal disputes over the relative probative value of documentary evidence versus oral testimony, (2) a sometimes extreme scepticism of judges concerning the evidentiary value of witness recollections, (3) a widespread reluctance of judges to take into account broader historical context as a form of corroborative evidence, (4) disputes over the legal status of expert evidence by historians, (5) highly abstract and sometimes speculative meta-evidentiary disputes about the relation between evidence and time, (6) legal disputes over what does or does not constitute substantially new evidence that can revive a so-called 'duty to investigate'.

Before going into these evidentiary disputes in more detail, however, let me first give a brief background sketch on the rise of historic justice in the UK.

2 Historic Justice in the UK: A Brief Background Sketch

I do not have the ambition here to answer the broad questions of 'why the struggle for historic justice' and 'why now'? In the context of this article it suffices to remark that the rise of historic justice in the UK does not happen in isolation and that it needs to be placed against a background of a transnationally increased focus on the righting of (colonial) historical wrongs (see Barkan 2001; Shelton 2003; Thompson 2002; Curthoys et al. 2008). It should also be remarked that (post-colonial) historic justice litigation generally emerges in combination with other forms of, often more straightforwardly political, activism including demands for public apologies, public inquiries, the removal of colonial monuments, the initiation of new commemorative rituals, etc.

It is hard to give a precise periodization for the recent shifts in the transnationally dominant sensitives toward colonial historical wrongs. Yet, when we focus specifically on their manifestation in the legal sphere in the UK, we are confronted with a phenomenon of the new millennium. Even with this specific focus in mind, however, different starting points can arguably be chosen to tell the story of the rise of historic justice.

One possible starting point is a series of lawsuits against a compensation scheme for British ex-internees of Japanese WWII camps announced by the UK government in November 2000. This scheme was heavily contested because it foresaw compensation only for victims with 'a close link with the United Kingdom'—which de facto meant having a European blood line—instead of including all those who at the time of their internment were British subjects according to the law. Several ex-POWs and citizens from the former Empire initiated lawsuits seeking judicial review of the scheme, claiming that the blood link criterion was discriminating. Some of these lawsuits were highly successful and resulted in important changes to the compensation scheme—most notably that by the Nepalese Gurkha soldiers.[3] Other claimants failed in their attempts to be included. Each of the lawsuits, however, involved complex historically oriented discussions.[4] Several of the lawsuits also referred to a statement by a historian, David Omissi.[5]

If one considers the series of lawsuits challenging the compensation scheme as a starting point, then the emergence of post-colonial historic justice in the UK appears as a side-effect of policies and political sensitivities concerning WWII. It should be noted, however, that although these lawsuits involve profound historical discussions, they are lacking an element that I believe is characteristic of more fully fledged historic justice: namely the challenging of statutes of limitation. Because the compensation cases concerned the judicial review of a contemporary governmental initiative,

[3]See *Gurung & Anor v Ministry of Defence* [2002] EWHC 2463 (Admin) (27 November 2002). As a result of the Gurkha litigation the compensation scheme was amended. See 'Written Ministerial Statements' of 5 November 2003 on www.parliament.uk.

[4]See for example *Association of British Civilian Internees Far East Region v Secretary of State for Defence* [2002] EWHC 2119 (Admin) (18 October 2002); And *Association of British Civilian Internees; Far Eastern Region v Secretary of State for Defence* [2003] EWCA Civ 473 (03 April 2003).

[5]Omissi was then a senior lecturer in Imperial history at the University of Hull. He gave evidence on racist divisions within the imperial armies. His witness statement was prepared for the *Gurung* case but was also relied on by the claimants in later cases. See *Mohammed, R (on the application of) v Secretary of State for Defence* [2006] EWHC 2098 (Admin) (11 August 2006). And *Dost Mohammed, R (on the application of) v Secretary of State for Defence* [2007] EWCA Civ 1023 (01 May 2007).

from a legal perspective they did not question the limits of law's temporal jurisdiction and were thus not about historic justice, strictly speaking.[6]

Another possible starting point of the rise of post-colonial historic justice is the series of compensation cases brought against the UK by former inhabitants of the Chagos Islands who were forcefully displaced during the 1960s and 1970s to enable the construction of a military base. The lawsuits by the Chagos Islanders were started around the turn of the millennium and their legal battle continues until today and has become extremely complex.[7] The Chagos Islands litigation is a prime example of the uses of legal means to deal with colonial injustices and it also did involve a limited discussion on statutes of limitations. Yet, because many of the claims of the Chagos Islanders involve so-called 'continuing torts'—many of them are still being denied a right to return, for example—the issue of time limitations again did not become a key issue in this legal battle.[8]

If one specifically associates the emergence of historic justice with the challenging of time of limits and looks for a case on colonial injustices where this was a key issue, then a good starting point is the litigation initiated in 2009 by five former Mau Mau insurgents against the Foreign and Commonwealth Office (FCO) for atrocities committed in Kenya in the 1950s. In two path-breaking judgements in 2011 and 2012, judge Richard McCombe ruled that the Mau Mau case should not be dismissed as expired.[9] Interestingly, McCombe's ruling was enabled by a judgement about 'historic sexual abuse' that shortly before created an important legal precedent concerning the disapplication of the time bar.[10] As a result of McCombe's judgements, the UK government settled the case and a compensation payment of nearly £20 m was made to over 5000 Mau Mau veterans (Hague 2013). From this perspective, post-colonial historic justice thus seems to have been facilitated by, and partly a (unforeseen?) side-effect of, changing sensitivities concerning historic child abuse.

---

[6]In a judgement on the compensation scheme judge Arden in this context tellingly claimed that "[although] the facts of this case are most unusual and concern a historical situation which occurred some sixty years ago […] it should not be assumed that as a result the decision of this court is outside the mainstream of discrimination cases." See *Secretary of State for Defence v Elias* [2006] EWCA Civ 1293 (10 October 2006), §263.

[7]Still in February and May 2019, the UK was scolded by the International Court of Justice and the UN general assembly that it should relinquish its colonial control over the islands (see BBC News 2019; Bowcott and Borger 2019).

[8]Judge Laws, who in November 2000 delivered a judgement on the first major, and largely successful, Chagos Islands lawsuit for example remarks that in this case the theme time limitations was not raised by the parties. Judge Gibbs similarly argued that: "It would be no answer to say that these documents reflected the standards of a different period. I venture to think that the impression on right thinking people upon reading them would have been similar, then as now." *Bancoult, R (on the application of) v Secretary Of State For Foreign & Commonweal Office* [2000] EWHC 413 (Admin) (3 November 2000), §1 and §72.

[9]*Mutua & Ors v The Foreign & Commonwealth Office* [2011] EWHC 1913 (QB) (21 July 2011). And *Mutua & Ors v The Foreign And Commonwealth Office* [2012] EWHC 2678 (QB) (05 October 2012).

[10]See *A v Hoare* judgement of 30 January 2008.

Although the well-publicized settlement of the first Mau Mau case in no way guaranteed the success of subsequent historic justice cases, it did certainly inspire other potential claimants. Soon after the settlement, for example, a second much larger litigation concerning the 'Kenyan Emergency' involving some 44.000 claimants was started in late 2012. Kimathi v FCO would be dismissed in late 2018 but by that time it had turned into an enormously extensive legal battle and, according to some commentators, one of the longest running trials in English legal history (Block and Holborn 2018).

Around the same time as the second Mau Mau case another series of litigations was initiated about the killing of 24 civilians in 1948 by British soldiers at the village of Batang Kali in what was then the Federation of Malaya. Over the years, several official investigations were initiated about this massacre, but these had been clear cover-ups. The main aim of the litigation was to force the government to initiate a public inquiry by requesting a judicial review and by attempting to establish a legal 'duty to investigate' via references to international law. The claimants were able to take their case through several courts between 2012 and 2018 but the litigation eventually failed.

In mid-2015 a lawsuit was filed from yet another part of the former empire. 34 Cypriot independence fighters sued the UK for colonial atrocities in the late 1950s.[11] Sophocleous v. FCO & Defence led to two judgements in 2018[12] but the case was settled out of court in early 2019 with a compensation payment of £1 m (Smith 2019).

Finally, there are some other, unsuccessful but interesting, recent civil cases that add another dimension since they sued the UK for its role in the decolonization process rather than for colonial injustices strictly speaking.

On 30 March 2015 the Queen's Bench Division rejected a claim brought against the FCO by seven claimants from an Indian minority in Malaysia.[13] The claimants contented that the interests of their ethnic minority had been ignored in the period between 1944 and 1957 when the independence of Malaysia was arranged, that as a result they still suffered disadvantages and discrimination, and that the British colonizer had played a key role in this process. The claimants held the UK liable for neglect because of the influence it had on the drafting of the constitution of the soon-to-be independent Malaysia.

On 5 November 2018, Queen's Bench stroke out a similar claim that was lodged by Makweley Lysongo, a secessionist activist of an Anglophone minority in the predominantly Francophone Republic of Cameroon.[14] Lysongo claimed the UK wronged his people in the late 1950 and early 1960s, when it decided to cede the 'British Southern

---

[11]The legal counsel of the Cypriot veterans took the successful settlement of the first Mau Mau case in 2013 as an important example (Pantelides 2013).

[12]See *Sophocleous & Ors v Secretary of State for the Foreign And Commonwealth Office & Anor* [2018] EWHC 19 (QB) (12 January 2018). And *Sophocleous & Ors v The Secretary of State for Foreign And Commonwealth Affairs & Anor* [2018] EWCA Civ 2167 (09 October 2018).

[13]*Ponnusamy & Ors v Secretary of State for Foreign and Commonwealth Affairs* [2015] EWHC 1760 (QB) (30 March 2015).

[14]*Lysongo v The Foreign And Commonwealth Office & Anor* [2018] EWHC 2955 (QB) (05 November 2018).

Cameroons' to the formerly French République du Cameroun instead of granting it independence. Here the UK was thus again sued for its role in decolonization process rather than for colonial injustices strictly speaking.

3 The Many Faces of Evidence in Historic Justice Cases

Discussions about evidence are an important aspect of most forms of adjudication. Yet, experiments with historic justice substantially sharpen some of these common discussions as a well as introduce some evidentiary challenges which seem relatively particular to this new type of litigation. I identify six major issues which pop up in diverse cases and which can form a major challenge for historic justice claims.

3.1 Oral Testimony Versus Documentary Evidence

One of the most noticeable evidentiary disputes in historic justice cases revolves around the relative value of oral testimony versus documentary evidence. In contrast to some other legal systems—such as the one in continental Europe—common law does not give preference to documentary evidence but rather sees oral testimony, given in court under oath and cross-examination, as the evidentiary 'gold standard'.[15] Documentary information generally is only accepted as evidence when it is formally entered as such during a hearing in court and ideally is presented by a witness who can contextualise it and be cross-examined about its authenticity, provenance and meaning. This preference for oral testimony often creates serious problems for the advancement of historic justice claims. Because several of the key witnesses are often already dead, seriously ill or untraceable by the time of the litigation, (post-colonial) historic justice cases can spark hefty discussions about the possibility of a fair trial in the absence of (extensive) oral testimony. How much of a stumbling block the scarceness of oral testimony forms greatly depends on the nature of the case (including the parties' litigation strategies) as well as on the inclinations of the judge(s).

One of the most prominent cases of successful historic justice litigation based primarily on documentary evidence is the first Mau Mau lawsuit. In Mutua & Ors v FCO, the defendant argued that a fair trial was no longer possible because too many key witnesses were already dead and thus no longer available to give oral testimony. The judge, however, ruled that the nature of the disputed issues and the shear extent

[15]For the expression that oral evidence given under cross-examination generally remains the evidentiary 'gold standard' of the British legal system see *Carmarthenshire County Council v Y* [2017] EWFC 36 (30 June 2017). Also see Wootten (2003, 23).

of the available archival material made it possible to have a successful trial based primarily on documentary rather than oral evidence.[16]

The prominent role of (historical) documentary evidence in Mutua was quite exceptional, however. There seem to be different reasons for the successfulness of the claimants' reliance on documentary evidence in this case: As I will explain in more detail below, the judge in Mutua, McCombe, appears exceptionally open to historical evidence as well as to working with historians. This had already become clear in the way McCombe dealt with the Gurung case of 2002 where he ruled in favour of the Gurkha claimants.[17] Together with Gurung, Mutua was indeed one of the few post-colonial historic justice litigations with an important presence of professional historians. The presence of historians greatly facilitated the way large amounts of documentary evidence could be introduced and processed in court. In Mutua the importance of documentary evidence was also increased and spectacularly highlighted after a large set of hidden archives had been discovered in state depots at Hanslope park.[18] Historian David Anderson played a key role in the discovery of these so-called 'migrated' or 'lost' archives and there is no doubt that the 'Hanslope disclosure' was an essential factor in the success of the Mutua case (see Anderson 2001; Badger 2012).

It is important to note, however, that the success of the claimants was by no means guaranteed after the Hanslope disclosure merely on the basis of the massive documentary evidentiary base it provided. Besides the factor of the historical mindedness of judge McCombe, the Hanslope and other documentary evidence could only play the prominent role that it came to play because of the particular (and with hindsight doubtlessly mistaken) defence strategy of the FCO. In the middle of the Mutua litigation the FCO announced that it no longer disputed the fact that the claimants had indeed been tortured and mistreated by the colonial administration in Kenya. Instead, the FCO chose to focus on a second line of defense. It argued that the UK government could not be held legally liable because the colonial administration was a separate government—the so-called 'division of the Crown'—and because the liabilities of the colonial administration had transferred to Kenya upon its independence rather than to London. As a result of the factual 'admission' by the FCO the focus of the judicial dispute moved away from the particular fate of the claimants in Kenya—for which less direct documentary evidence was available—towards the systematic nature of the abuses and the close relation between the local colonial administration and highest policy levels in London—and this changed focus indeed made the reliance on documentary evidence much more effective.

That the mere presence of extensive documentary evidence does not guarantee a successful litigation is clearly illustrated by the second Mau Mau case. In strong contrast to McCombe in Mutua, the judge working on Kimathi & Ors v. FCO, Stewart,

[16]McCombe in *Mutua & Ors v The Foreign And Commonwealth Office* [2012] EWHC 2678 (QB) (05 October 2012), §51.

[17]*Gurung & Anor v Ministry of Defence [2002] EWHC 2463 (Admin) (27 November 2002).*

[18]See *Mutua & Ors v The Foreign And Commonwealth Office* [2012] EWHC 2678 (QB) (05 October 2012).

was not impressed by the documentary evidence provided by the Hanslope disclosure and he did consider the absence of extensive oral testimony as an unsurmountable problem. Besides the disposition of the judge, the eventual dismissal of Kimathi can also be explained by the FCO's different defense strategy. The FCO this time made no factual admissions and kept the judicial dispute focussed on the particular claims by the individual claimants rather than moving it toward a more systemic level. This strategy, and the judge's receptivity to it, completely changed the evidentiary dynamics of Kimathi in comparison to Mutua: whereas Mutua had focussed on disputes that were more historical in nature, Kimathi primarily became a trial of memory—both in the sense that it was based on the memory of witnesses as well as that it put the evidentiary value of memory on trial. This brings us to a second major evidentiary dispute characterizing historic justice cases.

3.2 *Memory as Evidence*

While sworn and cross-examined oral testimony is considered the evidentiary gold standard in common law, this does not keep judges from being highly sceptical about this testimony when the recollection of 'antique' events is involved. One of the more remarkable features of historic justice cases is that they sometimes provoke quite far-reaching or even speculative meta-level discussions on the evidentiary value of memory.

The widespread scepticism among judges about the probative value of memory especially tends to be a major obstacle for parties who try to build their historic justice case primarily on 'live evidence'. As mentioned above, Kimathi is a good illustration of a case that to a great extent turned into a trial of memory, where the judge was highly sceptical of memory, and whose eventual dismissal was greatly influenced by that fact. In two of his main judgements in Kimathi, dated August 2nd and November 21st 2018, judge Stewart gives extensive commentary on the probative value of memory—thereby relying primarily on what has been said by colleagues in previous judgements, rather than on scientific research.[19] Stewart, for example, warns that memories are often believed "to be more faithful than they are" and that it is a common mistake to assume that recollections are more likely to be accurate when a witness experiences them very vividly or is very confident about them. "The authorities" (i.e. colleague judges that set legal precedents), Stewart argues, "make it clear that it is a well-known fact that memories become less and less reliable the staler an action becomes."[20] Citing some of these "authorities", Stewart claims that "with every day that passes memory becomes fainter and the imagination becomes more active" and that even in the case of shocking or traumatic events "memories

[19] *Kimathi & Ors v The Foreign And Commonwealth Office* [2018] EWHC 2066 (QB) (02 August 2018). And *Kimathi & Ors v The Foreign and Commonwealth Office* [2018] EWHC 3144 (QB) (21 November 2018).

[20] *Kimathi* (2 August 2018), §450.

are fluid and malleable, being constantly rewritten."[21] Courts therefore, according to Stewart, should constantly guard themselves against potential biases when working with witness recollections and he argues that "the value of oral evidence lies largely in the opportunity which cross-examination affords to subject the documentary record to critical scrutiny, and to gauge the personality and motives of a witness, rather than in testimony of what a witness recalls of particular events."[22]

Even the expert opinion by the forensic psychiatrist serving in Kimathi, prof. Mezey, could not dissuade Stewart from the radical scepticism about witness recollections that the authorities had imparted to him. Mezey had, for example, expressed strong confidence in the authenticity of two particularly traumatic recollections by TC34—the anonymized Test Claimant on which Stewart's first full trial judgement focused. These recollections concerned two horrific events whereby TC34 recalled the embodied experience of having the intestines of a dead inmate spilling over him and the psychological terror of being shown a set of severed heads during an interrogation by the colonial secret services. Based on the way TC34 emotionally and physically behaved while recounting his recollections, Mezey argued that her observations were "consistent with him actually experiencing a flashback in the room" and that is was "very unlikely that he could be hiding symptoms or the cause of the symptoms."[23] Judge Stewart claimed to have "due regard to Professor Mezey's expertise". Yet, after reminding himself of the authorities' view on recollection, he expressed being "sceptical as to the faith that Professor Mezey puts in what she saw on examination" and he did "not find [Mezey's expert opinion] to be very convincing evidence of what TC34 says occurred"[24] Stewart was especially glaubensunwillig toward TC34's recollection of the severed heads. Primarily referring to the alleged "inherent unlikelihood"[25] of the occurrence of "this sort of incident" the judge decided to ignore Mezey's expert evidence and to disregard it for evidentiary purposes. Stewart even added that he found it "tempting" to weigh in this "incident" against TC34's reliability.[26]

The highly sceptical assessment of witness recollections was absolutely devastating for the claimants in the Kimathi litigation as a whole. This was particularly so because the judicial dispute mostly focussed on largely undocumented events, because very little documentary evidence was considered relevant by judge Stewart, and because, as I will explain below, the judge was also very reluctant to allow corroborative contextual evidence and ruled against the use of expert witnessing by professional historians.

---

[21] *Kimathi* (2 August 2018), §96.

[22] *Kimathi* (2 August 2018), §96.

[23] *Kimathi* (2 August 2018), §405, §325 and note 289.

[24] *Kimathi* (2 August 2018), §325.

[25] Stewart suggested that "the incident is so bizarre that it is unlikely it ever happened". See *Kimathi* (2 August 2018), §408.

[26] *Kimathi* (2 August 2018), §408 and §409.

Another good illustration of the risks involved in relying heavily on victim's recollections is provided by the Chagos Islanders case which was dismissed by Judge Ouseley in October 2003.[27]

In this case the claimants chose to bring in live testimonies by former inhabitants of the Chagos Islands in order to testify about their living conditions before and after they were displaced. This litigation strategy backlashed badly. The testimonies were meant to support the case of the claimants by highlighting their suffering and giving greater visibility to their plea for a right of return. Yet, the judge rejected the use of courtroom testimonies for allegedly political purposes and also negatively assessed the trustworthiness of the witnesses—an element that played a key role in his dismissal of the case. In his judgement Ouseley elaborately discussed the contradictions, mistakes and silences of each of the witnesses whereby his most often repeated comment was that the testimonies first and foremost, and in some cases exclusively, demonstrated the untrustworthiness of memory when discussing old events.[28]

Although Ouseley admitted the problems with the witness testimonies may partly have resulted from issues of (linguistic and cultural) translation and a lack of understanding about legal procedures he primarily perceived these problems as reflecting 'unreliable memory'[29] The judge also complained that elements of "collective memory" or "folk memory" entered into many of the testimonies, whereby "evidence was also given, as if at first hand, about events which the witness could not have seen or heard."[30] Ouseley explained his vision on the issue as follows:

> There might be value in "collective" or "folk memory" evidence, or in a fairly sound general picture in which the individual details were more uncertain, if one were seeking a generalised or collective view for the purposes of an inquiry into the conduct of the UK Government. But I am concerned with litigation in which, on issues such as negligence and damages for personal injury, what happened to each individual Claimant would need to be measured with rather greater precision.[31]

3.3 *Historical Context as (Corroborative) Evidence*

Ouseley's references to the differences between the "generalised" perspective sought for in public inquiries and the more individualized approach of litigation, hints at

---

[27] *Chagos Islanders v Attorney General Her Majesty's British Indian Ocean Territory Commissioner* [2003] EWHC 2222 (QB) (9 October 2003).

[28] About one of the witnesses, Ms. Talate, for example, judge Ouseley remarked "it was the [bad] quality of recollection which, as with others, was the most telling feature of her evidence." *Chagos Islanders* (9 October 2003), §170.

[29] *Chagos Islanders* (9 October 2003), §160.

[30] In an analysis of the litigation by the Chagos Islanders, social anthropologist Jeffery (2006) argues that one of the key problems with the way the victims' testimonies were received in a legal context is related to cultural differences in how narratives are being told.

[31] *Chagos Islanders* (9 October 2003), §161.

another major evidentiary challenge often arising in historic justice. Due to the generally large scope of the claims and the sometimes enormous numbers of claimants, historic justice cases often raise heated discussions about the need for and value of (historical) contextual evidence. It is well-known that classical legal systems are generally rather ill-fitted when it comes to judging massive crimes that involve many victims, complex perpetrator networks and which have taken place over longer periods of time or broad geographical scopes. Due to their focus on individual crimes or torts and victims or perpetrators, legal procedures often tend to 'cut up' histories and have a hard time taking into account broader historical patterns—even when their existence seems obvious to historians or other academics. The procedures followed by the civil courts in the UK are no exception to this rule.

In most (post-colonial) historic justice cases the need to 'particularize'[32] claims, by tying them down to specific acts, perpetrators and victims and by providing directly corresponding evidence, forms a very difficult challenge. When little direct evidence can be found, claimants as a form of corroboration often try to submit evidence that relates not specifically to their own individual case but to similar cases within the broader historical context.

Whether or not claimants are successful in relying on historical context as corroborative evidence strongly depends on procedural rules and on the inclinations of the judge(s). Kimathi provides a good illustration of a case where the judge has been particularly unwilling to take into account contextual corroborative evidence and strongly rejected the introduction of 'historical' arguments which would threaten to turn litigation into 'inquiry' or worse a "historical seminar".[33] Whereas McCombe in Mutua was reluctant to strike out parts of the victims' claims because he considered it unreasonable to "divide the history up",[34] Stewart in Kimathi stroke out important parts of the victims' claims—e.g. false imprisonment, and psychological suffering—to reduce the history of the Kenyan emergency to one that was manageable in legal terms and came to revolve quasi exclusively around personal injury by physical assault.[35]

When the claimants' counsel, for example, made comments about "the broad historical background" and suggested "the Government had overreacted to the Mau Mau threat", Stewart replied that these were not matters he could or should judge.[36] The issue of contextual corroborative evidence also turned up when counsel tried to corroborate test claimants' allegations by showing how the abuses they testified about where also recounted by other witnesses in similar contexts and how they were part of broader historical patterns of abuse. Stewart generally rejected this evidentiary strategy.

A clear illustration of the low probative value Stewart attributed to contextual evidence can be found in his judgement of the case of TC20. The anonymised test

---

[32] Ouseley in *Chagos Islanders* (9 October 2003), §296.

[33] Stewart in *Kimathi* (2 August 2018), §22.

[34] *Mutua* (21 July 2011), §138.

[35] See for example *Kimathi* (21 November 2018) §4 and §15.

[36] *Kimathi* (2 August 2018), note 13.

claimant had suffered grave abuses in the process of so-called villagization whereby many Kenyans were forced to live in enclosed settlements. In order to corroborate TC20's allegations her counsel argued that each of the test claimants who had been villagized testified to similar abuses. Since the test claimants had been randomly selected from the database of 44.000 claimants, the lawyers argued, this showed a widespread historical pattern of abuse and thus had to be considered corroborative evidence. Stewart was not convinced by this argument, however. He replied that all test claimants individually suffered from the same evidentiary problems as TC20 because they could not produce documents to back up their claims. Mostly importantly, however, Stewart considered the probative value of the recurring testimonies "of very little, if any, weight", because the claimants "were in different villages at different times."[37]

Similarly, when the claimants in the trial of TC34 tried to corroborate the severed heads-claim (see above) by pointing to a series of documents which they saw as evidence of a widespread historical pattern of the use of psychological terror methods during interrogations, Stewart replied that:

> [...] these go nowhere near providing any sort of real corroboration for what TC34 alleges happened at CID Headquarters in Nairobi (in or about 1955). They are in different places and at different times and, on the Claimants' allegation, refer to enforced solitary confinement, sleep deprivation and spreading fear by rumours and beating people.[38]

Remarkably, the judge did accept a negative version of historical contextual corroboration about the same "incident" when he seemed convinced by the defendant's plea "that it had no knowledge and could find no record of British officers or Kenyan Police having severed a head during the Emergency, or of severed heads having been collected or kept in a cupboard or other storage medium, or having been shown to detainees."[39] Similarly Stewart seems to fall back on implicit notions of 'ordinary' historical context when he judges the severed heads claim as absolutely "extraordinary" and therefore "inherently unlikely".

Beyond the discussions about the 'core allegations' concerning the abuses during the Kenyan emergency, Stewart's rejection of evidence and arguments relating to broader historical context also extended to another important aspect of the Kimathi case: namely the discussion about the 'delay' in the filing of the claim. A key judicial dispute relevant to entire case was whether the claimants could justify why their lawsuit was not filed sooner after events took place. The claimants among other things referred to the historical context of a changed legal culture which made filing the claims possible now for the first time whereas earlier in history the claimants "could not reasonably be expected to believe that [they] could bring a claim against the British government, or that [they] would be compensated."[40] Moreover they argued

[37] *Kimathi* (21 November 2018), §34 and §36.

[38] *Kimathi* (2 August 2018), §404.

[39] *Kimathi* (2 August 2018), §401.

[40] Counsel of the claimants cited in *Kimathi* (2 August 2018), §145 and *Kimathi* (21 November 2018), §43.

that due to the different political culture and general adversity of the colonial administration and the UK government to engage into serious investigations of colonial abuses during much of the colonial and post-colonial period the claimants were not in a 'realistic position to bring a claim" earlier in history. None of these arguments convinced Stewart however. In both his judgements on TC34 and TC20 he found no evidence indicating good reasons for delay—something that strongly pleaded against them when they asked the judge to exercise his discretion to overturn the statute of limitations.

3.4 *Historians as Expert Witnesses*

Another important dispute in historic justice concerns the legal status of historians' expertise and the question of whether they should be allowed to give 'opinion evidence' as real forensic expert witnesses are allowed to do.

The presence of historians has been one of the more remarkable features of some high profile (and successful) cases such as Mutua and Gurung. The role of historians in historic justice litigation remains highly contested, however, and most cases proceed without historical expert evidence. In some cases historians' expertise is even explicitly banned from court.

Several witness statements were made for Mutua by three historians (Caroline Elkins, David Anderson and Huw Bennett) and their evidence was extensively cited by judge McCombe.[41] Yet, although the role of historians in Mutua was crucial, the evidentiary status of the their testimonies remained contested in legal terms. While McCombe was remarkably open to historians he also noted that the precise evidentiary status of this expertise still had to be decided if the litigation would proceed to full trial instead of being settled out of court. Moreover, in using the historians' evidence, McCombe was bound to rules set out in two preceding judgements in the same case by judges Tugendhat and Langstaff. These judges ruled that the scope of acceptable historical expertise had to be restricted to 'matter of fact' information and should not involve "opinion evidence".[42] Langstaff, for example, stated about the role of Caroline Elkins that:

> Her evidence has no particular value in this case, other than to identify relevant documents or to identify relevant witnesses who may be able to give effective and important testimony. Her position is very different from that of a witness who has herself directly seen something happen. It is also very different from the traditional role of an expert witness.[43]

[41]*Mutua & Ors v The Foreign & Commonwealth Office* [2011] EWHC 1913 (QB) (21 July 2011). And *Mutua & Ors v The Foreign And Commonwealth Office* [2012] EWHC 2678 (QB) (05 October 2012).

[42]*Mutua & Ors v The Foreign & Commonwealth Office* [2010] EWHC 2731 (QB), §12.

[43]Unreported judgement by Langstaff dated 13 December 2010 and cited by McCombe in *Mutua* (21 July 2011), §35.

While nominally claiming to be bound by these preceding judgements, McCombe doubtlessly went much further than his colleagues had foreseen in terms of allowing a broad scope of historical expertise and even opinion. Yet, the fact that the evidential status of the historians' expertise was never fully settled in Mutua heavily influenced the second Mau Mau case.

Very early in Kimathi, the FCO requested the judge to rule against the claimants' plan to (re-)use the historians' witness reports prepared for Mutua as well as a series of 'hearsay' testimonies recorded by Caroline Elkins in her book Imperial Reckoning (Elkins 2005). Judge Stewart only got to see a small sample of the historian's 'hearsay' evidence and historic witness statements, because the defendant objected to the judge reading them.[44] Based on this limited information, Stewart decided that the historians' evidence indeed had to be excluded. He judged that the historians' statements were 'essentially historical commentary' which included 'personal conclusions' and threatened to introduce inadmissible opinion evidence into the court. The judge also stated that "it is not the function of an expert to express opinions on disputed issues of fact which do not require any expert knowledge to evaluate" and he added the rhetorical question "what factual evidence can historians give which is not apparent from the documents themselves?".[45]

As noted above historians were not the only professionals in Kimathi whose expert authority was being questioned by the judge: forensic psychiatrist Mezey met a similar fate. This suggests a broader reluctance, by Stewart, to accept any expert authority which he may have perceived as threatening "judicial sovereignty" (Wilson 2016, 731). As Richard Wilson argues, perceived threats to judicial sovereignty can be a key factor in how judges respond to the presence of many types of experts in court. Yet, this reflex by judges to protect their judicial sovereignty seems particularly strong in relation to historians. This may be related to the fact that the reconstruction of (limited) chronological or causal histories is a core business not only of historians but also of judges and to the fact that many judges, like Stewart, seem to think historians have no special skills which they themselves cannot also master.

The guarding of judicial sovereignty of course does not necessarily lead to a total rejection of historical expertise. It can produce an ambiguous relation whereby historical expertise is relied on for certain judicial purposes while being rejected for others. Such an ambiguous reliance on historical expertise can be found in the Ponnusamy case of 2015. In that case the judge heavily relied on an article by historian Wade (2009) to sketch a factual background history about the fate of ethnic minorities in Malaysia before and after its independence in 1957. Yet, the judge rejected the claimants' attempt to use this same academic article to make their case that the discrimination against ethnic minorities in contemporary Malaysia is directly related to political decision-making around the time of independence for which British colonial power was co-responsible. As judge Blake puts it: "As a matter of academic opinion that may be a perfectly reputable view to take, but it does not amount to an

[44] *Kimathi & Ors v Foreign and Commonwealth Office* [2015] EWHC 3432 (QB) (26 November 2015), §13.

[45] Stewart in *Kimathi* (26 November 2015), §24.

assessment of legal responsibility for any discrimination and causation of damage."[46] Historical expertise was thus embraced by the judge for the purpose of reconstructing the chronology of historical events but rejected when it concerned the identification of causal relations and historical responsibility.

3.5 *Evidence and the 'Passage of Time'*

Another dispute that features prominently in historic justice cases concerns the relation between the 'cogency of evidence' and the 'passage of time'. This dispute can manifest high levels of abstraction. Rather than merely raising the issue of whether there is enough trustworthy evidence to have a firm trial, historic justice cases sometimes revolve around meta-evidentiary disputes about the 'evidence of evidence': how one can (dis)prove the (past) existence of evidence and its increasing or decreasing cogency over time.

Discussions about the relation between evidence and time especially arise when claimants request the disapplication of statues of limitations. The most important rules about time bars in England and Wales, are found in the Limitation Act 1980.[47] Besides providing time limits for legal actions concerning different types of wrongs, the Act also includes provisions where normal time limits can be extended or removed. Section 32, for example, includes a rule that the limitation period should be postponed when the defendant has deliberately concealed information. Section 33 specifically concerns personal injury or death and gives judges discretionary power to overrule time limits if this appears 'equitable'. To decide what is 'equitable', the Act demands judges to take into account several considerations. These include the reasons for the delay by the claimants and the conduct of defendant "after the cause of action arose"—for example in relation to requests for information. In the context of our discussion on evidence, however, the most important consideration is how the (dis)application of time limits could create an evidentiary 'prejudice' against either defendant or claimant when the evidence potentially has lost cogency over time. To cite the act: "the extent to which, having regard to the delay, the evidence adduced or likely to be adduced by the [claimant] or the defendant is or is likely to be less cogent than if the action had been brought within the time [normally allowed by the Limitation Act]".

Because of this rule, historic justice cases often do not only revolve around assessments of the evidence that is available at the moment of a legal action but also, or even primarily, around estimations or speculations about the evidence that would have been available if the action had taken place earlier in time. As a result, historic justice cases often involve highly speculative counterfactual reasoning or 'what if' histories.

---

[46] *Ponnusamy & Ors v Secretary of State for Foreign and Commonwealth Affairs* [2015] EWHC 1760 (QB) (30 March 2015), §58.

[47] See https://www.legislation.gov.uk/ukpga/1980/58.

Of all the post-colonial historic justice cases, Kimathi was probably the case with the most extensive and speculative discussions about the relation between evidence and time and the judge's eventual dismissal also essentially turned around these discussions. A large part of the Kimathi litigation specifically focused on what evidence would have been accessible to the litigating parties roughly half a century ago in comparison to today and how this difference has created legal 'prejudice' against either of them. These disputes were extremely complex because they did not only involve questions about which evidence is known to be lost but also about who could potentially have witnessed what and which documentary records could have existed and how to prove this. Concerning the 'loss' of documentary evidence an essential question was whether this happened due to legitimate 'weeding' procedures or rather illegitimate targeted destruction. If it could be demonstrated that the defendant purposefully destroyed incriminating evidence it could of course not claim that the absence of this evidence today creates a 'prejudice' against it. If, however, the loss of evidence resulted from legitimate archival policies, the defendants could claim that the overruling of the statute of limitations creates a prejudice against them because they (potentially) would have had a better chance to defend themselves in the past, when they still possessed the 'unweeded' records. In order to plead the latter case, the FCO introduced Robert Deane—the head of its knowledge management department—as an expert witness who could give evidence on the legality of its archival policies and on which archives would potentially have been at the FCO's disposal in the past but are now lost.[48] In response, the claimants argued that the majority of the documents no longer existing today were illegitimately destroyed by the FCO. Moreover they claimed that even if more evidence may have existed in Kenya in the past, it would not necessarily have been more accessible to the FCO (or rather its predecessor, the Colonial Office) in the UK because the general attitude of local administration was averse to any serious enquiry.

Judge Stewart was not impressed by the claimants' arguments. He seemed much more convinced by the FCO's argument that the passage of time had negatively affected the cogency of the evidence. Even if much remained unknown about why and when evidence was 'lost' and which evidence precisely had ever existed in the first place, the judge was convinced that the passage of time had created an unsurpassable prejudice against the defendant. According to Stewart this prejudice was so profound that it even involved "a prejudice in proving prejudice"[49]:

> To put the matter at its lowest, fifty plus years ago, the Defendant potentially could have found documents which could potentially have led to information about TC34 and to potential alleged tortfeasors or witnesses. At the very least it probably would have known which documents had been kept and which had been lost/destroyed. All these are, at a minimum, realistic possibilities; some are probabilities. After all these years, the position is that, apart from certain prejudice that the Defendant can prove, there is further prejudice in that it has been deprived in certain aspects from proving specific prejudice arising from lack of documentary or witness evidence.[50]

[48] *Kimathi* (2 August 2018), §183.

[49] *Kimathi* (2 August 2018), §204. And *Kimathi* (21 November 2018), §99.

[50] *Kimathi* (2 August 2018), §203.

Stewart's reflections on the effects of the passage of time on the cogency of evidence were strongly disputed by the claimants who in an intermediary appeal argued that the judge had been all too speculative and not even-handed in his judgement of TC34.[51] Yet, the claimants arguments were rejected. The appeal judges accepted Stewart's reasoning and argued that it is "no more than common sense" that the passage of time had indeed made evidence "less cogent than it might have been". They also argued that in the circumstances of "this very old case" it was "quite enough" for the defendant to argue that it was "prejudiced in being able to show prejudice" rather than having to prove which specific documents had been lost and what they would have revealed.[52] After the failed appeal by the claimants, Stewart repeated his arguments about the negative effects of the passage of time on the cogency of evidence in his judgement of TC20 and the issue played a key role in the judge's dismissal of the entire Kimathi case.

3.6 What Constitutes New and 'Weighty or Compelling' Evidence?

A final evidentiary dispute that seems quite specific to many historic justice cases revolves around the question of what kind of, and how much, information has to emerge before one can speak about the revelation of substantially 'new' evidence. The legal importance of this question stems from developments in international law, and more specifically Article 2 of the European Convention of Human Rights (ECHR) which, according to some interpretations, prescribes to its signatories a duty to investigate suspicious deaths which, within certain limits, can be retroactive and 'revived' beyond ordinary time limitations when new evidence emerges. This partially retroactive and conditionally revivable duty to investigate has been an important aspect of experiments with historic justice at the European level—most notably the case about the Katyn massacre of 1940.[53] Yet, it has also been relied on for cases in the UK—although mostly unsuccessfully. It, for example, has been used in attempts to (re-)open investigations into time barred cases of political killings in Northern Ireland.[54]

The ECHR was also used in Mutua. There the claimants argued that the history books on the Kenyan Emergency published in 2005 and the discovery of the Hanslope archives in 2011 provided substantially new evidence which on the European level would trigger a new duty to investigate and which according to the claimants

---

[51] *Kimathi & Ors v Foreign & Commonwealth Office* [2018] EWCA Civ 2213 (09 October 2018).

[52] Judge Longmore in *Kimathi* (09 October 2018), §11 and 16.

[53] *Janoview and Others v. Russia*, Applications nos. 55508/07 and 29520/09, ECtHR (21 October 2013). For an analysis of the discussion about retroactivity in this case, see Koch (2015) and de Broux and Staes (2018).

[54] See *McKenna, Re Judicial Review* [2017] NIQB 96 (27 October 2017); And *Finucane, Re Application for Judicial Review (Northern Ireland)* [2019] UKSC 7 (27 February 2019).

should also guide the British judge. The claimants' plea was unsuccessful, however. McCombe responded that the ECHR had no direct relevance because the law of England had not yet "progressed as far" as to create a domestic duty to investigate which would be similarly retroactive and revivable as the European one.[55] Yet, the judge did recognize that the Hanslope archives and especially the history books did indeed provide substantially new evidence and this strongly influenced his decision to overrule the statute of limitations.

The question of what kind of evidence could be considered substantially new, and thus revive a legal duty to investigate, was fundamental to the Batang Kali lawsuits which between 2014 and 2018 were brought before different courts in the UK as well as on the European level. In these lawsuits the claimants primarily referred to the airing in 1992 of BBC documentary In Cold Blood and the publication in 2009 of the book Slaughter and Deception at Batang Kali (Ward and Miraflor 2009) as new evidence allegedly triggering a renewed duty to investigate. The claimants legal struggle to force the British government to set up a public inquiry on the colonial massacre was unsuccessful, yet the question of what type of evidence would be "sufficiently weighty and compelling"[56] to revive a duty to investigate proved a difficult legal issue on which judges did not seem to find a consensus. The latter became very clear when the case, after having moved through the Queen's Bench Division[57] and the Court of Appeal,[58] was treated by five judges at the Supreme Court.[59] In the supreme court judgement of 25 November 2015 judge Neuberger (the author of the main judgement whose views were largely followed by judges Mance and Hughes) recognized that some revelations by soldiers involved in the massacre, dating back to around 1970, indeed did constitute a "classic example" of fresh evidence that at that moment would have justified a new investigation.[60] Yet, the crucial legal issue was whether any similarly new evidence had appeared after 1970 and recently enough to maintain that there still was a legal duty to investigate at the time of the legal action. Neuberger judged this was not the case. No recent "item of evidence", according to the judge, added anything to the basic insight that had already been "quite apparent" by 1970.[61] Neuberger especially rejected the claimants' argument that sufficiently weighty and compelling fresh evidence to trigger a new duty to investigate could be found in the documentary of 1992 and the book of 2009.

In the same judgement, however, another judge, Lord Kerr, was more positive about the evidence provided by the Slaughter and Deception book. The least this

[55] *Mutua* (2 August 2018), §142 until §151.

[56] *Keyu & Ors v Secretary of State for Foreign & Commonwealth Affairs & Anor* [2014] EWCA Civ 312 (19 March 2014), §74.

[57] *Keyu & Ors v Secretary of State for Foreign & Commonwealth Affairs & Anor* (Rev 1) [2012] EWHC 2445 (Admin) (04 September 2012).

[58] *Keyu & Ors v Secretary of State for Foreign & Commonwealth Affairs & Anor* [2014] EWCA Civ 312 (19 March 2014).

[59] *Keyu & Ors v Secretary of State for Foreign and Commonwealth Affairs & Anor* [2015] UKSC 69 (25 November 2015).

[60] *Keyu* (25 November 2015), §105.

[61] Neuberger in *Keyu* (25 November 2015), §107.

book did, Kerr pointed out, "was to collate material from various sources which supported the appellants' case that the government's claim that no further inquiry was necessary could not be sustained."[62] The judge also argued that the question of what evidence is sufficient to revive a duty to investigate should be "approached broadly". Referring to the jurisprudence by the judges in Strasbourg, Kerr claimed that:

> Clearly, therefore, it is not necessary that the new material take the form of hard evidence. Allegations, provided they are credible and have the potential to undermine earlier findings, will suffice. A reassessment of already existing evidence, if it is plausible and enjoys the same potential, will also be sufficient.[63]

Kerr's plea for a broader approach to evidence was seconded by Lady Hale. Hale's position dissented from the majority judgement. She favoured granting the claimants' demand for a public inquiry. Much like Kerr, Hale found the question of what constituted the revelation substantially new evidence "a much more difficult issue to resolve than does Lord Neuberger."[64] According to Hale the discussion primarily revolved around the concepts 'new' and 'coming to light'. Although Hale accepted the defendant's claim that the bare bones of the allegations were known by the 1970s due to two separate investigations, she argued that these investigations each only showed "one half of the picture", that these partial pictures were only brought together in Slaughter and Deception and that this book therefore did provide new evidence. Hale furthermore argued that the 'coming to light' of new evidence should not be interpreted as the moment when such evidence became available to particular authorities but rather when it entered into the broader public domain.[65] In this sense as well, Slaughter and Deception together with some other emerging information according to Hale indeed provided sufficient new evidence to trigger a renewed duty investigate. Since Hale expressed a minority opinion, however, it did not help the claimants to win their case and the case also did not make it when it was brought before the ECtHR in May 2016.[66]

4 Conclusion

Post-colonial historic justice litigation in the UK started around the turn of the millennium, significantly increased around 2010 and today still remains very dynamic and open-ended. Over the past two decades claimants coming from many different parts

[62] *Keyu* (25 November 2015), §261.

[63] *Keyu* (25 November 2015), §265.

[64] *Keyu* (25 November 2005) §296.

[65] *Keyu* (25 November 2005), §297.

[66] The ECtHR rejected the Batang Kali case in a judgement in 2018. See *Chong and Others against the United Kingdom*—29753/16 (Inadmissible—FIRST SECTION) [2018] ECHR 802 (11 September 2018).

of the former British Empire have obtained some remarkable successes as well as suffered drawbacks.

Some of the most successful cases were those of the Nepalese Gurkha soldiers, the first batch of Mau Mau veterans and the Cypriot independence fighters. Each of these cases led to substantial compensations payments and these success stories have undoubtedly had a lasting effect on the broader rise of post-colonial historic justice. The compensated cases have demonstrated that claims can sometimes be successfully brought against a former colonial power even if they concern events that date back several decades. This had long been sheer unthinkable. By making the unthinkable thinkable, the successful cases, at the very least, have signalled to potential claimants a change in legal culture which manifests a new openness toward historic justice claims and which makes them worth pursuing—even if outcomes remain unpredictable.

The success stories should not, however, make us overestimate the openness of the British legal system toward (post-colonial) historic justice. With some notable exceptions (e.g. judges McCombe and Hale) most judges therefore remain highly sceptical toward claims that challenge ordinary time limitations and in their perception primarily involve historical or moral issues rather than legal ones. Judges generally seems well-aware of the importance of a certain responsiveness to new moral and political sensitivities concerning historical injustices in order to safeguard the societal legitimacy of the law. Yet, most judges strongly fear the spectre of an open-ended justice[67] and they frequently remind their audience of the fundamental differences between trials and public inquiries or historical research.[68]

These differences indeed remain large. Even when there exists a large academic consensus that certain historical wrongs have taken place, claimants can face great difficulties to mount a successful legal case. These difficulties partly relate to technical matters of law but they also involve evidentiary challenges.

Although civil litigation is based on a 'balance of probabilities' rather than the 'beyond reasonable doubt' of criminal law, the evidentiary demands placed on claimants in civil procedures can still be very high. I have identified six major evidentiary disputes which together can form an enormous stumbling block for historic justice cases.

With the possible exception of the scepticism about memory, these evidentiary disputes would seems rather alien to most historians. Most historians are, for example, used to working with documentary evidence and in the absence of living witnesses and they generally attribute more evidentiary value to historical context than judges do. The difference between history and law is most clearly illustrated, however, by the last two evidentiary disputes I described in this article. One obvious difference between judges and historians is that the latter generally maintain a more positive view of the relation between the cogency of evidence and the passage of time. Although few historians will of course deny that information can get lost over time,

[67] See for example Neuberger in *Keyu* (25 November 2015), §116.

[68] See for example Judge Ouseley in *Chagos Islanders* (9 October 2003) §152. And Judge Stewart in *Kimathi* (02 August 2018), §20.

they generally also believe that the passage of time can have positive epistemic effects and that historical insight can increase with temporal distance. This because new archives can turn up, more systematic research can be done, and witnesses can become more willing to speak.

The idea of 'judicial prejudice' is also alien to historians. No historian would forfeit a historical investigation for which a reasonably substantial evidentiary base is available because of the observation that an even larger evidentiary base may have existed in the past. Similarly the legal question of what type of evidence is new and weighty enough to justify reopening an investigation is relatively alien to historians for whom the slightest bit of new information already warrants new research and who often revisit the same evidence to write new and sometimes radically revised histories.

This brings me to a last question: whether the presence of (professional) historians makes a difference for (post-colonial) historic justice? Here I am cautiously optimistic. There are too few post-colonial historic justice cases to settle the question statistically. Yet, I do not think that it is a mere coincidence that some of the most successful cases involved professional historians and I do believe that the presence of historians can make a difference—especially when they are allowed to give witness statements. The difference that can be made by historians is, in my opinion, for example, apparent in the radically different dynamics that appeared in the first and the second Mau Mau case. Yet, the Mau Mau cases also provide a good illustration of an important caveat: that the influence of historians is highly dependent on the particular litigation strategy chosen by the parties and the openness of judges toward historical research and expertise.

References

Anderson, David. 2001. Mau Mau in the High Court and the 'Lost' British Empire Archives: Colonial Conspiracy or Bureaucratic Bungle? *The Journal of Imperial and Commonwealth History* 39 (5): 699–716.

Badger, Anthony. 2012. Historians, A Legacy of Suspicion and the 'Migrated Archives.' *Small Wars & Insurgencies* 23 (4–5): 799–807.

Barkan, Elazar. 2001. *The Guilt of Nations: Restitution and Negotiating Historical Injustices.* Baltimore: Johns Hopkins University Press.

BBC News. 2019. Chagos Islands Dispute: UK Obliged to End Control, Feb 25. https://www.bbc.com/news/uk-47358602. Accessed 23 Mar 2020.

Block, Neil, and Jack Holborn. 2018. Kenyan Emergency Group Litigation Comes to a Close (Kimathi and Others v Foreign and Commonwealth Office). *LexixNexis.* https://1f2ca7mxjow42e65q49871m1-wpengine.netdna-ssl.com/wp-content/uploads/2018/12/Kenyan-Emergency-Group-Litigation-comes-to-a-close-Kimathi-and-others-v-Foreign-and-Commonwealth-Office.pdf. Accessed 20 Sept 2019.

Bowcott, Owen, and Julian Borger. 2019. UK Suffers Crushing Defeat in UN Vote on Chagos Islands. *The Guardian*, May 22. https://www.theguardian.com/world/2019/may/22/uk-suffers-crushing-defeat-un-vote-chagos-islands. Accessed 23 Mar 2020.

Curthoys, Ann, Ann Genovese, and Alex Reilly. 2008. *Rights and Redemption: History, Law and Indigenous People.* Sydney: UNSW Press.

de Broux, Pierre-Olivier, and Dorothea Staes. 2018. History Watch by the European Court of Human Rights. In *The Palgrave Handbook of State-Sponsored History After 1945*, ed. Berber Bevernage and Nico Wouters, 101–119. New York: Palgrave.

Douglas, Lawrence. 2001. *The Memory of Judgment: Making Law and History in the Trials of the Holocaust*. New Haven [CT]: Yale University Press.

Elkins, Caroline. 2005. *Imperial Reckoning: The Untold Story of Britain's Gulag in Kenya.* New York: Henry Holt and Company.

Golsan, Richard. 2018. The State, the Courts, and the Lessons of History: An Overview, with Reference to Some Emblematic Cases. In *The Palgrave Handbook of State-Sponsored History After 1945*, ed. Berber Bevernage and Nico Wouters, 513–534. New York: Palgrave.

Hague, William. 2013. Statement to Parliament on Settlement of Mau Mau Claims' by the Foreign Secretary, William Hague, to Parliament on 6 June 2013. https://www.gov.uk/government/news/statement-to-parliament-on-settlement-of-mau-mau-claims. Accessed 20 Sept 2019.

Jeffery, Laura. 2006. Historical Narrative and Legal Evidence: Judging Chagossians? High Court Testimonies. *Political and Legal Anthropology Review* 29 (2): 228–253.

Koch, Julia. 2015. The Difficulty of Temporal Jurisdiction in Janowiec and Others v. Russia. *Boston College International and Comparative Law Review* 38: 43–57.

Pantelides, Poly. 2013. Kenya Decision Paves Way for EOKA Fighters. *CyprusMailOnline*, June 7. https://cyprus-mail.com/old/2013/06/07/kenya-decision-paves-way-for-eoka-fighters/. Accessed 23 Oct 2019.

Shelton, Dinah. 2003. The World of Atonement: Reparations for Historical Injustices. *Netherlands International Law Review* 50 (3): 289–325.

Smith, Helena. 2019. UK to Pay £1m to Greek Cypriots Over Claims of Human Rights Abuses. *The Guardian*, Jan 23. https://www.theguardian.com/world/2019/jan/23/britain-to-pay-group-of-greek-cypriots-1m-after-claims-of-human-rights-abuse. Accessed 10 Oct 2019.

Thompson, Janna. 2002. *Taking Responsibility for the Past: Reparation and Historical Injustice.* Cambridge: Polity Press.

Wade, Geoff. 2009. The Origins and Evolution of Enthocracy in Mayasia. *The Asia-Pacific Journal* 7 (4): 1–38.

Ward, Ian, and Norma Miraflor. 2009. *Slaughter and Deception at Batang Kali.* Singapore: Media Masters.

Wilson, Richard A. 2005. Judging History: The Historical Record of the International Criminal Tribunal for the Former Yugoslavia. *Human Rights Quarterly* 27 (3): 908–942.

Wilson, Richard A. 2016. Expert Evidence on Trial: Social Researchers in the International Criminal Courtroom. *American Ethnologist* 43 (4): 730–744.

Wootten, Hal. 2003. Conflicting Imperatives: Pursuing Truth in the Courts. In *Proof & Truth: The Humanist as Expert*, ed. Iain McCalman and Ann McGrath, 15–52. Canberra: The Australian Academy of the Humanities.

On Fact Cognition and Legal Reasoning in Song Dynasty Justice from the Perspective of Intellectual Rationality

Focusing on the Narration of "Distinguishing *Shi* from *Fei*" in Qing Ming Ji

Jingliang Chen and Xiaokang Wang

1 The Shift of Paradigm of Researching Justice in the Song Dynasty: From Whether the Judgement Was Conducted in Accordance with the Law to Whether Intellectual Rationality Was Followed

It is a long-standing and controversial academic issue in the field of legal history whether traditional Chinese civil disputes were judged in accordance with the law or not. The earlier representative negative opinions came from Max Weber, a German scholar. He believed that the traditional Chinese judicial system was based on the ethics of kinship, which pursued the justice of individual cases, and thus it belonged to "Kadi Justice" (Weber 2010), which featured arbitrariness and unruliness. This view has been developed by a Japanese law historian named Shiga Shuzo. Based on his study of civil trials in the Qing Dynasty, Shiga held that traditional Chinese justice only mediated disputes according to ethical senses, which was a kind of "didactic conciliation" (Shiga 1998a, b, c). However, American scholar Huang Zongzhi expressed opposition to Shiga's view. He stressed that mediation based on ethical senses was only the representation of Confucian ideals and official discourses rather than the actual situation of local civil litigation in the Qing Dynasty. As a matter of fact, once the litigation procedure was initiated, local officials in the Qing dynasty

J. Chen (✉)
Research Institute of Legal Culture, Zhongnan University of Economics and Law, Wuhan, China
e-mail: chjliang@163.com

X. Wang
Law School, Zhongnan University of Economics and Law, Wuhan, China
e-mail: 2550369602@qq.com

B. Zhang et al. (eds.), *A Dialogue Between Law and History*,
https://doi.org/10.1007/978-981-15-9685-8_14

"generally adjudicated cases in accordance with the law". He believed that there was a "deviation" between the "practice" and the "representation" (Huang 2014).

The issue "whether traditional civil justice was conducted in accordance with the law or not" has been the subject of much further debate among scholars on Qing Dynasty legal history, represented by Shiga Shuzo and Huang Zongzhi.[1] The reason was that their theoretical judgments actually referred to the overall characterization of traditional Chinese judicial culture, although their research object was the legal history of the Qing Dynasty, which opened up a wide academic field and also sparked more controversies. For example, He (2005, 1–3) and Gao (2006, 98–109) generally supported Shiga Shuzo's judgment, holding that the law was not respected in traditional Chinese justice, which resulted in its illogic and irrationality. However, some scholars like Zhang (2006, 67–69) and Lin (2014, 155–157), disagreed with this criticism. They insisted that traditional Chinese justice was logical and principled, although it was different from modern western justice. Also, they thought national legislation played an active role in traditional Chinese justice. Therefore, traditional Chinese justice could still be regarded as being conducted in accordance with the law, rather than being so chaotic and arbitrary that "the public officials' power was above the law".

In the process of related discussions, the study of legal history in the Song Dynasty has gradually become a new hotspot for this controversy. Most scholars responded to the question of whether traditional civil disputes were conducted in accordance with the law based on the court verdicts of the Song Dynasty, represented by *The Analects of Court Verdicts of the Song Dynasty (Qing Ming Ji)*. According to Wang (1997, 118–134), judicial officials in the Song Dynasty were guided by an "instrumentalist legal view with the main purpose of following the principle of ethics and quelling the litigation". He believed that "those legal provisions were not rules in the strict sense, but tools for controlling people", and "rules could only exist in the consciousness of officials with ethnics as the value orientation" (Wang 1998, 117–130). It can be said that that was a confirmation of Shiga Shuzo's viewpoints from the perspective of the study of legal history in the Song Dynasty.

Of course, more scholars preferred to rethink Shiga Shuzo's judgment, in order to find out the logic and orderliness of justice in the Song Dynasty, such as Haruhito Sadate, Liu Xinjun, Chen Rui, Liu Liyan, Geoffrey MacCormack and Chen Jingliang. According to Haruhito (2016, 353–383), the civil trial in the Song Dynasty was "the alternative judgment and adjudication made on the merits of two parties' claims in accordance with the law, rather than the instructional mediation on the basis of the emotive reason". Liu (2002, 1–32) believed that the emphasis should be placed on the "legal principle" based on "morality", although the trial in the Song Dynasty was not based on the principle of "supremacy of legal provisions". Centering on *The Analects of Court Verdicts of the Song Dynasty*, Chen (2011, 36–47) indicated

[1]An international academic seminar was held in Kamakura, Japan from September 21st to 23rd, 1996. The theme of the meeting was "Law, Society and Culture in Late Imperial China—Dialogue between Japanese and American Researchers". The participants were Japanese and American researchers on the legal history of the Qing Dynasty represented by Shiga Shuzo and Huang Zongzhi.

that famous judicial officials in the Song Dynasty made full use of legal methods such as deductive argumentation, analogical argumentation and value measurement during the trail; and integrity was the common characteristic between traditional Chinese legal views, judicial views and legal methodology, which "didn't seem to be backward or illogical" compared with the Western model. Liu (2012, 153–178) analyzed judgment attitudes and methods on two major issues of heir establishment and property division from 28 court verdicts recorded by five famous judicial officials in the Southern Song Dynasty, namely Cai Hang, Wu Shiqing, Fan Yingling, Hu Ying and Wu Ge, in *The Analects of Court Verdicts of the Song Dynasty*, making a conclusion that those five judicial celebrities shared remarkably similar, universal and predictable reasoning methods and evidences. Therefore, he deduced that similar civil judgments were tried in similar ways in the Southern Song Dynasty. He added that the ethical and Confucian classics used by famous judicial officials in the trials "played a role of assisting rather than violating the law" (Liu 2013, 277–328). In addition, Liu also stated that the content of "heavenly principles" in trials of the Southern Song Dynasty were similar and consistent to some extent. "Heavenly principles" mostly referred to natural instincts, natural bonds and ethical relationships between members of a family and human relations according to feudal ethics, which were mostly applicable to family disputes instead of disputes between strangers. "Heavenly principles" had not given rise to judicial uncertainty or inconsistency, whether it was to safeguard the rights and interests of victims or punish perpetrators. Geoffrey (2013, 299–358) discriminated the meaning and function of several key words such as "law", "emotion", "reason", "human feelings" and "details and reasons of a case" frequently mentioned in the trial of civil cases in *The Analects of Court Verdicts of the Song Dynasty*. He insisted that "in most cases, 'law' was the basis of judgment. There were also some cases in which 'reason' could independently form the basis of judgment, and even in certain circumstances, 'human feelings' could independently form the basis of judgment." Chen (2008, 103–116) believed that the judicial tradition in the Song Dynasty was a tradition of the statute law. Its judgment was objective and definite, and its consideration and reason were only supplementary to the judgment in accordance with the law. Therefore, justice in the Song Dynasty was not "Kadi Justice".

To sum up, researchers have gradually deepened their understanding of the judicial tradition of the Song Dynasty from their respective perspectives, and have also basically responded to those classical issues arising from the study of Qing Dynasty legal history. However, it should be admitted that there are still gaps in the arguments between the two sides on this issue, with a lack of an inclusive theoretical framework to connect those two sides at a higher level. As a matter of fact, it depends on the definition of "law" to find the answer to the question of whether ancient China could try cases in accordance with the law. Zhang Weiren said, "there must be two basic elements for the law: a proper purpose and a set of detailed principles." The latter corresponded to logicality and systematism, while the former corresponded to fairness and justice. He added, "people who mastered political authority might not make the perfect law, so the foundation of the law should not be set according to their preferences, but be laid by a set of principles recognized by the public. This set of principles was called 'heavenly principles and human feelings' in Chinese traditional culture, and in modern terms is called 'legal principle'" (Zhang 2006, 59–67). According to this definition of "law", "legal principles" also included "heavenly principles and human feelings" above the national law. In this case, the observation of national law could not be the only criterion of whether traditional civil cases were tried in accordance with the law, since judgements under the principle of "heavenly principles and human feelings" were also made in accordance with the "law". Upon further consideration, this was also the basic position of Lin Duan, Haruhito Sadate, Liu Xinjun, Chen Rui, Liu Liyan and Geoffrey MacCormack. However, if this definition of "law" was not accepted and "heavenly principles and human feelings" were not considered as the "higher law" of ancient China, the reference to "heavenly principles and human feelings" would be the destruction of judicial justice rather than rational judgment in accordance with the "law". Gao Hongjun believed that the "heavenly principle" was an "essentialist ideology" that suppressed individual rights, while "human feelings" might have been a negative factor that interfered with judicial justice (Gao 2006, 98–109). Therefore, it fundamentally denied those efforts to seek logic and principles behind Song Dynasty justice (and even the entire traditional Chinese justice).

Thus, is it possible to respond to the definition of the traditional (civil) judicial culture based on the legal history of the Song Dynasty? If it is possible, what is the research direction (Zhao 2018)?[2] The author believes that the key to pushing forward this project lies in methods and perspectives rather than empirical evidences and historical data. A careful analysis of the previous related debates shows that although those two viewpoints have distinctions, they actually share the same logical thinking, that is, drawing conclusions on three issues—"whether traditional justice emphasized logic and rationality, whether it was arbitrary and whether it was reasonable" from perspective of "whether traditional civil cases were tried in accordance with the law". The difference between them is basically limited to the definition of the "law". There is no consensus of relevant discussions due to divergences between the two sides on whether "heavenly principles and human feelings" can be regarded as "higher law" in ancient China.

[2]In view of this, Zhao Jing has made a systematic reflection in his recent article "Chinese Traditional Judicial Culture in the Song Dynasty: Rethinking Japan's Research on *Qing Ming Ji*". He collected the research results of Japanese scholars on *Qing Ming Ji* and started his research from the definition of hearing litigation. He set three research directions: deepening the understanding of legal sources, differentiating the trial style of judicial officials and reflecting on the evaluation criteria of "litigiosity". Due to the gap in academic information caused by the language barrier, Chinese scholars have seldom cited the research results of Japanese scholars on *Qing Ming Ji* for a long time. As far as this is concerned, the collection by Zhao Jing is helpful for Chinese academic circles to enhance the understanding of Japanese related achievements. However, no matter how rich and detailed the research are, it is still the core theme of the traditional judicial research in the Song Dynasty to respond to "whether traditional civil cases were tried in accordance with the law" by deepening the understanding of legal sources and exploring the nature of hearing cases. Judging from Zhao Jing's collection, Japan's research on the history of the Song Dynasty also failed to bridge the gap between the two arguments.

Apparently, the definition of "law" turns out to be the essential issue. It is worth noting that there are two questions about the definition of "law" in the study of the history of the Chinese legal system: First, what was the traditional "law" in China? Did it include "heavenly principles and human feelings"? Second, what should Chinese "law" be from the modern perspective? Can modern people accept the value connotation of "heavenly principles and human feelings" in traditional justice, and is it necessary to completely rethink this issue? Obviously, the former is a factual judgement, which is a representation of "to be", while the latter is a value judgement, which shows what "ought to be". In the study of legal history, it is not easy to give equal consideration to those two aspects of "law" at the same time, because it requires both the factual experience and the construction of philosophical theory. Most of the time, people can place emphasis on only one side. Those who held affirmative opinions on the issue of "whether traditional civil cases should be tried in accordance with the law" were basically focused on the first issue, stating that the harmony of heavenly principles, human feelings and national law was the inherent logic of traditional Chinese "law", but they lacked sufficient reflection on the second issue, let alone the effective response. On the other hand, most of the discommenders were focused on the second issue, stressing that people must think about potential defects in the value connotation of traditional justice on the basis of "heavenly principles and human feelings" under modern logic, but they were not in view of the fact that the logic of heavenly principles, human feelings and national law was consistent and harmonious with the traditional Chinese legal system. Besides, they failed to offer solutions to transform the traditional law. This embarrassing situation shows that without consensus on the definition of the Chinese word "law", it is impracticable to judge the logic of "whether traditional justice emphasized logic and rationality, whether it was arbitrary and whether it was reasonable" from perspective of "whether traditional civil cases were tried in accordance with the law".

Through these statements, the author wants to emphasize that the transformation of the problem paradigm is necessary for the academic circle in the qualitative research of traditional judicial culture. The paradigm shift means that the connotation of Chinese "legal" order should be explored from the perspective of whether traditional justice emphasized rationality instead of judging "whether traditional justice emphasized rationality and whether it was arbitrary and rational" from perspective of "whether traditional civil cases were tried in accordance with the law". "Rationality" in Chinese was translated from Western philosophical discourse. It has multiple meanings. However, what does it mean here? The author prefers the meaning of "intellectual rationality".

According to Kant's critical philosophy system, "rationality" has three meanings: first, it refers to "intellectuality" (i.e. "intellectual rationality"), also known as "pure rationality", which involves human knowledge; second, it means the ultimate "rationality", which is similar to the universal spirit, that is, the "practical rationality" involving human's moral will; third, it generally refers to human's advanced mentality, including intellectuality (knowledge), practical rationality (will) as well as the reflective judgement (emotion) (Yang and Deng 2001, 14–25). Generally speaking, "rationality" is the core of human spiritual culture, while "intellectuality" or "intellectual rationality" is one of the important components. So, what is the connotation of intellectual rationality? Philosopher Feng Qi stressed that, "we carried out logical thinking on the basis of practical experience, and knowledge was the result of logical thinking." "There are two kinds of logic considering the relationship between form and content of logical thinking": one is formal logic with abstract concepts as its core, the other is dialectical logic combined with concepts and reality, while the essence of logical thinking is "the movement of judgment and reasoning" (Feng 2016). Feng (2016) added that "scientific knowledge" is the result of "rational thinking" which is featured with "universal validity". The "logical thinking" and "rational thinking" mentioned by Feng Qi refers to "intellectual rationality". It can be seen that the "knowledge rationality" has two major characteristics: it forms concepts then makes judgements and applies reasoning strategies through formal logic or dialectical logic, while it pursues knowledge with universal validity in the results.

According to philosopher Yang Guorong, in the context of Western philosophy, the realization of "intellectual thinking" provides "the premise to grasp the essence of things and to realize the rational concreteness" (Yang 1998, 39–48). "Intellectual thinking" means intellectual rationality, referring to "seeking the truth"; "rationality" is practical rationality, which is associated with "pursuing for the virtue". Intellectuality is the prerequisite of rationality. In other words, the construction of knowledge-based systems, logical reasoning and rational persuasion are the premise of explaining purposiveness and acceptability (desirability) of something in value. That is to say, in the context of western philosophy, "intellectual rationality" is the basic standard for examining the purposiveness and acceptability of things. In fact, the "rule of law" or "trial in accordance with the law" is justified in this cultural atmosphere in the West: in judicial activities, the law connects "to be" (case) and "ought to be" (judgment). That is to say, it connects the truth with virtue. Only by intellectual reasoning and persuasion can people outline a universally effective cognitive and behavioral pattern rather than a wantonly chaotic one, and can judicial activities be improved from seeking the truth to pursuing goodness. In judicial activities, the universal effectiveness of knowledge should be reflected in the stability and predictability of cognitive and behavioral patterns.

Nowadays, it is inevitable to consult and use Western discourses when people of Chinese legal culture want to promote heterogeneous civilization on the world stage, since the Western culture is strong and powerful in the world. This paper studies fact cognition and legal reasoning in the justice of the Song Dynasty from the perspective of "intellectual rationality" in the Western culture, and explores the issue of whether traditional justice emphasized logic and rationality, which is helpful to redefine the connotation of the order of Chinese "law". Specifically, some issues are discussed in this paper. First, did traditional Chinese justice stress logic and rationality? Second, how did it stress logic and rationality? Third, how were factual cognition and legal reasoning accomplished? Besides, this paper does not make an abstract assertion of the existence or absence of western-style "intellectual rationality" in traditional Chinese justice, but takes "intellectual rationality" as a theoretical frame of reference, thus to analyze whether there were stable and predictable logical reasoning or rational persuasion factors in traditional Chinese justice.

2 "Distinguishing Shi from Fei[3]": Pursuit of Truth and Goodness in Judicial Verdicts in the Song Dynasty

Based on the cases in *The Analects of Court Verdicts of the Song Dynasty*, this paper discusses the judicial tradition in the Song Dynasty. It is necessary to choose an entry point that can reflect the theoretical concern, since intellectual rationality has been taken as the perspective of investigation. The entry point chosen by the author is the narrative of "distinguishing *shi* from *fei*" in *Qing Ming Ji*. According to statistics compiled by the author, the words "*shi*" and "*fei*" appear 33 times in 27 pieces of verdicts in *Qing Ming Ji*, and they are often accompanied by the word "distinguish" (or "discriminate"). The author sorts out the verdicts and learns that some narratives of "distinguishing *shi* from *fei*" focus on the following aspects. First, there is the emphasis on evidence identification and facts cognition, such as "the judge must ascertain the transaction facts on the basis of the contract with the official seal, and distinguish *shi* from *fei* of the *didang*[4] relationship between the two parties" (Wu 1987c, 169). It required finding out the facts of the case and discriminating whether there was the "*didang*" relationship between two parties. Second, there is the emphasis on legal reasoning, value judgment or the pursuit of fairness and justice, such as "when hearing a case, the judge should distinguish *shi* from *fei* in accordance with the law instead of human feelings" (Zhang 1987, 215). In this situation, it refers to distinguishing who is right and who is wrong. Third, there is equal emphasis on the former two demands, for example, "the *shi* and *fei* of the civil lawsuit yesterday should be distinguished" (Zhen 1987a, 15), which means to find out the fact of the case, to make a value judgement and to pursue fairness and justice. Details are shown in the following table (see Table 1).

According to the above table, the words "*shi*" and "*fei*" were used in 33 pieces of court verdicts in *Qing Ming Ji*. In three cases, "*shi*" and "*fei*" focus on finding out facts of the case; in seven cases, they are used to make a value judgment and to pursue fairness and justice; while in 23 cases, they have all three demands for finding out the facts of the case, making a value judgment and pursuing fairness and justice. The above statistics show that there is a narrative of "distinguishing *shi* from *fei*" in the judicial verdicts of the Song Dynasty recorded in *Qing Ming Ji*. It tends to ascertain

[3]"*Shi*" and "*fei*" are Chinese characters. In Chinese, "*shi*" can not only express affirmation of fact, but also positive recognition in value and norm, namely "justice"; correspondingly, "*fei*" can not only indicate denial of fact, but also negative evaluation in value and norm, that is, "injustice". As a result, "*shi*" and "*fei*" have both meanings in the aspect of fact, namely "yes" and "no", and meanings in the aspects of value and norm, namely "justice" and "injustice".

[4]*Didang*, a particular transaction form in the Song Dynasty, referred to an informal pawn in the folk. There was a significant difference between "*didang*" and "pawn", and the distinction between "*didang*" and "pawn" was the core of the fact cognition in this case (see details below).

Table 1 The statistics of "*Shi*" and "*Fei*" in *Qing Ming Ji*

No.	"*Shi*" and "*Fei*" and their meanings in *Qing Ming Ji* (Each of the following cases has three sub-items: A. The source text; B. The meaning of "*shi*" and "*fei*" in the context; C. The related evidence.)	
1	A	(1) The judge should be of justice and fairness. According to historical materials, justice and fairness generate perceptiveness. Once the selfish motive is produced, *shi* and *fei* would be reversed. In this condition, it is impossible to make the judgement in accordance with the law (2) Both prefectures and counties are in the same executive branches, and officials at different levels all work in the same system. If the superior is arrogant and does not share messages with the subordinate, and the subordinate is not reporting to the superior, how can problems of governments and people be solved, with the blocking of information channels and no awareness of *shi* and *fei*? (Zhen 1987b, 2)
	B	"*Shi* and *fei*" in the first example focuses on the value judgement and the pursuit of justice and fairness: "*shi* and *fei*" refers to the standard of goodness and evilness In the second example, "*shi* and *fei*" stresses the importance of finding out the facts of a case: "*shi* and *fei*" means the situation of governments and people, as well as "neglected deficiencies of the administrative activities and people's sufferings"
	C	This court verdict is to exhort the official colleagues and the subordinates to follow administrative and judicial principles. The issue of evidence construction is not involved
2	A	(3) When officials deal with the public affairs, he should make the judgement of *shi* and *fei* based on the generally acknowledged truth and judge the extent of crime in accordance with the law. The official cannot violate the generally acknowledged truth at his own will, and cannot bend the law for the benefit of his relatives or friends (4) As a criterion of distinguishing *shi* from *fei*, the heavenly principle cannot be changed. As a standard of deciding cases, the national law cannot be broken. The reversing of *shi* and *fei* goes against the heavenly principle, and the improper punishment is contrary to the national law (Zhen 1987c, 6)
	B	"*Shi* and *fei*" in the third and fourth examples are to make value judgements and pursue justice and fairness. "*Shi* and *fei*" refer to the evaluation criterion of goodness and evilness, which is equivalent to "the principle", "acknowledged truth", "public law", "heavenly principle" and "national law"
	C	It does not involve the issue of evidence construction
3	A	(5) The *shi* and *fei* of the civil lawsuit yesterday should be distinguished. One who commits a crime should be imprisoned in accordance with the law (Zhen 1987a, 15)

(continued)

Table 1 (continued)

No.	"*Shi*" and "*Fei*" and their meanings in *Qing Ming Ji* (Each of the following cases has three sub-items: A. The source text; B. The meaning of "*shi*" and "*fei*" in the context; C. The related evidence.)	
	B	In the fifth example, "*shi* and *fei*" refers to finding out facts of cases, making value judgements, and pursuing justice and fairness. "*Shi* and *fei*" also has the meaning of rightness and falseness of a case or reason
	C	It does not involve the issue of evidence construction
4	A	(6) However, Li Keyi and Li Kegang engaged in a lawsuit at the government office. Now they are waiting for the judicial official to judge their *shi* and *fei* as well as rationality and irrationality (Zhang 1987, 45)
	B	In the sixth case, "*shi* and *fei*" has the meanings of finding out the facts, making a value judgement, and pursuing justice and fairness: whether Li Keyi pretended to be Li Shaoqing's direct descendant, and should he be punished
	C	The original copy of Li Shaoqing's certificate of honor awarded by the emperor and his epitaph; the examination of whether Liu Qi was beaten "to bleeding, and whether the scars still exist"
5	A	(7) They reported to the Department of State Affairs of the central government, and asked for the approvement and authorization. People almost know the *shi* and *fei*, and officials are aware of what people are exhorting (Wu 1987e, 60)
	B	In the seventh example, "*shi* and *fei*" has the meanings of finding out the fact, making a value judgement, and pursuing justice and fairness: whether Huang Lu, the magistrate of a county, committed the crime of corruption; whether Deng Xun, an official of a county, and other people lodged a false accusation against Huang Lu; whether Deng Xun would be punished
	C	The testimony of Deng Xun
6	A	(8) Xiao and Zhang went to court for the farmland. Although the official did not clarify the *shi* and *fei*, he settled the lawsuit in accordance with human feelings. For hiding the facts, he confiscated their money, and turned back the farmland to the owner. Why did Zhang refuse to be judged in the court, but gave the land to the educational official immediately? There must be a reason (9) The educational official accepted the land privately without learning about *shi* and *fei*, while the transport official questioned the educational official and asked if he should refuse or accept the land, and if he was worried about the result (Fang 1987, 93–94)

(continued)

Table 1 (continued)

No.	"*Shi*" and "*Fei*" and their meanings in *Qing Ming Ji* (Each of the following cases has three sub-items: A. The source text; B. The meaning of "*shi*" and "*fei*" in the context; C. The related evidence.)	
	B	In the eighth example, "*shi* and *fei*" has demands for finding out the facts, making a value judgement, and pursuing justice and fairness: Does the disputed farmland belong to Xiao or Zhang? Who is right? In the ninth example, "*shi* and *fei*" has the meanings of finding out the facts, making a value judgement, and pursuing justice and fairness: Does the disputed farmland belong to Xiao or Zhang? Is it legitimate for the educational official to accept the farmland given by Zhang?
	C	The official document issued by the local educational bureau
7	A	(10) Knowing this affair indirectly, the secretary agency recorded it yesterday. As for the adjudication, it confused the truth and falseness as well as *shi* and *fei*; why did the secretary agency not explain it in detail? (Jian 1987, 146–147)
	B	In the tenth example, "*shi* and *fei*" has demands for finding out the facts, making a value judgement, and pursuing justice and fairness: Was there a pawn relationship of land property between Jia Mianzhong and Jia Wenhu? Was it the truth that Jia Mianzhong allocated the land to Yan? Should Jia Xuan be recognized as the heir? Whose argument is right between Jia Mianzhong and Jia Wenhu?
	C	The testament and pawn contract held by Jia Wenhu, and the written document of adopting Jia Xuan as the heir for succession (the written document of household alteration issued by the government)
8	A	(11) The lawsuit of Yu Xingfu and Fu Sanqi for the boundary of a mountain was settled yesterday, but Xingfu asked his younger brother, Dingguo, to collude with the village head, giving false testimony that Fu Sanqi overstepped the boundary, to disturb *shi* and *fei* (Liu 1987a, 157)
	B	In the eleventh example, "*shi* and *fei*" has demands for finding out the facts, making a value judgement, and pursuing justice and fairness: Is the boundary of Yu Xingfu's forests and Fu Sanqi's farmland clear? Did Fu Sanqi overstep the boundary before the lawsuit? Is the mountain occupied by Yu Xingfu valid? Between Yu Xingfu and Fu Sanqi, who is right?
	C	Documents (with the office seal) held by Yu Xingfu, original documents held by Liu Decheng; the vice-magistrate investigated the boundary between the forest and farmland of these two people on the spot; it was found that Fu Sanqi bought the farmland from Liu Basi, and Fu Sanqi was managing the land property now
9	A	(12) Title: Collateral Evidences Should be Considered when Both Parties Hold Different Views of *shi* and *fei* (Zhang 1987, 160)

(continued)

Table 1 (continued)

No.	"*Shi*" and "*Fei*" and their meanings in *Qing Ming Ji* (Each of the following cases has three sub-items: A. The source text; B. The meaning of "*shi*" and "*fei*" in the context; C. The related evidence.)	
	B	In the twelfth example, "*shi* and *fei*" has the meanings of finding out the facts, making a value judgement, and pursuing justice and fairness: whether there has been a contract made in the second year of Jiading (in A.D. 1209); whether the content of the contract is true; and whether the Songjiayuan Mountain was the pawn in the contract; between Ceng Zihui and Fan Seng, who is right?
	C	The contract in which Fan Chong bought the mountain from Yang Sanliu in the first year of Shaoxi (A.D. 1190), the records that Fan Chengzhi, Fan Yuanzhi and Fan Seng divided up family properties and lived apart in the third year of Kaixi (A.D. 1207), the contract in which Zeng Daji bought the Huangzhi garden and the Songjiayuan Mountain from Huang, Fan Ba and Fan Seng as well as the contract in which Magistrate Zeng bought the Songjiayuan Mountain from Song Wu in the first year of Baoqing (A.D. 1225)
10	A	(13) The judgement of trade and business should be based on the contract with office seal. The judicial official must distinguish *shi* from *fei* of the *didang* relationship (Wu 1987c, 169)
	B	In the thirteenth example, "*shi* and *fei*" stresses finding out the facts of a case: whether the trade relationship of Luojiawu Mountain between Chen Siyou and He Taiying was "*didang*" or "selling-off"
	C	The contract in which Chen Siyou bought Luojiawu Mountain and the former contract with office seal in the second year of Baoqing (A.D. 1224), the contract in which He Taiying bought the Luojiawu Mountain from Chen Siyou in the second year of Shaoding (A.D. 1229)
11	A	(14) The dates of contracts are overlapping. Therefore, it is obvious that *shi* and *fei* need to be clarified (Zhang 1987, 181)
	B	In the fourteenth case, "*shi* and *fei*" has demands for finding out the facts, making a value judgement and pursuing justice and fairness: Sun Dounan sold each of his two gardens to two persons. What was the time order of these four deals, and which two deals were valid?
	C	The contract in which Sun Tui bought a piece of garden land from Sun Dounan in the fourth year of Shaoding (A.D. 1231), the contract in which Sun Lan bought the same piece of garden land from Sun Dounan in the sixth year of Shaoding (A.D. 1233), the contract in which Sun Lan bought two pieces of garden fields and three huts from Sun Dounan in the fifth year of Shaoding (A.D. 1232), the contract in which Sun Tui bought two pieces of garden fields and three huts from Sun Dounan in the sixth year of Shaoding (A.D. 1233); the confession of Sun Yanlie and Wang

(continued)

Table 1 (continued)

No.	"*Shi*" and "*Fei*" and their meanings in *Qing Ming Ji* (Each of the following cases has three sub-items: A. The source text; B. The meaning of "*shi*" and "*fei*" in the context; C. The related evidence.)	
12	A	(15) It is better to resolve the dispute by conciliation. If there must be a lawsuit, witnesses of the two parties must appear in court. In the dispute over the landed property, the critical point of distinguishing *shi* from *fei* lies in investigating the fact that the landed property belongs to whom, instead of considering which approach between conciliation and lawsuit should be chosen (Ye 1987b, 182)
	B	In the fifteenth example, "*shi* and *fei*" has meanings of finding out facts, making a value judgement, and pursuing justice and fairness: whether the property has been redeemed or not; whether it has been sold off if it has not been redeemed; who is right between Wu Wusan (Wu Fu) and Chen Shui Yuan
	C	The original records provided by Wu Wusan (Wu Fu), which mark the boundary line of the farmland, the ratification which proves the redemption of the farmland, Chen Shuiyuan's contract with the office seal which was delivered by Wu Yanlin, the pawn contract of hire made by Wu Yaxiu and Chen Shuiyuan's father Chen Xieyuan, the later contract of sale made by four brothers (Wu Chaoxing, Wu Duzheng, Wu Fu, Wu Gui) and Chen Xieyuan, the lease contract made by Wu Chaoxing, Wu Duzheng, Wu Fu, and Wu Gui
13	A	(16) Although *shi* and *fei* have not been distinguished, it seems that they are insatiable for the whole property and would be satisfied by 2 mu of the land, but they cannot bear to give up the land, therefore, the litigation would not end (Wu 1987a, 183–184)
	B	In the sixteenth example, "*shi* and *fei*" has demands for finding out the facts, making a value judgement, and pursuing justice and fairness: Who has the ownership of the land of over 6 mu sold by Hua Gang, Hua Wei and their sons Hua Weide and Hua Weizhong? Is the land the undivided heritage of Hua Yong or the heritage allocated to Hua Gang and Hua Wei? Between Hua Dachen and Hua Weide and Hua Weizhong, which party is right?
	C	Ten contracts in which Chen Shunchen bought land properties from Hua Gang, Hua Wei, Hua Weide and Hua Weizhong from the second year of Shaoding (A.D. 1229) to the third year of Jiaxi (A.D. 1239), documents recording the details how Hua Yong's four sons divided the properties in the second year of Kaixi (A.D. 1206), documents recording how Hua Gang, Hua Dacheng and his brothers divided the properties in the years of Jiading (A.D. 1208–A.D. 1224)
14	A	(17) Although owing a contract of sale signed by Zhang Xunzheng, Zhang Chengdao has never been managing the property, so he believes that he can win the ownership of the property, since it was he rather than others who has the contract of sale. Only with three transfer deeds from Zhang Mo and other people, Zhong Chengxin has managed the property for 28 years without the contract of sale, thus he insists that the property belongs to himself. The two parties hold different opinions, and the *shi* and *fei* cannot be judged (Ye 1987a, 191)

(continued)

Table 1 (continued)

No.	"*Shi*" and "*Fei*" and their meanings in *Qing Ming Ji* (Each of the following cases has three sub-items: A. The source text; B. The meaning of "*shi*" and "*fei*" in the context; C. The related evidence.)	
	B	In the seventeenth example, "*shi* and *fei*" has demands for finding out the facts, making a value judgement, and pursuing justice and fairness: Who has ownership of the three houses, Zhang Chengdao or Zhong Chengxin? Whose argument is right?
	C	The contract of sale provided by Zhang Chengdao, which bears the names of Zhang Xun and Zhang Chengdao, the transfer deeds provided by Zhong Chengxin, which bears the name of Zhangmo and others, the rent books, records of leasing and service principles as evidences of managing the three houses from Zhang Chengdao; The lessees all claim that they rented the houses from Zhong Chengxin
15	A	(18) The official nowadays judges the *shi* and *fei* of the affair first, then investigates the authenticity of the will (19) They want to discount the property in accordance with the contract, and ask Niu Datong to manage the property in accordance with the will. The public almost can distinguish *shi* from *fei*, and make a fair judgement (Wu 1987b, 198)
	B	The eighteenth case prefers to make a value judgement and pursue justice and fairness: "*shi* and *fei*" is the criterion of good and evil deeds, that is, "the reasonability of affairs" In the nineteenth example, "*shi* and *fei*" has demands for finding out the facts and pursuing justice and fairness: Does the mountain in Xiangqi Town belong to Qian Jumao? Is Qian Jumao's will held by Niu Datong fake? Whose argument is reasonable between Niu Datong and Qian Xiaoliang?
	C	The document that records details of how Qian Jumao and Qian Juhong divided properties in the second year of Jiading (A.D. 1208), Qian Jumao's will held by Niu Datong
16	A	(20) When hearing a case, the judge should distinguish *shi* from *fei* in accordance with the law instead of human feelings (21) If Youlong was adopted when he was a one-year-old baby, then he should be taken as the heir in accordance with the law. However, Wu Lin should not tamper with the will, turning "1" into "7" thus changing the identity of Youlong from a baby to an elder boy. It is clear what are the *shi* and *fei* from this action (Zhang 1987, 215–216)
	B	In the cases of No. 20 and No. 21, "*shi* and *fei*" has demands for finding out the facts, making a value judgement, and pursuing justice and fairness: whether the certificate issued by the county that Wu Youlong was taken as the heir is true. Should the government admit Wu Youlong as the heir? Whether Wu Youlong is qualified to inherit the property
	C	Two certificates issued by the government of the county in which Wu Chen adopted a child with different family name (Wu Youlong) as his son ("the certificate issued by the county")

(continued)

Table 1 (continued)

No.	"*Shi*" and "*Fei*" and their meanings in *Qing Ming Ji* (Each of the following cases has three sub-items: A. The source text; B. The meaning of "*shi*" and "*fei*" in the context; C. The related evidence.)	
17	A	(22) According to statements of two parties, the judicial official thought the administration of the heritage could be carried out by the government by collecting and sealing up the property, so as to ensure the young heir can inherit the heritage in the future. Therefore, the judicial official decided to use this method to deal with the dispute between Liang and Zheng and to judge *shi* and *fei* between them (Han 1987, 232)
	B	In the case No. 22, "*shi* and *fei*" stresses to make a value judgement and pursue justice and fairness: which arguments are right between Mrs. Liang, the principal wife or Mrs. Zheng, the concubine?
	C	The government has investigated and verified
18	A	(23) Title: Distinguish *Shi* from *Fei* (Ye 1987c, 232)
	B	In the case of No. 23, "*shi* and *fei*" has demands for finding out facts, making a value judgement, and pursuing justice and fairness: Does Dong Sanba have any evidence to prove that he is the son of Han Zhicheng, whether he should be recognized as the son of Han Zhicheng, and whether he supports Dong Sanba's claim to inherit Han Zhicheng's property
	C	The testimony of Han Shijian, Zhou Lanjie, Dong Sanba and Han Youpo; Through verification, the official learns about the lives and social relations of Han Zhicheng, Zhou Lan Jie and Dong Sanba
19	A	(24) These two people have submitted the written indictment to the government. The *shi* and *fei* are distinguished without convening them to the government office (Wang 1987, 248–249)
	B	In the case of No. 24, "*shi* and *fei*" has demands for finding out the facts, making a value judgement, and pursuing justice and fairness: Which of the two proofs that testify Yu Jili's identity as the heir is true, and should Yu Jili be recognized as the heir?
	C	The credentials of adopting a son as the heir which are held both by Governor Yu of the county ("the document issued by a county") and by the local county government ("the lawsuit document"); the written confessions of the Chief Housing Official, Yu Jigong, and Governor Yu's concubine, Liu Shier
20	A	(25) The county magistrate made the decision only considering whether the will was right or wrong and how to balance the righteousness and interests, regardless of the total quantity of the wealth and the amount of the division. However, the adopted son could inherit 3000 mu of farmland, while two daughters only got 260 mu of farmland from the 3000 mu of farmland (26) There is no need to distinguish *shi* from *fei* of the will (Fan 1987a, 291)

(continued)

Table 1 (continued)

No.	"*Shi*" and "*Fei*" and their meanings in *Qing Ming Ji* (Each of the following cases has three sub-items: A. The source text; B. The meaning of "*shi*" and "*fei*" in the context; C. The related evidence.)	
	B	In the examples of No. 25 and No. 26, "*shi* and *fei*" has demands for finding out the facts, making a value judgement, and pursuing justice and fairness: whether the will held by Zheng Xiaochun and Zheng Xiaode is true or not? Whether the distribution plan in the will is fair and righteousness?
	C	The will made by Zheng Yingchen before his death
21	A	(27) Wu Chun claimed that Wang Sheng dug and cut down trees to fill his ancestor's tomb. After that, Zhuo Qingfu said that Wu Chun and Wu Hui hit and injured Wang Sheng, discouraged Wang Sheng from holding the funeral, broke the tombstone and stopped him from burying his ancestor. Each party has described the scene of the mountain, but *shi* and *fei* cannot be distinguished (Pu 1987, 325)
	B	In the case of No. 27, "*shi* and *fei*" has demands for finding out the facts, making a value judgement, and pursuing justice and fairness: whether the contracts and other documents between two parties are true or not? Is the land in the northern part of the Daguang Mountain and the southern bank of the Fenshui River the ancestral property of Zhuo's family or bought by Wu? Between Wu Chun and Zhuo Qingfu, who is right?
	C	The contract held by Zhuo Qingfu in which Zhuo's ancestor gave the land to Wu Siwu and Wu Nianqi to bury their ancestors in the second year of Qingyuan (A.D. 1196); the contract held by Wu Chun and Wuhui in which their father, Wu Cheng, bought the mountain from Jiang Yan; the written documents dividing the property, held by Zhuo Qingfu; the map of the mountain painted by Wu Chun; the map of the mountain verified by the deputy governor, the subordinate of Governor Zhao; the testimony from the neighbors, such as Bao Zheng and Wei Qiqi. The deputy governor and a respectable judge named Pu Yang investigated the boundary line between the mountain and land on the spot, and checked and verified the authenticity of the mountain map with a compass
22	A	(28) If the official makes the judgement only based on the confessions, he can hardly get facts of *shi* and *fei* (Hu 1987d, 388)
	B	In the case of No. 28, "*shi* and *fei*" focuses on finding out the facts of whether there is a sexual relationship between Huang and her father-in-law, Li Qizong
	C	The confessions of Huang and Li Qizong; the official learned of rumors of an affair between Huang and Li Qizong through the verification

(continued)

Table 1 (continued)

No.	"*Shi*" and "*Fei*" and their meanings in *Qing Ming Ji* (Each of the following cases has three sub-items: A. The source text; B. The meaning of "*shi*" and "*fei*" in the context; C. The related evidence.)	
23	A	(29) The reason is that the governors and judicial officials sold the position of the head of government runners and developed them as their underlings. When there is one person needing to be arrested, they are anxious to go to his or her home with a flock of runners and take possession of all things regardless of any principles and *shi* and *fei*. That is the reason why Luo Run's family was suffering a lot (Hu 1987e, 438)
	B	In the case of No. 29, "*shi* and *fei*" refers to making a value judgement and pursuing justice and fairness: It means the criterion of good and evil deeds, that is, the "principle"
	C	The official verification
24	A	(30) The official would make a fair adjustment between *shi* and *fei*, reasonable or groundless, and never settle the lawsuit without any cause or reason (Hu 1987c, 506)
	B	In the case of No. 30, "*shi* and *fei*" has the meanings of finding out the facts, making a value judgement, and pursuing justice and fairness: whether Luo Bangchen and Luo Siliu took the property of Fan Rubin's family or not? Who was wrong among Luo Bangchen, Luo Siliu and Fan Rubin?
	C	The confessions of Zhong, Luo Bangchen and Luo Siliu; the relevant information of Lu Shiyi's estate and Fan Rubin's estate have been verified by the government
25	A	(31) After a careful review of the verdict, *shi* or *fei*, and reasonable or groundless deeds have been well known without omission (Hu 1987b, 527)
	B	In the case of No. 31, "*shi* and *fei*" has demands for making a value judgement and pursuing justice and fairness: what is the proper way to deal with Mr. He's relatives and neighbors who have bullied the widow?
	C	The official verification
26	A	(32) The official admires the upright and open-minded rather than the flattering and unfair. With the posted announcement nowadays, I want to let the public know his mind, make *shi*, *fei*, rightness and falseness public, and discuss it with talents and celebrities of the county. Please be aware of articles written in the announcement (Weng 1987, 551)
	B	In the case of No. 32, "*shi* and *fei*" has demands for finding out the facts and pursuing justice and fairness: Did Weng Haotang, the magistrate of the county, accept bribes? Was the act of posting an anonymous announcement justified?

(continued)

Table 1 (continued)

No.	"*Shi*" and "*Fei*" and their meanings in *Qing Ming Ji* (Each of the following cases has three sub-items: A. The source text; B. The meaning of "*shi*" and "*fei*" in the context; C. The related evidence.)	
	C	The anonymous announcement
27	A	(33) The behavior of disturbance has not been investigated or checked, but there is no opposite opinion about *shi* and *fei*. The troublemakers have been arrested into the government office, and the official has done conciliation with goodwill (Pei 1987, 555)
	B	In the case of No. 33, "*shi* and *fei*" has demands for finding out the facts and pursuing justice and fairness: whether Pei Yi has done something as Deng Si said? Whether Pei Yi's agreements held by Deng Si are true? Who is right between Deng Si and Pei Yi?
	C	The official verification

facts of the case or make a value judgment and pursue fairness and justice. As we all know, in the modern legal context, fact cognition and legal reasoning are two basic elements of judicial activities and legal methods. In modern judicial practice, the deductive method is the basic logic of judgement for judicial officials: judgements should be made based on legal norms as the premise at the macro level and factual cognition as the premise at the micro level. Similar to modern justice, justice in the Song Dynasty focused on concerns of fact cognition and legal reasoning.

Secondly, in terms of the whole reasoning structure of these judgments, it can be learned that finding out the facts was basically inseparable from making value judgments and pursuing fairness and justice. For example, in the earlier example of Luojiawu Mountain, the meaning of the phrase "must distinguish *shi* from *fei*" was to verify whether the transaction of Luojiawu Mountain between Chen Siyou and He Taiying was "*didang*" or "selling off". However, the purpose of finding out facts was to make a fair judgement, to whom the mountain should belong. Moreover, as far as the proven logic of this case, once the judicial official found the fact that the transaction was "*didang*" or "selling off", he could naturally deduce the value judgment in line with fairness and justice. The proven logic will be discussed in detail in the following sections.

Third, it is not to say that only verdicts with "*shi*" and "*fei*" place emphasis on "distinguishing *shi* from *fei*", while judgments without "*shi*" and "*fei*" do not require investigation of fact, value judgment or pursuit of fairness and justice. In fact, some studies have shown that these meanings of finding out the facts of a case (to be), carrying out value judgments and pursuing fairness and justice (ought to be) are mixed in "*shi*" and "*fei*", and this is prevalent in the verdicts of *Qing Ming Ji* (Geoffrey 2013).[5] Based on the above statement, it might be inferred that judicial judgment in the Song Dynasty has demands of facts and goodness, which are the internal motives guiding judicial officials' reasoning work in the Song Dynasty.

Given the judicial history of the Song Dynasty, this inference may not be false. First of all, the emphasis on evidence is indeed the basic principle of Song Dynasty justice, and the truth-seeking of fact cognition is the primary premise for judicial celebrities to make judgments. According to Song Ci, a famous arraignment official and forerunner of forensic medicine in the Southern Song Dynasty, "Death penalty is the most severe punishment for legal cases, so judicial officials must find out the fact of the case. Meanwhile, the top priority for finding out the facts is the examination and verification of injuries, diseases and corpses, since they are key factors to make a judgement on whether criminal suspects will be convicted or not, and whether criminal suspects will be sentenced to death or not"(Song 2016, 1).

---

[5]According to the research of British scholar Geoffrey MacCormack, "*qing*" (or "*renqing*") and "*li*" (or "*qingli*") in *Qing Ming Qi* have both descriptive function and normative function. In other words, each of the two words contains two meanings: the fact (to be) and the value judgment (ought to be). Specifically, "*qing*" sometimes refers to "fact" and sometimes refers to "feeling". "*Renqing*" can generalize "the realistic situation prevailing in the society", and more often refers to "behaviors that conform to the corresponding ethics requirements". "*Li*" is sometimes used to describe the "*daoli*" for the existence of things, and sometimes refers to "principles", "ethical principles" or "standards".

Obviously, Song Ci believed that special attention should be paid to the facts of criminal cases, especially capital cases, and that fact cognition was based on the examination and identification of evidences. Also, he regarded the examination and identification of evidences as a matter of human life and legal justice.

In fact, justice in the Song Dynasty also attached great importance to fact cognition in civil cases, which was embodied in the judicial celebrities' reflection on fact cognition activities and their emphasis on evidence. Famous judicial officials in the Song Dynasty had a profound critical reflection on cognitive activities of the fact, because they clearly knew that people's cognitive ability was limited and the cognition of fact could be in line with fact or could deviate from fact. They called the facts of a case "*shiqing*" in an example such as: "The testimonies of those two persons are quite different, and people who wrote this contract are dead and cannot bear witness here. On this occasion, it was hard for officials to make a thorough investigation of the facts from the source" (Zhang 1987, 161). On the other hand, fact cognition that was basically in line with the facts was called "*qingshi*", as in this example: "As the county magistrate, the judicial official should investigate and identify the facts and make a judgement in accordance with the law when there are troubles between two parties" (Huang 1987, 585). Judicial officials were fully aware that the difficulty in getting the "facts" was mainly due to the fact that the parties in the case were inclined to make statements of facts that were beneficial to their own parties, and thus, the parties' words might be either "true" or "false". Since it was difficult to distinguish "fact" from "falsehood", famous judicial officials in the Song Dynasty consciously scrutinized "facts" and "claims" of the two parties. As it is said in the verdict of "A Man Getting His Uncle's Land Property by a Forged Contract", "Something which looks right is wrong, and words which sound weak are strong. The investigation of testimony was beneficial for finding out the facts, thus judicial officials who are good at hearing the case would not be biased" (Jian 1987, 146–147).

Then how did famous judicial officials in the Song Dynasty discern the false from the genuine and find out facts? The answer was their emphasis on the evidence. In the process of judicial practice, judicial celebrities especially emphasized that fact cognition should be verified by "evidence". For example, there was a piece of verdict recording the following: "Jiang Wenhui, the direct descendant of Jiang Tongbao, wanted to redeem the land of Jiang Tongbao. One must show the pawn contract if one wants to redeem something. Now since there was no contract, it was difficult for this government to let him redeem the land" (Zhang 1987, 320). This case demonstrated that it was difficult to identify the pawn relationship without a contract as the factual "proof" for redemption. In another example, "Hua Yong's four sons divided up the family property and lived apart in the second year of Kaixi (A.D. 1206). Later, Hua Gang and Hua Dacheng divided up the family property again in the years of Jiading (A.D. 1208–A.D. 1224). Why was there still the undivided land after the first division of family property? Why did they not fight for the land when Hua Gang was alive 30 years ago? Why did they contend for this land rather than other undivided properties? Was there any evidence that this land had not been divided? If the undivided fields had been left by the ancestors, there would be numerous written agreements of the undivided land and the original dividing contracts which were consistent with each other. Therefore, people without the written contracts could not prove for themselves" (Wu 1987a, 184). According to Wu Ge (pseudonym, Shuzhai[6]), the judicial official, "evidence" was a must in order to prove whether the disputed land property was the undivided ancestral property or not. Therefore, it was necessary to provide documentary evidences for identifying and verifying, such as copies of agreements and contracts saved by each family. The attention to the "proof" of fact cognition reflected that famous judicial officials in the Song Dynasty attached importance to finding out facts of cases, and also showed their consciousness of ascertaining facts by evidence.

There are 17 pieces of documentary evidences like contracts, 8 pieces of testimonies of witnesses and 10 pieces of official verification records in 27 court verdicts (actually 24 court verdicts, since the first three verdicts were official admonitions) related to the narrative of "distinguishing *shi* from *fei*" in *Qing Ming Ji*, if the same kind of evidence in the same verdict is counted only once. There are 10 cases that use only documentary evidence as evidence, 3 cases that use only official verification as evidence, and only 1 case that uses only witness statements as evidence. In most cases, judicial officials used different types of evidences to make the fact cognition. Of course, it cannot be concluded that only the evidences mentioned in the verdicts were used in specific judicial activities, but people can imagine the cautious attitude of judicial celebrities in the Song Dynasty towards the fact cognition activities of the cases, based on the aforesaid evidences and their usages mentioned in those verdicts.

Secondly, the value of Song Dynasty justice was established in the pursuit of good will and justice in judgment results. Based on cognition of case facts, famous judicial officials consciously made value judgments and legal reasoning. Hu Ying (pseudonym, Shibi), a famous judicial official in the Southern Song Dynasty, once stated that "the official should investigate the fact of the property lawsuit based on contracts and written materials, and make a fair judgement of right or wrong in accordance with legal provisions" (Hu 1987a, 336). This viewpoint is quite in agreement with the judicial viewpoint nowadays that "facts are the basis, and laws are the criterion". Hu Ying's statement was of great significance. It showed that judicial officials in the Song Dynasty were fully aware of the distinction between fact cognition (the premise of legal deductive reasoning at the micro level) and legal identification (the premise of legal deductive reasoning at the macro level), which marked the epoch-making progress of China's local legal methods.

In fact, Hu Ying was not the only one who had consciousness of or made statements about distinguishing factual issues from legal issues in historical records about justice in the Song Dynasty. According to the verdict of the case of "A Dispute for the Land Property among Wu Su, Wu Rong and Wu Gui": "People all have their own *daoli*[7] for civil litigation, and the transactions should be based on the *ganzhao*. There is

[6]Wu is the family name; Ge is the given name; Shuzhai is the pseudonym. There are similar cases in contexts hereinafter.

[7]*Daoli*, also *li*, refers to some principles beyond phenomena, and also refers to the theory of moral, political and legal order. See below for details.

a criterion which distinguishes right from wrong. The one who is wrong will be punished while the one who is right will be rewarded. Thc reward or punishment would be implemented to break the plot" (Zhang 1987, 112). "*Ganzhao*" is a Chinese version of documentary evidence in Song Dynasty justice, namely, relevant deeds of the case. The verdict showed that the facts of the transaction case should be based on relevant documentary evidence, while the judge should make a fair judgement on who was right and who was wrong in accordance with "*daoli*". This was also a conscious distinction between issues of fact and issues of law in judicial activities (the "law" here is broadly defined and refers to the basis of judgment). This shows that it was the consensus of famous judicial officials in the Song Dynasty to make value judgments and to use legal reasoning based on fact cognition in order to pursue the goodness and justice of the judgment results.

Another issue is raised by the phrase "each party of the civil case should have their *daoli*". Both "legal provisions" mentioned by Hu Ying and "*daoli*" were taken as the criterion of judging whether the basis of judicial judgment or the result of judgement in the Song Dynasty was in line with standards of goodness and justice. The relationship between "legal provisions" and "*daoli*" in the legal reasoning of the Song Dynasty will be discussed in the following sections. Based on the above analysis of the narrative of "distinguishing *shi* from *fei*" in *Qing Ming Ji*, this paper can draw the following conclusions: First, judicial decisions in the Song Dynasty indeed attached importance to finding out facts and pursuing goodness, which constituted internal motives of the reasoning work of judicial officials in the Song Dynasty. Second, famous judicial officials in the Song Dynasty fully realized the distinction between fact cognition (the premise of legal deductive reasoning at the micro level) and legal identification (the premise of legal deductive reasoning at the macro level), based on which they could fully display their legal wisdom and develop legal ability. The above two points were the manifestation of rational persuasion factors in the justice of the Song Dynasty. So how did judicial officials in the Song Dynasty conduct factual cognition and legal reasoning? Further analysis of cases will be carried out to deal with this issue.

3 The Connection Between Fact and Law: Internal and External Justification Applied by Famous Judicial Officials in the Song Dynasty

Considering such statements as "investigating the facts based on documents, while making the judgement in accordance with legal provisions" and "each party of the civil lawsuit should have their own *daoli*, and the transaction should be conducted in accordance with written documents", people can see the core issues of judicial judgements in the Song Dynasty: how to verify basic facts of the case; how to choose judgment norms (law); how to make a logical and purposeful connection between the facts and the law. From the perspective of modern legal methodology, these issues involve "subsumption". "Subsumption" is the thinking process of determining the relationship between living facts and legal norms (Ruthers 2005, 295). In a broad sense, "subsumption" refers to "the inference process of attributing the fact to the constituent elements of legal rules in order to receive legal consequences". In a narrow sense, "subsumption" means "the equivalence between the specific pending case and the case definitely covered by the constituent elements of the statute law". The issue is how the famous judicial officials determined the relationship between living facts and legal norms, since judicial decisions in the Song Dynasty had the two demands of seeking facts and achieving goodness under the condition that they have fully realized the distinction between factual issues and legal issues.

This issue is not as simple as it seems. The simplest and ideal legal reasoning mode is Aristotelian syllogism. For example, the law stipulates that "the person who killed someone shall be sentenced to death" (the law, the premise at the macro level); the person killed someone (the fact, the premise at the micro level); therefore the person shall be sentenced to death (the conclusion, the judgment result). However, in judicial practice, legal reasoning cannot be so simple and clear. As a premises of modern legal deductive reasoning, the facts and the law should be recognized and required by virtue of legal wisdom and methods. As a result, a pair of concepts of legal justification theory has been created in order to connect the justification of fact and law with the ultimate legal deductive reasoning: "internal justification" and "external justification". "Internal justification" ensures that the desired judgment conclusion can be logically derived from the quoted premise, while "external certification" guarantees the correctness and reliability of the premise used for internal certification (Shu et al. 2018, 389–390). In other words, "internal justification" refers to the ultimate legal deductive reasoning, while "external justification" is the respective justification of facts and laws. As far as these are concerned, the connection between living facts and legal norms by famous judicial officials in the Song Dynasty was indeed realized through the comprehensive usage of internal justification and external justification. Therefore, the explanation of specific cases is a must.

Judging from the content of external justification, difficulties exist in the justification of the facts and the law. However, since the law has been established, it is often much more complicated to find out and justify the norms for decisions than to determine the facts. Since those famous judicial officials might encounter such problems in judicial practice in the Song Dynasty, this section will start with fact determination under established norms for decisions ("law" in a broad sense), leaving famous judicial officials' responses to the dilemma of establishing judgment standards to the next section. Various civil litigations in the Song Dynasty can be divided into the following three types based on the personal status relationship of the litigants: first, disputes between ordinary people ("ordinary people" refers to people who are not relatives or without the relationship of superior and subordinate); second, disputes between relatives; third, disputes involving scholars, government officials, rich and powerful people (Chen 2012, 1–28). The third category of cases will be discussed separately since it had a certain particularity under the background of the ancient social order and did not occupy a dominant position. This section mainly discusses the factual cognition and legal reasoning process of the first two kinds of cases.

First, a case between ordinary people is selected to be analyzed—the case of "*Didang* or Selling off" decided by Wu Ge (pseudonym, Shuzhai), which was mentioned in the preceding narrative of "distinguish *shi* from *fei*" (Wu 1987c, 168–170). The case took place in the second year of Li Zongchun's reign in the Southern Song Dynasty (A.D. 1242). Wu Ge, the presiding judicial official, was the magistrate of Lin'an at that time. It was ascertained through investigation that Chen Siyou spent 13,000 coins for the disputed Luojiawu Mountain in the second year of Baoqing (A.D. 1226), owning an original contract with office seal. Then he sold the original contract of Luojiawu Mountain to He Taiying at a price of 7000 coins and made a contract in the second year of Shaoding (A.D. 1229). "At that time, Chen Siyou had given the original contract with office seal to He Taiying, and He Taiying had paid the purchase tax. Five years later, He Taiying paid the property tax for the original contract." In the second year of Chunyou (A.D. 1242), Chen Siyou filed a lawsuit in the county government, insisting that the relationship between He Taiying and himself was "*didang*" instead of "selling off", so he intended to redeem the contract of Luojiawu Mountain from He Taiying. During the first trial, the magistrate of the county thought that "the transaction of *didang* was popular" in the local area. Moreover, it was illogical that Chen Siyou would buy Luojiawu Mountain for 13,000 coins in the second year of Baoqing (A.D. 1226) and sell it at the price of just 7000 coins in the second year of Shaoding (A.D. 1229). Thus, he suspected that the transaction between Chen Siyou and He Taiying was "*didang*". Therefore, "he asked He Taiying to return the pawnage". However, "He Taiying arrested the judgement and insisted that the county government made a wrong decision", then he appealed to a higher government. To sum up, the focus of this dispute lay in whether the transaction of the original contract of Luojiawu Mountain between Chen Siyou and He Taiying was a "*didang*" transaction or not, and whether Chen Siyou could redeem the land.

It is of course a matter of fact cognition whether this was a "*didang*" transaction or not, but it is an institutional fact—the determination of the fact depends on the interpretation of the legal system. As a judicial official of the retrial, Wu Ge believed that there were problems in the fact determination of the case in the magistrate's first trial judgment. According to Wu Ge, "the lawsuit of the transaction should be judged based on the contract with the office seal. The official must distinguish *shi* from *fei*, and make the judgement whether the transaction between Chen Siyou and He Taiying was '*didang*' or 'selling off'." He observed: "It was prevalent that villagers made contracts with their fields and pawned their rights to the rich in an informal approach, then paid back the money and got contracts before the appointed date. Besides, there were also some people who were rich and cruel that wanted to forcibly occupy the pawnage by paying the purchase tax to pretend they had purchased the property instead of receiving the pawnage. However, in order to avoid transaction risks, people who pawned properties in the informal approach often did not give properties to the lender and the lender often dared not pay taxes at once." What was the reason? According to another verdict "*Didang* without Leaving the Property" recorded by Wu Ge: "According to the law, one who pawned the land property should leave the property. One who pawned the land property and transferred ownership must pay taxes and get the contract with the office seal on time. The pawn transaction could be regard as legal only if people abide by this law" (Wu 1987d, 167). It can be seen that, in accordance with the law, both "transaction in the formal institution" and "legal pawn transaction" should meet the conditions that people who pawned property shall leave it and the other party of the transaction shall pay the tax. It was based on this legal norm that Wu Ge deduced the fact model of such cases: "The parties of the transaction had exchanged the money and property. Since one party had left the property to the other party, while the other party had paid the tax, it could be identified clearly as a sales transaction rather than a *didang* transaction." Furthermore, he confirmed the facts of the case that "Chen Siyou gave away the land property immediately after he sold it to He Taiying and made a contract. He Taiying paid the tax after buying this property. There was no doubt that it was a legal sales transaction rather than a '*didang*' transaction."

"*Didang*" in the verdict of this case was "an informal mortgage loan in the folk". Its connotation was that the property owner mortgaged the land to the rich to borrow some money. The land owner could redeem the property before the scheduled time, or the land would be in the possession of the lenders. If it was determined that there was no *didang* transaction between the two parties, it could only be inferred that Chen Siyou could not redeem the land in accordance with the rule of *didang*. In fact, selling-off and pawn were two kinds of land transactions in the Song Dynasty. According to the institution, the property could not be redeemed once it was sold off, while the pawn transaction just transferred the land usage right and preserved the ownership.[8] Then, was the Luojiawu Mountain transaction between Chen Siyou and He Taiying "selling off" or "*didang*"? Could Chen Siyou redeem the land in accordance with the rules of *didang*? Aiming at these questions, Wu Ge carried out a further analysis.

According to Wu Ge: "People doubted that Chen Siyou bought the land at a high price but sold it at a low price. However, they did not notice that the land price fluctuates in different years. In addition, in accordance with the law, once the pawn transaction has been completed for three years, the unredeemed property would be in the lender's possession, and the redemption would not be accepted. How could Chen Siyou redeem the land property when he sold it off and made a sale contract ten years ago?" Aiming at the statement of Chen Siyou that he spent 13,000 coins for the land in the second year of Baoqing (A.D. 1226) and sold it to He Taiying at the price of 7000 coins in the second year of Shaoding (A.D. 1226), Wu Ge made two kinds of speculations about the price difference. First, "the land price fluctuates over time", which meant that the selling-off transaction between Chen Siyou and He Taiying was completed in accordance with the law, and the price difference was the normal price fluctuation over time. On the premise of the completed sale transaction, Chen Siyou certainly could not redeem the land. Second, Wu Ge proposed another hypothesis

[8]The pawn transaction was different from the *didang* transaction in form although the real estate was allowed to be redeemed before the date required for the pawn transaction. The formal pawn transaction of farmland and houses must meet the requirements of leaving the property and paying taxes, while the *didang* was only a non-formal loan mortgage between private sectors. One of the starting points of the mortgage was tax avoidance, thus the mortgagor would not leave the property immediately. Therefore, the *didang* was an informal form of the pawn.

that if the transaction between Chen Siyou and He Taiying was a pawn transaction rather than a sale transaction, He Taiying took possession of the mountain of Chen Siyou as the lender, to let the borrower repay the loan by converting the real estate of the land, which was "converting the pawnage to repay the loan".[9] In this case, even if Chen Siyou and He Taiying made a pledge contract, Chen Siyou's redemption appeal should not be accepted in accordance with the law that "once the pawn transaction has been completed for three years, the unredeemed property would be in the lender's possession, and the redemption would not be accepted", because over ten years had passed when the lawsuit was initiated in the second year of Chunyou (A.D. 1242).

Summing up the verdict of this case, Wu Ge indeed used both internal and external justification to connect living facts and legal norms. This kind of legal reasoning included two stages: First, redemption was acceptable if it was a pawn transaction (this judgment standard was a commonly accepted transaction custom). It could be taken as the legal deductive reasoning framework based on internal justification to discuss whether there was the case fact as a corresponding premise at the micro level—whether it was justified to conduct the external justification. In this process, the judicial official Wu Ge reconstructed the facts of the case by explaining the legal norms, proving that there was no pawn relationship between the two parties, and that the two parties had "a legal transaction" in the form of "selling-off or pawning". It followed that Chen Siyou could not redeem the land according to the rule of the pawn. Second, in the case of "legal transaction", redemption was only acceptable if the property was transacted by the pawn transaction (redemption was unacceptable in the case of selling off, but acceptable in the case of pawning, which were generally accepted transaction customs). In addition, legal proceedings of redemption shall be instituted within three years after the transaction in accordance with the law, which was the legal deductive reasoning framework established by internal justification to discuss whether there was the case fact as a corresponding premise at a micro level—whether to institute legal proceedings within three years. In this process, Wu Ge reconstructed the living facts of the case once again by interpreting the legal norms, proving that there was no fact as the corresponding premise at the micro level, and Chen Siyou could not redeem the land according to the rules of the pawn. Therefore, the official finally decided that "He Taiying bought the contract with the official seal and took charge of the property in the second year of Shaoding. Chen Siyou sued He Taiying although he knew the facts, so he committed a crime of fraud." In other words, the judicial official rejected Chen Siyou's request of redeeming the land.

Secondly, a case of a dispute of an adoption of an heir and family property division between relatives will be analyzed in this part, namely, the case of "A Boy was Adopted as the Heir in Accordance with a Contract" (Zhang 1987, 215–217). This case also took place in the Southern Song Dynasty, but the exact time is unknown. The judicial official was "Mr. Justice". In this case, according to the genealogical records, Wu Chen had four daughters and one son. The eldest was called Mrs. 24 and married to Shi Gao; the second girl, Mrs. 25, was married to Hu Yan; the third

[9]"Converting the pawnage to repay the loan" was a term in the financial field in the Song Dynasty.

child was Wu Youlong, Mr. 26, who was adopted from another family; the fourth child was Ms. 27, and some said she had married Xu Shi, while some said she was sold to others as an adopted daughter; and the fifth child was Miss 28, who had not been married. Wu Youlong was adopted by Wu Chen before his death. Wu Chen and Wu Youlong were both dead at that time. Tu and Wu Deng, Wu Youlong's wife and his son, were in charge of the family property of Wu.

Mrs. 24 filed a lawsuit, claiming that Wu Youlong was only the adopted son from another family, rather than the established heir for succession of family properties, and thus the family of Wu had no male offspring as the heir for succession of family properties. According to Hu Yan, the husband of Mrs. 25, there was no male offspring in Wu's family, and the fortune of this family was mostly increased by the management of Mrs. 24's husband and himself with Wu's family's properties as the capital. Therefore, the fortune of Wu's family should be divided equally by the four daughters. Tu and Wu Deng did not approve of his view. They insisted that Wu Youlong was indeed the adopted son as the heir for succession, and the family of Wu had male offspring. It could be seen that the focus of the dispute in this case lay in whether Wu Youlong was the adopted son as the heir; whether Wu Chen had a male descendant; whether Wu Youlong or the four daughters of Wu Chen were eligible to inherit the property of Wu Chen.

It was a matter of fact cognition and also of fact at an institution level whether Wu Youlong was the adopted son as the heir. In other words, what exactly was an "heir" depended on the provisions of the law. In response, the judicial official, who signed "Mr. Justice", quoted legal provisions and made the following analysis: "According to the law, a child who was adopted under the age of three by another family with a different family name can use the family name of the adoptive father and be registered in the household of the adoptive family. Since then, the adopted child enjoys the same juridical status as a natural son. The judicial official should make a fair judgement in accordance with the law after investigation of the facts, even though the adopted child has not changed his household registration with the government." The law applicable here was actually the "adopted son" article of the *General Penal Law in the Song Dynasty: Law of Household Register and Marriage*: "Although the abandoned child under three years old has a different family name, he can take the family name of the adoptive family." It was on the basis of the above legal norms that the judicial officer deduced the essential fact model of such cases that the adopted child can be recognized as the heir for succession of the family line only if he was adopted when he was less than three years old.

As to whether Wu Youlong had adopted a son as the heir, the judicial official conducted various investigations and obtained evidences, including that Wu Youlong had been in mourning for Wu Chen for three years as the son after Wu Chen's death, while the four daughters had been in mourning for Wu Chen for nine months as the daughters; Wu Youlong "has nourished Wu Chen and his wife in their old age and buried their bodies, and totally did his duty as a son"; Mrs. 24 did not file a lawsuit when Wu Chen died but Wu Youlong was alive; two "documentary evidences issued by the county" concerning Wu Chen's adoption of Wu Youlong, namely, the credentials of Wu Chen's adoption of a boy with different family name

(Wu Youlong) as the heir issued by the county government that year. From the perspective of case fact construction, only the two "documentary evidences issued by the county" recording Wu Youlong's age at the time of adoption were connected with the legal argumentation. It was found that the credentials in the hands of Tu recorded that Wu Youlong was adopted at the age of one. Wu Lin (his identity was unknown in the verdict, but he was suspected to be one of Wu Chen's brothers, since his name has the same Chinese character component as Wu Chen; what was certain was that he was on the side of Ms. 24 and Hu Yan) had a documentary evidence which recorded that Wu Youlong was adopted when he was seven years old, but the number in the document had been tampered with.

As for the contradiction between the documentary evidences of Tu and Wu Lin, the judicial official indicated: "The identity of Wu Youlong was recognized by the public law. If he was adopted at the age of seven, then the county government had no reason to issue the documentary evidence that proved Wu Youlong was adopted at the age of one. If Wu Youlong was adopted at the age of one, then his identity of the heir shall be recognized by the law. But Wu Lin should not change the "one" in the documentary evidence to "seven" and mix Wu Youlong's identity of a baby with an elder boy. We could distinguish who was right and who was wrong from the documentary evidences." That was to say, according to the law, only when the child was adopted under the age of three could his identity as the heir be recognized by the government. Tu's documentary evidence recorded clearly that Wu Youlong was a one-year-old baby when he was adopted, which was in accordance with the law. However, the words have been changed in the documentary evidence issued by the county held by Wu Lin to state that Wu Youlong was a seven-year-old boy when he was adopted, which was not in conformity with the law. It could be inferred that Wu Lin's version of the county document had been tampered with in order to create the fact cognition against Wu Youlong's family, while Tu's county document was authentic and undoubtedly true. "Although Wu Youlong was the adopted son of Wu Chen, his family name has changed to Wu once he was adopted by Wu Chen. Although Wu Chen has died, he left documentary evidence to prove Wu Youlong was the adopted son." Therefore, Wu Youlong was indeed the adopted son as the heir, and Wu's family still had male offspring. The judicial officer's reasoning process was precisely based on the understanding of legal norms to estimate the essential facts model of the case. Then he reconstructed and joined the fragments of the living facts of the case, and finally realized the verification of the case facts.

Based on the fact that Wu Youlong was indeed the heir, the judicial official made a further judgment on how to inherit the property of Wu Chen. First, the judge recognized Wu Youlong as the heir, and that he could "inherit the family property in accordance with the legal articles". The "article" here referred to the article of "Division of Property" in the *General Penal Law in the Song Dynasty: Law of Household Register and Marriage*: "[Provision] Orders for households: the farmlands, houses and other properties shall be equally divided by the sons of the dead householder. The wealth brought from the daughter-in-law's family is not included. If a son of the dead householder is dead, sons of the dead son should bear their dead father's share. If all sons of the dead householder are dead, the property should be equally divided by all grandsons of the dead householders. The unmarried son should get another share for the marriage, and the unmarried sister and daughter of the dead householder should also get a share for marriage, but the share should be half as the unmarried son. If a son of the householder is dead without leaving his own son, the son's wife and concubines should bear their husband's share. If the husband and brothers of the householder's married daughter are all dead, the married daughter should get a share as much as the son of the dead householder." According to this regulation, Wu Youlong was eligible for inheritance, and his share of property would be inherited by his son, Wu Deng. Second, it was determined that the family of Wu still had male offspring, so Wu Chen's inheritance was naturally not suitable for the law of the family without male descendants. That was: "According to another law, for the family without male descendants, all the family's property will be given to all the unmarried daughters in this family, and the married daughter who was abandoned by her husband or whose husband was dead and returned home will get a share half as the unmarried daughter." The judicial officer stressed: "Hu Yan's claim was illegal, that the property of Wu's family was earned by the second son-in-law with the property of Wu's family as the capital, so that the property should be divided by the four daughters of Wu Chen. In accordance with the law, if the son-in-law ran the business and earned more for his wife's family, the son-in-law would get three tenth of the property when there was no male descendant of the family. Now that Wu Chen has adopted a son as the heir and the adopted son also had a son, the family of Wu cannot be taken as a family without male descendants. On this occasion, how can the family be divided as the family without male descendants?" Therefore, the official dismissed the lawsuit of Mrs. 24 and Hu Yan etc. Third, the judicial official also indicated: "There is no stipulation that the married can inherit the property of her parents, but the unmarried can get a share of the heritage in accordance with the law. The unmarried sister, son and daughter or daughter who has returned home after marriage can get a share of the property for marriage. The unmarried daughter will get another share of the property which shall be less than the share for marriage." In accordance with the law, the judicial official made a decision that Mrs. 24, Mrs. 25 and their husbands had no right to inherit the property. Miss 28 would get a share of property for marriage in accordance with the law, and Wu Deng and his mother shall treat Miss 28 with due respect. The arrangement of Ms. 27's property share was pending until the Tongcheng County verified the marital status of Ms. 27.

Summing up the verdict of this case, the judicial officer also used internal justification and external justification to connect the living facts and the legal norms. For this case, the issue of whether Wu Youlong was adopted as the heir was the core of the legal reasoning. The reason was that if Wu Youlong was not the heir, there would be no male descendant in Wu's family, and the heritage of Wu Chen should be divided by both unmarried and married daughters of the householders in accordance with the category of "Property of Family Without Male Descendant" in the *General Penal Law in the Song Dynasty: Law of Household Register and Marriage* and the provisions of "Regulations for Family

Without Male Descendant in the Years of Tiansheng[10]". However, if Wu Youlong was adopted as the heir and Wu Chen still had a male descendant, thc heritage of Wu Chen would be divided in light of the verdict of this case in accordance with the provisions of "Division of Property" in the *General Penal Law in the Song Dynasty: Law of Household Register and Marriage*. In other words, the above two decisions based on two kinds of factual possibilities constitute the presupposed framework for the internal justification of this case. Then, the judicial official carried out external justification after discussing the fact whether Wu Youlong had adopted a baby as the heir, which was the premise at the micro level. It was in the process of comprehensive application of internal justification and external justification that the judicial official realized the subsumption of the living facts to legal norms and completed the ultimate legal deductive reasoning.

In fact, it was common to use the comprehensive methods of internal justification and external justification in the justice of the Song Dynasty. For the cases mentioned in the narrative of "distinguish *shi* from *fei*", the determination of the cases were the results of internal justification and external justification through the subsumption of living facts to legal norms when the legal norms had been established while the facts of the case had not been verified. For example, there was the determination of the fact whether there was an amour in the case of "Fighting for Property and Suing His Wife for an Adulterous Affair" (Zhang 1987, 181), the determination of the identity of other male descendants returning to their ancestral homes in the case of "Distinguishing *shi* from *fei*" (Ye 1987c, 239–241), and the determination of the time when Wu Fang bought the land on Jiangyan Mountain in the case of "A Dispute for the Graveyard Between the Landlord and the Lessee" (Pu 1987, 325–327).

In conclusion, it was actually a superposition of deductive reasoning methods where famous judicial officials of the Song Dynasty comprehensively used internal and external justification to link up facts with the law when the judgment norms were relatively determined but the facts of the case were yet to be proved. To be specific, firstly, there was presupposition of one (or several) internal justification framework(s) according to the judgment standard, which was the usage of the deductive reasoning itself, i.e. taking the living facts as the premise at the micro level and the judgment norms as the premise at the macro level to obtain the (possible) judgment method. Secondly, the establishment of the facts as the premise at the micro level was a further usage of deductive reasoning for external justification, namely, taking the living facts as the premise at the micro level and judgement norms as the premise at the macro level, so as to realize the subsumption of legal norms into living facts in the circular interaction between facts and norms and to obtain a result consistent with the facts of

[10]According to the category of "Property of the Family without Male Descendants" in the *General Penal Law in the Song Dynasty: Law of Household Register and Marriage*, "[Provision] orders for the funeral: For those households without male descendants, all the myrmidon, maidservant, slaves, shops, houses, and their wealth will be sold by closed relatives. Apart from the money spent on the funeral and graveyard, all the wealth will be given to the dead householder's daughters. If the dead doesn't have a daughter, the wealth will be given to the closed relatives. If the dead doesn't have any relative, the government will verify the wealth. If the dead householder made a will to deal with the heritage. The heritage will be dealt with in accordance with the will once it is verified."

the case. Finally, the case facts confirmed by external justification were nested into the internal justification framework to obtain the judgment result of the case.

The preceding classification shows that there were some stable and regular logical reasoning and rational persuasion factors in the fact identification and evidence application of judicial activities in the Song Dynasty. The famous judicial officials had made full use of logical reasoning to collect evidence and construct fact cognition through analyzing evidence, persuading the two parties to approve the case facts for making a decision which was described by the judicial official in the form of preaching and reasoning. Besides the spiritual pursuit for facts and goodness and distinguishing the factual issue from the legal issue, judicial celebrities in the Song Dynasty had developed quite mature legal methods for determining the relationship between living facts and judicial norms. It should be noted that various types of formal logic, especially deductive reasoning, were frequently used as legal methods by famous judicial officials in the Song Dynasty. The above analysis is enough to prove that it is untenable to argue that traditional Chinese justice was illogical.

4 Law and Li[11]: The Response of Famous Judicial Officials in the Song Dynasty to Difficulties in Finding and Justifying the Norms for Decision

As mentioned above, besides proving the facts as the premise at the micro level, the external justification process of specific legal reasoning also includes the search for and justification of the law as the premise at the macro level. Where should judicial officials look for the judgment standard, and what is the appropriate judgment standard? The process of solving these problems is commonly known as "finding the law", which involves the "origin of law" theory in modern jurisprudence. It is worth noting that in the context of modern legal methodology, no matter how we define "law" or "origin of law", there is always a unavoidable problem—there are often cases where (appropriate) judgment norms cannot be found in specific judicial practices. Either there is no provision in the law at all, or there are practical difficulties in the application of legal provisions. In other words, there are difficulties in finding laws, conflicts of rules or loopholes in the law. This is the dilemma of finding and justifying the norms for decision. This kind of cases can be called "hard cases". In fact, although ancient China did not establish a disciplinary method of law, and there were no terms such as "conflict of rules" or "loopholes in law", judicial celebrities in the Song Dynasty also encountered similar difficulties in justifying the norms for decision. It was in the process of dealing with the dilemma of standardizing the

[11]The Chinese character "*li*" has rich meanings. As for the verbal meaning, it refers to handling and management, which means to keep the country and society stable and in good order. As for the nominal meaning, it refers to the vein, the logic, the principle beyond the phenomenon and things and the theory of describing this principle. The word "*li*" in this article is mainly inclined to the latter.

judgment and establishing the evidence that the famous judicial officials in the Song Dynasty applied legal methods, displayed their superb legal wisdom, and at the same time showed their limitations of thinking to some extent.

Judicial officials in the Song Dynasty believed in two sayings about fact cognition and legal reasoning. One was that "one must rely on documents to inspect the actual situation; one must be in accordance with legal provisions to justify right and wrong". The other was that "the civil lawsuit shall be based on *daoli* and the transaction shall be based on written documents". That was to say, both "legal provisions" and "*daoli*" were taken as norms of the judicial judgment in the Song Dynasty, or as the standard of whether the judgment result was fair or not. In that way, was the usage of "legal provisions" and "*daoli*" arbitrary in the process of establishing judicial norms in the Song Dynasty? In this regard, the answer must be found from famous judicial officials' responses to the dilemmas of standardizing judgments on the basis of judicial cases in the Song Dynasty.

Written by Zhou Mi during the last years of the Southern Song Dynasty (A.D. 1270–A.D. 1276), *Qi Dong Ye Yu* (*The Essays of Qi Dong*) is a masterwork of essays on the historical materials of the Song Dynasty. An essay titled "A Compulsory Divorce" recorded a case that occurred in Putian, Fujian Province during the period of Song Lizong's reign (A.D. 1205–A.D. 1264), which involved the issue of finding and justifying norms for decision. Since the text is short, the original text is shown here in order to present the original information:

Mr. Yang in Putian accused his son and daughter-in-law of being unfilial. The government arrested and questioned the two defendants, only to find out that Mr. Yang has participated in the murder of his daughter-in-law's father. Mr. Yang has been in prison for a short time. Being granted amnesty by the government, he was released with a reduced sentence. However, Mr. Yang's daughter-in-law was still at Yang's home. The officials did not convict him of other crimes since the death penalty has been pardoned. The public was not familiar with the law and did not think there was anything strange about it. After that, Yang sued his son and daughter-in-law again. The trial judge, Yao Bao, who served as the judge of Xinghua Army, believed that "although there was a gap between Mr. Yang and his son-in-law, the daughter-in-law still needed to be filial to Mr. Yang, since Yang's son has not been divorced from his wife." Therefore, Yao Xi intended to declare the couple guilty. However, the deputy magistrate, Chen Zhensun (courtesy name, Boyu), held different views and claimed that "father and son have a blood relationship, while husband and wife are connected by marriage. The marriage-constructed relationship shall be cut off if one party did something wrong to the other one. According to the law, a man and his ex-wife can marry each other again if the man repudiated the wife or the couple divorced by agreement, but a man and his ex-wife are prohibited to marry each other again if they had been divorced from each other compulsorily. This rule was applicable to this case. Furthermore, there have been killings on both sides, which was the most serious condition that led to compulsory divorce. Even though Yang's crime had been pardoned at the time of the initial interrogation, Yang's daughter-in-law shall be ordered to be compulsorily divorced from her husband, though the government failed to do this. If Yang's daughter-in-law were courteous to her husband's family, she would oppose her relatives and serve her enemies. She would take the risk of being charged with being unfilial by her parents' family if she was a little unpolite to them. It was illegal if they failed to be divorced, since the compulsory divorce shall be conducted in accordance with the law. According to the law, the husband-wife relationship was not recognized by the law if the marriage was illegal, and their relationship was equal to people without relative relationship. In this case, even if the so-called daughter-in-law did something offensive, she should be considered as an ordinary person without relative relationship with Yang instead of Yang's daughter-in-law. Now the case should be dealt with in accordance with this provision, and the woman should not be arrested and imprisoned." At that time, everyone admired that the judge really understood the meaning of the law. According to records in *Essays*, some person in Shouzhou killed his wife's parents and brothers. The state official made the decision to punish the murder's wife for being related to the murder who had committed a monstrous crime. The judge who was in charge of criminal affairs retorted that "A man who hit his wife's parents could be sentenced to compulsory divorce from his wife, not to mention the man who murdered his wife's parents and brothers. The woman should not be punished for being related to the murder." This case was the same as the previous one. One could not be considered as abiding by the law if he only stuck to the law regardless of *li* (Zhou 1983, 147).

In this case, Yang took part in the incident of beating his daughter-in-law's father, resulting in the death of his daughter-in-law's father. Yang was free from punishment because of the general amnesty at that time. Later, Yang accused his son and daughter-in-law of being unfilial. According to the trial judge of the case, Yao Bao, who served as the judge of the Xinghua Army, although Yang killed his daughter-in-law's father, they still had the father-daughter relationship in law. Therefore, Yang's daughter-in-law was convicted of the crime of being unfilial in accordance with the law because she was rude to Yang. However, the deputy magistrate, Chen Zhensun, who was in charge with the retrial of the case, held that Yang's daughter-in-law shall be compulsorily divorced from his husband because Yang beat and killed his daughter-in-law's father. Since the compulsory divorce was a must, the judicial official should order them to divorce. According to the law, the amnesty could certainly exempt Yang from the crime of killing, but it could not be applied to the compulsory divorce. He stated that "it was illegal if they failed to be divorced, since the compulsory divorce shall be conducted in accordance with the law. According to the law, the husband-wife relationship was not recognized by the law if the marriage was illegal, and the relationship between Yang and the women was equal to people without relative relationship. In this case, even if the so-called daughter-in-law did something offensive, she should be considered as an ordinary person without relationship with Yang instead of Yang's daughter-in-law. Now the case should be dealt with in accordance with this provision and the woman should not be arrested and imprisoned." That was to say, the marriage was ended after the compulsory divorce, and the father-daughter relationship was also cut off, thus the woman had no relative relationship with Yang. In this case, the crime of being rude and unfilial to the father-in-law was non-infringement, and the woman should not be punished.

In this case, the judicial official was confronted with the dilemma of finding and justifying the norms for decision. Specifically, several legal provisions were applicable to the same case. Thus, there were several possibilities for cognitive construction of the facts based on different laws and regulations. Obviously, the judicial official, Yao Bao, made his decision based on the article of "unfilial" crime stipulated in the "Ten Evils" of the *General Penal Law in the Song Dynasty: General Provisions.*[12] However, the deputy magistrate, Chen Zhensun, made his decision according to the articles of "Compulsory Divorce and Divorce by Agreement" and "Illegal Marriage" in the *General Penal Law in the Song Dynasty: Law of Household Register and Marriage.*[13] In fact, the difficulty in this case was not because of the conflicts between legal provisions, but because the trial judicial official (Yao Bao) omitted a major case fact (i.e. the couple should be compulsorily divorced), while the review judge (Chen Zhensun) successfully constructed the case facts between the circular interaction of law and facts. People at that time praised Chen Zhensun for "knowing the law well", which meant that his choice of judging norms and justification were in line with the purpose of the legislation. According to the recorder of this case, Zhou Mi, the case was similar to a case recorded in *Mengxi Bitan (Dream Pool Essays). Essays* recorded that there was a man in Shouzhou who killed his wife's parents and brothers. The judicial official of the state sentenced the man's wife and children for being related to the man who had committed a monstrous crime according to the article of "Immorality".[14] The judge who was in charge of criminal

[12]According to the article of "Ten Evils" in the *General Penal Law in the Song Dynasty: General Provisions*, the seventh evil is being unfilial. The cases are as follows: Accusations and curses against grandparents and parents; leaving hometown and dividing the property before the death of grandparents and parents when one cannot serve their grandparents and parents; Removing mourning clothes and marrying or pursuing pleasure within three years of the death of grandparents and parents; Concealing the death of grandparents and parents, and refusing to hold the funeral; Pretending grandparents or parents are dead.

[13]According to the article of "Compulsory Divorce and Divorce by Agreements" in the *General Penal Law in the Song Dynasty: Law of Household Register and Marriage*, "[Explanation and Amendment]: The compulsory divorce occurs when a woman's husband beats her grandparents and parents or kills her maternal grandparents, uncles' grandparents, brothers, aunts and sisters; when one of the couple's paternal grandparents, parents, maternal grandparents, uncles' grandparents, brother, aunts, or sisters kills the other's; when the woman kills her husband's maternal grandparents, uncles' grandparents, brothers, aunts, sisters, or has an affair with the husband's father, brothers, uncles, cousins, nephews, and thus intends to kill or hurt the husband. The divorce will be compulsorily conducted even though the crime could have been pardoned". The article of "Compulsory Divorce and Divorce by Agreements" also reads: "All those who were sentenced to compulsory divorce must be divorced, and offenders will be sentenced to prison for one year. [Explanation]: Compulsory divorce should be conducted only when the judicial official makes the decision. Compulsory divorce is not necessary if there is no official decision." According to the article of "Illegal Marriage" in the *General Penal Law in the Song Dynasty: Law of Household Register and Marriage*, people who marry illegally should be divorced and correct their action in accordance with the legal provision, even though they would be exempted from punishment.

[14]"Immorality" refers to two legal provisions in the sentence of "the state official made the decision to punish the murder's wife for being related to the murder who had committed a monstrous crime". One is "immorality" in the "Ten Evils" of the *General Penal Law in the Song Dynasty*. The other is "killing three people of a family or dismembering the body" in the *General Penal Law in the*

affairs dismissed the trial and claimed that a man who hit his wife's parents should be sentenced to compulsory divorce from his wife in accordance with the law. Since the man murdered his wife's parents and brothers, he shall be compulsorily divorced from his wife in accordance with the legal article of "Compulsory Divorce". Therefore, the woman shall not be punished because the compulsory divorce had ended the marriage.[15] The common ground between these two cases lay in whether appropriate legal norms have been chosen to cut out and reconstruct the facts of the case.

The case recorder, Zhou Mi, finally indicated that, "one could not be considered as abiding by the law if he only stuck to the law regardless of *li*." This sentence is worth pondering carefully. It was undisputed that the "law" here was the legal provision, but what was the meaning of *li*? It should include two meanings: First, "*li*" referred to the moral and ethical concepts beyond specific legal provisions. Just as Chen Zhensun said, "Father and son had a blood relationship, while husband and wife were connected by marriage. The marriage-constructed relationship shall be cut off if one party did something wrong to the other one. According to the law, a man and his ex-wife could marry each other again if the man repudiated the wife or the couple divorced by agreement, but a man and his ex-wife were prohibited to marry each other again if they had been divorced from each other compulsorily. This rule was applicable to this case. Furthermore, there have been killings on both sides, which was the most serious condition that led to compulsory divorce." That is to say, according to Confucian ethics, the relationship between father and son originated from nature, while the relationship between husband and wife was made by human beings. There was no doubt that the relationship between father and son was closer than that between husband and wife. If a woman's father was killed by the woman's father-in-law and the law required the woman to honor her father-in-law, it was obviously against the common sense of ethics. Second, "*li*" referred to methods and rules of explaining the facts by the law and incorporating the facts into the law. In the Shouzhou case recorded in *Mengxi Bitan* and the Putian case contained in *Qi Dong Ye Yu*, two trial judges committed deviations in the process of selecting

---

Song Dynasty: Law on Stealing. According to the "Ten Evils" in the *General Penal Law in the Song Dynasty: General Provisions*, "The Fifth evil is immorality. Those who kill three people of a family or dismember the body will be sentenced to death, and his wife and children will be exiled to a place 2000 li away."

[15]According to records in *Dream Pool Essays*: "Recently, each judicial official of Xingzhou and Shouzhou made a false decision. The two decisions were rejected by the judge of criminal affairs. In Shouzhou, one killed his wife's father and brothers. The state official made the decision to punish the murder's wife for being related to the murder who had committed a monstrous crime. The judge of criminal affairs disagreed, saying: 'A man who hit his wife's parents could be sentenced to compulsory divorce from his wife, not to mention the man who murdered his wife's parents and brothers. The woman should not be punished for being related to the murder.' A case of theft and homicide occurred in Xingzhou. A couple died instantly and their only son died the next day. All properties of this family were assigned to the married daughter. The judge of criminal affairs disagreed, saying: "The son of the couple was still alive when the couple were dying. Therefore, the property belonged to the son. Since the daughters were married, they could inherit the property." These two officials made similar mistakes, but one of them made false decisions for living people, the other made false decisions for the dead."

and justifying judgment standards, which resulted in the omission of pivotal facts—the compulsory divorces between husband and wife. However, the reviewing judges were able to find a balance between legal norms and living facts. The two reviewing judges (the judge of criminal affairs and Chen Zhensun) corrected the misjudgments of the two trial judges (the judicial officer of the state and Yao Bao), which not only reflected the reviewing judges' familiarity with the legal content, but also showed their superb quality in legal methods. Chen Zhensun made the judgment on the fact that the relationship between Yang and his daughter-in-law was destroyed because of the compulsory divorce, and the judge of criminal affairs made the decision on the fact that the marriage relationship was cut off by the compulsory divorce. The judgements on facts and final decisions were comprehensive applications of internal and external evidence.

The binary separation and interaction of "law" and "*li*" stated by Zhou Mi here could exactly respond to the above-mentioned questions. In the process of justifying judicial norms in the Song Dynasty, the application of "legal provisions" and "*daoli*" was logical instead of being random and arbitrary. In the case of Putian, Chen Zhensun questioned and condemned the judgment of the first instance based on Confucian principles of propriety and righteousness. He made a comprehensive use of internal and external evidence to draw a conclusion by incorporating facts into the law rather than make an arbitrary judgment under the guise of relative relationship. What can be concluded is that most famous judicial officials in *Qing Ming Ji* deduced judgment results in accordance with the law in the context of relatively well-developed judgment standards, although they often condemned immoral parties according to Confucian terms such as "heavenly principles", "human feelings", "ties of friendship", "three cardinal guides and five constant virtues", "propriety and righteousness" and "social status", and Confucian classics such as *The Analects of Confucius*, *The Book of Rites*, *The Commentary of Zuo*, *The Book of Songs* and *The Commentary of Gongyang*. On the other hand, "*daoli*" was often applied to prove the legitimacy of "legal provisions" without changing the judgment results. Some sayings in the cases above were made in similar situations, such as the saying that "the lawsuit was judged after considering the reasons" in the case of "*Didang* or Selling off" (Wu 1987c, 169); the statement of "to find out *Shi* and *Fei*, and to "line with human feelings" in the case of "A Boy was Adopted as the Heir in Accordance with a Contract" (Zhang 1987, 215); the irony that "the world turned vulgar; the social status was reversed; the courtesy and righteousness were destroyed" in the case of "A Dispute for the Graveyard Between the Landlord and the Lessee" (Pu 1987, 326); and the saying of "how to prevent this kind of lawsuit in the future if the bud was not broken at the beginning" in the case of "Distinguishing *shi* from *fei*" (Ye 1987c, 241).

It must be noted that the common ground of those analyzed cases was the relatively well-developed judgement norms. To be more specific, there were two situations for the judgement standard. First, the judgment standard was relatively definite and unitary, whose emphasis was on the proper use of implicative rules, such as the cases analyzed in the second section of this article. Second, the judgment standard was not unitary, but it did not involve deep questions about the judgment norm itself. Its difficulty lay in the extensive search for and proper explanation of the judgment standard, just like the case analyzed in this section. However, in actual judicial practice, what was really challenging was the "hard cases" that even threw the judgment norms into crisis, namely, where there were no relevant legal norms or suitable legal norms. These "hard cases" were beyond the limit of time and space, challenging the judicial celebrities in the Song Dynasty. It was in these situations that the binary separation and interaction between "law" and "*li*" proposed by Zhou Mi was further applied and highlighted.

First of all, taking the case of "Daughters Should Get the Heritage" (Fan 1987a, 290–291) in the narrative of "distinguishing *shi* from *fei*" as an example, this section will analyze the justification process of a famous judicial official. The judicial official in this case was Fan Yingling (pseudonym, Xitang). According to the original biography of *History in the Song Dynasty*, Fan Yingling passed the highest imperial examination in the first year of Kaixi (in D.C. 1205). Therefore, the case should have occurred in the reign of Ningzong or Lizong (about D.C. 1194–D.C. 1264) (Tuo et al 1977, 12344). In this case, Zheng Yingchen had no biological heir but two daughters, Zheng Xiaochun and Zheng Xiaode. Zheng Yingchen had adopted one of his brother's sons as his heir for succession before his death, named Zheng Xiaoxian. Zheng Yingchen had abundant heritages, with 3000 mu of farmland and 10 warehouses. He made a will before his death, giving each daughter 130 mu of land and one warehouse. Zheng Xiaochun and Zheng Xiaode asked to divide the heritage in accordance with the will, while Zheng Xiaoxian disagreed. The dispute of "the will's *shi* and *fei*" in this case included two aspects: One was whether the will made by Zheng Yingchen was true or false, and the other was whether the contents of the will were appropriate. As a result, the judicial official of this case encountered the dilemma of justifying both the factual cognition and the judgment standard.

Fan Yingling did not spend much time on verifying the authenticity of the will. What he analyzed at first was the issue of the justification of the norms for decision. Regarding the inheritance qualifications of the two daughters, Fan Yingling held that "they deserve it even though their parents did not make a will", which meant that the two daughters were legally qualified to inherit. According to the regulations at that time, "there is no clear stipulation on whether the married daughter can get the heritage, but all those unmarried daughters are definitely qualified to inherit in accordance with the law" (Zhang 1987, 215). It can be inferred that both of the daughters were unmarried. The basis was in the article "Division of the Property" in the *General Penal Law in the Song Dynasty: Law of Household Register and Marriage*: "[Provision] Orders for households: the farmlands, houses and other properties shall be equally divided by the sons of the dead householder. The wealth brought from the daughter-in-law's family is not included. If a son of the dead householder is dead, sons of the dead son should bear their dead father's share. If all sons of the dead householder are dead, the property should be equally divided by all grandsons of the dead householders. The unmarried son should get another share for marriage, and the unmarried sister and daughter of the dead householder should also get a share for marriage, but the share should be half as the unmarried son." That was to say, each of the two daughters could legally get half of Zheng Yingchen's marriage money. However, the problem was that the above provisions on "Division of the Property" could not cover some important facts, namely: Zheng Xiaoxian was the adopted son as the heir, while Zheng Xiaochun and Zheng Xiaode were unmarried biological daughters of Zheng Yingchen. In this condition, there was the possibility that Zheng Yingchen made a will to distribute some of his heritage to two unmarried daughters.

In addition, there was an operational problem in this case. Zheng Xiaoxian "wanted to be in possession of the heritage, but he has stated nothing but mean words". Given the limited amount of information in the verdict, it is necessary to speculate on the subjective reasons why Zheng Xiaoxian denied the authenticity and rationality of the will. According to common sense, under the premise of "unmarried daughters are qualified to inherit in accordance with the law", Zheng Xiaoxian might have argued that the two sisters got too much under the will, rather than completely deny the inheritance qualifications of Zheng Xiaochun and Zheng Xiaode. The verdict did not show whether Zheng Xiaoxian had been married or not, but it could be inferred that he was also unmarried in accordance with the law. If Zheng Xiaoxian had been married and spent money on the wedding, he must stress that his two sisters got more heritage than half of his marriage money. Since there was no such claim, it can be inferred that Zheng Xiaoxian was unmarried, thus there was no comparison standard of the marriage money (Liu 2012, 153–178). Therefore, even if there was no will, it would be difficult to apply the "Division of the Property" article in this case.

In this condition, how could one deal with the dilemma of justifying the judgement standard? The judicial official, Fan Yingling, cited two kinds of norms: One kind of norms were the customary rules and judicial precedents in other places, and the other was one of the Confucian classics—*Mencius* and the discourse of "the debate on righteousness and interests". Fan Yingling indicated: "If parents did not make the will, the two daughters still deserved the heritage. If they divided the heritage in accordance with the customary rules and the precedents of equal division in other counties, the adopted son would receive half of the heritage, while the two daughters would the get the other half." According to the verdict of "The Son-in-law Should Not Get the Heritage of His Wife's Family" recorded by Liu Kezhuang (pseudonym, Houcun) in *Qing Ming Ji*: "According to the law, the daughter could get half of the son's share when they divided the heritage of their dead parents" (Liu 1987b, 277). It showed that there was indeed a rule in another county that stipulated that "the daughter could get half of the son's share". To refute the view that the will distributed too much to the daughters, Fan Yingling cited this rule to illustrate that the two daughters would get more property than that given by the will if "the heritage was divided in accordance with the customary rules and precedents". However, Fan Yingling did not take this as the reference criterion. The reason was probably that this rule still could not cover the fact that the son was adopted as the heir and two daughters (possibly) had the will made by their father, to which Fan Yingling attached great importance.

Since "the heritage would not be divided equally in accordance with the customary rules of other counties", why should the authenticity of the will be questioned? The trial judge, the county magistrate, thought that the distribution to the two daughters was too much according to the will. In response, Fan Yingling explained: "The county magistrate made the decision only considering whether the will is right or wrong and how to balance the righteousness and interests, regardless of the total quantity of the wealth and the amount of the division. However, is it reasonable that the adopted son can inherit 3000 mu of farmland, while the two daughters only get 260 mu of farmland from the 3000 mu of farmland? There is no need to argue whether the will is right or wrong. In other words, the will is obviously appropriate no matter it is real or fake." He said, "Although the two daughters were born by Zheng Yingchen, they cannot benefit from the ancestral property, while the adopted son can get all the property. How to balance the righteousness and interests? What is the right decision to deal with the property? How to divide the heritage to follow the principle of righteousness rather than pursuit of interests? If the division does not harm the fundamental interests of the adopted son, and the two daughters' acquirement does not damage the righteousness, the judge should make the decision once he sees the will." Fan Yingling quoted the classics of *Mencius* and launched a "debate on righteousness and interests". He believed that Zheng Xiaochun and Zheng Xiaode, as unmarried daughters born by Zheng Yingchen, had closer relationship with Zheng Yingchen than the adopted son, Zheng Xiaoxian. Therefore, even if there was no will (assuming the will was forged), it was not excessive or too much to distribute the property to Zheng Yingchen's two biological daughters according to the plan in the will, which on the whole corresponded to the Confucian principle of adopting a son as the heir and leaning to people with closer blood relationship.[16]

On the contrary, if the will was true, there was no doubt that the property should be divided in accordance with the will made by Zheng Yingchen. As a matter of fact, there was a stipulation in the previous section quoted from "Regulations for the Family Without Male Descendant in the Years of Tiansheng" that "if the authenticity of the will was clearly verified, the property shall be divided in accordance with the will". In this case, Zheng Yingchen had two daughters but no son. He adopted a son as the heir to avoid the situation of having no offspring, but his situation was only a line away from being without offspring. In this condition, where the two daughters had gotten a will made by their father, the article of "to carry out in accordance with the will" could be applied in this case if the judgement were made after referring to "Regulations for the Family Without Male Descendant in the Years of Tiansheng". Although the judicial official Fan Yingling did not make the statement explicitly here, his thinking and reasoning were in line with this. According to the verdict recorded by Fan Yingling in "Disposing of the Farmland Property of Household Without Offspring": "Legal provisions: for all the households without offspring, the inheritor should be appointed by the closest and most senior relative of the dead householder. If there were only unmarried daughters of the dead householder, they should get a quarter of the entire property. If there were married daughters who

[16]According to Volume II of *Mencius*: Li Lou: "Mencius said, 'You can take it, and you can refuse to take it, but taking it hurts honesty. You can give it away, while you can refuse to give it away, and giving it away hurts your interests. You can die, while you can refuse to die, and going to die hurts the courage.'" The comparison and contrast of "can do" and "can refuse to do" is to explain that whether you can do something or not depends on whether the behavior is necessary or not and whether it conforms to rites and righteousness. Fan Yingling was just demonstrating that "daughters inheriting the property" conforms to righteousness.

returned home because of divorce or death of the husband, they should get one fifth of the whole property. Those daughters shall get their share in accordance with the law" (Fan 1987b, 288). This was different from the case of "Daughters Should Get the Heritage", since the heir was appointed after the death of the householder. However, the interference in this case was in accordance with the legal provisions for households without offspring. Therefore, in the case of "Daughters Should Get the Heritage", it was possible for Fan Yingling to follow the regulation of "Regulations for the Family Without Male Descendant in the Years of Tiansheng", judging from the decision that each of the two daughters "got 130 mu of the farmland and had the management right of the land property lawfully in accordance with the will".

To sum up, there were legal loopholes in the case of "Daughters Should Get the Heritage" under the premise that legal subsumption of the living facts was ineffective, even though there were the article of "Division of the Property" in the *General Penal Law in the Song Dynasty* and the regulation of "the daughter should get half of the son's" in another county. The famous judicial official, Fan Yingling, created or analogized the rule by citing Confucian classics, rite and morality. He held that in the case where the son was adopted and there was a will for distributing properties to unmarried daughters, the will should be carried out if the distribution of the will was consistent with *daoli* and legal provisions, even though one party doubted the authenticity of the will. The process of justifying the judgment standard was a part of the external justification. According to the binary division of "law" and "*li*" put forward by Zhou Mi, "law" referred to article of "Division of the Property" in the *General Penal Law in the Song Dynasty* and the regulations of "the daughter should get half of the son's" in another county, while "*li*" referred to *Mencius* and "the debate on righteousness and interests". Based on the understanding of "law" and "*li*", the judicial official in this case dealt with the dilemma of justifying the judgement standard by adjusting and improving the current "legal provisions" according to "*daoli*", namely, the inherent concepts of justice and moral belief. This kind of work is called "continued legal development" in modern legal science (Larenz 2003, 160).

Just as legal subsumption of living facts was often inefficient, there was another difficulty in the justification of judicial norms in the justice of the Song Dynasty. The law lacked relevant provisions for such living facts, thus no legal norms could be found for decisions. There is an example in the case of "The Compulsory Divorce Is Approved Because of the Ambiguous Affair" (Hu 1987d, 388–389) mentioned in the above narrative of "distinguishing *shi* from *fei*". The judicial official in this case was Hu Ying (pseudonym, Shibi). According to the original biography of *History of the Song Dynasty*, Hu Ying passed the highest imperial examination in the fifth year of Shaoding (in A.D. 1229), and then he was appointed as an official of Pingjiang Prefecture and the supervisor of judicial adjudication in Zhejiang Province (Tuo et al 1977, 12478–12479). This case should have taken place during this period. In this case, Huang was Li Qizong's daughter-in-law. At that time, Huang and Li Qizong seem to have a "Xintai Affair" (the term comes from *The Book of Songs*, satirizing an old man who has an affair with a young lady), namely, illicit sexual relations. However, Huang's husband did not want to be divorced from Huang. According to the article of "Compulsory Divorce and Divorce by Agreement" in the *General*

Penal Law in the Song Dynasty: Law of Household Register and Marriage, "If one had sex with her husband's close relatives such as father, uncles, brothers, cousins, nephews, she might kill or harm her husband. Even though her cheating could be pardoned, the woman should be compulsorily divorced from her husband." "Those who were sentenced to compulsory divorce must carry out the order, and offenders should be sentenced to one year in prison." If Huang and Li Qizong indeed had an affair, Huang and his husband should be compulsorily divorced, and both Huang and Li Qizong should be convicted and punished. However, there was a lack of evidence in this case. According to *Provisions of the Law in Qingyuan*, it was said that "the criminals of illicit sexual relations could be affirmed if the husband caught adultery in the act" (Yang and Tian 2002, 921). Naturally, there was no such evidence link in this case, and neither Huang nor Li Qizong had confessed. In order to avoid an unjust judicial decision, Hu Ying did not want to extract confessions by means of torture. Therefore, the adultery in this case could not be verified.

The difference between this case and the case of "Daughters Should Get the Heritage" was that rules could be created or introduced by quoting *Daoli*, though the legal subsumption to the facts of life was ineffective in the latter case, while the relevant judgment standard could not be found in the former case since there was no stipulation about the ambiguous affairs of the old man and his daughter-in-law. However, under the cultural atmosphere of ancient China, which attached great importance to ethics and discipline, it was impossible for judicial officials to be indifferent to such ambiguous situations, let alone refuse to judge on the grounds that there were no regulations in the law. Confronted with the dilemma of justifying the norms for decision, Hu Ying indicated that "such occasion occurred between the old man and his daughter-in-law. It was difficult to maintain the relationship from before the lawsuit, even if there was no affair between them. If one loved his wife, but his parents did not like the daughter-in-law, the daughter-in-law should be divorced. That is what *The Book of Rites* had taught people for so many years. Since Huang must have annoyed her father-in-law, was it possible for her to stay in this family because the couple wanted to live together until old age? In this case, the court made the decision that Hang should be compulsorily divorced from her husband and remarried to another. Li Qizong would not be punished. Here, the judicial official quoted *Provisions for Married Women of The Book of Rites* as the norm for decision: "If one loves his wife, but his parents do not like the daughter-in-law, the daughter-in-law should be divorced". At the same time, the judicial official firmly believed that Li Qizong must dislike Huang after the lawsuit, and the father-daughter relationship was hard to repair. As a result, Huang was sentenced to divorce from her husband, and the criminal responsibility was exempted because of the lack of the evidence. Therefore, Hu Ying also "improved the law" by quoting principles as legal provisions, just like Fan Yingling did.

In addition to the above two situations, there were also dilemmas in the justification of norms for decisions in the Song Dynasty. Although the legal rules at that time were sufficient to cover the facts of life, ruling according to the existing legal rules (as judicial officials believed) would lead to unjust consequences. Three cases mentioned in the above narrative of "distinguishing *shi* from *fei*" will be sited as examples, such as "Abolishment of the Father-Son Relationship Because of Selfish Desire", "An Anonymous Letter" and "Collateral Evidence Should be Considered when Both Parties Hold Different Views of *shi* and *fei*". Only the normative conflicts will be analyzed due to the large number of cases.

In the case of "Abolishment of the Father-Son Relationship Because of Selfish Desire", the County Magistrate Yu was the father of Yu Ai. He adopted his relative Yu Shengfu's son, Yu Ji, as the son of Yu Ai after the death of Yu Ai and his wife. County Magistrate Yu wanted to abolish Yu Ji's adopted son identity after being incited by his concubine, Liu. According to the category of "Adopted Son (as Heir)" in the *General Penal Law in the Song Dynasty: Law of Household Register and Marriage*: "One should be sentenced to be in prison for two years if he attempted to abandon the adopted son, in the condition that the foster parents still have no biological son. [Explanation]: according to the legal provisions for households, one who has no son is allowed to adopt a relative's son as his heir. One should be sentenced to be in prison for two years if he wants to abandon the adopted son, in the condition that the foster parents still have no biological son." Wang Liugeng, the judicial official, believed that the adoption of Yu Ji, "the son of a relative of the same clan", as the heir was legal and could not be abolished. According to the law, County Magistrate Yu and Liu should have received the penalty of "being in prison for two years" for their unprovoked abandonment. However, the judicial official Wang Liugeng thought: "As Yu's concubine, Liu had given birth to a son for Magistrate Yu. Liu and Yu Ji also have a relative relationship. Even animals love their children, let alone human beings. Children could discuss the parents' fault. Yu Ji was adopted as the son of Yu Ai to enable Yu Ai to avoid being without male descendent. Yu Ji should not pursue Liu's previous fault and create conflicts with Liu" (Wang 1987, 248–249). This view was based on the Confucian principle of patriarchal clan system, holding that Yu Ji, as a humble child, could not pursue the fault of his grandfather Yu Ji and his grandmother Liu. Therefore, the penalty of "being in prison for two years" should be cancelled.

In the case of "Collateral Evidence Should be Considered when Both Parties Hold Different Views of *shi* and *fei*", Zeng Zihui initiated a lawsuit against Fan Seng, questioning the authenticity of the content of a transaction contract for mountain land. However, the doubted land transaction contract was made in the second year of Jiading (in A.D. 1209), while the tax was levied in the second year of Shaoding (in A.D. 1229). Twenty years had passed when the lawsuit was launched. The judicial official indicated: "In accordance with the law: the pawn transaction has been made for more than 20 years (the doubtful words are as below). The owner of the pawn and the lender held totally different views. Besides, none of the contract writers were alive and could be present as witness". Therefore, "it was difficult for this office to find out the truth from the root, so it was unavoidable to let the two parties verify the facts by themselves". The quoted legal provisions have been used many times in the verdicts of *Qing Ming Ji*. For example, the verdict of "A Dispute for Land Property among Wu Su, Wu Rong and Wu Gui" stated that "according to the law, the lawsuit for land property without a clear contract would not be accepted if the pawn owner or the lender was dead and the transaction had been made for 20 years" (Zhang 1987, 111). Therefore, the government should not accept the lawsuit in accordance with the law. However, according to the judicial official, if the government made no interference, the two sides would fight for the property endlessly, causing losses to both sides and disturbing the government. As a result, he cited the allusions of "The situation Between Zheng and Xi" recorded in *The Commentary of Zuo* (*Zuo Zhuan*) and "The Triumph Between Yu and Rui" recorded in *Records of the Grand Historian* (*Shi Ji*) to illustrate the disadvantages of endless struggle and advantages for early litigation, thus demonstrating the necessity of government intervention. Thus, "the two parties insisted on their points and the judicial official could only make the decision impartially" (Zhang 1987, 160–162). The final decision was made by the government after further investigation and evidence collection.

In the case of "An Anonymous Letter", someone in the county posted an anonymous letter to accuse Weng Fu (pseudonym, Haotang), the county magistrate, for accepting bribes. This anonymous letter was obtained by yamen runners and presented to Weng Fu. In the verdict, Weng Fu declared that he did not take bribes and ordered his statement to be posted together with the original anonymous letter. According to the article of "Reporting Crimes by Anonymous Letters" in the *General Penal Law in the Song Dynasty: Law of Lawsuit*: "Those who reported crimes by anonymous letters would be exiled to a place 2000 li away." Also, according to the article: "Those who lodged a false accusation against county officials would be punished by a harsher penalty". The crime of accepting bribes was stipulated in the article of "Accepting Bribes from People Under Supervision" in the *General Penal Law in the Song Dynasty: Law of Official Position System*: "The official who took bribes from people under supervision would be punished. Officials who took bribes with value equal to a foot of cloth would be punished by flogging 40 times, a bolt of cloth by flogging 80 times, eight bolts of cloth by being exiled to a place 2000 li away. Officials who were engaged in bribery events would be convicted of a lighter crime with maximum sentence of flogging 100 times. Officials who asked for bribery would be punished by doubly harsher punishment. Officials who compelled someone to commit bribery would be convicted of the crime of breaking the law." Therefore, if someone was found to falsely accuse the county magistrate of taking bribes, he or she could be exiled for up to 3000 miles according to the law. However, Weng Fu did not track down the person who posted the anonymous letter, nor did he punish him or her in accordance with the legal provisions mentioned above. He just expressed his gratitude and criticism to the anonymous letter poster based on Confucian classics. He stated: "Confucius said, I was lucky because people would know my faults. As the saying went, those who dared to criticize me were my teachers." The sentence "Confucius says, I am lucky because people will know my faults" comes from *Elaborating Theories of the Predecessors* in *The Analects of Confucius* and could be used to express gratitude to the writer of the letter for his supervision and warning. At the same time, he also added, "It was a pity that the person did not point out my fault in the court but posted an anonymous letter. I was afraid it was not an honest action that people had been promoting" (Weng 1987, 550–551).

In the above three cases, the existing legal rules were sufficient to cover the facts of life, but judicial officials believed that ruling according to the existing legal rules would lead to unjust consequences. Therefore, they quoted Confucian classics or rites to prove that bypassing the current legal provisions was in line with justice. In this sense, the practices of several famous judicial officials all belonged to the justification of judgement norms by using "principles" as "legal provisions". Moreover, they all made arguments when they gave up the application of the current law, which showed their caution. The basic reason why they made the above judgments can be summed up by saying that they give up "law" and followed "*li*" since there was a conflict between "law" and "*li*". It might be similar to conflicts between legal rules and legal principles in the legal context nowadays. However, the crux of the problem lay in the fact that there was a certain "*li*" behind any specific "legal provision", and the conflict between "law" and "*li*" was essentially the conflict between different kinds of "*li*". In other words, under such a dilemma of justification of norms for decision, the task of judicial celebrities was actually to measure the interests and values represented by different kinds of "*li*" in individual cases. Although the value reference system for measuring work at that time had a certain range of stability, it was difficult to completely exclude personal preference factors. As a result, there was also a subjective crisis in the method of justifying norms for decisions.

To be specific, the measurement in the case of "Collateral Evidence Should be Considered when Both Parties Hold Different Views of *shi* and *fei*" was conducive to the stability and restoration of the transaction order at that time. However, its negative impact was that it was likely to cause the litigators to ignore the legal article of "lawsuit of land properties without a clear contract", thus inducing the booming of civil disputes over farmland and increasing the burden of hearing lawsuits. The measurement in the case of "Abolishment of the Father-Son Relationship Because of Selfish Desire" helped the adopted son as the heir of the case to smoothly integrate into the family and to maintain the order of ethics. However, according to this logic, it was unnecessary for the legal article of "adoptive parents who have no children but abandon the adopted son". There was the same problem of the measurement in the case of "An Anonymous Letter". Although the famous judicial official showed his image of being polite and open to suggestions through his tolerant actions, it also invalidated the provisions of "Crime of Posting Anonymous Letters to Accuse People" and "Crime of Falsely Accusing a Prefectural Magistrate" in the *General Penal Law in the Song Dynasty*. It was obviously a challenge to common sense that a criminal could potentially be sentenced to exile to a palace 3000 li away, while he was only criticized without any other punishment. In a word, in these cases, the sufficiency of the argumentation was questionable although the judicial officials demonstrated the choice of "*li*" over "law". The law needed to be abolished or amended if it had problems, which was beyond the reach of judicial celebrities. However, if the judicial official replaced "law" with "*li*" to uphold the justice of individual cases, it would lead to opposition between justice and legislation, which would certainly damage the authority of the legal system. It was in this conflict between "law" and "*li*" that people saw the dilemma faced by famous judicial officials in the Song Dynasty in the process of justifying judgment norms. In fact, overcoming these problems depended on the communication and consensus reached by the judicial professional community and on the precipitation of experience and acceptance of rational reflection over many years. What's more, this dilemma is beyond the time and regions. It is far from satisfactory for people nowadays to respond to these problems. How can we criticize the ancients?

Generally speaking, in the process of finding and justifying legal standard as the premise at the macro level, famous judicial officials in the Song Dynasty dealt with various problems by distinguishing "law" from "*li*" or making connections between "law" and "*li*". They realized that in order to find an appropriate norm for decision, they should not only pay attention to "law" but also to "*li*". There are two meanings of "*li*". On the one hand, it refers to the principles of social morality and national order other than specific legal provisions. Attaching importance to "*li*" means that the result of legal reasoning cannot violate the concept of justice and the moral beliefs inherent in the political and cultural community. From the perspective of judicial objectives, the conflict between "law" and "*li*" in this context is the same as the conflict between the trial in accordance with the law and the justice of individual cases. From the perspective of the response to get out of the dilemma of justifying the judgement norms, "*li*" can be used as a resource to supplement and improve "law". It is based on this principle that certain socially recognized principles and rules (such as the transaction habits mentioned in the second section of this paper) can become the normative basis for decisions. On the other hand, "*li*" refers to the methods and rules of legal subsumption to the facts, and the application of law in explaining or justifying judgement norms. The following requirement should be achieved to attach importance to "*li*". Certain principles should be followed in the process of adjusting or developing the existing "legal provisions" on the basis of the "*daoli*". That is to comprehensively apply the internal and external evidence, and to pursue the coordination of "law" (trial in accordance with the law) and "*li*" (the justice of individual cases). This binary interaction between "law" and "*li*" shows that famous judicial officials in the Song Dynasty had "continued legal development" in judicial activities, which highlights the special position of the Song Dynasty in the development of Chinese legal methods.

5 Conclusion: Legal Methods and Intellectual Rationality in the Justice of the Song Dynasty

The analysis above shows that famous judicial officials in the Song Dynasty attached great importance to evidence. They used evidence to identify facts and made value judgments and legal reasoning based on the fact cognition. There were regular logical reasoning and rational persuasion factors in these processes. This regularity was mainly reflected in three aspects. First, they had the demands of finding truth and pursuing goodness, and they consciously distinguished factual issues from legal issues. Second, they comprehensively used internal and external evidences to connect the facts and the law. Third, they coped with the difficulties of finding and justifying judgment norms through the binary interaction of "law" and "*li*". These three aspects actually reflect the great achievements in legal methods made by famous judicial officials in the Song Dynasty.

However, can such achievements prove that there were intellectual and rational factors in the justice of the Song Dynasty? According to Mr. Feng Qi, "intellectual rationality" has two characteristics: First, in terms of process, it forms concepts, makes judgments and applies reasoning through formal logic or dialectical logic. Second, in terms of result, it can produce knowledge with universal validity (stability in space and predictability in time) (Feng 2016). Taking these two characteristics as the standards, people can notice that judicial celebrities in the Song Dynasty did use formal logic or dialectical logic to make legal reasoning, and they also obtained knowledge with universal validity.

Specifically, when the judgment standard was relatively determined, famous judicial officials realized legal subsumption into the living facts in the circular interaction between the facts and the standard, obtained a result consistent with the facts of the case, and made decisions on the basis of deductive reasoning. That was the application of formal logic. However, when there was a dilemma in finding and justifying judgment norms, they explained and developed the law in the binary interaction between "law" and "*li*" to balance the relationship among the law, social ethics and the principle of national order—to amend and adjust the "law" by the application of "*li*" so as to create a new premise for deductive reasoning, which was the embodiment of dialectical logic. It was based on the application of the above legal methods that famous judicial officials indeed obtained generally effective intellectual results in judicial practice and outlined stable and predictable cognitive and behavioral patterns. It shows that although justice in the Song Dynasty was often labeled as "justice in accordance with human feelings" or "justice by morality" by scholars, it contained profound intellectual rationality rather than only moral rationality.

It should be noted that the self-consciousness in legal methods of famous judicial officials in the Song Dynasty was essentially a kind of knowledge. The knowledge connected the search for facts and the pursuit of virtue. The core issue of was how to pursue virtue on the basis of searching for facts. According to the analysis of this article, this intellectual issue has exerted influence on judicial practice in the Song Dynasty. However, more research should be conducted on the issues of how the intellectual rationality of the legal method grew up under the historical background, and what were the economic, political, ideological and cultural foundations and motivations.

References

Chen, Jingliang. 2008. Narrative of the Judicial Tradition in the Song Dynasty and Its Significance—An Investigation Based on Civil Trials in the Southern Song Dynasty. *Journal of Nanjing University* 4: 103–116.

Chen, Rui. 2011. Legal Methodology in the Song Dynasty—An Investigation Centering on *Qing Ming Ji*. *Modern Law Science* 2: 36–47.

Chen, Jingliang. 2012. Interpretation of "Ganzhao": Starting from the Litigation of the Real Estate in the Song Dynasty from Perspective of "Reforms in the Tang and Song Dynasties." *Journal of Henan University of Economics and Law* 6: 1–28.
Fan, Xitang. 1987a. Daughters Should Get the Heritage. In *Ming Gong Shu Pan Qing Ming Ji*, ed. Siwei Zhang, 290–291. Beijing: Zhonghua Book Company.
Fan, Xitang. 1987b. Dealing with the Land Property of Households Without Male Descendants. In Ming Gong Shu Pan Qing Ming Ji, ed. Siwei Zhang, 288. Beijing: Zhonghua Book Company.
Fang, Qiuya. 1987. Educational Officials Should Not Accept Bribes. In *Ming Gong Shu Pan Qing Ming Ji*, ed. Siwei Zhang, 93–94. Beijing: Zhonghua Book Company.
Feng, Qi. 2016. *Collected Works of Feng Qi*. Revised. Shanghai: East China Normal University Press.
Gao, Hongjun. 2006. Between Having Nothing to Say and Having Something to Say: Comments on Mr. Zhang Weiren's. *Chinese Traditional Justice and Law. Tribune of Political Science and Law* 5: 98–109.
Geoffrey, MacCormack. 2013. Legal Reasoning in the Southern Song Dynasty. *The research on ancient Chinese legal document* 7: 299–358.
Han, Sizhai. 1987. Wife Accusing the Concubine's Father of Illegally Occupying the Property. In *Ming Gong Shu Pan Qing Ming Ji*, ed. Siwei Zhang, 232. Beijing: Zhonghua Book Company.
Haruhito, Sadate. 2016. "Legal Meanings" and "Human Feelings" of in *Qing Ming Ji*—Traces of Legal Interpretation by Lawsuit Parties. In *Selected Works of Japanese Scholars on Chinese Legal History: The Volume of Legal History of the Song, Liao, Jin and Yuan Dynasties*, ed. Yifan Yang and Hiroaki Terada, 353–383. Beijing: Zhonghua Book Company.
He, Weifang. 2005. Three Traditions of Chinese Ancient Justice and Their Influence on Contemporary Times. *Journal of Henan University of Economics and Law* 3: 1–3.
Hu, Shibi. 1987a. A Question for Different Interests Between the Bank and Private Lending. In *Ming Gong Shu Pan Qing Ming Ji*, ed. Siwei Zhang, 336. Beijing: Zhonghua Book Company.
Hu, Shibi. 1987b. Conspiring to Bully the Lonely. In *Ming Gong Shu Pan Qing Ming Ji*, ed. Siwei Zhang, 527. Beijing: Zhonghua Book Company.
Hu, Shibi. 1987c. People of the Dong Nationality Being in Danger and Refusing to Chasing. In *Ming Gong Shu Pan Qing Ming Ji*, ed. Siwei Zhang, 506. Beijing: Zhonghua Book Company.
Hu, Shibi. 1987d. The Compulsory Divorce Is Approved Because of the Ambiguous Affair. In *Ming Gong Shu Pan Qing Ming Ji*, ed. Siwei Zhang, 388. Beijing: Zhonghua Book Company.
Hu, Shibi. 1987e. The Local Army Should Not Harass the Countryside. In *Ming Gong Shu Pan Qing Ming Ji*, ed. Siwei Zhang, 438. Beijing: Zhonghua Book Company.
Huang, Gan. 1987. A Dispute for the Graveyard Between *Zhang Yunshu* and His Brother. In *Ming Gong Shu Pan Qing Ming Ji*, ed. Siwei Zhang, 585. Beijing: Zhonghua Book Company.
Huang, Zongzhi. 2014. *Representation and Practice of the Civil Justice Since the Qing Dynasty—History, Theory and Reality (Volume I): Law, Society and Culture in the Qing Dynasty—Representation and Practice of the Civil Justice*. Beijing: Law Press.
Jian, Qian. 1987. A Man Getting His Uncle's Land Property by a Forged Contract. In *Ming Gong Shu Pan Qing Ming Ji*, ed. Siwei Zhang, 146–147. Beijing: Zhonghua Book Company.
Larenz, Karl. 2003. *Methodology of Law*. Trans. Aie Chen, 160. Beijing: The Commercial Press.
Lin, Duan. 2014. *Weber's View on Chinese Traditional Law: Criticism of Comparative Sociology of Weber*, 155–157. Beijing: China University of Political Science and Law Press.
Liu, Houcun. 1987a. A Dispute for the Mountain Land Boundary. In *Ming Gong Shu Pan Qing Ming Ji*, ed. Siwei Zhang, 157. Beijing: Zhonghua Book Company.
Liu, Houcun. 1987b. The Son-in-Law Should Not Get the Heritage of His Wife's Family. In *Ming Gong Shu Pan Qing Ming Ji*, ed. Siwei Zhang, 277. Beijing: Zhonghua Book Company.
Liu, Xinjun. 2002. On the Application of "Heavenly Principles" in the Litigation of the Song Dynasty. *The Study of Legal History* 3: 1–32.
Liu, Liyan. 2012. A Civil Adjudication in the Southern Song Dynasty: Making Same or Different Decisions for Same Cases. *Social Sciences in China* 8: 153–178.

Liu, Liyan. 2013. The Role of "Heavenly Principles" in the Trial of the Southern Song Dynasty. *Journal of the Institute of History and Language* 84: 277–328.

Pei, Yi. 1987. An Accusation Against *Deng Si* of Blackmailing and Beating. In *Ming Gong Shu Pan Qing Ming Ji*, ed. Siwei Zhang, 555. Beijing: Zhonghua Book Company.

Pu, Yang. 1987. A Dispute for the Graveyard Between the Landlord and the Lessee. In *Ming Gong Shu Pan Qing Ming Ji*, ed. Siwei Zhang, 325–327. Beijing: Zhonghua Book Company.

Ruthers, Bernd. 2005. *Jurisprudence*. Trans. Xiaochu Ding, Yue Wu. Beijing: Law Press.

Shiga, Shuzo. 1998a. An Investigation of Chinese Legal Culture—Based on the Form of Litigation. In *Civil Trials and Civil Contracts in the Ming and Qing Dynasties*, ed. Yaxin Wang and Zhiping Liang, 1–18. Beijing: Law Press.

Shiga, Shuzo. 1998b. An Investigation of the Civil Legal Sources of the Litigation System of the Qing Dynasty—Habits as Legal Sources. In *Civil Trials and Civil Contracts in the Ming and Qing Dynasties*, ed. Yaxin Wang and Zhiping Liang, 54–96. Beijing: Law Press.

Shiga, Shuzo. 1998c. A General Investigation of the Civil Legal Sources of the Litigation System of the Qing Dynasty. In *Civil Trials and Civil Contracts in the Ming and Qing Dynasties*, ed. Yaxin Wang and Zhiping Liang, 19–53. Beijing: Law Press.

Shu, Guoying, Xiahao Wang, and Lei Lei. 2018. *Methodology of Law*. Beijing: China University of Political Science and Law Press.

Song, Ci. 2016. *Record of Redressing Mishandled Cases*. Trans. Suijie Gao and Linsen Zhu. Shanghai: Shanghai Chinese Classics Publishing House.

Tuo, Tuo, et al. 1977. *The History of the Song Dynasty*, vol. 35. Beijing: Zhonghua Book Company.

Wang, Liugeng. 1987. Abolishment of the Father-Son Relationship Because of Selfish Desire. In *Ming Gong Shu Pan Qing Ming Ji*, ed. Siwei Zhang, 248–249. Beijing: Zhonghua Book Company.

Wang, Zhiqiang. 1997. A Preliminary Study of Legal Thoughts in *Qing Ming Ji*. *Chinese Journal of Law* 5: 118–134.

Wang, Zhiqiang. 1998. The Value Orientation in the Judicial Judgment of the Southern Song Dynasty—A Preliminary Study of the Verdict of the Southern Song Dynasty. *Social Sciences in China* 6: 117–130.

Weber, Max. 2010. *Confucianism and Taoism*. Trans. Tianfu Hong. Nanjing: Jiangsu People's Publishing House.

Weng, Haotang. 1987. An Anonymous Letter. In *Ming Gong Shu Pan Qing Ming Ji*, ed. Siwei Zhang, 550–551. Beijing: Zhonghua Book Company.

Wu, Shuzhai. 1987a. An Accusation Against the Nephew of Selling Stolen Land. In *Ming Gong Shu Pan Qing Ming Ji*, ed. Siwei Zhang, 183–184. Beijing: Zhonghua Book Company.

Wu, Shuzhai. 1987b. A Dispute for the Mountain. In *Ming Gong Shu Pan Qing Ming Ji*, ed. Siwei Zhang, 197–198. Beijing: Zhonghua Book Company.

Wu, Shuzhai. 1987c. *Didang* or Selling off. In *Ming Gong Shu Pan Qing Ming Ji*, ed. Siwei Zhang, 168–170. Beijing: Zhonghua Book Company.

Wu, Shuzhai. 1987d. *Didang* Without Leaving the Property. In *Ming Gong Shu Pan Qing Ming Ji*, ed. Siwei Zhang, 167. Beijing: Zhonghua Book Company.

Wu, Yuyan. 1987e. A County Official Accusing the Magistrate of the County of Corruption. In *Ming Gong Shu Pan Qing Ming Ji*, ed. Siwei Zhang, 60. Beijing: Zhonghua Book Company.

Yang, Guorong. 1998. *Reason and Value*. Shanghai: Shanghai Joint Publishing Company.

Yang, Zutao, and Xiaomang Deng. 2001. *The Essence of Kant's Three Criticisms*. Beijing: People's Publishing House.

Yang, Yifan, and Tao Tian. 2002. Miscellaneous Category, Sex Offenders, Arrest and Death Orders, In *China's Rare and Precious Legal Classics Volume I: Provisions of the Law in Qingyuan Volume 80*. Heilongjiang: Heilongjiang People's Publishing House.

Ye, Yanfeng. 1987a. A Dispute Between Uncle and Nephew. In *Ming Gong Shu Pan Qing Ming Ji*, ed. Siwei Zhang, 191. Beijing: Zhonghua Book Company.

Ye, Yanfeng. 1987b. Criticism on False Incrimination. In *Ming Gong Shu Pan Qing Ming Ji*, ed. Siwei Zhang, 182. Beijing: Zhonghua Book Company.

Ye, Yanfeng. 1987c. Distinguishing *Shi* from *Fei*. In *Ming Gong Shu Pan Qing Ming Ji*, ed. Siwei Zhang, 241. Beijing: Zhonghua Book Company.
Zhang, Siwei. 1987. *Ming Gong Shu Pan Qing Ming Ji*. Beijing: Zhonghua Book Company.
Zhang, Weiren. 2006. Chinese Traditional Justice and Law. *Modern Law Science* 5: 59–67.
Zhao, Jing. 2018. Chinese Traditional Judicial Culture in the Song Dynasty: Rethinking Japan's Research on *Qing Ming Ji*. *Academic Monthly* 9: 149–161.
Zhen, Xishan. 1987a. Advice for Some Affairs. In *Ming Gong Shu Pan Qing Ming Ji*, ed. Siwei Zhang, 15. Beijing: Zhonghua Book Company.
Zhen, Xishan. 1987b. To Magistrate and Duty Magistrate. In *Ming Gong Shu Pan Qing Ming Ji*, ed. Siwei Zhang, 2. Beijing: Zhonghua Book Company.
Zhen, Xishan. 1987c. To Officials of the State and County. In *Ming Gong Shu Pan Qing Ming Ji*, ed. Siwei Zhang, 6. Beijing: Zhonghua Book Company.
Zhou, Mi. 1983. *Qi Dong Ye Yu*, vol. IIX. Beijing: Zhonghua Book Company.

Can Truth Be Negotiated? Rethinking Plea Bargaining at the ICTY

Suhao Chen

1 Introduction

Almost all judicial systems are supposed to find the truth. Generally, legal truth in a judicial proceeding should be consistent with objective truth to the fullest extent. In this sense, the judicial proceeding should be governed by the correspondence theory. In the view of legal practitioners, evidence is the only bridge between legal truth and objective truth, and an accurate truth-finding process shall be based on sufficient investigations of evidence. It has been a global trend to avoid full criminal trials through consensual procedures. Thus, it is acceptable to simplify the evidence investigation and lower the factual requirement after a guilty plea has been reached under an agreement. In such a situation, negotiation, rather than a sufficient investigation of the evidence, has become the basis of factual ascertainment confirmed by the court. As an increasing number of criminal cases are concluded by consensual procedures, correspondence theory may give way to consensus theory.

What legal practitioners focus on is microscopic truths, such as somebody has committed a crime under a certain frame of mind at some time, rather than the historical impact of the crime. When the concerned truth is not so microscopic but is a major incident with a historical impact, can the truth be negotiated? In this regard, the ICTY can be used as a good research sample.[1] According to the resolutions of the UN Security Council, the purposes of establishing the ICTY included putting an

[1]The International Tribunal for the former Yugoslavia, known as the ICTY, was established in 1993 and has the power to prosecute and try persons responsible for serious violations of humanitarian law committed in the territory of the former Yugoslavia in the 1990s. By the end of 2017 when the ICTY closed, after which it would only operate as an appeal institute, it had tried 161 defendants and developed a unique jurisprudence.

S. Chen (✉)
School of Law, Nanjing Audit University, Nanjing, China
e-mail: suhaochen@nau.edu.cn

B. Zhang et al. (eds.), *A Dialogue Between Law and History*,
https://doi.org/10.1007/978-981-15-9685-8_15

end to crimes against humanity, taking measures to bring justice to persons who were responsible for such crimes, and contributing to the restoration and maintenance of peace.[2] Given such a background, cases before the ICTY were all related to historical incidents such as constant armed conflicts. Trials and judgments of the ICTY, which are international community records of these incidents, have historical significance. Thus, ascertaining the truth had great significance for this ad hoc tribunal. On the one hand, the retributive and deterrent effects could only be achieved by penalizing persons who were responsible for those crimes based on accurate truth. On the other hand, a complete historical record could only be established on the basis of accurate truth, and such a record would alter the bias and misunderstanding of people in the former Yugoslavia, serving as a warning for future generations.[3] Thus, at least in theory, the truth should be ascertained by the tribunal through trials and cannot be negotiated by parties. The ICTY accepted plea bargaining due to efficiency considerations and even allowed charge bargaining between the prosecution and the defense. This process inevitably included negotiations of truth and raised controversies.

This article starts with an overview of the practice of plea bargaining at the ICTY and continues by analyzing the positive and negative effects of plea bargaining on truth finding. Unlike a municipal court, the ICTY regarded establishing a historical record as one of its missions. This contributed to the overlapping of truth-finding processes in history and in law. Based on this, the author will further compare the truth-finding approach of history and law and discuss the question of whether truth can be negotiated through the lens of consensus theory.

2 An Overview of Plea Bargaining at the ICTY

Although the design of procedures at the ICTY was closer to the adversarial system of common law countries, the tribunal's attitude toward plea bargaining, which is still prevalent in common law countries, developed from absolute objection to gradual acceptance.

2.1 The Acceptance of Plea Bargaining

It has become a world trend to divide criminal procedures into contested procedures and consensual procedures (Thaman 2010). When the ICTY was established, it provided no special arrangement for the trial process of cases in which defendants pleaded guilty. Article 20, Sect. 3 of the statute stipulated that the Trial Chamber would set the date for the trial after instructing the accused to enter a plea, indicating

[2] United Nations Security Council, Resolution 827 (1993), 25 May 1993, S/RES/827 (1993).

[3] ICTY, *Prosecutor v. Momir Nikolić*, Sentencing Judgment, IT-02-60/1-S, 2 December 2003, paras. 59–60.

that the trial would not be avoided if the defendant pleaded guilty. On 31 May 1996, *Dražen Erdemović* became the first defendant to plead guilty at the tribunal. This was not the result of a plea agreement.[4] How the case should have proceeded turned out to be a difficult question for the chamber, as specific rules were missing. Consequently, Rule 62b is was added to the Rules of Procedure and Evidence in 1997, authorizing the Trial Chamber to enter a finding of guilt without a full trial and to instruct the registrar to set a date for the sentencing hearing when the defendant pleaded guilty.

This does not necessarily mean that a guilty plea could result from bargaining by merely allowing the chamber to accept guilty pleas. The jurisdiction of the ICTY included grave breaches of the Geneva Conventions of 1949, violations of the laws or customs of war, crimes against humanity, and genocide, which are the most serious crimes in human society. Considering the gravity of these crimes, the ICTY objected to the adoption of plea bargaining at first.[5] There were another 5 defendants who entered guilty pleas after *Erdemović*, all of which were the result of plea agreements. In response, Rule 62er was added to the Rules of Procedure and Evidence in 2001. This clause allowed the prosecution to amend the indictment and recommend a more lenient sentence in exchange for the defendant's guilty plea. The adoption of this rule indicated that plea bargaining had been formally embraced by the ICTY.[6]

2.2 *Rules of Plea Bargaining*

At the ICTY, Rule 62b is and Rule 62er were the statutory basis of plea bargaining, consisting of a plea agreement and a guilty plea. In addition, the mitigating effect of guilty pleas has been developed by case laws.

According to Rule 62er, when the accused entered a plea of guilty based on a plea agreement, the prosecution could apply to amend the indictment accordingly, submit that a specific sentence or sentence range appropriate or not oppose a request by the accused for a particular sentence or sentencing range. This means that bargaining content included both the sentence and the charge. To secure a guilty plea, the prosecution might withdraw several charges or decide to pursue a charge of a lower degree instead of a more serious one. It should be noted that the Trial Chamber was not bound

[4] ICTY, *Prosecutor v. Drazen Erdemovic,* Sentencing Judgment, IT-96-22-T, 29 November 1996, para. 3.

[5] The then president of the ICTY stated, "We always have to keep in mind that this tribunal is not a municipal criminal court but one that is charged with trying persons accused of the gravest possible of all crimes. The persons appearing before us will be charged with genocide, torture, murder, sexual assault, wanton destruction, persecution and other inhumane acts. After due reflection, we have decided that no one should be immune from prosecution for crimes such as these, no matter how useful their testimony may otherwise be." See Judge Antonio Cassese, President of the ICTY, Statement Made at the Briefing to Members of Diplomatic Mission, U.N. Doc. IT/29, February 11, 1994.

[6] ICTY, *Prosecutor v. Momir Nikolić*, Sentencing Judgment, IT-02-60/1-S, 2 December 2003, para. 46.

by such an agreement under Section B of this clause. The Trial Chamber could reject a plea agreement or impose a sentence beyond the range suggested. Section C further stipulates that the Trial Chamber required the disclosure of a plea agreement in open session at the time the accused pleaded guilty except for when good causes existed.

Rule 62er set 4 conditions for a valid guilty plea, whether it was reached on the basis of an agreement or not: the plea was made voluntarily, it was informed, it was not equivocal and there was sufficient factual basis for the crime and the accused's participation in the crime. Except for the requirement of "not equivocal", this clause is almost identical to Rule 11 of the US Federal Rules of Criminal Procedure. An unequivocal plea could not be qualified by statements that appeared to present a legal defense for the crime.[7] Thus, an Alford plea was not acceptable at the ICTY.[8] This was intended to prevent an innocent person from pleading guilty. In terms of the way to examine the sufficiency of the factual basis, the language of this clause was "either on the basis of independent indicia or on lack of any material disagreement between the parties about the facts of the case". This meant that the chamber could simply rely on the agreement between parties to confirm case facts. A guilty plea accepted by the Trial Chamber was a conviction itself, which was followed by a sentencing hearing directly.

Case laws show that the rationale for reducing the defendant's sentence after the guilty plea included the following: relieving the pressure on witnesses and victims to testify before the tribunal; saving time, effort and resources[9]; helping to establish the truth[10]; encouraging other perpetrators to come forward and accept responsibility[11]; and promoting reconciliation in the post-conflict area by showing the defendant's remorse and contrition.[12] Some chambers have held that the importance of conserving resources should not be overestimated, and international courts should not be awarding sentencing reductions merely for efficiency purposes.[13] In addition, substantial cooperation with the prosecution was regarded as a mitigating factor under Rule 10, Section B of the Rules of Procedure and Evidence. According to the less rigid standard, providing information to the prosecution or testifying in other

[7]ICTY, *Prosecutor v. Drazen Erdemovic*, Joint Separate Opinion of McDonald and Vohrah, 7 October 1997, para. 8.

[8]In the Alford case, the defendant who pleaded guilty claimed he was actually innocent. The plea was accpteted by the court. See *North Carolina v. Aflord*, 400 U.S. 25, 37.

[9]ICTY, *Prosecutor v.Stevan Todorović*, Sentencing Judgment, IT-95-9/1-S, 31 July 2001, paras. 80–81.

[10]ICTY, *Prosecutor v. Duško Sikirica* etc., Sentencing Judgment, IT-95-8-S, 13 November 2001, para. 149.

[11]ICTY, *Prosecutor v. Dragan Nikolić., Judgment on* Sentencing Appeal, IT-94-2, 4 February 2005, paras. 55–56.

[12]ICTY, *Prosecutor v. Biljana Plavšić.*, Sentencing Judgment, IT-00-39&40/1-S, 27 February 2003, para. 76.

[13]ICTY, *Prosecutor v. Momir Nikolić*, Sentencing Judgment, IT-02-60/1-S, 2 December 2003, para. 67.

cases under a plea agreement sufficed for substantial cooperation, which could be rewarded with a sentence reduction.[14]

2.3 Reasons to Adopt Plea Bargaining

At the ICTY, almost every guilty plea came from an agreement between the prosecution and the defense. The justification for sentence reduction as a result of the guilty plea reflect the attempt to connect to the adoption of plea bargaining with higher ends, such as establishing the truth or promoting reconciliation. This sort of hindsight cannot replace a more convincing explanation: plea bargaining was accepted mainly due to efficiency considerations.

One rationale behind establishing the ICTY was that domestic judicial systems of countries from the former Yugoslavia did not have the capacity to handle war crimes at that time.[15] When these domestic courts gained the capacity, there would no longer be a need to run an expensive international court. Thus, the ICTY was designed to be an ad hoc tribunal rather than a permanent tribunal. In fact, the ICTY started working on a completion strategy in 2003 that said that the tribunal should finish all its work by 2010.[16] As we have witnessed, this plan was not accomplished until 2017. In the process, the ICTY was confronted with consistent pressure from the UN.[17]

The stress coming from such a rigid time schedule was enhanced by the caseload volume and complexity of procedures at the tribunal. Conflicts in the former Yugoslavia resulted in the death of tens of thousands of people and the forcible displacement of millions, accurate numbers of which are almost impossible to determine. Against such a background, even prosecuting the most serious crimes would bring a considerable caseload volume to the tribunal and burden its limited resources. The complicated commanding structure, numerous victims and widespread locations of war crimes made the investigations and trials extremely time-consuming. Apart from these factors, reluctance to cooperate and the unstable political atmosphere in the former Yugoslavia increased the difficulty even further (Tieger and Shin 2005, 668–669). In the extreme case such as that of *Slobodan Milošević*, the defendant was indicted on 12 May 1999, but the judgment was not delivered even after a marathon-style trial, as *Milošević* died in the detention center on 11 March 2006.[18]

---

[14]ICTY, *Prosecutor v. Stevan Todorović,* Sentencing Judgment, IT-95-9/1-S, 31 July 2001, paras. 83–88.

[15]United Nations Security Council, Resolution 827 (1993), 25 May 1993, S/RES/827(1993).

[16]United Nations Security Council, Resolution 1503 (2003), 28 August 2003, S/RES/1503(2003); Resolution 1534(2004), 26 March 2004, S/RES/1534(2004).

[17]The ICTY was required to report on the progress of the completion strategy in its annual report. In addition, the tribunal had to submit special report on the completion strategy to the UN Security Council every six months.

[18]ICTY, *Report of the President Death of Slobodan Milosevic*, 30 May 2006, paras. 5–18.

As mentioned above, a guilty plea helps to save courts time, effort and resources by accelerating the proceedings.[19] It seems that plea bargaining was an unavoidable choice for the ICTY if it wanted to fulfill its mission. In a report to the UN Security Council, President Meron said, "The more accused plead guilty, thereby obviating the need for a full trial at the Tribunal, the more likely it is that the Tribunal will be able to complete its work on time."[20] Regardless of the hesitancy to embrace plea bargaining, it became an important part of the ICTY practice. Twenty defendants reached plea agreements with the prosecution by the time the ICTY closed. As a consequence, the dispute on the correlation of plea bargaining and truth-establishing was raised. Such an arrangement is in conflict with the traditional idea of truth finding, since charge bargaining and the omission of trials indicate that the truth that is confirmed is incomplete. However, there exists an opposite opinion, which says that important information can be secured by a plea agreement: the acknowledgment of guilt has indispensable value in establishing a historical record, and the loss of depth in facts can be seen as a necessary sacrifice to expand the breadth due to resource constraints; therefore, plea bargaining helps in establishing the truth. Both opinions will be discussed below.

3 The Conflict Between Plea Bargaining and Establishing the Truth

In essence, plea bargaining at the ICTY consisted of the following factors: the omission of the trial based on the guilty plea, which was the result of the plea agreement between the prosecution and the defense. This mechanism was in conflict with truth-establishing in at least three aspects.

3.1 Negotiable Charges

In plea bargaining, the prosecution can amend or withdraw certain charges in exchange for the defendant's guilty plea. At the ICTY, it was common for the prosecution to drop charges in two ways. First, the prosecution could withdraw several counts of crime. The prosecution withdrew 7 counts of rape and torture (violations of the laws or customs of war) after *Dragan Zelenović* agreed to plead guilty to 7 counts of crimes against humanity; the prosecution also withdrew 27 counts of other crimes

---

[19] ICTY, *Prosecutor v. Stevan Todorović,* Sentencing Judgment, IT-95-9/1-S, 31 July 2001, paras. 80–81.

[20] Completion Strategy Report, 24 May 2004, S/2004/420.

after *Stevan Todorović* agreed to plead guilty to 1 count of crime against humanity.[21] Second, the prosecution could decide not to pursue genocide charges after the defendant pleaded guilty to less severe crimes. In the cases of *Biljana Plavšić* and *Momir Nikolić*, the remaining counts of indictments, including genocide, were dismissed after they pleaded guilty to persecution, a crime against humanity.[22]

The above practice has been widely criticized for undermining the historic mission to establish the truth. As Scharf points out, the "dropping of charges has the effect of editing out the full factual basis upon which a conviction rests and thus has the potential to distort the historic record generated by the Tribunal." Since *Plavšić* did not provide evidence related to the dropped genocide charges, the dropping of those charges may, according to Scharf, "be erroneously viewed in Serbia as an admission by the prosecutor that those crimes did not take place (Scharf 2004, 1080–1081)." Considering the severity of genocide, Clark maintains that "prosecuting a defendant for a crime against humanity does not have the same symbolic and moral significance as prosecuting him for genocide. The ultimate crime against humanity, to prosecute genocide as anything less than genocide is to do a fundamental injustice to the victims and their families (Clark 2009, 428)." Judges at the ICTY expressed similar concerns when they accepted guilty pleas. In the *Nikolić* case, the Trial Chamber noted that "in cases where factual allegations are withdrawn, the public record established by that case might be incomplete or at least open to question, as the public will not know whether the allegations were withdrawn because of insufficient evidence or because they were simply a 'bargaining chip' in the negotiation process."[23]

3.2 Unexamined Accuracy of Self-Admission

In addition to dropping charges, another feature of plea bargaining is sentence reduction. In most cases, the Trial Chamber sentenced defendants within the range suggested by the prosecution. Compared with those who pleaded not guilty, the defendants who reached agreements with the prosecution received more lenient sentences. For example, *Plavšić*, one of the major leaders in Bosnia and Herzegovina, was accused of being responsible for persecutions against the non-Serb population in B&H. The prosecution withdrew genocide charges against her and submitted that an appropriate sentence in this case was a term of imprisonment of not less than 15 years and not more than 25 years after *Plavšić* agreed to plead guilty. Taking her position and the positive effects of her remorse on future reconciliation into consideration,

[21] ICTY, *Prosecutor v. Dragan Zelenović*, Sentencing Judgment, IT-96-23/2-A, 4 April 2007, para. 10. ICTY, *Prosecutor v. Stevan Todorović*, Sentencing Judgment, IT-95-9/1-S, 31 July 2001, paras. 7–8.

[22] ICTY, *Prosecutor v. Momir Nikolić*, Sentencing Judgment, IT-02-60/1-S, 2 December 2003, paras. 12–13. ICTY, *Prosecutor v. Biljana Plavšić.*, Sentencing Judgment, IT-00-39&40/1-S, 27 February 2003, paras. 1–5.

[23] ICTY, *Prosecutor v. Momir Nikolić*, Sentencing Judgment, IT-02-60/1-S, 2 December 2003, para. 63.

the Trial Chamber finally sentenced her to 11 years' imprisonment.[24] Conversely, her co-accused, *Momčilo Krajišnik,* who had a much lower rank in the leadership hierarchy, was sentenced 20 years' imprisonment after a long trial and a successful appeal against the initial sentence of 27 years' imprisonment.[25] The appeal judgment was delivered on 17 March 2009, which was 7 years after the indictment. Only 6 months later, *Plavšić* was granted early release.

Did these defendants plead guilty sincerely on a factual basis or merely for sentence reduction and early release? In answering this question, it is not enough to judge from the guilty statements, since almost all defendants express sincere remorse.[26] It should be kept in mind that a large part of defendants at the ICTY are political elites. Thus, it seems to have been an acceptable choice to use guilty pleas as a compromise strategy for the defendants who knew very well about cost–benefit comparison. Thus, it was not surprising to see *Plavšić* publicly renounce her admission of guilt and stated that she had pleaded guilty simply to get a break on her sentence (Simic 2011, 1400). In the view of some victims, these defendants were not actually sorry for what they had done. As one study showed, the consensus among interviewed victims was that the defendants who claimed they were sorry for what they had done were being disingenuous and were simply seeking to get a reduced sentence(Clark 2009, 432).

3.3 Omission of Trials

When a defendant pleads guilty according to the agreement, he or she also waives the right to a public trial. Thus, the trial can be omitted, and the sentence hearing then follows. In this regard, a guilty plea is the equivalent of a conviction, as in the adversarial system in common law countries. For example, in the 1927 *Kercheval* case, the US Supreme Court stated that "a plea of guilty differs in purpose and effect from a mere admission or an extrajudicial confession; it is itself a conviction. Like a verdict of a jury, it is conclusive. More is not required; the court has nothing to do but give judgment and sentence."[27] Different from this approach and under the influence of the idea of material truth, judges in Continental countries place more emphasis on the obligation to find the truth. Even when defendants plead guilty, judges are still required to ascertain the truth, and trials can be shortened rather than omitted. For example, according to the German Constitutional Court, based on the guilty principle, criminal court judges have an obligation to seek the truth, and a

---

[24]ICTY, *Prosecutor v. Biljana Plavšić.*, Sentencing Judgment, IT-00-39&40/1-S, 27 February 2003, paras.128,132.

[25]ICTY, *Prosecutor v. Momčilo Krajišnik.*, Appeals Chamber Judgment, IT-00-39-A, 17 March 2009, para 827.

[26]These statements are available online at https://www.icty.org/en/features/statements-guilt.

[27]*Kercheval v. United States,* 274 U.S. 220, 223 (1927).

mere formal admission of guilt is never sufficient to meet the court's obligation to investigate the truth (Weigend and Turner 2014, 97).

Judges in the *Nikolić* case expressed their concerns related to the avoidance of a public trial. The sentencing judgment reads that "when convictions result from a guilty plea, certain aims of having criminal proceedings are not fully realized, most notably a public trial. A public trial, with the presentation of testimonial and documentary evidence by both parties, creates a more complete and detailed historical record than a guilty plea, which may only establish the bare factual allegations in an indictment or may be supplemented by a statement of facts and acceptance of responsibility by the accused."[28] Interestingly, all three judges in this chamber came from jurisdictions with a civil law tradition.[29] This may not be coincidental since the belief that "guilty plea is conviction" is obviously in contrast with the idea of material truth, which is deeply rooted in the minds of judges from civil law traditions.

3.4 Analysis from the Microscopic Perspective

Restricted by ideas and procedural rules, the ICTY focused on certain parts of the truth, namely, the case facts. One of the primary goals of the tribunal was to end sovereign impunity and hold individuals responsible for the crimes they had committed. The tribunal pointed toward individuals, not peoples, as perpetrators of war crimes, so that the guilt of a few would not be shifted to the innocent. Consequently, the tribunal had to focus on individual criminal responsibilities, and its judgments could only reflect parts of the whole conflict event. Judges at the ICTY had to concentrate on events that were singled out by the prosecution against individual perpetrators and could not focus on the larger picture of the event as historians may do. Meanwhile, the judges had a duty to exercise strict self-constraint to relevant evidence only. Aimed at providing a good model for domestic criminal justice, the tribunal granted numerous procedural rights to the accused according to a quite high standard, which may have limited its capacity to seek material truth.

Obviously, a trial before the ICTY was not the best way to establish a historical record. When contrasted with the long history of constant armed conflicts occurring in that area, facts covered by investigations of the ICTY were extremely limited. Thus, when we talk about the conflict between plea bargaining and truth finding, we shall point to case facts, which are the basis of individual culpability. As long as the negotiated factual basis could reflect the totality of the accused's criminal conduct, the ICTY's mission to punish individuals responsible for the crimes would not be undermined, at least in theory. Considering that the accused enjoy great freedom in giving up their rights, it is not hard to meet the above requirements of factual basis.

---

[28] ICTY, *Prosecutor v. Momir Nikolić*, Sentencing Judgment, IT-02-60/1-S, 2 December 2003, para. 61.

[29] The three judges are Liu Daqun from China, Volodymyr Vassylenko from Ukraine and Carmen Maria Argibay from Argentina.

At the same time, dropping charges and avoiding trials does not directly lead to destroying or sealing relevant archives or evidence, so such actions will not impede further research by historians.

4 The Counterbalancing Mechanism Between Plea Bargaining and Establishing Truth

As mentioned above, the use of plea bargaining due to efficiency concerns, inevitably impedes the establishment of the truth in certain cases. Nevertheless, a theory of counterbalancing evolved in the practice of the ICTY, maintaining the idea that plea bargaining was not in conflict with establishing truth and may even have promoted the process.

4.1 Reliable Factual Basis

The Trial Chamber was not bound by the plea agreement between the prosecution and the defense. If the chamber thought that there was no sufficient factual basis, it could reject the agreement. Like the US Federal Rules of Criminal Procedure, the ICTY Rules of Evidence and Procedure did not mention how the factual basis should be determined and what standard should be met. In this regard, the ICTY case laws set two specific requirements that could help to counterbalance the loss of case details due to dropping charges.

First, it was necessary that the dropping of certain charges would not remove factual allegations of the case. The Trial Chamber of *Nikolić* stated that "in cases of plea agreements where the Prosecution has expressed its intention not to proceed to trial on certain charges, such motions are generally granted; a trial chamber may seek to satisfy itself that the remaining charges reflect the totality of the criminal conduct of the accused."[30] Moreover, "in this case, the Trial Chamber notes, with interest, that while the Prosecution moved to dismiss numerous charges against *Momir Nikolić*, including genocide, it did not seek to remove any of the factual allegations underlying these crimes. Thus, the factual basis upon which the remaining charge of persecutions is based can be found to reflect the totality of *Momir Nikolić's* criminal conduct."[31] At least in the views of some judges, it was necessary that prosecutors would not amend the factual basis substantially when they decided to dismiss certain charges.

Second, supporting evidence was required by the chamber. Judgments often include as much factual information from plea agreements as do the reasoning parts

[30]ICTY, *Prosecutor v. Momir Nikolić,* Sentencing Judgment, IT-02-60/1-S, 2 December 2003, para. 50.

[31]ICTY, *Prosecutor v. Momir Nikolić,* Sentencing Judgment, IT-02-60/1-S, 2 December 2003, para. 51.

of conventional judgments based on in-court confessions in civil law countries. In some cases, judges paused after each particular description of a criminal act in the indictment and asked the defendant whether the description was accurate instead of waiting for the defendant's plea after reading out the whole indictment (Damaška 2010, 108). This practice reflects judges' careful consideration of the factual basis. In addition, chambers also required the submission of statements and documents that supported both the acknowledgement of guilt by the defendant and the indictment to which he or she pleaded guilty. In the case of *Darko Mrđa,* for example, prosecutors submitted detailed testimony and had two witnesses testify in the court, even though an agreement had been reached.[32] Tieger and Shin commented that "in smaller cases, these submissions may reflect virtually the sum total of witness information on which the prosecution intended to rely. Even in cases dealing with several offences and multiple counts, the prosecution's submission of supportive material is likely to focus on the heart of its case (Tieger and Shin 2005, 671)."

4.2 Indispensable Value of Acknowledgement by the Defendants

It should be noted that cases prosecuted before the ICTY were not normal cases. They were related to serious violations against humanitarian laws in constant armed conflicts as a result of complicated political, ethnic, religious and historic factors that had not been discovered completely by the international community. A large part of defendants before the tribunal were elite politicians who still enjoyed strong support and had influence on domestic politics at the time of the trials. Against such a background, defendants' acknowledgement of guilt had two types of indispensable value in establishing the historical record.

First, acknowledgement of guilt by the defendant can provide a perpetrator's perspective on the event, helping outsiders understand the reasons behind it. After the massive armed conflict in the former Yugoslavia, both victims and historians were eager to know why the former neighbors chose to destroy the community in which they had lived in harmony. This question can be better answered by insiders, perpetrators and persons who participated in policy making. For example, in her statements, *Plavšić* said, "A blinding fear that led to an obsession, especially for those of us for whom the Second World War was a living memory, that Serbs would never again allow themselves to become victims... In this obsession of ours to never again become victims, we had allowed ourselves to become victimizers."[33] According to Tieger and Shin, it marked the first time that a leader charged with war crimes against humanity referred to the role still played by the memories of the atrocities of the Second World War as a motivation, albeit not as justification, for the commission of the crimes in which she had been involved (Tieger and Shin 2005, 672).

[32] ICTY, *Prosecutor v. Darko Mrđa,* Sentencing Judgment, IT-02-59-S, 31March 2004, para. 8.
[33] The statement can be found at https://www.icty.org/en/sid/221.

Second, the acknowledgement of guilt by the defendant can promote reconciliation. For the ICTY, the discovery of the truth was a fundamental step toward reconciliation and the prevention of all forms of revisionism.[34] However, reconciliation cannot be achieved unless the truth discovered by the tribunal is widely accepted in the former Yugoslavia. Acknowledgements of guilt shows a defendant's remorse and contrition, which will help to secure forgiveness from victims and increase acceptance of the ICTY's judgment among them. For example, a survivor of the Srebrenica Genocide stated that "the confessions (of *Dragan Obrenović and Momir Nikolić*) have brought me a sense of relief I have not known since the fall of Srebrenica in 1995. They have given me the acknowledgement I have been looking for these past eight years. While far from an apology, these admissions are a start. We Bosnian Muslims no longer have to prove we were victims. Our friends and cousins, fathers and brothers were killed—we no longer have to prove they were innocent."[35] On the other hand, the acknowledgement of guilt from former political leaders also helped to change their supporters' minds and encouraged national governments to cooperate with the ICTY. In addition, acknowledgement of guilt can help to establish the truth and undercut the ability of future revisionists to distort what historically happened.[36]

4.3 Improvements in the Total Quality of the Truth

In terms of individual cases, facts that come from plea bargaining based on mutual agreements are not as complete as those that may be produced by a full trial, even though they can be supported by some evidence. If we take crimes against humanity in the former Yugoslavia as a whole event, plea bargaining can be understood as a sacrifice of depth for breadth in truth, making the bigger picture of the event clearer. Thus, plea bargaining helps to establish the truth. This can be explained in two ways.

First, resources saved by plea bargaining can be used to prosecute more crimes. As mentioned before, the major reason to embrace plea bargaining is to balance the conflict between limited resources and the high cost of international criminal proceedings. Without plea bargaining, the tribunal could not have completed its work. Thus, the efficiency of the plea-bargaining process results in a greater number of completed cases, which definitely provide additions to the historical record. The expansion of the breadth of the truth can make up for the loss in depth within certain cases and help the international community to have a bigger picture of the whole event.

---

[34] ICTY, *Prosecutor v. Milan Babić,* Sentencing Judgment, IT-03-72-S, 29 June 2004, para. 68.

[35] ICTY, *Prosecutor v. Dragan Obrenović,* Sentencing Judgment, IT-02-60/2-S, 10 December 2003, para. 112.

[36] ICTY, *Prosecutor v. Miroslav Deronjić,* Sentencing Judgment, IT-02-61-S, 30 March 2004, para. 260.

Second, plea bargaining encourages defendants to cooperate with the prosecution by providing key information and testifying in other cases. With the evolution of transnational crime, organized crime, and white-collar crime, the increasing complexity of crimes has made prosecutions more expensive and time-consuming. In response, gathering inside information through plea bargaining has become quite common at the domestic level. In fact, the US government suggested that the tribunal permit plea bargaining as a way of eliciting evidence against the most important defendants at the very beginning of its establishment, but this proposal was rejected (Scharf 2004, 1073). In the practice of the ICTY, the information-eliciting function of plea bargaining played a very important role. For example,*Dragan Obrenović* agreed to cooperate with the prosecution as a result of plea bargaining. In October 2007, he testified in court against his former co-accused for 7 days.[37] This case and other related cases helped the tribunal and the international community discover what happened during the Srebrenica Genocide, adding an indispensable part to the historical record.

4.4 Analysis from the Macroscopic Perspective

Considering the features of the cases set before it, the tribunal had to take on the task of establishing an accurate and complete historical record.[38] Admittedly, the long proceedings of the tribunal produced thousands of witnesses, pieces of documentation and physical objects, all of which contributed to the important historical record. Actually, the creation of a historical record was not perceived as a primary objective by the creators of the tribunal, and there was no relevant clause in the statute. The rationale for the emphasis on establishing a historical record was based on the potential value of such a record. As the UN Security Council pointed out, such a historical record would prevent a cycle of revenge killings and future acts of aggression.[39] In this way, establishing a historical record served the tribunal's mission of maintaining peace.

In individual cases, the tribunal gave up the pursuit for certain parts of the historical truth by approving the dropping of charges and avoiding trials without the substantial review of the accuracy of the guilty pleas. However, the tribunal still required the factual basis to reflect the totality of the crime. Thus, the search for case facts that consisted of the basis for criminal responsibilities was not undermined. It was merely achieved in a different way due to resource constraints. The objective to convict and punish those individually responsible for their crimes could still be fulfilled without

---

[37] ICTY, *Prosecutor v. Dragan Obrenović*, Sentencing Judgment, IT-02-60/2-S, 10 December 2003, paras. 121, 126.

[38] ICTY, *Prosecutor v. Momir Nikolić*, Sentencing Judgment, IT-02-60/1-S, 2 December 2003, para. 60.

[39] See Provisional Verbatim Record of the 3175th Meeting of the Security Council, 22 February 1993, New York, and Provisional Verbatim Record of the 3217th Meeting of the Security Council, 25 May 1993.

a full record of the whole event. In the bigger picture, if the prosecution selected right cases, the goal of achieving breadth over depth would prevail. Two factors improved the quality of the historical record: more cases were prosecuted with resources saved by plea bargaining, and plea bargaining was always accompanied by a factual basis that consisted of the basis for criminal responsibility. Therefore, the author thinks that the argument that plea bargaining helps to establish the truth is right if three conditions are satisfied: first, the truth is divided into case facts and historical records, and case facts are defined as an objective basis for individual criminal responsibility; second, the factual basis of the plea agreement reflects the totality of the criminal conduct; third, the prosecution has selected the most representative cases.

5 The Influence of Plea Bargaining on the Acceptance of the Truth

From the microscopic perspective, negotiations of case facts that do not undermine the basis of individual culpability are acceptable. From the macroscopic perspective, acknowledgement by the defendant has a unique value in the establishment of the historical record, and the resources saved and information gathered by plea bargaining improve the total quality of the truth-finding process. Therefore, the truth can be negotiated even at the ICTY, which dealt with cases with a historical impact. A further question that deserves exploration is how the acceptance of truth confirmed by the tribunal was influenced by plea bargaining. Although judges and historians have different perspectives and methods in exploring historical events, their conclusions need to be accepted to be valued and achieve initial exploration purposes.

5.1 Missing Details Are Inevitable

Although historians have some advantages in seeking the truth, for example, they are granted the privilege of using historical archives (evidence) without the restraints of judicial procedure, this does not mean that they are more likely to get closer to the objective truth. Missing or omitting certain details is inevitable in both historical writing and judicial investigations. An incomplete truth is not necessarily a false truth, and the ignorance of some details due to negotiation will not automatically undermine the acceptance of the relevant truth.

In this regard, the misunderstanding of historians' approach to finding the truth will be corrected. Hayden White has pointed out that "in their research, historians typically try to determine not only 'what happened' but the 'meaning' of this happening, not only for past agents of historical events but also for subsequent ones. And the principal way meaning is imposed on historical events is by narrativization. Historical writing is a process of meaning production. It is a delusion to think that historians wish only to tell the truth about the past (White 2000, 396–397)." Thus, "when it is a matter of trying to assess contending representations and interpretations of the meaning of the same event proffered by historians of roughly equal erudition and wisdom, the facts cannot be invoked to decide the matter. First, because what is at issue in contending interpretations is not only, what are the facts?, but also, what is to count as a fact and what is not. And secondly, because, when it is a matter of contending interpretations, what counts is not the truth of fact so much as the meaning that is to be ascribed to the events under discussion (White 2000, 399)." Therefore, there are preferences in selecting materials and value judgments in historiography. It is also impossible for historians to rebuild the past. They may even reach contradictory conclusions. In terms of finding the truth, legal practitioners should not envy historians for their freedom. The approval of the truth negotiation process at the ICTY cannot be interpreted as legal practitioners having placed less emphasis on truth finding than historians do. As with disagreements among historians, this only reflects differences in priorities. As long as the factual basis of plea bargaining can reflect the totality of the defendant's criminal conduct, plea bargaining is acceptable for legal practitioners.

5.2 *Negative Effects of the Misinterpretation of Sentence Deduction*

At the ICTY, the search for case facts served the purpose of punishing war criminals and ensuring that international humanitarian laws are respected through the retributive and deterrent function of penalties. On the other hand, the historical record that resulted provide a basis of consensus for reconciliation and helps to maintain peace in the concerned area. The realization of this purpose depended on a more significant pre-condition—case facts, and the historical record confirmed by the tribunal are now widely accepted and internalized in the area that was formerly Yugoslavia (Clark 2009, 426). If the judgments of the tribunal are not interpreted appropriately, they may even have negative effects on the realization of the above purpose.

Unfortunately, the legitimacy of international criminal courts has been subject to question, and these courts are regarded as the "victor's justice" (Peskin 2005). In related counties, protests and demonstrations against the proceedings of the ICTY were quite common (Clark 2009, 426). Case facts and the historical record confirmed by the tribunal have not been widely accepted by the public in the former Yugoslavia due to the complicated domestic political atmosphere. This may be a common problem for international courts (Zacklin 2004). In terms of plea bargaining, sentence reduction received by defendants has raised misunderstanding and objection among victims. In the case of *Deronjić*, for example, a witness stated, "I saw *Miroslav Deronjić* plead guilty and I felt glad that he admitted his guilt. I do not however understand how it is possible to give him any lenient term of imprisonment after what he himself has confessed."[40] This attitude was common among victims. Many victims would have preferred to face the ordeal of a court appearance rather than see the offender receive a significant sentence reduction in return for a guilty plea (Henham 2003, 103). Thus, sentence reduction resulting from plea bargaining may further undermine the acceptance of judgments and the truth established by the tribunal among a large number of victims.

5.3 The Potential Benefit is Undermined by Limited Participants in the Negotiation

Essentially, the establishment of the ICTY is an effort to promote reconciliation in a post-conflict society via judicial or quasi-judicial processes. Similar mechanisms include other international tribunals and truth commissions. This sort of practice has changed the concepts of truth and evidence. The Truth and Reconciliation Commission of South Africa claims that there are four notions of truth: factual or forensic truth, personal or narrative truth, social or dialogue truth, and healing and restorative truth.[41] This goes beyond the dichotomy between objective truth and subjective opinion and puts more emphasis on how to promote the acceptance of truth and fulfil its potential values. The TRC further claims that factual truth is the familiar legal or scientific notion of bringing to light factual, corroborated evidence and of obtaining accurate information through reliable procedures, which can reduce the number of lies that can be circulated unchallenged in public discourse. On the other hand, social truth is the truth of experience that is established through interaction, discussion and debate. Its goal is to try to transcend the divisions of the past by listening carefully to the complex motives and perspectives of all those involved. Social truth makes a conscious effort to provide an environment in which all possible views can be considered and weighed, one against the other. In addition to finding the truth via a reliable process, the TRC also values the importance of promoting the acceptance and varied understanding of the truth, which reflects a process of interaction and negotiation.

In comparison, the ICTY paid more attention to the truth-finding procedure than to the interaction between conflict parties. In the former aspect, the ICTY achieved prominent results. For example, no governments denied the Srebrenica Genocide after it was confirmed by the ICTY, which helped in reducing lies. However, due to procedural constraints, the number of victims who had the chance to make statements and express their opinions was quite small. ICTY, whose main working language was English, was located in the Hague, quite far from where most of the victims lived. This exacerbated the gap between the victims and the tribunal. As the victims could not participate in the plea negotiation, their chance to express themselves was

[40] ICTY, *Prosecutor v. Miroslav Deronjić*, Sentencing Judgment, IT-02-61-S, 30 March 2004, para. 239.

[41] Truth and Reconciliation Commission of South Africa Report, Vol. 1, pp. 110–114, 1998.

further limited after the procedures were abbreviated due to plea agreements. In this sense, the plea negotiation controlled by the prosecution and the defense deprived victims of their right to participate. At the same time, the ICTY did not distribute enough resources for its outreach work. Thus, the ICTY procedure was inadequate in promoting the abovementioned social truth.

6 Conclusion

Humans' investigation of historical facts varies in its approaches and priorities based on which values the investigators hold. This is the theory of multi-form truth. After analyzing plea bargaining at the ICTY from both microscopic and macroscopic perspectives, we reach the preliminary conclusion that the case facts were basically reliable and the historical record was enhanced. In this sense, plea bargaining at the ICTY promoted truth finding. At the very least, it provided important materials for future historical research. However, only accepted truth has realistic value. The questioning of the tribunal's legitimacy and misinterpretation of sentence reductions after plea bargaining has undermined the acceptance of the judgments and the historical record, making related purposes unfulfilled.

Thus, we continue to ask, how can we guarantee that the result of a truth-finding process is accepted? In this regard, our analysis is not confined to the correspondence theory. Against the background of reconciliation in a post-conflict society, the relevant truth will be negotiated among a larger group to promote its acceptance and build a basis for consensus. Historians may be in a better position to lead such a negotiation since they are more likely to have direct contact with audiences.

In Bosnia and Herzegovina, Serbs, Croats and Bosniaks are allowed to maintain separate education systems. Accordingly, three versions of history about the recent conflict are taught in B&H. In 2000, the Parliamentary Assembly of the Council of Europe passed a resolution on "Education in Bosnia and Herzegovina" that proposed a moratorium on the teaching of the last war of 1992 to 1995 so as to enable historians from all the communities in B&H, with the help of international experts, to develop a common approach. In other words, in terms of reconciliation, having no history education is better than having contradictory history education. Similar policies were adopted in Rwanda and South Africa. The international community made numerous efforts to bring historians from different communities together for discussions. Finally, the Guidelines for Writing and Evaluation of History Textbooks for Primary and Secondary Schools in Bosnia and Herzegovina was adopted by all Ministers of Education after several rounds of exchanges and debates. The guidelines state that authors of textbooks should decrease the amount of information relating to political history and that textbooks should be objective, scientifically based and aimed at building mutual understanding, reconciliation and peace in the country. However, the guidelines do not say how certain events should be written about. In July 2019, it was reported that as part of an ongoing project to unify school curriculums with Serbia, Republika Srpska was ready to introduce new history textbooks for high school pupils that would include the 1992–95 war in Bosnia and Herzegovina. The previous history textbooks in Republika Srpska only included a few general facts about the war. This decision was criticized as being a nationalist move aimed at creating a homogeneous Serb identity (Lakic 2019). However, the new textbook was supposed to provide different views about the war, featuring stories from both Croats and Bosniaks. This is a good example for showing that a consensus basis for reconciliation is extremely hard to reach or negotiate since different parties always have different narratives and memories.

As shown, reaching a consensus on certain parts of historical events through interactions and negotiations is much harder than reaching a plea agreement. This reflects the different concepts of negotiations in the judicial process of finding the truth and in writing history. In this regard, more dialogues between history and the law are needed.

References

Clark, Janie Natalya. 2009. Plea Bargaining at the ICTY: Guilty Pleas and Reconciliation. *European Journal of International Law* 20: 415–436.

Damaška, Mirjan. 2010. Negotiated justice in international criminal courts. In *World Plea Bargaining: Consensual Procedures and the Avoidance of the Full Trial*, ed. Stephen C. Thaman, 81–106. Durham: Carolina Academic Press.

Henham, Ralph. 2003. Some Issues for Sentencing in the International Criminal Court. *International of Comparative Law Quarterly* 52: 81–114.

Lakic, Mladen. 2019. Bosnian Serb schoolbooks to teach same war history as Serbia. https://balkaninsight.com/2019/07/22/bosnian-serb-schoolbooks-to-teach-same-war-history-as-serbia/. Accessed 11 Nov.

Peskin, Victor. 2005. Beyond Victor's Justice? The Challenge of Prosecuting the Winners at the International Criminal Tribunals for the Former Yugoslavia and Rwanda. *Journal of Human Rights* 4: 213–231.

Scharf, Michael P. 2004. Trading Justice for Efficiency: Plea-bargaining and International Tribunals. *Journal of International Criminal Justice* 2: 1070–1081.

Simic, Olivera. 2011. Bringing "Justice" Home? Bosnians, War Criminals, and the Interaction Between the Cosmopolitan and the Local. *German Law Journal* 12: 1388–1407.

Thaman, Stephen C. 2010. *World Plea Bargaining: Consensual Procedures and the Avoidance of the Full Trial*. Durham: Carolina Academic Press.

Tieger, Alan, and Milbert Shin. 2005. Plea Agreements in the ICTY: Purpose, Effects and Propriety. *Journal of International Criminal Justice* 3: 666–679.

Weigend, Thomas, and Turner Iontcheva. 2014. The Constitutionality of Negotiated Criminal Judgments in Germany. *German Law Journal* 15: 81–105.

White, Hayden. 2000. An old Question Raised Again: Is Historiography art or Science?. *Rethinking History* 4.

Zacklin, Ralph. 2004. The Failings of the ad hoc International Tribunals. *Journal of International Criminal Justice* 2.

A Historical Retrial of the Socrates Trial: Who Was the Victim of Guilt Presumption?

Jinpeng Feng

"Taking facts as the basis and law as the criterion" is the basic principle of the modern judicial trial, and it was also the fundamental principle of the judicial trial in classical Athens. However, as there are many human factors involved in the process of making a judgement, this principle is not always well implemented in practice, which can inevitably lead to presumption of guilt and then result in some clearly misjudged cases, of which the most famous is the trial of Socrates.

In 399 BCE, under a plan created by the democratic leader Anytus, three accusers—Meletus, Anytus and Lycon—jointly prosecuted Socrates for "corrupting the young, and … not acknowledging the gods the city acknowledges, but new daimonion instead" (Plato, *Apology*, 24b-c). In other words, they suggested that Socrates had committed the crimes of solicitation and impiety.[1] In the court, which had 500 jurors, Socrates was first convicted by 280 votes and then was sentenced to death by 360 votes (Diogenes Laertius 2.41–42). The world, especially the followers of Socrates, was unwilling to accept the result and perceived it as an unjust case based on a presumption of guilt. Because Socrates is a crucially important figure in the history of Western thought, his trial gradually became the evidence used to criticise Athenian democracy as mob rule, and was even elevated to a broader issue by later

[1]It is not clearly evinced that anyone in Athenian history other than Socrates was sentenced to death for solicitation ("corrupting the young") and/or impiety. Because there was no clear, unified definition of impiety in Athenian law or the relevant provisions were lost, scholars summed up the impiety in this case and characterized Socrates' heterodoxy as an example of this (Parker 2005). Although it is recorded that the philosopher Anaxagoras, a metic in Athens, was accused of impiety for calling the sun a stone and was eventually expelled by the Athenians, due to conflicting records, scholars believed that the charge of impiety was most likely invented for the trial of Socrates (Plutarch, *Pericles*, 32; *Nicias*, 23; Diogenes Laertius, *Lives and Opinions of Eminent Philosophers*, 2.12).

J. Feng (✉)
Institute of European Civilization, Tianjin Normal University, Tianjin, China
e-mail: taiji309@163.com

B. Zhang et al. (eds.), *A Dialogue Between Law and History*,
https://doi.org/10.1007/978-981-15-9685-8_16

scholars who asserted that it showed how philosophy was unjustly judged by politics. Therefore, thinkers wishing to defend Athenian democracy have had to make concessions on this point. The famous American journalist I. F. Stone is the representative of this line of thought. He claimed that the purpose of his writing *The Trial of Socrates* was not to rehabilitate the reputation of Athenian democracy but rather to “remove some of the stigma the trial left on democracy and on Athens” (Stone 1989).

However, should the Athenians and Athenian democracy really bear the indelible stigma of the trial of Socrates? To answer this question, this paper employes the historical method to set Socrates’ trial against the background of the period and analyses the particularities related to Socrates’ presumption of guilt, reconstructs the context of his trial as realistically as possible by combining the records of Plato and Xenophon, and explores three possibilities regarding his acquittal and the reasons for his seeking death. The paper concludes that the conviction and death sentence of Socrates resulted from a trial that he deliberately planned himself, in which the Athenians and Athenian democracy were the real losers and victims.

1 Discrimination Between Fact-Findings of History and Law

Facts are the core of history and law. However, once an event has occurred, it cannot be repeated, and so historians and jurists (including juries and judges) can only consider the facts related to an event on the basis of historical material or legal evidence. Both history and law (or judicial trials) are based on the identification and interpretation of evidence. The former emphasises “making argument based on historical material” and the latter follows the basic principle of “taking facts as the basis”. Through this commonality, history and law are closely related to each other. This point is particularly obvious in Chinese history.

Unlike the West, law and history are deeply rooted in each other in Chinese history, and one can even draw the conclusion that “history and law are of the same origin,” or “history and law are of the same methodology”. Xu Shen (许慎), a Chinese philologist in the Han dynasty, argued that history and law are of the same origin, or that law develops from history. In the preface to *Shuowen jiezi* (说文解字), he mentioned that “tying the rope is for governance, and for unifying the affairs (结绳为治, 而统其事)” (Xu 1963, 65).[2] In early Chinese society, the state was governed by the records of historiographers, who also acted as legal officials. Xu Shen also stressed that historiographers and legal officials should make objective and just judgements: “Historiographers are those who record the facts. The character *shi* (史) is made of *shou* (又) and *zhong* (中). *Zhong* means justice”; “Law (*fa*) is the criterion of punishment for crime. Law should be equal as still water (*shui*) is flat and even, and

[2]There is a similar viewpoint expressed in *The Book of Changes*: “In ancient times, tying the rope is to rule; and the later sages replaced it by books and inscriptions” (Chap. Xici xia).

so the character *fa* (法) is made of *shui* (水)" (Xu 1963, 202). Chinese traditional historiography, then, not only pursued truth but also fairness and justice, as the law did.[3] In the evolution of China's official administrative hierarchy, it can be seen that legal officials were originally historical officials. Wang Guowei (王国维), in his *On History* (《释史》), mentions: "The historiographers are the officials in charge of documents, and the offices have been important since the ancient times. … Many official titles and their offices come from the historiographers" (Wang 2004, 269). During the Shang and Zhou dynasties, the prime ministers of kings and princes were called *Yu shi* ("御事"), which came from the historical official title *Yu shi* ("御史") found in inscriptions on bones or tortoise shells from the Shang dynasty (Wang 2004, 269–271). During the Spring and Autumn and the Warring States Periods, the official *Yu shi* often exercised their functions as legal officials (*Shi Ji*. Chap. Huaji Biographies). Later, the *Yu shi* became judicial officials rather than historical ones, with the duty of supervising and impeaching other officials, and this office lasted into the Ming and Qing dynasties: "In the Qin Dynasty, the imperial court appointed *Yu shi da fu* (御史大夫), in charge of the deputy prime minister and very respectable; and appointed the censors (*Yu shi*) having the impeachment authority, to supervise the prefectures and counties. After the Han Dynasty, there were changes in the office of the *Yu shi*. The Tang Dynasty established *Shi yu shi* (侍御史), *Dian zhong yu shi* (殿中御史) and *Jian cha yu shi* (监察御史, supervising censor). During the Ming and Qing Dynasties there remained only the office of supervising censors (*Jian cha yu shi*), independently exercising their authorities in different districts" (He et al. 2005, 1442).

In terms of methodology, Chinese textology, one of the branches of Chinese history, has been inspired or influenced by judicial trials. Hu Shi (胡适) posited in his article "The Methods of Scholarship" (《治学方法》) that the terms *Kao ju* (考据, evidence-finding) and *Kao zheng* (考证, proof-finding) are both legal terms, and that "our textology is originally a kind of law of evidence that those who have been junior officials in the earlier time learned from their experience in judgement of litigations" (Hu 2005, 221–222). Chinese historians should therefore use the principle of the law of evidence to examine historical facts as carefully as Western juries or judges would examine legal evidence. It was under the influence of Western evidence law that Hu Shi put forward the historical research principle of "bold hypothesis and cautious verification".

[3] From the time it came into being, Chinese historiography took on the responsibility of punishing evil and promoting good. There is the famous example of Zhao Dun killing his king (赵盾弑君). During the Spring and Autumn Period, Zhao Ling-gong wanted to kill Zhao Dun, so Zhao Dun fled. Before he reached the border, Zhao Ling-gong was killed by Zhao Chuan (赵穿). Soon, Zhao Dun returned, to continue in his role as prime minister of the state of Zhao. Dong Hu (董狐), the historical officer at that time, recorded the incident as "Zhao Dun killed his king". He accused Zhao Dun of being in the state and being the prime minister, but of not doing his duty to catch the murderer. Dong Hu's deed was praised by Confucius, who called him "a good historiographer of ancient times, recording the history without hiding anything" (*Zuozhuan*. Chap. The 2nd year of Xuan Gong).

The viewpoints that "history and law are of the same origin" and that "history and law are of the same methodology" are based on the rationale that historical research and the judicial trial both emphasise the authenticity of evidence and adopt some similar methods. However, there are obvious differences between them in the finding of facts or the interpretation of evidence, and in the degree of authenticity of the confirmed facts.[4]

First, the nature of the evidence is different, and the circumstances related to fact-finding are even more diverse. The jury and the judge consider partial evidence that both parties in litigation have consciously filtered. Moreover, when judging the facts, they have to face the induction and even the instigation of lawyers (cf. Foster and Huber 1999). Finally, public opinion outside the court can also put some pressure on the jury and the judge. All these factors may influence their judgement of the facts. However, historians deal with evidence that often has not been filtered, or has been less consciously filtered. Their materials have multiple sources, rather than just two sources, and so these evidences seldom deny but often support each other. At the same time, historians tend to work in isolation when sorting through historical materials, with little external interference, so they tend to make a more accurate judgement and interpretation of the evidence.

Second, the jury or the judge is more restricted by the law in fact-finding, while historians have more freedom. When judging facts, the jury or the judge should not only consider the authenticity and the relevance of evidence but also abide by the provisions of relevant laws (cf. Anderson et al. 2005). Due to these professional restrictions, legal facts tend to reflect a partial or limited truth rather than a whole truth. In contrast, the goal of historical research is the whole truth. To achieve this goal, historical study does not make such strict requirements on the relevance of evidence; hence, historians can adopt direct or indirect evidence, evidence proved or to be proved and so on. In addition, historians only need to follow the relevant criteria of the historical discipline to identify evidence, and do not need to comply with any legal requirements. In a word, more restrictions in law may lead one to believe that the authenticity of legal facts is inferior to that of historical facts, and even that some correct legal judgements can be considered by historians as misjudgements. For example, there is a notable case in which Aaron Burr, the third vice president of the United States, was prosecuted and acquitted for treason in 1807.

Third, there are time constraints for finding and interpreting facts for a judicial trial, while historians are not bound by time restrictions. The judicial trial must take into account factors such as economic cost and public opinion, which results in cases needing to have a judgement within a certain time frame. Theoretically, with less time, the collected evidence would be less complete, and fact-finding would be hastier, which would eventually lead to proven facts being further away from truth. For historical research, however, proven historical facts are often the result of

---

[4]I should give my thanks to Professor Thomas Man (满运龙) for his inspiration, through which I have finished the following content on the discrimination between fact-findings of history and law. I should also like to express my gratitude to Professor Zhang Qiusheng (张秋升), with whom the conversations improved my knowledge of historiography.

long-term research by a historian or even generations of historians. Thus by virtue of the advantage of the passage of time, the facts proved by historians are theoretically closer to the truth than those by a jury or a judge. At the same time, because the judicial trial needs to make a timely judgement, its fact-finding is often affected by the zeitgeist, which is bound to separate the determined facts from the real situation to some extent. However, historians have a certain distance from the time when an event happened, so they are not bound by time, but can discriminate the evidence more objectively and rationally, and draw more objective conclusions.

Finally, the purposes of historical and judicial fact-finding differ markedly. Recovering the truth is a basic goal for historians, while upholding justice is the duty of the jury or the judge (cf. Anderson et al. 2005). With the objective of serving justice, the law has certain provisions concerning facts which differentiate legal facts from historical facts. At the same time, in the name of justice, the Western jury is usually composed of amateurs, though they are guided by judges who are professionals (cf. Anderson et al. 2005), and they are still confined by their own cognitive capacity, psychological emotions and other factors, which can inevitably affect their fact-finding. Historians, by contrast, are professionals with academic training. Objectivity and rationality are their basic qualities; collecting as much evidence as possible is a basic step in their research; multi-angle and multi-level thinking is a basic paradigm; and the facts should reflect an overall picture. Therefore, in the pursuit of a goal, historical facts are closer than legal facts to indicate what actually happened.

To sum up, judicial trials are restricted and influenced by many factors in the fact-finding process, with the result that legal facts must be limited and partial facts. This issue can cause and certainly has caused the results of some judicial trials to be inconsistent with or even contrary to the truth. To find out the truth is a basic goal of history, and historians tend to investigate as many historical materials as possible and frame their research results as close to the truth as possible. Therefore, judging from the requirements of the two disciplines of history and law, it can be said that historical facts are more authentic than legal facts. The methods of history can be a useful supplement to legal research, and their introduction to legal cases can, to a certain extent, overcome certain shortcomings of law in terms of fact-finding. I shall take the trial of Socrates as an example to demonstrate this.

2 Particularities of Socrates' Presumption of Guilt

According to the existing historical evidence, individuals presumed guilty in classical Athens were either public figures who were actively involved in politics or officials who held important posts. Besides, all of them came from the upper class of society, and had noble birth or financial resources. Second, the presumption of guilt was often found in cases tried in unusual times, when the general emotion of the Athenian public became so agitated that some people used it to attack their enemies through legal methods. Finally, in the case of Socrates, the fundamental reason why he was convicted was not due to the instigation of his accusers but due to the fact that, as the accused, he intentionally provoked the jury. Judging from the status of the accused, the context of the trial and the reasons for the conviction, the trial of Socrates does not accord with the general presumption of guilt in classical Athens.[5]

First, the status of Socrates was different from that of others who were wrongly convicted. Those persons were basically active politicians, and they came from the upper class of society. Due to their different class origins, the Athenian jury, which mainly came from the lower and middle classes, tended to make a presumption of guilt against members of the upper class (cf. Hammond 1977). In classical Athens, politicians were often associated with wealth. Because of the liturgy system, anyone who wanted to succeed in politics needed to perform the liturgies, spending his own wealth to benefit the whole citizen community, so as to win public support. The liturgies cost so much that only the rich could afford them. Therefore, both democratic leaders and aristocratic leaders almost always came from the upper class, such as the famous democratic leader Pericles and the aristocratic leader Cimon. Socrates, by contrast, was neither an active politician nor a man of great wealth. Although Socrates discussed with his disciples how to be an excellent politician and expressed his own views on politics, he did not intend to put these thoughts into practice by himself; therefore, he rejected political life in fact. He remained unknown in political life, except for performing his civic duties, serving as a soldier three times and presiding over an assembly as a member of the presiding committee.[6] Because he did not participate in politics, Socrates never faced the danger of being attacked or accused by his political opponents.

The population of classical Athens was divided into four classes. The first two were wealthy classes, who acted as cavalrymen in military service. The third was the middle class, who served in the army as hoplites, that is, heavy infantry soldiers. The fourth class was *thetes*, that is, the poor, who did not have the money to equip themselves as members of the heavy infantry and even had to work as labourers

---

[5]There were three kinds of presumption of guilt in classical Athens. The first was presumption of guilt under the principle of supremacy of national interests, such as a vote of *ostracism*, which was applied in the trial of the two generals who helped Thebes in 379 BC. In certain periods, the Athenian community would maintain the interests of the whole polis at the expense of the individual citizen, finding innocent people guilty without conclusive evidence of a crime, or even any evidence at all (cf. Aristotle, *The Athenian Politeia*, 22.2-9; Xenophon, *Hellenica*, 5.4.1-19). The second was the presumption of guilt under the procedures of *euthyna* and *eisangelia*, such as the trials of the famous historian and the Athenian general Thucydides in 424 BC and the famous general Timotheus in 373 BC, and others. In classical Athens, each citizen had the right to prosecute any official for malfeasance, bribery or treason (Thucydides, *The Peloponnesian War*, 3.115.2-6, 4.66.1-4; Xenophon, *Hellenica*, 6.2.11-13; Pseudo-Demosthenes, *Against Timotheus*, 6-21). The third kind resulted from instigation of prosecutors and was derived from the second kind of presumption of guilt, the most notable example of which was the trial of the eight generals who led the Battle of Arginusae in 406 BC. At a time when Athenians were generally in a state of agitation, some politicians made use of this approach to attack their opponents or evade legal responsibility (Xenophon, *Hellenica*, 1.6.26-7.34; Diodorus Siculus, *Library*, 13.100.1-103.2; Kagan 1987, 354 n.1).

[6]Plato, *Apology*, 28d-e, 32b; Xenophon, *Hellenica*, 1.7.15. However, Socrates probably held public office during the time of the Thirty Tyrants. The Thirty Tyrants ordered him, along with four other men, to arrest the innocent Leon, but he abandoned his mission on the way (Plato, *Apology*, 32c).

to maintain themselves and their families (Aristotle, *The Athenian Politeia*, 7.3-4). Socrates was from a middle class Athenian background, and served three times as a heavy infantry soldier.[7] However, he then later fell into poverty because he pursued the philosophical life for a long time instead of paying attention to family affairs (Plato, *Apology*, 23b-c, 31b-c). So, in terms of status, Socrates was neither a politician nor a wealthy man, and therefore, under normal circumstances, he would not have been falsely accused so that he would not have been presumed guilty.

Second, the presumption of guilt often occurred during critical periods, and defendants were directly involved in major events and often accused of treason, bribery and other felonies. For example, the Athenians frequently held votes of *ostracism* in the 480s BCE and around 460 BCE, when the Athenian democratic constitution faced serious threats. The eight generals were charged and condumned for failing to retrieve fallen soldiers or their bodies in the Battle of Arginusae in 406 BCE around the festival of the Aparturia, which was celebrated to consolidate the common relationship of the *phratry* (clan).

The case of Socrates was completely different. He was charged and the trial took place in 399 BCE, when the Athenian democratic regime had been rebuilt for four years and was stable. The international situation at that time was also quite peaceful and secure. Athens was neither at war with other city states nor threatened with invasion from outside. In 404 BCE, Athens had been defeated in the Peloponnesian War. With the support of Sparta, the government of the Thirty was established in Athens, which was called "the Tyranny of the Thirty". Eight months later, the Democrats defeated the army of the Thirty Tyrants, re-established the democratic regime, proclaimed amnesty, and the reconciliation and stability of the Athenian *politeia* was realised (cf. Aristotle, *The Athenian Politeia*, 34.2-40.4; Xenophon, *Hellenica*, 2.3.1-4.43). Even if Socrates did not leave Athens during the time of the Thirty, his disciples Critias and Charmides were the leader and a major member of the Thirty, respectively. However, the amnesty decree prohibited any person other than the chief criminal suspects, such as the Thirty Tyrants, from being held legally liable; and even these types of suspects could prove their innocence through the legal process (Aristotle, *The Athenian Politeia*, 39.6). As the amnesty law had been passed and violators would be severely punished, Socrates could not at all be accused of what he had done under the Tyranny of the Thirty (Aristotle, *The Athenian Politeia*, 40.2). Anytus and his friends clearly understood that they had to prosecute him for other crimes to successfully remove him as a hidden danger to democracy. So they charged Socrates with "corrupting the young, and … not acknowledging the gods whom the city acknowledges, but new daimonion instead". These three crimes or faults more or less fit the Athenian impression of Socrates. "Corrupting the young" referred to Socrates' teaching of debate skills, dialectical thinking and especially *elenchus*, that is, logical refutation to the young men, who followed Socrates' example and challenged the ideologies of their parents and the traditional values of the Athenian *politeia* (Plato, *Apology*, 19b-c, 23c, 33c; Xenophon, *Memorabilia*,

---

[7]In *Laches*, Sophroniscus, Socrates' father, was called "a most honorable one", which implies that he was a man of high social status, of certain wealth and of noble character (Plato, *Laches*, 181a).

1.2.40-46). Among these students were the notorious traitor Alcibiades, who had brought disaster to the city of Athens in the Peloponnesian War; Critias, the leader of the Thirty Tyrants; and the son of Anytus himself (Xenophon, *Apology*, 29–31). This was also one of the reasons why Anytus accused Socrates: to prevent his son from following Socrates down an evil path. "Not acknowledging the gods whom the city acknowledges" refers to Socrates' early natural philosophical thought and his rationalistic religious conceptions and moral philosophy (Plato, *Apology*, 18b, 19b-c). In Aristophanes' comedy *Clouds* (366–408), Socrates proves that Zeus does not exist because thunderbolt strikes not the evildoers but the temples, the mountain peaks and the tall oak trees. The new god, the *aethereal vortex*, has replaced Zeus as the force of nature and can drive the clouds, rain and thunder. Although Aristophanes' description of Socrates is somewhat exaggerated and misrepresented, there is no doubt that Socrates, a member of the sophists, had a strong sense of rationalism and moral preaching in his religious conceptions. Believing in the "new daimonion" refers to Socrates' faith in a highly moral god, who is invisible and only makes sound. The divinity, whom Socrates called his "daimon", guided him to avoid doing wrong and to do only what was right (Plato, *Apology*, 31c-d). Thus, Socrates' religious beliefs preceded those of his contemporaries in Athens, who believed in the Olympian gods, who had the same appearance and character as human beings. Because common Athenians would not and could not understand Socrates' ideas, he was regarded as an "alien" and became an object of ridicule. But in the eyes of Anytus, who supported the democratic constitution and traditional morality, Socrates was an abettor, encouraging the young to challenge the traditional moral beliefs and the current democratic regime (Xenophon, *Memorabilia*, 1.2.9). However, the crimes they charged Socrates with were not prescribed clearly in Athenian law, and when the charges were brought, the jury would cast their vote in consonance with their sense of "what is most just" (Hansen 1991). Further, the lower—and middle-class Athenians constituted the main body of the jury, which inevitably brought Socrates a greater advantage in the trial.

Last, unlike any other case wherein a person was presumed guilty, Socrates' conviction resulted from his infuriating the jury with his own proud attitude and speech. In the classical Athenian court, litigants (and more often the accused) dressed up as the vulnerable, emphasised that what they said was true and pleaded for sympathy and justice. However, Socrates never relinquished his dignity in court by bending down to plead for sympathy from the jury. According to Plato's and Xenophon's accounts, Socrates did not write his speech in advance or even conceive of it beforehand. He was confident that his good conduct was his best defence, so he improvised his court speech. Additionally, he stressed to the jury that he had never before been in court because he had never sued anyone else or been sued; therefore, he was unskilled in making a lawcourt speech. He could only defend himself through his usual way of speaking and begged or reminded the jury to judge him on the basis of what he said, rather than how he said it (Plato, *Apology*, 17b–18a). But as is known to all, Socrates was a master of rhetoric and oration, and that he had not previously appeared in lawcourt did not mean he had not studied how to make a lawcourt speech or become skilled in it. Regarding this point, Socrates was obviously lying, and the jury certainly knew this. Therefore, from the very beginning, Socrates showed "contempt" towards the court and the jury, and his lofty integrity and uncompromising attitude were bound to cause disgust on the part of the jury. Next, he set out to clear up the long-held misunderstanding of the Athenians about him, by correcting Aristophanes' and other dramatists' portrayals of him as a ludicrous and loathsome intellectual who "philosophises things in the sky and beneath the earth and makes the weaker into the stronger argument" (Plato, *Apology*, 19b-c). And then he pointed out that the sophists knew nothing, as they were a group of tricksters who cheated for money by presenting ignorance as knowledge or wisdom. Socrates acknowledged that he was equally ignorant, too, yet he admitted that he knew nothing. Being ignorant, he had no knowledge or skill to impart to others, and was essentially an "interlocutor", so he never took a fee from any of his followers. However, Socrates is known for his wisdom. Even the oracle of Delphi, which the Greeks most trusted, admitted that Socrates was the wisest man, but he himself thought he knew nothing. To clear up his doubt, Socrates interviewed statesmen, poets, craftsmen and other people with a reputation for wisdom, only to prove that they were ignorant or had little wisdom. This demonstration by Socrates was imitated by young Athenians, who exposed the "ignorance" of the so—called wise men.

Consequently, Socrates was detested and vilified for these "uglifications" and accused of being a sophist who confused right and wrong. Socrates, however, not only believed there was nothing wrong with his conduct but also considered it divine, ordered by Apollo, and saw himself as a gift from Apollo to the Athenians, a gadfly who could criticise and persuade the Athenians, who were becoming lazy, to pursue virtue and truth (Plato, *Apology*, 30b–31b). In the end, he suggested that he was virtuous and had never done anything wrong or unjust because he had a "divine daimon" to guide him. Socrates' remarks caused several instances of commotion in the court, and the jury believed he used *megalegoria*, i.e. big talk (Plato, *Apology*, 20d4–5, e5, 30c1–6). Nevertheless, 220 of the 500 jurors voted for his acquittal. However, in his second speech, Socrates continued to display his previous attitude, expressing that he was not supposed to be punished with death or exile, but should be rewarded and given free meals at the city hall and regarded as a hero of the city. Although, through the persuasion and guarantee of Plato and others, Socrates was willing to pay a fine of 30 minas as a counter-penalty to the death sentence, he eventually infuriated the jurors who had supported him. Eighty of them voted against him, so he lost the case disastrously by 140–360.

3 Possibilities of Socrates Being Acquitted

Socrates was convicted and sentenced to death in court, and died a month later by drinking hemlock in prison. However, this result was not inevitable. As long as Socrates defended himself according to the established tradition of the Athenian court and did not deliberately offend the jury, he, as such a heretical intellectual, would be tolerated to a certain extent without being convicted.[8]

In Plato's A*pology*, Socrates made it clear more than once that the jury would not convict him if he gave up his position of "justice" and flattered the jury to win their sympathy and support, or if he admitted that he was wrong or guilty and that he would change his ways. This assumption or judgement of Plato or Socrates is correct. In the court, Socrates stood on the opposite side of the court and even of the whole Athens, insisting that the Athenians were depraved, only pursuing money, fame, honour and other things, without concerning themselves with the soul and virtue, and thus, god had appointed him to live in the pursuit of *philisophia*, examining himself and others (Plato, *Apology*, 28e5–6). And at the all-important end of the speech, he attacked and satirised the traditional practice of the Athenian court. Litigants brought their relatives and friends with them to court to cry for sympathy. As a result, serious trial affairs became funny performances and the jury did not decide where justice lay but rather dispensed justice as a favour (Plato, *Apology*, 29d2–30c1, 34b7–34d2). Nevertheless, only 280 jurors voted against Socrates. If he had won 30 more votes, he would have been acquitted. Judging by this vote, the jury should be believed to have remained remarkably calm and restrained. Repeatedly shocked or angered by Socrates' lofty words and deeds, the jury did not vote overwhelmingly against him.

Based on this fact, we can draw the following three possible conclusions. First, if Socrates had admitted his mistake, he would likely have been acquitted. During his speech, Socrates suggested, in the tone of a juror, that the jury would acquit him if only he would "no longer spend time in examining or *philosophia*" (Plato, *Apology*, 29c5–d1). His view was not fanciful, because it was based on a solid reality. The reasons are as follows: first, the body of the jury was very favourable towards Socrates. As a former member of the middle class and now of the lower class,[9] Socrates drew much sympathy among the jury, because the main body of the jury was composed of the middle and lower classes.[10] Although the Greek city states, including Athens, were defined as civic communities, there was a universal sense of identity among the citizens. However, due to the polarisation between the rich and the poor in every city state, a stronger sense of identity existed among different classes than the collective identity of citizen. The jury would thus have identified strongly with Socrates based

[8]In the same year, Meletus and Anytus planned not only the joint accusation against Socrates but also that against Andocides. In contrast to Socrates, Andocides was active in politics and more obviously guilty, but Andocides followed the tradition of the Athenian court in defending himself and was acquitted. (Andocides, *On the Mysteries*, 1–149.).

[9]Plato, *Apology*, 22b8-23c1. Xenophon also mentioned Socrates' poverty more than once (Xenophon, *Memorabilia*, 1.2.1, 1.3.3, 1.6.10, 3.14.1).

[10]Aristophanes, *Wasps*, 303–311; Pseudo-Xenophon, *The Athenian Politeia*, 1.18; Isocrates, *Areopagiticus*, 54; Demosthenes, *Against Timocrates*, 123. Aristotle also argued that due to receiving subsidies, the poor participated in politics in greater numbers than the rich: "All the citizens have a share in the government because of the superiority of the multitude; all actually take part in it and exercise their citizenship because even the poor are enabled to be at leisure by receiving pay. Indeed the multitude in this kind of state has a very great deal of leisure, for they are not hampered at all by the care of their private affairs, but the rich are, so that often they take no part in the assembly nor in judging lawsuits" (Aristotle, *Politics*, 1293a2-9).

on their class instinct. In contrast, the common masses had different degrees of hatred or suspicion towards the upper class, which can be seen from the fact that defendants were often sentenced to death or sent into exile in political cases. Anytus, the mastermind behind the accusation against Socrates, was a democratic leader and played an important role in overthrowing the Tyranny of the Thirty and rebuilding the democratic regime, yet he came from the upper class, and the other two accusers did, too. Therefore, compared with Socrates, Anytus and his friends did not have the advantage of jury members identifying with them, and perhaps were even at a disadvantage.[11] Second, the object of Socrates' instruction was generally the children of the upper class rather than those of the common people. Socrates' instruction had little impact on the common people, and they did not feel deeply or were particularly concerned about his "corrupting the young". Although there were many supporters of elite politics among Socrates' disciples, even including traitors like Alcibiades and crazy oligarchs like Critias, their evil deeds had no direct connection to Socrates' instruction. Although Socrates himself criticised the disadvantages of democracy and advocated the elite politics, he rejected politics in practice, as he did not participate in the camp of oligarchs, nor did he involve himself in any plot to overthrow democracy. In the end, the Athenian legal tradition favoured Socrates, because Athens had strict rules on the judicatory adjudgement in which collective trials and punishment were prohibited. In 406 BCE, the Athenians, in a state of extreme anger, and violating the decree of Kannonus, held a collective trial of eight generals who had led the Battle of Arginusae (Xenophon, *Hellenica*, 1.7.20). This was the only example that can be verified, and there is no other evidence that the Athenians ever held a collective trial. In 462 BCE, the Ephialtic reforms deprived the Council of Areopagus of important powers. As a result, he was retaliated against by the aristocrats and murdered by a metic (cf. Aristotle, *The Athenian Politeia*, 25.4; Plutarch, *Pericles*, 10.7). However, the mastermind behind the murder was not brought to justice. It follows then that, although the Athenian jury treated politicians more harshly, it treated non-politicians in a more lenient way. So, taking all these three factors into consideration, if Socrates had admitted that he was wrong and promised to refrain from the offending behaviour, he would very likely have been acquitted.

Second, even if Socrates had not admitted his mistake or guilt, he would have been able to win the support of the jury through pleading for mercy and get acquitted. Based on the existing sources, there were two kinds of mercy-pleading. One was that the defendant brought his wife, children and parents and had them cry in the court, presenting a pathetic appearance and leading the jury to intuitively sympathise with him. The other was that the defendant stated in his speech if he had been convicted it would bring misfortune to himself, his family, his friends and even the whole community of citizens, thus describing a tragic scene to win the jury's sympathy (cf. Isocrates, *On the Team of Horses*, 47–48; Aeschines, *On the Embassy*, 179). The playwright Aristophanes, in his *Wasps*, described exaggeratedly and criticised vividly the mercy-pleading phenomenon, ironised the defendant who was guilty of

[11] Xenophon also mentioned this advantage of Socrates in his memoirs; unlike his accusers, "he showed himself to be one of the people and a friend of mankind" (Xenophon, *Memorabilia*, 1.2.60).

doing anything possible to escape punishment, and pointed out that members of the jury were not all men of integrity, kindness and justice (cf. Aristophanes, *Wasps*, 547–575). To prevent the defendant's mercy-pleading from influencing the jury, the accuser would often remind the jury not to be confused by it, and not to be partial but instead impartial (cf. Isocrates, *To Philip*, 35; Lysias, *Against Alcibiades II*, 40; Demosthenes, *On the Dishonest Embassy*, 57; *Against Timocrates*, 76). Yet for all that, mercy-pleading could help the defendant win at trial. Dinarchus mentioned an extreme instance in which a certain member of the Council of Areopagus who claimed a subsidy illegally was fined and expelled, but the verdict was overturned by the popular court, and thus the man was acquitted (Dinarchus, *Against Demosthenes*, 55–59). Judging from the practical effect of mercy-pleading, if Socrates had done this, he would probably have been acquitted.

Third, even if Socrates had not admitted his fault or pleaded for mercy, he could still have won the litigation and been acquitted by virtue of his excellent rhetorical skills. As is known to all, rhetoric played an extremely important role in court speech, which was also a fundamental reason for the flourishing of rhetoric in classical Athens. From Plato's account, Socrates' accuser did not match Socrates in rhetorical skill. With his rhetorical skill alone, Socrates could crush his opponents. The court in Athens also had a question-and-answer session, but the speaker could only ask questions of the opponent, not of the opponent's witnesses (Todd 2005). Socrates was a master debater who always proved the absurdity of his opponent's point of view by putting him into a trap of logic through *elenchus*. In court, Socrates also did this. Against the charge of "corrupting the young", Socrates questioned Meletus by first forcing him to draw the false conclusion that all the Athenians were making the young men better, but that Socrates alone was making them worse. And then he led Meletus to admit that Socrates was deliberately corrupting the youth, after causing him to admit that evil men always did evil to those around them and that no one wanted to be hurt. Based on this, there was a logical, irreconcilable contradiction between these two conclusions: Socrates proved that if he did corrupt the youth, there was only the possibility that he did so unintentionally, because no one would deliberately teach anyone around him to do evil to himself. An unintentional mistake was not a crime, which only required criticism and instruction, not legal punishment (Plato, *Apology*, 24c4–26a7). Against the charge that he did not acknowledge "the gods the city acknowledges, but new daimonion instead", Socrates first induced Meletus to admit that Socrates had poisoned the young with the unorthodox *daimon*, and then to acknowledge that Socrates was an atheist. And then Socrates managed to make Meletus admit that Socrates' *daimon* was a god or child of a god in whom the Athenians believed. Through the second round of questioning, Socrates revealed that the accuser understood neither theism or atheism nor religiosity or heresy and finally justified his own belief. From the question-and-answer session, it can be seen that Socrates triumphed over his opponent (Plato, *Apology*, 26a7–28a1). Through a series of logical traps, he proved how absurd the accusation was, and he also proved his innocence. Therefore, if he had wished, Socrates could have won the support of the jury by his rhetorical skills alone.

Among the three possible choices above, the first two both give the impression of being weak to a certain extent and are inconsistent with Socrates' lofty personality. However, the third is compatible with who he was, suggesting he could have won the litigation without damaging his dignity. Socrates, however, still gave up this choice, chosed to use *megalegoria* to make the jury angery instead and lead to his being first convicted and then sentenced to death. So why did Socrates want to die? Was it to defend the dignity of philosophy, as asserted in Plato's *Apology*? Or was it to avoid the miseries of old age, as expressed in Xenophon's *Apology*?

4 Two Explanations of Socrates' Desire for Death

Regarding the trial of Socrates, the basic historical sources come from the works of his two disciples, Plato's *Apology* and Xenophon's *Apology*. Concerning the process of Socrates' trial, Plato's and Xenophon's records are exactly the same. They have minor differences regarding the content of his speech at court, but their reasons for why Socrates was sentenced to death are very different. Plato thought Socrates died to defend the philosophical life, but Xenophon believed he did so to avoid the various miseries of old age and pursue eternal fame. As Plato had a wide and far-reaching influence on the history of thought, and later scholars who studied Socrates' trial were basically philosophers and thinkers, Xenophon's record of Socrates' death has been dismissed as a misunderstanding and defacement of Socrates.[12]

In his *Apology*, Plato portrays Socrates as a steadfast martyr, a man with noble wisdom, willing to cost his life for the pursuit of truth and virtue. In the first speech, based on which the jury would vote for his conviction or acquittal, Socrates started speaking in a unique way, and then insisted that he would stick to his life of philosophy—examining himself and others, standing on the moral height and regarding himself as a gift of god, and criticising various kinds of people in Athens, such as the sophists, politicians, poets, craftsmen and even the common people, because they pretended to know the unknown and abandoned the virtues of life. In this process, he was aware of the potential danger of being convicted and sentenced to death, but he held firmly to his position, saing "I shall not change my conduct even if I am to die many times over" (21c3–23c1, 30a5–31c3). Although he knew his defence had angered the jury, he still hoped to be acquitted. First, after proving the absurdity of his accusers' charge by means of *elenchus*, Socrates tried to prove his innocence by himself. Based on the statement "I know nothing", he appears to have insisted that he had never been anyone's teacher, but was merely an interlocutor (32e6–33b8). And through his own view of the court and his own performance in court, he tried to prove his sincere faith in god (34b6–35d7). Second, both in the opening and at

[12]For a long time, there has been a tradition in academic philosophy that has respected Plato and neglected Xenophon, with the result that Xenophon's *Apology* is regarded as superficial and incredible, while Plato's *Apology* is considered the most authentic record of Socrates (cf. Mueller 1933; Dorion 2006). Although Leo Strauss (1972) emphasized the historical value of Xenophon's works, he chose to ignore the part about the cause of Socrates' death.

the end of his speech, Socrates begged or asked the jury to judge impartially, which was the usual practice in court speeches. In the opening, he reminded the jury that it was the speaker's virtue to say the truth, and that the juror's virtue was to judge according to the truth. And at the end, he reminded the jury once again to judge the case impartially (17d4–18a5, 35c2–d3). Facing the conviction voted on by the jury and the death penalty proposed by the accusers, Socrates showed an ambivalent attitude. On the one hand, he expressed his satisfaction with the result of conviction—he lost by only 30 votes; and on the other hand, he expressed his dissatisfaction with the death penalty—he should be rewarded with a meal at the city hall like a hero who has won glory for the city (35e1–37a1). After that, he chose the last among the three counter-punishments: imprisonment, exile and fine, with the sum being 1 mina. Soon, under the guarantee of Plato and others, he raised the sum to 30 minas. But the jury nevertheless sentenced Socrates to death by an overwhelming majority (37b3–38b8). According to Plato's *Apology*, Socrates was virtuous and innocent, while the whole city of Athens was corrupt, and he was sentenced to death merely because of his loftiness. This narrative style, that "there is not a righteous man but Noah", causes us to doubt its historical authenticity. Some scholars have pointed out that Plato wrote his *Apology* to avenge his spiritual mentor Socrates against Athens. As Gustav Mueller wrote: "He is in a position similar to Orestes or to Hamlet. The father of his soul has been murdered and his mother, the city, is guilty" (Mueller 1933), and revenge was Plato's unshirkable responsibility.

In addition to Plato, Xenophon gives us another image of Socrates. In his *Apology*, Xenophon clearly points out that Socrates employed *megalegoria* to anger the court, and to realise god's arrangement of his fate through the hand of democracy. He died at the most appropriate moment in life, in the most appropriate way, so as to achieve "immortality", that is, to be remembered and eulogised forever. We can see from Xenophon's *Apology* that Socrates was a wise man who could make right decisions and choices all the time. Xenophon begins his record by writing that Socrates was known to have used *megalegoria* in court, and this was rather ill-considered if he did not desire death (Xenophon, *Apology*, 1). He employed *megalegoria* because his "daimon" had instructed him to do so. He had planned to prepare his speech to win the case twice, but the daimon had prevented him from doing so each time, which reinforced his belief that death was his destiny as planned by god (Xenophon, *Apology*, 4–5). At the age of seventy, he was unjustly sentenced to death by the jury and died by drinking hemlock, which Socrates regarded as a favour granted by god. This method of dying had three advantages: It was timely, it was the most comfortable and dignified, and it was the most memorable (Xenophon, *Apology*, 6–9). First, for most ancient people, the age of seventy marked the end of old age. Socrates knew this very well. As he said: "the frailties of old age will inevitably be realised,—that my vision must be less perfect and my hearing less keen, that I shall be slower to learn and more forgetful of what I have learned" (Xenophon, *Apology*, 6). When he could not enjoy the pleasures of life and was living in pain, he wished to die rather than live. Second, drinking poison was the least painful and the most humane method of Athenian execution; it caused much less pain than beheading, being beaten to death and other criminal punishments. The body also remained intact and could be buried in his family cemetery after death, rather than in a foreign land, which would make him a homeless ghost.[13] For Socrates, even if acquitted, it was still painful to die at an old age, suffering from various diseases. By comparison, death by taking poison was easier. Last, a wrongful death would arouse the world's constant sympathy and he would be remembered forever. In the eyes of the ancient Greeks, there were two ways to achieve immortality. One was to have eternal life like the Olympian deities, which mortals could never achieve. But there was another way to immortality that was to be remembered and live in the memory of one generation after another and to be constantly eulogized, which could be achieved by mortals.[14] When talking about the third advantage, Socrates emphasised that "when a person leaves behind in the hearts of his companions no remembrance to cause a blush or a pang, but dissolution comes while he still possesses a sound body and a spirit capable of showing kindliness, how could such a person fail to be sorely missed?" (Xenophon, *Apology*, 7) Placing this sentence in the context of ancient Greece, can we see Socrates' intention to pursue the second means of achieving immortality? Given these three intentions, especially the last, the opinion of Xenophon was that Socrates was consistent in court. He was always lofty, still insisting on his innocence in the second speech, based on which the jury would vote on the punishment, and rejecting the counter-penalties put forward by his disciples, and eventually leading to the result that he was sentenced to death (Xenophon, *Apology*, 22–24). In a word, what creates the greatest impression in Xenophon's *Apology* is that Socrates' death sentence was the result of a careful plan of his own or the god he believed in.

However, the evidence that Xenophon provided did not attract the attention of scholars, and even Leo Strauss (1972), who believed highly in the historical value of Xenophon's works, completely ignored this information. Did Xenophon provide a piece of false evidence? No! Although it is a single piece of evidence, it has unquestionable authenticity. We can find supporting evidence in other historical sources to prove its authenticity. In particular, it is important to note that the aspiration to have a reputation in history is part of the record shared by Plato and Xenophon, who were on bad terms with each other. First, Socrates made himself seem special and divine. Plato and Xenophon recorded the Delphic oracle, the metaphor of a gadfly and the guide of the daimon. The Delphic oracle said Socrates was the most wise man, and based on

[13]The ancient Greeks attached great importance to the burial of the dead. They believed that if the dead could not be buried, their soul would not succeed in entering Hades. Athens also had a criminal penalty of "everlasting banishment", according to which criminals were put to death and their bodies thrown abroad, as it was forbidden to bury them within their homeland (Aristotle, *The Athenian Politeia*, 1.1).

[14]In Homer's *Iliad*, Achilles strongly expresses a desire for the second form of immortality, preferring to die early rather than live long without any reputation in later ages (Homer, *Iliad*, 9.410-416). Later, Alexander the Great also longed for eternal fame, and he expressed his admiration for Achilles, who had acquired everlasting fame through Homer's eulogy (Arrian, *Anabsis Alexandri*, 1.12). In ancient Greek society, notable persons and prominent families usually hired poets to write eulogies for themselves and their families to be immortal. Herodotus, the father of Western historiography, wrote his *Histories* to preserve the exploits of heroes so that they would not be forgotten by later generations (Herodotus, *Histories*, 1.1.1).

the oracle, Socrates began to examine himself and others, to be a hard-working "gadfly", "biting" the Athenians to cause them give up the wrong way of life in pursuit of money, fame and office, and to choose to pursue wisdom, truth and virtue. Moreover, he gave his own examining activities legitimacy and sanctity in the name of the guide of the daimon, who directed Socrates to do right from wrong. Second, both Plato and Xenophon recorded that Socrates mentioned Palamedes, who was wrongly sentenced to death and for whom he expressed his admiration. In Plato's *Apology*, Socrates argued that he would be perfectly happy after death and also be "immortal", standing alongside Palamedes.[15] In Xenophon's *Apology*, Socrates pointed out that Palamedes was praised far more than his unjustified murderer Odysseus (Xenophon, *Apology*, 26), and that to be remembered and praised means immortality. These two sources suggest to different extents that Socrates wanted to achieve immortality by becoming a Palamedic figure. A divine identity, a divine mission and an unusual death are similar to the story of Jesus, who came into the world, redeemed it and then ascended to heaven after death. Taken together, there is no reason to doubt Socrates' intention to achieve the second kind of immortality by creating his own unjust case.

Was Socrates' image as a moral personification not damaged when he gained immortal fame by creating his own unjust case, and made the Athenians and democracy notorious in this way? Did Socrates himself not consider this way immoral? Not necessarily. Socrates' political ideas were based on elitist politics and technocracy, and it was also his duty to expose and criticise the disadvantages of democracy. Therefore, he guided the young people in private conversation to pursue the true virtue, truth and ideal polity, to deconstruct the traditional Athenian knowledge and values. By creating his own unjust case, he could not only prove the defect in democratic politics but also achieve his expected goal. Was this not a wise approach in Socrates' opinion? From a neutral point of view, using his own experience in the trial, Socrates proved the correctness of his political ideas and the fault of Athenian democracy: A man, without being proved guilty, was sentenced to death, only because of his proud attitude and for refusing to bow to the jury to apologise. Did this not just demonstrate the absurdity of Athenian democracy? Even if there was a moral flaw in Socrates' practice, it was always ignored because of his great dedication, and this was the reason why the information Xenophon provided was not valued by later scholars. Therefore, in the memory of later generations, Socrates has always maintained a great and brilliant eternal image.

The subjects in historical activities are human beings with their consciousnesses. Those who want to win fame in history are just like both parties in judicial trials. They would choose to keep records that are favourable to them and even present false information. Facing these one-sided records and false information, historians can judge their authenticity and restore the historical truth only through careful analysis of the relevant sources. The jurors or judges in a judicial trial are in an environment

[15]Plato, *Apology*, 41b1-41c7. The word "immortal" in the text can be understood in two ways. First, according to the religious concept of the ancient Greeks, after death, the dead enter Hades, where they exist in the form of ghosts forever, and they will not suffer a second death. Second, the wronged Palamedes gained immortal fame, and so will Socrates standing alongside him.

similar to that of historians, but are not as fortunate as historians. They not only face conflicting testimony and persuasion and the restraint of relevant legal provisions, but also are affected by the zeitgeist and other factors of their age, so there is a certain gap between the facts that they find and the truth of the case, and the former is sometimes even contrary to the latter. Based on the records of Plato and Xenophon, this paper has analysed Socrates' status, the accusations against him, the course of his speech and the reasons why he angered the jury, and concluded that, although defending the philosophical life was an important reason for his being sentenced to death, his intention of seeking immortality was also a key factor. We can further conclude that the Athenians appeared to have judged Socrates, but in fact, Socrates judged the Athenians, who declared themselves guilty by convicting Socrates. In this double trial, Socrates won an everlasting reputation for himself through the unjust judgement of the jury and became the winning party and the beneficiary, while Athenian democracy bore everlasting notoriety for this and became the losing party and the victim. In a word, through analysis of the trial of Socrates, this paper reaches its final conclusion: as judges of history, historians can get rid of certain dilemmas of the jury or the judge and reveal facts beyond the law in some judicial cases; therefore, the introduction of historical research methods would help promote legal research and uphold justice in judicial trials.

References

Anderson, Terence, David Schum, and William Twining. 2005. *Analysis of Evidence*. Cambridge: Cambridge University Press.

Dorion, Louis-André. 2006. Xenophon's Socrates. In *A Companion to Socrates*, ed. Sara Ahbel-Rappe and Rachana Kamtekar, 93–109. Oxford: Blackwell.

Foster, Kenneth R., and Peter W. Huber. 1999. *Judging Science: Scientific Knowledge and the Federal Courts*. Cambridge, Ma.: The MIT Press.

Hammond, N. G. L. 1977. *A History of Greece to 322 B.C.* Oxford: Clarendon Press.

Hansen, Mogens Herman. 1991. *The Athenian Democracy in the Age of Demosthenes*. Trans. J. A. Crook. Oxford: Blackwell.

He, Jiuying, Wang Ning, and Dong Kun. 2015. *Cihai*. Beijing: The Commercial Press.

Hu, Shi. 2005. *The Voice of Hu Shi: Spheeches of Hu Shi 1919–1960*. Guilin: Guangxi Normal University Press.

Kagan, Donald. 1987. *The Fall of the Athenian Empire*. Ithaca and London: Cornell University Press.

Mueller, Gustav. 1933. Another Approach to Socrates. *International Journal of Ethics*. 43: 429–429.

Parker, Robert. 2005. Law and Religion. In *The Cambridge to Ancient Greek Law*, ed. Michael Gagarin and David Cohen, 61–81. Cambridge: Cambridge University Press.

Stone, I.F. 1989. *The Trial of Socrates*. New York: Random House.

Strauss, Leo. 1972. *Xenophon's Socrates*. Ithaca and London: Cornell University Press.

Todd, S.C. 2005. Law and Oratory at Athens. In *The Cambridge to Ancient Greek Law*, ed. Michael Gagarin and David Cohen, 97–111. Cambridge: Cambridge University Press.

Wang, Guowei. 2004. *Guantang jilin*. Beijing: Zhonghua Book Company.

Xu, Shen. 1963. *Shuowen jiezi*. Beijing: Zhonghua Book Company.

Seeking Truth in Law and History

How We Get to Know What Aaron Burr Did? Ascertaining Past Facts in History and in Law

Thomas Yunlong Man and MengXuan Lu

1 Shades of Truth About Aaron Burr in Two Events

Aaron Burr (1756–1836), the third Vice President of the United States (1800–1804), was an atypical member of the "Founding Fathers" club. This prestigious club is normally exemplified by such towering figures as George Washington, Thomas Jefferson, Benjamin Franklin, John Adams, Alexander Hamilton and James Madison who, in a span of one half century from the 1770s to the 1820s, led the British colonies in North America to gain independence from the Great Britain, created a federal republic for the newly independent United States and guided the young republic through its turbulent years of early existence. Son of the second president of the College of New Jersey (later Princeton) and grandson of the noted theologian Jonathan Edwards, Burr, at the onset of the colonial revolt against the British rule, suspended his budding legal career to join the Continental Army at age 20 and rose to the rank of lieutenant colonel through dedicated military service. After the independence, he resumed his law practice in New York City and quickly developed a successful political career in state and national politics. He ran with Jefferson on the Republican presidential ticket in the election of 1796 (which was won by Adams) and again 1800, which was decided in favor of Jefferson by the House of Representatives after 36 ballots when Burr and Jefferson had received equal number of votes from the Electoral College. Burr became Vice President during the first Jeffersonian administration (1800–1804) (Isenberg 2007).

T. Y. Man (✉)
Peking University School of Transnational Law, Shenzhen, China
e-mail: tman@stl.pku.edu.cn

M. Lu
China University of Political Science and Law, Beijing, China

B. Zhang et al. (eds.), *A Dialogue Between Law and History*,
https://doi.org/10.1007/978-981-15-9685-8_17

Despite his swift ascent to the top of national politics, Burr managed to become the common enemy of the nation's political archrivals Jefferson, leader of the Republican party, and Hamilton, leader of the Federalist party. Jefferson accrued strong aversion to Burr through the 1800 election when Burr declined to step aside when they received the same number of Electoral College votes. Hamilton, a fellow New Yorker, and Burr had long developed mutual animosity in local and national politics entangled with personality clashes. Both Jefferson and Hamilton seemed to view Burr as lacking in principle, motivated only by expediency and desire to satisfy his large personal ambitions. Unfortunate to Burr, as history turns out, he has been remembered primarily neither for his devotion in military service to the American independence nor for his brilliance in court advocacy or his extraordinary talent in political organization, but for his bitter antagonism with Jefferson and Hamilton that culminated in two events that captivated the young nation during the first decade of the nineteenth century: the duel with Hamilton in 1804 and his treason trial in 1807 orchestrated by Jefferson (Wood 2009, 382–383).

1.1 The Burr-Hamilton Duel

In 1804, towards the end of his term as Vice President in a Republican administration, Burr was enlisted by some Federalists, the Republicans' political foes, to run for New York governor. Hamilton was the most respected leader of the Federalist party, and he openly opposed Burr's candidacy. Burr lost the Federalist nomination but continued his campaign as an independent. Hamilton was widely quoted by media to have attacked Burr on numerous occasions. Burr requested Hamilton to retract these remarks and issue an open apology, which Hamilton rejected. Burr believed that Hamilton's public comments about him had exceeded the boundary of political disagreements and amounted to personal attacks as a matter of "gentleman's honor," which, according to the custom of that time, can only be resolved by a duel. On June 27, he challenged Hamilton for a duel, termed as an "interview," which Hamilton readily accepted.

On the early morning of July 11, Burr and Hamilton met at the agreed spot on the bank of the Hudson River on the New Jersey side. In accordance with the negotiated procedures and customs, they fired pistol shots at ten paces. Hamilton was hit and collapsed to the ground. Burr was not hurt. Hamilton died the next day in a friend's house in New York (Ellis 2001, 20–47).

Because duel was illegal under the laws of New York and New Jersey, both states charged Burr with murder. Burr left New York and returned to Washington to finish his remaining term as Vice President. Neither state started actual prosecution, but contemporaries and historians ever since have continued to debate the "facts" of the duel, focusing on two questions: (a) Did Aaron Burr kill Alexander Hamilton? and (b) Did Aaron Burr murder Alexander Hamilton? While there seems to be a near uniform answer to the first question, there is by no means any accord on the answer to the second question.

1.2 The Burr Treason Trial

Although emerged unhurt from the duel, Burr's reputation and public life virtually ended with the duel. He was widely disliked and even hated by members of the both parties, and Jefferson excluded him from the second Jeffersonian administration (1804–1808). Upon departure from Washington in March 1805, Burr immediately embarked on a secret and ambitious enterprise involving the vast the territory west of the Alleghenies that included both the settled areas comprising the states of Ohio, Kentucky and Tennessee and the Indiana Territory, Mississippi Territory, Orleans Territory and West Florida and the newly acquired area between the Mississippi River and the Rocky Mountains through the Louisiana Purchase in 1803 (Wood 2009, 365–374). From April 1805 to late 1806, Burr made several trips to this area during which he met, often secretly, with local leaders, military officers and wealthy individuals to discuss plans to invade the Spanish territories and to organize the Western states and territories into a country separate from the United States. He solicited support from the British and Spanish ministers to the United States and raised funds and provisions to assemble armed forces for a large scale "expedition." After President Jefferson learned Burr's activities, he publicly denounced them in November 1806. Burr was arrested in Alabama in February 1807 (Stewart 2011, 88–207).

Burr was indicted by a federal grand jury for treason and misdemeanor for carrying on war against Spain. He was tried at the federal circuit court in Richmond, Virginia, from August 3 to September 1, 1807, presided by Chief Justice John Marshall of the Supreme Court sitting on the circuit court as a trial judge. After Chief Justice Marshall made some important rulings on evidentiary issues and interpretation of the Constitutional provision on treason, the jury acquitted Burr (Hoffer 2008).

Burr's exoneration from the capital crime of treason ended his legal trouble but did not stop his contemporaries and historians of successive generations from pondering the "facts" of his activities that led to his treason trial. After all, do these "facts" support the allegation that Aaron Burr committed treason against the United States?

2 Fact-Finding in the Court of History and of Law

2.1 Reckoning with Past "Facts"

People live in different places and times. No matter where they live, people engage in social and political activities as "political animals" (Miller, et at. 1991, 20–21). They also engage in cultural and intellectual activities as "the most intelligent species" (Toothman 2010). In these pursuits, people invariably face the need to achieve resolution or at least understanding of social and intellectual problems of various nature and magnitude. Oftentimes resolution or understanding of a present-day social or intellectual problem requires knowing, to a variety of level of certainty, what happened in a given past time and place.

Historical studies and judicial trials are two kinds of human activities that rely heavily on ascertaining the relevant "facts" or "truth" in the recent or distant past to fulfill their respective core social functions. For this reason, historical research and writing, as an intellectual and, at least since the late nineteenth century, academic vocation, and judicial trials, established by the state as the statutorily ordained process to resolve legal disputes, have the common task of determining past facts at a very high level of certainty. Therefore, it has long been recognized that in terms of seeking past facts by evidentiary proof, history's use of evidence is "the most closely akin to that of the law"(Rescher and Joynt 1959).

At the same time, because of the fundamental differences in the nature of historical and judicial fact-finding, they approach fact-finding in vastly different ways that are in large part defined by their social functions and conditioned by their institutional and disciplinary contexts.

2.2 *Shared Needs and Tools of Inquiry*

In at least three respects, writing history and reaching a judicial decision share the need to determine historical facts with confidence in assured certainty.

2.2.1 Foundational Role of Fact-Finding

First, to perform their social functions, either expected or self-imposed, both judicial trial and historical writing must build their analytical enterprises on a solid foundation of factual accuracy.

A judicial trial endeavors to resolve a legal dispute. Every judicial decision to solve a legal dispute consists of primarily two components: ascertaining facts in dispute and applying legal rules and principles to these facts. The process of judicial fact-finding, or judicial proof, is fundamental and antecedent to any just adjudication of legal disputes. As noted by a legal scholar, "[F]acts are prior to and determinative of rights and obligations. Without accurate fact finding, rights and obligations are meaningless." (Allen 2014, 16) Justice, in this sense, is inseparable from factual truth (Ho 2008, 6).

In a similar vein, the craft of historical research and writing concerns explicitly with human past. In the Western world, it can be traced at least from Homer's Iliad and Odyssey of the sixth century B.C., two of the epics composed by the bards that have been preserved because they were in written form (Breisach 1983, 5–6). Keeping human memory remains the primary goal of historical writing, which is fundamental to all other social functions, despite the generational changes in articulating the related social functions of historiography (Novick 1988, 8), such as identifying the law of human progress, tracing the origins of contemporary institutions, customs, and, above all, proving "the existence of an inescapable link between past, present and future." (Breisach 1983, 2).

2.2.2 Fact-Finding Based on Indirect Information

"[W]hile the past is manifestly important," as aptly observed by a historian,

> "it is also impossible to apprehend directly (as one might apprehend the mountain and river system of Europe, the production and collection in a laboratory of H_2S gas, or the functions of the heart in pumping blood round the human body): it can only be apprehended through memories, myths, and, most important, through the relics and 'sources', archaeological, written, printed, painted, etc., etc., – which it leaves." (Marwick 1989, 2–3)

What is true to historical fact-finding is also true to judicial fact-finding. Like historians, judicial fact-finders have no personal experience or knowledge of the past facts to be ascertained. Instead, they rely entirely on the personal knowledge of others (i.e. layman witnesses who acquired personal knowledge for being physically present at the time and place of the particular past event) or the interpretations of certain real, documentary or "scientific" evidence (e.g. objects or results of scientific testing or experiments) provided by others (layman or expert witnesses) who are qualified as witnesses due to personal knowledge (Capra 2015, 92) or legally recognized special "knowledge, skill, experience, training or education." (Capra 2015, 133).

Therefore, both historical and judicial fact-finders have no direct contact with the past facts. They access these facts *indirectly* through information furnished by others in different forms. In historical writing, such information is normally referred to as "sources," and is known in judicial process as "evidence."

2.2.3 Evidence-Inference Reasoning

Because of the indirect nature of historical and judicial fact-finding, fact-finders in these two disciplines have to resort to "inference," the epistemological device by which rational fact-finders derive belief in past facts to be ascertained from "evidence" or "sources." Modern historical and judicial fact-finding undertakings explicitly or implicitly adopt the same "Evidence-Inference Reasoning" process. As observed by the editors of a book pioneering the interdisciplinary comparison of judicial fact-finding and history, both disciplines "involve … drawing inferences from evidence to test hypothesis and justify conclusions, and the logic of this kind of enquiry is governed by the same principles." (Twining and Hampsher-Monk eds. 2003, 5).

Before the scientific revolution of Western Europe in the sixteenth and seventeenth centuries, with some notable exceptions, most human societies enlisted the help of super-natural or divine forces to discover and explain past events (Breisach 1983, 12–65). Historians across different ages and civilizations had used the will of god(s) and miracles to record and interpret history (Marwick 1989, 31). By contrast, judicial trials had relied on various forms of "divine" judgment to sort out conflicting facts underlying legal disputes (Lea 1870). The main reason for historians and judges alike in the pre-scientific revolution age to seek truth by divine guidance was the fact that humans of ancient and medieval times had no trust in the human ability to know what had happened in the past. Based on this belief, they had to rely on some force outside the human cognitive faculties, either god(s) or other supernatural beings, to meet the social needs of reckoning with past occurrences (Arnold et al. 1981, 111).

The scientific revolution introduced fundamental changes. People began to develop a firm belief in the human ability to know its own past by themselves. The key to this realization was the nascent scientific method, by which people, without resorting to supernatural or divine forces, were able to understand their natural and social environment, both presently and in a given time and place in the past. Thus, all human acts that lay behind historical events became knowable phenomena, just like all sorts of natural phenomena. There were no longer mysteries or myths that would permanently defy human cognition, but only yet-to-be observed and cognized phenomena (Lerner ed. 1962, 11).

Central to this scientific method that would enable people to know their own past is the "Evidence-Inference Reasoning" process. What happened in the past are unique and incapable of being replayed (Lerner ed. 1962, 20), unlike the VAR (video assistant referee) and other instant replay technologies that have become widely used in sports competitions. But they have left traces of their occurrence in innumerable forms such as oral and written records, anthropological customs and archeological relics that inform people of later generations of their occurrence. Such traces of the past are commonly referred to as "evidence" due to their ability to evidence—prove—the occurrence of the past events (Longman 2001, 469).

Under the Evidence-Inference Reasoning model, it is believed that people are able to use verifiable evidence to make rational inferences of things and events for which they are unable to perceive directly through the five human senses. By intuition and natural thinking, people perform inferential reasoning based on generalized understanding of the natural phenomena and societal affairs from well-developed body of knowledge and experience (Allen et al. 2016, 138). Inferences can be either reasonable or unreasonable for various reasons (Strong et al. 1999, 173), but an explicit articulation of the reasoning process enables others to understand, evaluate and, if necessary, pass judgment on the conclusions. In an environment where human knowledge becomes public information open to all, this "Evidence-Inference Reasoning" process of scientific proof enables people to ascertain historical facts through a three-step process: (1) propose propositions or hypotheses; (2) make rational inferences based on all available evidence; and (3) use commonly recognized human knowledge to verify the inferences (Lerner ed. 1962, 9).

In accordance with the modern epistemological theory of fact-finding, historical facts, like most past and present natural and societal phenomena, are knowable, but not necessarily known (Lerner ed. 1962, 11). One central reason is that it is not possible, theoretically and practically, to obtain all evidence and the quality of the available evidence is neither perfect nor sufficiently credible (Twining and Hampsher-Monk eds. 2003, 33–34). Therefore, it is not possible to achieve complete certainty for past facts based on incomplete and imperfect evidence. Instead, people utilized the concepts of probabilities, a field bordering mathematics and logic that experienced rapid development from the first several decades of the twentieth century (Lempert 1986), to quantify the degree of certainty in fact-finding. Thus, in the prevailing discourse of modern fact-finding, while the concept "fact" denotes occurrence of events or state of affairs, past or present, that have become known, the concept "truth" represents "the closest statistical approximation to the observed occurrence of events." (Lerner ed. 1962, 13) In addition to this conception of "truth" based on the correspondence theory of truth through the probabilistic lenses, a growing syntheses of judicial proof centered around the inference to the best explanation model (IBE) (Pardo and Allen 2007) is competing with the probabilistic model to provide an alternative analytical framework (Allen 2014, 407–410). The IBE model is at least partially based on the coherence theory of truth (Kaptein et al. 2009), which in practical terms emphasizes consistency with known and verifiable explanations (Amaya 2013, 24).

2.3 *Contextual Constraints on Selecting Evidence and Making Rational Inferences*

Whereas historians and judges (and jurors in jury trials), as designated fact-finders in their respective fields, have implicitly or explicitly used the "Evidence-Inference Reasoning" method to derive rational conclusions of truth in fact-finding from available evidence, they nevertheless face vastly different external constraints in their respective fields. For our purposes, the following differences are particularly relevant.

2.3.1 Legally Authorized Decision-Makers V. Private Intellectuals

In judicial trials, the fact-finders, either the judge in a bench trial or the jurors in a jury trial, are individuals with legal authorization to ascertain the case facts through the formal judicial proceedings. They have no freedom to collect evidence outside the judicial process. Instead, jurors are forbidden from either actively gathering or passively learning evidence other than the information presented to them during the trial strictly according to meticulously formulated procedural and evidence rules. Judges have more access to evidence than jurors, but they are either deprived of the power to decide on factual issues in jury trials or censured by law in bench trials not to consider evidence outside the legally admissible scope. Thus, fact-finders in judicial process, while empowered by law to perform fact-finding as an official function, are at once severely limited by the same set of legal rules in exercising this official function.

In comparison, a historian has neither formalized legal definition nor legal authorization to carry out fact-finding in history. Everyone who writes about history, with or without a professional title or position in an academic institution, is recognized as a historian. As a practitioner in a specialized field of intellectual discipline, she relies on no legal authorization to express her opinion on historical facts. Nor is she restricted by legal rules of any kind from gathering evidence from any source and drawing conclusions on any factual issues. In practicing her craft, she is only restrained by her own sense of professionalism and voluntary submission to recognized ethical standards of the relevant professional community.

2.3.2 Limitations of Time

Judicial trials are structured in a strictly confined timeframe. A legal dispute, no matter how important by whatever standards, must be resolved within prescribed time limits because judicial resources are not infinite, thus must be distributed among different legal disputes. It follows that judicial fact-finders are required to complete fact-finding within legally prescribed timeframes, which in recent decades have become increasingly compressed as the increase of legal disputes has outpaced the expansion of judicial resources.

Unlike judicial fact-finders, historians are not equally pressured by legally prescribed time limits to complete their historical fact-finding. Unless driven by the self-imposed deadlines (e.g., for publication of an article in an academic journal), a historian is otherwise free from externally imposed timeframe to collect evidence and draw inferences from the evidence.

2.3.3 Scope of Facts to Be Proven

In addition to being free from legally prescribed such external constraints as time pressure, a historian is not under any legal requirement to select her subject of study. The historical facts she chooses to ascertain thus are not limited in any way by external factors, legal or otherwise. Instead, she is free not only to select the subject of study according to her own intellectual interests but also to define the scope of study, including what specific "facts" or historical "truth" to be unearthed or ascertained.

In sharp contrast, the scope of judicial fact-finding is strictly confined to "facts of consequence" (FOC), referring to facts in a legal dispute material to the legal resolution of the dispute. They are essentially elements prescribed by the substantive law to comprise the legal action (Allen et at. 2016, 135). Any other facts, unless directly related to or otherwise connected with any fact of consequence in a given legal dispute, are not within the purview of the fact-finding process.

2.3.4 Finality of Fact-Finding

As part of the formal dispute resolution process, a judicial fact-finding by the trial court is legally binding on the parties to the process and considered final with respect to the legal dispute in question. The appellate courts usually respect the trial court's fact-finding by strongly deferring to the trial court in factual determinations (Coffin 1994, 35).

Despite the often noted and not infrequently held popular belief that history renders the final judgment (Dershowitz 2004, 266), most historians do not subscribe to the idea that their profession is either legally authorized, as the judicial fact-finders in judicial trials, or properly equipped to have the final say on the subject matter of historical studies. "[I]n the court of history, there are no final judgments." (Resta and Zeno-Zencovich 2013, 844).

2.3.5 Free Proof V. Rule-Based Proof

At the practical level, there exists a more fundamental and consequential difference between the use of the "Evidence-Inference Reasoning" model in historical fact-finding and judicial fact-finding. This relates to the issue of whether formalized, legally prescribed rules and standards perform any meaningful role at the working level of the "Evidence-Inference Reasoning."

For historians, amateur or professional, there are no legally prescribed procedures, rules and standards. Since the beginning of historiography in the ancient times, fact-finding associated with historical research and writing has always been guided by loosely constructed vocational and, from the late nineteenth century professional, standards. Each historian is generally free to perform her fact-finding according to her own understanding of the contours and soft requirements of these standards. No legal consequence would ensue if any of these informal, unsystematic standards are deemed to be not strictly complied with. Any consequence would be reputational within the disciplinary community.

As compared with judges and legal scholars who practice judicial fact-finding in judicial trials and related legal writing, other than the "soft law" type of professional standards (Snyder 2019), historians are not legally constrained from exercising free proof in historical fact-finding. To some, this is a benefit, but also a drawback in terms of lack of disciplinary roadmap: "There is no historiographical Wigmore, Stephen, or Thayer and no body of precedents which is recognized as a reliable guide." (Fischer 1970, 62).

Unlike historians, judicial fact-finders are closely guided and tightly restricted by a complex web of legal rules, standards and procedures in performing the "Evidence-Inference Reasoning" to derive case facts in judicial trials (Twining 1994, 211). Under the common law tradition, this process is centered around the adversarial control of evidentiary proof on the basis of reliance on the inferential reasoning of lay fact-finders (Allen, et at. 2016, 688). It features a two-stage structure dealing with, respectively, issues of admissibility of evidence and sufficiency of evidence.

The first stage focuses on issues of admitting evidence into the pool of information made available to fact-finders as the evidentiary basis to make rational inferences of facts of consequence—factual matters material to the legal dispute. It is a heavily rule-based process, each aspect of which is defined and controlled by a complicated set of rules. These rules defining and controlling the admission of evidence constitute a major part of the body of legal rules and standards commonly referred to as the rules of evidence, such as the Federal Rules of Evidence that are applicable mainly to the U.S. federal courts (Congress 1975).

Striving to strike an appropriate balance among three sets of core values of seeking truth, procedural fairness and judicial efficiency underlying judicial proof in the U.S. courts, the rules of evidence, based on both statutes and case law, provide detailed requirements and procedures on the admissibility of evidence divided into functional categories (testimonial evidence, real evidence, documentary evidence, demonstrative evidence, etc.). In addition to a series of "positive" rules of admissibility based on established criteria of relevance, materiality and competence, there are also a diverse group of "negative" admissibility rules, commonly known as "exclusionary" rules, devised to exclude relevant and probative evidence based on articulated concerns on reliability (e.g. hearsay), fairness (e.g. character evidence), juridical economy (e.g. Rule 403 balancing test) and compliance with related Constitutional and legal requirements outside the judicial proof process (e.g. privileges; exclusion of illegally obtained evidence in criminal trials; subsequent remedial measures).

Once passed the admissibility thresholds, all evidence is presented to fact-finders through adversarial trial proceedings. The law becomes much less involved in the second of stage of judicial proof to determine the sufficiency of the evidence. Fact-finders are largely given a free hand to decide on the issue of sufficiency by evaluating the credibility of competing evidence and making rational inferences based on "natural reasoning." (Allen et al. 2016, 127–131) The law is satisfied with merely providing the legal standards of "sufficiency" and allocating the burden of proof to meet the applicable standard among different parties in different types of lawsuits, e.g. the prosecution in criminal cases bearing the burden of proving each element of the crime beyond a reasonable doubt and the plaintiff in civil cases generally bearing the burden of proving elements of the legal action by preponderance of the evidence (Giannelli 2009, 45–54).

3 Judicial "Truth" of Burr in Two Events

3.1 Two Events, Different Judicial Fates

Judging by the results of his encounters with criminal justice following his 1804 duel with Hamilton and his secretly planned "expedition" to the Western states and territories two years thereafter, Aaron Burr should be pleased with his luck. Although indicted for criminal offenses in both cases, he was never prosecuted for killing

Hamilton in either New Jersey or New York. He returned to New York to resume his law practice in May 1811, after the state had formally dropped the murder charge against him (Stewart 2011, 293). While he escaped prosecution for actually causing the death of a human being with national statue in an activity expressly outlawed by both New Jersey and New York, he was rigorously prosecuted by the federal government for his activities that had resulted in no loss of life or property.

3.2 Drama Played—The Treason Trial of Burr

The trial of Burr for treason in the federal district court in Richmond during the summer of 1807 provides us with a classical example of judicial fact-finding. Like all other judicial trials, the Burr trial was aimed to resolve a legal dispute—the dispute between the federal government under President Thomas Jefferson and an individual, Aaron Burr, over the question of whether Burr had committed the crime of "treason." Organized as a trial by jury, a federal jury of 12 men selected from the local community wielded the legal authority to ascertain facts and apply the law to the facts in order to make a judicial decision that would determine the fate of Burr—in this case, a life-and-death issue as treason is a capital offense.

Despite of the grave consequences of their decision, the jury, as fact-finders, had only limited time to make a decision. As it actually played out, the trial officially started on August 3, 1807 and lasted for 30 days until September 1 when the jury announced its verdict (Hobson 2006). The judicial decision in the form of a jury verdict was final as judicially affirmed "facts" of the case, which is not subject to review by anyone, including any appellate courts.

With the legal power to make final determination of case facts under a limited timeframe, the scope of the jury's fact-finding mission is strictly confined to "facts of consequences," i.e., the facts material to the essential elements prescribed by substantive law that comprise the underlying legal action. In this case, it was the crime of treason as defined in Article III, Sect. 3 (1) of the U.S. Constitution:

> Treason against the United States shall consist only in levying war against them, or in adhering to their enemies, giving them aid and comfort. No person shall be convicted of treason unless on the testimony of two witnesses to the same overt act, or on confession in open court

Accordingly, the Constitution has provided both the essential elements of "treason" as a federal crime and the unusually restrictive ways that such a crime can be proved in judicial proceedings. In terms of the essential elements of treason, there are basically two kinds of "treasonous" acts: "levying war against" the United States or "adhering to" the enemies of the United States by "giving" the enemies "aid and comfort." In the Burr case, the "adhering to" theory was apparently not applicable; the prosecution's charge was thus based on the "levying war" theory (Hobson 2006, 46–48). Regarding the ways of proof, because Burr rejected confession by pleading not guilty, the prosecution was left with the only option: testimony by two witnesses "to the same overt act." Therefore, the prosecution had to convince the jury that (a) Burr levied "war" against the United States; and more specifically (b) in levying such war Burr carried out "overt act" testified by two witnesses.

These constitutional constraints forced the federal prosecutors to build their case on selected evidence from Burr's diverse activities over a span of two years, focusing heavily on the "assemblage" of a group of armed men at Blennerhassett's Island, Wood County, Virginia (now West Virginia) on December 10–11, 1806, as evidence of "overt act" to levy war against the United States. They argued that, following the English common law, Burr could be considered to be legally or "constructively" present at Blennerhassett's Island on December 10–11 regardless of whether he was physically present. However, their efforts were dealt with a fatal blow by Chief Justice Marshall's interpretation of the meaning of "overt act" in the Constitution. Building on the courts' power of judicial review that had been emphatically pronounced in *Marbury v. Madison* (1803) four years ago, Chief Justice Marshall rejected the government's interpretation of "overt act" and accepted the defense's argument that no person may be held guilty of treason unless actually present when the "overt act" of "war" took place.

From the perspective of judicial proof, Chief Justice Marshall's interpretation of the "overt act" language effectively prevented the jury from making the inference of Burr undertaking any "overt act," thus disabling the prosecution from proving an essential element of the charged offense. Consequentially, even if the jury was able (and appeared to be ready) to use the "Evidence-Inference Reasoning" to infer, from the testimonial and documentary evidence showing a vast conspiracy involving U.S. military officials, private financiers and even foreign powers, intentions as well as preparatory acts of Burr that could be reasonably held to be "treasonous" in nature, such as plotting to seize Western territories by armed force and separating them from the union and especially his secret meetings and correspondence with the British and Spanish ministers to the United States to seek financial and military support for his plan to "render" the Western territories "independent of the United States" (Stewart 2011, 89), they were prohibited by Chief Justice Marshall's definition of "overt act" to convict Burr. Thus, the unusual language of the jury's verdict, reached after only 25 min' deliberation, hinted that they might have decided the case differently, if not for the court's instructions: "We of the jury say that Aaron Burr is not proved to be guilty under this indictment by any evidence submitted to us. We therefore find him not guilty." (Hoffer 2008, 171).

Therefore, it was the jury who formally determined the "facts" of the case by freely conducting the "Evidence-Inference Reasoning" as an internal, cognitive exercise. But their reasoning process had been meticulously conditioned by external legal rules and standards permeating the judicial fact-finding process. Chief Justice Marshall, who was not a fact-finder under the system, was nevertheless able to shape and even control the outcome of the fact-finders' reasoning process by various evidentiary rulings (Hoffer 2008, 143–171) and, above all, his interpretation of the meaning of "overt act."

4 Drama Never Played—The "Trial" of Burr for "Murdering" Hamilton

Shortly after Burr's fatal "interview" with Hamilton on July 11, 1804, he was indicted by the two states having jurisdiction over the incident. In early August, a coroner's jury in New York charged him with "murdering" Hamilton, which was followed in October when New Jersey indicted him with murder (Stewart 2011, 41–42). For the next several years Burr had to stay away from these two states, which partially explained his single-minded involvement in the Western territories that led to his treason trial of 1807. But New York and New Jersey never followed through with their indictments; neither sought to extradite him for trial. In 1807 the Supreme Court of New Jersey quashed his indictment. New York finally abandoned the murder prosecution in 1811, clearing the way for his return to the state to resume his law practice until his death in 1836 (Stewart 2011, 272, 293–294).

Without a trial, there has never been a judicial determination of whether Burr "murdered" Hamilton. But we may try to stage a virtual "trial" to demonstrate the possible reasoning process by which a state jury would have found the "truth" in the state's 'murder" charge. To be sure, this exercise lacks any judicial or historiographic value but may help illustrate some salient points in comparative judicial and historical fact-finding.

Based on the extant evidence from historical sources, there is no serious doubt about the "fact" that Burr killed Hamilton, or more specifically, Hamilton died of the wound inflicted by Burr's gunshot in their duel on July 11, 1804. However, there is hardly any agreement on the question of whether Burr "murdered" Hamilton. This would be the exact question that a jury, as judicial fact-finders, must answer in a hypothetical trial.

For instance, under New York law, the statutory definition of "murder" was killing a human being "with malice aforethought." (Stewart 2011, 41) The prosecution, charged with the burden to prove Burr's guilt beyond a reasonable doubt, would likely present the following evidence to induce the jury to make reasonable inferences of Burr's "malice aforethought":

1. Burr challenged Hamilton to the duel, *thus was the instigator*.
2. Burr fired the first shot, *thus was eager to kill*.
3. Burr aimed and shot Hamilton in his abdomen, *thus intending to inflict fatal harm*.

The defense would want to present evidence or dispute the prosecution's evidence to refute possible inferences of Burr's "malice aforethought":

1. Burr challenged Hamilton to the duel (prosecution's claim), but it was issued after repeated requests from Burr for Hamilton to retract his derogatory remarks on Burr.

    a. Hamilton was given ample time and opportunities to resolve the dispute without a duel, *thus Burr did not "plan" the duel.*

2. Hamilton picked the weapons to be used and the position. His second (Pendleton) called out the signal to shoot, *thus Burr was a "passive" participant.*
3. Burr fired the first shot (the prosecution's claim).

   a. This was Hamilton second (Pendleton)'s claim. But Burr second (Van Ness)'s recollection is to the contrary. At best it is not clear who fired the first shot. The only agreed point is that both parties fired shots within a few seconds time, *thus there is no basis for the inference that Burr was eager to kill by firing the first shot.*

4. Burr aimed and shot Hamilton in his abdomen (prosecution's claim).

   a. Hamilton fired first (based on Burr second's recollection), which caused Burr to sway slightly (Ellis 2011, 20), *thus his shot was the result of an impulsive physical reaction instead of a deliberative aim.*

5. Burr made no specific preparation for the duel, *thus there was no sign of any "malice aforethought" for intentional killing.*
6. Burr believed that no one would be seriously hurt from the duel, *thus, like most other duels of the time in which both parties would walk away from the duel without be seriously hurt* (Ellis 2011, 24) *his state of mind before the duel was not to go for a kill.*

   a. In the pre-duel negotiations, Burr readily accepted Hamilton side's proposal that only one doctor (i.e., Hamilton's doctor) would serve as physician for bother parties and said, "even that unnecessary." (Ellis 2011, 31)

7. Burr was genuinely shocked at Hamilton's collapse to the ground after the exchange of shots; *thus, the result of the duel was inconsistent with Burr's expectation of a "normal" duel in which no one would be seriously hurt.*

   a. Despite their disagreement on who fired the first shot, both seconds (Pendleton and Van Ness) – the only two witnesses at the site – agreed that after Hamilton's fall, Burr took a step toward Hamilton. Both seconds thought Burr's movement was "expressive of regret." (Stewart 2011, 34)
   b. After Van Ness intercepted Burr from approaching the fallen Hamilton for fear of arrest by the authorities, he took Burr to the waiting boat. According to Van Ness, Burr still tried to return to the dueling ground, saying, "I must go and speak with him." (Stewart 2011, 34)

On the critical issue of who fired the first shot, the prosecution might want to use the following evidence to lead the jury to draw the inference that Hamilton could not have fired first:

1. The evening before the duel, Hamilton wrote a personal statement expressing the desire to "throw away my first shot;" (Ellis 2011, 23) *thus Hamilton never intended to fire the first shot and could not have fired the first shot.*
2. On the trip back the New York, Hamilton recovered consciousness for a moment and said to his doctor, "Pendleton knows I did not mean to fire at Colonel Burr

the first time." He then warned, "Take care of that pistol; it is undischarged and still cocked; it may go off and do harm;" (Ellis 2011, 26) *thus, Hamilton did not realize that his pistol had fired, which supported the inference that Hamilton had never intended to fire at Burr, which in turn infer that Hamilton could not have fired first.*

Under the rules of evidence against hearsay that had well developed by the 1800s, it is very likely that the prosecution's first piece of evidence (Hamilton's pre-duel written statement) would have been ruled as inadmissible hearsay. The second piece of evidence (Hamilton's statements during the boat ride after the duel) might be ruled to be admissible dying declaration as an exception to hearsay. In either case, however, the evidence would have not been strong enough to enable the jury to draw the far-fetched inferences that Hamilton had not fired first or had not fired at all, especially in light of contrary evidence, both testimonial and physical, that both parties had fired.

In all likelihood, it would be almost impossible for a rational jury to have found Burr "murdered" Hamilton beyond a reasonable doubt.

5 Historical "Truth" of Burr in Two Events

5.1 Two Events, Same Disagreements

While Burr has been officially vindicated in at least one judicial trial to stay clear from the capital crime of treason, he has not received any definitive "verdict" from historians for his conduct in either of the two events. For over two centuries, historians have continuously debated the true facts of these two incidents. Unlike their counterparts in the judicial fact-finding process, historians are neither restricted by statutory procedure and standard of proof nor are required to affirm one version of the "facts" in order to render a "final" decision to solve a live dispute. Instead, freed from the practical necessity to reach a decision within strict time constrains, they seek historical "facts" as part of their intellectual and academic pursuit. In this pursuit, they respond to no legal or judicial authority and the only constraints on historical fact-finding are intellectual integrity and individual sense of excellence and reputation in the academic community.

5.2 Burr: "Murderer" in History?

Ever since the death of Hamilton in 1804, there have been countless historians, like most of the contemporaries of Hamilton and Burr, who believed and continue to believe that Burr killed Hamilton with malicious intent. Thus, many historians continue to describe Burr as "murderer" of Hamilton. (Hall ed. 2002, 75) Based on this belief that Burr was the "villain" who had "trapped Hamilton in his diabolical web," (Ellis 2011, 21) these historians are not hesitant to present the "facts" of the duel in a way that is consistent with this perspective:

> as the sun rose above the Weehawken dueling ground, Aaron Burr's first shot struck Hamilton just above his hip and tore through his body to lodge in his spine. Hamilton convulsively clutched his trigger when the bullet hit, and his shot struck a tree limb high over Burr's head. (Fleming 2009, 251)

Clearly, this narrative has firmly subscribed to the claim that Burr fired first, which, as noted in the previous discussion of the "virtual trial" of Burr for murdering Hamilton, is by no means a settled fact. Thus, this narrative starts from an unsteady foundation. Further, this narrative's statement that Hamilton "convulsively clutched his trigger when the bullet hit, and his shot struck a tree limb high over Burr's head" is on even shakier ground. First, there is no extant evidence of any kind that supports the claim that Hamilton "convulsively clutched his trigger when the bullet hit." Second, although both duelists' seconds had said that they discovered, days after the duel when they revisited the site, that some tree branches behind Burr were hit, there was no further proof (something like a modern ballistic test or eyewitness testimony) that it was Hamilton's shot that hit these branches because Weehawken was a popular duel ground and many shots had been fired there.

Other historians, especially modern scholars who have carefully examined all available evidence, tend to be much more prudent in presenting the "facts." Here is a good example:

> On the morning of July 11, 1804, Aaron Burr and Alexander Hamilton were rowed across the Hudson River in separate boats to a secluded spot near Weehawken, New Jersey. There, in accord with the customs of the *code duello*, they exchanged pistol shots at ten paces. Hamilton was struck on his right side and died the following day. Burr found that his reputation suffered an equally fatal wound. In this, the most famous duel in American history, both participants were casualties. (Ellis 2011, 20)

Like most modern historical writing, this narrative states only the "facts" that are reasonably supported by extant evidence (such as Burr and Hamilton "exchanged pistol short at ten paces") but leaves out those "facts" that lack reasonable evidentiary support (e.g. the omission of the "fact" of who fired first). With this, the historian moved on to explore the significance of the event (i.e. the last two sentences), which seems to be the ultimate focus of this particular historical writing. Similarly, a modern biographer of Hamilton also bypassed the issue of whether Burr murdered Hamilton, probably for the same reason of lacking evidentiary support to reach a conclusion. "By accident or design," wrote this biographer, "Burr's shot struck Hamilton in the right side and passed through his liver." (McDonald 1979, 361).

5.3 Burr: "Traitor" in History?

"Was Burr... guilty of treason...?" (Hoffer 2008, 189) This was surely the fundamental question posed to the federal district court convened in Richmond 1807. It remains an important question after more than two hundred years for historians, despite the federal court's determination in the negative on August 31, 1807 that once for all disposed of this question, adjudicatively. Apparently, the "final" conclusion of a judicial fact-finding is not equal to a historical fact-finding.

It was President Jefferson who not only took active part throughout the Burr trial, albeit behind the scenes away from the court, but also put into motion the train of judgement by history from the beginning of the trial proceedings. Shortly after the formation of a federal grand jury to consider an indictment in April 1807, he wrote in a letter to Senator William Branch Giles, a Republican ally from Virginia: "The nation will judge both the offender and the judges for themselves." (Smith 1996, 360) He was enraged by the outcome of the trial and blamed Chief Justice Marshall and the judiciary for their arbitrariness (Meacham 2013, 423). He sent the trial record to Congress with an appeal for impeachment of Chief Justice Marshall or amendment to the Constitution: "You will be enabled to judge whether the defect was in the testimony, in the law, or in the administration of the law, and wherever it shall be found, the Legislature alone can apply or originate the remedy." (Smith 1996, 373) But Congress took no action. Jefferson must have to find satisfaction in the thought that history would render the right judgment.

But two hundred years thereafter, historians are still hopelessly divided. Even though most historians tend to believe Burr was "guilty" of something, they are unsure of him guilty of "treason." In seeking the historical truth, they are not constrained by the legal definition of the concept of "treason," at least not as so stringently constructed by Chief Justice Marshall. Instead, they probably are guided by the dictionary definition of this concept, such as the one in the Longman Dictionary of Contemporary English: treason is "the crime of being disloyal to your own country or its government, especially by helping its enemy or trying to remove the government using violence." (Longman 2001, 154).

Free from the need to identify an "overt act" at which Burr must be physically present as Chief Justice Marshall had instructed the jury back in 1807, historians are not legally required or even eager to find out whether Burr had committed treason. For them, the not-guilty verdict of the 1807 jury is but one historical fact related to Burr, which has no binding effect on their intellectual pursuit. With access to much more evidence than the jury was allowed to access, historians are enabled to draw multiplying inferences thus gaining the ability to know more about the related facts in greater detail. However, their objectives are not limited to provide richer narratives of the related events, but more importantly to gain better understanding of these events by contextualizing them within the relevant frames of reference. Therefore, a historian' craft is not depended on reaching a final determination on one "fact," like the judicial trial. Instead, he is perfectly fine with leaving historical facts in indeterminate condition to move on to discovering larger historical meaning or significance.

In the Burr case, modern historians find Burr's actions hard to explain but their efforts of trying to provide reasoned explanations have been continuously enriching our understanding of Burr and his time. For instance, based on the existing evidence, it appears that Burr had engaged in "a conspiracy to sever the Western portions of the country from the Eastern states." (Hoffer 2008, 201) If the historical fact-finding stops here, it is probably not hard to form the belief that Burr's acts were "treasonous" in its dictionary sense of being "disloyal to [his] own country," especially taking into account the largely undisputed facts that Burr (a) secretly assembled and equipped some armed forces; (b) secretly met with the English and Spanish ministers to the U.S. to seek military and financial support; and (c) secretly met and discussed various plans of military nature, sometimes by coded letters, with James Wilkinson, U.S. Army General and Governor of the Louisiana Territory, who at that time was also serving as a Spanish agent.

But historians' contextual analyses have made this belief based on the dictionary definition of treason less convincing. First, Burr's activities were not truly "secretive." He had acted as though secretive (such as using coded letters to communicate with General Wilkinson), but his visits to most places in the Western region and many of his meetings were known to others or even reported by the local newspapers. Second, there is no evidence showing that Burr was aware of the fact that Wilkinson was a Spanish agent. There were unconfirmed rumors during Wilkinson's lifetime, but it was only confirmed one century later after the opening of the Spanish archives (Hobson 2006, 27). Third, unlike the post-Civil War time, disassociating from the United States during the early Republic time was frequently discussed in public by political parties losing a political battle within the union (Wood 2009, 696). Viewed in these contexts, Burr's activities appear to be less "treasonous" than through the lens of later generations.

In any event, historians, despite disagreements on almost everything about the question of whether Burr had committed treason, probably share this assessment that "[T]he ultimate version—if anyone ever writes it—will be massive, full of fact and conjecture … yet it will still fall short of the truth, for the truth died with Burr." (Melton 2002, 235) The judicial verdict notwithstanding, the historical quest continues.

6 Proving Facts by Evidence-Inference Reasoning

6.1 What "Fact" to Prove?

As noted earlier in this article, for our purposes, a "fact" is defined as an event or thing that is believed as having happened or having existed (Anderson et al. 2015, 382). Any fact is already known and capable of proving an inferred proposition is "evidence," also referred to in different contexts as "data" or "*factum probans*." (Anderson et al. 2015, 383) In conducting an "Evidence-Inference Reasoning" analysis, fact-finding starts with the need to prove an unknown "fact," which is presented as a "proposition" or "hypothesis," (Anderson et al. 2015, 383–385) or in legal disputes, as a "claim" of a party to the dispute.

For instance, the statements "Aaron Burr killed Alexander Hamilton" and "Aaron Burr murdered Alexander Hamilton" are both "fact" statements the truthfulness of which is to be proved (either affirmed or denied). In this sense, they are both propositions and hypotheses. In the latter case, the proposition was also a legal claim alleged by the New York and New Jersey prosecutors against Burr, just like the statement that "Aaron Burr committed treason" contained in the grand jury indictment against Burr in the Burr treason trial of 1807 (Hobson 2006, 46–48).

To prove either proposition, information from known or established facts, i.e., evidence, must be used by rational reasoning to reach another fact, i.e. inference (Wigmore 1935, 383). For instance, the proposition "Aaron Burr killed Alexander Hamilton" can be proved by such established facts ("evidence") as "Burr and Hamilton exchanged fire," "Burr's shot hit Hamilton" and "Hamilton died the next day." Here, a critical inference must be made ("Hamilton died from Burr's gunshot") in order to complete the proof that Burr "killed" Hamilton. If there were evidence indicating that Hamilton died from other causes not related to Burr's gunshot, then the proposition that Burr "killed" Hamilton would be disproved.

Now, compare the statement of "Aaron killed Alexander Hamilton" with that of "Aaron Burr murdered Alexander Hamilton," a major difference emerges. While the proposition "killed" contains a relatively simple, action based "fact," the proposition "murdered" contemplates a much more complicated, intent-centered "fact." To prove Burr "killed" Hamilton, the evidence and related inferences may take the form of objective actions or status (such as "Burr shot Hamilton" and "Hamilton died the next day") without referring to the state of mind or intent of the related individuals.

By contrast, the proposition that Burr "murdered" Hamilton would require proof of Burr's intent when he fired the shot at Hamilton in addition to affirming that he "killed" Hamilton. This seemly very simple change adds tremendous complexity to fact-finding. In the first place, in addition to action-based human activities perceivable by human senses, proving intent requires the fact-finder to look inside the human mind to find out the thought process, which is generally incapable of being perceived by human senses. In criminal law, all crimes require both a bad act (*actus reus*) and a culpable mental state (*mens rea*) for criminal liability to attach. Accordingly, fact-finders in criminal cases need to ascertain not only the culpable act but also the "guilty mind," which in most cases would require jurors or judges to decide "what some stranger, who stands accused of criminal behavior in the past, was thinking about at the time of his alleged crime." (Ginther et al. 2018, 242).

Secondly, adding the intent element to the proposition transforms the proposition from a "descriptive fact" in the sense that it simply describes an objective activity or status to an "interpretative fact" in the sense that the proposition itself incorporates elements of interpretation by the proponent. Therefore, a proposition, as an unknown "fact" to be proven, becomes a complex entity consisting of objective and subjective components that require satisfactory proof before it can be affirmed to be a "fact."

In practice, fact-finders in both historical studies and judicial trials are called upon to prove or disprove both "descriptive" and "interpretative" facts, which we refer to as "Elemental Fact" and "Compound Fact" respectively. Some scholars use the concepts "primary" and "secondary" facts to denote these two types of facts. A "primary" fact depicts the physical action of a person, which exists "as a matter of common sense" perceivable by human senses. This can be "a *state of affairs* (for example, the state of jealousy or insanity), a *process* (a 'going on' like continuous stalking or gradual poisoning), or an *event* (a 'taking place' such as a vehicular collision or an act of stabbing)." (Ho 2008, 7) A "secondary" fact goes beyond the physical dimension of a person's action (e.g. A bumps into B; Burr killed Hamilton) and asserts a mental dimension (e.g. A *intentionally* bumps into B; Burr killed Hamilton *with malice aforethought*), thus a "composite of the physical and the mental." (Ho 2008, 7).

Further, more often than not, fact-finders are expected to either affirm or deny propositions in the form of Compound Facts which are far more complex than our examples (A *intentionally* bumps into B; Burr killed Hamilton *with malice aforethought*) have demonstrated. Oftentimes, elements of a Compound Fact will require further interpretation during the course of proving the fact, and such interpretation may become subject of subsequent disputes. Chief Justice Marshall's interpretation of the meaning of "overt act" during the Burr treason trial is a handy example. In this sense, a Compound (or "secondary") Fact ceases to be a pure question of fact but a "mixed question of fact and law." (Ho 2008, 8) Chief Justice Marshall's interpretation was dispositive with respect to the Burr's case but has become a subject of legal and academic discussion ever since.

For fact-finders in historical or judicial fact-finding, it is much easier to apply evidence to an Elemental Fact to make a rational inference than to do the same with a Compound Fact. (Allen 2012, 717) Thus, it would greatly facilitate accurate fact-finding by devising a process that enables the fact-finders to treat multiple Elemental Facts as integral components of a Compound Fact. We will attempt to propose such a process in the next section.

6.2 A Modified Analytical "Evidence-Inference Reasoning" Model

Historians and the legal profession have developed in their respective disciplines guiding principles and methodologies to facilitate fact-finding at the practical level. Each has produced sophisticated studies of data (evidence; historical sources) analysis. For historians, an elaborate system of theories and methodologies relating to using different resources (e.g. primary and secondary sources) to ascertain historical facts has evolved over centuries (Marwick 1989, 196). Facts are not assumed but are established by "source [evidence] criticism" by which "persuasive exposition of inferences have been drawn from that evidence." Next, such facts are to be "validated" through objective valuation (Marwick 1989, 197).

Compared with historians, legal professionals are more concerned with immediate practical use of the fact analysis and reasoning because factual conclusions in judicial decisions will decide immediate outcomes of legal proceedings. Thus, they have devoted relatively more concerted efforts to develop "generalized set of procedures … that … may be applied in any method of analysis." (Anderson et al. 2015, 113) Ever since John Henry Wigmore formulated the "chart method" in the early twentieth century, successive models of analytical methods and devices have been proposed, argued and refined. Taken together, they have enriched the "Evidence-Inference Reasoning" process as used in judicial fact-finding. Contemporary representative of these efforts is the monograph Analysis of Evidence (First Edition, 1991; Second Edition, 2005) by Terence Anderson, David Schum and William Twining. In this book, the authors presented several methods of analysis (principally the "chart method" and the "outline method") and analytical devices (mainly the "chronologies" and the "narratives") (Anderson et al. 2015, 113).

In one sense, these methods and devices can be viewed as concrete working "protocols" or "procedures" to guide fact-finders in conducting case-based, specific "Evidence-Inference Reasoning" analysis. They endeavor to provide practically useful methods to (1) use available evidence ("recording and organizing data"), and to (2) draw rational inference(s) ("specifying the logical relationships among the propositions"), which is in essence a process of using evidence to "support or negate a fact of consequence." (Anderson et al. 2015, 113).

Central to these methods and devices is the process that "simplifies the complex proposition that is the *ultimate probandum* into simple propositions." (Anderson et al. 2015, 113) The ultimate objective is to convert the analysis thus conducted "into a coherent narrative" that (1) "[is] consistent with the theory of the case," (2) "accounts for the available evidence" and (3) "does not rely on facts for which there is no evidence." (Anderson et al. 2015, 114).

We believe these insights and efforts can be profitably applied to both historical and judicial fact-finding. Based on the models designed for lawyers as advocates in judicial process by the authors of Analysis of Evidence (Anderson et al. 2015, 112–158), we outline below a modified analytical model to enable historical and judicial fact-finders to apply the "Evidence-Inference Reasoning" process more conscientiously and, hopefully, conducive to producing more coherent narratives. Equally important, with such a "known and systematic protocol," (Anderson et al. 2015, 114) others not involved in the fact-finding process but having either the official or professional duty (such as judges of an appellate court called upon to review the fact-finding of the trial court, or legal counsel in the subsequent appeals) or intellectual interest (such as fellow historians, legal academics) can also use this analytical tool to review, test, or criticize the fact-finding process and its conclusions.

Like in the context of a legal dispute, at the start of an "Evidence-Inference Reasoning" process, three questions must first be addressed:

(a) What is the ultimate proposition (Elemental Fact or Compound Fact) to be proved?
(b) What is the available evidence?
(c) What are the plausible and defensible relationships between the evidence and the ultimate proposition? (Anderson et al. 2015, 114)

Next, the "Evidence-Inference Reasoning" analysis will proceed in the following steps:

(1) Formulate the Ultimate Proposition (*Ultimate Probandum*).
(2) Divide the Ultimate Proposition into Intermediate Propositions (*Penultimate Probanda*), if any.
(3) Sub-divide each Intermediate Proposition into Sub-intermediate Propositions (*Sub-pemultimate Probanda*), if any, until each Intermediate Proposition or Sub-intermediate Proposition takes the form of an Elemental Fact.
(4) Apply available evidence to each Intermediate and Sub-intermediate Proposition by drawing rational inferences between the evidence and the Elemental Fact.
(5) Use each Intermediate and Sub-intermediate Proposition that has been proven in Step 4 as newly acquired evidence to support the Proposition at the level immediate above until you reach the Ultimate Proposition; the Ultimate Proposition will be deemed to have not been proven if any of the Intermediate Proposition or Sub-intermediate Proposition has been disproven.
(6) Summarize all findings in a coherent narrative that takes into account all available evidence, all Intermediate and Sub-intermediate Propositions that have been proven or not proven.

We attempt to illustrate this process by three examples from the Burr events:

1. *Proposition: "Aaron Burr killed Alexander Hamilton"*
   (a) This ultimate proposition takes the form of an Elemental Fact.
   (b) The ultimate proposition can be divided into the following Intermediate Propositions:
      I Burr fired a shot at Hamilton.
      II Burr's shot hit Hamilton.
      III Hamilton collapsed to the ground immediately after being hit.
      IV Hamilton was carried away by his second Nathaniel Pendleton and Dr. David Hosack to a friend's home in New York City.
      V Hamilton died the next day from the gunshot wound.
      VI Others, as necessary.
   (c) If necessary, any of the Intermediate Propositions can be sub-divided into Sub-intermediate Propositions. For instance, Intermediate Proposition e. can be subdivided into:
      I The gunshot inflicted by Burr on Hamilton was of such nature and severity that it could cause Hamilton's death.
      II No intervening event between the time Hamilton was shot by Burr and died the next day that could have caused Hamilton's death.
      III Others, as necessary.
   (d) Apply the available evidence to each Intermediate and Sub-intermediate Proposition by drawing rational inferences between the evidence and the Elemental Fact.
      I *Illustration*: To prove Intermediate Proposition b. (Burr's shot hit Hamilton), (i) the accounts by two eyewitnesses, Burr's second Van Ness

and Hamilton's second Pendleton, can be used to make the rational inference that Burr's shot did hit Hamilton; and (ii) one may also take into account that there is no evidence negating this inference.

II *Illustration*: To prove the Sub-intermediate Proposition a. (The gunshot inflicted by Burr on Hamilton was of such nature and severity that it could cause Hamilton's death), (i) available evidence about the nature and severity of Hamilton's wound (for instance, Dr. Hosack's accounts and Hamilton's own words), (ii) information about the medical knowledge and technology in general at that time (the 1800s) and place (New York area, United States); (iii) information, if available, about the death rate from such wound; and (iv) information about the specific medical knowledge, technique, equipment, medicine, opportunities, etc. that were available to treat Hamilton between the moment he was shot by Burr and the time of his death the next day, can be used to draw rational inference that Hamilton did die from the gunshot wound inflicted by Burr. Notice will also be taken that either (i) there is no evidence negating this inference or (ii) evidence tending to contradict this inference, if any, is insufficient to negate this inference.

(e) Use the confirmed inferences from Intermediate Proposition b. and Sub-intermediate Propositions, respectively, as partial support for the Proposition at the level immediately above until all Intermediate Propositions listed in Step 2 have been proven.

(f) Summarize all findings in a coherent narrative.

2. Proposition: "Aaron Burr murdered Alexander Hamilton"

(a) This Ultimate Proposition takes the form of a Compound Fact, as the term "murder" incorporates an "intent" element and requires specific definition in each particular fact-finding context.

(b) The Ultimate Proposition can be divided into the following possible (depending on the specific elements for the crime of murder in the relevant jurisdiction, if the fact-finding takes place in a judicial context (Dressler 2009, 509) Intermediate Propositions:

I Burr killed Hamilton.

II Burr intended (e.g. "malice aforethought" under New York law) Hamilton's death.

III Others, as necessary.

(c) Sub-divide each Intermediate Proposition into Sub-intermediate Propositions. For instance, Intermediate Proposition b. (Burr intended Hamilton's death) can be sub-divided into Sub-intermediate Propositions at descending levels until each Sub-intermediate Proposition takes the form of an Elemental Fact:

I Burr hated Hamilton.

(1) Burr told others that he hated Hamilton.

(2) Burr did not speak to Hamilton when they sat at the same table in a party on July 4, 1804, seven days before he shot Hamilton in the duel at Weehawken.
(3) Others, as necessary.

II Burr used a deadly weapon against Hamilton.
(1) Burr shot Hamilton using a pistol.
(2) The bullet Burr fired at Hamilton was a large 0.54-caliber ball, known to others to be deadly.
(3) Others, as necessary.

(d) Apply available evidence to each Intermediate and Sub-intermediate Proposition by drawing rational inferences between the evidence and the Elemental Fact.

I *Illustration*: To prove Sub-intermediate Proposition b. (Burr used a deadly weapon against Hamilton), evidence affirming Sub-intermediate Propositions (i) (Burr shot Hamilton using a pistol) and (ii) (The bullet Burr fired at Hamilton was a large 0.54-caliber ball, known to others to be deadly) can be used to draw rational inference that Burr did use a deadly weapon against Hamilton.

II *Illustration*: From the newly proved fact that Burr did use a deadly weapon against Hamilton, rational inferences may be drawn to support an inference that "Burr intended to kill Hamilton" on the basis of the generalizations about human behavior: (i) ordinary people intend the natural and probable consequences of their actions; (ii) Burr was an ordinary person; and (iii) therefore, Burr intended the natural and probable consequences of his action (Dressler 2009, 513).

(e) Use the confirmed inferences from Intermediate Proposition b., as partial support for the Proposition at the level immediately above until all Intermediate Propositions listed in Step 2 have been proven.

(f) Summarize all findings in a coherent narrative.

3. *Proposition: "Aaron Burr committed treason against the United States"*

(a) This Ultimate Proposition takes the form of a Compound Fact, as the term "treason" incorporates an "intent" element and requires specific definition in each particular fact-finding context.

(b) The Ultimate Proposition can be divided into the following possible (depending on the specific elements for the crime of treason in the relevant jurisdiction, if the fact-finding takes place in a judicial context such as the Burr treason trial under Article III, Sect. 3 of the United States Constitution) Intermediate Propositions:

I Burr levied war against the United States.
II Burr adhered to the enemies of the United States, given them aid and comfort.
III Others, as necessary.

(c) Sub-divide each Intermediate Proposition into Sub-intermediate Propositions. For instance, Intermediate Proposition a. (Burr levied war against the United States) can be sub-divided into Sub-intermediate Propositions at descending levels until each Sub-intermediate Proposition takes the form of an Elemental Fact:

I Burr levied war.
 (1) Burr assembled armed forces and provisions.
 (2) Others, as necessary.

II Burr intended to levy the war against the United States.
 (1) Burr secretly met with the British minister to the United States.
 (2) Others, as necessary.

III Burr committed overt act of treason, which was witnessed by two witnesses.
 (1) At least 30 armed persons assembled at the Island of Blennerhassett on September 10, 1806.
 (2) Burr was present at the Island of Blennerhassett on September 30, 1806 (a proposition derived from Chief Justice Marshall's interpretation of the Constitution).
 (3) Others, as necessary.

(d) Apply available evidence to each Intermediate and Sub-intermediate Proposition by drawing rational inferences between the evidence and the Elemental Fact.

 I *Illustration*: To prove Sub-intermediate Proposition c. (Burr committed overt act of treason, witnessed by two witnesses), evidence affirming Burr's physical presence at the Island of Blennerhassett on September 30, 1806 must be presented according to Chief Justice Marshall's interpretation of the term "overt act" in the Constitution. Failure to prove Burr's presence would prevent fact-finders from making rational inference on the existence of "overt act." This is precisely what actually happened in the Burr trial. The prosecution acknowledged Burr's absence from the island. This, in turn, prevented the jury from finding an overt act.

 II *Illustration*: From the newly proved fact that Burr did not commit overt act, no rational inference may be drawn to support the finding that "Aaron Burr committed treason against the United States."

(e) Use the confirmed inference that Burr did not commit overt act of treason from Intermediate Proposition c., as rejection of the Proposition at the level immediate above until the Ultimate Proposition is denied.

(f) Summarize all findings in a coherent narrative.

7 Comparative Advantages

There seems to be an interesting mutual reliance between judicial fact-finding and historical fact-finding. Losing participants of a judicial process often find comfort in the belief that history would ultimately render the right judgment, as President Jefferson had expressed at the conclusion of the Burr treason trial. By contrast, modern professional historians tend to recognize that there is no "final judgement" in the court of history (Resta and Zeno-Zencovich 2013, 844). However, the inherent human desire to find certainty in social life by reaching conclusions on human behavior has prompted many historians to leave that task to the judicial process. "When the scholar has observed and explained," wrote Marc Bloch, "his task is finished. It yet remains for the judge to pass sentence." (Block 1953, 884).

The reality, as it appears to be through generations, would often betray the trust vested by one camp to the other and vice versa. Until technology has, if ever, advanced to the stage of producing commercialized "memory" scanner as depicted in the British futuristic TV series "Black Mirror" (Banner 2018) that can faithfully record and securely restore all human acts, thoughts and emotions which can be simply replayed whenever there is a need to find out what has happened in relation to the issue to be resolved (such as an insurance claim arising from a car accident), ascertaining past "truth" by drawing rational inference from existing and inevitably incomplete evidence will continue to perform its social and intellectual functions for the human society. Furthermore, even after the memory scanner becomes available, there would be the continued need of finding out what had happened in the pre-memory scanner times.

As a general matter, historical fact-finding has the virtue of preserving to a larger extent the natural reasoning process than judicial fact-finding. Aside from losing access to evidence for reasons of not their own making, such as destruction of historical records by natural force or blocking access to public archives by governments, historians, as fact-finders, are not restricted by law from accessing useful evidence. Thus, they have much more information at disposal to perform the Evidence-Inference Reasoning, which is conducive to more complete and accurate fact-finding.

By comparison, judicial fact-finding is "an unnatural decision-making process." (Allen et al. 2016, 129) For instance, the American system of judicial proof is based on reliance on lay fact-finders; at the same time, its rules of evidence have developed through centuries mainly because of a deeply rooted distrust of the anointed lay fact-finders, the jurors. As a result, as perceptively described in a study of jury deliberation process,

> it seems more plausible that the system is set up to promote misunderstanding. Factors blocking the serious jury trying to perform its task include: the convoluted, technical language; the dry and abstract presentation of the law following the vivid, concrete, and often lengthy presentation of evidence; the requirements that jurors interpret the evidence before they know what the verdict choices are; the fact that juries usually do not get copies of the instructions to take with them into the jury room; the lack of training in the law for jurors as part of their jury duty; the general failure to discover and correct jurors' preconceptions about the law; the failure to inform jurors that they are allowed to ask for help with the instructions; and the fact that those who do ask for help are often disappointed by a simple repetition of the incompressible paragraph. (Ellsworth 1995, 128)

Apparently, judicial fact-finding practices *intentional* exclusion of evidence, much of which is relevant and probative information. While such systematic exclusion of useful evidence may be justifiable for various legitimate policy reasons and competing social values other than ascertaining truth (Allen 2014, 17–20), it does make judicial fact-finding an artificial reasoning process. This result, seemingly undesirable, serves larger social purposes. In general, society holds the highest standards for doctors and lawyers (Anderson et al. 2015, 112) presumably because their decision-making exerts immediate impact on concrete human lives. For this reason, complex rules for judicial fact-finding have been developed to reduce the risks associated with natural reasoning and channel the fact-finding process to reach the best conclusion practicable within the timeframe and other institutional and procedural constraints of a judicial trial. This practical necessity in turn incentivized legal academics and practitioners to sharpen the conceptualization of, and more importantly, realistic procedure for performing the Evidence-Inference Reasoning. From this development in judicial fact-finding historians may gain some insights to enhance historical fact-finding by conscientiously avoiding risks associated with natural reasoning and utilizing more rigorous Evidence-Inference Reasoning in historical studies.

References

Allen, Ronald J. 2014. *Professor Allen on Evidence*, vol. I. Beijing: People's University Press.

Allen, Ronald J., et al. 2016. *An Analytical Approach to Evidence: Text, Problems, and Cases*. New York: Wolters Kluwer.

Amaya, Amalia. 2013. Coherence, Evidence, and Legal Proof. *Legal Theory* 19: 24.

Anderson, Terence, et al. 2015. *Analysis of Evidence*. New York: Cambridge University Press.

Banner, Adam. 2018. *'Black Mirror': Sci-fi Technology Exists, but is the Evidence Admissible?* Podcast Series: ABA Journal.

Breisach, Ernst. 1983. *Historiography: Ancient, Medieval, and Modern*. Chicago: University of Chicago Press.

Capra, Daniel J. 2015. *Federal Rules of Evidence (2015–16 Edition)*. St. Paul: West Academic Publishing.

Coffin, Frank M. 1994. *On Appeal: Courts, Lawyering, and Judging*. New York: W.W. Norton and Company.

Dershowitz, Allan M. 2004. *America on Trial: Inside the Legal Battles that Transformed Our Nation*. New York: Warner Books.

Dressler, Joshua. 2009. *Understanding Criminal Law*. New York: Lexis Nexis Matthew Bender.

Ellis, Joseph J. 2001. *Founding Brothers: The Revolutionary Generation*. New York: Alfred A. Knopf.

Ellsworth, Phoebe. 1995. Are 12 Heads Better Than 1? Law Quadrangle Notes 38:56–64.

Fleming, Thomas. 2009. *The Intimate Lives of the Founding Fathers*. New York: HarperCollins.

Giannelli, Paul C. 2009. *Understanding Evidence*. New York: Cambridge University Press.

Hall, Kermit. 2002. *The Oxford Companion to American Law*. Oxford: Oxford University Press.

Ho, H.L. 2008. *A Philosophy of Evidence Law: Justice in the Search for Truth*. Oxford: Oxford University Press.

Hobson, Charles F. 2006. *The Aaron Burr Treason Trial*. Washington, D.C.: Federal Judicial Center, Federal Judicial History Office.

Isenberg, Nancy. 2007. *Fallen Founder: The Life of Aaron Burr*. New York: Viking.

Kaptein, H., et al. (eds.). 2009. *Legal Evidence and Proof: Statistics, Stories, Logic*. Aldershot: Ashgate.

Lea, Henry C. 1870. *Superstition and Force: Torture, Ordeal, and Trial by Combat in Medieval Law*. New York: Barnes and Noble Books.

Lempert, R. 1986. *The New Scholarship of Evidence: Analyzing the Process of Proof*. Boston University Law Review 66:439.

Lerner, Daniel (ed.). 1962. *Evidence and Inference: The Hayden Colloquium on Scientific Concept and Method*. New York: Cambridge University Press.

Longman Dictionary of Contemporary English. 2001. London: Longman.

Marwick, Arthur. 1989. *The Nature of History*. London: Palgrave Macmillan.

Matthew R. Ginther, et al. 2018. Decoding Guilty Minds: How Jurors Attribute Knowledge and Guilt. *71 Vanderbilt Law Review* 241: 242.

McDonald, Forrest. 1979. *Alexander Hamilton: A Biography*. New York: Norton.

Meacham, Jon. 2013. *Thomas Jefferson: The Art of Power*. New York: Random House.

Melton Jr, Buckner F. 2002. *Aaron Burr: Conspiracy to Treason*. New York: John Wiley.

Michael S. Pardo, Ronald J. Allen. 2008. Juridical Proof and the Best Explanation. *Law and Philosophy* 27(3):223–268.

Miller, David, et al. (eds.). 1991. *The Blackwell Encyclopedia of Political Thought*. New York: Blackwell Publishers.

Morris S. Arnold, et al. eds. 1981. *On the Laws and Customs of England—Essays in Honor of Samuel E. Thorne*.

Novick, Peter. 1988. *That Noble Dream: The "Objectivity Question" and the American Historical Profession*. Cambridge and New York: Cambridge University Press.

Peter Charles Hoffer. 2008. *The Treason Trials of Aaron Burr*. Lawrence: University Press of Kansas.

Rescher, Nicholas, and Carey B. Joynt. 1959. Evidence in History and in the Law. *The Journal of Philosophy*. 56: 561.

Resta, Giorgio, and Vincenzo Zeno-Zencovich. 2013. Judicial Truth and Historical Truth: The Case of the Ardeatine Caves Massacre. *Law and History Review* 11: 844.

Smith, Jean Edward. 1996. *John Marshall: Definer of A Nation*. New York: Henry Holt.

Stewart, David O. 2011. *American Emperor: Aaron Burr's Challenge to Jefferson's America*. New York: Simon and Schuster.

Strong, John W., et al. 1999. *McCormick on Evidence*. St. Paul: West Group.

Toothman, Jessika. 2019. *Are Humans the Smartest Animal?* https://science.howstuffworks.com/life/inside-the-mind/human-brain/humans-smartest-animal.htm. Last visited October 25, 2019.

Twining, William. 1994. *Rethinking Evidence: Exploratory Essays*. Chicago: Northwestern University Press.

Twining, William, and Lain Hampsher-Monk (eds.). 2003. *Evidence and Inference in History and Law: Interdisciplinary Dialogues*. Evanston: Northwestern University Press.

Wigmore, John Henry. 1935. *A Students' Textbook of the Law of Evidence*. New York: The Foundation Press.

Wood, Gordon S. 2009. *Empire of Liberty: A History of the Early Republic, 1789–1815*. Oxford-New York: Oxford University Press.

Chasing Truth from the Perspective of History

Luping Zhang

1 An Overview of Cui Yingjie Case

1.1 Multiple Versions About the Case Facts

This paper takes a criminal case which had caused a sensation throughout China as an example. First of all, let's take a thorough observation of the case and its evolution.

On August 11, 2006, at the outside of Kemao Building in Zhongguancun, Beijing, vendor Cui Yingjie, had a dispute with Li Zhiqiang, vice captain of City Administration Group of Haidian District of Beijing Municipal Bureau of City Administration and Law Enforcement. The conflict led to the death of Li Zhiqiang. Cui Yingjie was subsequently arrested and prosecuted to Beijing First Intermediate People's Court. The case facts directly determined the conviction and penalty of the defendant, which was also the main issue of contention among all relevant parties in the case and people outside the court at all trial stages. Multiple versions of case facts came into being in the debate and narration of the pending case. The author will scrutinize four relatively palpable and representative versions hereof.

It should be noted that firstly, the four versions of texts are within professional scope in order to ensure the quality of the analysis and the persuasiveness of the conclusion. In general, texts with obvious literary characteristics are excluded, such as media reports and folktales.[1] Those texts are derived from The Written Opinion Recommending Prosecution issued by the Public Security Department, Indictment

[1] The narrow sense of "literature", as mentioned in the introduction chapter, is generally considered as the narrative that embraces features like conspicuous and overt emotional exaggeration and imaginative plots.

L. Zhang (✉)
Department of English, School of Foreign Languages, China University of Political Science and Law, Beijing, China
e-mail: lupingz@cupl.edu.cn

B. Zhang et al. (eds.), *A Dialogue Between Law and History*,
https://doi.org/10.1007/978-981-15-9685-8_18

issued by the Prosecution, the defense opinions of the defender, the confession made by the defendant and the advisory opinions of legal professionals outside the court. Secondly, the four versions are the summary of author's analysis rather than the indiscriminate copy of existing narrations. Specifically, this paper quotes and analyzes the original texts of the Written Opinion Recommending Prosecution, the Indictment and the final judgment which described the facts. And the stories that the defender and the defendant attempted to narrate might be mingled with their contentions towards factual details.

1. **Version One**: On the afternoon of August 11, 2006, vendor Cui Yingjing was selling barbecued sausages without license by the street of the northwest corner of Kemao Building in Zhongguancun Science Park of Haidian District, Beijing. The law enforcement officers of City Administration Group of Haidian District of Beijing Municipal Bureau of City Administration and Law Enforcement punished Cui Yingjie for unlicensed business activity and confiscated his tools including tricycle and stove. Cui Yingjie violently impeded the law enforcement in the process of confiscation and held a knife to threaten the officers. After the confiscation, Cui Yingjie held grudge against the officer and intended to revenge, so he thrust the leaving officers with his knife and gave a fierce stab on Li Zhiqiang's vital part between the neck and the collarbone. The stab injured the victim's right brachiocephalic vein and the right upper lobe and caused Li's death.[2]
2. **Version Two**: On the afternoon of August 11, 2006, ……. The law enforcement officers ……., punished Cui Yingjie for unlicensed business activity and confiscated his tools including tricycle and stove. During the process of confiscation, Cui Yingjie fought for the tricycle with the officers and kept holding the knife that he used to cut sausages. After the tricycle was confiscated, Cui Yingjie rushed to the officers' truck but was chased by the officers. When Cui Yingjie was escaping, he stabbed the vice leader of the City Administration Group, Li Zhiqiang, and the officer was dead after being sent to the hospital.[3]
3. **Version Three**: Born in a small village of Pingyang Town, Fuping County, Baoding City, Hebei Province, Cui Yingjie was a poor farmer and earned his living by working as a temporary security guard in an entertainment in Kemao Building in Zhongguancun Science Park, Beijing. Since April 2006, the employer had been behind in payment for four months. Be cornered by poverty, Cui Yingjie chose to be a vendor and sell barbecued sausages to make a living. On the afternoon of August 11, 2006, the law enforcement officers of City Administration Group of Haidian District punished Cui Yingjie for unlicensed business activity and confiscated his tools. Since the tricycle was bought by borrowed money, Cui Yingjie begged the officers to leave behind the tricycle but only to find out the indifference of the officer. Cui Yingjie left the scene and went back again to find the girl who sold sausages with him, and happened to see his tricycle being loaded

[2]From the Indictment Opinions of Beijing Public Security Bureau and the Indictment of the Beijing People's Procuratorate.

[3]From the Indictment of the Beijing People's Procuratorate.

on the officer's truck. Cui Yingjie rushed to the truck for a final try to get his property back but was prevented by the officer. Being afraid of the compulsion in the disarray, Cui Yingjie was anxious to escape and carelessly scratched his knife to the side, resulting in a stab on the vice leader Li Zhiqiang who was dead after being sent to the hospital.[4]

4. **Version Four**: Born in a small village of Pingyang Town, Fuping County, Baoding City, Hebei Province, Cui Yingjie was a poor farmer and earned his living by working as a temporary security guard in an entertainment club in Kemao Building in Zhongguancun Science Park, Beijing. Since April 2006, the employer had been behind in payment for four months. Be cornered by poverty, Cui Yingjie borrowed money from his friends to buy tools including tricycle and stove to make a living by selling barbecued sausages on the street. On the afternoon of August 11, 2006, the law enforcement officers of City Administration Group of Haidian District punished Cui Yingjie for unlicensed business activity and confiscated his tools. At that time, the officers neither wore uniforms nor presented any identity document. What's worse, they failed to produce any official documents including the written decision of administrative penalty. There even wasn't any oral explanation. Cui Yingjie mistakenly thought he was robbed or extorted. Failed to get his tricycle back by imploration, he left the scene and went back to find the girl Zhao who sold sausages with him. Then, he saw his tricycle being loaded onto the truck. When Cui Yingjie made a final try to get his property back, he carelessly stabbed the vice leader of the City Administration Group Li Zhiqiang by the knife in his hand. The victim was dead after being sent to the hospital.[5]

1.2 Which Version Tells the Fact?

In accordance with legal common sense, the four versions would lead to entirely different judicial results under criminal law. Therefore, they could not be valid at the same time. To find the only "truth", firstly people would think of evidence. The credible evidence listed in the court judgment is as follows.

I. Survey and Authentication Report along with Physical and Documentary Evidence

   (a) According to thc Record on Forensics Examination and photos on spot provided by criminal and investigation team in Haidian Sub Office of Beijing Municipal Public Security Bureau the site was located on the right lane of the southeast side of the main road on No. 1 Bridge in Zhongguancun Science Park, Beijing. The central scene was on the right lane 30 m southwards of the main road intersections from south to north park lane on the southeast side of No. 1 Bridge in Zhongguancun Science Park.

[4]From the trial record of the Cui Yingjie Case. https://tiebabaidu.com/p/226845523.

[5]See Foootnote 4.

In the scene, there was a 1.7 meter-long blood on the ground (had been extracted) and a red plastic handle (had been extracted) aside. In the office of City Administration Group of Haidian District on the underground floor in Hailong Building, there was the tricycle (had been used by the defendant) with a red plastic scabbard (had been extracted) under stove, pan and other items. In the emergency room in Haidian Hospital, a 10.5 cm-long and 2.3 cm-wide-blade (according to the briefing, the blade was removed from Li Zhiqiang's in emergency rescuing) was extracted from Yin Zhaojiang in City Administration Group of Haidian District.

A piece of cloth, which has been submitted for inspection, was found in the 79th locker in the hallway of the monitoring room of the security department in Minggui Club on the eighth floor of Kemao Electronic Mall in Zhongguancun Science Park, Haidian District in Beijing.

(b) The Forensic Report in "Beijing the Public Law of Pathological Character (2006) No. 676 Autopsy Certification" issued by Forensic Identification Center in Beijing Municipal Public Security Bureau proved that there was a 10 cm long visible diagonal stripe wound on the left side of the laryngeal prominence, with slightly right direction below the subcutaneous superficial muscular layer, which led to the phleborrhexis on the right brachiocephalic from Right thoracic cavity to the superior lobe of right lung. Li Zhiqiang died from the hemorrhagic shock caused by stabbing (like blade) hurt on the right brachiocephalic vein and the right upper lobe.

(c) The Forensic Report in "Beijing the Public Law of Physical Evidence Character (2006) No. 2747 Biological Evidence Certification" issued by Forensic Identification Center in Beijing Municipal Public Security Bureau proved and strongly supported that the two submitted blood stains at the scene and the blood stains on the blade and the cloth (the 79th locker in the hallway of the monitoring room of the security department in Minggui Club) was from Li Zhiqiang.

(d) The photos of tricycle, blade, and knife handle and scabbard produced in the court were proved by the defendant Cui Yingjie as the items and lethal weapon he used.

(e) Registration Form of Criminal Cases issued by Criminal Investigation Detachment of Haidian Sub Office of Beijing Municipal Public Security Bureau proved that at 5:10 p.m. of August 11, 2006, crime reporter Cui Gonghai stated that during the law enforcement with Li Zhiqiang and other colleagues at the north corner of the Kemao Building in Zhongguancun Science Park, Haidian District, a man stabbed Li Zhiqiang in the neck. Li died after being sent to the hospital.

(f) The Notes of Capturing the Accused and the Statement of Work issued by Criminal Investigation Detachment of Haidian Sub Office of Beijing Municipal Public Security Bureau proved that by investigation, Cui Yingjie had a major suspicion of committing a crime. At 3 p.m. of August 12, 2006, the Police summoned Zhang Lei, a friend of Cui Yingjie, from Jinbohan International Business Club in Haidian District, Beijing. According to

Zhang Lei, Cui Yingjie claimed that he stabbed a city administration officer and needed money to hide away. Afterwards, Cui Yingjie took the money provided by Niu Xuming and Duan Yuli and went to the hideout that Zhang Lei and Zhang Jianhua arranged. At 4 a.m. that day, Zhang Jianhua was arrested by the police at Jinbohan International Business Club in Haidian District. At 5:30 a.m., Cui Yingjie was arrested by the police at the fifth floor of the 72th Building in Wanlian Villa in Tanggu Development Zone, Tianjing. At 4 p.m. August 31, 2006, Niu Xuming was arrested by the police at Hengchang Technology Co. Ltd in Zhongguancun Science Park in Haidian District, Beijing. On 9 a.m. September 1, 2006, Duan Yuli contacted with the police and voluntarily surrendered himself. The police came to Kemao Building in Haidian District and took Duan Yuli away for further investigation.[6]

(g) The Household Register Certificates issued by the relevant Public Security Departments verified the information including the name, date of birth and address etc. of Cui Yingjie, Zhang Lei, Niu Xuming, Zhang Jianhua, Duan Yuli and the victim Li Zhiqiang.[7]

The aforementioned evidence mainly takes the form of historical traces and tangible materials, such as the bloodstain and fingerprints left at the criminal scene, on the knife and the cloth. The wound on the victim's corpse, the type of lethal weapon as well as the severity of the injury speculated from the wound are also evidence. And their most important role is to prove the existence of the case and to prove the relations between the case, key points, key events and the litigants (such as the defendant and the victim). For example, the defendant was on the scene, and the knife that injured Li Zhiqiang belonged to the defendant who did use the knife at the scene.[8]

Those punctuate traces left by history displayed punctuate events and the relation between the events and somebody. Although this kind of empirical existence and relation are one of the sections in the process of cognition, they don't have to be present through everyday language. Therefore, they could not form a factual text concerning the case because they are part of the "non-narrative" experience. Admittedly, physical traces left by history like material evidence and crime scene investigation could provide evidence that is more credible than subjective memory and recollection in the perspective of natural science. However, for case facts which could only be understood and accepted through narration, this kind of evidence could only take supplementary effect.

[6]From the Indictment of the Beijing People's Procuratorate.

[7]From The Criminal Judgment of the No.1 Intermediate People's Court of Beijing.

[8]Moreover, unnecessary details on subordinated evidence in the reorganization of the facts would not be given, such as historical documents used to verify the identities of people involved in the case.

As a matter of fact, people would come up with fragmented and punctuate impression once saw the following evidence: some bloodstains, a knife, a corpse, a suspect and so on. However, people could not derive any narrative text about everyday discourse from the evidence (a complete story with characters, plots, causes, details, results and thematic meaning). Therefore, the case and the things happened still remain unclear.

II. The video at the Crime Scene
The Criminal Judgment of the No.1 Intermediate People's Court of Beijing rule that, "the live recording of the law enforcement proved: the officers punished Cui Yingjie for unlicensed business activity, but Cui Yingjie first held a knife to obstruct the officers' legal enforcement and then rushed to the officers' truck when they left."

III. The Testimony of the Witness and Defendant's Confession

(a) the Indictment of the Beijing People's Procuratorate states that: the testimony of the witness Cui Gonghai (a member of the City Administration Group of Haidian District, Beijing) proved: on the afternoon of August 11, 2006, when he and his men cleaned up unlicensed vendors at the northwest corner of Kemao Building in Zhongguancun Science Park, they saw Li Zhiqiang was chasing a man who was running after the law enforcement truck. So Cui Gonghai joined the chasing. Later the man stopped and walked fast toward them. Li Zhiqiang was talking to other colleagues as the man walked behind them. When Li Zhiqiang turned back, the man rushed toward him a dagger in his right hand, giving a stab on Li Zhiqiang's neck and running away.[9]
The Identification Notes issued by the Public Security Department proved: after recognizing 12 photos of different male faces, witness Cui Gonghai identified that the man (Cui Yingjie) on the Photo No.2 was the man who killed Li Zhiqiang by dagger.

(b) The testimony of the witness Di Yumei (a staff in City Administration Group of Haidian District, Beijing) proved: on the afternoon of August 11, 2006, she and her colleagues were cleaning up unlicensed vendors in Zhongguancun Science Park. When they came to the northwest corner of Kemao Building, they saw a man and a woman were selling barbecued sausages by the street.[10]
The vice leader Li Zhiqiang led the officers to seize the vendor's tricycle, but the male vendor kept holding a dagger in his right hand to obstruct law enforcement. He pushed and shoved with the officers to prevent them from confiscating the stall. Then some officers loaded the vendor's tricycle on the truck. To protect it from being confiscated, the female vendor cried, yelled and held the front wheel of tricycle. After several officers dragged the female vendor away, Li Zhiqiang stood at the right side of the truck

[9]From the Indictment of the Beijing People's Procuratorate.
[10]See Foootnote 4.

she was sitting in and told the driver to leave. When Li Zhiqiang turned back, the male vendor jumped over the guardrail and gave a head-on stab on the left side of his neck. Then the male vendor swung his hand, and the blade was broken. After throwing the dagger on the ground, the male vendor turned around and ran into an alleyway.

The Identification Notes issued by Public Security Department proved: after identifying 12 photos of different male faces, witness Di Yumei recognized that the man (Cui Yingjie) on the photo No. 10th was the man who killed Li Zhiqiang by dagger.

(c) The testimony of the witness Lu Fucai (the assistant manager of the City Administration Group of Haidian District, Beijing) proved: on the afternoon of August 11, 2006, they were cleaning up unlicensed vendors in Zhongguancun Science Park. At about 5 p.m., when Li Zhiqiang and five assistant managers went on patrol to the alleyway on the north side of Kemao Electronic Mall, they saw a man protected a tricycle with a fruit knife in his hands. Li Zhiqiang told the man to put down the knife and pulled the tricycle, but the man refused. Failed to protect his tricycle, the man ran toward a courtyard. Then Li Zhiqiang told the officers to load the tricycle on the truck. After a while, the man with knife went back only to find his tricycle had been taken away. So he went straight toward Li Zhiqiang to give him a stab on his neck and ran away.[11]

(d) The testimony of the witness Zhang Jianguo proved: at about 4 p.m. of August 11, 2006, when they carried out law enforcement activities with City Administration Group to the north side of Kemao Electronic Mall in Zhongguancun Science Park, they found two unlicensed Xinjiang vendors selling cantaloupe and a male vendor selling sausages at the entrance of an alleyway. They confiscated the tricycle cart of one of the Xinjiang vendors. But they had not gone far before they heard loud noise behind. When they turned back, they saw Li Zhiqiang standing by the street side covered in blood with more blood squirting from the front part of his neck. (from the trial record of the Cui Yingjie Case. https://tiebabaidu.com/p/226845523).

The Identification Notes issued by Public Security Department proved: after identifying 12 photos of different male faces, witness Zhang Jianguo recognized that the man (Cui Yingjie) on the first photo was the vendorwho sold sausages at the scene.

(e) The testimony of the witness Zhao Qiaoran proved: one of her father's friends told her that Cui Yingjie worked as a security guard in Kemao Building in Zhongguancun Science Park of Haidian District, Beijing. At other times, Cui Yingjie would sell barbecued sausages on the streets and wanted someone to assist him. Since she would like to have a job in Beijing, Zhao arrived at Beijing on the afternoon of August 10, 2006. The next afternoon, she and Cui Yingjie made sausages at Cui's residence. At about 4 p.m., she and Cui Yingjie was selling barbecued sausages near the Kemao

[11] From the Indictment of the Beijing People's Procuratorate.

Building in Zhongguancun Science Park. Afterwards, the officers of City Administration Group intended to confiscate their tricycle and sausages, so Cui Yingjie took a knife to threaten the officers from confiscating the tricycle. When the officers loaded the tricycle on a truck, she begged them and pulled the tricycle. Later, she saw Cui Yingjie running away. Standing for a while, she left the scene as well.[12]

(f) The testimony of the witness Jia Fengxiang proved: at about 8 p.m. on August 11, 2006, he got a call from his friend Zhang Lei and was told that Cui Yingjie, one of Zhang's friends, wanted to find him. Zhang Lei also asked for his address in Tianjin and told him to meet Cui. At about 10 p.m., Cui called him to set up a date place. Then, he took Cui back to his dormitory. The next morning, the police came to the dormitory and arrested Cui.[13]

(g) The testimony of the witness Fan Baoshan proved: at about 5 p.m., he heard from his friend who worked in Kemao Center that Cui Yingjie wounded a city administration officer. Then he met Duan Yuli at the first floor and told Duan that Cui seemed to wound a city administration officer.[14]

(h) The testimony of the witness Fang Wenqi proved: at about 5 p.m. on August 11, 2006, Duan Yuli borrowed his mobile phone and did not give it back until next morning. His mobile phone model was Siemens S65.[15]

(i) The defendant Cui Yingjie made the confession during the investigation: at about 4 p.m. of August 11, 2006, upon he set up his stall, the officers came and wanted to confiscate his tricycle. He refused and took a knife as a threat. Later, the officers loaded his tricycle on the truck. He wanted to get his tricycle back but the truck had driven away. Failed to catch up, he felt so enraged and intended to revenge, so he stabbed the foremost officer by the knife.[16]

People with some judicial common sense and experience could easily understand that both the testimony of the witness and the confession by the defendant are evidence of vital significance. Such significance does not lie in the substantive law or procedural law, but in cognition. As mentioned before, although natural objects have already provided relatively reliable evidence concerning experience, they hardly make contribution to the complete picture of the formation of facts. Since the testimony and confession are narrative and belong to everyday language, people would not be conscious of the emergence of the events or start to ponder the case before reading the above evidence carefully. And only then the physical evidence could come into play to support or deny people's different imaginations concerning the case.

---

[12] From the Indictment of the Beijing People's Procuratorate.

[13] See Foootnote 4.

[14] See Foootnote 4.

[15] See Foootnote 4.

[16] From the Criminal Judgment of the No.1 Intermediate People's Court of Beijing.

Of particular note is that every testimony of the witness and the confession of the defendant is one paragraph of narrative text which reproduces historical scenes. Although they have gone through the construction of rhetoric, they are different from the factual texts that are proved by the court verdict. Meanwhile, they are actually the narrative texts of the writers of court verdict, rather than the original words of the witnesses or the defendant. It is widely known that the descriptions of the case made by the witnesses and the defendant are mainly in the form of question and answer in the trial. And an important work of the judges is to extract raw materials from the trivial dialogues and adopt them into statement. Certainly, when looking back upon the nonverbal historical situation, the interlocutors remold the recalled historical context in the form of language. To say the least, let us temporarily omit the aforementioned factors, and regard those testimonies and confessions as original evidence, and see what on earth they can bring to us.

To be safe, part of the rhetoric in the testimony and the confession should be excluded. The confession made by the defendant here is far different from that he made in the court. Moreover, the description that "he felt so enraged and intended to revenge" in the confession was vehemently denied by the defense during the trial. However, since there is no evidence for such words, we will leave out this line. We will also exclude some words with obviously story–telling feature in some testimonies and some detailed narration which cannot be supported by other evidence, like the vivid expression of "he swung his hand" in the testimony of the witness Di Yumei.

In fact, the testimony of Di Yumei, the city administration staff, was the most detailed and the most expressive compared with other evidence. In her testimony, Li Zhiqiang had already foreseen the impending danger, so he warned her to drive the truck away. And she also somehow "saw" that Cui Yingjie jumped over the guardrail and went at Li Zhiqiang directly. According to her, Cui Yingjie did not only give a stab on the vital part of Li Zhiqiang, but also deliberately "swung his hand" to break the blade. When reading the story, readers will definitely think that the defendant would not deliberately select a special victim and commit such brutal crime if it were not for his extremely intense hatred and evil mind.

However, judging from the video at the scene, if Di Yumei did sit on the driver seat of the truck, how did she clearly see what happened at the rear in just few seconds? How did she "see" many details that were not mentioned by other witnesses in the chaos? By contrast, people would definitely raise a rather alarming doubt.

Certainly, we do not doubt that Di Yumei perjured in the testimony. But since narrative is much more complicated, it cannot be evaluated by lie or right and wrong. The author would like to remind readers that even the basic argument that "case facts are the outcome of narrative and rhetoric" is acknowledged, the process should not be simply regarded as single-line activity where a certain narrator (e.g.: the judge) creates stories (case facts) directly based on materials (evidence). As material, evidence sometimes is a story told by the narrator. Different narrators provide various narrative texts through different ways in the legal process. Actually, justice is a platform where many narrators confront, communicate, integrate and split up with many stories.

Next, based on all the evidence, we could see a fairly clear and incontrovertible sequence of the case.

First of all, the clues of the case are chronologically listed as follows:

In the early 2004	Cui Yingjie came to Beijing
In 2006	Cui Yingjie spread things for sale without license in Zhongguancun Science Park
On August 11, 2006	Cui Yingjie's business was stopped
	Cui Yingjie had a dispute with people who stopped his business
	Cui Yingjie left the scene
	Cui Yingjie went back to the scene
	Li Zhiqiang was stabbed by the knife in Cui Yingjie's hands
	Li Zhiqiang was dead after being sent to the hospital
On August 12, 2006	Cui Yingjie was arrested by the Public Security Department

Subsequently, the case is composed with several core events which were adopted by the procedure of examining witness in the court. Also, all parties concerned had no controversy over the above events:

(1) Cui Yingjie was a farmer who worked town, living in a plight as of four months of salary arrears.
(2) Cui Yingjie borrowed money to buy tools like tricycle and sold barbecued sausages by the street side of Zhongguancun Science Park without business license.
(3) At about 5 p.m. of August 11, 2006, City Administration Group officers came to Cui Yingjie's stall to investigate and penalize vendors without business license.
(4) The first group of officers didn't wear uniforms or present any written documents or certificates, even without oral explanations.
(5) Cui Yingjie had a dispute with the officers for his tricycle with a knife in his hand.
(6) The tricycle was confiscated, and Cui Yingjie left the scene and was lost from Zhao who set up street stall with him.
(7) Cui Yingjie went back to the scene and rushed into the crowd with a knife in his hand.
(8) The vice leader of the City Administration Group was stabbed by Cui Yingjie in the neck and was dead after being sent to the hospital.

Then, if we compare the four versions of case facts mentioned at the beginning of the paper, it's not difficult to find the following points: the four versions are within the framework of the above-mentioned case clues; the four versions are included in the above-mentioned eight events. However, readers would easily recognize the great differenccs from the list of clues to the list of events and finally to the factual texts. Although arrangement of the events makes them visually clear, closer scrutiny would reveal that they almost make no sense in specific judicial activities as there is no applicable law to draw a judgment. Many of these important legal issues are not resolved at all. On the other hand, although four versions all seem to be derived from the irrefutable eight events, they are quite different from each other. And this kind of difference would technically engender sever judicial divisions. But what are the reasons hidden behind these phenomenon? What factors lead to the vertical differences between the lists and the factual texts and the lateral differences among those texts? The study is going to answer these questions.

2 Why Evidence Does not Equal to Fact?

Broadly speaking, the reorganization of the reality of a past case can certainly be regarded as the recollection, record and representation of history. But the representation of history here embraces specialty, which means it can only be completed in the context of law. Also, it has to actively and openly cater to specific legal targets, such as to meet the definition of the criminal charge and the criterion for imposing penalty. Different from imagination, people are not inclined to firstly find an external, objective and self-fulfilling history and then to judge whether it is in accordance with the rules that the law has set for a certain problem. Actually, the order is reversed. The law has laid down what ways and what patterns we should follow to observe, search and compile this part of history. For example, since Cui Yingjie Case is a criminal case, people's acts of searching for the case facts in the criminal tribunal were in the extent permitted by the adjective law. People are trying to fit the plot frame related to such a murder case in substantive law. The primary purpose of the situation where both writing and thinking mode of the facts have been already prescribed in the value and structure, is to ensure the authenticity and the justice as far as possible. However, in reality, the special requirements for narrative and rhetoric may destroy and create the facts at the same time.

2.1 The Manifestation Mode of Case Facts and Historical Facts

Since case fact is generally about the representation of history, the author will discuss the issue by adopting some terms and theories of historiography only to provide clear and concise discussion. As to the controversies in other subjects and the consequent influence on the adoption of theories in the study, the author will indicate and make explanations.

First of all, it should be noted that two groups of terms will be frequently employed in the study. The classification here only serves to provide a concise content rather than correcting people's habits of diction in other situations. Therefore, the implication and the usage of the two groups of vocabularies are confined to this study only.

The first group: evidence—event—fact.

To provide a convenient and clear discussion, the author intends to make a distinction among the evidence, event and fact. As to the evidence in the study, it points to the relatively stable traces left after a case, such as historical sites (crime scene, body and physical evidence), documentation (written evidence), and witness recalls (witness testimony and client statement). Meanwhile, Xu Jingcun, Criminal Evidence: Division and Reversion, PEOPLE'S PROCURATORIAL MONTHLY 2005, (3) holds that "evidence in litigation should be a unity of its formation and content." The evidence used as analysis materials in Cui Yingjie Case (and Deng Yujiao Case) in the study are undisputed and admitted by court.

Event, the primary language record of the conditions in a case, is a historical circumstance which is directly reflected from evidence and an intuitive statement of the content. It also possibly excludes obvious literary rhetoric (not all rhetoric) according to people's common sense, such as the statement that "Cu Yingjie did not have business license" and the direct answers to questions like "whether Cui Yingjie had a dispute with the officers".

The fact in the study is the final mature narrative text. It described the case and provides basis for court to make judgment. More importantly, fact, different from event, is a melodramatic panoramic view of the case with beginning, ending, plots, characters, fate and definite meanings (of litigation and law).

The second group: annals—chronicle—history (narrative history).

This group belongs to the general concept of history, which respectively refers to three kinds of genres of written history. As a basic type of historical records, annals uses short phrases or sentences to record events and lists those items with time order. It is also called chronology or chronicle of events and is now frequently used as appendix of long compilation of history usually with annual time unit. Chronicle is more detailed than annals in the record of events and shows an incomplete narrative tendency. History, also called "narrative history", is complete narrative story with consistent relations, structures and meanings in event and time. The case facts required in judicial judgment is a case in point.

Although the above three words are commonsense notions, the study specially refers to the article written by Hayden White: *The value of narrativity in the representation of reality* and the essay written by German scholar Hershel: *The new chronicle: An outline of historical theory*. Admittedly, Hayden White's philosophy of history is one of the author's sources of inspiration and is valuable for the formation of the basic views in the study. Readers can also find that the author draws lessons from the analysis methods used in *the value of narrativity in the representation of reality* in this section. However, as to the actual argument and discussion, the author is not intended to (and cannot) follow Hayden White's thinking mode of relying on Structuralism, especially when he narrowly regarded rhetoric and the factual narrative of history as metaphors (i.e. the narrowest result of the development of rhetoric from middle ages to modern times) after pointing out that the rhetoric had constructed the history. His understanding toward rhetoric is what the author criticizes. On the other hand, the specialty of the characters of legal issues is the focus of the study.

Moreover, it should be noted that the three genres are the results of basic and cursory classification with relatively strong cross–culture. Almost every civilization had undergone a process from complication to simplification after it had learnt to record history by words, and Chinese are no exception. Meanwhile, genres can be classified in many other ways. For example, Lao Ai, in An Overview of the Historic Meaning of Chinese Civilization to the twenty-first century Academic Monthly 2004 (6), subdivided the process of textualization of early Chinese history into: oral statement—fragmented record of events (such as inscriptions on bones or tortoise shells) – individual record of events (bronze inscription)—consecutive record of events (such as state history of Spring and Autumn Period)—historical compilation (*The Spring and Autumn Annals*)—historical narrative (such as *Zuo Commentary on the Spring and Autumn Annals*)—human narrative (such as *Historical Records*). However, the standard of the classification is not based on the maturity level of narrative development, because the word of mouth is regarded as a primary prehistory inferior to the record of events. But actually, at the time when writing habit had not emerged, stories that were passed from mouth to mouth for widely spreading family history had borne more practiced narrative construction and skills than consecutive record and historical compilation. We can even say that it is easier to find flourishing and refine epics and legends among the crowd in the absence of words. The author chooses this classification not only for its merit of cross-culture, but also because it reflects the evolution that written records have experienced in the narrative refinement.

2.2 *Failed or Incomplete Formation of Fact*

Let's review the sequence of Cui Yingjie Case in the first section of this paper. In comparison, the chronological list the author adopted when summing up the clues of the case in the last section can be seen as annals. The list of the eight core events belongs to typical chronicle, while the four different versions of the case facts at the beginning of the paper are mature narration of historical texts. The author intended to "restore" the list of clues and events, but it neither mean that such texts did occur in the trial nor all the narrative related to the trial must include the above three steps. Yet in practice, the author did find that judges write similar draft to help sort out their thoughts when carefully reading the files. Narrative text can directly draw its conclusion in individual cases. The author restores the above list with the purpose of giving necessary discussion. Readers who agree with the view of narrative construction in the study should be cautious about all texts in the study.

Case clues:

In the early 2004	Cui Yingjie came to Beijing
In 2006	Cui Yingjie sold things without license in Zhongguancun Science Park
On August 11, 2006	Cui Yingjie's business was stopped
	Cui Yingjie had a dispute with people who stopped his business
	Cui Yingjie left the scene
	Cui Yingjie went back to the scene
	Li Zhiqiang was stabbed by the knife in Cui Yingjie's hand
	Li Zhiqiang was dead after being sent to the hospital
On August 12, 2006	Cui Yingjie was arrested by the Public Security Department

After examining all the evidence (including trial record) used in the court verdict, the author arranged the acts of the main character—Cui Yingjie in the time order to produce a record format similar to annals. From the clues, it is not difficult to find almost all of Cui Yingjie's acts related to the case, the death of Li Zhiqiang and every record in the case can be directly obtained from the evidence that were examined and finally adopted by the court without reasoning and explanation. However, we are unable to find any information that can make conviction and evaluation on the defendant's acts from the clue. Whether it is the problem of fact itself or it is the way of writing that caused the problem?

Let's make a comparison with classical historical texts of annals. Hayden White in The Content of the Form: Narrative Discourse and Historical Representation used German historical document *Saint Gall Annals* as example. The document is fairly consistent with the typical form of annals. Take the entries that had been recorded since A.D. 709 for example.

709. Hard winter. Duke Gottfried died.
710. Hard year and deficient in crops.
711.
712. Flood everywhere.
713.
714. Pippin, mayor of the palace, died.
715.
716.
717.
718. Charles devastated the Saxon with great destruction.
719.
720. Charles fought against the Saxons.
721. Theudo drove the Saracens out of Aquitaine.
722. Great crops.

723.
724.
725. Saracens came for the first time.
726.
727.
……

(The author wants to remind the readers that although Hayden White had analyzed annals and narrative in *Narrativity in the Representation of Reality*, the author's selection of the record is not a repetition but for the keynote of the study. White's analysis focused on how to write history, but the author gives priority to the content that can conclude theories related to legal practice.)

There is nothing wrong when giving a look at the excerpted list. It's proper to use such a simple way to record the world where we live in. Clearly, it is not a story format that the daily language familiar with, because it has no beginning, no plot and no end. The number of year in the left column can be extended indefinitely forward or backward as long as the annals calendar has not changed. The events in the right column are not only monotonous but are also recorded in an almost indifferent tone by the anonymous recorder. Therefore, the events seem to have nothing to do with the recorder, readers or any other people.

However, the events actually provided some information according to White. When readers faced the impassive record, they would be placed "in a culture hovering on the brink of dissolution, a society of radical scarcity, a world of human groups threatened by death, devastation, flood, and famine" (from the Content of the Form: Narrative Discourse and Historical Representation). It may be somewhat exaggerated, but we did see that the content was full of wars, disasters or death. Then come the problems that readers start to raise queries about the record, reliability, significance and purpose of the events happened in the past out of curiosity. Readers would find later that the queries play a key role in the trial of the case.

According to the people's daily experience, it's impossible that only few things happened in life, details lie in every nook of our lives. Then, why the annals only recorded only one thing in a whole year? Why there are lots of blank spaces in the annals? It's impossible that nothing had happened in the blank years. According to our common sense, the history of a tribe would never be blank as long as its people kept producing offspring. And this kind of questions can go a step further: what are the standards that the recorder followed when selecting the events that he or she believed should be written in the history? White in The Content of the Form: Narrative Discourse and Historical Representation believed that "All of the events are extreme, and the implicit criterion for selecting them for remembrance is their luminal nature. Basic need—food, security from external enemies, political and military leadership—and the threat of their not being provided are the subjects of concern; but the connection between basic needs and the conditions for their possible satisfaction is not explicitly commented on" (from the Content of the Form: Narrative Discourse and Historical Representation).But the author thinks it is only a conjecture, because the recorder did not pay attention to annual agriculture and missed many important wars in the period. Since the series of fragmented events may be random, it remains unclear that whether "intentional" historical record exists.

Continuity and the standards of record are followed by purpose—what is the purpose of writing such an annals? The intentional standard cannot be determined without a certain purpose. However, it is frustrating that this point still remains unclear. History recorders are always claiming to comply with a supreme purpose of leaving descendants a real document about what happened in the past with emphasis on comprehensiveness and reality. Yet they are consciously or unconsciously limited to smaller or more specific purposes, such as a particular time, nation, culture and regime.

In the above annals, we cannot find any concept concerning the country at all. Phrases like "Duke Gottfried" and the "subordinate with power" suggest that there was at least some certain power structure. And the several fights against the Saxons and the Saracens suggest the national position that the recorder might hold. However, what are the relations between the departed duke and Pippin, Charlie and Theodore who fought against invaders? Do they belong to the same country or the same regime? What is the nation that perennially had conflicts with the Saxons and the Saracens? The Saracens who were expelled from Aquitaine first came to here, and where is "here"? What geographical relation does the place have with the nation represented by the recorder? What role did the characters and the events recorded in the annals play in the destiny of the nation? Questions can go on endlessly.

If readers know something about the history of medieval Europe, they can make a guess based on the broken record that the recorder might write the annals from the standpoint of Frankish Kingdom. "Pippin, the subordinate with power" should be the famous Mayor of the Palace of Merovingian Dynasty in Herstal. And "Charlie" was the illegitimate son of Pippin—Charlie Matt, who took over the Mayor of the Palace in A.D. 715. He was the kingmaker of Clovis IV who was really a puppet of the Mayor of the Palace. At that time, Frank was internally divided into three small states with frequent wars. The north was invaded by the Saxons while the south was oppressed by the Arabs. From A.D. 715 to A.D. 718, Charlie gave a counterattack against the Saxons and the Saracens who attacked from the east bank of the Rhine. He conquered the Saxons and forced them to bow down and pay a tribute. However, the annals missed many crucial events like the Battle of Soissons that started the unification process of Frank in A.D. 719, Iconoclasm in A.D. 726 and the Annexation of Burgundy later, which makes people feel confused about the recorder's standpoints.

Annals, as a recording method, fail to adequate serve the people who try to find out the truth. The questions that the annals could not answer can be summarized as follows:

1. What are the relations between recorded events?
2. How to present the integrity and the continuity of the sequence of the events?
3. As an entirety, what central theme does the recorded content describe?
4. As an entirety, what meaning (experience, reasons and moral judgment) does the recorded content embrace?

Readers will find out later that the emergence of narrative is to solve the above questions.

2.3 *The Crux of Failed Texts*

(1) Case clues in the way of annals

The above analysis can be consistently applied to the clue list of Cui Yingjie Case. What we see are independent lines of characters and acts.

As to the relevance, the left and right columns have an obvious correspondence in time, but the lines up and down have no relation except the sequence of time. Especially, in the key part of the case from line four to line seven, what is the relation between Cui Yingjie's dispute with the people who stopped his business and his act of leaving the scene? Was it because Cui Yingjie failed to get his property back and gave up or he was driven away by the stronger officers? What is the connection between Cui Yingjie's acts of leaving and returning back. Whether it was something happened that forced the defendant to go back? Was it the victim or other irrelevant reasons? Any reader would feel an obvious fracture between Cui Yingjie's back and the death of Li Zhiqiang. Whether Cui Yingjie's back has direct association with his act of injuring people to death? Are there any events that have been omitted between the two acts? What is the exact circumstance when Li Zhiqiang was stabbed by Cui Yingjie's knife?

As to the integrity, records similar to annals do not have neither beginning nor ending. From the perspective of recording events, every entry could be a completely corresponding record of "time–event". But when they were combined together, none of them could be regarded as a standard measurement for integrity. It would not bring much influence if they start, end or break at any time. In the aspect of story, however, there is no recognizable story. Although characters appeared, there is no discernible plot or ending that concluded whether characters and their acts had achieved a common effect in the text. Certainly, the integrity of the story is no longer a problem.

As to the meaning, it should be noted that different from historical record activities like *Saint Gall Annals*, the meaning of the text has been clearly defined in the context of justice, which must be finished by speakers involved. This is a kind of legal meaning, and recorded texts related to facts need to first cater to the perspective that legal order adopts when observing historical facts. For example, the text may pay no attention to Cui Yingjie's financial situation like income, but it has to show Cui Yingjie's subjective attitude when he had dispute with others and caused someone's death. Meanwhile, it should also accommodate the evaluation system adopted by the legal order towards historical facts, i.e., the text should enable its readers to figure out that what type of legal review should be made at the judicial level, and that what relationship does it have with the rights and obligations in current law or the content concerning convictions, moreover, enable its readers to make a clear judgment based on the texts and decide on which side could win or lose and whether the defendant is guilty or not. This list of clues certainly failed to finish the above tasks. Thus it's safe to consider them as pointless sentences in judicial context.

(2) The influence that subjective requirement has on the formation of narrative

We can make the conclusion here that it is the features of the activities of legal practice that decides the unavoidable manifestation of narrative texts. If we go into the features seriously, we would find that although the case facts and historical facts claim to be objective and real, their deep motivations of telling stories are subjective.

First of all, the texts related to the facts must be "meaningful". From a broader perspective, this is actually people's inner desire of recognizing, understanding and mastering the world and the social environment they are living in. It is also an aspirated nature to ensure a safe life through the establishment of (cognitive, intellectual and actal) orders. Therefore, faced with the large amount of existing non-narrative representations of things that had happened, people will instinctively believe that they are not perfect and still need to be finished. With regard to history, White in The Content of the Form: Narrative Discourse and Historical Representation states that "And the official wisdom has it that however objective a historian might be in his reporting of events, however judicious he has been in his assessment of evidence, however punctilious he has been in his dating of *res gestae,* his account remains something less than a proper history if he has failed to give to reality the form of a story." As to the justice, people would be more eager and strict to require a story format of facts to answer all of the queries against the characters and plots, to satisfy their emotional desires for truth and justice and to meet their requirements for a stable life.

The next point (which also needs more explanations) is that after reading the nameless annals and the list of clues in Cui Yingjie Case, readers would realize that both of them lack clear theme. Although individual entries are clear, the combination of all of them fails to express a theme. Different from the cognitive desire reflected from the requirement that a text must have its meaning, people's strong desire (what meanings and lessons that you expected me to get when you tell me a story) for theme is more likely the result of their culture education. The theme of a story, though objective on the surface, is an issue with strong political and moral overtones. In his introduction to his *Lectures on the Philosophy of History*, Hegel states:

> In our language the term History unites the objective with the subjective side, and denotes quite as much the *historia rerum gestarutn,* as the *res gestae* themselves; on the other hand it comprehends not less what has *happened,* than the *narration* of what has happened. This union of the two meanings we must regard as of a higher order than mere outward accident; we must suppose historical narrations to have appeared contemporaneously with historical deeds and events. It is an internal vital principle common to both that produces them synchronously. Family memorials, patriarchal traditions, have an interest confined to the family and the clan. The *uniform course of events* which such a condition implies, is no subject of serious remembrance; though distinct transactions or turns of fortune, may rouse Mnemosyne to form conceptions of them—in the same way as love and the religious emotions provoke imagination to give shape to a previously formless impulse. But it is only

the state which first presents subject-matter that is not only *adapted* to the prose of History, but involves the production of such history in the very progress of its own being.

Hegel goes on to distinguish between the kind of "profound sentiments," such as "love" and "religious intuition and its conceptions," and "that outward existence of a political constitution which is enshrined in... rational laws and customs."The latter, he says, "s an *imperfect* Present; and cannot be thoroughly understood without knowledge of the past."This is why, he concludes, there are periods that, although filled with "revolutions, nomadic wanderings, and the strangest mutations," are destitute of any "*objective* history." And their destitution of an objective history is a function of the fact that they could produce "no *subjective* history, no annals."

We need not suppose, he remarks, "that the records of such periods have accidentally perished; rather, because they were not possible, do we find them wanting." And he insists that "only in a State cognizant of Laws, can distinct transactions take place, accompanied by such a clear consciousness of them as supplies the ability and suggests the necessity of an enduring record." When, in short, it is a matter of providing a narrative of real events, we must suppose that a subject of the sort that would provide the impulse to record its activities must exist.

Although the author has always disagreed with Hegel on his view of philosophy and his imaginations of the spiritual immanence of national states and the existence of nation and its consciousness, the author holds the opinion that the above paragraph penetratingly pointed out the key points: country, nation and clan (or other group titles that can be used to describe the cohesive affinity in an excursive group of people). Concept is a prerequisite for narrative history. State or other group titles are the subjects of the narrative. Once claimed that a certain narrative text was the history of a country or a nation, the writer must take the country's or the nation's stand to select events that were closely bound up with the country's or the nation's fate as well as the events that can show the origin, growth, prosperity, decline, collapse and extinction in the anthropomorphic life process of the country or the nation. Readers who have been trained are quite familiar with this kind of thinking mode. When we fail to take the country or the nation's stance, we would feel confused and unsatisfied with the historical records presented for us.

As the theme of narrative and the stand of narrator, group titles like country, nation, tribe and family, along with their systems, law, "clear and conscious acts" have already borne defined political nature, then what about its morality? According to Hegel in Lectures on the Philosophy of History, "a nation is moral, kind and robust when it is devoted to realizing its will and when it protects itself from the external violence in the process of objectification."

It is not important whether Hegel's opinion is true or false. What comes first is that almost all the generations of history writers have firmly believed the similar doctrine. If a historical text has clear theme, the image of political community (which country, nation or group and what kind of fate will the history facts talk about) is supposed to be obvious (at least, it won't be as confusing as the annals mentioned above). During the writing, whether the author basically agrees with the attitude toward the political community,[17] or disagrees,[18] or remains distant neutral apparently,[19] all of them convey the messages in an obvious or an underlying way: how should the political community of people survive and develop? How should a country or a nation organize or take actions so as to become stronger? What situation or what choice would lead to the end of a country or a nation? And this is the existence of social system and the concept that people cannot realize their meanings of living without the system. Despite its conceit, the concept is still widely accepted nowadays. As the most common language mode in people's life, "every historical narrative has as its latent or manifest purpose the desire to moralize the events of which it treats."[20] "Narrativity, certainly in factual storytelling and probably in fictional storytelling as well, is intimately related to, if not a function of, the impulse to moralize reality."[21]

In comparison, case facts are supposed to have more clear value standpoints than common historical facts. Different from historical facts where writers can claim to simply record history and do not have to be responsible for what readers conclude from his record, the case facts must follow a judgment of being true or false, lenient or punished. The facts, together with the judgment will be present to the public, and people can take part in the evaluation system. At the same time, the narrative in judicial practice, with simpler and more straightforward political nature and morality, openly gives official propaganda to implement a act even an ideological criterion that are required to be generally followed:

> Where there is ambiguity or ambivalence regarding the status of the legal system, which is the form in which the subject encounters most immediately the social system in which he is enjoined to achieve a full humanity, the ground on which any closure of a story one might wish to tell about a past, whether it be a public or a private past, is lacking.[22]

The description of case facts in the court have to aim at the system evaluation and moral criterion, or it will be regarded as null narrative.

The author would like to kindly remind readers again that though the narrative theme bears high morality, it has a tricky pattern of manifestation. On the face of it, the narrator would firstly tell a story to the audience, and suggest that everything he/she said is an objective description of the case. Then, the narrator would tell people what lessons they should draw from the story. It seems that the facts and lessons are independent with each other, but actually the latter has already infiltrated into the former. In other words, the latter decides what the former will be. And this point will be further analyzed in the later part of the study.

---

[17] Such as the national history composed by historians in different countries.

[18] Such as the American writer of *The Rise and Fall of the Third Reich*, William L. Shirer who is definitely an anti-Nazi.

[19] Such as *Decline and Fall of the Roman Empire* finished by Edward Gibbon about two thousand years after the collapse of Ancient Rome.

[20] From Hayden White, The Content of the Form: Narrative Discourse and Historical Representation.

[21] See Footnote 20.

[22] See Footnote 20.

3 The Trial Requires What Type of Text?

3.1 *Fragmented Case Information*

The previous section has summarized the features of failed record of facts: the linkage between recorded events is hardly recognizable; the combination of events fails to show the familiar integrity, recognizable theme and meaning. These features are conspicuous in the annals of clues in Cui Yingjie Case. What about the other texts (the sequence of events of the case) that the author has present?

Through careful comparison with the evidence materials in the court verdict, we can conjecture the events as follows:

(1) Cui Yingjie was a farmer who worked town, living in a plight as of four months of salary arrears.
(2) Cui Yingjie borrowed money to buy tools like tricycle and sold barbecued sausages by the street side of Zhongguancun Science Park without business license.
(3) At about 5 p.m. of August 11, 2006, City Administration Group officers came to Cui Yingjie's stall to investigate and penalize vendors without business license.
(4) The first group of officers didn't wear uniforms or present any written documents or certificates, even without oral explanations.
(5) Cui Yingjie had a dispute with the officers for his tricycle with a knife in his hand.
(6) The tricycle was confiscated, and Cui Yingjie left the scene and was lost from Zhao who set up street stall with him.
(7) Cui Yingjie went back to the scene and rushed into the crowd with a knife in his hand.
(8) The vice leader of the City Administration Group was stabbed by Cui Yingjie in the neck and was dead after being sent to the hospital.

The eight events are directly got from the evidence the court verdict present. "Directly got" means that the information was in the simplest language without any thinking or linguistic process like reasoning, speculation, explanation and imagination.

If we firmly uphold the traditional concept of litigation, we will find that the eight events above should be the "case facts" required by justice. They are also derived from the proved and adopted evidence that have gone through the examination of witness and trial. Theoretically, we can call the end of the trial of facts and work out a judicial conclusion based on the case facts. But is this really the case?

Obviously, people who have legal knowledge would feel confused after reading the above events. It's impossible for them to get any information from the narration to guide them to make judgment. What are the reasons behind?

3.2 From Chronicle to Narrative History

To make a foreshadowing of the narrative analysis of Cui Yingjie Case, it is necessary to take some historical texts as examples to make a comparison with the crucial differences between the simple list of events and the complete factual narrative.

(1) Insufficient chronicle

To address the question, we need to first make a comparison between the list of core events and the previous list of case clues. If the list of clues can correspond to a narrative format like annals in history, the list of events can correspond to the narrative format like chronicle. Compared with annals, chronicle is more widely-known and embraces more comprehensive details, plots and narrations, but it also lacks something when compared with the "historical" texts that people like most and frequently read.[23]

The author will skip issues like writers, politics, law, philosophy and culture that have been widely discussed in the fields of literature, history and philosophy, trying to regard the above annals as a historical document and observe its narrative issues from the perspective of readers without any academic background and stereotype. Compared with *Saint Gall Annals,* the annals above is more interesting, because it at least bears a theme—the chronicle events of Lu State in the Eastern Zhou Dynasty (actually, many states were involved in the recorded events, and some people believe that historiographers at that time would exchange information on official record of events), which is also a theme with clear and typical political position. Every entry is clear based on the year unite of reign of the dukes. With seasons as child entries, the writer recorded the events that he or she thought necessary. Since it is the history of Lu State, some important events were recorded, such as food production, natural disasters, special weathers, aspect astrology, diplomacy, wars, duke families and governments in states.

Hayden White in the Content of the Form: Narrative Discourse and Historical Representation, made a more profound comment on the drawbacks of chronicle: "the chronicle, like the annals but unlike the history, does not so much conclude as simply terminate; typically it lacks closure, that summing up of the "meaning" of the chain of events with which it deals that we normally expect from the well-made story. The chronicle typically promises closure but does not provide it." Probably, as a complete text, *The Spring and Autumn Annals* is expected to convey some reflective thoughts and principles according to its original writer and writers who later recompiled the text. However, they did not use understandable language or make any explanation to readers. The story lost its meaning because the ending that expressed thoughts

[23] In some circumstances, the "chronicle" in Chinese and English are widely used to describe all of the obvious methods of recording history in time order. In that case, annals or time line is also seen as one of the chronicles. But the study makes a distinction between chronicle and annals. Moreover, it should be noted that there is no sharp line between the two. As all of the classification made by human being, the ambiguous dividing line is inevitable. We can only make a general convention, because it's impossible to naturally classify what is annals and what is chronicle based on simplicity and complexity.

and principles had been missed. And this made the recorded content scattered and pointless, making the chronicle unable to meet people's curiosity about the "truth".

(2) Narrative history

Since *The Spring and Autumn Annals* provided oversimplified and confusing record on history, many descendants have written biography for it to interpret the meanings to readers. In the chronicle, *Zuo Commentary* bears more specialty than *Gongyang Commentary* and *Guliang Commentary*, because it narrated another history with corresponding time and detailed content and put it under the original text as annotation, rather than adopting the well-known way of discussion. The annotation served to give supplementary details to events that had not been recorded in the original text. In *The Spring and Autumn Annals*, the record of the Second Year of Duke Huan of Lu was less than one hundred words (without any punctuation), but *Zuo Commentary* added about one thousand words for the entries in the year, including some events that had never appeared in the original text.[24]

In *The Spring and Autumn Annals*, the Prime Minister of Song State, Hua Fudu, killed the senior official and the duke of Song State. The related diplomatic incidents provoked by the above events were recorded in *Zuo Commentary* as follows:

(THE FIRST YEAR OF DUKE HUAN'S REIGN) Hua Fudu of Song happened to see the wife of Kong Fu on the way. He gazed at her as she approached, and followed her with his eyes when she had passed, saying, "How handsome and beautiful!".

In the Duke's 2nd year, in spring, Hua Fudu attacked the Kong family, killed Kong Fu, and carried off his wife. The duke was angry, and Hua Fudu, in fear, proceeded also to murder him.

Man with noble character believed that Hua Fudu committed such unforgivable crime because he had no respect for his Duke. Therefore, the Spring and Autumn Annals wrote that he committed regicide. The Duke Huan of Lu, the Marquis Xi of Qi, the Marquis Huan of Chen and the Earl Zhuang of Zheng met in Ji to discuss how to put down the civil strife in Song State. Since Duke Huan was bribed, he agreed Hua Fudu to set up his own regime.

During the 10 years of Duke Shang's rule in Song, he had fought 11 battles, so that the people were not able to endure the constant summonses to the field. Kong Fu Jia was the minister of War, and Hua Fudu was the premier of the State. Taking advantage of the dissatisfaction of the people, Hua first set on foot a report that the constant fighting was owing to the minister of War, and then, after killing Kong Fu he murdered Duke Shang. Immediately after, he called duke Zhuang from Zheng, and raised him to the dukedom; in order to please Zheng, bribing also the Duke Huan of Lu with the great tripod of Gao. The Marquis of Qi, the Marquis of Chen and the Earl of Zheng all received bribe, and so Hua Fudu acted as chief minister to the duke of Sung.

[24]If we regard *Zuo Commentary* as historical document, we would face the problem that whether it belongs to chronicle or narrative history. From single passage, its words meet the basic definition of narrative history. But on the whole, it records intermittently by year. The author will take single passage as sample and will regard it as narrative history when comparing it with typical chronicle text.

In April, Duke Huan of Qi took the tripod from Song State and put it in the Imperial Ancestral Temple This act of the duke was not proper, and Zang Aibo remonstrated with him, saying, “He who is a ruler of men makes it his object to illustrate his virtue, and to repress in other what is wrong, that he may shed an enlightening influence on his officers. He is still afraid lest in any way he should fail to accomplish these things; and more over he seeks to display excellent virtue for the benefit of his posterity. Thus the roof of the Imperial Ancestral Temple should be thatched, the chariot for worship should be bedded by mat made by cattail, gravy should have no spices, main food should have no rice that has been husked for twice, all of which are in order to show thriftiness. Ceremony robe, hat, knees-cover, jade pendant, belt, dress, puttee, shoes, hair clasp, the rope of the jade on earlobes, the rope of hat and the cloth of hat have their own rules to show caste system. Jade mat, scarves, sheath, ornaments on the sheath, leather belt, ornaments on the belt, ribbon and horse collar have their own hierarchies to show the number that each class has set up. Drawing dragons and fire, embroidering white and cyan square pattern and white and black square patch are used to express decorations. Five hues are used to picture different images to express colors. Tin bells, chariot bells, Heng bells and bells on the flags are used to express sounds. Flags with sun, moon and stars are used to show brightness. The code of conduct should be thrifty and systematized with a certain amount of increase and decrease. Use decoration and colors to record it. Use sounds and brightness to promote it so as to convey messages to all officials. Therefore, all officials would be alert and afraid and dare not break the rule. However, you abandon morality but worship evil, and put the bribe in the Imperial Ancestral Temple. If you openly show the officials, they would follow the same act. Then who should be punished? The collapse of a state can be resulted from the evil of officials. The misconduct of officials is caused by preference and open corruption. The tripod of Gao State in the Imperial Ancestral Temple obviously show corruption. And what can be worse? King Wu of Zhou beat Shang Dynasty and took the Nine tripods (九鼎) to Luoyi. At that time, people thought he was improper because he apparently put the bribe in the Imperial Ancestral Temple. What should be done?” However, the Duke Huan of Qi refused to adopt his suggestion. After hearing the matter, in *Zuo Commentary, the first year to the eighteenth year of Duke Huan of Lu*, Hisotry, an official of Zhou Dynasty said: “the descendants of Zang Sunda may enjoy their high position and great wealth for a very long time, because he does not forget to dissuade his misconducted duke.”

As to the civil strife in Song State, *The Spring and Autumn Annals* only gave simple description that Hua Fudu killed his duke and Kong Fu. While in *Zuo Commentary*, Hua Fudu ran into Kong Fu’s beautiful wife, then he killed Kong Fu and looted his wife, which incurred his duke’s displeasure. So the whole event turned into: Hua Fudu coveted Kong Fu’s wife and had some political disagreements with Kong Fu, so he decided to kill Kong Fu. But he was afraid that his duke got angry, so he committed regicide. And this story has one of the important plot structures in typical narrative: the beginning of a story. The beginning here is not referred to the natural start of words, but an initial pattern that is decisive to the condition for unfolding the story.

Hua Fudu's act in the chronicle seemed to be unprovoked. His act only stayed at a certain point of time with arbitrariness. His act was not resulting from any events beforehand. And the same are to later events that Duke Huan of Qi and other noblemen put down the civil strife or Duke Huan of Qi took the tripod of Gao State has any connection with Hua Fudu's act. If it has, what are the connections among events? On the contrary, in narrative history, everything is clear and in order:

Trivial cause: being covetous of beauty.

Results: murdering, looting other people's wife, committing regicide which resulted in turbulence in state and a series of changes in diplomacy.

Primary causes: (1) after Duke Shang of Song took the throne, Song State has suffered from perennial strife. The Minister, Hua Fudu was covetous of the wife of Kong Fu, so he charged Kong Fu for provoking strife. Hua Fudu killed Kong Fu and looted his wife, but he was afraid of being punished by his duke. Therefore, he committed regicide, bringing about more disarrays in politics. (2) Later, dukes of many states like Lu, Qi, Chen and Zheng were bribed by Hua Fudu.

Results: Duke Huan of Lu formed alliance with dukes of Qi, Chen and Zheng, and the status of Hua Family in Song State was admitted. Duke Zhuag of Zheng, who was recalled from Zheng State, had been actually a puppet duke of Hua Family. A new political frame was formed where Song State got closer to Zheng State and positively won over other States, such as Lu, Qi and Chen.

Moreover, we can also find another "ultimate pattern that is different from the initial one and includes the results of the story". Other events are placed between the beginning and the ending of the story to form the plots, i.e. the progress and the evolution from the beginning to the ending. "And this kind of argument means that every event in the story is confined within a generally speculative circumstance from which the events obtain their meaning. In other words, the historical meanings of events consist in their origins and the results derived from the origins."

Apparently, the beginning of the initial pattern is a functional rhetoric structure, which serves to inform readers in narrative that it was the things happened that caused the following series of plots and actions. If the things could be avoided, the story would be no longer existed. The rhetoric function of the ending of the ultimate pattern bears obvious political features that the things happened together with the following actions finally led to a certain fate. If different choices took place at some points in the process, there would be another abruptly different fate and ending. If people could bear the story in mind, they could weigh the advantages and disadvantages and make their own judgment when faced with the similar circumstances.

In other words, the rhetoric structure of narration which is from the beginning to the end implies a concept of "causality" for readers and imbues them a philosophical or political mode of thinking that world, history, social condition as well as people's life are not random and disordered. The reason why they present the way they are is that they are driven by some certain power. Good narrative texts are able to reveal such power, making people understand and grasp the world and human being present by the stories.

In this way, three of the four questions concluded in the second section of paper have been solved by narrative history:

1. The relevance between events: recorded events are closely connected with each other by a causality (part of it is imaginary), and the next event is triggered by the last one;
2. The integrity of the story: according to Hershel, with initial and ultimate pattern, each recorded event was put on their own position in a reasoning chain to finish the evolution from initial pattern to ultimate pattern together so as to form an entirety;
3. The theme of the story: as mentioned before, the general theme of chronicle was about the "history of Lu State". At this stage, the theme of narrative history can be concluded as the "influence of the regicide on Lu State and geopolitics".

And the fourth question is the meaning or the comment on the story. What comment does the narrator give on plots and characters? What meaning does the narrator convey to the readers? And this content is usually demonstrated in two ways in narrative process: being hidden in the plots or being positively described to the audience by the narrator. The latter is generally seen as less mature works in the field of literature, such as crude children' literature and folk fables. In this kind of stories, structure of "this story tells us......" is followed after the fate of the characters to advise people to learn from the characters in the story or warn people of not following the step of the characters in the story. As to the story with hidden comment, it does not have obviously didactic content but leave the mission to readers and audience who are supposed to find out the meaning from the story by themselves. However, we need to be cautious that some narrators would claim that there is no comment on the story, and what they are doing is just to record or narrate. But the author thinks this is a deception because purposeless language cannot construct narrative. And the purpose is nothing but the desire that the narrator tried to exert influence on the audience, so it can only be successful or failed.

In *Zuo Commentary, the second year of Duke Huan of Lu*, the comment that the narrator tried to express is quite obvious, but it is technically processed and conveyed by one of the characters. Zang Aibo gave a long speech about cloth, ornamentation, tonality and hierarchy to point out that Hua Fudu's case was a malicious crime out of moral order. However, Duke Huan of Qi not only accepted bribes and acquiesced Hua Fudu's act, but also displayed the tripod in the Imperial Ancestral Temple. What officials and people would do after seeing all of this? From the political perspective in narrative history, Zang Aibo's words are exactly standard Confucian materials of politics and ethics.

3.3 Completed Case Facts: How Do Different Versions Remedy Fractures in Information

(1) The fractures in case events

With discussion over chronicle to narrative history, we can give answer to the question proposed in the first part of this section: why do people still feel confused about what judgment should be given even though the eight events related to the case are displayed clearly? And the reason is that the eight events in time order are like the unsatisfying chronicle. Although every entry is clear, irrefutable and better than the annals, it still cannot meet people's requirement for facts and truth.

Irreparable fractures and ambiguity can still be found among events. For example, as to the event (6) and event (7) where Cui Yingjie left the scene and came back, readers would doubt what are the relations between the two events? Although they are connected with each other, they are apparently incoherent and have blank space in time, because the defendant left the scene for a while and then came back. There is also blank space in environment, because the defendant came back for something happened or he might came up with something. We cannot find something important based on the above discussion because of curiosity. However, we can discover the key problem in the defending words of the attorney of the defendant in the court. According to the trial record of the Cui Yingjie Case. https://tiebabaidu.com/p/226845523, "The second time that Cui Yingjie ran out was to find the girl who set up street stall together with him, rather than committing revenge……the second time that he came back was to get back his living tools, rather than killing Li Zhiqiang." And this sentence suggested that the fracture between event (6) and event (7) was of great importance to the defendant, and how did narration fill in this gap would decide on the validity of the constitutive element of the crime as well as the life and death of the defendant.

Similar problems occurred between event (7) and event (8). Cui Yingjie ran into the crowd with knife in his hands, and then he stabbed Li Zhiqiang to death. However, the series of actions are incoherent, what was the specific circumstance? Whether the defendant ran into the crowd purposelessly or to find a particular target? If he did it purposely, was the target Li Zhiqiang or someone else? What psychological state was Cui Yingjie in when he stabbed Li Zhiqiang? All of the questions are the central points of the prosecution and defense arguments in the trial.

Only Cui Yingjie himself knew the reason why he came back to the scene again after leaving. And he claimed in the court that when he found Zhao, the girl setting up stall with him was lost, he came back to search for her. His attorney actively defensed on this point. While the prosecution was reluctant if the statement was adopted by the judge, because they believed the defendant returned to the scene with the purpose of revenge, so the Criminal Judgment of the No.1 Intermediate People's Court of Beijing rules that: "Cui Yingjie had no personal conflict with Li Zhiqiang, and he had the idea of revenge because he was punished for unlicensed business activity. So his idea of revenge was not only directly against Li Zhiqiang, but against all the officers present".

As to the specific situation of the death of Li Zhiqiang, the record present in the court could not provide details because there were blocked by obstacles. Therefore, the recall of the litigant and witnesses were the only way to restore the scene, but most of them did not notice it. According to Cui Yingjie, it was chaotic, and he was eager to escape so he gave a purposeless cut randomly behind him. According to the officer Di Yumei, who claimed to see the process, Cui Yingjie stabbed Li Zhiqiang intentionally and "swung his hand, and the blade was broken".[25]

However, another officer Cui Gonghai claimed that the defendant gripped the dagger reversed and gave an upward stab. (the Criminal Judgment of the No.1 Intermediate People's Court of Beijing) Although this case has insufficient evidence at this point, objective act, at least its appearance, can be exhaustively reflected through evidence. The problems are the subjective factors behind the objective acts. Unfortunately, people cannot directly understand others psychological activities. They can only depend on indirect ways, such as deduction and imagination based on objective acts.

The reason why fractures in chronicles would raise contentions is that they are key factors directly influenced the judgment. And the reason why contentions could happen and there could be possibilities for contentions is that the evidence failed to provide a clear answer to the court (or anyone else).

At the same time, there has already been a predetermined requirement in the context of law for how to remedy such fractures. And this has given the case facts less choice but more rhetoric than common historical texts. In the case facts, mode of thinking, cognition and language are prescribed. For history, if we free some doctrines that were not strict before, we can totally admit that although the annals or chronicle are relatively unsatisfying, they can still be seen as truth in some ways, though they are not observed or present through the language or mode of thinking that people are familiar with. But in the field of law, especially in justice, the rhetoric format of truth is prescribed. If required details are missed, the whole text would be considered as unclear and doubtful, especially in criminal cases.

(2) Established factual narrative

In any case, it is inevitable that case facts with high-level historical narrative will occur in various written document and oral statement present to the court and the public in the judicial process. In Cui Yingjie Case, there are at least four narrative texts of case facts. See the example at the beginning of the first section in this paper.

Version One: On the afternoon of August 11, 2006, vendor Cui Yingjing was selling barbecued sausages without license by the street of the northwest corner of Kemao Building in Zhongguancun Science Park of Haidian District, Beijing. The law enforcement officers of City Administration Group of Haidian District of Beijing Municipal Bureau of City Administration and Law Enforcement punished Cui Yingjie for unlicensed business activity and confiscated his tools including tricycle and stove. Cui Yingjie violently impeded the law enforcement in the process of confiscation and held a knife to threaten the officers. After the confiscation, Cui Yingjie held grudge against the officer and intended to revenge, so he thrust the leaving officers with his knife and gave a fierce stab on Li Zhiqiang's vital part between the neck and the collarbone. The stab injured the victim's right brachiocephalic vein and the right upper lobe and caused Li's death.[26]

[25] See Footnote 4.

[26] From the Indictment Opinions of Beijing Public Security Bureau.

The above versions give concise information and actually fill the gaps between events in chronicle and replenish the information that the evidence failed to show.

1. The theme of narrative: since the judicial prosecution in Cui Yingjie Case is the narrator, the story has two themes under special context. One is obvious while the other is latent. The obvious theme described a story where a scoundrel publicly committed a crime and violated the law and social order. The key words of this text that remind the readers all the time are country, law, order, justice and security. With such guiding theme, all the events in chronicle can be correspondingly explained and organized. While as to the latent theme in the context of law, evil peoplc will surely be punished, the disrupted order will be restored and the offended will of the nation and people will be pacified.
2. The integrity of narrative: the reason why such criminal case would take place is that Cui Yingjie defied law and sought personal interest. He made money by carrying out illegal unlicensed business activities, and what he sold was prepared food that is in great need of safety supervision and standardized management. When defendant's illegal act was stopped, his nature of evil and defiance against the law became aggravated. Thus he threatened the officers by holding a knife and killed one of them for revenge. The ultimate pattern (ending) of narrative, on the surface, was resulted from a vicious case in the form of the death of a law enforcement officer; while as to its deep meaning, the real ending is hidden. The case was so vicious that everyone could imagine that if the country or the society still embraced justice, the most satisfying ending was to give severe punishment for the criminal. In other words, the real ultimate pattern of the story was given to the judge and readers who spontaneously showed it.
3. The connection between events: at this point, events in the chronicle of the case are no longer occasional or respectively independent. On the contrary, they are closely connected with each other and perfectly developed through definite causality and the mode that "specific act is guided by concrete thoughts". Finally, they will come to the ending that reveals the entire meaning of the story.[27]

Since Cui Yingjie carried out illegal business activity, he was and should be stopped and even be punished by law enforcement officers (city administration officers). Cui Yingjie threatened the officers by holding a knife because of the punishment and his nature of evil and lawlessness. Cui Yingjie ran into the officers with a knife in his hand and killed Li Zhiqiang because of the confiscation of his living tools and his hatred and the idea of revenge on the officers. Then, readers can reasonably estimate that Cui Yingjie would be arrested, prosecuted and appeared in court. What is more, a severe sentence will befall him. In this case, the narrative related to the case facts is almost flawless without any fracture in chronicle. As to the event (7), there is nothing doubtful that Cui Yingjie rushed into the crowd to kill someone for revenge (and event (6) was unintentionally deleted in this narrative text). Meanwhile, there

[27]It is easy to find that the narrative text we are talking about did not adopt all the events in the chronicle. The missing events actually include important rhetoric purpose which will be given specific discussion in the future.

is also nothing unclear in event (8). The motivation of revenge murder has decided the subjective aspects of the elements in the crime. The defendant had been aware that he would cause someone's death, but he still positively carried out the crime. Since the subjective factors of the defendant are quite clear, we don't have to delve into the details of his acts, even if no one had witnessed the reality.

Now, let's take a look at the version four:

Version Four: Born in a small village of Pingyang Town, Fuping County, Baoding City, Hebei Province, Cui Yingjie was a poor farmer and earned his living by working as a temporary security guard in an entertainment club in Kemao Building in Zhongguancun Science Park, Beijing. Since April 2006, the employer had been behind in payment for four months. Be cornered by poverty, Cui Yingjie borrowed money from his friends to buy tools including tricycle and stove to make a living by selling barbecued sausages on the street. On the afternoon of August 11, 2006, the law enforcement officers of City Administration Group of Haidian District punished Cui Yingjie for unlicensed business activity and confiscated his tools. At that time, the officers neither wore uniforms nor presented any identity document. What's worse, they failed to produce any official documents including the written decision of administrative penalty. There even wasn't any oral explanation. Cui Yingjie mistakenly thought he was robbed or extorted. Failed to get his tricycle back by imploration, he left the scene and went back to find the girl Zhao who sold sausages with him. Then, he saw his tricycle being loaded onto the truck. When Cui Yingjie made a final try to get his property back, he carelessly stabbed the vice leader of the City Administration Group Li Zhiqiang by the knife in his hand. The victim was dead after being sent to the hospital.[28]

Likewise, in the above text, the events in the chronicle were formed into a story like narrative history with sophisticated rhetoric skill. However, the version gave an abruptly different story. First, the theme was changed. In the first version, a vicious criminal killed a law enforcement officer. While in this version, Cui Yingjie was a poor worker who was bullied and humiliated by the outrageous city administration group. When the defendant ran to his tricycle to try to protect his own property, he stabbed (maybe by accident or because of wrong judgment) Li Zhiqiang in chaos by the knife for cutting sausages in his hands, leading to the death of Li Zhiqiang. In the context of justice, the latent theme of this version is that the accident was not a vicious criminal case but a tragic unforeseeable event or circumstance. There was no evil scoundrel who committed intentional homicide but a poor farmer who was driven to desperation and unintentionally injured someone. Therefore, what the court needs to take into consideration is that how to deal with such contradiction in the complicated and unbalanced social relations so as to avoid the great shocks caused by the intensification of the persistent social problems.

Due to the changes in theme, the same chronicle would be interpreted and organized in totally different ways. Under this theme, the unlicensed business activity in event (2) is no longer a lawless act but a helpless decision forced by life according to event (1). As for the event (5) that Cui Yingjie had dispute with the officers, the

[28]From the Mistake of Misperception, https://www.lawyerluo.com/law/309.html.

first version regarded it as a violent confrontation against laws and threatening law enforcement officers by holding a knife. While in this version, his dispute was interpreted as a misunderstanding caused by improper law enforcement. And the fracture between the event (6) and event (7) is refilled as follows: failed to get his property back, Cui Yingjie actually gave up and planned to leave the scene. He went back to find the girl who setting up stalls with him. When he saw his tricycle was taken away by the officers, he attempted again to get his tricycle back so he rushed into the crowd. Due to the disordered situation, he accidentally injured someone.

Possibly, those who have the experience of judicial practice would forecast that this version would hardly be accepted by the court. But we have to admit that it completed the same task as the first version did, i.e. it constructed a narrative story that is consistent with historical language and court language that people are familiar with when faced with the same evidence, case clues and events of chronicle (and all of the four version in the first section of this paper have finished the same task).

The process of evolution of narration of case facts will call an end. And it is meaningless to give answer to the question proposed at the beginning of this paper: which version of the case facts is the truth? What really confused us is that different narrative can be generated from the same information, including (non-narrative) evidence. Moreover, in the context of justice, the differences between texts can lead to far different judicial judgments.

Charlemagne's Imperial Title: From the Perspective of Evidence Science

Longguo Li

1 Imperial Coronation

In April 799, Pope Leo III (796–816) was attacked suddenly and arrested by a group of conspirators when he was leading the procession for the great Litany from the Lateran palace to St Peter's basilica at Rome. The leaders of the conspirators, the *primicerius* Paschal and the *sacellarius* Campulus, threatened to blind the pope and cut out his tongue, who only saved himself by fleeing at night down from the Wall of the City. Under the escort of the Frankish legates stationing at St. Peter's Basilica, Leo went to Spoleto, whence he journeyed northward, across the Alps and met Charlemagne in Paderborn, not far from Aachen, the capital city of the Frankish kingdom.

Charlemagne received the Pope with full honors, but we do not know in any detail of the talks between them. After the meeting Leo III returned to Rome, accompanied by the Frankish legates and a group of soldiers, while Charlemagne went back to Aachen. The next spring, Charlemagne took an itinerary to the coastal region of northern Francia. On the way, he visited many famous churches and monasteries, with whose abbots and rectors he spent time and might well have conversed. Among them were Angilbert, abbot of Saint-Riquier, Alcuin, the abbot of St. Martin in Tours, and Theodolf, bishop of Orléans. In August 800, Charlemagne convened a general assembly of the kingdoms at Mainz, and from there he marched to Rome with a large army.

At Rome, Charlemagne held another great assembly for a week to reach a resolution of the accusations made against the Pope. By taking an oath before the altar of St Peter's with a manuscript of the Gospels held in his arms, Leo III was cleared

L. Li (✉)
Peking University, Beijing, China
e-mail: llguo@pku.edu.cn

B. Zhang et al. (eds.), *A Dialogue Between Law and History*,
https://doi.org/10.1007/978-981-15-9685-8_19

successfully of the allegations against him. On Christmas day of that year, Charlemagne was crowned by Leo III as the emperor of the Romans. According to Professor Matthias Becher, that seminal ceremony went as follows: On Christmas day of 800, Charlemagne went to St. Peter's to participate in the third Christmas mass. When he stood up from prayer, 'Leo III took a crown and placed it on the head of the Frankish king. The Romans who were present immediately understood the significance of this act. They appealed to the saints and acclaimed Charlemagne as emperor, calling out three times.' (Becher 2003, 7). They acclaimed, 'Charles, the most pious Augustus, crowned by God, the great and peaceful emperor, long life and victory! (*Carolo augusto, a Deo coronato magno et pacifico imperatori, vita et Victoria*).'

As Emperor, Charlemagne brought the opponents of the Pope to trial, who were then condemned to death by lèse-majesté. Through papal intercession, they saved their lives and were exiled into Francia. The new emperor sojourned at Rome for a few more months and then returned to Francia via Spoleto, Ravenna, Bologna and Pavia in turn in the autumn of 801. It is a general consensus that from 29 May 801 onward, Charlemagne utilized probably at Ravenna the wordy titulature *Carolus serenissimus augustus deo coronatus magnus pacificus imperator Romanum gubernans imperium qui et per misericordiam dei rex Francorum atque Langobardorum* ('Charles most serene augustus, crowned by God, great peacemaking emperor governing the Roman empire and also by God's mercy king of the Franks and of the Lombards') (Mühlbacher 1906, 265). Three different parts made up the titulature: the imperial title 'emperor governing the Roman Empire' (*imperator Romanum gubernans imperium*) and the two royal titles, 'king of the Franks' (*rex Francorum*) and 'king of the Lombards' (*rex Langobardorum*). Charter evidence suggested that Charlemagne never abandoned the above imperial title until his death, although he also used other imperial titles on several occasions. It is with these imperial titles that I shall be concerned in this article.

2 From 'Rex Romanorum' to 'Imperator Romanum Gubernans Imperium'

'*Imperator Romanum gubernans imperium*' has been exhaustively discussed elsewhere (Peter Classen 3, 187–204). What concerns me is the other two fairly short-lived imperial titles which Charlemagne had used, before the wordy title and after, respectively.

Historians have admitted that '*Imperator Romanum gubernans imperium*' is not the first imperial title of Charlemagne. In 1931 Max Kössler argued that the first imperial charter had been issued by Charlemagne with a strange titulature, 'with the grace of God, king of the Franks, of the Romans and of the Lombards' (*Carolus Dei gratia rex Francorum et Romanorum adque Langobardorum*) (Kössler 1931, 3). Carl Heldmann in 1928 argued as well that Charlemagne was created as Roman emperor in order to settle the case between the papacy and his opponents, when Heldmann investigated the reasons why the imperial coronation happened at the end of 800 at Rome (Heldmann 1928, 438–439). After decades of scholarly debate, Kössler's opinion was received generally by historians. In his classical study of the term '*Romanum gubernans imperium*', Peter Classen provided a very succinct overview of the history of the debate and recognized the imperial title of that document as true. He further conceded that the charter with its imperial title had posed a challenge to the scholars; he evaluated it nonetheless only 'as a testimony to a temporary embarrassment' (Classen 1983, 199).

Roger Collins also discussed the first imperial title in his biography of Charlemagne, although he concentrated on the reasons why it was soon replaced by the normal imperial title mentioned above. He suggested that Charlemagne had been crowned under the title of *Imperator Romanorum* or 'Emperor of the Romans' (Collins 1998, 150). Mainly based on the study of the sources of titulatures, Eckhard Müller-Mertens recently discussed to some extent the first imperial title 'rex Romanorum' (Müller-Mertens 2009, 50–92). Recently, from the perspective of the audience, Ildar Garipzanov pointed out that the imperial title addressed the Romans whose political assumptions and suppositions were influenced by the late Roman and early Byzantine past (Garipzanov 2017, 138).

These researches remind us of the importance of the first imperial title. It is still wanting to study the imperial titles of Charlemagne as a whole, by which we may illuminate the contending opinions among the advisers of the emperor promoting the transformation of these imperial titles.

From the perspective of evidence science, the first imperial charter is also too precious to be neglected. The charter was edited by Engelbert Mühlbacher as no. 196 of the early Carolingian charters in *Die Urkunden Pippins, Karlmanns und Karls des Grossen*, the first volume of the MGH charter series. It was issued to Aribert, bishop of Arezzo, by Charlemagne on 4th March 801 when he sojourned at Rome. For a long period, the bishops of Arezzo and the bishops of Siena had contended for the ownership of the monastery of Saint Amsanus. Under the advice of pope Leo, Charlemagne settled the case and confirmed the rights of Aribert. The charter recorded the judgement of the court and the confirmation of Charlemagne and his chancery. In the beginning of the charter, as usual, is the *titulature* or the titles of Charlemagne, which runs as 'With the grace of God Charles the king of the Franks, of the Lombards and patricius of the Romans' (*Carolus gratia dei rex Francorum et Langobardorum ac patricius Romanorum*). Here, the notary used the old and yet normal form of Charlemagne's titulature before his imperial coronation. But a copy (B) written in the late ninth century or early tenth century from the archive of the church of Arezzo utilised another form of Charlemagne's titulature, in which there is the first imperial title as we have mentioned above (Mühlbacher 1906, 264).

'Rex Romanorum' is probably a literal translation of the imperial title of emperor at Constantinople, who is called '*Basileus*' or '*Basileus Romanorum*' (literally 'king' and de facto 'Emperor of the Romans'). In idiomatic Latin usage, the emperor of the Romans was officially called 'Imperator Romanorum'. The *Annales Regni Francorum*, the official chronicle of the Carolingians, provided a clear case to support the above understanding. In the entry of 812, the chronicle recorded that Charlemagne received the legates from Constantinople in the church at Aachen, and the latter loudly praised Charlemagne as 'emperor and king' (*imperatorem et basileum*), which signified the official recognition of Charlemagne's imperial title (Pertz and Kurze 1905, 136).

If 'rex Romanorum' is an equivalent expression of 'imperator Romanorum', then there exits today much more evidence on the first imperial title of Charlemagne. In the above official chronicle, Charlemagne's courtiers offered a detailed description about the celebration of the imperial coronation in St. Peter's. 'At that day the people who were present there celebrating the key Christian festival hailed Charlemagne as "emperor of the Romans". On the most holy day of the Lord's birth, when the king, at Mass before the confession of St. Peter, rose up from prayer, Pope Leo placed on his head a crown; and he was acclaimed by the whole populace of Rome: "To Charles, Augustus, crowned by God the great and peaceful emperor of the Romans, life and victory!"' (Pertz and Kurze 1905, 112). Charlemagne's courtiers remarked that their king was crowned by Leo III under the title of 'imperator Romanorum'.

The papal curia offered another detailed record of the ceremony. This is contained in the biography of Pope Leo III, which is generally considered as composed shortly after his death, circa in 816. Although the biography was composed from different viewpoints, it mentions in like manner the first imperial title of Charlemagne. 'Then all the faithful people of Rome, seeing the defense that (Charlemagne) gave and the love that he bore for the holy Roman Church and his Vicar, by the will of God and of the blessed Peter, the keeper of the keys of the kingdom of heaven, cried with one accord in a loud voice: "To Charles, the most pious Augustus, crowned by God, the great and peace-giving Emperor, life and victory." While (t)he Pope was invoking diverse saints before the holy confession of the blessed Peter the Apostle, it was proclaimed three times and he was constituted by all to be Emperor of the Romans. Then the most holy pontiff anointed Charles with holy oil.' (Duchesne 1892, 7). Charlemagne was acclaimed by the Roman people as 'imperator Romanorum'.

After his imperial coronation Charlemagne's new titulature was still created from three various titles. By introducing the new imperial title into the titulature, Charlemagne abandoned one of the old titles, '*patricius Romanorum*'. It is curious that the imperial title did not simply occupy the same place of '*patricius Romanorum*' and remained in the third or the last place. In addition, the new imperial title was not yet promoted to the first rank; instead '*rex Romanorum*' was put into the second place among his three titles, before '*rex Langobardorum*' but after '*rex Francorum*'.

Nearly two months later Charlemagne, once again changed his titulature when he sojourned at Ravenna after his departure from Rome. He used a more acceptable form of the wordy titulature we have already mentioned above. Compared with the first imperial title, the new or the second imperial title used '*imperator Romanum gubernans imperium*' in place of '*Rex Romanorum*' or '*imperator Romanorum*', and its rank was promoted further forward as well. The new imperial title thus occupied the first rank, before 'king of the Franks' and 'king of the Lombards'. Given the adjustment of the titulature, it is the imperial title which changed completely, both its expression and its rank.

The rules by which the three titles were ordered in Charlemagne's imperial titulature must have changed at about the end of May. The new wordy title emphasized the honour of the imperial title, which was considered to be the highest one. Compared with 'king of the Franks' and 'king of the Lombards', 'imperator' was exalted to the most prestigious, and as a result occupied the first rank. At the same time, with the participle '*Romanum gubernans imperium*' as a modification, the imperial title signified a concrete state, 'Roman empire'. The modification indicates that the new imperial title closely connected with the first imperial title, '*rex Romanorum*'. The connection is conducive to understanding the nature of the imperial title in the second imperial titulature of Charlemagne.

As a titulature, '*Rex Francorum et Romanorum adque Langobardorum*' may simply unite three individual *regna* (kingdoms) into a system. It probably coordinates its three parts in terms of their political importance or even the size of their territories. 'King of the Franks' is most important in the series on account of the huge territory under his control, while 'king of the Lombards' is the least for the same reason. The place of 'rex Romanorum' may imply that as a state or commonwealth, the Roman Empire is larger than the Lombardian kingdom and smaller than the Frankish kingdom.

3 Roman Empire as a Geographical State

Over which territories could Charlemagne reign as emperor of the Romans or by governing the Roman Empire? The question is to some extent neglected by historians partly because the first imperial title soon replaced by the second one, and partly because a very closely related question, what was the nature of Charlemagne' empire, has drawn more of historians' attention. Notwithstanding that the change of the imperial title in May 801 created a title of emperor relatively independent from the Roman Empire, the first imperial title expressed itself clearly that Charlemagne was a Roman emperor.

In the late eighth century, there existed only one Roman Empire, which is now generally called the Byzantine Empire. In the literature, there was a varied terminology referring to the Empire, with the preferred name being *respublica*, which was an inheritance from the ancient Roman republic. The emperors at Constantinople were naturally the rulers of the Roman Empire, although the territories they controlled had changed greatly from that of the ancient Roman empire. They had lost forever the provinces of North Africa and western Europe beyond the narrow coastal regions of the Mediterranean. In the western part of the empire, the emperor at Constantinople only ruled de facto central and southern Italy with its many islands, while they influenced the barbarian kingdoms largely by conferring legitimate honors on the ambitious barbarian rulers.

Charlemagne took his first tour to Rome in 775. After his meeting with Pope Hadrian I, he began to introduce the title of '*Patricius Romanorum*' in his titulature (Ganshof 1950, 263). As *patricius*, Charlemagne acted as a protector of the papacy, while as a new conqueror of the northern part of Italy, he was acclaimed as the king of Lombardy or Italy. From December 775 onward, Charlemagne utilized the prototypical form of his titulature, 'Charles, by grace of God, being crowned by God, king of the Franks, King of the Lombards, and Patricius of the Romans.' Charlemagne shared the rule of the western part of the Roman Empire with the emperor at Constantinople.

While contemporary narrative sources seldom tell us the geographical components of the western territories of the Roman Empire, a forged document created during that period sheds precious light on the problem. The *Donation of Constantine*, one of the most famous forgeries in the Middle Ages, offered a geographical list of the provinces of the Roman Empire. The forged document is generally believed to have been created in the period from the mid-eighth century to the early ninth century, although there exist at least four various schools of interpretations on its date of fabrication (Gericke 1957, 1–88). Most historians agree that the *Donation of Constantine* was composed with the involvement of the Roman curia, although recently, Johannes Fried has argued in favour of its origin from Franconia (Miethke 2010, 36–37). The fabricated text is contemporary roughly with the life of Charlemagne, and it involves the participation of the notaries of the papacy, so it may be helpful in illuminating the concept of the Roman Empire prevailing in the Roman curia during the reign of Charlemagne.

The *Donation of Constantine* provides a list of the territories of the whole empire: "Through our sacred imperial orders as much in the east as in the west, and both in the north and the south, that is, in Judea, Greece, Asia, Thrace, Africa and Italy with its various islands, we conceded our generousness to them." (Fuhrmann 1968, 85–6). According to the same document, the western part of the empire only included the provinces of Italy: 'We conceded as much our palace before mentioned as also Rome and all provinces, locations and cities of Italy or of the western regions to that blessed bishop, our father Silvester, universal pope.' (Fuhrmann 1968, 93).

The above document clearly indicated that the western regions of the Roman Empire were equivalent to 'all the provinces of Italy', which had been donated to the universal pope. Besides the literary analysis of the text, a similar conclusion may be drawn another way. The eastern part subtracted from the total territories of the Roman Empire equals those areas which belonged to the western part of the empire. Judea, Greece, Asia and Thrace constituted absolutely the eastern part, while Africa may subject to either part of the Empire. Furthermore, continental Africa had already been under the control of the Arabs for nearly a century, although one plausible explanation may be that there were many islands of Africa owned by the Roman Empire, especially those lying off the southern coast in the eastern Mediterranean. If this explanation is acceptable, the western part of the Roman Empire included, therefore, mainly, the whole of Italy and its islands.

This concept of the Roman Empire in the west is further illustrated by Charlemagne's practice of imperial administration in Italy. The Italian Capitulary (*Capitulare Italicum*) was one of the documents issued by Charlemagne when he sojourned in Italy in 801. It bore witness to the imperial administration. In the capitulary, Charlemagne acted only as emperor, and avoided making any reference to the other two titles in the normal titulature. The persons whom Charlemagne addressed were those officials serving the Roman Empire in Italy, which corresponded with the imperial title of Charlemagne. The preface of the document reads as follows: 'In the name of our lord Jesus Christ, Charles, crowned by divine will, reigning over the Roman Empire, the most serene August, to all dukes, counts, the owners of the castles, and all the officials of the Roman Empire throughout Italy under our law' (Mühlbacher 1906, 204).

It is notable that in the capitulary, Charlemagne talked about the reasons why he came in Italy. He said, 'We came to Italy on account of the benefit of the holy church of God and for regulating the provinces.' 'The benefit of the holy church of God' must refer to the rebellion against Pope Leo III and the trial of those conspirators. By these enactments, Charlemagne secured the peace in the Roman Church. If the first reason mainly concerned the religious aspect of the Roman Empire, the second one, 'regulating the provinces' of Italy, stood behind the imperial administration in Italy, or dealing with the secular aspect of the Roman Empire. The Italian Capitulary represents thus one of the attempts to regulate the administration in imperial Italy made by Charlemagne as the new emperor.

The date of the Italian Capitulary is also remarkable. The notary used a unique imperial dating method. It reads: 'in the year 801 of our lord Jesus Christ's incarnation, the ninth Indiction, the 33rd year of my reign in Francia, 28th year in Italy, and the 1st year of my consulate'. Compared with the famous charter No. 196 of Charlemagne which bears the second imperial title, the dating method of the Italian Capitulary provides a clue for its place in the chronology of Charlemagne. The dating method in the charter is: 'Give in 29th May at the first year, by support of Christ, my rule (*imperium*), 33rd year of my rule in Francia and 28th year in Italy'. In contrast to the dating method of the Italian Capitulary, the dating of the charter arranged the three dating systems in reverse order—first the date of the reign of the empire, then of Francia and then of Italy—but also began to use the normal form of the imperial dating method, 'imperium'. The dating method suggests that the Italian Capitulary had been issued before the charter No. 196, in other words, before the end of May.

The consular date shows that the quaint honour was ever appealing to Charlemagne. With the recreation of an emperor in the west at Rome, there occurred a strong revival interest in the antique Roman honour and its political culture. Against this background, we may suppose that within the first five months of Charlemagne's imperial period, his imperial title was still flexible, just as Mühlbacher more than one century ago had commented (Mühlbacher et al. 1908, 167).

It is probably at the end of May that Charlemagne changed his imperial title, signifying that the nostalgic mood began to wane. The charter evidence shows that from 29 May, the notary of the new emperor began to use '*imperator Romanum gubernans imperium*' as the normal imperial title, which would be kept in usage until the end of Charlemagne's rule. It is better, nevertheless, to consider the 'normal' imperial title as one link in a longer chain of evolution. Considering the period from 800 to 814 as a whole may help not only to view the history of the imperial titles more thoroughly, but also shed new light on the motives behind its evolution.

4 From 'Imperator Romanum Gubernans Imperium' to 'Imperator'

In the second imperial titulature, the imperial title occupied the first rank among the three titles, preceding both 'king of the Franks' and 'king of the Lombards', while in the first imperial titulature, the imperial title, 'rex Romanorum', was put in the second rank, between 'king of the Franks' and 'king of the Lombards'. The imperial title 'imperator' was recognized by Charlemagne as the highest honour. With such an adjustment, the honour of emperor was transferred to a general title, which would to some extent provide unity for the three *regna*. In the 1950s, Peter Classen argued convincingly that the emperor and the empire were united into a paradox title, by which Charlemagne included the Romans within the Frankish realm without centring the Empire upon them, while the core of the empire was Italy (Classen 1983, 201). The imperial title thus no longer meant an emperor of the Roman Empire, one of the three kingdoms, but instead denoted an emperor of all three kingdoms.

At the same time, the new imperial title took a modifying phrase, 'governing the Roman Empire', which referred particularly to the remaining lands of the Roman Empire in the West, or the provinces of Italy and their islands. With such a modifying participle, the second imperial titulature not only kept its connection with the first one, but also hinted at its Italian origin. The empire was a Roman Empire.

That the highest honour, 'emperor', was separated somewhat from the empire was in effect the result of the change of the imperial title, although it may be considered as a compromise of two extremities: the generalized imperial title and geographical probably the smallest kingdom, the Roman Empire. In the 1950s, Walter Ullmann insisted on the universal nature of the empire, which would prepare the political stage for the struggle between the papacy and the emperors in the middle ages. He considered 'Roman empire' as 'of course nothing else but Latin Christendom', and thus equal to the whole territory which Charlemagne governed (Ullmann 2010, 114). Attempting to trace the history of the Papal state, Thomas Noble claimed that Charlemagne's empire was 'Christian and Frankish' (Noble 1984, 296). These researches remind us of the eclectic style of the imperial title, a mixture of the universal idea of emperorship and the geographical polity of the Roman empire.

Notwithstanding that Alcuin was one of the leading proponents of the concept or even theory of the universal imperium, his idea was not prevailing at Rome. On that subject, the monks from the Lorsch monastery articulated another theory of universal emperorship instead of universal imperium. The *Lorsch Chronicle* (*Annales Laureshamensis*) is the only existing narrative source today which in some detail records the discussion of the general assembly, which was held at Rome before the imperial coronation, on the issue of imperial coronation. According to the chronicle, on that occasion, a concept of the universal emperorship was put forward: 'Since there was no longer an emperor in the land of the Greeks and they all were under the domination of a woman, it seemed to Pope Leo and to all the fathers who sat in the assembly, as well as to the whole Christian people, that they should give the name of emperor to the king of the Franks, to Charles, who occupied Rome, where the

Caesars had customarily resided, and also other capitals in Italy, Gaul, and Germany. Because Almighty God had consented to place these lands under his authority, it seemed right, according to the desire of the whole Christian people, that Charles should also bear the imperial title.' (Pertz 1826, 38–39).

There are three points worthy to be mentioned. The above quotation did hint that Charlemagne's empire was closely related to the ancient empire, however the author expressed this idea in a discursive way, for he talked about the ancient capitals, instead of the territories of the Roman Empire. Even if the land under Charlemagne's control was relatively small in comparison with the ancient Roman Empire, Charlemagne owned most of the ancient capitals such as Rome, Ravenna, Milan and Trier, not to mention that there was no emperor at Constantinople, the eastern capital.

The second point is that the Lorsch Chronicle was indeed talking about the Roman empire, though it did not mention directly the word 'empire' (imperium). In its place, the author talked about the emperor. The chronicle mentioned indeed the ancient emperors, to whom Charlemagne is equal, and the key term in its persuasion is the title of emperor (*nomen imperatoris*).

The last but not the least is that the author cautiously avoided using any word related to 'romanus'. Charlemagne was equal to the ancient emperors, he controlled the ancient capitals, although these emperors and capitals were Roman. As a result he was protected and supported by the grace of God, so that all Christians persuaded him to accept the title of emperor.

Charlemagne did not accept this advice. He used the first imperial title, 'rex Romanorum', but he gradually conceded to the pressure of this group of advisers. After five months of hesitation and experimenting with tentative titles, he finally changed his imperial title. He accepted on the one hand the universal concept of emperorship, while he maintained the idea of Roman Empire by adding a modifying participle to the title of emperor, '*imperator Romanum gubernans imperium*'.

The second imperial title became the normal title for Charlemagne. The normal titulature based on the second imperial title was generally used in official documents. However, in the letters written to him by his advisers, he was called only by his imperial title, 'emperor' (*imperator*), without the modifying participle or the other two royal titles. For example, Magnus, the Archibishop of Sens, wrote to Charlemagne with addressee as 'the most glorious emperor' (*gloriosissime imperator*) (Duemmler 1895, 534). Alcuin provides a vivid witness of the transformation from the old customised addressee to the new one. In his letter-collection, there exist today about 10 letters to Charlemagne after the latter's departure from Franica and before his own death in 804 (Dummler 1895, 351–471).

These letters may be divided into three groups in terms of Charlemagne's titles, which roughly advance with time. In five letters (No. 211, No. 229, No. 231, No. 238 and No. 240) written at the end of 800 and the beginning of 801, Alcuin insisted on hailing Charlemagne as 'king David' (*David rex*).

Alcuin was hesitant to use the new imperial title, so he adhered to the private and intimate salutation, 'David'. Ernest Dümmler, the editor of Alcuin's letters, once commented that Alcuin was accustomed to calling the emperor by his surname, 'David' (Dümmler 1895, 383, note. 1). Since David in the Bible was only a king, never an emperor, Alcuin had to make a compromise between David king and emperor. In letters No. 249 and no. 257, he called Charlemagne 'king and emperor augustus' (*Karoli regi imperatori atque Augusto*) and 'king Augustus' (*rex Augusto*) respectively. But he also used the vocative case of the emperor, 'holy emperor' (*sancte imperator*).

Unfortunately, the last two letters of Alcuin to Charlemagne, No. 307 and No. 308, do not permit us to know the imperial title of the addressee on account of being incomplete. Alcuin had used, nonetheless, the vocative case, 'most excellent emperor' (*excellentissime imperator*), and did not mention his preferred surname 'David' (Dümmler 1895, 351–471).

In 806, Charlemagne determined to deal with the problem of how he could pass on the empire and kingdoms to his three lawful sons while maintaining the stability of 'imperium et regnum'. He employed the rule of division of his domain. In order to maintain peace among the three successors, he convened a general assembly and issued a capitulary to regulate their relationship and to let them obey the rules guiding their actions toward each other. In the capitulary '*divisio regnorum*', there are two types of titulature. Some of the manuscripts utilize its normal form, 'Charles, the most serene Augustus, crowned by God, the great peaceful emperor governing the Roman Empire, who under the mercy of God is also the king of the Franks and of the Lombrads' (*Karolus serenissimus augustus, a Deo coronatus magnus pacificus imperator, Romanum gubernans imperium, qui et per misericordiam Dei rex Francorum atque Langobardorum*), while Manuscripts 2 and 3 provide another unusual form of titulature, 'Charles, Emperor Caesar, invincible king of the Franks, the rector of the Roman Empire, the pious, happy, victorious and always triumphant Augustus' (*Imperator Caesar Karolus, rex Francorum invictissimus, et Romani rector imperii, pius felix victor ac triumphator semper augustus*) (Boretius 1883, 126).

By comparing these two types of titulature, we find that the latter titulature is composed of two titles, in contrast to the three titles of the normal form. The modifying participle of the imperial title disappeared, while an individual title was added, 'rector of the Roman Empire', which has similar meaning to the modifying phrase, 'governing the Roman Empire'. The new title for the ruler of the Roman empire followed behind the royal title of the Frankish king, '*rex Francorum*', and indeed took the place of 'the king of the Lombards'. The separation of 'imperator Caesar' from '*Romani rector imperii*' is in line with the tendency of the transformation of Charlemagne's titulature, so that the imperial title stood for the first time in the official documents independently as an individual title without any modification. It became a general title for Charlemagne who ruled the two kingdoms and the Roman Empire.

After a series of difficult negotiations with the emperors at Constantinople, in 812, Charlemagne's imperial title was recognized by them. One of the effects was that Charlemagne may be legally called 'emperor' (*imperator* and *basileus*), which is similar to the imperial title in manuscripts 2 and 3 of the Capitulary '*Divisio regnorum*'. The letter of credence to emperor Michael at Constantinople written in early 813 illuminated the last imperial title of Charlemagne very clearly. Charlemagne called himself 'In the name of the holy father, son and spirit, Charles, by the plentiful divine, emperor and Augustus, and also king of the Franks and the Lombards' (*In nomine patris et Filii et spiritus sancti. Karolus divina largiente gratia imperator et Augustus idemque rex Francorum et Langobardorum*) (Ernest Dümmler, epistolae vol. II, 556).

In 813, Charlemagne called from Aquitaine to Aachen Louis the Pious, the only surviving son of the three lawful successors, and at the general assembly created him as emperor and his co-ruler. One year later, Charlemagne died at Aachen. Louis the Pious arrived quickly at the palace of Aachen and began to rule the whole empire. Correspondently, he put in use his new titulature, which was the same as his imperial title, 'In the name of the Lord God and our Saviour Jesus Christ, Louis, emperor Augustus ordained by divine providence' (Boretius 1883, 261), although on very rare occasions Louis also used the modification, '*Romanum gubernans imperium*'.

5 Conclusions

In 1928, Carl Heldmann published his detailed review of the scholarship on the imperial coronation of Charlemagne. There were generally two great academic traditions upon this historical event: the universal theory and the local theory, although he could have discovered nine various schools (Heldmann 1928). The universal theory argued that the imperial coronation was a natural outcome both of the growth of the power of Charlemagne and the expansion of his kingdom, while the local theory articulated that it was the local factors at Rome that instigated that famous historical event (Ganshof 1949, 5–6). Nearly one century later, Steffen Patzold commented as well that researchers may be grouped into two different schools by this criterion (Paztold 2012).

The study of the imperial title has consequently two different trajectories: the universal nature of the imperial title and the local characterise of that title. We may nevertheless find a middle way between them if we view the title as changeable and therefore take the whole evolution of Charlemagne's title into view. The general tendency of its evolution is from the localised title, 'emperor of the Roman Empire', to a universal one, 'Emperor'.

From Christmas Day 800, when Charlemagne was crowned as the Emperor of the Romans, to 814, the year of his death, the imperial title of Charlemagne was subject to frequent changes. The first imperial title 'Emperor of the Romans' was designed as an equivalent honour as his two other titles: 'King of the Franks' and "King of the Lombards', although it ranked between them. All of them had the meaning of a ruler of a kingdom (*regnum*). As 'Emperor of the Romans', Charlemagne's political domain was the provinces of Italy and their islands. About five months later, Charlemagne started using his second imperial title 'Emperor governing the Roman Empire'. This title is a compromise between the universal concept of the emperorship and an emperor who ruled a limited territory, 'the Roman Empire'.

The imperial title thus ranked in the first position and became the highest honour in Charlemagne's titulature. In 806, for the first time, the imperial title was separated from its modifying participle, and occupied still the first rank, while an independent title, 'rector of the Roman Empire', stood behind the royal title of the king of the Franks, occupying the third rank in the titulature. The imperial title in the capitulary of 806 on the one hand corresponded to the daily usage in the letters written to Charlemagne by his subjects, where he was hailed as emperor; and on the other hand, it predicted the appearance of the third imperial title, 'Imperator Augustus'. The third and last imperial title was created in 812 when Charlemagne's imperial title was finally recognized by the emperors at Constantinople.

Viewing the three imperial titles as a whole, the imperial title was gradually generalized, from referring to a ruler who reigned over Italy, the western part of Roman Empire, to a ruler who controlled the three kingdoms (*regna*): the Frankish kingdom, the Lombardian kingdom and the Roman Empire.

Appendix

(Table 1).

Table 1 Imperial titles and titulatures

	1st Imperial title	2nd imperial title	3rd imperial title	
Title	Rex (Imperator) Romanorum	Imperator Romanum gubernans imperium	Imperator	
Titulature	*Carolus Dei gratia rex Francorum et Romanorum adque Langobardorum*	*Carolus serenissimus augustus deo coronatus magnus pacificus imperator Romanum gubernans imperium qui et per misericordiam dei rex Francorum et Langobardorum*	*Imperator Caesar Karolus, rex Francorum invictissimus, et Romani rector imperii, pius felix victor ac triumphator semper augustus*	In nomine patris et Filii et spiritus sancti. *Karolus divina largiente gratia imperator et Augustus idemque rex Francorum et Langobardorum*
Time	4 March 801	From 29 May 801 onwards	806	812
Sources	Diploma no. 196	Diploma no. 197	Capitul. 45 Manus. 2 and 3	Epistolae Variorum Carolo no. 37

References

Becher, Matthias. 2003. *Charlemagne.* Translated by David Bachrach, New Haven: Yale Universtiy Press.

Boretius, Alfred. 1883. *Capitularia regum Francorum,* tomus I, Monumenta Germaniae Historica (MGH.), Legum Sectio II., Hannover: Hahn.

Classen, Peter. 1983. 'Romanum gubernans imperium: Zur Vorgeschichte der Kaisertitulatur Karls des Großen', *Vorträge und Forschungen: Ausgewählte Aufsätze von Peter Classen,* ed. J. Fleckenstein, Sigmaringen: Jan Thorbecke Verlag, 187–204.

Collins, Roger. 1998. *Charlemagne.* Basingstoke: MacMillan Press LTD.

Duchesne L. ed. 1892. *Le Liber Pontificalis: Leo III,* Paris.

Dümmler, Ernest. 1895. *Epistolae Karolini Aevi,* tomus II, Epitolarum tomus IV, MGH., Berlin: Weidemann.

Fuhrmann, Horst. ed. 1968. *Das Constitutum Constantini Text,* MGH. Fontes iuris germanici antiqui, in usum scholarum, X. Hannover: Hahn.

Ganshof, François-Louis. 1949. *The Imperial Coronation of Charlemagne: Theories and Facts.* Galsgow: Jackson, Son and Company.

Ganshof, François-Louis. 1950. *'Note sur les origines byzantines du titre, Patricius Romanorum", Annuaire de L'institut de Philologie et D'histoire Orientales et Slaves,* 261–282. Bruxelles: Secrétqriqt des éditiones de L'Institut.

Garipzanov, Ildar. 2017. *The Symbolic Language of Authority in the Carolingian World.*

Gericke, Wolfgang. 1957. "Wann entstand die Konstantinische Schenkung?" in *Zeitschrift der Savigny-Stiftung für Rechtsgeschichte.* 1–88.

Heldmann, Karl. 1928. *Das Kaisertum Karls des Großen: Theoiren und Wirklichkeit.* Weimar: Hermann Böhlaus Nachfolger.

Kössler, Max. 1931. *Karls des Großen erste Urkunde aus der Kaiserzeit.* Graz: Leuschner and Lubensky.

Miethke, Jürgen. 2010. *„Die „Konstantinische Schenkung" in Der mittelalterlichen Diskussion: Ausgewählte Kapitel einer verschlungenen Rezeptionsgeschichte,* 36–37. Heidelberg: Universitätsbibliothek Heidelberg.

Mühlbacher, Engelbert. ed. 1906. *Die Urkunden Pippins, Karlmanns und Karls des Grossen,* MGH., Diplomatum Karolinorum tomus I., Hannover: Hahn.

Mühlbacher, Engelbert, Johann F. Böhmer, and Johann Lechner. 1908. *Die Regesten des Kaiserreichs unter den Karolingern: 751–918.* Innsbruck: Verlag der Wagnerschen Universitäts-Buchhandlung.

Müller-Mertens, Eckhard. 2009. Römisches Reich im Frühmittelalter: Kaiserlich-päpstliches Kondominat, salischer Herrschaftsverban. *Historische Zeitschriften* 288: 50–92.

Noble, Thomas. 1984. *The Republic of St. Peter: The Birth of the Papal State, 680–825,* Philadelphia: Press of Pennsylvania University.

Paztold, Steffen. „Karl der Große: Geheimnis eines Weihnachtstages", *Spiegel,* Geschichte, Heft 6, 2012, 11, 27.

Pertz, George H. ed. 1826. *Scriptorum Tomus I.,* 38–39. MGH., Hannover.

Pertz, Georg H. und Kurze, Friedrich. (eds.). 1905. *Annales Regni Francorum.* MGH., in usum scholarum, Hannover: Hahn.

Ullmann, Walter. 2010. *The Growth of Papal Government in the Middle Ages: A Study in the Ideological Relation of Clerical to Lay Power.* Oxon: Routledge.